TimeOut

Interviews 1968-1998

Edited by Frank Broughton

Penguin Books

PENGUIN BOOKS

Published by the Penguin Group
Penguin Books Ltd, 27 Wrights Lane, London, W8 5TZ, England
Penguin Putnam Inc, 375 Hudson Street, New York, New York 10014, USA
Penguin Books Australia Ltd., Ringwood, Victoria, Australia
Penguin Books Canada Ltd, 10 Alcorn Avenue, Toronto, Ontario, Canada M4V 3B2
Penguin Books (NZ) Ltd, Private Bag 102902, NSMC, Auckland, New Zealand

Penguin Books Ltd, Registered offices: Harmondsworth, Middlesex, England

First published 1998
10 9 8 7 6 5 4 3 2 1

Copyright © Time Out Group Ltd, 1998
All rights reserved

Colour reprographics by Precise Litho, 34–35 Great Sutton Street, London EC1;
and Westside Digital Media, 9 Bridle Lane, London W1

Printed by Jarrold Book Printing Ltd, Norfolk

Time Out Interviews 1968-1998

Contents

**Edited and designed by
Time Out Guides Ltd
Universal House
251 Tottenham Court Road
London W1P OAB**

Tel: **0171 813 3000**
Fax: **0171 813 6001**
www.timeout.com

Editorial
Editor Frank Broughton
Managing Editor Peter Fiennes
Assistant Editor Bill Brewster
Copy Editors Lily Dunn, Kevin
Ebbutt
Editorial Assistant Jane Babb
Librarian Jill Tulip
Text Input Giovanna Cellini,
Jonathan Heaf, Angela Lim, Jane
Marlow, Richard Wilkinson
Proofreaders Ian Cunningham,
Sarah Halliwell, Sophie Blacksell

Design
Art Director John Oakey
Art Editor Mandy Martin
Designers Benjamin de Lotz, Scott
Moore, Lucy Grant, Paul Mansfield
Scanning/imaging Chris Quinn
Picture Editor Kerri Miles
Picture Researchers Kit Burnet,
James Clarke, Rupert Nightingale,
Nicola Rawlings, Fiona Thomson,
Emma Tremlett

Marketing
Marketing Director Gill Auld
Marketing Manager Christine Cort

Administration
Publisher Tony Elliott
Managing Director Mike Hardwick
Financial Director Kevin Ellis
General Manager Nicola Coulthard
Accountant Catherine Bowen

**The Editors would like to thank
the following:**
The past and present Editors and staff
of *Time Out*, especially Brian Case,
Simon Garfield, Steve Grant, Greg
Miller, Andrew Shields, Xanthe
Sylvester, Tanis Taylor, Dominic
Wells; also Arthur Davidson QC,
Sarah Guy, Angela Jameson, Ruth
Jarvis, Pete Kidd, Tony Lacey, Raz
Mireskandari, Zoë Sanders; and all the
contributors to this book.

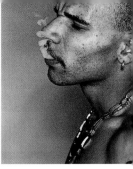

Picture Credits

pv David Bowie by **LFI**, Yoko Ono by **Sheridan Davis/Redferns**, George Best by **SK Fraser/Camera Press**, Jimi Hendrix by **David Redfern**; pvi Naomi Campbell by **Dave Hogan/Rex Features**, Michael Caine by **J Sutton-Hibbert/Rex Features**, Cher by **Rex Features**, Zoe Ball by **Andrew Hobbs**, Warren Beatty by **Paul McNicolls**, Martina Navratilova by **Leo Mason/The Image Bank**, Boy George by **Rex Features**, Bjork by **Gavin Evans/Retna**; pvii Chris Eubank by **Sam Teare/Sky TV**, Steve Coogan (as Alan Partridge) by **Trevor Ray Hart**, The Spice Girls by **Ralph Perou/Retna**, Robert De Niro by **David Gadd/Sportsphoto**, Spike Lee by **Graham Whitby/Sportsphoto**, Joanna Lumley courtesy of **BBC**; p10 Yoko Ono by **Sheridan Davis/Redferns**; p14 Jimi Hendrix by **David Redfern**; p16 Jimi Hendrix by **Joel Axelred/Redferns**; p18 John Peel courtesy of **BBC**; p23 John and Yoko by **Alex Agor/Camera Press**; p24 John and Yoko by **LFI**; p29 Mick Jagger by **The Kobal Collection**; p34 Lou Reed by **Barrie Wentzell**; p36 Captain Beefheart by **LFI**; p37 Ravi Shankar by **Shuhei Iwamoto**; p38 Tuppy Owens by **Tuppy Owens**; p40 Football gangs by **Hulton Deutsch**; David Bowie by **LFI**; p46 Gary Glitter by **Gered Mankowitz**; Jeff Beck by **David Redfern**; p49 'Day for Night' courtesy of **The Kobal Collection**; p52 George Best by **S K Fraser/Camera Press**; p54 Ali V Foreman by **Corbis-Bettmann/UPI**; p55 Ali V Foreman by **Corbis-Bettmann/UPI**; p56 Muhammad Ali by **Camera Press**; Car bomb by **Roger Perry**; p58 Bombers by **PA News**; p59 Uri Geller by **Roger Perry**; p60 New York nightclub by **David Redfern**; p62 Playboy by **Camera Press**; p66 David Hare by **Roger Perry**; p68 Warren Beatty by **Paul McNicolls**; Gay bikers by **Robert Workman/GAZE**; p74 Erich Von Daniken by **Klaus Aarsleff/Fortean Picture Library**; p75 Reading Festival by **Popperfoto**; p76 JPR Williams by **Bob Thomas/Popperfoto**; p78 Punk by **Peter Mazel/LFI**; p79 Punk by **Ebet Roberts/Redferns** and **Caroline Greville-Morris/Redferns**; p80 Johnny Rotten by **LFI** and Punk by **Gamma**; p83 Adam Faith by **Bob Vincett/Redferns**; p83 Miss Piggy courtesy of **PolyGram**; p84 Tom Waits by **Joseph Stevens**; p86 Arnold Schwarzenegger by **Keith Morris**, David Stone and Arnold Schwarzenegger by **Keith Morris**; p89 Peter Pan courtesy of **Mary Evans Picture Library**; p89 Elvis courtesy of **Liaison**; p90 Steven Berkoff by **Nobby Clark**; p92 Richard Pryor by **Roger Perry**; p93 Richard Pryor by **Roger Perry**; Skateboarding by **Rex Features** and **Bill Coward/Camera Press**; p95 Robert Mitchum courtesy of **Channel Four**; p96 The Royal Jubilee by **Cecil Beaton/Camera Press**, Ian Berry/Magnum, Bruno Barbey/Magnum; p98 The Clash by **Adrian Boot/Retna**; p101 Carl Perkins by **David Redfern**; p102 Disco by **David Redfern**; p106 Derek Jameson by **Phil Loftus/LFI**; p108 Norman Mailer by **Karsh Of Ottawa/Camera Press**; p110 Tom Wolfe by **Jerry Bauer**; p112 Jorge Luis Borges by **SIPA Press**; p112 J G Ballard courtesy of **Granada Publishing**; p114 The Slits by **Mark Rusher**; p114 Chrissie Hynde by **Adrian Boot**; p114 Maggie's Farm by **Steve Bell**; p116 John Cooper Clarke by **Rex Features**; p117 James Baldwin by **Valerie Wilmer**; p118 The Jam by **Jill Furmanowsky/LFI**; p119 Sir Les Patterson as Dame Edna Everage courtesy of **BBC**; p122 Heavy metal by **Simon Fowler/LFI** and **Dave Ellis/Redferns**; p123 AC/DC by Geoff **Swaine/LFI**; p124 Martina Navratilova by **Rex Features**; p125 Martina Navratilova by **Rex Features**; p126 Joseph Beuys by **Caroline Tisdall**; p127 Roland Barthes by **Fabian/Sygma**; p128 John Lennon by **London Features**; p130 Grace Jones by **Adrian Boot**; p134 Brixton Riots by **David Hoffman**; p134 The Royal Wedding by **Rex Features**; p135 Phil Lynott by **Adrian Boot**; p136 Martin

Amis by **Paul Tozer**; p138 Rollerskating by **Rex Features**; p140 Lemmy by **Paul Slattery**; p144 Laurie Anderson courtesy of **WEA**; p146 The Jam by **Paul Cox/LFI**; p147 Germaine Greer by **Bruce Rae**; p148 Falklands by **Jeremy Nicholl**; p149 Sergio Leone courtesy of **National Film Archive**; p150 William Burroughs by **Robert Mapplethorpe**; p152 Malcolm McLaren by **Bob Gruen**; p153 Malcolm McLaren by **Adrian Boot**; p154 Kathy Acker by **James Hamilton**; p156 Julie Walters courtesy of **Rank Film Distributors Ltd**; p156 Alan Bleasdale courtesy of **Royal National Theatre**; p159 Dirk Bogarde by **Christopher Cormack**; p164 Roman Polanski by **Paul Yule**; p170 Al Pacino courtesy of **Cinema International Corp**; p172 Samuel Beckett by **Orde Eliason/Link**; p177 Bob Geldof by **Brian Aris**; p178 Cher by **Lazic/Rex Features**; p179 Ken Livingstone by **Barry Marsden**; p180 Issey Miyake by **Richard Young/Rex Features**; p180 Alexis Sayle by **LFI**; p184 Oliver Reed by **Richard Young/Rex Features**; p186 James Brown by **Rogan Coles/Link**; p188/9 Watchmen by **DC Comics**; p190 Lee Marvin by **Terry O'Neill**; p193 Bono by **Granitz/LFI**; p195 Bette Midler by **Michael Putland/LFI**; p196 Gilbert and George courtesy of **Anthony d'Offay Gallery**, London; p198 Don McCullin by **D Rogers**; p199 Spitting Image by **Barry Marsden**; p200 LL Cool J by **Ron Wolfson/LFI**; p201 LL Cool J by **Angie/LFI**; p202 Beastie Boys by **Ross Marino/LFI**; p206 Harry Enfield courtesy of **Channel Four**; p207 Jerry 'Gobshite' Sadowitz courtesy of **ICA**; p208 Boy George by **Simon Fowler/LFI**; p210 Acid House by **David Swindells**; p212 Clint Eastwood courtesy of **Warner Bros**; p226 Mia Farrow courtesy of **Rex Features**; p228 Tom Waits by **Peter Anderson**; p229 Elvis Costello by **Steve Double/Rex Features**; p230 Roseanne Barr courtesy of **Channel Four**; p232 Nigel Benn by **Chris Goddard**; p233 Richard Harris by **Michael Birt/Katz Pictures**; p236 Robert de Niro by **Jill Furmanovsky/Retna**; p243 Victor Lewis-Smith by **Terra Fimna**; p246 AWB by **Gideon Mendel/Network**; p248 Michael Caine courtesy of **Guild Films Distribution**; p251 Sharon Stone by **Firooz Zahedi Carolco**; p252 Robert Altman by **David Fisher/LFI**; p254 Julie Burchill by **Sillitoe**; p257 Jarvis Cocker by **Colin Bell**; p259 Graham Whitby/**Sportsphoto**; p261 Derek Jarman by **Allan Titmuss**; p262 Natasja Kinski by **Lance Staedler/Outline**; p264 Harold Pinter by **Jill Furmanovsky**; p267 Camden Bombing by **Oliver Gillie/Independent**; p269 Tony Curtis by **J Self/All Action**; p271 Jon Ronson by **Barry J Holmes**; p271 Naomi Campbell by **Dave Hogan/Rex Features**; p272 Quentin Tarantino by **Rankin**; p275 Joanna Lumley courtesy of the **BBC**; p278 Chris Eubank by **Sam Teare/Sky TV**; p280 Woody Allen by **The Douglas Brothers**; p284 David Bowie by **Doralba Picerno**; p285 Brian Eno by **Martyn Goodacre**; p287 Miranda Sawyer courtesy of the **BBC**; p290 Oasis illustration by **Vanessa Dell**; p292 Bjork by **Gavin Evans**; p294 Tricky by **Gavin Evans**; p295 Tricky by **Gavin Evans**; p296 Spike Milligan by **David Gamble/Sygma**; p297 Trainspotting by **Liam Longman**, courtesy of **Polygram**; p298 The Spice Girls by **Ralph Perou/Retna**; p300 Alexander McQueen by **Philip Poynter**; p302 Diana, Princess of Wales by **Dominic Dibbs**; p304 Swampy by **Ginger**; p305 Steve Coogan (as Alan Partridge) by **Trevor Ray Hart**; p306 Damien Hirst by **Ginger**; p308 Wu-Tang Clan by **Gavin Evans**; p310 Helen Mirren by **Nigel Parry/Katz**; p313 Jean Paul Gaultier by **Gavin Evans**; p313 Jack Nicholson by **Luc Roux/Studio/MPA**; p313 Tony Blair by **Rex Features**; p314 Zoe Ball by **Andrew Hobbs**; p318 Jeremy Clarkson by **Barry J Holmes**; p320 The Lady and the Wimp by **Kipper Wiliams**.

Introduction

When magazines made a living from their content rather than their nipple count, there was a simple rationale behind the interview. It was a chance for the reader to engage with the experience of those who had lived a life less ordinary, and it was an opportunity, given access to swollen characters and intriguing ready-made dialogue, for a writer to shine. Even today, when magazines are spangled full of middle-shelf microcelebs and the interview is often just badly-disguised product placement – a blatant plug for a film, some tales of sex and drugs to make you shell out for the rock and roll – the form itself can still deliver the goods.

Here are nearly 200 encounters with the people who have entertained us over the past 30 years, selected with an eye on the above definition of what an interview can be. Most are people removed from us by virtue of their fame; all, I hope, have an interesting story to tell, whether in their lives or in their words.

This book is also a time capsule. Turning the pages of 1,500 issues of *Time Out*, I quickly realised how well it reflected changing attitudes and obsessions. As a weekly entertainment guide, aiming to list everything diverting in the world's busiest capital, few magazines can boast such a close relationship with the now.

The articles and interviews are arranged chronologically, and I have let them speak for themselves, with just the date and issue number to set them in context. Each year is introduced with a page detailing the events and pop-cultural quirks which defined it, as well as that year's movies and albums and what *Time Out* thought of them at the time.

In short, this book is about life lived in the past three decades, something I did and something you probably did too. I hope you enjoy it.

Frank Broughton, Editor

● ●

I remember in the very early days of *Time Out*, sitting in our windowless basement office on a Saturday night at midnight, thinking 'Why on earth am I doing this?' as I attempted to ring yet another vaguely coherent jazz musician in a vain attempt to find out who was playing at some tiny venue somewhere in Soho. Right from the magazine's inception, *Time Out* was insatiably hungry for information, and the events we strove to cover seemed to multiply daily. I felt that I'd created this monster that I had to feed. Sitting in that basement, the only thing that kept me going was the thought that eventually I would make something of it and the quality of my life would improve and I'd meet everyone in the world…

I never considered myself to be intrinsically part of the late '60s 'scene'. Although I was deeply sympathetic, I wasn't completely behind it. I never enjoyed smoking dope, and I was too impatient to go along with all that peace and love crap completely. However, there was this whole new way of experiencing the world, all these new things which were incredibly important: the films of people like Warhol, Steve Dwoskin, Kenneth Anger, or the theatre groups that sprang up in the wake of the Living Theater's visit to London, all the rock music that everyone was buying and talking about.

This exciting new way of life was reflected in the underground press – in fact it was in *OZ*, *IT* and *Black Dwarf* that I first read about what was happening in London – but these publications didn't have much interest in packaging actual information because they were too wrapped up in it all and wanted to use their page space for their polemics. I thought there was a job to be done.

And in the 30 years since then, *Time Out* has done this job and grown successful, to the extent that we have consolidated our presence in Europe and launched *Time Out New York*. I am now told that I don't own a magazine, I control an international *brand*.

I am very proud that, in its time, the magazine has managed to affect the cultural life of London as well as simply report it. *Time Out* gave a name to 'fringe' theatre, it was a loud voice in battling censorship, in supporting the defendants in the OZ trial, in informing people about feminism, gay liberation, sexual freedom, drugs. We broke big news stories from time to time, like the famous eavesdropping case of GCHQ which at the time seemed incredibly boring and innocuous, but heavily embarrassed the government. In the '80s we campaigned against the archaic licensing laws and battled to make weekly television listings freely available.

These things were all arguably political, but I supported them because they were a statement of allegiance to a certain way of life. To me, *Time Out* has always been a magazine geared to the consumer, telling people what's out there. But by taking an interest in certain areas of life, and having a vehicle to tell people that these things existed and by providing free publicity for them, you actually gave them a chance to survive.

I'm a very pragmatic, feet on the ground person, so I suppose I'd like to use the word 'efficient' here, in saying that *Time Out* has been a very 'efficient' reflection of the last 30 years. The fact of having done so much does surprise me, and it's amazing how much has been covered. I don't think there's much of any importance that has happened in London in the last 30 years that hasn't been through the pages of *Time Out*.

Tony Elliott, Founder and Publisher, Time Out

NB. *Some early interviews are taken from Time Out's predecessor,* UNIT, *Tony Elliott's magazine at Keele University. Others are taken from* Time Out'*s sister publication,* Time Out New York (T.O.N.Y.)

1968

Man the barricades. After the '67 Summer of Love, Vietnam splashed blood on our pretty faces and our acid-educated ideals had to face the real world. We were young and we were loud, and peace and love began to mean more than long hair and a pop festival. The hippie music explosion met with a sexual revolution and Paris-led intellectual insurrection. Our parents gave up hope.

January
The Viet Cong Tet Offensive commences.

March
Protestors gather in front of the US Embassy calling for withdrawal from Vietnam.

April
Martin Luther King assassinated.

Abortion legalised in the UK.

May
Unrest in France begins with clashes between students and police.

The tower block, Ronan Point, collapses, killing four people.

Manchester United beats Benfica 4-1 at Wembley in European Cup final.

June
Andy Warhol is shot in New York.

Two days after Warhol is shot, Bobby Kennedy is murdered in Los Angeles.

August
First issue of *Time Out*.

Soviet tanks roll into Czechoslovakia to crush the 'Prague Spring'.

September
Marlon Brando is the first white member of the Black Panthers.

First Boeing 747 flight.

October
Troubles in Northern Ireland begin with confrontations between Catholics and police on a civil rights demonstration.

During an awards ceremony at the Mexico Olympics, sprinters Smith and Carlos clench fists in a Black Power salute.

November
Richard Nixon elected as President of USA.

2001: A Space Odyssey
This tripartite sci-fi look at civilisation's progress to a visionary future is beautiful, infuriatingly slow, and pretty half-baked.

Once Upon A Time In The West
Long live Leone's timeless monument to the death of the West itself. Critical tools needed are eyes and ears – this is Cinema.

Rosemary's Baby
A supremely intelligent and convincing adaptation of Ira Levin's Stalinist thriller. Sexual politics, urban alienation, and a deeply pessimistic view of human interaction permeate it.

The Band – Music From The Big Pink (Capitol)
'Music From The Big Pink' may well come

to be regarded as one of the most important records for a very long time. Don't ignore it.

The Beatles – The White Album (Apple)
Far out and freaky-deaky. The Beatles continue to make the studio their own with progressive pop for the Now People. Listen to this.

Jimi Hendrix Experience – Electric Ladyland (Track)
The whole recording is a virtuoso performance in guitar playing by Hendrix, proving once and for all that he is the greatest manipulator of the instrument in the pop field. So completely individual that few try to play his work or even can.

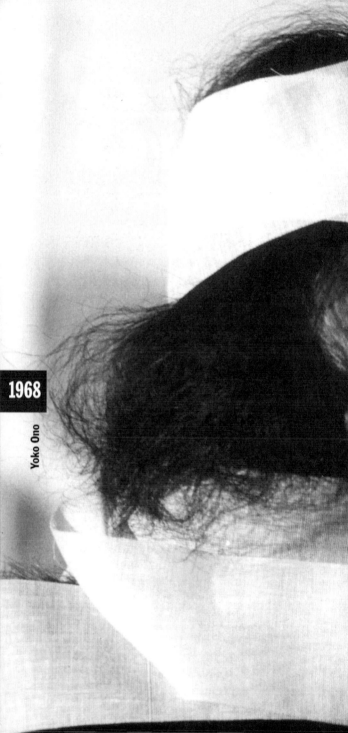

1968

Yoko Ono

YOKO ONO: a reputation as diffuse and diverse as the things she does. She will be remembered by most for her 'bottoms' film, cherished by others for her kite flying or her 'Painting to let the evening light go through'. Like a bee she never rests in one place, disseminating her pollen, nurturing the conception of her ideas and attitudes in others before flying elsewhere to begin again.

Her biography runs as follows:

Born: bird year

Early childhood: collected skies

Adolescence: gave birth to a grapefruit, collected snails, clouds, garbage, cans etc. Have graduated many schools specialising in these subjects.

At present: travelling as a private lecturer of the above subjects and others; recipient of Hal Kaplow Award.

She is a composer, artist, poet, creator of events and philosopher. She has made films; thirty minute studies of the striking of a match, the blinking of an eye, the movement of a smile. 'Number four' was about bottoms.

'I'm on the stage usually and asking people to come and fly or something. I don't fly.'

Her works include an all white chess set and 'A painting to be stepped on'. She has had various exhibitions with exhibits including an unfinished painting added to by each visitor and a totally white room called 'The Blue Room Event'. Recently she held a thirteen-day-long dance festival, taking place 'in your mind'.

'People think that I'm doing something shocking and ask me if I'm trying to shock people. The most shocking thing to me is that people have war, fight with each other and moreover take it for granted. The kind of thing I'm doing is almost too simple. I'm not interested in being unique or different. Everyone is different. No two persons have the same mouth shape for example, and so without making any effort we're all different. The problem is not how to become different or unique, but how to share an experience, how to be the same almost, how to communicate

'Basically I am interested in communication and therefore participation of everybody. I'm just part of the participation and the thing to participate should be basically a mind sort of thing. I can express it in any medium, just as you use water in everything for cooking.

'I'm on the stage usually and asking people to come and fly or something. I don't fly. I'm just sitting there and watching them fly. I might bring out huge very high ladders and ask people to fly off them. They can jump off the middle, they don't have to go from the top. Part of my pieces is imaginary. There are many people who don't actually jump off, but they do so in a way, because they see the ladder and see themselves go up there and jump off.

'All my pieces are white because I think that white is the only ▶

"1968"

"As I look ahead I am filled with foreboding. Like the Roman, I seem to see 'the River Tiber foaming with much blood'."
Enoch Powell, doing his bit for race relations in Birmingham

"If you take the game of life seriously, if you take your nervous system seriously, if you take your sense organs seriously, if you take the energy process seriously, you must turn on, tune in and drop out."
Timothy Leary.

"This is not a cricket team, but a team of troublemakers for South Africa's separate development policies."
SA Prime Minister John Vorster, after cancelling the MCC tour of his country for containing Basil d'Oliveira, a 'Cape coloured'

"Let us commit ourselves to the truth, to see it like it is and to tell it like it is, to find the truth, to speak the truth and live with the truth. That's what we'll do."
Richard Nixon, accepting the Republican Party nomination for Presidency

"I would not necessarily say that every single member of the British Government is a practising Communist. Perhaps that would be stretching things a little."
Ian Smith, Prime Minister of Rhodesia

"Do not adjust your mind – there is a fault in reality."
Graffiti, Paris, May

"Pop is the perfect religious vehicle; it's as if God had come down to earth and seen all the ugliness that was being created and had chosen pop to be the great force for love and beauty."
Donovan, obviously 'on one'

"Unfortunately, not everybody believes in computers yet."
An investor complains about Luddism on Wall Street after the first computers are installed

"Don't hurt me."
Sirhan Sirhan, after gunning down Robert Kennedy

colour that allows imaginary colour to be put on. In the Lisson Gallery I'm going to have a one room environment that's called 'The Blue Room Event'. The room is completely white and you're supposed to stay in the room until it becomes blue.

'I consider my shows, and especially this one, like giving an elephant's tail. When a blind man says "what's an elephant", you lead the man to an elephant and let him grasp the tail and say "that's an elephant". The existing material in the gallery is like an elephant's tail and the larger part is in your mind. But you have to give a tail to lead into it. The thing is to promote a physical participation that will lead you into this larger area of mind.

'I think that art is good just as anything is good in a sense that it's better if anything happens than nothing. So what I'm trying to do is make something happen by throwing a pebble into the water and creating ripples. It's like starting a good motion. I don't want to control the ripples and everything.

'When I made the bottoms film, people said why don't you make one where you not only make them walk but run as well, or include the part where they take off their pants. These are good variations. But I have so many ideas that I can't afford to get hung up on variations. All I do is give an elephant's tail, the inkling of the thing, the basic format, and then after that people can do it themselves. My things tend to be just basic. Somehow I feel the natural trend today is not to be just basic, but decorative as well. I have friends where everything is rainbow coloured and when they come here they ask why everything is white.

'The white chess set is a sort of life situation. Life is not all black and white, you don't know what is yours and what is theirs. You have to convince people what is yours. In the chess situation it is simple if you are black then black is yours. But this is like a life situation, where you have to play it by convincing each other.'

'Cut Piece' – a Yoko Ono event – involved an audience who cut off pieces of Yoko's clothing while she sat calmly on stage. 'It was a form of giving, giving and taking. It was a kind of criticism against artists, who are always giving what they want to give. I wanted people to take whatever they wanted to, so it was very important to say you can cut wherever you want to.

'It is a form of giving that has a lot to do with Buddhism. There's a small allegorical story about Buddha. He left his castle with his wife and children and was walking towards a mountain to go into meditation. As he was walking along, a man said that he wanted Buddha's children because he wanted to sell them or something. So Buddha gave him his children. Then someone said he wanted Buddha's wife and he gave him his wife. Someone calls that he is cold, so Buddha gives him his clothes. Finally a tiger comes along and says he wants to eat him and Buddha lets the tiger eat him. And in the moment the tiger eats him, it became enlightened or something. That's a form of total giving as opposed to reasonable giving like "logically you deserve this" or "I think this is good, therefore I am giving this to you."

'There was an event that I did for a programme on Japanese television. I just went out into the street and gave away flowers. They thought it was pretty stupid. The other happening makers on the programme did very surrealistic, fantastic dramatic things, "very meaningful" things and there I was just giving out flowers.

'The happening is like a theatrical thing, where you use people to do things that are like abstract theatre and that have nothing to do with spontaneity and experience. A good example is an event I did in New York, where people had to get into a small bag, take their clothes off inside and contemplate. There was this very beautiful dancer, who was in a very in-crowd, and who was very used to doing happenings and things like that. She went into the room and in just two minutes dashed out and said 'I did get into the bag and I thought of taking my clothes off. Then I suddenly realised that there was no point in taking my clothes off because no-one would see me anyway'. So in a happening you're always being an exhibitionist in a way. That's typical of a happening maker because she didn't have that personal urge.

'I'm very social conscious. when I make a painting I just don't want to leave it at home. I think it has to evade all the phases of life. The ultimate goal for me is a situation in this society, where ordinary housewives visiting each other and waiting in the living room will say, "I was just adding some circles to your beautiful de Kooning painting", or "I was just adding some colour to your Peter Blake." There's this strange false value that people create on art work. Art should be almost free like water and light.

'Television was going to do something on the dance festival. I went there and said that the first instruction is breathing. Breathe and do it in any way you want to. The television people got very upset. They wanted something more visual.

'If anybody wrote in, they just sent some flowers. Others thought I got a lot of pounds out of it. I received letters saying that they didn't mind if I was an eccentric, but would I keep it to myself and not ask a pound for my nonsense? I'm not asking for a pound even. Flowerwise a pound's worth of flowers could mean just one flower. The point is that it is very nice to do the thing together. I usually wake up at dawn just to watch the sky or breathe. This time, I thought maybe some other people are breathing with me. It goes on to the thirteenth day and the instruction is then that you're the best. I just can't wait until the thirteenth day comes.

'I think that gradually many of the hippies will turn their backs on me. I don't believe in limited turning on like LSD. They think that's the only turning on there is. I believe that there are ways of turning on like walking barefoot in the park or dancing in the wind.

'This swinging age is now in its beginning stage, like in jazz where you had hot and cool jazz. The hot jazz first and then the cool jazz. It's terribly hot now and I hope it will soon cool off. That's the way I want to go. I am dealing with the age I hope will come.' ●

> ## 'The room is white and you're supposed to stay there until it becomes blue.'

1969

January
LSE closed by governors after gates smashed by students.

March
Kray twins receive 30 year sentences.

Jim Morrison is arrested in Miami after displaying his penis at a concert.

First Concorde flight.

April
First British troops sent to Northern Ireland

May
Strikes break out in protest against government white paper 'In Place Of Strife'.

18-20 year-olds allowed to vote for first time.

June
Judy Garland dies in London. Riot at Stonewall bar ensues. Gay Lib is born.

July
Brian Jones of the Rolling Stones dies.

Neil Armstrong walks on the moon.

Mary Jo Kopechne dies when her car crashes on Chappaquiddick Bridge. Edward Kennedy admits to leaving scene of accident.

August
Charles Manson and his followers murder five people, including Sharon Tate.

Woodstock festival takes place.

September
Coup led by Colonel Gadaffi against King Idris in Tripoli.

October
Leader of Beat Generation, Jack Kerouac dies.

First episode of Monty Python is broadcast.

December
Half-crown ceases to be legal tender.

Revolution! We had all the answers, but with the oldies growing wary, we had to start fighting for them. The underground press battled censorship, nakedness became political, the LSE was occupied, Northern Ireland was 'Britain's Vietnam' and you couldn't go down the shops without tripping over an action or a demonstration. Concorde took off and Apollo 11 landed, but many at Woodstock never came down.

Easy Rider
The colourless acting of Peter Fonda and Dennis Hopper is only redeemed by the appearance of Jack Nicholson as an eccentric Southern lawyer.

Midnight Cowboy
Dustin Hoffman's Ratso reflects his position as a leading actor on the off-Broadway stage, only recently been discovered by the cinema.

Butch Cassidy And The Sundance Kid
You could do worse than catch Redford and Newman in one of the funniest if slightest Westerns of recent years.

Captain Beefheart and his Magic Band - Trout Mask Replica (Straight)
The first thing I heard was, 'A squid eating dough out of

polythene bag is fast and bulbous. Got me?' After that it made a kind of sense.

Crosby, Stills And Nash - Crosby, Stills And Nash (Atlantic)
It is remarkable that refugees from three groups should manage to produce an album of such intense discipline.

Led Zeppelin - Led Zeppelin II (Atlantic)
The fact that Led Zeppelin happen to be a groovy-looking group is not entirely unconnected with their success. But, it's almost worth buying for Plant's voice and Jimmy Page's guitar, which at times sounds as disturbing as car tyres screaming to a crash.

Jimi Hendrix

Jimi Hendrix interviewed in *UNIT*, by **Steve Barker**

The blurb on your first LP says you are trying to create, create, create. Are you satisfied with what you are creating?

We like to have our own sound, but we're not satisfied, not yet. You might be pleased with what you're doing once in a while, but never really satisfied. We're pleased with the LP we've just finished for instance. But the ideas we got out of it could go on to our next one.

How does the Experience get such fusion when you are basically a bluesman, Noel a rock man and Mitch a jazzman?

I don't know! Actually this is more like a free-style thing. We know what song we're going to play and what key it's in, and the chord sequence and we just take it from there.

How far can you go with the music that you're playing now?

I don't know. You can go on until you bore yourself to death I guess. You got to try something else. I think I'll start all over again and come back as a king bee.

You write all your own material, where does it come from?

Just from me. We go to clubs a lot and go all around in taxis and you happen to see a lot of things. You see everything, experience everything as you live. Even if you're living in a little room, you see a lot of things if you have imagination. The songs just come.

'Loneliness is such a drag'?

That's what it really is sometimes. That was the song I liked best of all we did. I'm glad it didn't get big and get thrown around.

Does this mean you're an introvert?

Well, sometimes. Right then when I wrote 'Midnight Lamp' I was. I was feeling kind of down like that. But really I have to catch myself and find out. So you go into different moods and when you write your mood comes through. So you can go back and listen to your records and know how you were feeling then and how your moods change at different times.

But 'loneliness is such a drag' is a whispery quiet thing. How come you put these words in among powerful extrovert stuff?

I like to play loud. I always did like to play loud. The words of the song just come. I don't know how it comes about, it starts off quiet until we get into it.

How much do you owe to a blues background?

Not necessarily anything! I went south and just listened to the way the people played blues guitar and I dug it. But then

I like a lot of other things too. That's why we try to do our own stuff, make something new.

There's a lot of controversy over the responsibilities of pop stars. Do you yourself feel any?

That's silly. Whatever a cat does in his private life should be his own business. Everybody knows this, but you can say it a million times and it still won't get through to some people. I don't really feel responsible too much to myself. Maybe that's all.

"*The News of the World* is as British as roast beef, and we intend it should remain so."
NOTW editor Stafford Summerfield, on the potential sale of the paper to the Czech, Robert Maxwell. It was sold to Australian Rupert Murdoch instead

"That's one small step for a man, one giant leap for mankind."
Neil Armstrong

"This is the greatest week in the history of the world since the Creation."
Modest Richard Nixon after the moon-landing

"I will see you later."
A member of the Kray brothers' gang offers an ominous goodbye after sentencing at the Old Bailey

"We have the enemy licked now. He is beaten. We have the initiative in all areas. The enemy cannot achieve a military victory: he cannot even mount another offensive."
Admiral John S McCain, C-in-C of US Pacific Forces, on Vietnam

"As far as criticism is concerned, we don't resent that unless it is absolutely biased, as it is in most cases."
SA's John Vorster offers a measured view of free speech

"The performers are severely burdened. Naked, you have to be beautiful as well as talented."
Critic John Simon, on 'Oh, Calcutta!'

"These chicks are ready for anything. Eventually most of them are going to get married to regular workers. These guys are lucky to be getting girls like these, girls who have attained some level of sexual adventurousness. These guys will be happier, do their jobs better, and the economy will reflect it."
Frank Zappa with his Groupie Theory

"We sold off a small yacht and I may have to give up polo. We may have to leave Buckingham Palace next year if we go into the red."
Prince Philip complains of his meagre civil list allowance of £475,000 per annum on US TV

1969

Jimi Hendrix

Do you ever feel like going away and sorting yourself out like maybe Dylan did?

I think that's going to have to happen soon anyway because everyone's getting so tired and you work so hard sometimes and it gets to be really frustrating.

How come you got caught up in the hippie scene.

It just happened to come about that we were around at the time of psychedelia and all the in-clothes. I dug that scene, but not necessarily what you call the hippy scene, because I don't like classification anyway. Regardless of the scene, we just happened to be playing freakout and psychedelic things, but it does bother us because psychedelia only means mind expansion anyway. I can't hear a single word the Pink Floyd are saying. There's so many other types of music. We just happened to be in that groove, that bag right then.

Do you try to communicate by words or sound when you're on stage, or both? Because the words never usually come out.

Most of the songs we're doing now, people know the words, I think, but it probably doesn't mean much to them. They just want somebody to break their neck on stage.

Does that mean you write primarily for yourself?

Oh definitely. One song we did called 'I Don't Live Today' was dedicated to the American Indian and all minority depression groups. All I did was just use a few words and they said 'what does that mean. That doesn't mean anything', because there was only three or four lines in there anyway.

How about Donovan and his little scene?

He's nice, kinda sweet! He's a nice little cat in his own groove, all about flowers and people wearing golden underwear. I like Donovan as a person, but nobody is going to listen to this 'love' bit. I like Dylan's music better because it's more earthy and live. 'Mellow Yellow' is slang in the States for really groovy. 'Sunshine Superman' means that he can get his girl. Anyway that's my interpretation. I'd like to play some sessions with Dylan, his group ought to be more creative. These days people think that everyone else ought to have trips and everyone is singing about trips.

How about straight piss-taking like the Mothers?

I like to listen to them, but we do our own thing. You know we had a chance to go into that bag because everybody's mind is still open. But we decided that we didn't want to go that way completely towards strict freak-out.

Are there any pressures on you as to what material you record?

No none at all. We're just writing and playing what we want. But our moods change, like once we wanted to do a Dylan song as one of our singles. Then we wanted this and that, but we always wind up doing our own regardless whether they flop or not. At least we're doing our own thing. If you do someone else's

song every fifth single, it shows something is missing. But you just don't throw anything out on record. I like to be involved and I like music. The same old story. All that goody goody stuff. Music is a love to me. The money's great too.

What level are you aiming for when you make a record? The kids?

No not necessarily. We quite naturally want people to like it. That's the reason for putting the record out. You see I have no taste. I couldn't say what's a good record and what's a bad one really. I don't have no feelings about commercial records. I don't know what a commercial record really is. So what we do is write and try to get it together as best as possible for anybody who'd really dig it. It doesn't make any difference who.'

How big a part do visuals take in your stage act?

I get a kick out of playing. It's the best part of the whole thing. You just do it when you feel like it sometimes. I used to feel like it. But not any more man, you would have a heart attack if you were doing it every night like we were doing three or four months ago. We'd be dead by this time. You can't do it right unless you feel it. Half of the things I do I don't even know it because I just felt like it at the time. If you have everything planned out and one little thing goes wrong you think 'Oh, what am I supposed to be doing now. Oh yeah, I'm supposed to be going like this... Hi everybody, I'm doing it'.

At this point a young lady from the Manchester Independent asked Mr Hendrix as to whether there was anything he wanted materially. This question was slightly distorted by an outburst of primitive laughter from the male section of the gathered assembly. She asked if there was anything left.

There's a whole lot of things left. Thousands of them. I see them downtown everyday. Millions of them! Marvellous!

What about the Beatles and the things they're doing now?

I think it's good. They're one group you really can't put down because they're just too much and it's so embarrassing, man, when America is sending over the Monkees. I am so embarrassed that America could be so stupid as to make somebody like that. They could have at least done it with a group that has something to offer. They've got groups in the States that are starving to death, trying to get breaks and then these fairies come up.

Do you ever think of going back to the States?

I think about it every single day. I really miss it. Like the West Coast. Nothing has to happen to me. I just like to be out there. I like the weather, the scenery and some of the people. You can have a chocolate milkshake in a drug store, chewing gum at a gas station and soup from little machines on the road. It's great, it's beautiful. It's all screwed up and nasty and prejudiced. And it has everything. ●

1970

Hendrix and Joplin bought the farm, The Beatles split, rubber bullets stalked the streets of Belfast and real ones brought death to anti-Vietnam protesters at Kent State. Germaine Greer told girls to go out and get some, and city parks everywhere were trampled by hotpants and kaftans in the post-Woodstock rush to turn a guitar, a couple of joints and some naked children into a free festival.

January
George Best is banned by the FA for 'disreputable behaviour'.

February
Timothy Leary is jailed for ten years after offering a plain-clothes policeman a joint.

April
Paul McCartney announces his departure from the Beatles.

May
Four students are killed by state troops at Kent State University in Ohio.

Ulrike Meinhof leads a successful raid to spring Andreas Baader from prison.

Bobby Moore is charged with stealing a bracelet in Bogota, Colombia.

June
Police bust *Oz* after infamous Schoolkids Issue.

England loses lead against W Germany in quarter-finals of World Cup, after Alf Ramsey makes disastrous substitutions.

July
EM Forster dies.

August
Portests break out in Notting Hill, after police harassment at the Mangrove Restaurant.

Timothy Leary escapes from jail.

September
Jimi Hendrix dies in London.

October
Oil strike by BP kicks off North Sea oil rush.

Inspired by Hendrix, Janis Joplin dies of an overdose.

November
Author Yukio Mishima commits suicide.

Germaine Greer's 'The Female Eunuch' is published.

M*A*S*H
There were parts that a Milligan or Cleese might have been proud of. It's good to see that somebody can still make war funny.

Catch 22
Aside from the background shots of airplanes crashing and some good flying footage, there is little on screen to explain why 'Catch 22' cost so much.

Zabriskie Point
Zabriskie Point has its faults, but its clarity and accomplishments cannot be faulted. Antonioni makes beautiful images only to discover their irrelevance.

Van Morrison - Moondance (Warner Bros)
Morrison towers so high above 99% of all

the rubbish currently forcing themselves upon us with their half-learned musical ability, their pseudo-drug-influenced and political-activist lyrics, and their stupid freaky album covers.

Neil Young - After The Goldrush (Warner Reprise)
Seems to me NEIL YOUNG could just be

one of the more sensitive valves to MANKIND'S soul, that's signalling to us to understand.

Miles Davis - Bitches Brew (CBS)
The sound Miles gets here is incredible. Something between Bartok night music and a zonked-out Stax rhythm section. Ethereal chugalug, you might call it.

John Peel

John Peel interviewed in *UNIT*, by **Bob Harris**

Pop music seems to be splitting in two. In one direction Englebert and his mimics rush away with their adoring fans, whilst towards the other extreme, various groups and individuals led by the Beatles progress to a freer, improvised and distinctly creative sphere. Though most people seem content with the 'wallpaper' and fab forty Radio 1, a freer and creative presentation is creeping in under the figure-head of disc-jockey John Peel.

John Peel, with his 'Perfumed Garden' programme on Radio London, a mixture of records, poetry, letters and conversation, immediately satisfied a demand for intelligent listening and 'involvement' from the public. He will shortly have another

'Perfumed Garden' on Radio 1 and at present is joint host on Sunday's 'Top Gear'. In a conversation with Bob Harris he talks about the way pop music is evolving and about his career and attitude to pop resulting in his becoming Britain's first really creative DJ. Perhaps one day, when the oldish DJs at present monopolising the network are eventually pensioned off, John Peel will be seen as a prototype for the future.

I think it is unfortunate to have a concept of what pop music is because it is expanding so much now. It is difficult to say whether the principal writers at the moment are song writers, poets or what they are. Groups are veering towards the theatre and all kinds of elements are being introduced into popular music, which I think can only result in the improvement of all of them.

I think eventually it'll all just become one; everything will become fused. Pop music will become television will become pop music will become theatre will become poetry will become whatever... Things are progressing in this direction. The theatre is becoming involved, for example the light show type ideas and the film clips groups are doing, and the Beatles' 'Magical Mystery Tour'. Already pop music, poetry, films and TV are getting mingled in with one another until eventually you won't be able to say where one begins and the other ends.

There are some nice trends at the moment, one being that record companies are now prepared to issue LPs by new groups and singers before they release a single, because they figure they've got that much to say. That's a good thing because for years they've been doing that with Jazz and blues.

Groups need LPS

I think the Cream thing saying they don't want to do any more singles is good in a way, because a lot of groups need an LP to develop their ideas; they can't get them across in two and a half minutes on a single.

It would be nice if the record companies would get round to issuing some LPs without instantly thinking of the profit thing

> ### 'Donovan is getting so good now. The incredibly delicate things he does are so nice.'

at the end. Elektra records have only made a profit on one LP they have released in this country, which is incredibly sad when you think of some of the beautiful records they've issued, but they are still prepared to issue this type of thing in Britain.

Unmechanical Floyd

A lot of the groups have some good ideas too. The Pink Floyd are knocked a hell of a lot now, but they really have some superb ideas. I think the point is that they rely a lot on collective improvisation, so if one guy is off, it throws everyone else off. So sometimes when you go to see the Floyd they are very bad and then other times they are incredibly good. But if a group is consistent it usually means, to my mind, that they are a bit of a drag because they are just mechanical.

If you do go and see the Troggs or Dave Dee, for example, you know they are going to sound exactly like their records. But the Floyd music is ultra-pop. It is really sensational music. The Soft Machine are superb too, and if anything, are even more into electronic improvisation than the Floyd.

Relaxed Hendrix

Then of course, Hendrix has some superb ideas. It is interesting really because Hendrix is more relaxed now. The first LP was incredibly exciting but at the same time a bit frightening too, because there was a sort of anger and violence in it. I must admit, though, that Hendrix, on stage, is a drag. I don't like all ▶

this erotic crap because I don't think it's necessary. You can play the guitar a hell of a lot if you're not pretending to be stuffing it. I just think that he is enough of a musician to be able to stand up without doing it.

Donovan is getting so good now. I don't know what he is like as a person, and I think this is important, but I think his songs are just exactly right. It doesn't seem to be fashionable at the moment to like Donovan, which is a great pity. The incredibly delicate things he does are so nice, things like 'Guinevere', the dream sequence, fantasy-type ideal situation things. I think Donovan is just beginning to get on the same sort of thing that Paul McCartney is on now, which is simplicity.

Beatle simplicity

'Hello Goodbye' is incredibly simple and yet at the same time very effective, because there is an awful lot happening in it and a great deal of depth to it. I have heard it said that Lennon is leaving McCartney behind now, but I think this is absolute rubbish. I don't think Lennon is leaving McCartney behind or vice-versa, I just think that they are going in opposite directions.

But I think we are reaching the stage now where pop music is splitting in two. Like on one side you have the good groups like the Family, Nice, Traffic and Tyrannossaurus Rex (who incidentally are really incredibly good) and these groups will obviously go on doing better and better things. Then on the other side you've got the backwater of dirge-like things.

Frankie Vaughan dead

I really thought Frankie Vaughan was dead or working as a bus conductor or something, but they found him, so you really can't tell from where you are. But the really nice thing is that, with very few exceptions, everyone in the group-scene in England is incredibly cooperative. They don't have this 'I'm a pop group' thing that so many American groups seem to have and they are helping in different ways to get people involved in nice ideas and this will continue to get stronger.

I only wish that when I was younger there was a 'Perfumed Garden' scene, because I was so incredibly hung up and I'm sure it would have taken less time to get my ideas straightened out.

When I started to work for Radio London, I began by doing the 'fab forty' stuff and then I volunteered to do the late night show (12-2am), because no-one else wanted to do it. After a time I began bending the format a little more each night until, by the time the attention of the station management had been drawn to it, it was already an established fact.

'The perfumed garden'

The other disc-jockeys reacted against it to begin with because this is something a disc-jockey has always wanted to do, to have this freedom thing, but the Radio London programme administrator, Alan Kein, was quite jazzed about the idea, so I started doing the whole 'Perfumed Garden', just bringing in more stuff as I thought of it, whatever happened to come up or whatever was suggested.

Letters played an important part in it. People would say, 'Hey will you try to do this?' and I would try to do it. I think it is the way a radio programme should be, although not all radio pro-

grammes because obviously you have to have some of the wallpaper music that Radio 1 is providing so well at the moment.

But you also need, somewhere in your day or in your week, a programme where the people who are listening are not treated as though they are totally moronic. I don't know why I called the programme 'The Perfumed Garden'. I didn't know about the book at the time, it was just a nice idea, wandering at night through a perfumed garden. As far as I was concerned it was a state of mind.

I would like to think that it was more than just a pop record show because it did, I suppose, try to influence people into at least sitting up and thinking about the ideas that I think are important. It doesn't mean that I thought that everyone had to believe in them, it was more a question of 'here you are – do what you like with them'.

Involvement

But so many people became involved with it. I got incredibly involved myself and I think that if you're doing that regardless of what you're doing, it communicates to other people. But you have got to know that as you get involved in something, people are going to appreciate your involvement and perhaps try to become involved also and in this way the whole thing can just spill over. I really think that it can have consequences beyond anyone's wildest hopes, because if people become really strongly involved in something and they really believe in it and can get other people involved as well, you've got the start of something very important.

You see, the people who were deeply involved with 'The Perfumed Garden' weren't, in the main, people who were involved with the music scene. They were just very ordinary people living very ordinary lives in very ordinary places. The ideas behind it and the sense of involvement I felt may have communicated something new to them and they became involved. Something existed for them to become involved in, whereas previously nothing had.

I think that as Radio 1 progresses, always assuming that it is going to progress, the personal involvement will become greater because they'll realise that a pop radio thing, if it is going to work, has to be rooted in the community to a far greater extent than it is at the moment.

The 'non-hear' station

The really depressing thing, though, is that 98% of the people listening to Radio 1 really don't hear it, I mean they really don't. A disc-jockey could get up there and say 'That was a fucking good record' and I swear people wouldn't know he'd said it because they really don't hear.

'Top Gear', although obviously far from being ideal as a musical thing, is the best programme on Radio 1, purely and simply because no-one else, with the exception of Kenny Everett, is trying to play nice music. But when BBC television first started, it was a lowest common denominator thing then, all westerns, and gradually they realised that it wasn't necessary to do this all the time and that you could afford to put some nice programmes on. Ultimately I hope the same will be true of Radio 1. ●

1971

January
Open University goes on air.

66 people die at Ibrox in Glasgow when barriers collapse at an Old Firm match.

February
First British soldier shot dead in Northern Ireland.

Britain goes decimal.

April
Composer Igor Stravinsky dies.

May
Schoolchildren in East End strike protest at sacking of teacher Chris Searle.

Phillips launches the first VCR, retailing at nearly £400.

June
Mick Jagger marries Bianca.

July
The Doors' Jim Morrison finally breaks on through to the other side.

August
George Harrison's prototype 'aid' benefit, Concert For Bangladesh, takes place.

Oz editors convicted of publishing an obscene article (later quashed on appeal), but cleared of conspiracy charges.

October
Tycoon Robert McCulloch purchases London Bridge and re-erects it in Lake Havasu City, Colorado.

November
Angry Brigade activists Jake Prescott and Ian Purdie go on trial at Old Bailey.

Miss World competition disrupted by protestors throwing flour bombs.

December
Former Nazi officer Kurt Waldheim becomes Secretary-General of the United Nations.

The wages of sin went decimal, and while scientists were inventing the microchip and VCR, everyone else was busy being liberated. Women's Lib, Gay Lib, children's, animals' and vegetables' Lib raised questions and made headlines as did the *OZ* magazine obscenity trial and the bombs of home-made anarcho-terrorists the Angry Brigade. Beating Prince by a quarter century, Andy Warhol changed his name for reasons of Art.

   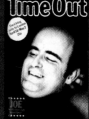

French Connection

Director Friedkin has made a fast, tasty, tight little thriller without sociological meanderings.

Performance
Apart from the censor's cuts, the full rich texture of the film can be experienced for the first time, since in other countries the cockney accents have been dubbed. Don't miss 'Performance'.

Clockwork Orange
The film is very hard, very harsh, very fast and totally abstract. 'Clockwork Orange' is not a revelation, it's just brilliant entertainment.

The Stooges - Fun House (Elektra)
No drawn-out incom-pleted-sentence hashi doldrum high, but Detroit Romilar

squads violating violent inviolates, daily deviation, confessions of Perverso. D'ya feel it when ya touch me?

John Lennon - Imagine
This album is enough to make you glad the Beatles broke up. Lennon could never have done anything so urgent and

desperate and uplifting as this while McCartney was still around.

Isaac Hayes - Shaft
I'd expected computerised funk, however, it reveals Hayes as an excellent writer, an adventurous arranger; generally one of the brothers soul needs most right now.

John – go to the

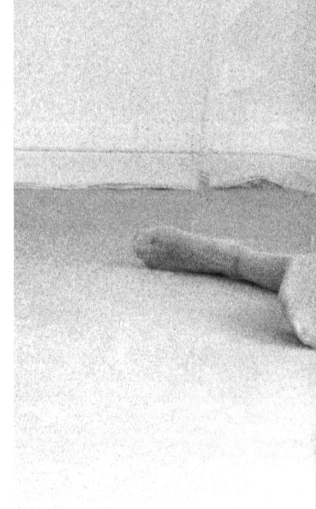

John Lennon and **Yoko Ono** interviewed in T.O.77 by
Tony Elliott

*'Grapefruit' is the Yoko Ono paperback just pub-
lished by Sphere Books. To launch its publication the
publicity conscious John and Yoko were interviewed
by virtually every newspaper in the country (The press
officer called to say did we want to interview Yoko
Ono? 'John Lennon's wife you know?' He promised
John would be there if we wanted to go). The interview
was done two weeks ago at the Lennon's Ascot home
as just one of a tightly scheduled day of similar encounters with the media.*

1971

John Lennon & Yoko Ono

John: We've had tons of shit thrown at us over the last two
years. I'm getting sick of it. It's just like I'm some guy who got
lucky and won the pools and that's me Hawaiian prize! So anyone who's met her before like you won't have that attitude about
her being a Hawaiian actress, etc!

Yoko: 'Grapefruit' is being published five or six years after
the first printing and I was afraid that it would be kind of
dated, so I read it again. I saw that things like my Touch
Poems have been translated into the Esslen psychiatric thing.
But there are still loads of things that have not been picked
up at all.

I think 'Grapefruit' is still relevant because it's like a frame
of mind and once you get into it it's easy for anyone to be an
artist. Everyone could start thinking like that and start doing
creative things. People would then forget about being violent
because it's a form of resentment, a way of showing to people
that they are not communicating. Violence is the saddest form
of communication because it's the kind that doesn't make it at
all. The best way to communicate is to open up your mind and
show what you're thinking.

John: *(reading through a previous interview with Yoko)* So
you were quite intelligent before I met you, love!

Yoko: You've got a very good deal and well you know it.
What I'm doing is to use a way of communication and if everyone picks it up it could promote peace.

Time Out: *The forms have changed though from the earlier years. Are you still doing the sculpture pieces and things like
the dance cards?*

Yoko: Yes. 'War Is Over If You Want It' posters was my idea.
I would have done that before if I had had the money. It was
possible because John was on my side. It's still like the dance
thing, but on a larger scale.

Time Out: *So you are conscious that financially you have the
opportunity to achieve more than most people can?*

Yoko: Yes. But it still isn't really very different. I want
'Grapefruit' to be pushed and I came back specially from New
York to do so.

John: It's a beautiful book that's more relevant than the
I Ching or the fucking Bible.

Yoko: I was poor and doing things like earning bread at
the time of writing 'Grapefruit'. Instead of getting a job where
I would have to work eight hours a day, I would get a janitor's job or something so that I could spend my time writing.
I used my head like that. In this society if you relieve yourself from thinking properly then you can do things better.
People inhibit themselves and every day spend energy and

oilet...

time killing themselves as human beings. John and I have a lot of energy because we don't kill ourselves and spend our energies.

John: The only thing we make money on is records. I can't help that and I'm not going to throw it down the drain now it's happening. The peace poster cost us £30,000. We subsidise ourselves like people used to subsidise classical music. We give relatively large sums of money away. It used to be to relatives, but now it's to people like gypsies. I try to get it or somehow cheat it from Apple Films or some angle. Once you get money people know it and charge you twice for everything. We think that's a fair peoples' tax!

Yoko: It means I can't make films cheaply any more, which was my pride and joy. So many things I used to get a kick out of I can't do any more, like I tried to live on nothing and tried to outdo the establishment by surviving like that.

John: I certainly don't agree with the philosophy that you can't be left-wing because you're rich. I just happen to be rich by a rather dubious process called show business. We're artists, so we're revolutionaries too. The other revolutionaries we meet, whether it's Jerry Rubin, Abbie Hoffman or Tariq Ali, agree that our place is as artists. We're revolutionary artists. All we're doing is exactly the same as when we met only instead of me being another poor artist I'm a rich artist. I was reading this other interview to see how she's changed, but she hasn't. We might get some museum shows for her in New York in the fall. She has plenty more ideas and concept shows to put on. It was hard to get them to do anything before she was Mrs Lennon.

The bed event was the result of us lying in bed together for a few months. When we first met we didn't get out of bed and we wanted to find something we could do together. She wanted me to go down to Trafalgar Square and stand there in a black bag like she used to. I said if I go down there I'll get killed and said let's go and do the most comfy thing. What we really like is being in bed, so we'll develop from things like that.

Yoko: We have to make money every day let's face it because we live in a society where money counts. But gradually we're doing various things. Everybody can be an artist, there's no necessary specialisation. The way we live here is exactly like I've always lived except that there's more people here and the place is larger.

John: It's a very large council house. It's got three bedrooms! Yoko hasn't changed at all. Here she is putting out 'Grapefruit' with the Dance Events in again. In the Syracuse exhibition, apart from some brand new ideas, there'll be a section with her past work from the Indica shows etc. I don't think the money will have changed her development as an artist.

Yoko: You know the art world is very snobbish. For instance I tried to do a show at the ICA. We went there and they were so snobbish! We said please give me a show exactly as you would another artist who you think is good. I made that point clear. But they had to go round saying that John was offering them some money so I could get into the ICA! 'World In Action' asked John to do a programme. I said why don't you include me and push my work because I felt it was important. They said how could she have the nerve! The whole atmosphere was terrible in those days – you know 'Yoko trying to use John's name' etc. I would have used any other circumstances.

John: Or any other lover… I'm her favourite husband you know.

Yoko: Even Sphere Books said are we going to get John Lennon as well for the autographing session? It's like sometimes I am just a way to get to him. Unless John goes to the toilet or something no-one speaks to me.

John: I turned on to rock and she turned me on to avant-garde or whatever you call it. In the early days she would be sitting in the Beatle sessions and would say 'Why is everything always four in the bar?' I would say that that was what we liked. To get there she had to do it intellectually. You know – a form of art that's a heartbeat, heartbeat is primitive, primitive means it's okay that's great. She really turned me on to film-making. I was just messing around with 8mm, but she made me do it properly. I love it. I want to have them on at the Odeon.

Yoko: We concentrate our minds in trying to free ourselves to do whatever we want and for that we need some money. It's like having a baby. It's a great drag for a woman, taking nine months and after eight you just count the days to go! Similarly some of the most beautiful things that happen take a slow time to work, and most impatient people just try and use violence instead of being patient and doing it like a woman has a baby. Do it gradually and then the whole world would really be peaceful.

John: It's got to be like natural law, Mother Nature or whatever. Our duty is to keep the balance rather than let it go the other way. The main problem today is to keep the balance.

Yoko: The next generation is going to be better, just an inch better. I know my generation is better than my mother's. 'Grapefruit' could help indirectly in the way my Touch Poems and concerts may have helped people to communicate better. If I've turned one person on then I'm happy. John and I have turned each other on and that's enough in a way.

Time Out: *Do you follow through completely? Like 'Cold Turkey' was about drug addiction, so have you done anything to help junkies?*

John: I'm not here to help junkies. Don't you see I have my own problems. I can't go around setting up schools for junkies, I have my own day to day problems with that scene. Singing 'Cold Turkey' is my contribution to junkies. I'm not telling people not to do it. All I'm saying is that it hurts. That's my contribution. I'm an artist – I'm not anything else so I sing about the pain I had with that situation. I can't give any more than art. Setting up a rehabilitation centre would be like sending a bag of rice to India.

Yoko: We're not that rich and the money we can give is relatively small. We give more in our songs and our work.

John: We have to go. How about just one more question?

Time Out: *Why don't you ask me one for a change?*

Yoko: Well what are you going to write about 'Grapefruit'? How much space do you think you'll give it? ●

Hollywood Babylon

Kenneth Anger interviewed in T.O.91, by **Tony Rayns** and **John DuCane**

'**M**y relationship with Hollywood began when I was four years old, when I realised that they had let my option drop. I saw myself with a future as a child actor, and decided they had made a terrible mistake by not signing me up for a lifetime contract. I'd be a willing capitalist slave to Jack Warner to this day, if they wanted it, the way lots of artists worked for Lorenzo de Medici – just, uh, bread and butter. Fuck politics, whether they're left or right-wing is immaterial to an artist, period.

The creative artist is divinely unscrupulous, and will accept any political creed that will allow him to express himself, no matter what form of subversion is necessary. We've seen this brilliantly illustrated in films this century by the 'Bolshevik' Eisenstein and the 'Nazi' Riefenstahl. Both of them were strictly only interested in themselves as creative artists.

So my relationship with Hollywood smacks of Aesop's fable of the Fox and the Grapes: over thirty years (and then some) I have developed a case of enormous, petrified, extremely sour grapes over the subject of Hollywood. There's that marvellous German word that explains the essence of the German soul – *Schadenfreude* – that particularly Hunnish pleasure in seeing your enemies fall to pieces in front of your eyes. All I've had to do is sit back and wait thirty years to see the whole empire of Hollywood Babylon crumble into dust.

I am a conservative, meaning that I cherish things of value. This places me at the antipodes of a cheap hustler like Andy Warhol, who is the garbage merchant of our time. And more power to him – he's got a lot of garbage to choose from, it's not very hard. He's chosen to paint pictures that he's very proud will chip off and fall to pieces in ten years.

My approach to art is the Egyptian one, and I am building for eternity. You might as well make it in steel or carve it in the hardest granite. If it's the statue of the god or goddess you adore and it takes you twenty years to make, the chances are that an eye, a smile, a wrist or something of that figure is going to survive, maybe even when mankind is just a question mark in future archaeology.

Before I started making movies, I made puppet shows, and I'd do Chinese legends that I wrote myself – they were always Oriental. One was called 'The Banana' – that was my first script. I may still be making it, I think you're doomed to repeat yourself in that department, the first love somehow lingers.' ●

Oh, really?

Andy Warhol (& friends) interviewed in T.O.59, by **Terry Krueger**

In case you hadn't noticed, Andy Warhol, complete with friends and superstars, was in London last week to open his show at the Tate. This interview was controlled, or rather non-controlled, in the typical Warhol manner. He once said, 'The interviewer should just tell me the words he wants me to say and I'll repeat them after him'. Warhol is like the eye of a hurricane, calm, quiet but the reason for and source of all activity around him. You begin to confess to him or rather define your role in this particular movie, much the same way his films were conceived. The following is a case in point.

Time Out: *The show that's at the Tate, has that been going around?*

John Coplans: [Editor of *Art Forum* magazine] We never put on the same show twice. Thirty-two Campbell soup cans are missing, which are very key, and a lot of other paintings as well, and the space is very bulky, and they chopped it up a lot, I don't know what they've done with those Brillo boxes, I would have liked to have done them myself, but I couldn't interfere. Where the cows are should be where the Brillo boxes are, and they should have been expanded. I hollowed out the center of the boxes and sort of let them spill right out; now they look like a piece of cake. I mean they tried very hard, given the kind of people they really are, you know, they're very lazy, but they have tried.

Time Out: *How do you feel when your paintings get shown in places like the Tate?*

Andy Warhol: Well, Irving…?

John Coplans: That's exactly where they should be, shown for as good as they are, Andy's a good artist.

Time Out: *But what about the movies?*

Irving Blum: [New York art dealer] But it's another thing, they have their own consequences, they aren't together…

John Coplans: They should be seen another time in the right way, and to confuse the two is to denigrate from his act as a

Stagestruck

from T.O.58, by **Tony Allan**

Witchcraft arrived on the English stage with a heavy thud at the Hendon Classic late last Saturday night, when Alex Sanders, 'The World's Greatest White Witch', performed a couple of rituals before an audience of around 1,000 people. The posters had promised 'a night you will never forget', and for once they weren't far wrong.

The programme started with Sanders and his wife, accompanied by a troupe of lesser witches, performing one of the most important of their rituals, the Drawing Down of the Moon – though as there weren't any programmes or explanatory messages, very few people had any

idea what was going on. The ritual itself was slow-moving and quite beautiful, accompanied by Gregorian chants and tape-recorder invocations to bring the moon-power down. The atmosphere was suitably Dennis Wheatley, and apart from a few nervous giggles, the audience seemed attentive and quite impressed.

The second half was less predictable. As the audience settled back in their seats an announcement came over the PA speakers that the Sanders would be under great stress during the next ritual and warning that witchcraft was not for those of a nervous disposition. Then the curtains swung back to the sounds of 'Thus Spake Zarathustra', revealing a small man in a big goat-head devil mask

painter; that is my view and I took that very strictly, that view.

Time Out: *Are you still painting now?*

Andy Warhol: Uhhh no...

Time Out: *Why? Do you like films better?*

Andy Warhol: Oooo ya...

Time Out: *For what particular reason ?*

Andy Warhol: Uhhh, mmmm, I don't know?

Time Out: *Would you go back to painting?*

Andy Warhol: No, mmm, I think the art in New York now is so great, so different!

Time Out: *Did you choose all those images originally, you know, soup cans?*

Andy Warhol: Mmmmm, ya...

Time Out: *Most of the things in the show?*

Andy Warhol: They were just from magazines.

Time Out: *We were wondering, when you work in the film media, do you choose people for an image?*

Andy Warhol: No, they were just pictures from magazines and the people were people we just used for movies...

Time Out: *Doesn't it worry you that your films don't get shown as well as your paintings?*

Andy Warhol: Mmmmmm, no ...

Time Out: *Do you decide what is to be shown?*

Andy Warhol: Mmmmm, noo ...

Time Out: *Do you like to be famous? I mean the BBC and all.*

Andy Warhol: You're on television one night, then they know you the next two nights, otherwise they don't know you at all.

Time Out: *Do you feel hassled by people still?*

Andy Warhol: No, not at all...

Time Out: *Would you do things for other people, helping them produce their works of art?*

Andy Warhol: We have some, ah, you know, mmmmm, ummm, it's hard thing to do because there are so many people that don't pay, so I mean any money we get we put into the movies.

Time Out: *What's the highest one of your paintings ever sold for?*

Andy Warhol: Uhh, what was the highest?

Irving Blum: I would say sixty thousand.

Time Out: *Does the value mean anything to you?*

Andy Warhol: Mmmmm, no. Wasn't it a rigged job?

Irving Blum: No not at all, well it might have been in some way rigged. Finally it worked! Had it not been rigged it would have been sold for something very close to that.

Andy Warhol: No, I mean there are auctions that... I just know three or four people that work for... and when you really try to buy something they really do try to make the prices go up; it's all so funny. No I mean anything, it's all so funny the way they make the prices go up, but it's certainly exciting!

Time Out: *Do your films make money?*

Andy Warhol: Mmmm, not yet... they just make enough to do other films.

Time Out: *Do you construct them within a certain budget?*

Andy Warhol: Oh they're very cheap, about 4,000 dollars.

Time Out: *If one of your paintings was sold for a million dollars, what would you think of that?*

Andy Warhol: I guess I don't think about it 'cause we never get any money out of it, or anything.

Time Out: *Just the premium put on it; does that mean anything to you at all?*

Andy Warhol: Mmmmmm, noooooo, because you can't do another picture and sell it for the same amount anyway, so it doesn't matter.

Time Out: *So in a sense they're worthless?*

Andy Warhol: Mmmmmm, yaaaa...

Time Out: *Can I have one?*

Andy Warhol: Ahh, ohh, I don't have any... but we can uhh just make one... I think someone is making some, you know posters and that... ●

sitting on a black throne. In front of him a celebrant was making obeisance. The 2001 soundtrack faded into silence. Then, incongruously, amplified guitar rang through the speakers and the stage was suddenly full of dancing girls in multi-coloured transparent robes and men in little black cache-sexes, freaking to Black Widow's 'Come to the Sabbat'. With the Demon God behind, it all looked a bit like the worship of the Golden Calf as seen by Cecil B DeMille. Next, Maxine Sanders made her appearance. A blue spotlight caught her, apparently in a trance, halfway down the cinema's central aisle. She slowly found her way up the ramp leading to the stage, where her husband was waiting inside the protected circle to meet her. It was at this point that things started to go wrong.

According to Alex Sanders afterwards, what happened was that, fearing that his wife in her trance was going to fall down the ramp, he made the mistake of coming out of the circle in order to catch her. What the audience saw was a sudden upping of the tempo of events on stage. The Sanders and the other witches ran wildly round and through the circle, candles and incense burners were knocked flying, one girl fled down the ramp and ran shrieking up the central aisle, and Maxine, wielding a flail, began to beat her husband viciously, who seemed to be on the point of retaliating with the ceremonial sword. Then she slumped to the ground, apparently straight onto one of the upturned incense burners, and at this slightly hysterical point the music was cut off abruptly and the curtains closed.

The house lights came up and for a minute or more the audience sat waiting for something to happen. Then the management announced over the loudspeakers that Maxine Sanders was hurt and receiving medical attention and would the audience please leave. At the back of the hall somebody started slow hand-clapping and others took it up nearer the front. Gradually people began to filter out into the foyer, where, under the eyes of the local constabulary, a mixed crowd of shocked citizens and disappointed thrill-seekers gathered, demanding their money back. ●

Mick Jagger

It was taken for granted that I would do anything

Mick Jagger interviewed in T.O.63 by **Tony Elliott**

'Performance' was written by Donald Cammell and directed by Cammell and Nick Roeg. Mick Jagger's role in the film as an ageing rock and roll recluse inevitably provoked debate as to just how much of Jagger himself is revealed in Turner's character. Here Mick Jagger talks openly about the film and himself.

I think Turner is a projection of Donald's fantasy or idea of what I imagine how I am. The thing is that it's very easy for people to believe that's what I'm like. It was easy to do – in a way – because it's just another facet of me – if I felt inclined to go that way. But now when I look at it there's so many things I could have done to make it stranger, or to make it more real – to my mind – of how Turner would be and how he would live. I think it was a bit too much like me in a few ways. But he's not quite hopeless enough.

I don't think there's many people like that individual. I found his intellectual posturing very ridiculous – that's what sort of fucked him up. Too much intellectual posturing in

'I get very aroused by music, but it doesn't arouse me violently.'

the bath when you're with two women is not a good thing. That's not to be taken too seriously! It made me skin go all funny! I know people like that.

It isn't me really. You just get into the part – that's acting isn't it? You just get into the feeling of that person and I got into feeling like that. You know you don't want to make any decisions, and there's certain things you know you've got to do, and there's certain things in your fate that you know. Some people like to sit down and get really involved in the things that they know and some people just want to take what they are and just carry on. Turner was just a person who'd stopped all that and

become very tuned in to it. After a while you really get into thinking like that and driving everyone crazy. I drove everyone a bit crazy, I think, during that time. It was all taken for granted that I would do anything!

At the time I couldn't see the film because I was very hung up about it. I'd rather it had come out. It should have been out years ago. I still think it's a good film. But I think it was a better film two years ago.

I feel I did create something. It was enjoyable as far as that's concerned. That's what made it such hard work. Although you can say it was contributing something creative, it wasn't shot with one camera taking Anita [Pallenberg] and I out into the middle of nowhere for three days and saying this is the sort of feeling we want you to have. It was shot just like a regular movie. You had to know what you were doing before you got on camera. It wasn't just a question of improvising for hours and hours. We had to work it all out before otherwise you just got in a mess. We'd suddenly stop shooting one day because I'd say I wasn't going to say those lines. There were all kinds of situations like that and the regular technicians would go 'Blimey I've never seen anything like it!' and all that. Donald's whole thing is casting people for what they are and how they fit into the part, to make them work out and create the part, rather to work on things that were already in their minds.

There's two important things about the film to Donald. There's the sexual thing – not only physically sexual, but the interrelating of the sexes and the interchanging of roles. And the role of violence and the role of women, vis-a-vis the role of violence of a man. How the two things can balance each other out. And the ritualistic significance of violence. That's one of the main themes if you can gain any conclusion out of it. Donald's really hung up on the ritual of violence not being the thing anymore where certain people can go through certain moods – like a tournament or a small war – but now that that's not being used anymore that's very dangerous.

He's deploring the lack of ritual in violence. The way of coping with the violence is to sort of act it out theatrically. I personally

don't feel I have to do it. Part of me does. But some people do. There are some people in our society who have to do so to deal with it or to deal with that part of you and therefore that part of the majority need to stage some kind of violence.

I don't understand the connection between music and violence. Donald's always trying to explain it to me and I just blindly carry on. I just know that I get very aroused by music, but it doesn't arouse me violently. I never

"Unscrew locks, smash tannoys, paint blackboards red, grind all the chalk to dust."
Children's Angry Brigade at one with the education system

"It is a very good thing the line has been drawn."
Mary Whitehouse on the *Oz* trial

"You won't outlive this, old man."
Charles Manson advises the judge after his trial for murder

"Dangerous drugs – explosives – immigration – law and order – just a few of the interesting subjects you could meet in clerical work at the Home Office."
Home Office recruitment advertisement

"Clunk click every trip."
Department of Transport ad for safety belts

"In extreme cases marijuana can so destroy a man's character that he mixes freely with persons of another race."
Extract from a South African textbook on criminology

"What we get is closer to rock bottom than rock opera."
Critic John Simon on 'Jesus Christ Superstar'

"The only way to get an all-volunteer army is to draft it."
F Edward Herbert, Chairman of US House Armed Services Committee

"Things will never be quite the same again."
An anonymous French government official after the UK joins the EEC

"Politics is the art of the possible."
RA Butler, paraphrasing Bismarck

"General Amin, a beefy, soft-spoken man of the Madi tribe, sets an example of self-restraint. First reports seem to suggest... a military which, with any luck, may turn out to be of like nature and ambitions to those which have successfully brought law and order and relatively clean administration to Ghana and Nigeria."
The *Daily Telegraph* gets it badly wrong

went to a rock and roll show and wanted to smash the windows or beat anybody up afterwards. I feel more sexual than actually physically violent. I get a sexual feeling and I want to fuck as soon as I've been playing. I cool down very quickly. I can come off the stage and be back to normal in five minutes. You can only really get into the feeling if you're with a group of people like that. The only time I've felt violent was in some street demonstration and you really get the feeling of being in with a crowd which wants to do something and you get really carried along whether they're right or wrong. Whether the policeman is doing his job or whether the cause that you're hitting the policeman for is really right, what's it fucking matter? The point is that the act of violence is more powerful than the intellectual political act. I never felt that feeling in a crowd with music although I've felt very turned on but not like that. ●

balls on the rail

'We're the only rock band on the face of this planet that knows what rock and roll is all about.'

Pete Townshend interviewed in T.O.80, by **Al Clark**

How has your encounter with Meher Baba affected your writing?

Well, the effect has become very clear. I mean, 'Tommy' has got a mystical thread flowing through it, and it's about the spiritual evolution of a man rather than about the sub-teenage frustrations I used to write about before. But most of all it's affected my writing by changing me as an individual, by making me less panicky and more committed to living my life minute to minute. Previous to being involved with Meher Baba I tended to weigh things up very carefully whereas now I'm much more impulsive, I just sort of chase my karma around with the feeling that Baba's got his thumb on my head, so everything's all right. At the same time I haven't

changed that much, I've still got a bad temper and I'm fairly aggressive as a musician.

On the visits I've made to the Baba Centre, I've always been very struck by the general irreverence of everybody and that mixture of amusement and terror that you get when you realise you're in a place and something just might happen… like committing yourself

That's part of the excitement of course. The point being that you make that incredible gesture. I *commit myself.* There. Done. Right. All right then, take me wherever it is I'm going. But of course you're going nowhere, nothing changes and all you're doing is committing yourself to yourself. If you really work at it and

sustain a solid focus, you can get a fantastic amount of just straight exhilaration and amusement out of life, because you're in a position to see things from the ideal point of view, which is your own, instead of always looking at things from other people's point of view.

I'm always roaring with laughter when I find myself doing something that I've decided I'm not going to do anymore. I mean, I was once in a hotel room halfway through an American tour, very sexually frustrated, masturbating away, and suddenly realised what I was doing and roared with laughter. I just found that very funny and thought that it brought right into perspective what may be the blight of a lot of people's lives.

Have the other members of the Who at any stage become involved with Baba in their own way?

(Laughs) No. It's very weird to be in a group like the Who and feel that you're at a totally different stage of spiritual evolution from the others, and yet at the same stage of physical evolution. We're all very similar as physical bodies, we enjoy the same degree of self-punishment, the same music, we enjoy playing together and so on, but we have different basic ethics of how to live our lives and they don't cross. Deeply written in Who philosophy is the fact that each member thinks the other guy's way is total bullshit but-it's-all-right-by-me. I may be putting words in people's mouths, but that's probably true.

So let's say I'm tolerated in my mystical beliefs, although I should imagine there's a bit of a fear in the group that I might grow my hair down my back and start putting out solo

'...if you could say what I'm going to do is go and live on a rock farm.'

albums about... do a George Harrison basically. I don't really think there's any danger of that because I would never broach the subject of self-awareness as close to my work as Harrison has. A prime example is Inayat Khan who wrote the Sufi literature, started the Sufi indoctrination in the States, and was also a master musician who played the vina. He was *the* bloody master musician. When you went to one of his concerts, you were taken out of your body, I mean that's literally what happened, ridden and riddled and taken out of your ego and removed from yourself and GOD, GOD, GOD. Well he stopped and just started to teach, but he never tried to teach or preach while he was a musician. He stopped being a musician and then went to teach and preach. I don't think I've ever heard a man who has spoken more truth to me than Dylan, but he's never preached in a song and yet I'm sure he's got a lot of good sense that he could lay on me. I'm not knocking Harrison incidentally, 'cos he's a sincere guy.

OK. What are the Who going to be up to next?

For a start we're going to wind up for ourselves the cycle that Tommy created, rather than have it wound up by other people on our behalf. What we've naturally tended to do is say that 'Tommy' can go on and become whatever it wants to do, and we'll remain being the 'oo and come up with another incredible first.

But really I think the time is too delicate to do that now in rock because it's at a period in which

a first ain't gonna come unless it's embodied in a different way of living rock music. People are looking to a different area of rock for their answers, and that's the music itself, which they're finding more and more is completely empty. And that's basically because one of the problems of any creative form is that someone starts something off, and by the time you get to the end, everyone's bastardised each other so much that they've created a very solid format from which they can't escape.

And worse than that is the bastardisation by rock of things that were dying in other show-business forms. Like the theatre: going and paying your money, queueing outside, going in and seeing the group from 7.30 till 9.30, and then going home. That's *terrible*, right? Yet rock picked it up and said well this is good. I mean, good riddance to fucking Bill Graham, much as I love him, and hopefully to Woodstock and all its other boogaloos. I think what needs to happen now is some rock situation, possibly paid for by a film company, some rock situation which is real, which it creates itself and which because it happens on film will show the way if you like. But rock has got to be taken out of concert halls and football stadiums, and off records, and Radio One and AM radio and FM radio in the States which began well but is now incredibly distorted and corrupt.

I really look on the Who as one of the few bands that could ever pull it off. We've pulled it off before and I think we can pull it off again. We want to make a film. I'd like to get 2000 people and just live with them for six months, feeding and clothing them, and not as a power trip, I mean, I'd be included too.

Didn't your project at the Young Vic embrace a little of that, in that the audience were meant to be a part of it and remain with you for long periods?

Yeah, but what actually happened was that we got on the stage and people wanted to see the Who's new *act*. The Young Vic is after all a theatre, it's not a field. It would strike me as being an incredible scene if you could say: I'm not going to buy a rock album, I'm not going to go and see a rock movie, I'm not going to go and hear a rock opera, what I'm going to do is go and live on a rock farm. A tattooist friend of mine round the corner has written a script called 'Guitar Farm' which will be an island somewhere, and you go there and you live fucking rock and roll, you bang the walls and it comes out. I think that's what it's going to have to be all about.

People can still tour, like a circus does, but rock has used up its audience, the sideshows have got predictable, and what eventually is going to to happen is that the circus is going to come into town and it's going to pack out as usual. But everybody's going to sit there bored, because that's the way it used to be, the circus came to town and you automatically went to it.

And yet you knew what was going to fuckin' happen, the geezer was going to fight with a lion, and the clown was going to come out and throw a bucket of confetti over you, and the same old things over and over again... until eventually one day the circus doesn't come to town.

That is what is happening to rock. I admit it'll take six years or more to finish up, but it's inevitably going to happen unless it's steered off in another direction.

The next stage in rock must embody itself, not just four new guys with a different kind of haircut playing Moog synthesizers – the thought of which horrifies me – but a whole new way for creative people to reach their audience, a new form of performance, the way that performance happens, the way musicians are remunerated, what people pay and everything. It's difficult to be optimistic about rock when most of it sounds like it's been conceived around tables in managers' or accountants' offices. Its possibilities may be boundless but its actual state is terrible. This is absolutely true.

In fact, sometimes I really do believe that we're the only rock band on the face of this planet that knows what rock and roll is all about. It's not understanding the technicalities of it, it's doing it, and the Who have done it all the way down the line. There are thousands of great groups and thousands of great rock people, but most of them have got tied up somewhere.

To put it another way, we want to be a rock band. If there ain't no rock and roll, you can't be a rock band, you've got to be cabaret artists. If it's possible for us in our position to create any sort of push or excitement in the rock business which is going to allow us to remain a rock band, we're going to do it. We don't care if it's the biggest fucking disaster of all time, and that we end up looking like total cunts, and that we never make another penny playing music in our lives. Somebody's got to do it, and until you put your balls on the rails it really isn't going to happen.

I'd do anything to make a living, but I can't do anything as a rock musician. I can't go on playing for much longer with things as they are, not so much because I don't like the set-up – I mean the idea of being a bastard and flashing about in a yankee car was what originally gave me my ambition – but because somewhere along the line somebody has taken away the audience that stands in front of you at a concert and feeds you the information you need to do a good show.

The Who are rapidly becoming a circus act, one of those who always get good reviews in the *Melody Maker*'s 'Caught in the Act' because they are simply going through the motions. Because we're a very expert group, we don't make mistakes, we know what they want. We do what we've always done, it's good in its way, but it's like a good circus act. I'm not deriding the Who for fuck's sake, but when it was real it was a lot better. Yeah, we're going to put our balls on the rails I think. ●

Sweet Sweetback's Baadassssss Song

Melvin Van Peebles interviewed in T.O.97, by **Jim Pines**

You bled my momma…
you bled my poppa…
but you won't bleed me!

Melvin Van Peebles' latest right-on film 'Sweet Sweetback's Baadasssss Song' hit the US like a Nuclear Black Bomber. The Black Panther newspaper devoted a whole issue to it and Huey P Newton made the book required reading for all Panthers. Embarrassed Knee-Grows got together to boycott 'Sweetback' and one cinema owner went as far as to cut the film at his personal convenience. He was sued of course.

'Sweetback' is a unique film, black and otherwise. It's also an impressive example of a 'do-it-yourself writer/director' blowing the scene wide open with complete disregard for conventionality.

Typically, Britain has banned the film through its bullshit censorship, and unless people here kick up a storm, it won't ever get here.

Hollywood has now realised the commercial potential of a growing black audience. And obviously 'Sweetback' had some kind of effect.

Fuck, what do you mean 'Sweetback' had some kind of effect… 'Sweetback' *was* the effect, it was the cause man.

How would you define that cause? In what way would it work?

There's goddamn nothing to define man. The film hit like it was out of your fuckin' mind. I did it. Now everybody says, 'Oh, you know there's a black audience'. No shit.

Do you see this as some kind of movement that could…

…Fuck the movement. I just hope they gonna get together and start making their own films. Yeah, I hope so. Hey, you know, I just do it. Muthafuckas still mumbling and talking about 'We gonna do this…' Shiiit, I hit 'em before they get the news. That's it, it's done. And then they are all discussing on my territory now. Ahhh man, you see, if we used the audacity we do in chasing pussy… in business, then we'd be something else. Where I bogard my bread from, cats would kill me if I don't pay out. How can you take a risk like that! Say man, I climb in some husband's wife and get killed on the humble, huh. Dig what I'm saying? If you want it man… you know… goddamn slave minds we have. The whole thing is decolonising the mind. I looked in the mirror one day and I said 'You are the studio.' I am the studio. 'Sweetback's outgrossing muthafuckin' Columbia man, with all them people running around there. And tell you another muthafuckin' thing, I own the film a hundred percent… Ain't nobody owns a major film… I own the muthafucka a hundred fuckin' percent. Nobody say nothing. You can laugh, it's alright. Making a film and making them call it 'Sweet Sweetback's Baadasssss Song' and putting it up. That's revolution; that's saying 'We're somebody!' Not 'The Ballad of the Indomitable Sweetback'. Hey! And that's where kickin' ass and taking names comes in. All the rest is bullshit… all the rest is fuckin' bullshit. ●

The *OZ* trial

from T.O.61

The *OZ* magazine obscenity trial has been postponed until early July, but not without some more hassles for *OZ* personnel. Judge Mervyn Griffith-Jones allowed the postponements, 'before he saw our haircuts,' as *OZ*-men Felix Dennis and Richard Neville laughingly put it. As the two left the Old Bailey they were photographed by *Time Out* photographer Keith Morris, though Old Bailey minions rushed up shouting 'No, no, stop, no pictures.' With pre-planned efficiency, the fruit of bitter experience, the camera was rapidly passed around allowing the film to be removed to safety.

Felix Dennis then laid verbally into the minions and one proceeded to drag him into the Old Bailey and then backed him against a wall. 'He stank of drink,' said Felix, 'and kept shouting at me, "I wish we weren't in here. I'd like to get you down a dark alley and kick your fucking face in, you dirty hippie".' ●

1972

We officially waved goodbye to the '60s and said hello to David Cassidy, The Osmonds and the silver shoulders and platform shoes of glam rock, as well as the computer, which, though slow and unhealthy-looking, had finally turned up at work. While we sat in candlelight waiting for the power cuts to end, Nixon was busily (and secretly) bombing Cambodia and Idi Amin was kicking people out of Uganda. We had a 'war' over cod.

Deliverance
Terrific boy's own adventure stuff with adult ingredients of graphic mutilation and buggery, but Boorman is never content either to leave it at that or sub-scribe to the ecological concerns of James Dickey's novel.

Dirty Harry
'Dirty Harry' isn't a film to celebrate; it's too uncomfortable for that.

The Godfather
Like the 'Ten Comm-andments', 'The God-father' shows us the wielding of power like we've never seen before. It's not conc-eivably an action or gangster movie, more of a spectacular.

Tim Buckley - Greetings From LA (Warner Bros)
This is the most spectacularly sung,

played, arranged and produced record I've heard this year.

David Bowie - The Rise And Fall Of Ziggy Stardust And The Spiders From Mars (RCA)
This confirms that David Bowie is one of the few performers capable of tearing to shreds the predo-minant aesthetic preconceptions:

an album of undeniable hair-raising brilliance.

Rolling Stones - Exile On Main Street (RS)
Another improbable yet hugely successful double LP, with the Stones making their own definitive state-ments on how it feels. 'Exile' is the great monument to lethargy and disease.

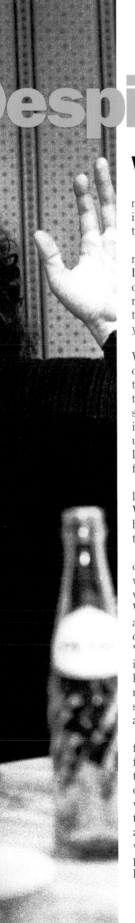

Whatever else Lou Reed may be, he's certainly a rock 'n' roller. He started out professionally by writing 'tons of shit' for cheap labels after playing Top Ten numbers in various bands for a few years. From that to forming the Velvets with John Cale seems quite a jump. What was the link with Cale?

'We both liked rock 'n' roll… and we were the only people running around with long hair; we kinda had to stick together. In those days old women would avoid you on the bus. If you could get a seat it was kinda nice. Now there's a lot of vipers running around with long hair', he says, looking me straight in the eye. Ask him why Cale left the group, and he doesn't waste your time: 'That's private'.

After Reed and Cale had got the band working, they met Warhol. 'Friends of ours were involved in the art scene… and one of the people they brought round was Andy. And he heard the music and he said "Oh, wow!" Which is what he kinda says to everything so it doesn't really mean very much. But then he said "It would be really nice if I showed movies and you played in front of the movies…" and from there it was "Why don't we use strobe lights" and "Why don't we use slides?"… and the light show was born as far as New York was concerned. The first rock 'n' roll light show'.

'The whole thing was fabulous,' he says. But there were problems. 'First of all, people thought we were a put-on: Andy Warhol's a put-on so we must be a put-on. We must not know how to play, the whole thing's gotta be camp… it just seemed that we'd never be able to break that, it just went on for ever.'

He denies that the Velvets were conscious of themselves as outrageous or as innovators. 'It seemed so logical to do what we were doing. We couldn't understand the reaction. People would tell us it was violent, it was grotesque, it was perverted. We said – "What the fuck are you talking about? It's fun. Look at all these people having fun" – And these reviews would come out and say "Warhol-Velvet-Underground electro-shock-New York", and violent, depraved. And we'd say, "Jesus Christ, what is this, what are we doing? We're playing rock 'n' roll with some lights going on". So we didn't pay attention to them and we didn't think of ourselves as originators – although later in retrospect, I can look back and say, "Hey, as a matter of fact we were and we did".'

But an awareness of being a bit unusual was to some extent forced on them. There was MGM's distinct lack of enthusiasm, for a start. 'The record company never did shit for us… and that, of course, is one of the reasons that we could put out some of the songs we put put, precisely because (1) they didn't know we existed, (2) they couldn't listen to our albums for more than three records. They would just listen to it and say "Oh my God" and take it off and ship it out… But the "evil" image, I suppose was because we came out with an overt drug song that wasn't pro or con, it was just there. And because we did "Venus in Furs", I suppose… feedback, it sounded violent. So I can now

amputations

understand, now that I have some kind of perspective, why people might have been a little taken aback.'

The records were consistently banned by the radio stations, of course. 'We put out "Here She Comes Now" in San Francisco and they said "That's about a girl coming", and I said "Well, no it's not, it's about somebody coming into a room". And then I listened to the record and I realised it probably was about a girl coming as a matter of fact, but then again, so what? But we were banned again… Half the time I really don't know what I'm writing about. I won't know till it's all over and I have a bit of time to take a look back at it'.

Most of the ironies and ambiguities in his lyrics are carefully calculated, however, and he's keenly aware of other kinds of detail. Take 'The Gift': 'One of the things I've always regretted is that when Waldo gets stabbed in the head I put a wrench into a canteloupe on the track and you can't really hear it. It's supposed to go 'squish'. It wasn't loud enough. Then some people have said to me the timing is wrong for the squish. It should have been before you said the line or it should have been after. And other people have said the hippest thing would be not to have it at all. You just get it from all sides.' He calls the track 'a funny case history of paranoia'.

There's a line in 'The Gift': 'It was more than human mind could bear', which comes pretty close to summing up the whole character of the 'White Light/White Heat' album, particularly the second side, and I asked him if he ever saw the Velvets' heavier stuff as a kind of musical image of a prolonged scream. 'Yeah, well… yeah, right. We wanted to go as high and hard as we could. And then finally we went as far as I thought we could go with that. So the third album was a turnaround. People said to me it was a sell-out, or 'They censored you'. I know we could have continued in the vein of the first two albums… put out another drug song, another violent song. I just said no'.

When he began work on his solo LP he came to the Morgan studios in London in search of the kind of sound achieved there by Rod Stewart, Cat Stevens and the Kinks, among others. It's the first on which he's been happy with the production, and he regrets that the Velvets' records were so weak in that respect (he says he thinks their third album sounds like it was recorded in somebody's bathroom). 'But they have a nice rough quality… it's got all that energy, and if you happen to listen to the lyrics they'll take you someplace you may not have been. You may not want to go there, but if you want to, it's there.'

He has no intention of going back to 'White Light' himself. 'That's an album that I listen to as rarely as possible. "Sister Ray" can really clean you out if you're in a certain mood. But I try to avoid those moods if I can'. '"The Murder Mystery" was a track that suffered particularly from the recording quality, but he can't imagine re-recording it. 'It's about so many things that I don't want to… I mean I couldn't go through the lyrics again 'cause the trip they would put me on would be… I just couldn't handle it. 'Cause that was then and I'd rather stay

where I am now than go back to where that was. I mean, if you follow the albums it's a gradual straightening-out in a way.' He can't listen to 'Heroin' now either: 'John's viola was so furious and anguished and excruciating… that track tears me apart and I don't want to know about it any more.'

Nevertheless, there's a cut on the new LP called 'The Ocean'. 'It evokes the ocean in a fairly unpleasant manner', he says, 'A guy goes mad on the track, and obviously goes mad. The ocean engulfs him. You can hear, like, witches in the background saying "Here come the wa-a-a-ves". It gets very eerie'. But he doesn't see himself as a kind of spokesman for social cripples and outsiders, as has been suggested. 'All I really mean is that the person on that track is one example of a mad person, in a mad situation… like a lot of my friends are mad, but aren't we all? Who isn't? Especially in cities… My God.

'I don't think we've ever taken a moral stance. We present characters and situations and however you look at I them I guess is your stance. My stance is to put them out of the way. I see them the way they are. But I keep my views of them to myself, except I express the way I think they are. For instance there are some characters that I wouldn't allow in my house – if I had a house'. The guy in 'Heroin', for one: 'I wouldn't be too interested in having him around. He'd probably, rip me off.'

He describes how in the early days, people would come up to him and tell him how 'Heroin' really turned them on to heroin. 'So my reaction to that is, what if I wrote a song about suicide, schmuck?… All I meant to be was like a channel, like information about certain things… Music can entertain, music can do this and it can do that; the things that I get kind of interested in

> **'People would tell us it was violent, it was grotesque, it was perverted. We said – "What the fuck are you talking out?"'**

are (1) dancing and (2) introducing to a story, a set of characters that might involve them and get them to meet somebody else.'

In 'Sweet Jane', there's a line 'Me, I'm in a rock 'n' roll band. Huh!' Everyone leapt on it: there'd been a big switch in his attitude to what a musician could or should do, right? 'Everybody goes through their changes', he says. 'I don't even know if change means you move forward or anything. All I kinda know is that change just means… you change'. To most people 'Loaded' seemed a lot more buoyant than the earlier stuff; but he demurs. 'Not "up" exactly; just the passage through different scenes that everybody goes through who's in an urban life. And it works its way finally to a point like where I've got it now, where I don't have to concentrate on any one area'. So where does he think he might go next? 'I don't know. I'll be intrigued to find out'. ●

Captain Beefheart
interviewed in T.O. 120,
by **Ian Pollock**

'Everyone should go fly a kite'

Captain Beefheart feels that much of the poverty of modern life is connected to the divorce between ourselves and natural things like organic shapes and colours. He commented some time ago on the decline in kite-flying as a clear indicator of this malaise. Well, as he was staying near Hyde Park, I mentioned the kite-flyers that played there.

– I've been watching them, they're real nice. Everybody ought to go fly a kite. You feel the wind and that strain. Put a brush in your hand and do the canvas like the wind does the kite.

– They have some beautiful kites, one is like a huge hawk.

– Well, if they do that maybe they'll appreciate how beautiful the hawk is and won't shoot him out of the air. You know, if they can feel the way that feathers feel… It's a good way to see over the hill, you know what I mean, you put your eyes in the kite and you can see over the hill.

– To see?

– Without seeing with your eyes. I think the hill is eye consciousness, you know just seeing everything with your eyes, like interpreting who a person is on first glance without feeling them, with your eyes shut. You don't have to shut your eyes physically, but I mean you should look deeper than just the way they look.

– But everyone has their own hills, don't you think?

– Anthills, or own hills… no, I'm only teasing. I think that a lot of those hills have been put there out of fear. I think that the long blackdress and fear of the female ankle and the worry about private parts and all these things are ridiculous. Now I don't say that everyone should jump out of their clothes and run around naked, I think that's really ridiculous, they'd freeze to death and get sunburnt, but I think that everybody that's taking a shower shouldn't be that embarrassed. The rain when it falls hits everybody, everybody takes the same shower. Water is the cheapest drink, now, but the glass is the lowest.

Beefheart seems to be entranced by vacuum cleaners. He is shown holding one in the little photo on the sleeve of Zappa's 'Hot Rats' and there is a photo of him performing in Washington with several huge industrial cleaners draped in and out of the sound equipment. It emerged that these pleasant creatures had important lessons for us too.

Procol Harum

in T.O. 111, by **Al Clark**

There's little doubt, even now, that 'A Whiter Shade of Pale' was the descant of its day, the all-purpose reference point, the popular funeral march of wiped-out, candlelit melancholia. But at the same time, many regarded it as complete in itself, the beginning and end of Procol Harum's effective contribution to music. And drool-hungry reporters and disc-jockeys used to find Procol Harum so unresponsive that their interviews have become a legend, comparable in their obtuseness to Dylan's famous mid-'60s confrontations.

Remember this one?

Interviewer: What do the rather obscure lyrics of 'A Whiter Shade of Pale' mean?

Gary Brooker: Nothing in particular, man.

Interviewer: Do you regard what you wrote as good music?

Gary Brooker: It's just a song.

Interviewer: I suppose everyone will have forgotten about it in two weeks.

Gary Brooker: Sure, man.

Interviewer: Doesn't that worry you?

Gary Brooker: No.

Ravi Shankar

interviewed in T.O. 140,
by **Jan Murray**

'There was a period of about two years, after the Beatles business, that everywhere I went I was mobbed. I even had what you call groupies. My God, I like women very much, but I did not like those groupies – absolutely I did not. They were so forced, so artificial. Now the hysteria has died away and only the people with a serious interest in Indian music are left.

'I like many of the rock musicians and certainly my friendship with the Beatles helped to attract young people to my music. I am very grateful for that. George no longer plays the sitar but we are still good friends and he continues to study the religious philosophies of my country. (I was very angry with the Beatles over that silly business with the Maharishi, but that is finished now, thank goodness.) But it isn't true to say that the Beatles' influence brought me a new audience. I had been building a following among the young for a long time before I met George in 1966.

–I think that you can look at a vacuum cleaner and find out a lot of things, like the dust, you know, they collect a lot of dust and dirt and everything. You can find out what somebody's had for dinner, or you can find out what they do, or how they walk, which is far out.

–You've never written a song about them; because they'll be in the Smithsonian someday.

–Sure will, and one day I will, like it's... to see the world, in an Oldsmobile.

At this point, the Captain began whistling a tune that sounded awfully familiar, but which I couldn't place until he continued:

–Remember that. Holiday 88 (a TV show I think). That was when everything got real pointed. Like the DC3 as opposed to the F104 or the Boeing. I mean, like the Sabre jet, emulating the shark as opposed to now they're emulating needles and things.

An important figure in the Captain's cosmology at the moment is Jean-Pierre Hallet, a Belgian animal lover who tried unsuccessfully to start a zoo in an area of California near the Captain's home. He was unsuccessful because people were frightened that the animals would escape. Hallett is also the author of two books which his wife is presently reading to him. I asked him if he didn't like zoos.

–Yeah, it's terrible that they have to lock them up in zoos. But man hasn't learnt to communicate with animals yet. He isn't very intelligent.

–That's why people are frightened of them.

–I'm not. I used to go into cages with lions. You know the MGM lion, Leo, their emblem lion? I used to go into cages with him when I was five, down at Griffith Park Zoo in Los Angeles, to sculpt him with a friend of mine. And do you know what happened? He was very old, the lion, and some idiot threw a cigar on him and it burned through and killed him. It burned through his skin while he was asleep. Made me sick. It was one of the most traumatic things I remember from my childhood. Isn't that awful, that sonofabitch.

Of course, the extension of his concern for animal life takes him straight to the ecological conundrum. But not for him a trendy preoccupation with plastic bottles. Beefheart's solution is quite clear – just love, cherish and care for the things of nature.

'All you new dinosaurs
Now it's up t'you t'choose
'Fore your feet hit the tar, you
better kick off them old shoes.'
The Captain explained:

–Well, that's about the La Brea tar pits in Los Angeles, because if they don't change, then they're gonna sink into the tar pits. I've been saying it for years. Look at 'Safe as Milk'. I'll tell you what that meant: the mother's breast that's going to be unfit for the child because of Strontium 90, the hot juices of the breast. Everybody thought I meant acid, but I wouldn't talk about an Aspirin at that length. I was inferring that the feeling that something is 'safe as milk' can't be a feeling any more because milk isn't safe.

The Captain creates a kaleidoscope of thoughts when he talks, and the only response is to lie back and enjoy it. Perhaps the deepest impression is left by his reluctance to think in words but rather in images. On one occasion as he was talking, his wife Jan was reading a book and the turning of the pages was distracting him. Gently he turned to her and said:

–Jan, Jan... I can't really hear with those pages going, you know, I want to pick up an instrument to that percussion.

A question that may be answered by 'yes' or 'no' is very often answered by a short little image culled from some past glimpse of the world. The Captain carried a large book wherein these glimpses are recorded (which may one day be published under the title *The Day My Typewriter Went Daaaaaaaaa.* There was an obvious question for the conscientious interviewer:

–Do you use a typewriter?

The Captain replied:

– What type of writer do you mean? A flesh writer or a flesh writer with buttons? ●

'I realise that westerners may find Indian music difficult because it is primarily melodic and concentrates on one mood or emotion. This is established in the first movement of a raga, the alap, a solo exposition which provides the basis for improvisation. Audiences here usually prefer the next section, the jor, as the element of rhythm is added by the tabla drum. In the last section, the jhala, we build speed and excitement to the climax. A raga is an aesthetic projection of the artist's inner spirit – he breathes life into the notes through embellishments and ornamentation.

'I enjoyed absolutely some of the pop festivals in which I participated. The Monterey Festival was my greatest experience with a young audience – it was very beautiful for everyone. I played for over four hours and the communication was complete.

'Now I refuse to play in pop festivals because their atmosphere has changed. I have often become very angry with the audience. They neck and smoke pot and roll around. They do not pay attention to the music as they should. I have to stop and lecture them, explain that our music is as serious as, say, Bach, and deserves the same concentration. There is sometimes an element of eroticism in the music, this can be an important element, but there is so much more. ●

Tuppy Owens

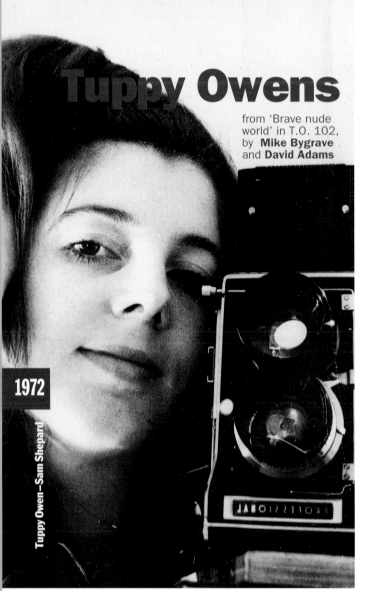

from 'Brave nude world' in T.O. 102, by **Mike Bygrave** and **David Adams**

1972

Tuppy Owen – Sam Shepard

'I have to be terribly inspired to write them, in the right frame of mind,' she explains. 'I can't write them if I'm too randy and I can't write them if I'm not feeling sexy'.

She used four different couples 'because just one gets boring.' The girls she gets passed on to her from other girls or through an agency ('Not if I can help it. Too expensive'). The men are a problem. 'Finding a really super-looking bloke is very difficult'. For the Open Air books she told the girls to bring their own men 'because they're so difficult to photograph – it's freezing cold and so on – and anyway the man doesn't matter very much'.

She thinks she is the only girl photographer in the sex market. She is coquettish and self-deprecating in a university sort of way, sounding like a sexual lamb to the slaughter on occasion. She talks about sex the same way most girls talk about nature: 'The Summer book's all in the sea and that's very way out, the positions are absolutely ridiculous. Very bizarre. Floating sex and things. The Autumn one's the most beautiful of all really because it's all in autumn leaves and everything, all oral positions and in front of bonfires – really fantastic.'

She doesn't care who buys the books but would like to think they're young couples looking to enrich their sex lives. Would she buy one? 'Only to make sure I was better than anybody else. That would be the reason. You never really know because everybody always says you're the best'. (Some confusion ensues. I think she means the best photographer. She means the best lover).

Like everyone I met working the sex market, she feels pornography does no harm and would collapse if it wasn't illegal. But she doesn't think increased sexual freedom in, say, the underground press will undercut her: 'Papers like *Suck* are for young people who want to read naughty things. And the secret of pornography is that it is naughty, yes. But it has to be seriously naughty, not fun naughty.'

'There are a lot of people who don't know about hard-core. I mean, you get down to the average people, they don't particularly want to see other people's organs over the place. They want a more healthy attitude to it, which isn't just looking at page after page of fanny. Which is what a lot of hardcore magazines are. So I'm showing them lots of different things. Like in "Summer" I've got a couple, she's in one of these barrows like in a farmyard and he's running around with it and that's really an incredible thing because he's only got to tilt her up a bit. And they're running over this ground that's uneven, you know, ploughed. And that's a really way out thing. I mean, if people actually went to try that, they'd have quite a ball, wouldn't they?' Her eyes light up. It is a nice thought: 'England's green and pleasant land, covered with couples having it away in wheelbarrows.' ●

Tuppy Owens is a nice university girl of 26 who photographs people making love. Well, they don't actually make love, except for 'one couple I used who couldn't stop. I don't like them doing it. I hate watching it'. Which seems strangely squeamish for a professional voyeur.

She drifted into the sex field via a company that manufactured lampshades. The lampshade market is not what it used to be, so on the side, they printed sex books. One day an American walked in with a sex manual – known in the trade as 'Love Position Books' – and said, redo this for the British market. Tuppy, an amateur photographer and ex-anthropologist, took on the job for nothing. The result was called 'Sexual Harmony' and sold 50,000 copies.

Her conversion to the sex market was complete. But all that anthropology must have left its mark and she has set her own series of books firmly in the open air. The first, 'Spring' must be one of the funniest ever. Here's a sample photo caption:

Normal Position in the Mud: the soft mud provides a sensuous substratum into which the female body moulds itself like a huge soft down mattress. The man is quick to lie upon her and drive into her from above. At first his tender concern makes him seek to protect her hair from the mud but soon the total abandonment of their position causes them both to throw caution to the winds and roll in the clean red earth.

Sam Shepard

from 'Free form playwright' in T.O. 124,
by **Naseem Khan**

He's tall and slim and cool, Sam Shepard. He's like a cat to look at because he's got that same kind of amiable, relaxed detachment. Ask him about America, his plays, life, theatre, and he'll answer with gentle self-mocking seriousness with a hint of a high behind the words.

Shepard is possibly the most important playwright working at this moment. His plays are extraordinary and deeply stirring; beginning from sharply written and recognisable situations, they can take off into flights of fantasy that are both strange and very real at one and the same time. The nearest equivalent is in music, in free-form jazz.

'I just tried tried things that were musically orientated', Sam explained, 'It was like, y'know, listening to it as you write it. Like the way jazz is put together – Charlie Mingus's early music for instance, a kind of collage of rhythms and sounds-rather than thinking in terms of plot and character and development and... what are the other things you're supposed to think about? Because that takes away a lot of the excitement from it, when you know exactly what a play's going to be about. When you know exactly how it's going to develop and you keep shooting for this ideal model in your head. It just seems a really boring thing to do. Where, as if you start out with hardly anything – and you improvise the language and the movement that the people are involved in, it's a lot more interesting to write.

'Theatre to me is like... as acoustic rhythm and blues is to electric music, that's what theatre is to movies. Theatre just seems more of an immediate thing. It's funkier in a lot of ways because you're dealing with this stripped down reality. You can't pull so many tricks. In a movie you can trick people all over the place. And you can lose yourself a lot easier in a movie. You can dream, you can just go to sleep. Whereas in the theatre it's very hard. And I like the whole make-shift thing of having just a space and people and not having to have a lot of costumes and props and so on. They're just using real simple things.

'It's harder to bullshit, and that's the way I like it. It's just harder all round.' ●

12-foot prick in Islington

from T.O. 125

Asked by the local Social Services Department whether they would like to take part in the Islington Festival procession, a group of kids from the Action House decided they would like to make a 12-foot high ejaculating prick. They got the use of the van and were just erecting the prick when the police turned up, claiming the object was indecent. The children claimed it was a mushroom, but the police were adamant, and so the chiildren transformed it with tissue paper, into a rocket. The police then went away, off came the tissue paper and the great prick joined the procession. On arrival at the Town Hall the prick started heaving – and the climax came as white emulsion paint was pumped from a tin which had been concealed in the balls.

"1972"

"I am fed up with a system which busts the pot smoker and lets the big dope racketeer go free. I am sick and tired of old men dreaming up wars for young men to die in."
Senator George McGovern, US Presidential candidate

"I don't think pornography is harmful, but it is terribly, terribly boring."
Sir Noel Coward

"I hate the kids most of all. You can't shoot them, can you? But I'd love to beat the hell out of them."
An anonymous British soldier in Northern Ireland

"We have the happiest Africans in the world."
Ian Smith, head of rebel state Rhodesia

"We always thought that Amin was a decent chap. After all, he served in the British Army for more than 15 years."
A spokesman for the British Home Office offers a measured opinion of the expulsion of Ugandan Asians from Uganda

"I'd much rather have that fellow inside my tent pissing out, than outside my tent pissing in."
Lyndon B. Johnson explains White House etiquette regarding Edgar J Hoover

"I can say categorically that no-one in the White House staff, no-one in this administration, presently employed, was involved in this bizarre incident."
President Nixon on the Watergate break-in

"If Jesus, at the Last Supper, offered his body and blood to all the apostles, He was giving us to understand that we must do the same."
Alfredo Delgado, one of the survivors of the Andes plane crash, who ate the bodies of the crash victims

"Avoid missing ball for high score."
The only instruction on the first mass-market video game, Pong

in T.O. 115, by **Chris Lightbown**

Football gangs

Every football club in the League in London has a recognised 'End', an area marked in geographic terms by the goalposts (because there are usually no seats behind the goals at football grounds, only open terraces broken by crush-barriers). When you read that '20 youths were escorted from the ground', it means that the kids came out of The End.

An End is like a castle, held and fortified against invaders – the representatives of the visiting team's home End. To 'take' an End means to push – ie, fight – the resident supporters out of their patch, thereby disgracing them, diminishing the vocal support for the home team and, possibly, affecting the outcome of the match.

Every End at each ground has its own name: the North Bank at Arsenal and at West Ham, the Shed at Chelsea and the Park Lane at Tottenham; and each End has its own identity. Sometimes, as at West Ham, there may be several End gangs who will agree to join together in the interests of The End. Sometimes, as at Arsenal, it's basically one big gang, with a horde of hangers-on. An End might consist of between 200 and 20,000 people, depending on the success of the club and the nature of the surrounding area.

The gangs themselves are usually territorial, exercising physical control over the young people in their immediate area (as in central-north London or the East End) where the support for a particular football club is simply an element in local youthful fashion. Though there are some anomalies – in Croydon, deep in the heart of the Chelsea suburbs and overrun by the Shed white and blue, the actual Croydon support West Ham.

But don't kid yourself and romanticise all this. It's not as hunky-dory and good-old-time-London homeliness as it sounds. It is violent and people get hurt. It isn't chic; it isn't funny. Heads should remember, before they get any more involved, that this the kind of life that they left behind.

The North Bank v The North Bank or Arsenal v West Ham

11.30

Waiting for the cheap seats in the comfortable stands, waiting for the gates to open, Arsenal football lovers are already assembling in doleful queues around the back of the Highbury North Bank. The North Bank Boys meanwhile are coming together at a pub called 'The Gunners' around the corner. The North Bank terrace looms over 'The Gunners' – its influence fleshed amply out with posters of Arsenal players and teams. By 12.15 the long, low saloon bar of 'The Gunners' strains full of boozing kids, most of them aged between 12 and 18. As the room tightens and the clamour rises, three big men in their twenties watch on ever more silent and distant from their eyrie round the right-angle of the bar. The juke-box hammers away and the talk is all West Ham. The Mile End gang, the West Ham mob, is known to be meeting at 12.45; their concerted arrival is expected between 1.15-1.30.

1.00

About 200 half-cut kids fall out of 'The Gunners' into the street and set up a swaggering parade around the Arsenal ground, chanting and clapping in awesome unity. By the time they've gone halfway round the rectangle and arrived at Arsenal underground station, they're all as high as the sky and looking to kick the shit out of the Mile End gang, which is now due. Having picked up some bashful extras, they are now about 350 strong. A few police are moving visibly scared along their flanks; ahead of the gang and behind are horses and Land Rovers.

The police bluster the gang away from the station and they swing up the road to parade around the remaining half of the rectangular streets surrounding the ground.

Meanwhile… The Mile End gang arrives. They form outside the station as the North Bank boys turn out of sight around the corner at the top of the street, at the opposite end of the ground. Moving parallel with the doleful queues, and across the back of the North Bank (the territory that they had come to take), clapping and chanting 'U-Ni-Ted; Tra-La-La; U-Ni-Ted; Tra-La-La', the West Ham kids turn into Avenell Road along the length of which is built Arsenal's main stand. The North Bank boys arrive at the other end of Avenell Road at precisely the same time. There's about twenty seconds of bloody hell for the onlookers as, shouting their lungs out, the gangs slowly approach each other.

Then the North Bank charges. The Mile End turns about and sprints off without a thought of a fight. Protected by the police, they go down to the ground entrance by the Arsenal station. The North Bank boys go into the ground from Avenell Road. That takes about three-quarters of an hour and 60p. They all seem very excited about something.

2.00

The rivals have marked out their patches. Looking at the North Bank from the centre of the pitch, you have West Ham (the Mile End mob) to your left: Arsenal (the North Bank) is to your right. A rank of nervous policemen extends from top to bottom of the terrace. The gangs occasionally scuffle with the police or make unconvincing runs at each other. But mostly they shout. The chanting goes on and on, a constant reworking of about three themes, which are roughly 'We are good; you are bad'; 'We like us; we hate you' and 'Our team is better than yours'. When 20,000 people keep that up for an hour you start to think you've been trapped in a time-warp. There must be something else to talk about.

2.55

The teams come on. West Ham have fielded three West Indians. The Arsenal crowd takes the racist advantage, setting up a chant of 'We-Are-The-White-Men'.

3.00-4.45

It's a drag, relieved only by the irony of Arsenal substituting a spade for their injured captain. The outcome of the match is secondary to the major issue, which has already been settled. More Arsenal supporters have come than West Ham followers.

The North Bank has been held. An irrational conflict has been temporarily settled; a Saturday afternoon has passed, there's something to talk about tonight, something to hoist the adrenalin during the week. Artificially sustained, the high might carry through to next Saturday. And if you can't wait that long, Manchester United come on Tuesday night. ●

1973

February
Government approves a plan for a motorway to encircle London.

March
The first mainland IRA attacks occur as two car bombs explode outside the Old Bailey and Great Scotland Yard.

Noel Coward dies.

The last US troops leave Vietnam.

April
VAT introduced.

Picasso dies.

July
Kung fu king Bruce Lee dies suddenly at the age of 32.

August
'Rocky Horror Show' is an unlikely summer theatrical hit.

September
Chile's socialist president, Salvador Allende, commits suicide atfer General Pinochet comes to power during a bloody coup.

November
State of Emergency declared by government because of energy crisis.

Princess Anne marries Mark Phillips.

December
Government announces introduction of three-day week in the New Year to save power.

Speed limits of 50 mph are imposed across most of Europe. Driving is banned in Holland on Sundays.

Homosexuality is taken off the American Psychiatric Association's list of diseases.

Shocked? Betrayed? Get real! Watergate broke and we were truly shaken at the idea of a politician lying and breaking the law. We would soon get used to it. The Arabs turned off the oil tap and the resulting energy crisis brought a state of emergency. London got commercial radio and 'The Rocky Horror Show'. We joined the EEC. Plus VAT.

Super Fly
'Super Fly', if not everything it was cracked up to be, is still a great film. A poem of the street that dances along from tacky prologue to no-shit ending.

The Exorcist
All 'The Exorcist' does is take its audience for a ride, spewing it out the other end, shaken up but none the wiser.

The Sting
'The Sting' is a bit soulless; but all those who liked George Roy Hill's earlier 'Butch Cassidy...' should enjoy this as much.

Marvin Gaye - Let's Get It On (Tamla Motown)
The best ever Marvin Gaye album and solid confirmation that these days he and

Stevie Wonder are in a class of their own when it comes to music from Motown.

Mike Oldfield - Tubular Bells (Virgin)
It is pure music, created by an absolute musician, and I can't see how anyone could listen to it unmoved. This is the most brilliant and frighteningly

original music to have ever appeared as 'pop'.

Wings - Band On The Run (Apple)
The best post-Beatle effort, and one which may do a lot to overcome the prejudices of those who see him only as a middle-of-the-road writer, drastically reducing the tweeness quota here.

And *now* for something completely different

The Monty Python team interviewed in T.O. 167, by
John Collis, **Bob Wilson** and **John Lloyd**

John Cleese

Will there be another Python series?

I think there'll be more Python television. I'm rather the fly in the ointment. The others are keen to do another series. We've now done forty shows; to do another thirteen doesn't seem to prove anything. I think without a very big break now to recharge it'll begin to go downhill, and it'd be a pity if Python just faded away like that.

Before we started recording you said that you're very lazy, and only write when you have to. But there must be a certain amount of over-writing.

We certainly have different styles of writing. For instance, Mike and Terry are much more prolific than Graham and I; they really provide the backbone to a lot of the shows. One thing that has slightly changed is that in the first series we tended to mix the writing partnerships up more. But now, anyone who knows us can usually pick who's written what. Except when we write parodies of each other. If Graham and I are feeling wicked we write something that starts with a slow pan across open countryside with music in the background, because that's the way that Mike and Terry's things always start. If they do a parody of us they'll have two old ratbags screaming abuse at each other, and discussing weird subject matter in technical terms. Eric is word-obsessed, and writes stuff about anagrams and people who speak backwards and so on. I think in retrospect it's a shame we haven't broken it up more, and written with people we don't normally write with.

Where do the Accountants spring from?

Well, yes, that's a personal thing, because I so nearly became one. Occasionally our private obsessions creep through, and I've got one about accountants. Because I genuinely do believe it to be one of the more dull and boring jobs. And yet one of the contricks at school was that if you went into accountancy you were all right. In five years' time you can have a qualification after your name and you're set up for life. I suppose I had a slight social purpose just to try and suggest that perhaps this might not be quite the right angle on accountancy.

You said that you'd like to do writing that involved more investigation...

Yes. I'd love to produce something that sustained itself for an hour-and-a-half or two hours. The trouble with comedy is that it's safer to do short things. Which is possibly where I'm slightly at variance with Mike and Terry, who write masses of short things, and keep moving on to something else. But maybe if I'd written three or four plays in the last four years, what I'd really want to do is a short, sharp television series.

It's an approach particularly suited to television, though, because you don't have to tie things up.

I think so, and yet it struck me the other day that in fact *Private Eye* have been doing it for years... you know, that thing 'continued on page 94'. If you have a nice little funny in three or four paragraphs that doesn't really end then it's a great device.

Do you ever toy with the idea of bringing more people into Python, as guest appearances?

We've once or twice thought about bringing people in to do very specific things. We had a magnificent sketch for Kenneth McKellar, but I think in the end he was a little bit worried about appearing on the show. It was a superb idea. It was a thing where a lot of old ladies came out of the audience and were blindfolded and then beaten up by stage, screen and television personalities. They had to guess who was beating them up. And we wanted him to come on, and we'd have dressed Terry Jones up, because we give him all the really rough parts, and Kenneth would have beaten him up, and Terry would have laid on the floor saying 'Oooh... is it Des O'Connor?'... and so on. In the end Kenneth felt rather uneasy about doing it, and more through oversight than anything, because we kept him waiting, in the end I don't think we did that sketch.

Richard Baker seemed to enjoy his bits.

Yeh. Well, my private Python award of the year would have gone to him for that newsreader. I mean, I just couldn't believe how funny he was. It's very interesting how many actors are bad at comedy, and how many people who aren't actors are good at it.

I remember that Harold Wilson came on after one of your shows, and I was waiting for him to do something funny…

Yes. The two nicest things said about the show… one was said to Terry Jones by a teacher, and I think it's possibly our proudest claim. He was a teacher in the East End, and was with some kids who weren't easy to control, and he said that their behaviour pattern had changed… that they'd become sillier and less violent. The other nice thing is that people say when Python finishes and they start watching the next programme they can't take it seriously. In a strange sort of way, I think that's rather satisfactory.

Michael Palin

What is it particularly that you want to do before the next series, if there is one?

God knows. I'd like to do some longer writing just to see if I can. You put down on your passport 'writer' but with Python it's terribly difficult: what does it mean really? It's just six people with a complementary sense of humour really enjoying themselves, it's like sitting around in a pub and telling stories.

Do you have time to watch much TV?

No, I watch very little. It's a kind of paradox. You've suddenly got this era where there is so much information, so many books available, new magazines. There's going to be another TV channel; it's all there and yet one has got less and less time to look in. I find that one of the things I try and miss out on is TV.

Because there's a good proportion of it that's derivative and dull, and yet I watch it if it's on. So I just try and watch things I like, which is football, and spend the rest of the time reading.

What do you do for kicks?

Well, I drink a lot of milk. It's a very dull life really. My kicks are having the work done and just being able to have time to do exactly what I want to do. Taking the kids out somewhere, reading a book I wouldn't normally have time for, seeing someone I don't see very often. I like to think of Python as something that's very enjoyable to do, but basically it's a job. It makes you a little bit of money with which you try and buy a little bit of time for yourself.

Do you ever feel that living in London puts you out of context with the rest of the country?

Yes. I was born and brought up in Sheffield and when I go up there it's very different. You feel a bit out of water and it takes a bit of adjusting to. It's easy to forget what people themselves are like, and that's the main thing. If you have a drink with them they're much more extrovert. In London there's this slightly controlled feeling about people, not wanting to give too much away, you know, keep their cool. I like to think of myself as still being from Sheffield.

Python seems subversive in an ideal way. The worrying thing about the radical left is that it's often so humourless.

The awful thing is, not to give the feeling that people are being preached at. 'These are London media people saying that we should think this, that or the other.' You should keep doing *Time Out*, we should keep doing Python, because they are attempts to put forward a critical point of view. The difficult thing is to try and combat a general feeling of complacency, and that we're all quite happy to live in a Tory-controlled society.

What are your feelings about the BBC and the way in which they've treated you?

The BBC is a strange organisation: I think there is more concentration of intelligence, well-informed thinking people in the BBC than in probably any other large organisation, but they all become a bit bogged down in bureaucracy. The BBC is very conformist in its light-entertainment taste.

The great thing though, is that they gave Python virtually a free brief to do what we wanted. Because they knew us all, for a start… it wasn't as if we all suddenly appeared as radicals from the underground saying 'We want our show, we want to say what we want to say, man, right on'. Then they would have been scared stiff, very wrongly. But because they knew us they were lulled into it, until this last series when we had a three page letter saying we should cut this, that and the other.

The thing is they have been very good, and when they did make cuts it seemed rather ridiculous. It suddenly seemed strange to be cutting a word like masturbation when you're allowed to say 'Screw the Bible.'

We're not a nation of prudes, whatever anyone thinks. It's only when you come on television that you're led to believe the people of Britain are very delicate flowers who must be nurtured and not offended. Unfortunately, the people who dislike us or who are critical of the BBC are very vocal and well organised, viz. Mary Whitehouse. She says, 'I have 800,000 people who all agree with me, this is obscene.' But it's nothing against the 18 million who actually enjoy 'Till Death Do Us Part'. They don't fill in questionaires and say 'yes, I'd like to see more filth on television.'

Terry Jones

I think one of your distinguishing marks as humorists is that you explore a joke's mechanics.

Yes, I agree. We often do this sort of 'meta-comment,' as someone once called it, a sort of commenting back on the joke constantly, which can get tedious, perhaps we've done it too much. It is formula, I suppose.

Will there be another Monty Python series?

No, definitely not, absolutely impossible, quite out of the question. John Cleese is very anxious to do one, but… you know, we're not really interested – my feet have to grow a bit, just speaking personally

Yes, but he is quite… big, isn't he?

A lot of people say that about him. He isn't, actually.

Well, we interviewed him in bed, so we couldn't really tell.

Yes, well you see, he's really quite small, the rest of us have to stoop, and bend our knees, and so forth, in order to make John look bigger.

Can you think of any sketches where this deformity was particularly obvious?

We don't like to talk of it like that, actually. And then it's really more the drink problem with John, you know.

Ah, yes, the drink problem, where is the drink problem?

Just behind you.

Has he been a lush long?

Well, I wouldn't put it as strongly as that… but of course it does mean he relies on regular employment more than we do.

One thing that's emerged from the other tedious interviews we've done, is that you and Mike write a lot of the Python material.

We do write the vast bulk of Python, that's true, yes, quite true, I can't deny it.

You and Mike worked together before Python, did you not?

We were at Oxford together – we did a revue there, though we didn't write it together. Then when I was writing for the BBC, I met Michael.

(Voice from the kitchen): Hey, what about a plug for me?

Ah yes, at that time Michael was working with a very brilliant writer called Robert Hewison.

(Voice from kitchen): H-E-W-I-S-O-N

Who?

(V from k): HEWISON!

Who's that?

Oh, he's the one in the kitchen.

What, the one cleaning the potatoes?

Yes, the one with the apron on.

He was doing some comedy act, duo thingy, was he?

Yes, that sort of thing, you know…

(V from k): Yeh, then Sir came along an' nicked it.

Yes, I took it off him very cheap.

I think it's awfully enlightened, keeping him on as a butler. It's a terrible problem, isn't it, just how to treat old friends when one moves on, so to speak?

Yes, it is. Well, you see, he just insists on coming round in the evening and cleaning the potatoes, you know.

Can you think of any sketches – I'm sure you can – that you and Mike have written, that have been in the series, that everyone's liked, that are particular favourites of yours.

Well, for instance, Mike and I wrote 'Silly Walks', but… it was an idea I think of Graham's – Mike and I wrote it – and it was really only remembered because John did it.

But John said he doesn't like doing it. Do you think he doesn't like doing it because he didn't like it?

No, I don't think he likes doing it because he's exposing himself to ridicule – he does look extremely silly doing it.

Yes, it's a pity he said he doesn't like doing it, because it is extremely funny.

Yes, but the thing is, you've got no escape from it. It's not you being clever, or being witty and intelligent, it's just you being silly.

Graham Chapman

We understand making a series involves a fair bit of travelling?

We did a lot of filming in Jersey in the last series and quite a lot in Scotland, both very oppressed areas I must say. I got thrown out of the first hotel in Scotland. The manager let me in later, largely because I'd spoken to a group of mountaineers, because I used to do a lot of climbing. They were four pretty butch people, I'd been talking to them and found out, in fact, that I'd done rather more difficult climbing than they'd done, so I thought right, here goes, as an experiment, 'Hey, blokes, I'm gay' and their reaction was, fine. That's okay, that's all right.

But meanwhile there was a very county-type girl over the other side of the bar who'd been eyeing me up for a long time that evening and after having made this revelation to these people and they're all thinking that it's fun and exchanging climbing stories, I think I stood on the table and told her to fuck off, or at least that's what I was told later that I'd done, because she wouldn't get anywhere with me darling, 'cos I was a poof. She called the manager and I got thrown out, and eventually the other people managed to persuade the manager that I wasn't totally insane and I could stay in the hotel and I was allowed back in and eventually ended up chatting with the man and he ended up giving me a cigar and a free drink.

It was like I'd come in from a concentration camp or something. Mind you, I must have been fairly drunk because I do remember falling out of bed later and thinking that I was on the ceiling.

This was on alchohol?

This was alchohol, yes. It seems to work for me.

Are there tensions in Python? Do you find one person's ideas coming out more strongly than another's?

John's bigger than the rest of us. I can be fairly fierce, but I don't think there is any friction in that way. I find I tend to align with John as far as choice of material is concerned, we have a much more aligned sense of humour and Mike and Terry tend to go along the same way, and Eric, poor thing, is on his own. I think we've now reached a point where we can be fairly honest with each other about what we think of something, I can say I think that's rubbish or that's good and nobody gets hurt. I think when we started off in the first series, we were a little bit conscious of 'Oh, we've got to use him for something', but now I don't think that applies.

Do you ever feel that where programming is concerned, the nature of what you're doing is making it a little easier for somebody else to do something similar?

I don't know. I suppose it does help people and other programmes. That's one of the worries of the heads of light entertainment, they think, 'Oh if you allow Monty Python three bloodies, a bugger and a fuck you've got to give Dick Emery at least two,' you know, not realising that that's not our method of working. If we have a word we want to use, it's there for a reason, it's there because it's an integral part of what you've written. Like when we had the 'Spanish Inquisition' – there was only one word that could really finish up that programme. They were busily trying to get to the court on time, and we had the sort of Dick Barton music playing and things and he didn't arrive on time of course and everyone was waiting around for the Cardinal, the screen faded to black and all you heard was 'Oh bugger'. There was no other word that would do, I mean, it could have been 'Oh fuck', I suppose, but it couldn't have been damn, bother or any of the other suggestions that people might have had.

You got away with 'bugger', but not 'fuck'.

Yes, the Turkish influence of the BBC.

How much did you owe to the Goon Show?

Oh, a lot, a great deal to Spike Milligan. I think we were all of us active Goon listeners and ever since, avid Spike Milligan fans, he's a marvellous man.

You've been lucky in a way, I suppose, in that you started right from the beginning on BBC 1, whereas Spike still seems to get shunted off onto BBC 2.

Yes he does, it's a real pity.

And he's still doing very good things now. There was a series, I don't know if you remember it, called Q5. One of the strongest things about it was that it started to bring in all the things about the studio, people would wheel on doors and break down all those assumptions of situation comedy, and you carried on from there.

Well, I suppose our biggest thing was getting rid of the punch line. For years people had been doing a punch line, and we had to do it too as writers. The producer would look quite blank if there wasn't a punchline, because how can he end if he can't cue the audience to applaud, you've got to have something there. Well, we don't worry about the audience particularly, let them get on with it.

In fact they get in the way sometimes, particularly at the beginning of this series – because they would over-react, you know. I remember one instance where the studio audience was so pleased when a particular line was got right that there was a cheer, which was quite wrong for that line because in fact that line wasn't warranting a cheer, so you had to cut that and do it again, by this time you're forgetting your lines like mad and so then there's another cheer when you get it right. They did get in the way and we actually had to ask a few of them who seemed

to be appearing each week to keep a little bit more quiet.

Do you get any comments when you do something on the police force, the courts, a judge or the army?

We haven't had many complaints from authoritarian figures. A bishop wrote to us once, saying why didn't we do more on the Church. We had no official reaction from the police or the army, although I gather that there's a lot of army messes that are fairly avid viewers.

Do you watch a lot of TV?

I watch quite a bit at the moment. I normally don't. I went through a couple of years having been a butch, hetero young doctor and before that a medical student, I finished up at the age of 25 finding that I was other than that, and so I felt that I had a lot of ground to catch up on. I tended to go out every night and I must say it was quite successful. I've seen quite a lot of action in the last few years, but I've calmed down a little bit now.

John seemed to dominate the first series, but he doesn't any longer.

No he doesn't. That was partly a conscious decision of his own because he didn't want to appear in so much film. It's also probably because we all know John is very physically distinctive. I mean he's six foot five for a start and he's got a huge chin and he's a very strange shape altogether, therefore people tended to recognise John Cleese. The rest of us are a little amorphous as faces and do tend to wear beards or moustaches or drag or whatever. I personally like that, because you don't get pointed at in pubs or stared at or whatever and you can go in and have a drink somewhere. It's a bit awkward occasionally – you're going into a pub and somebody will say 'Mr. Gumby' behind your back. It doesn't happen very much, it's only late at night, the rest of the time you just get stared at occasionally.

Isn't your life dependent on people recognising you?

Yes, it is dependent on that, but it's not dependent on people loving us. A lot of people, comedians in particular, really want not only the laughter from the crowd, they also want a little bit of adulation. Obviously it's a necessary part of their makeup. I don't think we mind if we get contempt. ●

David Bowie

Somewhat slightly sane

from 'Judy Garland comes to N4' in
T.O. 154, by **Connor McKnight**

While I was on holiday in Italy this summer,
I met a girl who expressed interest in
Bowie. Now, to this girl Bowie was a cross
between Rod Stewart and Pete Townshend. I
asked her why she had become interested. Her
only reaction was to voice further uncertainty.
'Everyone seems to be talking about him.' She
seemed almost ashamed about her curiosity. I
wanted to make something with her so I offered
to take her to the gigs that he was planning to
do later that month. When I got back to London,
I rang to confirm our date. She told me that she
already had tickets. I was pretty pissed off at this
since tickets were meant to be very hard to get
hold of, but she said that her sister had given
them to her. Bowie had come into her sister's
shop to buy some clothes.

Bowie had bought two suits for about £120.
When I asked about the clothes I was told that
they had been made by a fellow called Kansai
Yamamoto, who is the darling of those people to
whom money is a gimcrack. Bowie's wife had

come into the shop at odd intervals throughout
the day, toying with various garments. She finally bought two jump suits, one in ordinary
leather, and the other in painted chamois.
Bowie's wife tried them on, and when asked
whether they were OK, she said that they had
identical bodies so it would be all right. Bowie
was delighted by the suits when his wife took
them to the recording studio where he was
recording Ziggy. When I talked to this girl's sister after a few weeks she was confused as to
whether it had been Bowie or his wife that had
been into the shop.

The Rainbow, August 18 1972. The lobby is
crowded with people, and as a collective mass
they exhibit a tenseness, the almost breathless
anticipation that heralds a real star. It's David
Bowie tonight and everyone is here. And I mean
everyone. I took a tape recorder up there. One or
two remarks helped.

Elton John: 'What'll I see tonight? I think I'll
see an amazing show. I've followed him since he
was doing gigs at the Marquee – years ago. I
remember him from the lower third and all that
rubbish. I just think he's great. I think "Hunky
Dory" and "Stardust" are masterpieces. The

lyrics and the story in Ziggy? Well I don't know
too much about that. I just enjoy the music.'

Me: 'Could you say what you expect tonight?'
Lou Reed: 'Well, I'm friends with him.'
Me: 'The guy who runs this place thinks it
could advance rock music by ten years.'
LR: 'That's a pretty good guess.'
Iggy: 'Sure I've seen Bowie before. I've seen

- -

Plastique phantastique
romper rock

The Rock nostalgia wave is bringing back the show-biz style of the early sixties

from T.O. 152, by **Music Star**

Mao's millions could learn a thing or two from Gary Glitter. The
numerous parents at the Rainbow last week must have been relieved
to see him leading their unhealthy children through a rigorous programme
of physical jerks – arms UP two, three, four, DOWN two, three, four, OUT
two, three, four and CLAP!

The godless youngsters, swaying energetically in the aisles, must surely have been inspired by the ancient virtues that their hero represents.
Faith – anyone who sports such tight costumes must have loads of it.
Persistence – in the face of a really monumental and lengthy rejection by
the record-buying public, now so well rewarded. Self-sacrifice – the staring eyeballs and contorted features which accompany his movements have
earnt Gary the title of 'King of Cardiac Rock'. Modesty, Stamina, Clean-
Living… one could go on and on.

From the start of his Rainbow show he had the entire audience in a state
of shock. Even the cooler critics were mesmerised by his cheek. First the

Bowie face to face. I've seen Bowie naked. I've seen him any way you want it. I think we're gonna see the David Bowie super Limey, ultra-fag, semi-repro Rock and Roll show.'

Ted Way (Manager of the Rainbow): 'I've seen many groups rehearse here, but I've never seen anyone to match these people's sheer dedication to what they're after. Honestly, Connor, I went home last night at six o'clock in the morning, and they were still at it. At about three, after four hours of rehearsal, they decided to change it. So they all sat down and figured out what to do. For simple professionalism, I've never seen anything like it.'

A nervous fellow from Newcastle (who wouldn't look me in the eye): 'I don't really know why I'm here. I love his records, and I want very much to see someone who can write the songs that he does. I'm not queer. "Ziggy" is very heavy but, at the same time it's funny. It's a joke about someone like Bolan.

Tony de Fries (Bowie's manager): 'No I can't talk to you. Why? Because the relationship between artist and manager is too delicate.'

De Fries smokes large cigars (honestly) and at those gigs, wandered around the audience asking them questions about the show. He carried a clip board wherein all the replies were entered. Doubtless they would come to be analysed at some kind of de-briefing session following a show.

One of the indices of the star is the number of people who 'knew him before it all began to happen for him'. Mary Finnigan was one of the people who shared Bowie's early fumblings towards art. She has written this personal recollection.

'Evening meetings in the pub garden – 50 of us gawping at each other, fighting lovingly, an almost unbelievable hello. Sometimes the pale man with curly hair and a weird eye spoke up and it usually made sense. But Bowie was different. Wise beyond his years, in private an enigma, publicly a mannered, charming fellow with an eye for the birds.

'We called ourselves an Arts Lab because it was fashionable and found it poster-splashed by the local newspapers. It didn't start that way, but the alternative was a fan club, which it was anyway, but nobody cared because we were all so stoned, man. The whole of disaffected Beckenham, Bromley, Penge and points north, south, east and west, dropped acid that summer.

'Most of us are still catching up on the experience, while Bowie's seen-it-all, done-it-before, sussed-the-trip-wires, maturity had him ready for lift-off.

'It was easy to knock on all those tender enthusiasts and say "Hi, would you like to rehearse some street theatre on the hill in the park today – have some fun and get it on?" Yes, you know the rest. The grooving around was such a buzz, but everyone was too stoned, man,

too far out, man, too amazed just Being. Street theatre never hit the streets, but some jewellery got made, some posters sold, some printing done and a newspaper happened.

'Bowie loving Beckenham less and success more. "Space Oddity" – 15 of us watching Neil Armstrong on TV. Angela flipped out and a flash of understanding cut through the amazement. Visconti said they looked like each other in drag. Dr Calvin Mark Lee, cool Chinese San Franciscan, sold pictures to finance "Space Oddity", organised Rolls Royces, gave away bounty, loved David. Lionel Bart came by.

'Someone said, "wouldn't it be a groove to put on a free concert in the local park?" The council said yes, the money materialised, candy floss machine, side-shows and our own newspapers. Angie's wheelbarrow barbecue, Calvin's posters, Chas's herb shop, someone else's candles and the prettiest girls in town on the tea stall. Clem and his Indian guru playing sitar on the grass, Bowie, Strawbs, Keith, Bridget, local rock bands belting it out from a gazebo-style bandstand.

'Flower children, families, old ladies, discreet policemen, skinheads, rockers and young reporters found more than a little magic that day. We made over £100 on our free concert and got high on the achievement. A brief and enjoyable episode for the Beckenham people involved and the beginning of a planetary journey for David Bowie.' ●

solitary echoing drum in the darkness, an invitation to human sacrifice at some Molochian temple in the jungle, then the awesome roar of seven gleaming choppers, lining up on stage with their headlights blinding the audience. Finally the appearance of Gary himself, lying on the pillion of the last cycle like a zombie about to be given its charge, while the wall of fanatically singleminded noise resolved itself into 'I'm the Leader of the Gang'. Other moments stand out. The elaborate histrionics of 'I'm Just a Lonely Boy' and 'Donna' (these presumably accepted as 1973 songs by the young audience). The coy flashing of a hairy nipple in 'Do you Wanna Touch Me' – this last being a good example of Gary's confidence in his abilities. Crouching on the edge of the stage in his black matador's outfit he held out the possibility of a million-volt Weenage Esalen Orgy.

'Do you wanna touch?'

'YES!'

'Who do you wanna touch?'

'YOU!'

'Why?'

(Puzzled sussuration as weeny brains confront themselves with the problem.) Then straight back into the wall of sound before things get out of control. This is a good example of how near Gary skates to the edge of the black hole. It was as if he was deliberately deflating the situation so that he could test his skill by rebuilding it. He succeeded of course, within seconds.

If a lot of today's music looks back to the early 1960s, so does the presentation, and more important, the accompanying business style. The teeny-bop magazine, or fanzine, has come back with a rush and now flourishes on the private likes, dislikes and breakfast habits of the stars. Page after page of colour pictures, with the text between acting only as a filling, and behind them the whole collection of agents, managers, promo

men, pluggers and session men who crawled so neatly into the woodwork during the denims and sweatshirt progressive period of two years back and more. In the wake of the glam explosion, a thousand faces peer out hopefully from the pages. Make-up, diamante, sequins and a chord. You can be a big star, son, just sign here. Of course it would be foolish to pretend that this has not always gone on, even at the height of the 'Rolling Stone' telling-it-like-it-is journalism, but it is depressing to see the con-men regaining their control so completely, and flaunting it so openly.

Some of the product is clean like the Osmonds, who actually went to a Mormon temple on their last tour here to give thanks for the golden rain, but all are plastic and phantastique.

Rock is the new Hollywood. A star system and a billion dollar industry, not free of disreputableness, and the record producers taking on the role of the auteur, so much loved by the *cahiers du cinéma* school of film criticism. Unfortunately the disreputable side has been getting out of control, and the pop industry is now having its own mini-Watergate.

Withholding of royalties and much more is being alleged in the lawsuits which are springing up like unsightly boils on the smooth face of the music industry in the States. Two of the ex-Monkees are suing Screen Gems, their management company, for $20m; the Mamas and the Papas are suing ABC-Dunhill for $3.5m; David Clayton Thomas is suing Columbia for $2.5m; the Stones are suing Klein-Abko for $75.5; and these are just the courageous few.

With more than fifty artists and performers in the United States earning well over two million dollars a year and a serious critic writing in the *New York Times* that 'a lyric poet like Paul Simon could be as essential to the economy as Harold Geneen' (President of ITT), it's easy to see why the boys want to get their hand in the till. Not only that, but if there's a trend to be exploited, flog it to death. There is actually a group being formed in ▶

LA at the moment composed of five eleven year olds!

In the face of these recent revelations, and the enormous earnings of the Rock aristocracy, the public have reacted with the same kind of cynicism that they display in politics. In both fields the sense of betrayal is identical. In politics it is fashionable to say that 'they're all as bad as each other', while the idealism of the late sixties record buyers has been rather crushed by a pile of coke, tequila and Lear Jets. The identification of rock 'n' roll with revolution – 'Rock 'n' Roll, Dope and Fucking in the streets' – is largely dead, although a dedicated few like Hawkwind still struggle to burnish the blackened image. Many bands reacted to business problems by setting up their own labels and in the beginning it was thought that this would lead to less dependence on the businessmen. Bands would have complete control over material, packaging, marketing and promotion. Of course these inflated ideals have collapsed. but even more modest ambitions – such as the freedom not to be pushed around too much – have proved difficult to achieve. In practice most musicians get rather confused and bored if they are asked to do a lot of auditing of accounts and they settle for a larger royalty cheque and that's about it. Sometimes they pick out a particular accountant and say 'Look man, you sort out the bread hassles, we'll get on with the music'. This is what the Stones did with Allen Klein – but the honeymoon didn't last long.

Even the Grateful Dead, the most recent band to launch their own label, have scrapped their original plans. These included distributing through head shops, a fleet of 'Good Humour' trucks to take the records to outlying areas not well-served by retail chains, and a whole series of head spinoffs. But surprise, surprise, we find that in Europe at least, 'In the Wake of the Flood' is being distributed in a completely conventional manner by Atlantic. The involvement of the average head, through the fan club, seems to be to check up on whether the album is arriving in his friendly neighbourhood store. Well, free labour can't be bad can it?

Meanwhile the hardware gets more and more complicated. From Hi-Fi to Stereo to Quadrophonic. Cylinder, disc, cassette, eight-track. More and more live albums are being made, because the equipment to do them justice is at last on the market and more and more people are listening to them – in their living rooms. Venues get bigger and bigger, roadies multiply, PA systems need articulated lorries to haul them about, ticket prices soar. Suddenly it all seems a long way from the Shadows with their AC 30s at

the Empire Pool. While, back in the real world, pigshit politics intrude and through a doped haze it seems that things are running out. Unfortunately it's soon going to be difficult to find solace in music as the oil shortage is affecting not only juggernauts but also the record industry. Vinyl, from which records are made, is a by-product of oil, and the position in the States at the moment is so critical that record company executives admit quite openly that they are having to pass inferior product at the pressing plants simply because the quality of the raw materials is deteriorating every week.

Difficulties with raw materials do not only affect the distribution end of the business. United Artists admitted last week that from now on they would only be producing the records they knew they could sell. Not only would the print order be limited but the company would be very reluctant to sign up new artists unless they were guaranteed sellers. So we can expect a fine crop of Great Soundtracks and Ray Conniff anthologies. The smaller independent labels, who normally employ the pressing facilities owned by the giant conglomerates, will be turned away from the plants, just as the small petrol operators are being given the cold shoulder at this minute by the big Oil companies. Budget labels will suffer and we will all sink into a morass of middle of the road, mid-Atlantic schmalz. Music for western civilisation to collapse by.

Rock is a billion dollar industry now – the new Hollywood.

Despite these problems, however, the Industry is expanding in the timehonoured capitalist tradition. In the boardrooms brandy-veined cheeks quiver with excitement at the thought of the Japanese market. (It has expanded 10 times in the last two years.) At last we'll pay the little buggers back for those Sonys! Beyond stretches the Third World – Music will win it all back.

The final word shall remain with Gary. Fresh from winning back Australia for us, he leads his class in a mass workout. Then the PT instructor becomes Hollywood choreographer. Slowly the curtain at the back of the stage rises, revealing a gigantic white staircase lined with swaying silver-clad beauties – looking strangely (and one suspects deliberately) frumpish and out of time. A feast for the fags and a sincere thank-you to the fans at one and the same time. He ascends to the heavens, blowing kisses, turns and disappears. Perhaps such gestures will be harder to manage in future – but let's hope not. ●

Jeff Beck

from 'Unbalanced' in T.O. 156, by **Andrew Furnival**

'I'm pretty unbalanced, I know that. Where all this started was the violence on the guitar bit, that's where people sewed me up as a villain. You see, when all these dudes came out with guitars and started thrashing about on stage it took on a completely new dimension. Instead of going round punching people's heads in I used to play guitar, and it came out that way because I was around about the time of the late rockers.

'The guitar's the very hardest instrument there is and I took this challenge saying, "right, let's see how hard it is" and I fooled around on a friend's zither, which was like the nearest thing I could get to it. I couldn't afford a guitar

and I plunked around and I was knocked out with the sounds I got out of that thing.

'I made my first guitar, made it out of plywood. I bought a mike pickup for it. It had a great sound but my dad chucked it out in the garden and it wasn't waterproof glue and the whole thing fell to bits and that was it.

'We went to America for a threeweek tour. In fact Hollywood was on fire when we left because they were all on acid, the superhippies, and this feedback stuff that we were playing, and ghastly noises, that would bring them in.

'One party was the best thing I've ever been to, oh boy. There were just a lot of nice people.

Bob Dylan was there – and Natalie Wood. I nearly pulled her. I could have done but I didn't have the bottle. There she was sitting there and I could have carted her off down the road – I just didn't have the bottle to do it.

'I don't smoke pot. It probably looks like it, but I don't. I used to drink on tour. I was getting through a bottle of vodka a day, more than that because on the plane they dish out the drinks liberally and when they bring me a drink they'll bring me two doubles. As it gets to about 5 o'clock in the evening, you start getting excited about the show and you have a drink and you calm down and that wears off and you have another one and it goes on and on until you are just about to go on, then you down half a bottle and start getting really pissed. You've got to, I mean people just don't realise that you've travelled so many thousands of miles, and the audience, they don't care what the hell you've done. They just want you in good shape and sometimes it's the only way to get in good shape.' ●

Duvets/Continental quilts
from T.O. 161

Like anything different, the duvet is viewed with the utmost suspicion by the British public. We find it hard to believe that a bag of feather or (now) terylene fibres is an acceptable substitute for any number of blankets, eiderdowns, not to mention bedsocks and of course, pyjamas. Since we first looked at duvets only 18 months ago, the market has expanded tremendously – so much so that even Woolworths, Marks and Sparks and Tesco now market both down and the new terylene filling. *Which*, February 1971, did a really extensive survey of duvets, comparing the quality of fillings and dispelling a lot of very fundamental fears like 'will it fall off?'

Watergate
from T.O. 199

The trouble with books that attempt to produce 'instant history' is that they are inclined to be outstripped by events. For all the anecdote, detail and reconstruction, the *Sunday Times'* first stab at the 'full inside story' of the Nixon conspiracy was written too soon to contain some of the most significant developments of the scandal.

It is in the area of what, politically, Watergate is about that the 'Insight' team is at its weakest. The catalogue of intrigue, deception and subversion make disturbing, even frightening, reading, but it is no more, really than many people always suspected. Nixon did, after all, authorise the greatest war crime of modern times – the dropping of four million tons of high explosives on North Vietnam. We must look elsewhere for answers to the most important questions: sure Nixon had to win the election, but for who? The Mafia? Or was Watergate, as has been proposed, the prelude to an executive coup?

Francois Truffaut
from T.O. 197

In your new film 'Day for Night' you show the cinema to be quite brutal. There's an actor who dies but the main concern of the crew is that the film has to go on. Everything has to be subjected to budgets and deadlines.

That's no contradiction. It's the end result which has to have charm. And anyway, I think the shooting of the film is fairly good-humoured, and not at all cruel.

Well, I find it a bit alarming that an actor is killed and the first thing people think about is how to patch up the film.

But it's the truth. If an actor dies in a plane crash or has a skiing accident, the first thing a director will think about is how he can finish his film.

I know, but it comes as a kind of shock.

Ah, I knew in doing it that it was a bit shocking. But sometimes a leading actor is forbidden by his contract to travel by plane throughout the shooting, for example. When we are shooting near the mountains the actors sometimes go skiing on Sunday and I'm sick all day with worry.

For the actors or for the film?

For the film.

"If no-one can understand our decision, it's up to other people to look for meaning in what we say, and not for us to explain what we mean."
A spokesman for the Department of the Environment spearheads the campaign for Plain English

"This is a very fine country to be acutely ill or injured in, but take my advice and do not be old and frail or mentally ill here – at least not for a few years. This is definitely not a good country to be deaf or blind in either."
Keith Joseph, Secretary of State for Social Services, reassures the public

"Labour will tax the rich until the pips squeak."
Denis Healey gets his priorities temporarily right

"There can be no whitewash at the White House."
President Nixon promises to get to the heart of the matter

"I made a terrible mistake. I pressed the wrong button but Mr Nixon said it didn't matter."
President Nixon's secretary Rose Mary Woods admits she erased 18 minutes of vital information from the Watergate tapes. Oops

"President Nixon has an unusual sense of humour."
Psychiatrist's report after Nixon had laughed at war scenes during the movie 'Patton' and apparently giggled during an announcement for a bombing raid in Vietnam

"Homosexuality in itself merely represents variant sexual preference which our society disapproves of but which does not constitute mental illness."
The American Psychiatric Association changes its position after 100 years

"Who loves ya baby?"
Lieutenant Theo Kojak, NYPD

Pinball London

The world of silver balls and golden geese

from T.O. 173, by **Duncan Campbell**

Hips swaying gently in the half-light, tiny beads of sweat hovering delicately on his pencil-thin moustache, forefingers twitching feverishly, he heaves his bulky fifteen stone slightly to the left. Seconds later he is spinning in orbit, burners lit, moon rocket flashing dimly below. He lets his breath out slowly. A slight smile of triumph spreads over his ashen face. He nods quietly to himself, unaware of the rest of the universe. John M Dobie, pinball wizard, has won another replay on the Bally Cosmos.

The Cosmos is just one of the thousands of London's pinball machines. John M Dobie is just one of the proud successors to Tommy who play the tables in the cramped arcades of Soho and the West End, who dedicate their spare hours and spare change to the heady magic of pinball.

Pinball. Glass-topped temple to twentieth century ennui. Fourlegged father of the finest rock opera of the sixties. The game that President Lincoln played while the Union Army lost at Bull Run. The device with the strangest banners. And the progenitor of a mighty money-making industry.

Since the first machines eased their way across the Atlantic after the war, they've sent so many silver balls a-spinning that they now need special arcades to house them.

The very first literary reference to pinball, according to *Playboy* magazine, comes in the 'Pickwick Papers' with tales of how they 'beguiled their time chiefly with the bagatelle board' at the Peacock Tavern.

Gottliebs actually invented mass-produced pinball machine way back in 1930 when you got seven balls for a cent; they can still be relied on for a mean game. Check out their double-flipper King Kool if you come across it.

Bally played their part in pinball history by adding the sophistication of the Tilt in in 1935. Now you won't see a machine without it.

The New Pinball Wizards

They speak, they see, they feel.

'I started playing in Greece. Flippers – that's what they call them on the continent – are illegal there now, have been for seven years. So when I first came to London I started playing for, well, nostalgia,' says Stavros Georgopoulos who can knock up the maximum of 15 replays at Playland in Piccadilly.

What do you need to be a wizard?

'Time. Time and money, that's all,' he stroked a thick beard. 'It takes me about a quarter of an hour to pick up a new machine. But once a machine has been "learned", they change it because it isn't making them any money... you soon find out how to shake a table without tilting. That's the key. You see, I used to have my own table in a basement in Athens.'

What does he think of his fellow players?

'Pinball,' sighs the 25-year old expatriate, 'pinball is a dark game. Most of the people who play have nothing better to do.'

The flipper-kings of Victoria, Marcel Moules and Pandolis Ashiotis, take a less sanguine view of the game. Marcel looks like a Welsh seaside comic, all grin and good cheer. He's just knocked up a record 420,000 on the King Kool machine. Pandolis is a big bear of a man who's been playing ever since he could shove a drachma into the tables of his native Cyprus. They're the two rivals for the roost at the Victoria Golden Goose. Both agree that you need good reflexes and loads of practice to succeed. As they play, the only sound is the relentless click of the 'replay' numbers piling up.

They've never played the wizards of Soho, men like Mick Papodopoulos, a lanky long-hair who's perfected the tables in Las Vegas. But both are anxious for a showdown competition.

The burly John M Dobie – never did find out what the M

stood for – plays lunchtimes at Lots O Fun and sees the game as a battle against The Machine.

'It's you,' he says, pulling back cautiously and letting another ball fly off on its replay mission, 'against It.'

In Soho, it's you against more than It.

The Chinese players there got so good at the new machines at the Golden Goose that they got 'discouraged' from playing there. Later after an argument about whether they had jammed matchsticks in the one-armed bandits, a 'bit of a battle' broke out, according to one former employee who still hangs out there.

The Chinese, the Cypriots, the West Indians all have reputations for wizardry. Dig that, Eysenck. But why, apart from the joy of skill and the aesthetics, do they play?

'Masturbation', says Tom McMahon, a 33-year-old Scottish plumber now living in Marylebone, self-styled loner and dreamer. 'Masturbation – that's what this game is all about. Look – you pull your balls out and play with them. Then you pull your plonker back. And you know what?' he asks, banging a knotted Edinburgh fist on the glass top, 'the woman wins every time. You get nothing back, do you?' Those are the wizards. But they make up a tiny proportion of the pinballers.

The rest are tourists who have found out that London really swings for the very rich or the very stoned; and the lonely who would rather play the balls than sit looking spare in a pub; and the time-killers who drop in at the peak times of noon and six. Plus, of course, all the pinball pimps. Most arcades have their share of dealers and dealt-to, runaways and hookers. One reason for the dope-dealing is that it's easy to strike up a conversation without looking suspicious and if the police arrive, it's easy to drop the evidence under a pair of passing platform heels.

Women & Pinball

'He ain't got no distractions'

You don't see many women playing pinball.

In fact, in the Soho Golden Goose, they're positively discouraged. A sign tells unaccompanied women that they're not welcome after 10.30pm. So the pros-

titutes, the inhabitants of what Henry Miller, himself a great pinballer, calls 'the slaughterhouses of love', are shooed off by red-jacketed attendants before they can suggest to tourists that there are other ways of balling than with a Klondike or an Apollo.

I asked Anna Raeburn, out-spoken Projects Editor at *Forum* magazine, why so few women played. 'Well, they're much more likely to be raking the dance-halls and discos looking for a bloke. And it's bloody hard on the nails. You need a strong right arm too.'

A member of the Women's Movement that I talked to said she thought that it was just because women couldn't bothered with something as 'silly and competitive'.

The machines

Two flippers to fantasyland

The three makes of machine you'll run across in the arcades, pubs and shops all come from Chicago and Miami. The names to look for are Gottliebs, Williams and Bally (as mentioned in the 'Tommy' opera, kids).

Each of these manufacturers bring out three or four new models every year, models that give a strange, funky impression that they're designed by some genius electrical engineer a giant step away from reality. For out of 145 tables in the central London arcades, 33 had themes related to card-games like Straight Flush and Poker. 30 were to do with other games like baseball, American pro-football or snooker. 25 were space-oriented – Cosmos, Apollo, Outer Space. 14 had a musical or dance theme. Six featured guns, like Lawman. The rest were a surreal mixture of Flying Carpets, Spanish Eyes, Crescendoes, Aquarius, Klondikes, Jack-in-the-Boxes (decorated with tit-swinging art-nouveau ladies) and so on ad nauseum.

What pinball experts reckon to be the finest goddam machine in the world is the Bally Fireball, now alas sadly defunct. Send me a postcard if you ever run across one. The best game I've run across in London is the Bally Cosmos. In this, the ball actually leaves the horizontal surface and goes into 'orbit' in the vertical section of the table before coming back to light up some more burners. Instead of replay signals, a Fuel Pod flashes up. OK?

Flipping Tips

Watch out for the tilt!

Before you commit your 5p piece – most pinball games cost 4p, 5p or 10p for a doubles match – there are some things you should check. Are all the lights working? If some of the rollovers aren't lit, you may not get the full score you're entitled to. Are both flippers working? Is it a newish machine? Some of the pre-1969 models don't have the most modern tilt system: so if you tilt, you lose the whole game, not just that ball.

There is in pinball, as in cricket and love, no substitute for for experience. But if you've never played before, here are a few tips. Don't send the ball speeding off too fast. Pull the plunger back slowly and then release it. It's called 'slow-balling'.

Do let the ball run onto the end of your 'flippers' – the two little arms at the bottom of the table which you activate by the buttons on your side. This enables you to flip the ball much further and back up to the top of the table where the big scores are to be had.

Don't flip frantically away with both flippers at once. Practise the 'single-finger-flip' which will give you greater accuracy.

Do try 'shaking' the table. This is the real key to pinball success and if you don't master the art of 'shaking' you might as well go back to dominoes and darts. It's an expensive business to learn because you have to test each machine to see how far you can shift them before they tilt.

But once you've learned this essential skill you'll be knocking up the 'replays'. You'll hear a magical, climactic 'click' and the figure 1 will pop up in the replay box. Your first replay is like, well, your first anything.

Pinball Competition

Find the Pinball Wizard of London

Time Out is exploring the possibility of running a Pinball Wizard of London competition. We'd like to hear from any potential wizards and pinball-freaks who would be interested and any pintable manufacturers who would like to lend out their machines for posterity. And don't worry, Tommy, we'll make sure all the application forms will be printed in braille. ●

George Best

from 'Georgie! Georgie! Who is this Georgie?' in T.O. 194, by **Peter Ball**

More words have been written about George Best than probably any other footballer in history. Possibly more than about any other 'pop idol', including Jagger, the Beatles or Bowie. The latest addition to the library is a book by John Roberts, Best's ghostwriter for his articles in the *Daily Express*. It's subtitled 'Fall of a Superstar'.

It's a well known story. After an apparent rejuvenation of United under their new manager, Frank O'Farrell, it's the story of United's decline to bottom of Division One, punctuated by Best's absences from training and games, fights in nightclubs, two retirements, and the final sacking of O'Farrell and the announcement that Best would never play for United again. Yet, paradoxically, the more written about George Best, the less we seem to know about him.

Like all the others, John Roberts' book looks mainly for the answer in Best's off-the-field activities. On the pressures for a pop idol of his magnitude. On all his birds (lots of sexy pictures), his staying in bed rather than training, his business adventures. It's mainly a gossip columnist's book. Yet one would have thought that someone as close to him as his ghost-writer would have had some insight. But no. And we shouldn't blame John Roberts too much. Because significantly, Michael Parkinson, who John Roberts sees as a close friend of Best's, is in the same boat.

For those who don't remember, Parkinson was helping Best with his autobiography. Yet a week before Best returned to Manchester United this season with the papers full of rumours to that effect, Parkinson went in print categorically denying that George would return. And a week later wrote an abashed article confessing that he still didn't understand George: and was still waiting for the phone call Best had promised he would make before taking such a decision.

Parkinson's book will not now be published, because it reveals too much. David Meek of the *Manchester Evening News* is writing one. He should have seen a lot of George at close quarters, in his job as the Manchester United reporter for his paper. But what hope for him to reveal the Best enigma?

Perhaps the answer is a simple one. That there is no enigma. George Best is a footballer – which many people seem to have forgotten. A genius of a footballer. He does it on the field. He reveals himself on the field as an artist. An artist who can take a generally earthbound game, like football is, and lift it to the plane of high art. In popular terms, he makes it the greatest of all art forms. More people, in Manchester or Wigan, the Potteries or Tyneside, or even in sophisticated London, have

'I'm not saying who he is, but his name is Bobby Charlton.'

been uplifted, have been given a vision of beauty by George Best, more than by Rembrandt, Shakespeare, Beethoven or even Mick Jagger. The beauty of incredible balance, speed and ball control allied to a wiry strength and bravery which confronted and defeated big and ruthless opponents. Which for a time carried a very undistinguished team to the top of the league.

And that perhaps is the whole answer to the George Best question. That he expresses himself in his art. And that it was football problems which led to his apparent final retirement. And John Roberts, amid the mass on his private life, does reveal some indications that this might be so. He quotes Best as saying so himself:

'I've got nothing against the management. It's the team. It's just not good enough. It's just not going anywhere. I could go right through the team and find things wrong. People knock me when I'm not doing it, but when I'm not doing it, who is?… Sammy McIlroy could be a great player in five years. But I can't wait five years …

'If I'm fouled, it's not the pain that bothers me. It's the frustration about a good move being ruined because some clogger has just taken the legs from under you.'

There are hints that it was also trouble with other players. A dissatisfaction with fading stars like Bobby Charlton, who in their turn moralised about his behaviour. When John Roberts asks Best how the other players welcomed him back after his January 1972 absence, Best says 'They've been great. All except one. I'm not saying who he is, but his name is Bobby Charlton.'

Which all seems to add up to the same conclusion – that it was artistic dissatisfaction which caused him to retire. Easily understandable. Of course other players have their legs kicked from under them; other players have to play for poor teams; other players have trouble with team-mates. And answer the problems by a transfer. But George Best wasn't another player. He was the supreme artist of our century. And now he's back. Again, simply, because, 'I was missing the game more than I expected.'

And on Saturday, all being well, he will be playing for Manchester United at Tottenham. On Saturday, George Best will probably be appearing in London. One of the places which has inspired him to his greatest displays. Don't go expecting that. It's too early, even if he can recommand his genius ever again. But go. Even if you've never been near a football ground in your life before. Because when an artist of his dimensions is in reach, he must be seen. Seen doing his thing. Not snapped having a punch-up in a nightclub or leaving Tramps with Miss Great Britain. But bringing grace and vision and magic to the lives of thousands of people. That's what George Best is about. Football. The rest is bullshit. ●

1974

Bombs, bombs and bombs, as internment and military occupation spurred the IRA to bring Northern Ireland's troubles to the mainland. Lord Lucan vanished, Nixon finally resigned and Evel Knievel failed to make it over the Grand Canyon. Ted Heath shortened the working week to three days to stave off the effects of oil shortages and the miners' strike. 'The Sweeney' rocked the box, as did 'Kojak'.
– 'Who Loves Ya Baby?'

February
Prime Minister Ted Heath dissolves Parliament.

Miners' overtime ban turns into national strike.

General Election proves inconclusive as Labour leader Harold Wilson forms minority government.

March
Miners return to work, country returns to five-day week.

Lieutenant Onoda surrenders on Filipino island of Lubang, but only after receiving the order from his commanding officer, Major Taniguichi, now an elderly bookseller.

May
Duke Ellington takes the great A-Train in the sky.

August
President Richard Nixon resigns as a result of Watergate scandal.

September
Parliament dissolves in preparation for another General Election in October.

Haile Selassie deposed.

October
Five killed and 46 injured in Guildford pub bombing.

Labour returned with tiny majority in Election.

Muhammad Ali defeats George Foreman in Zaire. Zairean government bans wigs and Christmas in attempt to regain its African culture.

November
Covent Garden market moves to Nine Elms.

Lord Lucan disappears after murder of his nanny.

John Stonehouse MP fakes suicide at a beach in Florida.

December
Tom Baker is the new Doctor Who.

The Parallax View
'The Parallax View' is inexorably agora-phobic: excellent performances; fascinating film.

Monty Python And The Holy Grail
Python's delightful and, on the whole, consistent *reductio ad absurdum* of the Grail legend.

Chinatown
Classic detective film, with Nicholson's JJ Gittes moving through the familiar world of the Forties *film noir* uncovering a plot whose enigma lies as much within the people he encounters as within the mystery itself.

Eric Clapton – 461 Ocean Boulevard (RSO)
50,000 words won't even begin to to tell you why I'm still

starry-eyed and smil-ing: buy this record and watch the law of diminishing returns stand on its head.

Brian Eno – Here Come The Warm Jets (Island)
What might, in other hands, turn into an indulgent hotchpotch is saved by a really inspired overall sound production.

Joni Mitchell – Court And Spark (Asylum)
A further chapter in the emotional disquiet of Joni Mitchell who, in her quest for fulfilment, continues to record the details of abortive encounters with enviable insight, veracity and conviction. Witty, authoritative and undeniably great.

ALI VS FOREMAN

At 3am on September 25, George Foreman and Muhammad Ali will step into a ring in Zaire for the latest in an incredible series of fights, all called 'The Fight of the Century'. Foreman is World Heavyweight Champion, and this will surely be Muhammad Ali's last chance to recapture the title taken from him in 1967 in an outright political manoeuvre. Sponsoring the fight, not surprisingly, is a curious syndicate businessmen: Risnelia, a Swiss investment firm with 'major interests in Zaire', and David Frost's Hemdale Enterprises. Predictably too, Viewsport is running the British closed circuit TV operation. Sport seems a curious word to use in that company. But in spite of the background there are a few people involved about whom the word sport does not have a hollow ring. We have had a look at a couple of them: George Foreman, the defending champion, and Muhammad Ali's 'number one fan', Paddy Monaghan, an Abingdon labourer.

George Foreman

from 'An American dream', in T.O.236, by **Ruby Stolbof**

'**I**'m going to beat your Christian ass, you white flag-waving bitch you!' Muhammad Ali screamed at George Foreman at a boxing writers' banquet at the Waldorf Hotel in New York recently. A reference to when Foreman won an Olympic Gold medal, and paraded around the ring waving an American flag.

George Foreman grew up in Houston, Texas's Fifth Ward, one of the oldest established ghettos in the South. He mixed with criminals and dope addicts, and always thought he'd end up the same. There didn't seem to be any way for kids like George. He has said that he really tried hard to be tough, that he even worked hard to be good at it, wanting at one time to be a great thief and hustler, but he failed.

He was always in trouble with the police and juvenile authorities, who say that it was taken for granted that Foreman was a dead cert for Huntsville State Prison. In 1963 he dropped out of junior high school without telling his mother. She'd give him lunch money, he'd spend it on cheap wine. He was one of seven children. There was no father around the house, so Mrs Foreman raised them alone. Every Sunday after church she would sit and talk to George, trying to straighten him out. Afterwards they, would pray together.

Nancy Foreman had to work long hours to make enough money for herself and her children. She worked every day as a cook and then went on to do a second job in the evenings. George says he got to thinking of his mother as someone made of iron. 'Then one day it just got to be too much for her. In the Fifth Ward we used to call it "bad nerves", but really it was a case of total exhaustion'.

While Mrs Foreman stayed at home recovering from her illness, George was urged to join the Jobs Corps – a government training programme for drop-outs. After several weeks of carpentry lessons he wrote home to his mother saying that he was going to build her a house. 'That was the greatest feeling I ever had. I felt I was somebody, it meant I could earn a good living as a carpenter if I wanted to.'

However, when Foreman finally returned to Houston he discovered that no one wanted to hire him, despite his skills. George says he thinks it was discrimination, but can't prove it. He spent his days hanging around the streets of the Fifth Ward again with the old crowd. They'd drink some wine and smoke some grass, then they'd look for some pills. Sometimes they'd wander around at night just looking for something to do. George was just 18 at that time and has since said how glad he is that no one ever came up and said, 'Hey George, let me shoot some of this stuff in your arm, you'll feel great!'

Finally he was sent to Pleasanton, California, where he was met by Doc Broadus, an ex-lightweight whom he had first met through the Jobs Corp Centre. It was Broadus who first taught him to box. He told Foreman that he considered him to be the finest amateur heavyweight in the world, and encouraged him to work towards the Olympic Games. 'When he told me that, I

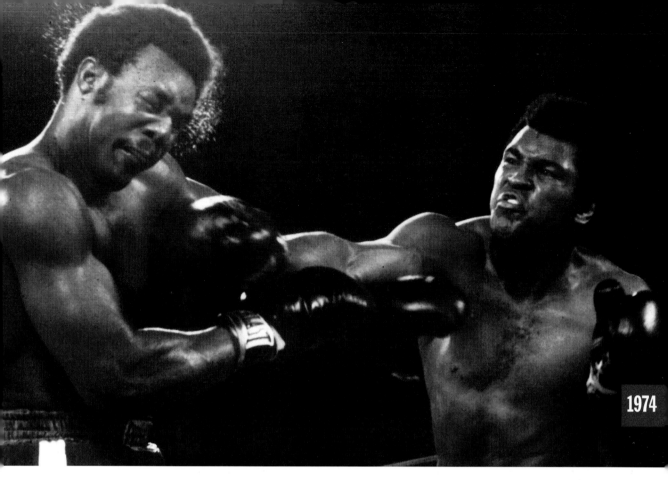

1974

couldn't believe a man I respected that much, thought so much of me. I said I would do anything to get that gold medal. When I won it, I just pulled that flag out of my pocket. I knew that I was proof the American system could be made to work'.

Much of the interest and enthusiasm from boxing fans is racist in nature, particularly in a championship fight. Muhammad All and George Foreman are both black, but the same aspect is present because of their different religious beliefs. Foreman is Christian and upholder of the American system, and as such is a National Hero; Ali as a Black Muslim sees the system as rotten, and says that it will be changed by the liberation of the blacks from their white slave masters. These differences are very much in focus now and will obviously go a long way in promoting the sale of tickets for the fight in Zaire. The 100,000 seat stadium is expected to be sold out even though the fight is to be at 3am to accommodate TV.

'If Muhammad Ali wants the Championship he can run for it, although the ref may have to tell him to go get it. You got to bring some to get some, that's an old saying, and I sure won't be telling him "please take my title". How would I stop All from running? By knocking him out, that's how. Once a man gets in the ring he does what I let him do.

'From what I can see Muhammad Ali can't hurt anyone except by his talking. Like when he almost made Joe Frazier cry because he called him ignorant. Joe didn't know what the word meant, and I don't think Ali knows what the word means either. It just means you don't know a few things. So I'm ignorant too, I'd be stupid if I didn't admit it, but let anyone try and call me stupid!

'I know Ali is a fighter, and no one works as hard as him. There's no way you can tamper with what's been given to a man. I didn't give it to him and I can't take it away. I won't say anything bad about him, besides, I've learnt that two people you can't ever knock are John Wayne and Muhammad Ali.

'I'm not trying to fool nobody, I'm just interested in making a good living. Ali – he's a politician. I could go out and kiss babies, but I don't go in for all that. He seems to get turned on by it, he needs it, I don't. People have to accept me the way I am. You stick your feet into the sands of time, but the sea comes and washes it away. I accept this. This should be an easy fight for me, my style is to get it over with quick. I'm a good defensive fighter, and I can really hit. Yes I get cut, but I'm not particularly susceptible. I'm just a regular guy, no different than anyone else. Just a basic fellow. I'm not the greatest!' George Foreman has had 40 professional fights, winning 37 of them inside the distance and gaining decisions in the other three. Of his last nine fights, eight of them have ended inside two rounds, the other in one. In his last three fights he has had his opponents down onto the canvas at least ten times. This has to be some kind of record. The last man to fight him was Ken Norton, famed for busting Ali's jaw. After getting destroyed by Foreman in the second round, Norton exclaimed, 'I made the mistake of trying to defend myself by holding my arms out in front of me. He just punched his way straight through them'.

Dick Sadler is Foreman's manager. A one-time vaudeville song-and-dance man, Sadler learned about boxing through working with Archie Moore and Sonny Liston. He is very much a father figure to Foreman and has helped him through various financial

▶

problems and legal actions concerning the ownership of of the champion. Foreman had such a devastating punch that Sadler once said to him, 'Watch out, George, or you won't be box office!' George, however, has been guaranteed 5,000,000 dollars for fighting Ali, and has talked about sending him and his mouth into retirement.

'Ali has no punch. You know at that second fight with Frazier when Ali caught him on the jaw at the end of round two? That was a punch in a thousand, you couldn't repeat that. Ali knew he'd hurt him and he suddenly thought he had a strong punch and went dancing back to his corner full of glee. I was there with a girl, and I said to her, "Ali's gonna come out steaming in the next round because now he thinks he can really hurt Frazier, and he's gonna get himself into a lot of trouble." Which he did.

'I'm getting to be a family man now, although my first obligation is to boxing. I've gained all I can, I'm a millionaire and I have a child. I don't want to tamper with all this now. I realise being heavyweight champion of the world is only a temporary position. I'm not the owner, only the caretaker.

'The best fights are the fights you have have to fight, not the routine ones. I can jab better than Ali, and as for the holding business, I'll be my own referee, my own judge. All I have to worry about is him trying to win the fight. He has to worry about getting hurt.'

Muhammad Ali

from 'Ali's number one fan', in T.O.236, by **Chris Lightbown**

Muhammad Ali has turned on a hell of a lot of people, but no one more than Paddy Monaghan, a 30 year-old labourer and boxing fan from Abingdon, Berkshire. For Monaghan, as for many, the crucial date in his love of the Champ was April 28, 1967. On that day Ali was stripped of his World Heavyweight Championship title because of his refusal to be drafted for the Vietnam war. The action was unique – people in Ali's position are usually sent over to entertain the troops, at most – and it was viciously vindictive. It is now universally acknowledged that it was Ali's politics that lost him the title.

Monaghan was stunned at the news, and started raising a petition – destination undetermined – to protest. Monaghan's angry activism very painfully taught him what the media and organised sport think of ordinary fans, but he persevered until he had over 22,000 signatures, stopping only when Ali's boxing licence was returned in 1970.

But Monaghan's fortunes were mixed in the early days of the campaign. Ali has always excited tremendous following in this country, far beyond boxing itself, and Monaghan was deluged by letters from mums, pensioners, kids, gentry and working men, all wanting to sign up for the Fan Club he was starting for the Champ. So great was the response to Monaghan's petition that he gave up his job to work full time for the Champ's return.

The other factor that led Monaghan's working full time for Ali's return was his obsession with the press treatment of the case. Although free from the patriotism which prevented the US press from giving Ali any chance of a fair hearing, the British sports press never attacked the injustice of the title-stripping. Nor did it

News blues

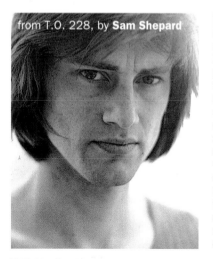

from T.O. 228, by **Sam Shepard**

Right now I'm wondering what kind of significance a play can have in the face of these last few days. From LA to Ireland to Israel and back here to cosy little England, I'm going to rehearsals. I'm watching something take shape. I'm trying to concentrate and then running off to the Who concert to see a hundred thousand people clapping their hands over their heads while Roger Daltrey whips his microphone and Townshend does the splits and Ken Russell does a tracking shot of the whole shmear. Then I'm looking up at the sky and feeling myself in this jammed-in mass of bodies at £2.50 a throw and I'm thinking 'What is this?' Am I doing research? I'm 30 years old and I'm at a rock concert in the middle of nowhere?' Everyone's covered in red dust and chugging on wine bottles and the Who are

cranking out 'Summertime Blues' like nobody's business. They'll always be this great. They were great then and they're great now but what the fuck time is it? Didn't I do this in '68? The sun goes down and they whip into the first three notes of 'Pinball Wizard'. I counted them. The first three notes and everybody in the joint knows what song it is. Not only that but they all know the words! A hundred thousand people singing in unison to some very tricky lyrics. I was stunned. Now this here is an audience to beat all. It took me a long time to give up the fantasy that a play could ever have the same unanimous impact as a piece of music but this really drove it home. Then I'm turning and looking around me at this audience and something new comes in. Everyone looks ecstatic and hypnotised as though the same emotion has put everyone out to lunch. 'Pinball Wizard' has released something and there's no going back. You could've lowered an atom bomb on the place and no one would've cared. Each new discuss the extraordinary official conspiracies that arose to block Ali every time he came near to negotiating a return to the ring in backwater states which were prepared to take the gamble.

Most British coverage of Ali was on the news pages: the sports press treated him, at best, as some super-cuddly Teddy Bear who had a nice line in limericks.

With no press coverage of the issue, Monaghan's campaign to draw attention to Ali's situation started to take on elements of vaudeville. Monaghan and his 'Ali is our Champ' banner became a routine sight at Hyde Park Corner and Trafalgar Square, before showing up under the noses of Frazier and Foreman when they appeared as World Champions in England. Frazier, and Foreman's Dick Sadler, were barely restrained from eating Monaghan alive. Undeterred, Monaghan exhorted a whole clutch of celebrities into the campaign: George Best, Bobby Moore, Prince Philip and Henry Cooper.

Monaghan might have given up by this time had he not come into contact with the man himself. Ali had heard of Monaghan's campaign, and summoned him to an audience while the Champ was over on a flying visit in 1971. Monaghan found that Ali behind the scenes was very different from the raging extrovert we were all seeing. 'He was so humble, and so straightforward with people. He read all his fan mail. I found out he had been reading all the letters I had been sending on to the States, and would help anyone in a spot of trouble.'

The last remark is a clue to the extraordinary friendship that sprang up between the two men. Ali is as straightforward as a boys' comic hero; in the world of hustlers and hangers-on that inevitably surrounds a champion, Ali's generosity has brought him close to financial ruin more than once. Monaghan would never ask him for money. He came from the same pre-sportsman stable; he had been shocked at the unfairness of Ali having lost his title, and his efforts to draw attention to Ali's fate all but bankrupted him and made him a laughing stock in the media.

Monaghan's friendship with Ali became a Magical Mystery Tour: he visited the States four times as Ali's guest, addressing student meetings at which the Champ spoke, working in Ali's corner during exhibition bouts: he was treated as a confidant in Ali's otherwise all-black inner circle. When All steps out against George Foreman in Hemdale's early morning beanfeast, Monaghan will be watching at one of the Viewsport venues in London.

Monaghan is constantly being stepped on by fly-by-night merchants after a quick route to Ali. Sport, he realises, is about big guys and big money. A sports fan who is turned on by the greatest sportsman anywhere, devoting all his energies to however futile a cause, would not even rate a sneer down Hemdale way. Which is funny. I thought that was what it's supposed to be about. ●

Streaking - a political movement?

letter in T.O.216

Dear Time Out,

Being as the enlightened habit of 'Streaking' seems to be catching on, maybe it's going to be an exciting summer.

After all why should it just be confined to the stage or films.

After witnessing brutal treatment to two streakers (knocking one unconscious) by the police in the Kings Road on Saturday afternoon; it seems the police and authorities fear 'Streaking' as much as they fear political dissent, or bombs. Maybe in sympathy with 'Streakers' we should have a 'Streakers Rally' in Hyde Park. I think we will find people streaking everywhere.

Roddy Barm, Orme Court, Bayswater Road, W2

---

song comes like that. Like a rush then a fall back to nothing then another rush. On and on like that until finally it's time to go back to some kind of life.

Then I flash forward a couple of weeks to an imaginary opening of this play of mine at the Royal Court. A whole different kettle of fish. Different people coming for different reasons than they'd go to see the Who. But what reasons? It's got music in it. There's a reason! From the title 'Tooth of Crime' they may suspect it's got something to do with urban problems. Maybe everybody's having a good time. But then it's got these 'significant overtones', these 'implications', these 'mythic' heroes, this fancy language. Somehow it's got to be analysed and put in the right perspective. Somewhere between the Who concert and the Royal Court there must lie another possibility. Maybe not. Maybe that's just the way it is. You either get wiped out emotionally or you sit back and make judgements. In any case it depends on the event. I start to verge on a weird cynicism. I start to feel this play is just a drop in the bucket. The news makes me empty. The news set next to an opening night or even a rehearsal. My values go swimming around. I'm writing this half knowing it's an advertisement. What does the other half know? When I wrote this play something was going on. Something urgent. At times I can still feel it. A kind of deadliness. Like letting off some poison. Is that what an audience comes for? To take in somebody else's poison? Is that what rock music has become? Who are these monsters crashing around the stage yelling at each other through microphones? Then I think 'Oh yeah, it's an exciting piece of theatre'. What does that mean? The rhythms get to me. My own rhythms. The music works. Then there's a boring patch. My stomach gets all tight. I wish I hadn't written that. Oh I wish I really hadn't written that. I wish I'd used one less 'fuck'. It's not too late to change it. I could change the whole thing. Take out the whole scene. No. It's the actor. He doesn't know what he's doing. No. It's the 'fuck'. Too many 'fucks'. I mean one 'fuck' is enough to get the thing across, you don't need six 'fucks' in the same sentence. Now I'm censoring myself. Think I'll go out and buy a paper. No! Not the news again! I'll stick it out. It's only rehearsals. It's a process. You can't expect results like that. Try to be objective. Watch it evolve. Remember what you originally had in mind. What was it? These two guys. No, this one guy who gets challenged by this other guy. No, this world of weird people playing a murder game. I dream about LA. In the middle of the Royal Court, in the middle of rehearsals I dream about LA. That burning house. 500 cops shooting it out for two hours with an ex-con and some armed women. Five hundred cops at the same place at the same time, firing on one little house in California. Things have really changed. ●

THE YEAR OF THE
BOMBS

from T.O. 210

The elusive bombers photo-fitted by the police. After a year, bombs are now accepted as a part of political life.

Exactly a year ago, on Friday March 8 1973, London gained first-hand experience of car bombs. Two of the four bombs planted by an active service unit of the Provisional IRA exploded, one at the Old Bailey, the other off Whitehall. Suddenly the reality of life in Northern Ireland hit the streets of London.

Carrier Bag/ Car Bombs 1973

Mar 8: four car bombs in London, in Westminster and Old Bailey.

Aug 2: bomb at Portuguese Consulate in Cardiff claimed by 'Freedom Fighters For All'.

Aug 19: petrol bomb at Aldershot claimed by 'Freedom Fighters For All'

Aug 20: carrier bag bomb at shopping arcade, Hampstead.

Aug 24: bomb at Baker Street tube.

Aug 31: bomb at Marble Arch.

Sep 1: two bombs in Solihull.

Sep 8: bomb at Victoria Station; five hurt.

Sep 9: bomb, Sutton Coldfield; one serious injury.

Sep 10: bombs at Kings Cross and Euston; 13 hurt.

Sep 12: Bomb at Comm and O Association, in Lower Sloane Street; five hurt.

Sep 12: bomb in Oxford Street offices of Prudential Assurance Company.

Sep 17: two bombs at Army's Rhine HQ School in München Gladbach, West Germany.

Sep 17: bomb at Perry Barr factory.

Sep 17: bomb at Household Cavalry camp in Purbright.

Sep 18: bomb at offices in Witton Birmingham.

Sep 18: bomb in Edgbaston, bomb disposal officer killed.

Sep 20: bomb at Duke of York Barracks, Kings Road, Chelsea, 5 hurt.

Sep 28: bomb at West London Air Terminal, 8 injured.

Oct 1: bomb at Westminster offices of Allen International, a security firm.

Oct 5: bomb at Army Careers Office in Surbiton.

Oct 5: plastic bomb disarmed in British Army truck in Hanover.

Oct 27: bomb near Moorgate tube station.

Dec 18: car bomb outside Home Office building, Westminster, 54 hurt.

Dec 18: car bomb outside Pentonville Prison, 5 hurt.

Dec 18: bomb at same Hampstead shopping arcade hit in August.

Dec 20: carrier bomb at French Embassy.

Dec 21: two bombs at and near Hilton Hotel.

Dec 22: three bombs in London (one in Leicester Square; two near Charing Cross).

Dec 22: three bombs in London Cinemas (Swiss Centre; Cinecenta; Jacey).

Dec 23: bomb at pub near Centre Point.

Dec 23: bomb at Kensington police station.

Dec 23: bomb at Wimpey offices in Hammersmith.

Dec 24: two bombs at Swiss Cottage.

Dec 26: Bomb at pub in Victoria.

Dec 26: Bomb at Sloane Square tube.

1974

Jan 2: two bombs in Birmingham stores.

Jan 5: bomb at Madame Tussaud's.

Jan 5: bomb at Boat Show.

Jan 5: bomb at Burns Security Offices.

Jan 6: bomb at Chelsea home of Major General Ward.

Jan 6: bomb at Kensington home of General Sir Cecil Blacker.

Jan 24: bomb at Chelsea home of Oscar Murton, Tory MP.

Jan 24: bomb at Chelsea home of Sir John Newton Smith.

Jan 24: bomb in First Street, Chelsea

Jan 25: bomb at Israeli bank in City.

Feb 4: bomb in Army coach in Yorkshire kills twelve.

Feb 12: bomb at National Defence College, Bucks; 10 injured.

Letter Bombs 1973

Apr 11: letter bombs – four explode (Min of Defence; Royal British Legion; CO1; Union Jack Club; Old Bailey; Stock Exchange; Downing Street).

Aug 21: letter bombs at British Embassy, Washington.

Aug 28: letter bomb at British Embassy, Paris.

Sep 18: letter bombs at Embassies in Kinsnasa (Zaire), Lisbon and offices in Gibraltar.

Sep 18: letter bomb to 2 British Government Offices, Brussels.

Dec 17: two letter bombs at London post offices, 6 hurt.

Dec 17: Brigadier O'Cock receives letter bomb.

Dec 17: letter bomb at British Home Stores offices.

Dec 19: letter bomb to home of George Drayson, Tory MP.

Dec 19: Parcel bomb at Oxford Street post office.

Dec 22: Letter bomb at Shooters Hill Police Station; one policeman injured.

Dec 23: three bombs found in post offices.

1974

Jan 22: Bishop to Armed Forces receives letter bomb.

Jan 25: letter bomb at Pilkington Glass in Lancashire.

Jan 30: Judge John Buzzard injured by letter bomb.

Feb 1: Reg Maudling receives letter bomb.

Feb 4: security guard injured by letter bomb at 'Daily Express'.

Fire Bombs 1973

Jul 12: Wakefield Army Stores burnt down.

Aug 18: 14 incendiary bombs in West End stores.

Sep 1: three fire bombs in Birmingham.

Sep 8: three fire bombs in Manchester shops.

Sep 13: three fire bombs in Manchester.

Sep 27: two fire bombs in Welwyn Garden City shops.

Oct 2: fire bomb causes £3m damage at Woolworths, Colchester.

Oct 8: Woolworth's in Faversham, Kent damaged by arson.

Oct 23: three fire bombs in Wembley shops.

1974

Jan 10: two fire bombs at Heals.

Uri Geller

from 'Pinball wizard', in T.O.249, by **Ian Pollock**

Uri Geller was on a lightning tour. Greased lightning, bolting through a series of regional TV spots and publicity outlets. The object was to promote the latest Geller project, an album of his poetry which he talks over a fairly syrupy backdrop of lush string and choral arrangements. He has recorded the album in French, German, Italian and Japanese, as well as in English, which is some indication of the spread of the Geller phenomenon.

Most of the TV appearances included part of the album track entitled 'Mood', in which Uri's velvety tones hypnotically coax the listener into trying to bend metal or start up a broken watch. 'Everything is possible to you who truly believe.' These appearances precipitate an incredible response, jamming the switchboard with a flood of miraculous claims from viewers. Birmingham's 'Pebble Mill' programme, which goes out at lunchtime, received around three thousand calls after their session with Uri. Most of these were claiming broken watches that had ticked back to life and two of these cases seemed of particular interest. The first was a lady who claimed that her digital battery clock had started, minus the batteries. The second stated that a broken watch had not only started but had also set itself to the right time, untouched by human hand.

If you're a believer then you're already converted but the scientific mind is not so easily convinced. 'Uri Geller and Science', the lengthy article by Dr Joseph Hanlon in *New Scientist*, concluded that Geller is simply a good magician. I asked Dr Hanlon how he would explain the results claimed by members of the public in their own homes. His answer is that people tend to exaggerate; they fail to properly observe and accurately recount such occurrences. He cites the experiments where witnesses to a staged road accident give widely contradictory evidence, in some cases going so far as to invent an extra car. He drew a parallel with the reaction to a Dutch TV show by magician David Berglas. Berglas sat his subjects around a table and asked them to concentrate on a wine glass which was in the centre, trying to shatter it by thinking destruc-tive thoughts. The glass shattered and was soon followed by viewers' reports of various glass objects broken at home. But Berglas admits that he is using a trick.

Geller's reply is simple. 'Everything could be duplicated by magicians but it doesn't have to mean that I did it the way they did.'

If he isn't a conjuror then what is he? According to his authorised biography written by Andrija Puharich, the man largely responsi-ble for bringing Geller out of the land of Israel, he is the intermediary between intelligent ener-gies in outer space and us simple earthfolk. 'Our helper sent to help man.' Puharich's book lists numerous paranormal happenings, psychoki-nesis, materialisations, UFO sightings and direc-tives from these intelligences. Uri is painted as a cross between a somewhat flippant and ego-tistical Superboy and the latest in a long line of messianic figures.

Disappointingly Uri Geller opens the door before walking through it, a little late for our interview. The BBC had him bombing around in a Ferrari for a forthcoming series. 'They want-ed something fast.' A supercharged pinball. Talking to him is a little like holding a conver-sation with a man in a revolving door.

Uri won't be specific about personal UFO sightings but only generalises about a belief in life in outer space and adds, 'Well I don't know why I believe in them, since I was a kid I always went to all the films.' (I didn't ask about Frankenstein.) But I can't talk about it. I'm going to spill out things without permission that have happened in the last two years. Defence Department things, Government things, You don't know what I've done there (at the Stanford Research institute). I've done incredible things that are suppressed. I've erased video tapes, I've levitated things. Who told them to leave it out? I never know who's financing all those experi-ments. Who is? NASA? I don't really know who's behind them.'

What is the Defence Department's interest?

'If they think this guy has powers they want to control it, they want to know what he can do with his powers. They know and the Russians know that very soon there is going to be psychic warfare. People are going to knock out radio sys-tems and spy by telepathy. Everyone's trying to be the first.'

But he said that his powers cannot be used at all negatively?

'There is a positive force controlling my pow-ers. I cannot turn it to evil. I went to a casino three days ago to win money and I lost, yet at SRI I knew what the dice was going to fall on ten times in a row.

'So what! Who cares about the sceptics? I couldn't care less about them. There are enough people converted without me challenging and facing everybody. Look, I became known because of this and now I'm in it. There's no way out for me and so I demonstrate. I don't want people to think that I'm here to say "Hey look at Uri Geller, believe in me." I don't want people to believe I have a mission here. I don't want to be messianic figure. Maybe I'll convert people but I don't want to fight. I have to work with some scientists.

'Everybody's trying to cash in,' he says.' The magicians are trying to get publicity. Let them. I'm earning money. I'm not rich. I hope I will be rich.'

One of Puharich's concerns about Geller's character in the book was that he just seemed interested in money and fame.

'OK I admit it. Three or four years ago I was interested in money. My mother was pulling expresso things in a coffee shop for twenty years. I wanted to earn money to let her be free, and I wanted to buy a nice house and a nice car. Goddammit where does it say that a guy who has powers has to lock himself up on a mountain and eat herbs? Now I know that this is so impor-tant that you can't even talk about money here.'

Why does he think he has these powers? 'Why?' sighs Uri as though a little weighed down by his burden. 'Why was I born on the date that Jesus was born, it's a mystery to me also.' Will we ever plumb the depths of these great cosmic secrets? I wondered. 'Who cares?' whispered the White Rabbit, 'the kids love it.' Later I checked Uri's birthday. December 20. ●

A very glandular pub

from T.O.219, by **Duncan Fallowell**

There's a pub in the East End where the reek of lust addles the brain and where you might be asked to hold a flick-knife while someone takes a leak

'**O**h boy, we took this mescalin from a witch doctor and the ship went adrift along the Spanish Main for a day or so – that's when I had the tattoo done I showed ya in the pissa!'

'That one will go down well. They'll like that.' And so I put it first to be rid of it, in case you might think it a little too pat, and then –'Fantastic grass in Jamaica. Five bob and they'll fill up ya pillow case.' He produced a neat spliff and lit it, jauntily working the nostrils, fingers à la Bogart: the modern merchant matelot, stoned. Me, I was just louche, hoping to cop a drag. Beneath his David Cassidy hair-do slops the brine. Dress: Harry Fenton Upper Spiv but softened and subtly fancy, apart from the thonging through his fly – definitely a carnivore, yet not a cannibal. And I know of no other pub where it is possible to smoke spliffs in such a friendly, unparanoiac atmosphere.

'What's his cock like?' someone murmurs.

'Like a tooth pick, dear, with a baked bean on the end,' someone replies, for this is a very good night in a very glandular pub in a very avoidable part of the Isle of Dogs – ah, another Venice du Nord and gasworks where St. Mark's might be. In fact the place is almost impossible to find from directions, even when the streetlights are on. Your arrival can only be guaranteed if you are taken personally by one in the know, which at the very least makes it chic. Here the reek of lust addles the brains like sweet ammonia, the two bars (both noisy from talk and records, one inadvertantly nautical minus the yachting caps, the other darker with a plaster cave ceiling dropping off and brothel lighting) quickly assuming mythological proportions. When I took a tiny American redhead, Rita Rocks, she was drawn in with the question 'Do you want any tom?' Her answer was 'I have rather a lot already' – no neophyte in the slaughterhouse this babe, and she continued shaking her hands in the air while a lot of other people were socked in the balls by Zeppelin Rock and Roll very loud, switching to the Staple Singers at their most vertiginous funky (Respect Yourself) for the self-appointed go-go-soubrette, a desperate-looking girl with loose mouth, voice like a hod of bricks, incredibly flash clothes and one lugubrious tit hanging out like a sulky schoolboy, spattered with Advocat. Forgive the salvo of metaphors but when it comes to the quintessence of the essence and you're in at the birth of shazam, well, holding back can send you half blind, inducing an effect similar to delirium tremens.

Five Years ago the City Arms attracted outsiders to the drag show but driving past it last week one saw a huge prig sign 'Under Entirely New Management'. A two-second check-out saw that it had been done up like a fish and chip shop in Lloret de Mar and was empty. The same applies to the Waterman's Arms, castrated by a naïve understanding of 'trade', the Londoner (winkles Americani but sometimes OK when there's a local ted group and you're feeling down in the *boue*), the Earl of Aberdeen – despite the unisexuals standing around in blood-red underpants this is really just a teen boozer for the local towers. If you're lucky you might be asked to hold a flick knife while someone takes a leak, more likely you will be deafened by the snapping of ankles as they try to lift their multicoloured platform feet along with Noddy Holder. Plenty of lager and beans, often visually bizarre as particularly East End kids are these days, and a feeling that they would all do much better at the Sundown, Charing Cross Road: low brow.

Believe me, go further East where the Thames sucks at foundations, the denim bites deeper, and there is a strange sensation of driving along a dark road humpy with bridges over undisturbed black water, zig-zags of rusting cranes, collapsing warehouses, untenanted dockyards and occasionally a cargo ship climbing hundreds of feet above you, picked out in yellow bulbs almost near enough to touch. An alarming juxtaposition of scale. Yes, my place is the real place. It was busted one New Year's Eve when the mari-

New York nightclubs

from 'Carry me back to New York City', in T.O. 226, by **Anita Schnee**

The scene was a place called the Dom, in the East Village. Black people would come down to it from Harlem and up from Brooklyn, but since it was in the East Village, it was reasonably OK for white folks to escape with their lives intact, even to be tolerated as something of a curiosity.

The dance floor was wall to wall; table space was grudgingly restricted to the corners. The furniture was light, for easy hurling, and indestructible, to do more damage to whomever it landed on than to the management's property. There was none of your psychedelic nonsense. Light was furnished to see and be seen by.

When you dressed for the Dom, you dressed for work. You don't run the four-minute mile in stilettos. Similarly, elaborate coiffures wouldn't stand up at the Dom. Floorlength chiffon was inappropriate. Makeup was kept to a minimum.

In any case, feminine gewgaws were irrelevant. It didn't matter how you looked; the criterion for women and men alike was how well you shook your moneymaker. Not how intelligent or what a good conversationalist or what amazing numbers of drugs you could take.

You got out there on that floor and you got down to it. There was none of your self-indulgent hippy shake going on; it was tight, disciplined work, and out of it came all the imagination, creativity, and infinite variation on a theme to be found in the best ballet or the most brilliant football. God knows where the dances were laid down, but everybody knew them, and every month or so they would change. Songs were even written in homage to them – 'King of the Cool Jerk' and 'Funky Broadway', for example.

time drag queens rustled out of their galleys, handbags solid with drugs, attar of roses and bacon fat, and precipitated an orgy. One of them, Lesley, sits on a bar stool reminiscing through his maquillage. His language too has a natural tendency to *crotte*, lyrical one might say in its concern for the organs of love and the sphincters of passion. 'He screwed me so hard I thought his prick would come out through my mouth. And there was Africa slipping by on our left'. From time to time he applies cover-up to the intertwined anchors on the back of one hand, irksome relic from the days when he was a cabin boy pushover. 'Me landlord moved across the water to the Ship and Whale after the riot but it didn't make so much difference. That fucking stripper is no artiste but she can sure fill a bar.' Breasts so grand she supports a gin and tonic on each before flipping her bra: twenty minutes twice a week including the Sabbath. Some big under-sixteens are jacking at her and by closing time the little latrine will be awash with their impatient discharges green as phlegm. Several are on the bash, the carousel of Piccadilly. For teenagers they are already subculturally very advanced, effortlessly take their place among the petty crooks, local heads and hookers, fish faggots, fruit flies and ferns, the corner of pensioners who like to come in to moan at the roaring disco, and physiognomies more enigmatic still. It isn't at all oppressive but one faint visiting spirit referred to 'a whiff of Jack the Ripper and Edwin Drood, eh?' Well: beer, musk, new sweat, parma violets, blue with smoke and something else which makes you want to lean against a juke box wearing a hard-on.

Slued beyond redemption, I naturally lose my bearings. The roads are a mess of stomach-churning bends and at the best of times all look alike. After wasting ten minutes trying to grasp directions given through a car window by three boys it is decided that they should squeeze in the back with Rita and we all go off to the Blind Beggar for shellfish, and from there to the DOK Club where it occurs to nobody that our companions are under age except for the one who works in the City 'in an office that sends tea all over the world.' The second is a bit fresh and showing off his fly buttons while the third plays spot the sex through my bins. 'Nanti polone, kiddo,' says a blue-chin battleship in rhinestones. They giggle.

And the pub? You might want to know its name. A rush of West End would kill it and I cannot afford to have that on my conscience. Besides I don't want to feel like Judas when I next go over, having to explain what we're all doing in Egon Ronay with our doylies. ●

● ●

Everyone would do the same basic – what, step? movement? – and the flair and style would come in the interpretation. Everyone did the Boogaloo, the Philly Dog, the Funkys Chicken and Broadway, and the Camel Walk differently.

We literally danced ourselves out of our minds. I remember once I wore a wrist-watch, and when I fell into bed at five in the morning and attempted to take it off, I found that I had taken my skin along with it. I did not wear watches to the Dom thereafter.

In many ways it was a tough scene – the ultimate tribute, awarded to only the very most inspired, was a spontaneous melting away of the crowds, leaving one couple alone out there, showing everyone what it was all about. I only saw it happen once and I'll never forget it. But that was exceptional. Most of the time the feeling was that expressed by The Man James Brown in one of his songs: 'There was a dance/they call the Boogaloo/I may not do the dance/as well as you /I do the best/that I can do.' The irony of that song – James being one of the most amazing dancers in the world – was not lost on the listeners. ●

Dope shortage

from 'Smoke to snow' in T.O.218, by **Adam Symes**

'It's all the same these days: mirrors, mirrors everywhere, but not a joint to smoke,' commented an acquaintance as he bent his bleeding nose to the mirror for yet another line of coke and sympathy, His was, perhaps, a hyperbolic voice from the road of excess, but his sentiments confirmed what every doper knows: cocaine and pills are plentiful, while hash is both scarce and expensive. London, as a land of dope and glory, has had its day.

There is no hash hillock to match the butter mountain; the price is up, the quantity and quality available is down. The reasons behind this fact, and its consequences, are various; but most importantly the major thrust has been at the centre – against the dealer. Nine tons of hash were seized by customs in 1973.

A survey commissioned by the government in 1969 and leaked in 1971 postulated at least one million smokers. It is recognised in the trade, nevertheless, that the police have put a stop to several of the major importing rings. Simultaneously cocaine has become more widely available, at an average price of £20 to £25 a gram, as have certain downers, Mandrax in particular.

The total effect of the assault on dealers has been severely to diminish the political force behind the pro-pot lobby. By police concentration on dealers, the majority of middle-class users have found fines for possession to be relatively minimal in both financial and social terms. Thus they have complacently allowed a situation to develop in which their suppliers have been hounded down, and their own supplies reduced.

Many have turned to the demon alcohol – the problems and numbers of alcoholics increase yearly – or to more dangerous pills and powders. Dealers are not anticapitalist heroes of the underground economy; stereos, choppers and fine food claim their allegiance also. But only they provide the desired service.

Home Office gossip revealed that the Conservative Government had no plans to initiate pro-hash legislation. Not that hash was thought to be dangerous, merely that it was felt to threaten the work-ethic and thus diminish productivity. But this merely disregards the Dionysian desire in all of us to get really out of it. By forcing the harmless and socially useful hash market to wither, the authorities will find that they have created a new monster.

Ours is a culture already attuned by the ministrations of the NHS to drug usage to combat the horrific problems of modern life. To remove the innocuous cannabis from the scene is but a prelude for the grotesque squalor of a downers, drink and coke mentality.

PLAYBOYS

from 'Total frontal erotica… a good investment', in T.O. 206, by **Ronnie Mutch**

My first encounter with Hugh Hefner was at a press conference held when he flew into London in 'The Big Bunny' (not the ultimate Playmate, but a large black DC9). All previous press conferences paled into insignificance next to this one – brilliant sunshine, a huge fluffy pink marquee with sparkling chandeliers, hordes of beautiful smiling bunnies (of which more later), lakes of Moët, acres of breasts, miles of beautiful legs and finally and most fittingly, Food by Freud. Oh Sigmund, even I could not have dreamt up that alliteration had it not been true. Clement and I, sadly, discussed Irish stew.

Framed by a halo of red-white-and-blue-clad bunnies, Hugh, or Hef as he prefers being called, sat on the Masculine Throne, his lady friend or rather his 'steady, Barbie', on his left and all around a group of besotted journalists, asking the usual besotted questions. There was a slight edge of tension when one young lady, palpably sober and angry, asked about his views on women. 'Womensh lib' ventured a man from the fourth estate. Hef fielded the question cautiously, almost automatically. Indeed, he replied to all questions as if he had written answers to them. I remembered a phrase from an ex-colleague of his – 'the only man I know who is a walking press release.' That, to me, summed him up. Bright but cautious, the smiles all a little too fixed. Indeed, as the questioners droned on and on, I became a little worried that the immobile bunny-girls, still painfully smiling, would succumb to some new type of facial ailment, brought on by too much fixed and stony joy.

I was then introduced to Hef's entourage. It went something like this. 'Hi there, this is Stu. He's a famous artist. This is Dave, he's a famous author. That's Ken, he's a famous musician. Ah, what did you say your name was?'

I couldn't resist it: 'Ronnie. I'm just famous.'

I was later introduced to Vic, or Victor Lownes III, Director European Playboy (to accord him his full title). I had heard a lot about Vic: 'Man, he's the real Playboy,' 'He's really something else' and so on. I do not know what I expected, a combination of Don Juan, Errol Flynn and Rothschild, I suppose. The reality was a charming, middle-aged man, well kept and tonsured, infinitely accommodating, and best of all, honest and amusing, although like all Americans I've met who have made a great deal of money, he was very serious about one thing – money.

'What are your hobbies, Vic?'

'Collect art.'

'You like good pictures?'

'Naa, it's a good investment.'

'What sort of pictures, Vic?'

'You know, straight stuff, representational art, a bit of surrealism.'

'Hmm.'

'Ah yes, something that will interest you. I collect erotic art.' Here at last was something. He was a Playboy after all.

'You collect erotic art… it interests you, turns you on?'

'Naa, it's a good investment.'

Vic gave me the run of the Playboy Club for more 'homework'. This sounds glamorous, but sadly it isn't. I find gambling a bore, even at £10 a chip, and since the club is run on the lines of an efficient combination of a nursery school and IBM the tinsel behind the glitter left me cold.

And the bunnies, I hear you say. Well now… with a few exceptions, they were all cheerful, good looking, much of a muchness, monosyllabically named Annes, Jeans, Mays. Many names with but one face and figure.

It was at the Club that I was introduced to the Order of Flagellants. These are the aspirant bunnies. They come from all over, 30 at a time, at their own expense, week after painful week, lured by the glamour of being selected as a bunny. A sort of glamorous Universal Standards Stamp of Approval on their personalities and looks, is what they are after. They strip to their bras and panties, and troop, bounce, smile and stalk their way into the interview room in front of the 'Hutch Mother'.

'Name, address, stand up please, turn left, smile, sit down… I'm afraid there are no vacancies.' The tension for so short an interview is enormous, and the defeat swift and often devastating. I particularly remember one woman of about 28. She came in smiling like death, lied about her age, lied unnecessarily about her marital status and then uneasily remembered the ring she had forgotten to remove from her left hand. Her ambition was written all over her. She was not going to be trapped in a surburban semi by a husband and two or three snotty, screaming kids. She was young enough, she was pretty enough, she was going to be a bunny. She smiled and smiled and thrust her already sagging mother's breasts forward. The verdict was swift and as gentle as could be managed. 'Sorry, dear, we've nothing to offer you.' The faintly motherly selector of bunnies, herself an ex-bunny, smiled benignly. The result was a death sentence, and the woman, her smile frozen horribly on her face, made for the door. I noticed that her legs were faintly varicosed. At the door she stopped, half turned and tried to mouth thanks, but the tattered, shattered dreams and the tears were too much in the way. She walked on, mother, wife, forever and irrevocably trapped. I left and had a drink.

I then asked Vic whether I could see his home, which I was told was a prototype Playboy mansion. Vic acceded, even though he was not going to be there. 'Certainly, make yourself at home.' The First Lady would show me around. 'First Lady?' 'Ah yes, I date extensively, but she's the most important.' The word 'date' sounded most incongruous coming from a middle-aged man.

The house was superb, a cross fertilisation of Mies van der Terrible, Golders Green Renaissance, and Harper's Bizarre. When Vic mentioned that he collected pictures and erotica he was not using the word loosely. Every square inch of wall space was covered. The First Lady and I were alone in this unending fornicatorium. She was an ex-playmate, by name Connie, and was inordinately proud of Vic's possessions. Everything was expensive. The master bedroom was an expanse of inlaid wood. Bedstead, tables, chairs, dressing table, even wonder of wonders, the box holding Kleenex tissues was inlaid. By comparison with Hef of course, Vic is in the junior league, but display and competition are the essence in the Playboy world. On the way out I caught a glimpse of a cartoon which did interest me. It was a good likeness of Vic berating a secretary in the *Playboy* office. The caption ran: 'At home you can call me Mr Lownes. In the office you call me *Baby*, is that clear!'

It is easy, even fashionable to knock Hefner and his cronies. The man is this century's most conspicuous consumer and he enjoys it (horrors!). He owns two mansions and has two first ladies. A midwestern, ex-Puritan American's fantasy turns out to be every man's fantasy. This is not an indictment of him, but of society.

And yet I wonder. In the last analysis, is it not the fact that he is into fairly old-fashioned male-oriented sex that I envy. After all, he does not deal in death or destruction, he is into fucking, and that can't be all bad. But is it worth all the shouting and cymbal clanging? In 50 years' time, partly because of him, it will all be passé.

But then, so will he. ●

"1974"

"I am now called Tania."
Heiress Patty Hearst adopts a new name after being spotted robbing a bank on behalf of her kidnappers, the Symbionese Liberation Front

"I have never issued an inflammatory statement in my life."
Rev Ian Paisley after supporting a seven-day Protestant Workers' Strike and paralysing the Northern Ireland Assembly

"Every time someone shakes my hand I feel they are trying to take my pulse."
An ailing French President Georges Pompidou. He died later that year

"I urge the Congress to join me in mounting a major new effort to replace the discredited president."
President Nixon's Freudian slip. He meant to say 'precedent'

"I have no intention of resigning."
President Nixon, January

"I shall resign the Presidency, effective at noon tomorrow."
President Nixon, August

"Hey everybody. The fucker quit."
David Crosby of Crosby, Stills, Nash & Young announces the news of Nixon's resignation at Roosevelt Stadium, NJ

"Our long national nightmare is over. Our constitution works."
Gerald Ford, on being sworn in as President

"That Gerald Ford. He can't fart and chew gum at the same time."
Lyndon B Johnson

"Oh dear, what a pity. Nannies are so hard to come by these days."
A concerned Belgravia resident responds to police questions about the murder of Lord Lucan's nanny, Sandra Rivett, and his subsequent disappearance

"We are, without doubt, the most abused, the most unfairly criticised and the most silent majority in this country."
Sir Robert Mark, Metropolitan Commissioner of Police

Harlem in tutus

Arthur Mitchell interviewed in T.O. 232, by **Jan Murray**

'I'm a man who happens to be black; not a black man. There's a big difference. I founded the Dance Theatre of Harlem, but I'm the company's messenger, its instrument. I receive spiritual guidance – call it intuition if you like – but I know it comes from up there, and I don't belong to any particular religion. If I turn the company into some kind of ego-trip, it's changed, maybe ruined. That's not going to happen'.

There is no point in arguing with Arthur Mitchell. His record is too impressive, his critics too envious, his energy almost overwhelming. He's had the star treatment, as a brilliant soloist with the New York City Ballet for ten years. In 1968 he decided to form his own school in a garage. From those beginnings have evolved a professional ensemble of 27 dancers, all black, and a school of 1,500 students based in its own centre in Harlem. The school already teaches music and dress making as well as most kinds of dance. It is in the process of becoming an accredited independent University of Allied Arts.

America has produced a number of black dance companies, most notably Alvin Ailey's. But the foundation of Mitchell's is classical ballet, and the repertoire contains war horses like the 'Le Corsaire' pas de deux (a favourite party piece for Fonteyn and Nureyev) plus modern 'classics' by George Balanchine and, planned for the future, a black 'Giselle'. So what are a bunch of kids from New York's most infamous ghetto doing in tutus?

'The black militants were always asking me that. "Why are you teaching a 19th-century European art form?" they wanted to know.

'As a start, I'd be perpetuating a hoax on the public if I concentrated on other dance styles because classical ballet is what I know. And I believe it gives the best all-round training, a technique that provides a basis for every other kind of dance. Black people need education and I want the best for them. Why limit ourselves?

'Okay, I was their first black dancer to break into a major classical company. So-called authorities have always said that blacks can't do ballet because their feet are flat, their bodies are the wrong shape. Well, I happen to think that people should be given the freedom to choose, that people can accomplish anything they want to do, given the chance. When you see my kids dancing, you'll understand. The proof of this particular pud-

ding is right there on stage. That's black power'.

Three of Mitchell's own works will be performed during the Dance Theatre's London season. His 'Rhythmetron' is based on an African ritual. Black choreographers Louis Johnson, Talley Beatty and Geoffrey Holder are represented too, and there's lot's of 'black' music. Plus pointed shoes.

'I think the Dance Theatre is making classical ballet relevant for today – that's very exciting to me. The steps may be the same but we give them a shot of our own kind of energy. None of that 'tip-toe through the tulips' stuff. My kids come from tough backgrounds, they don't have preconceptions about what ballet should be, so we have a freedom all our own. And they can dance anything. It's mind-blowing to see them jump from one style to another during the course of a programme. It's not the style that matters, it's the concepts!

'What I want to do is give opportunities to black kids. Even if they don't become dancers, they work out some of their frustrations through the physicality of dance, walk better, think straighter. We show them there's an area of the arts that is no longer closed to blacks.' ●

1975

Are you coming out tonight? Gay folk figured the time was overdue to make their presence felt and joined in with the recent years' penchant for liberation. The Sex Discrimination Act was passed but Tammy still told us, 'Stand By Your Man'. Mini skirts went maxi, it snowed in June, 'Jaws' made it snappy, and the 'Sloane Ranger' was identified in the wild for the first time.

January
Margaret Thatcher elected leader of Conservative Party.

Crash at Moorgate tube station kills 43 people in the worst London Underground disaster to date.

April
Khmer Rouge come to power in Cambodia.

May
Tube drivers refuse to drive trains containing Scotland fans to Wembley.

June
First ever UK referendum produces a vote (by 2-1) to stay in the EEC.

Elizabeth Taylor and Richard Burton re-marry, two years after divorcing.

The first North Sea oil is piped ashore.

August
Third cricket test abandoned after protestors fighting to clear the name of jailed pal George Davis pour oil on the wicket.

September
Spaghetti House siege begins after gunman takes seven Italians hostage.

October
Figure of one million reached on unemployment register for first time since war.

November
Ross McWhirter, publisher and right-winger, is shot dead at his home by IRA.

Spanish dictator General Franco dies.

December
The first pop video is shown on Top of the Pops. Unfortunately, it's 'Bohemian Rhapsody' by Queen.

Jaws
Spielberg shoots the old fashioned monster movie with considerable flourish and only gets bogged down in an intractably cold performance from Robert Shaw.

Picnic At Hanging Rock
The film is dominated in turns by vague feelings of unease, barely controlled hysteria and a swooning lyricism.

One Flew Over The Cuckoo's Nest
For all the film's painstaking sensitivity and scrupulous chartings of energies and repressions, one longs for more muscle which only Nicholson consistently provides.

10cc - The Original Soundtrack (Mercury)
The level of musicianship and thematic

content places 10cc in the highest echelon of rock innovators.

Bob Dylan - Blood On The Tracks (CBS)
From somewhere Dylan has rediscovered the supreme creative resources that he has funnelled into his best work in the past, and has produced a perfect

collection of songs. A staggering performance.

Rod Stewart - Atlantic Crossing (Warner Bros)
Depending on how many albums you already have, this will either be a welcome event or merely the latest development in the familiar singalong soap opera.

David Hare interviewed in T.O. 285, by **Ann McFerran**

The acid dream is over

'The acid dream is over, it said so in the *Daily Express*,' says Arthur, the songwriter in David Hare's new play 'Teeth 'n' Smiles'. As 'Kennedy's children' skewered the US of the '60s, so Hare's play tells the story of his generation in England. The hero of the play is a rock 'n' roll band, that shooting star of English culture in the sixties. With Helen Mirren as the self-destructive lead singer, and with specially written music played by a real five-piece band, this play should, at the very least, awaken the Royal Court theatre, where it opens next Tuesday, from its summer in the doldrums of revivals. At best it could wean rock audiences from the heady world of pop to a theatre which needs an injection of youth-blood.

At 28, Hare is probably the most mainstream of the generation of new writers. After going to Cambridge, he founded the Portable Theatre, a writers' touring company, with Tony Bicat and Snoo Wilson. Since those early pioneering days, Hare has been resident dramatist at the Royal Court where, in 1971, his play 'Slag' (a play about three teachers in a school) was produced in the Theatre downstairs. His play 'Knuckle' was produced two years ago by a West End management.

'Teeth 'n' Smiles' relies heavily on his experience at Cambridge. About a rock group who are playing a May Ball gig in the Cambridge of 1969, the play tells of the expectations, the exploitation and the exhaustion at the end of the sixties acid dream, as experienced by a band on the run. Against this background of music and exhaustion hovers a three-cornered relationship. Maggie, the whisky drinking, self-destructive and raunchy lead singer, played by Helen Mirren, is discovered and bedded by Arthur, played by Jack Shepherd, an ex-Cambridge music student turned songwriter. After an ecstatic affair, the couple part; Arthur goes to write songs, and Maggie to sing with the band, always wanting to keep on the move. Meanwhile, Arthur has been 'having it off' with Laura, played by Cherie Lunghi, the group's hard-working and resilient PR girl. However, unlike traditional plays, this three-cornered relationship is only a background for the real story, the star of which is the band. It's a minor cult, middle-range band, the kind of band who've probably blasted a few glorious gigs in

1968 and been on the road ever since, trying to re-capture these moments, aiming ultimately at survival. The band are played by musicians who are actors and actors who are musicians. All the actors in 'the band' have experienced being on the road, and in the play, places become hazy – to them Cambridge could be Canterbury and vice versa – and they play nonsensical games to pass the time.

Rehearsals with a director who is also the writer, means, as Dave King – who plays Saraffian, the band's crooked, manipulating manager – says, 'You can't blame the dialogue when you get it wrong.' It also disposes of all those tedious arguments about what the writer is really saying. Hare, wearing a T-shirt and baggy trousers, sits on his hunkers watching intently and leaping to his feet to explain the feelings behind the words of his characters. Sometimes, when an actor feels a line isn't clear a change is made with little fuss. Hare explains his characters as hard as he works his actors.

Your last play was 'Fanshen', a documentary about the revolution in China. Before that you wrote 'Brassneck' with Howard Brenton, a play about postwar corruption in the Midlands. 'Teeth 'n' Smiles' is about English rock culture in the '60s. It's our own history. How did you come to write the play?

I'd been writing about figures in public life and people who were far removed from me and everyone kept saying why does your generation of writers never write about yourselves, why do you always batten onto the weaknesses of other generations or go back into history to exploit the general decadence of other ways of life. But it takes a long time to assimilate autobiographical material. If you write about something directly within your own experience, as this play is, then it's best to do it eight years on. It's just taken that long to get the perspective I wanted on that particular series of events.

The play is set at a May Ball in Jesus College, Cambridge, in 1969. You were at that college. How much was it based on your own experience?

Quite a lot. I think it's so boring and dishonest when writers dress up their own experience. They think that by changing a few details they distance themselves. Then you get all those endless plays about why your wife is having all affair with the milkman. To write about yourself in disguise is a form of grotesque self-pity which the English stage is sick with. So I thought, if you were going to write about something you'd experienced, it was much better to be honest and not change *any* of the critical details. Like I *did* go to to Jesus College, Cambridge and there *were* rock groups visiting at the time. Everything on the surface is documentarily accurate. The rock groups were fantastically aggressive and they hated having to play those dates, and they were extremely rude to the audience. And, by and large, their audiences disliked them very much too. It was an extraordinary clash of two worlds; these May balls with people dressed up and performing a complete parody of a life that was over many, many years ago, and into that crashed these rock bands, like travelling trouble on the move.

How did you feel about Cambridge?

Cambridge has a totally narcissistic community because it has no standards to judge itself by. There are no actions, only words, and if there was to be an aerial strategic bombing of England, I would start with Cambridge.

You've researched thoroughly the whole business of a rock group on the move. Why did you want to write about rock musicians?

There is this wonderful comedy of rock musicians. It *is* intrinsically very, very funny that so many rock musicians are so pretentious and so thick and they lead such bloody awful lives that they just go catatonic with the sheer exhaustion and exploitation. There's that side to it and then there's the other side that they *are* often very good musicians and they *do* just live through their music. They feel that, having played their music, that their music says everything that they have to say. But the other side of their lives has this funny numb quality about it. Words have a numb value. Deliberately through the play you see completely spaced out characters and you can't believe that they can actually get a sentence out, but they leap up, pick up a bass guitar and are so completely transformed when they hit the stage. In many ways the play is about whether talking has any point at all. There are the bands who believe in music and keep saying things like 'it's not worth discussing' and there are the figures like Arthur the songwriter and Anson the student who believe in articulating things, and these two worlds jam together as they did in the '60s, and they do in the play.

Maggie, the female lead singer, is a self-destructive alcoholic. How did you come to write about such a person?

I didn't understand masochism. Suddenly I was very struck with the thought of somebody living a life in which they avoided all opportunities of being happy. It wasn't that they couldn't find themselves, or relate to any of those boring things that people said in the fifties and sixties, it was because they were actually frightened of being happy because they felt it was wrong. I think this is a fact about living in the West, in this part of the century. People are conscious of the absurdly over-privileged lives they've led, that nothing has ever been really difficult for them. In the middle classes, there's very little experience of suffering at all except on a level of personal bereavement or personal failure. It struck me so much that I wanted to write about it.

At the end of the play Arthur says 'I can see us all. Rolling down the highway into middle age. Complacency. Prurience. Sadism. Despair.' Do you believe this?

The characters in the play either believe protective things; that's to say they surround themselves with zen or with the belief in the class war, or a belief in art, and they say inside my skull I've got the whole world worked out but of course there's nothing I can do about what's going on outside. Or like Maggie, they try for pure action which just moves you on into the next square. If you have a period like in 1968, when you believe in a revolution and then afterwards, the objective criteria for a revolution are missing, indeed definitively absent as they were in this country, you're soured with the impossibility of change. And if what you believe bears no relation on how you act, people go mad. I *do* believe that people do go clinically mad if what they believe bears no relation to how they live. ●

Sex, politics and 'Shampoo'

Warren Beatty interviewed in T.O. 269, by **Dave Pirie** and **Chris Petit**

Warren Beatty's new film 'Shampoo' opened recently at the Odeon Haymarket after mixed reviews and good business in the States. Apart from starring in the film, Beatty also wrote it (with Robert Towne, responsible for 'The Last Detail'and 'China Town') and produced it.

'Shampoo' offers an ambitious examination of sexual and political hypocrisy in modern America. American critic Pauline Kael discovered in the film 'the most virtuoso examination of kaleidoscopic farce that American movies have ever come up with'. Others were less impressed, refusing to see anything more than Beatty exploiting his own personal lifestyle to box-office ends. David Denby asked whether we were expected to believe that 'sex and careerism in Beverly Hills are the kind of behaviour that made the constitutional debaucheries of the Nixon-Agnew era an inevitability?' Here, Beatty talks frankly about his career, his lack of regrets and his opinion of Richard Milhouse Nixon.

Where did the idea for 'Shampoo' come from?

I had always wanted to make a film about a compulsive Don Juan or a hyper-sexual character whose condition didn't necessarily emanate from misogynistic or latent homosexual feelings, and thereby challenge in some way the established Victorian and Freudian assumptions. I developed a script many years ago called 'What's New Pussycat?' with Woody Allen which dealt with this area. But I had a lot of disagreements with the producer and so Peter O'Toole did it. The film was changed very drastically. Robert Towne and I began working on this project around '67-'68. We were very good friends, so were able to be insulting to one another without destroying the impulse to work.

What do you think of George as a character?

He's a kind of sex object, a dumb blonde, who's manipulated. He's quite compliant with everybody and I would imagine that he can hardly get it up.

What about the ending of the film where Jackie turns down George. Are we meant to view it as tragic?

The Beach Boys song comes up very quickly at the end which I had always hoped would show most people that we are not going into some funeral dirge. There's no doubt in my mind that in two hours George has got his address book out and thumbing through the numbers. At one time we considered putting in an epilogue showing where the characters had got to. Lester gives George the money for his shop which he opens and runs badly. Jill lives at Malibu for about three months with Johnny Pope then moves out because he won't marry her. Lester gets another mistress pretty soon and Jackie takes a series of younger lovers, while Lorna becomes a feminist.

I thought at one stage the film was going to be a straight comedy. At what point did you put in the political background?

I don't think you can separate politics from sexual politics. Nixon, Agnew… that's so practical it's not even political. To me you can't make an unpolitical movie. Your politics are going to show by permission or omission, so that the best you can do is to try and focus on them in some way in your movies, organise it so that it doesn't happen totally by accident. I mean the fucking system has hardly a leg left to stand on and so it's almost impossible to avoid it in movies now. I think we are at the complete end of an era of public trust in America.

In 'Shampoo' the politics proceed out of character and the characters' sexual are evident. There's been some change between 1968 and 1975, particularly the area of self-concept in women. George would have changed much less over the years because he's such an example of non-sublimated libido.

You've now written, produced and acted but you've never realised a long-standing intention to direct.

'Shampoo' I was going to direct for years, just as I was going to direct 'Bonnie and Clyde'. But when I produce a film as I did with both those, I'm what you call hyperactive. There's nothing in a film that I produce that I don't like. With both films I thought, well, as long as I'm going to work with the cameraman, the editor, the writer and the other actors, why don't I get myself what we call a director. And I never know what a director does in movies because it changes with every director in every film. I see films as movements involving groups of people who share a kind of sense of humour about something, or a lack of sense of humour. I would never work with a director I didn't really respect, but I do believe in the group experience in making films, very very strongly. I am very antagonistic to the *auteur* theory promulgated by the *Cahiers du Cinema*. Bullshit.

Do you think it's done harm to Hollywood?

Tremendous harm. I think it stamped out the creative ego of many writers, actors and producers. It really conjured up antagonisms between directors and producers, actors and writers, developing all kinds of phoney respect for people who were for some reason or other called directors. A respect that was due to other craftsmen on the film. It's turned the directorial star system into something that's exceeded the old one with actors

We definitely thought 'Shampoo' was on one level a statement on the movie industry: it's set in Hollywood, you've cast several film producers as fund raisers, and in a sense the George character is like an actor or a star, a hunk of meat that has been cast around. Was that on your mind?

Well you never know what's on your mind. Those producers – Bill Castle, Brad Dexter and Tony Bill – had all acted before and I knew them. They were part of the Hollywood I knew, but to make some specific statement about their presence in the film is difficult. To overarticulate is a mistake because making a film is an attempt to express the unconscious.

When I'm hyping a film, as I'm doing now, I try not to get too smartass and articulate. I'll skirt a lot of issues, talk a lot about film-making, politics, sex, I'll talk about a lot of things, but I try to avoid talking about my intentions in the film, because I don't want to limit an audience's reaction. In a way, film hype is counter-productive to the perception of film. I think the best thing to do is to try and give some indication where your feelings lie and let people know that you worked hard and weren't sloppy about the film.

Beatty's rise as a film actor came in the early '60s as a discovery of Elia Kazan, who had also made Dean and Brando. Unlike most of his contemporaries, he served no long apprenticeship in B-movies or television. For most of that decade he was not taken particularly seriously by the critics, ▶

although in retrospect his choice of films looks shrewder than a lot of other actors. Yet since 'Bonnie and Clyde', which confirmed his box-office status all over the world, he has made only a handful of films.

If you compare your credits with say Nicholson or Redford and Eastwood it turns out that you've made relatively few films, and almost none of them genre films.

What was the first name you said?

Nicholson.

I thought you said Nixon.

They've all done westerns and horror movies, but you haven't got into that hardcore popular cinema very much.

Everyone has done more movies than I have. But I've been what they call financeable longer than any of them except for Marlon Brando and Paul Newman who are both 14-15 years older. But of my age range, that is Nicholson, Redford and those guys, I've been around roughly twice as long as them and I've made about half as many films. So in analysing what I've done, a lot of it has to do with what I haven't done. A lot of it has to do with – what were you doing with all that time? I've never been interested in going from one film to another as an actor – it just never interested me. I've turned down a lot of movies and a lot of hits in the process.

Do you regret it?

I don't regret any of it. I don't regret turning down 'The Sting', or 'Gatsby', 'Butch Cassidy', 'The Way We Were' or 'The Godfather'. The film I would come closest to regretting is a film that Pontecorvo made which eventually became 'The Battle of Algiers' which he offered to me years before he made it. He sent the script to New York and wanted me to play a Frenchman in Algeria which I couldn't see myself doing. The film that eventually came out I thought was very good, but I would never regret not doing a film because it became a big money-maker.

Have you ever taken on films that you subsequently wished you hadn't done?

I didn't have to do anything. There were pictures that I did because I felt maybe I could get away with them and it would be convenient at the same time. There was a period when I wanted to make movies in England for personal reasons and I made a couple of rather silly films…but I never did a film because I had to.

What attracted you to 'Bonnie and Clyde'? You've described them as glamourised.

There was a socio-economic undercurrent that in itself allowed a segment of the population to glamourise Bonnie and Clyde. That's what they did. Like a segment of the population has glamourised Huey Newton or Patty Hearst.

Nevertheless, when you compare how you looked in the film with how Bonnie and Clyde really looked, it's a very heroic conception of them. Don't you consider yourself too attractive for the part?

Attractive? I don't consider that a serious problem, I really don't. Well, they were made more romantic than they were. The poor all thought that Bonnie and Clyde robbed from the rich and gave to the poor. They robbed from everybody and kept everything.

What was your initial point of interest in the film?

It was really something in the style of Benton and Newman's script. They deserve the primary credit for what epitomised for me the casualising of violence in the '60s: I thought the juxtaposition of violence and humour was very important. It was of course that which alienated so many old-timers. I'm not talking about the casualising of violence in films, but in society. You had a Democratic President in Lyndon Johnson, who was a very violent man, wreaking havoc in Southeast Asia. At the same time the man was a liberal domestically. He appointed liberals to the Supreme Court. He was very much a defender of civil rights and individual rights. So you had black people whose civil rights would be defended by the Administration before they were packed off to Vietnam to be annihilated. It was something that we were not used to.

'It was intolerable to live in a country where Richard Nixon was President.'

Outside of films Beatty has become increasingly involved in American politics to the extent of taking two years off to devote himself to George McGovern's campaign for the Presidential Election of 1972. McGovern said of him: 'He has a political maturity astounding in someone so inexperienced – the instincts of a man who has spent a lifetime in politics.' Already there are rumours about his contribution to the Democratic party's challenge for the Presidency in 1976.

How did you get involved with McGovern's Presidential Campaign?

I knew George McGovern from when I had worked for Bobby Kennedy. I also knew Muskie pretty well and liked him. He wanted me to participate in his campaign and I almost did. But finally he seemed so indecisive and middle-of-the-road that I felt it would be a waste of time, so I began working with George.

What sort of chance do you think he had of winning the elections?

None. Once Wallace had been shot it made a big difference. If Wallace had been in the campaign, a lot of his supporters who went over to Nixon would have otherwise stayed with the Democrats. You would then have had close to the same percentages as in the 1968 elections between Humphrey and Nixon, one of the closest elections in history. But to try and beat an incumbent President, as we were trying to do in 1972, is pretty tough. The fact is that it wound up being the first grass roots political campaign in American history, and as such I don't consider it a failure. Moreover, for me it was intolerable to live in a country where Richard Nixon was President. It wasn't possible to be very interested in movies at that period. ●

The last Hollywood starlet?

Valerie Perrine interviewed in T.O. 260, by **David May**

It is 11.15 in the morning and in complete conformity with the style of the 'new' Hollywood Valerie Perrine is still in her night-dress. She is in London to promote her third film 'Lenny'. The one that earned her the 1975 Cannes Film Festival Best Actress Award.

Ms Perrine's London visit is spent arranging lunches at smart restaurants with old friends, being interviewed, modelling for the *Sunday Times*, and being interviewed on the Michael Parkinson Show. The latter proving to be an irritant in an otherwise fun time. 'It didn't go as smoothly as I thought.' Apparently she thought he was going to be 'gentle and get fun things out of me', but the bluff Barnsley entertainer proved to have a mean streak beneath his jovial mask.

'People said I said some very good things – like he was trying to make me out to be scheming and conniving and I said "I just take what God gives me" and a lot of people liked that, but do you know what the first question he asked me was? "How does it feel to be a sex symbol at 32?" I mean…! What does it feel like to be an asshole at 50?'

The unpleasantness is forgotten however as she explains how karma determined that after eight years as a burlesque dancer she should go west for what turned out to be a classic introduction to Hollywood:

'I was living here! Right here! In London! I was out of money saying, well… I could get a job or I could go back to dancing at the Lido in Paris but I didn't want to work that way again… so I woke up one day with the feeling that I should go to Hollywood and be a movie star. No training, no experience. They're crazy. Ha ha. I was staying with a friend in LA living off food stamps and unemployment and one night this girlfriend of mine gave a small dinner party for about five or six people. A simple party and this agent, who didn't handle anyone big, was there and he said "Would you like to be in the movies?" I said "Sure". Three months later I was starring in "Slaughterhouse Five" and here I am.'

To be strictly accurate she only 'starred' in the last ten minutes of 'Slaughterhouse Five'. She played Montana Wildhack, time traveller Billy Pilgrim's celestial *Playboy* centrefold; a sweet, simpering, horny, maternal, muscular, harmless, siliconed sexual stereotype.

'They were looking for a beautiful girl with long blonde hair. A typical model type really, but when George [director George Roy Hill]

interviewed me I weighed 150 pounds, which is what I weigh now. I was really hefty, very zoftig (Yiddish for 'well built'). I think we should bring back zoftig. I really do. Men like it better in bed. They like to look at women on the streets who are really thin but in bed they like fleshy women. It's unbelievable. I mean I like men for the very hardness they have…'

She followed up her first big break with 'Last American Hero' playing a groupie for a gang of stock car drivers led by Jeff Bridges. 'The studio didn't want me to do it because there is a scene with me talking about how, when I was in college, I was invited to a fraternity party. But when I get there I realise that only ugly girls have beeen invited. It was called a "pig party".

'It was a very touching and emotional scene but the studio went Ohhh! We don't want you saying you have ever been anything but a raving beauty. I said I am not a raving beauty and I was an ugly duckling and it's the only acting scene I have been offered for a long time. You know the studio is really mad that I'm not lying about my age. They're really upset. Everyone tells me to lie about my age. 28 is a good age, 29 perhaps, but keep it in the 20s.'

'Everyone tells me to lie about my age.'

The first two roles led to 'Lenny' and the part of Hot Honey Harlow – who became Bruce's wife. How did she prepare for the film?

'I didn't.'

But surely Dustin Hoffman spent hours with Bruce's mother before filming started? 'Look Dustin had to play a person who people had seen or listened to. He had to pick up his mannerisms, speech patterns, his way of moving,

the way he looked. I played Honey Bruce. Nobody knew who she was. Goldie Hawn could have played her. When we decided she would be a junkie, I would be a junkie. When she was crying, I would cry. Sexy? I'd get sexy. I would do whatever came naturally.'

She admits both Lenny and Honey were made a lot more presentable for public consumption. 'We cleaned them up a lot. It would be very depressing if you don't. It wasn't sanitised though, it's just that there is a lot that you don't see. One of the things we changed was that Honey was apparently living with a girl when Lenny met her and in the movie it made it sound as though he talked her into going with girls.'

However much fate has prepared her for her 'marvellous' life over the last four years, Valerie Perrine is hard-headed enough to know that her well deserved success in 'Lenny' will not last forever. The movie business can be a tough proposition for an ageing actress.

'There is a period, between 40 and 50, when a woman is not used. Being a liberated woman in Hollywood doesn't mean a thing. They're just not writing roles for older women and I know that I like to have a definite dialogue going down. I work with love and affection and understanding and so forth. I wanna produce as well but I'm not ready. I figure in a couple of years I will be.' ●

The case of the disappearing closet

It started out as a tough night for our ace reporter ('Just the facts ma'am'). And it got tougher.

from T.O.255, by **Len Richmond**

It was a tough assignment. I had been hired to report on London's gay pub and club scene for *Time Out*. I had to dress for the part: a heavy overcoat, dark sunglasses, and an old hat pulled down low. I guess I'd better tell you the whole story from the beginning. The whole incredible story. It all started one night last November. At the time, I thought this would be just another feature story like all the others I'd covered as an ace reporter. I decided to start gathering information for the article at one of the monthly Jean Fredricks Fun Balls, held at Porchester Hall.

The place is packed when I arrive. Hundreds of female impersonators, some in women's clothes. It doesn't take me long to size things up. It's a drag ball. I had heard about such things in the army. I lean up against a wall, light up a cigarette, and look around the room. I see two Arabs dancing Sheik to Sheik. A pretty young drag queen looking like Marlene Deitrich in 'The Blue Angel' saunters up to me. She's a knockout.

'You wanna dance, big boy?'

'I can only lead,' I say.

'That's alright. I'll teach you to follow.' She pulls me out onto the crowded dance floor. We dance close. Awful close. I try and make conversation.

'Come here often?' I ask.

'Yeh. Jean has the biggest balls in town. I love 'em. Her parties are really a drag. Of course, half the people that come here look like a night of a thousand face-lifts. But what the hell, it's all in fun. Listen, honey, you're leading.'

'Oh, sorry sweetheart.'

'Just relax and trust me.' She pulls me closer and whirls me around. Then she whispers in my ear: 'If you guess who I'm dressed up as tonight, you can come home with me.'

'I'd say… a horse.'

'That's close enough.' Just then, a tatty little drag queen dressed up like a pirate breaks up our little love nest. Marlene snarls:

'Well, if it isn't Jean with the light brown teeth. What's on your little mind?'

'Gimme a cigarette.' She demands. Marlene turns to me and says:

'She's dressed up tonight as Captain Kidd 'cause she's got a sunken chest.' Captain Kidd seems to be having some trouble lighting her cigarette. I can see she is drunk as a skunk.

'I'm afraid liquor mortis has set in.' Marlene explains. Then she gives Captain Kidd a gentle push in the direction of the door. 'Now, why don't you go down to the morgue and tell them you're ready?' Captain Kidd staggers off into the crowd. Marlene puts her arm around me again and whispers:

'Now, where were we?' We begin to dance again slow. Awful slow.

'Listen Marlene, I could dance with you all night, but I got a story to do. I got a deadline.'

'I'll show you places that'll make your banana split.'

'Such a busy man. What kind of story?'

'I gotta getta line on the gay pub and club scene in London for *Time Out*.'

'For that tacky rag?'

'Listen Marlene, I think you're swell, but I've got an assignment to finish and…'

'Who the hell do you think you are? The Maltese Faggot? Listen, you want a story, right? Stick with me tonight and I'll show you places that'll make your banana split.' She grabs my hand and pulls me through the crowd.

'Where are you taking me?'

'We're gettin' out of this dive. Tonight we're gonna paint the town pink!'

I get this terrible feeling that I shouldn't go. I know this crazy dame's poison to me. But it's too late to turn back now. In a few minutes Marlene and I are gettin' out of a taxi in front of a place called the Union Tavern at 146 Camberwell New Road. We go in. It's packed with a lot of men all standing around like they're waiting for something to happen. Then it happens. A big guy comes out on a little stage. I think he's a guy. He's dressed pretty weird. He looks like the Queen Father. His name's Mark Fleming.

'We've got a lot of visitors here tonight,' he says as he grabs the microphone. 'They're all from Sweden. A whole coachload. This Swedish lesbian brings in fifty people in a coach. She says: "Now, we have to visit to the typical English Pouff pub." She's doing okay with these tours. She's got a house in the south of France, and a cottage in Leicester Square. Did you know, my dears, that these pearls I'm wearing are of royal origin? Yes, they are. These pearls belonged to our old Queen Mary before the war. I was a lady in waiting and when she died I thought I'd waited bloody long enough. Mind you, she ran out of her box twice trying to get them back. I sold her to Hammer Films eventually. Once Queen Elizabeth was going out of the palace gates and all the guards came to attention. Well, they came. I'm not sure they were at attention. Charles thanked them. The Queen that day was wearing this lovely diamond choker. Phillip said: "I hope it does". Do you know Princess Ann? A lovely woman. It's Ted Heath in drag. If I get hung for treason, I do hope there's a few sequins on the rope.'

He lifts up his skirt and marches off stage. He sure ain't no lady.

'Well, love…' Marlene sighs. 'Come on, let's move. We got a big night ahead of us. Next stop's a sleazy pub called the Colherne.' On our way to the Colherne on Old Brompton Road, Marlene insists we stop off at her flat so she can change her clothes. It sounds a little fishy to me, but I wait in the taxi. After what seems like ages she finally comes down the stairs. Only, I hardly recognise her. She's dressed completely in black leather, wearing studded boots, and a motorcycle cap. She's grinning from ear to ear.

'You like my new look?'

'Gosh, Marlene, you look swell.'

'Of course I do. If I'm goin' to the Colherne, I gotta look the part.' Her voice drops two octaves as she continues: 'And listen, you bastard, my name's not Marlene anymore, it's Marlon. Got it?'

'You are dangerous.' I laugh, but I know I'm falling deeper and deeper under her spell. Pretty soon, it'll be too late.

The Colherne's a popular pub in Earls Court. It's a warm night and the sidewalk in front is filled with the overflow. Marlon tells me that the coppers come by almost every night to chase the guys off the sidewalk at closing time. But they never bother the people on the sidewalk in front of the straight coffee house next door. It seems like a raw deal. Marlon takes me right into the part of the pub 'dominated' by the leather crowd.

'Ya know…' He begins as he leans against the bar. 'Most gays in London seldom go to gay pubs and clubs. They don't like 'em, and they got a point. Most of 'em are pretty exploitative. Overcharging for drinks, stuffy and depressing atmospheres. I don't think they've got much respect for their clientele. I know for a fact that some clubs even play their music really loud 'cause

Outrage
from T.O. 279

Monday July 7 saw 15 members of the Campaign for Homosexual Equality assemble in Trafalgar Square to illegally engage in public displays of affection. The group was demonstrating against current law, which forbids male homosexuals to kiss or embrace in public on the grounds that 'public decency would be outraged'.

Seeking to show that displays of homosexual affection are 'no more distasteful than those by heterosexuals', CHE General Secretary Alan Clarke asked Police Constable A805 if outrage would result if members of his group were to kiss.

PC A805 replied that he would be outraged, and that they had been warned. The policeman then departed and the group embraced in front of about a dozen newsmen. Few passers-by seemed unduly disturbed, although one older woman declared the display 'sinful', and a tourist from Birmingham said he thought it was 'not very nice'.

The demonstration was part of CHE's campaign for homosexual law reform to 'introduce the general principle that no conduct of a homosexual nature shall be an offence except where similar heterosexual conduct would be an offence'. The organisation has prepared a draft bill to lower the age of consent in homosexual relations to 16; permit homosexuals to advertise for partners; safeguard homosexuals from police entrapment and legalise homosexuality in Northern Ireland and Scotland, where all male homosexuality is still prohibited.

they know it makes people nervous and they buy more booze. That's all they seem to care about; pushing the drinks and pulling in the money. It's enough to keep anybody in the closet. Look around the room. Most guys are just standing around, not doing anything but looking at the other guys that aren't doing anything. It's like, once in a while I see somebody I wouldn't mind tickling my fancy with. I stare at them. They stare back. I look away, then I look back to see if they're still looking. They're looking but then they get embarrassed and they look away. It can go on like that all night. It's such a boring game.' Marlon grabs my arm and pulls me through the leather crowd.

'Come on, I'm getting depressed. Let's get the hell out of here. I'll take you to someplace a little more liberating.'

'Where?'

'I'll change into my Levi's and we'll go the the gay liberation disco at the Prince Albert pub.'

By the time we arrive at the disco, Marlon has changed his clothes in the cab. He's now wearing a pair of faded Levi's, a Mao-Tse-Tung sweatshirt, and a lot of gay badges. They say things like: 'Avenge Oscar Wilde' and 'How Dare You Presume I'm Straight?' It must be a full moon, 'cause everybody there seems all steamed up. They're dancing like there's no tomorrow. Marlon hands me a drink.

'What's your name now?' I ask him.

'Merlin… the magnificent!'

'Do you live up to your name?'

▶

'Try me.'

We begin to dance to David Bowie.

'Try to loosen up,' he says. 'Let yourself go.' I do the twist. I think he's impressed.

The dance ends. Merlin walks around the room visiting with friends, kissing and hugging them. I check out the place. It seems like a friendly crowd. Of course, some guys are standing around, looking like they're in a gay pub. But Merlin tells me that they're mostly newcomers, and they'll loosen up. Then he recites a little limerick he wrote:

Gay bars can be terribly boring
Love's reduced to 'see you' next morning
At Gay Lib you'll find, someone with a mind
And a purpose in life that's rewarding.

Merlin smiles and puts his arm around my shoulder. 'I'm afraid it's time to move again. I've still got to take you to the Black Cap, the Champion, the Boltons, the Ship and Whale, The Pig and Whistle, the Gigolo, The Masquerade, the Catacombs, the…'

'Wait a minute. Couldn't we go someplace quiet and…'

'Well, we could go back to my flat. I could show you the dirty postcard I got from Mrs Whitehouse.'

'Queer we didn't think of that before.'

I wake up the next morning in a strange room. Merlin is sitting on the edge of the bed smoking a cigarette. He's pouffing the smoke out of the corner of his mouth, casual like. He looks at me and smiles, then gets up to make some coffee.

'Come and get it,' he yells from the kitchen. I stagger out of bed and wander into the kitchen. It's then I notice: I'm wearing a dress.

'How did I get into this thing?' I plead with Merlin to set me straight.

'One leg at a time, the same as the rest of us.'

'Gosh.'

'Did you ever read the SCUM manifesto?'

'Not lately,' I say, adjusting my hemline.

'SCUM is the Society for Cutting Up Men. Their manifesto is quite interesting. It says that straight society has everything

Chariots of the gods?

from T.O. 258, by **Jerry Palmer**

Four years ago I was lent a copy of 'Chariots of the Gods?' After a few pages I was uttering strangulated grunts and twitching compulsively. The third chapter left me shuttlecocking between rage and hysterical mirth, and when I reached mathematical speculations about the Pyramid of Cheops ('Is it really a coincidence that the height of the Pyramid of Cheops multiplied by a thousand million corresponds approximately to the distance between the earth and sun?'), amazement finally stood down in favour of disgust and only an entirely unreasonable respect for the printed word stopped me heaving it in the fire.

In retrospect, my reaction was interesting: why didn't I just discard it straight away? Rage was an index of unwilling fascination. Largely, I have to admit, because I was totally unfamiliar with the things he was writing about. In that respect, I guess I'm typical of von Daniken's readers.

Fascination has eventually brought me back to von Daniken, who in the meantime has written three more books: 'Return to the Stars', 'Gold of the Gods' and 'In Search of Ancient Gods'. In the process he has sold 25 million copies in 26 languages, and the film 'Chariot of the Gods?' has been applauded in every major country, including the USSR and China. He has sparked off a rash of imitators and acquired the status of a genuine cult figure. Even *Time Out* praised him for the 'painstaking research' behind his central thesis: that at the dawn of civilisation earth was visited, perhaps repeatedly, by travellers from another galaxy who used their superior technology to construct a series of monuments which clearly could not have been constructed by the cultures of the time. Awed by such architectural feats, humanity – von Daniken argues – arrived at the notion of deity.

Von Daniken finds mysteries and makes them more mysterious. He makes them more mysterious by propounding theories that explain nothing else. He feeds on the desire that people feel for things that defy reason. His theories are the perfect incarnation of bourgeois culture. They are of no use to anyone – except the book trade – for they can not be used to produce any new knowledge at all. They are the meanderings of a mind bemused, but certain of one thing: the public's craving for the inexplicable.

ass-backwards. That men are really the weak, meek, mild, camp half of the species. They just don't want to admit it, so they pretend that women are. But the butch image that most men like to portray is really the true nature of women. If you think about it, you'll realise that drag queens and leathermen can enlighten straight society by showing them how absurd those stereotypes really are.'

'Yeh? Well, bedfellows make strange politics, I always say.'

'There was once a straight from the press
Who woke up one day in a dress
He wasn't amused, and said "I'm confused"
But his friend said "Coming out's best".'

Merlin reaches over and takes my hand in his. We stare at each other across the breakfast table.

'You know…' he says, 'the drag queen, the leatherman, the liberationist and all the other roles I play, they really are me. I'm all those people and so are you.' The next thing I know we're kissing, and crazy as it may seem, I know this is the beginning of a beautiful affair. ●

Festivals deflowered

from T.O. 275

Outdoor music is not what it used to be and it may never be the same again. The idea of a temporary tribal community at a three-day festival died twice in the mud at Bickershaw and Lincoln, and the events are now one-day extravaganzas held mostly in stadia designed for spectator sports.

The great festivals were charged with a collective consciousness, with a sense of identity and purpose. But once we returned from the open fields, the test of city living exposed the lack of stamina. A few struggled to develop communities embodying the new spirit; the rest became a new breed of consumer, burning up the fresh resources and providing very little.

Rock festivals reflect the changing barometer. As the record market has become larger and more categorised, festivals have become music events of huge financial proportions. Security is now the overriding factor in choosing venues. But the terraces are no place to house a music audience. Not after the trails of blood left by the regular rampages of today's manic football supporters.

End game

Alarming news from Manchester. It seems that Manchester United fans have been availing themselves of a new variety of LSD before matches; the acid, called 'Stretford End Acid' in honour of that part of the Old Trafford ground, is thought to be a possible contributory factor to some of the more eccentric behaviour of the United fans. No truth in the rumour that Arsenal supporters have been taking elephant tranquillisers.

"1975"

Fidel Castro:
"I read 'Jaws'. It's not a very good book, but I think the movie must be good because it's a Marxist picture."
Francis Ford Coppola:
"Oh?"
Fidel Castro:
"Yes. It shows that businessmen are ready to sell out the safety of citizens rather than close down against the invasion of sharks."
Francis Ford Coppola:
"Oh."

"If there's a hell, I've seen it."
Doctor working in the tunnel after the Moorgate tube disaster

"I owe nothing to Women's Lib."
Margaret Thatcher, on becoming the first woman leader of the Tory Party

"This going into Europe will not turn out to be the thrilling mutual exchange supposed. It is more like nine middle-aged couples with failing marriages, meeting in a darkened bedroom in a Brussels hotel for a Group Grope."
Historian EP Thompson on the EEC

"Television brought the brutality of war into the comfort of the living room. Vietnam was lost in the living rooms of America, not the battlefields of Vietnam."
Marshall McLuhan, Canadian sociological guru

"Let our children grow tall, and some taller than others if they have it in them to do so."
Margaret Thatcher, on her first speaking tour of the USA

"I hate shit. I hate hippies and what they stand for. I hate long hair. I hate pub bands."
Johnny Rotten sits on the fence

"Inherited wealth is not unearned – it is earned by somebody other than the person who has got it."
The *Daily Telegraph* has its finger on the pulse

"George Davis is innocent."
The graffiti of the year, seen everywhere

JPR Williams

from 'The mad buccaneer' in T.O. 257, by **David Jenkins**

catch its collective breath. Unleashing Williams on a rugby field is like letting an arsonist loose in a match factory.

'Yes, I know this physicality appeals to lots of people. It allows me to get away with being a bit foolish from time to time, with the crowd behind me. For instance, if I'm five yards from touch, with two or three huge forwards thundering down on me, well I should run into touch, but I'll take them on.'

Through 30 appearances for Wales, eight for the British Lions and countless for London Welsh and others, he has indulged his form of martial art to huge success; and, remarkably, he has emerged relatively unscathed.

'If you go in hard, it's less dangerous because your muscles are tensed.' That's Williams' own view, and he's a doctor who intends to specialise in sporting injuries so he should know. But what of the fractured jaw he suffered against Scotland last year? 'Oh, that was bad luck, I just slipped as I went into the tackle and his boot went into my face.' Or of the injury incurred by Danny Hearn, a notoriously uncompromising tackler, that led to a life in a wheelchair? 'Just tough luck.'

This physical confidence has allowed Williams to develop the anarchic brilliance of his full-back play. 'Ten years ago, a full-back just had to kick goals, now it's the ideal position from which to attack and counterattack.' In this evolution Williams has led the way, blessed by spending his formative footballing years under the great captaincy of John Dawes. In the golden era of '68-'72, Dawes led London Welsh, Wales and the British Lions to triumph via attacking, fluent rugby. Now Dawes has become Wales' coach, and Welshmen hope his arrival will end the team's recent lean spell. 'No, we've got the same approach. It's down to basics. Any half-backs, any three-quarters, if your forwards don't win the ball, you can't compete. John Dawes is just a change of face, a few new ideas. People forget that most of the Welsh team are only just starting. We call ourselves the Oldies, that's Mervyn Davies, Gareth Edwards, Gerald Davies and myself, we're the only ones left from 1971.' (1971 being the year Wales grand-slammed the championship.)

1971 and the British Lions versus New Zealand in Christchurch, the seething home of All Black rugby. The Lions were one up in the series, and the All Blacks were hungry for poofta pom-bashing revenge. Suddenly John Williams, the best, the craziest, the bravest full-back in the world of Rugby, fielded a kick deep in his own 25. In the circumstances, with a horde of rampaging forwards bearing down, there was a definite case for caution and a safe kick to touch. But, typically, Williams ran at the All Blacks, sold an exquisitely outrageous dummy and set up a 70-yard move to create one of the tries that myths are made of. He was, incidentally, totally concussed at the time.

'Well, I've always felt the harder you play, the less likely you are to be injured,' commented Williams in his Welsh-inflected lilt. 'Most injuries are caused by top-class players making half-hearted tackles and not going in hard enough in games they consider unimportant.'

Williams could never be accused of being half-hearted. (Except, perhaps, in the matter of drinks. 'I've got a squash match tonight,' he muttered and paused. 'Alright, a bottle of light ale.') He is intensively and physically competitive, seeming to relish the challenge of impossible odds. With the bone-jarring fierceness of his tackling and the thrilling spontaneity of his counter-attacks, Williams' involvement causes the crowd to

Given Williams' individualism and relish for close-quarter conflict, it is strange that Rugby League has not made more effort to sign him. 'They've only made me one offer, when I was only 19, never again. Maybe it's because I'm a doctor. Mind you I don't blame those who do turn pro. But you do need a good contract. All this stuff about someone signing for £15,000 – it's usually only half down; and then if you get injured in the first match, well you're out.'

But the temptation exists, particularly in Wales, where Rugby is the working-class sport.

'Some sort of payment has got to come. If someone's got to miss a shift for training or playing, he ought to be paid. It's unfair to be an entertainer and not get paid. Mind you, with all the international squad training sessions, trials, county games etc, if rugby were a professional game, the clubs would be up in arms. But as it is, the internationals are your showpiece, so they've got to be good; and to be good, you've got to be professional in approach. Because once you know the laws, and the conditions are good, it's a wonderful spectacle.' ●

1976

January
Agatha Christie dies. Hercule Poirot does not investigate.

March
Harold Wilson announces retirement; Jim Callaghan becomes Prime Minister.

Princess Margaret and Lord Snowdon separate.

May
Jeremy Thorpe resigns as leader of Liberal Party after allegations of homosexual affair with Norman Scott.

July
David Steel elected new leader of Liberals.

August
First mass rally held by Northern Ireland Women's Peace Movement. Its organisers, Betty Williams and Mairead Corrigan, receive Nobel Peace Prize.

Hundreds of people injured at Notting Hill Carnival after riots break out.

Nikki Lauda badly injured in West German Grand Prix.

22 African nations boycott Olympics in protest at New Zealand's continued sporting links with South Africa.

September
Mao Tse-Tung dies.

October
National Theatre on South Bank opens.

November
Peanut farmer Jimmy Carter defeats Gerald Ford in race for Presidency.

December
Sex Pistols appear on TV with Bill Grundy. Outbreak of swearing occurs; sales of 'Anarchy In The UK' leap.

Hot-hot-hot-fuck-fuck-fuck. The heatwave flamed through and made us all a little crazy, then punk screamed in and finished the job. Old rockers like Bowie (facist salutes) and Clapton (pro-racist stage-talk) pissed us off so much we formed Rock Against Racism. (Bowie and Clapton later atoned by smooching black supermodels.) By December Johnny Rotten was our favourite antichrist and music would never sound the same again.

The Man Who Fell To Earth
This hugely ambitious and imaginative movie transforms a straight-forward science fiction story into a rich kalei-doscope of contemporary America.

Taxi Driver
The film's strength lies in the way it absorbs the viewer totally. Though flawed, 'Taxi Driver' has unmistakable power.

The Shootist
Wayne, Bacall and Stewart manage to suggest a sense of lives drawing to a close while keeping graveyard morbidity firmly at bay.

Patti Smith – Horses (Arista)
Patti hits the occ-asional bum note but she has one of the great rock voices.

Steely Dan – The Royal Scam (Anchor)
Are Walter Becker and Donald Fagen the Bacharach/David of the seventies? Their genius lies in the fact that even in this glossy context their music remains provocative, not only to the brain but hips also. A formidable return to form and a great album.

Stevie Wonder – Songs In The Key Of Life (Tamla Motown)
Wonder remains one of black music's great eclectics, but still has his limitations. His lyrics are coloured by a soft-centred romantic escapism which finds its musical counterpart in the surfeit of tepid, smooth tunes, lacking edge and urgency.

The politics of punk

A dozen years ago Mick Jagger, Brian Jones and Bill Wyman pissed against a garage wall and the national papers asked if you'd let your daughter marry a Rolling Stone. Now punk rock has made the same lightning transition, and last month's minority cult provides today's headlines. **Mandy Merck** investigates the alleged political stance of the movement's followers, **Mark P**, Editor of the punk fanzine *Sniffin' Glue*, gives the inside view, and *Time Out*'s Music Editor, **John Collis**, puts the case for those who rolled with the Stones but can't handle the Pistols.

Rebel with a swastika?

from T.O. 352, by **Mandy Merck**

'Do not ask us for the word that squares off, every side, our shapeless life-urge, and in characters of fire proclaims it. Nowadays we can tell you only this, what we are not, what we do not want.' – Eugenio Montale.

'Tax. Electricity bills. VAT. Rules. Regulations. Routine. Tom Jones on TV. Politics. The Media.' Debra sits in Louise's Club about 1.30 one Saturday a.m. telling us what she does not want. She's 18, does jazz dancing when she can get the work, and is positively evangelical about Punk Philosophy. She is also friendly (a necessary Punk Paradox *vis-à-vis* the despised Media since the Phenomenon depends on PR like vampires depend on plasma) and almost embarrassingly gracious about our offer to go a round of sweet martini and lemonade for her and her friend, who's learning to be a model.

Debra's an object of great interest to us because she's drawn a swastika on her shirt. Does she espouse Nazi views? Well, she's not keen on supporting others with her taxes ('Why should I work hard for their benefit?') but that not very exceptional observation is as far as she'll go towards the Orthodox Right. Like a lot of other people, many of them neither 18 nor punks, she pronounces a number of our major parliamentary figures 'shit' and 'rubbish'. *Kirche, kuche, kinder* also fails to garner enthusiasm, and she declares herself 'bisexual' (a state-

ment I cherish more for its boldness than its sincerity – there are more bisexuals this year at Louise's than when it was a gay club). For her, as for another Louise's habituée, Calina (18, newly employed in telephone sales after 14 months on dole that Debra so objects to forking out for), swastikas are just something she likes. And then, of course, there's the fact that others don't.

Among these is the club's regular DJ, Caroline, into soft soul herself, but dressed in the punk informal de rigueur on Friday nights: hennaed red crop, blackened eyelids, python-patterned pegs. Caroline, a survivor from the club's gay days, also wears a Star of David, and asks patrons to kindly remove their swastikas. 'I say to them, do you know what the Nazis did? What they did to Jews and to gays?'

Trouble is, they don't know much. There seems little point, I suppose, in getting conversant with grown-up discourses like history or politics when admission is closed to their traditional rights and privileges. The modern prolongation of adolescence is a sociological truism that must itself be on the shady side of 20, like 'Rebel without a Cause'. But as my colleague Mark P. observes, unemployment (and the sacrifice of educational and training funding to the requirements of private profit) now places most kids in a limbo that stretches to the horizons of their twenties and beyond.

The alternative to that, or the anonymous labour of their parents ('My father sells furniture, works until four in the morning sometimes, and he has nothing'), is notoriety. 'If you don't get yourself noticed, who'll care what you have to say?' With the bourgeois consensus impossibly remote, what's wrong with raising a few hackles with the odd swastika or Cambridge Rapist's mask? (Real surprise is displayed when we ask whether the bondage gear means they're sexually into that.) 'Punks just like to be hated,' Calina observes amiably, offering us some gum.

They certainly like to be noticed. The flamboyant attitudes struck by everyone who hears the press is here is only surpassed by the outright advances of people plugging their own instant groups: 'Don't forget now, Gnat's Piss and the Buggers. We're going to piss all over the Pistols. Got it?' Only the older instant groups, like Siouxsie and the Banshees (one gig, but already a cover pic on a national daily) play hard to get. The Banshees' violinist, who's giving us ominous hints of their new version of the Lord's Prayer, is admonished by Siouxsie not to say anything 'until you've talked to your manager'.

So what's politically special about dole queue rock? 'Nothing,' Calina confides, 'it's just something kids can get into.' Despite the celebration of the audience, and the brief spate of publicising and signing virtual amateurs, punk hasn't stifled that terrible desire to climb out of the stalls onto the stage. There haven't even been many of the usual gestures towards 'alternative' control of production and distribution. Instead of posing a genuine challenge, punk treads that well-worn, if confining, trench of outrage politics so dear to the tabloids. (Remember that revolutionary Malcolm Muggeridge's 'Does England Really Need a Queen?') And while the politics remain the same the problems worsen...

When Montale wrote the lines above, his native Italy was working its way past class conflicts and post-war humiliation into fascism – a move prepared, at least in part, by artists and intellectuals who'd decried Italy's 'stagnation', national diversions and underdevelopment and called for a purge of violence, glory and blood. Anything, as a young Bowie fan declared to *Let It Rock* last year, 'even into destruction... If you stagnate, you're bound to get bored, you're bound to get people getting bored of life and seeing the faults in it.'

(Of course, there are ways to change things like unemployment without the delights of the Duce and his punctual trains, ways that don't even necessitate arms caches in W11. And when a big corporation pays someone a five-figure advance to sing about them, that will be a Phenomenon.)

Teenage repression

from T.O. 352, by **Mark P.**

No way are the Sex Pistols gonna be filed under 'Pop Groups': EMI will have to think up a new category. Rock music has been 'light entertainment' for too long: it's safe, and it's not scaring parents. The Pistols are the most important rock group in Britain at the moment. Not because they're playing five nights at Wembley or releasing a 'Best Of…' triple set, but because they've just chucked out the most relevant rock single since 'My Generation'. The group will cause an immediate reaction, good or bad, in everyone who sees and hears them.

Most kids have never experienced a feeling of unity with the performer; they've never had an idol on their level. Even the Who: they were an important group once, but what does 'My Generation' mean sung by a thirty-year-old? The audience for the Pistols is waiting… out there in the discos, the football terraces and the boring council estates. The Sex Pistols are not a new 'fashion craze', they're reality.

Life is about concrete, the sinking pound, apathetic people and the highest unemployment figures ever. The Pistols are helping kids to think; that's why everybody's scared. They reflect life as it is in the council estates, not in the fantasy world that most rock artists create. Yes, they will destroy, but what they destroy will be replaced by a more honest creation. Led Zeppelin, Queen and the Pink Floyd belong in the 'classical music' section. They've got to make way for real people, and the Sex Pistols are the first.

The original group (Steve Jones, Glenn Matlock and Paul Cook) used to rehearse in a Hammersmith warehouse. The future wasn't very interesting until they met Malcolm McLaren. He ran the Sex boutique in King's Road, and used to be the manager of the New York Dolls. Johnny Rotten was brought in as vocalist after they saw him in the Sex shop, looking bored. The early gigs a year ago were shaky, but by April '76 they had a loyal following and were playing regularly at the 100 Club. This soon became the only place they could play, after being banned from the Marquee, the Nashville and Dingwalls. In July they played Manchester and 'Anarchy in the UK' for the first time; their audience grew steadily.

By this time other bands were forming – the Clash, the Damned, the Buzzcocks, Subway Sect, Siouxsie and the Banshees. They came together for a 'festival' at the 100 Club in late September. The second night was marred by the throwing of a glass during the Damned's set. It smashed on a pillar and one of the fragments blinded a girl's eye. It could have happened anywhere but the management blamed 'punk rock' and so the music was banned. Now the Pistols had nowhere to play, but interest from record companies still grew. They talked with Polydor for two weeks but EMI zapped in and signed them.

Johnny Rotten is the most honest performer performer around at the moment, saying 'up yours' to everyone. It's the same with the rest of the group; they don't apologise to an audience like most 'small' bands. This is the reason the group will make it, on the honest level rock should be; the level that pleases the kids on the street.

▸

This is what's bothering kids today – they feel restricted in everything. All those giant security guards at the big halls stop them dancing. With the Pistols they get some kind of freedom.

It doesn't even matter if 'Anarchy in the UK' sells well or not. The Pistols have won the first battle. From now on they'll move forward and smash every rock 'n' roll law there is. Even now they're in the record business, they won't play by the rules. They'll be nasty and mean because that's the only way to get anything positive done. As Malcolm McLaren said: 'In order to create, you must first destroy'.

Media manipulated

in T.O. 352, by John Collis

Elderly archeologists are forced to bite their tongues and shuffle their feet awkwardly at the mere mention of Piltdown Man. The argument continues among scholars, as to which skull defines the elusive link between ape and man. In an inexact science the dilemma will perhaps remain a matter of individual interpretation; one expert will see a particular set of bones as justifying his own vision of evolution, another will prop up a different skeleton. All of them could be disturbed by the unexpected, but almost undeniably human, forms of life which have recently been shaken out of the woodwork and onto the front pages of the music papers and national press.

Every significant development in the popular music of the past 25 years has worried the older generation and produced the charge of being musically illiterate. Bill Haley taught teenagers to dance, Elvis to be aware of their sexuality, Eddie Cochran defined the generation gap, Dylan encouraged political awareness, the Rolling Stones preached the arrogance of youth. Even the Beatles weren't 'lovable mop-tops' to begin with, and every new direction taken in their later career was a betrayal of this clever Epstein image. The only difference with the Sex Pistols and their playground ilk is that they are indeed musically illiterate. Any signs of competence (for example the sheer force of the Damned's single 'New Rose') are swamped by the endless mind-crunching inanities of lesser lights… check out the Hope and Anchor on a bad night.

When the Sex Pistols first began to appear on the front pages of the pop weeklies, their faithful audience could probably be counted in dozens. The press were desperate for something to happen: rises in their sales over the years can be directly linked to 'phenomena'. If something, however tiny, is stirring deep in the forest which shows signs of providing a source of easily-workable copy, then why not hype it? The Pistols rose to the top of the heap because of the shrewd media-manipulation of their manager: one can only hope for the group's sake that he is working in their best interests. The saddest aspect of the affair is that one or two journalists of proven ability (as well as several with none) have heaved their jaded limbs onto the bandwagon. Any image, given enough exposure, can be milked into creating its own charismatic ghost. A sense of rock 'n' roll dignity will inoculate one against being fooled.

One interesting aspect of pop's development is that it now remains in the forefront of one's life at an ever greater age. The jivers of 20 years ago got married, raised a family and stored their records in the attic; the Woodstock generation still buys albums every week. It could be argued that punk rock is the first genre to cut itself brutally away from the roots of rock, and yet this seems to apply with greater force to the music that developed in San Francisco ten years ago. The difference is that a large part of rock's audience is the same crowd who were around ten or more years ago, and this time the 'revolution' seems arid and unrewarding: it was easier to accept the singer/songwriter, the rock 'n' roll revival and the rise of discotheque soul. Like every aging music fan before me I mutter that the kids have a right to their own music, that there would be something wrong with them if they didn't arrogantly reject what has gone before, and that there is something wrong with them for embracing something so shoddy. When they said rock 'n' roll was a passing phase they were obviously short-sighted, but punk rock will have the life-span of a scab. It has this in common with all previous rock noise – in spite of the half intelligible statements of its practitioners, it is designed simply to make money.

Presumably *Time Out* is giving coverage to this subject for the benefit of readers who have been in a coma for six months. Now that the magazine has recognised what is a small movement on the ground, but a phenomenon in the music business, perhaps it can quietly wait for it to go away, or to develop into something more worthy of note. ●

The girl can't help it

Rock's first real woman?

Patti Smith interviewed in T.O. 322,
by **Giovanni Dadomo**

Patti Smith grew up on rhythm 'n' blues. At 16 she had her allegiance to black music brutally transferred to the Rolling Stones, her father's horror at seeing the group on TV provoking an entirely opposite reaction: 'Mick Jagger is the greatest performer since Nijinsky.'

Soon after, she fled to New York in 1976 where she met up with the artist Robert Mapplethorpe, becoming a resident of the Chelsea Hotel, then a hive of creativity where artists and film-makers rubbed shoulders with rock'n'roll stars. She also began to construct poems, as well as writing about rock 'n' roll for Rolling Stone, Creem, and Rock magazines. She also began to perform her poetry, accompanied, as often as not, by fellow rock 'critic' Lenny Kaye on guitar.

Over the next couple of years Smith continued her involvement with the New York underground, appearing in the movie 'Robert Having His Nipple Pierced'.

Urged on by her manager Jane Friedman and boyfriend Allen Lanier (for whose group Blue Oyster Cult she'd written some lyrics) she began to sing. In late '74, accompanied by Kaye on guitar and pianist Richard Sohl, she cut her first record, a privately financed limited edition 45 featuring a 'version' of 'Hey Joe', with 'Piss Factory', an original, on the flip. 'In the beginning we were doing all these oldies,' she explains, 'because we couldn't play very well.'

'Piss Factory' is an autobiographical piece with the young Patti dreaming of escape: 'I'm gonna get on that train and go to New York City/and I'm gonna be somebody/ I'm gonna be a big star and I'm gonna be so big I will never return.'

The group added drummer Jay Daugherty and began to work regularly, the culmination of which was a deal with Clive Davis' Arista label. A debut album, 'Horses', appeared in November.

If you can imagine Burroughs, Genet, Artaud and Rimbaud getting together to form a rock'n'roll band then you have a glimpse of what 'Horses' is like. They're all present in spirit, Genet in particular: 'I'd read Sartre's 'Saint Genet' just before we did the album and I was very influenced by it. The idea of Genet in prison getting himself off by writing down his fantasies impressed me.'

The record was produced by John Cale and carries his icy thumbprint throughout. It features a version of Them's classic 'Gloria', Smith's intense delivery completely obliterating the fact that it's a woman singing about another woman.

Having transcended the sex barrier in such an uncompromising fashion with the first song, Patti's already vaulted into a world that is completely her own; she's the first real rock'n'roll woman.

Patti Smith may have all the right credentials but she's not a superstar yet. They've certainly been cautious about her latest recording, a live cut of 'My Generation'. For a start it's gone on the b-side of 'Gloria'. Secondly, it's been censored. To Townshend's 'People try to put us down/just because we get around', Patti's added 'we don't need that fucking shit/hope I die because of it', only English record buyers have to make do with 'We don't need that bleep-bleep-bleep'.

Why this was done remains a mystery, particularly as only a few weeks ago Dylan was allowed to say 'shit' on 'Hurricane'. Nobody consulted Patti Smith, that's for sure. She says she'll bring a couple of cases of the uncut version over with her. She also says she'll find out whose responsible for the censorship and 'break his balls'. ●

Glenda JACKSON

Through many of her roles, her work to elect a women's rights MP, and her support for the National Abortion Campaign, the actress has acquired something of a feminist reputation.

from 'A role in the fight' in T.O. 335, by **Mandy Merck** and **Angela Phillips**

'It is her right'

'The Select Committee are evading the central, basic issue, that if a woman says she doesn't want to have this child, it is her right. In any other form of operation, if you say I don't want my arm off, don't want this cancer removed, there won't be any acts of Parliament saying this should be stopped. It's ridiculous.

'One of the prime remarks of these ladies who are so adamant that there should be no abortion, is that the safest form of birth control is the word "no". But when a woman actually exercises her right and says no they think it's appalling. Why must you say say yes to sex and yes to pregnancy? Why can't you say yes to sex and no to pregnancy?'

'Because childbirth is allied to sex, if you have your cake you've got to pay for it and if you get pregnant, that's the punishment. If you don't want it, tough bunny, kid. You've had the fun… the fact that a great many people get pregnant because they observe the law of obeying their husbands, nobody thinks of that.

'I am extremely suspicious of people who on the one hand say we must protect the sanctity of life and at the same time say we must increase our defence budget. It just strikes me as being a ruthless sentimentality which someone else has to pay for. How dare they condemn a child to be born to a mother who doesn't want it? How dare they take that upon themselves?'

'A women's movement ticket'

'Getting more women elected to parliament on a women's rights platform is going to take a great deal longer than any of us originally thought. I spoke at a rally in support of Una Kroll's nomination as a parliamentary candidate in 1974. She stood on a women's movement ticket, and that's why she only got 430 votes. I'm surprised she got as many as that. She was an ideal candidate: she spoke specifically about problems that everybody would like to think of as merely female problems, and she also gave

extremely balanced attitudes to the old thing of 'How do you deal with defence being a woman?'

But then, like all these things, I could do nothing more during the campaign because I wasn't actually here. It's a time conflict, not a conflict of ideas. Quite often that is why I don't do things that I'm asked to do or would indeed like to do.'

'The absurd characters one is asked to play'

'What is hard is that one is increasingly aware of the absurd characters purporting to be female that one is asked to play. I can see that this is going to become more of a clash in the future, partly because I think most writers have been totally turned upside down by the Women's Movement. And therefore what was already an underwritten field – I mean there are very, very few good parts for women – is going to become less. The writers don't know what is acceptable, what people would like any more. Which is why, of course, so many women's parts are becoming men's parts – because they know where they are.

'What I do find depressing is that none of the younger writers are actually very much concerned about feminism. If they are interested at all it seems to be on the level of political or social violence. That there is something revolutionary about the Women's Movement doesn't seem to have actually penetrated their minds.

'Hopefully there will be more writers who will actually want to say something, even if they are against it. I think that would be valid if you had somebody who wrote a really terrific plot or film which was opposed to it. But not opposed on a totally emotional level, the way Lawrence is. I think the Lawrence sex-pol thing is total rubbish. Although I was indeed in 'Women in Love'. I wasn't in a position to turn down work and I thought Gudrun was amazing. She's such a horrible person, trailing around the the world telling everybody how sensitive she was, yet there is a sort of truth in her somewhere. She is trying to find a basis for herself, an actual root that she can attach herself to.'

'Their comeuppance in the end'

Reading 'The Female Eunuch' in 'A Touch of Class'? I think that was my idea. There are lots of things that one affected in the actual weighting of the script. Melvin Frank's original had this lady who left her children in cinemas and launderettes and with anybody while she had her assignations. And I said, I don't know if you know women like this, but I don't. I think you're going to have to make it as difficult if not more difficult for her to have assignations than for him, because he doesn't have to have anybody look after the kids, etc. So changes were brought in.

'But then of course as with all films, a great deal ends up on the cutting room floor. And all the women I've ever played always have to get their comeuppance in the end.

'There are films that do have marvellous parts for women in them, but they're still carrying through a rather prehistoric view of how women react. I'm thinking particularly of Bergman, who is a director I admire enormously. In all his films there's usually not just one central female but three or four and their inter-relationships and their relationships to the outside world are very tellingly defined; but they are still within the area that presumes a woman's responses to be a specific thing. It's very difficult as a woman to break out of that. It's very difficult to actually realise that so many of one's responses are invisibly, indelibly programmed.

'It's amazing listening to the conversations of relatives like my mother and aunt. They are women who have worked every, single day of their lives. They know just how hard it is for women. They know that in most working class homes, it is the woman who keeps family and household together. And yet they would no more think of expecting my father to go out and bring in a bucket of coal after work than they would fly to the moon, although they've worked all day and will probably work all night. They accept that that is a woman's lot. What is terrific now is that women are not accepting it.' ●

Adam Faith

interviewed in T.O. 311, by **Duncan Campbell**

Nine years ago Adam Faith and his roadie were quietly cruising through the countryside past some holiday cottages. He waved, as one does when one's chiselled Prince-of-Denmark face is as familiar as his, to a woman sitting with her friends in the sun.

Months later, the woman arrived at his dressing-room in London with her suitcase. She had divorced her husband, left her children with her mother and come to join Adam. She knew he wanted and expected her, had even dropped him a confirmatory note the day before, because, after all, he had sent her all these special messages in his records. 'And all I ever did was wave at her once. The window wasn't even down.'

The character that Faith plays in 'City Sugar', the play in which he makes his West End acting debut, would have both relished and despised such devotion. There are similarities between Lenny Brazil, the play's sharp-witted, cynical DJ, and the former Terry Nelhams (the name was changed in the days when any singer worth his salt was called Wilde or Fury or, if you looked a bit sensitive, Faith). There are also differences.

'Len is completely disillusioned with his life,' says Faith, 'because he feels he's compromised himself. He's sucked into the whole idea of being a star. He didn't know when to quit. I could have gone on playing 'Budgie' on TV, but then I'd never be doing this.' Faith nearly didn't have the chance to decide to branch out. A 1973 car smash almost killed him. The song 'I Survive' was his rather self-conscious reaction to it. 'That was a one-off aberration. It was done for all the wrong reasons. I thought I was seeing everything so much clearer than I ever had before. It's a bit like what I imagine it's like to be on acid.'

The acid trip, like any other drug experience, would have to be imaginary. 'I have never tried them, never even smoked a joint. Only ever taken Valium medically. It's not for any moral or health reasons, I just believe you should be able to carry on without any kind of crutch.' Among such crutches he numbers God. Which inevitably brings up the name of Cliff Richard.

'Cliff hasn't changed much has he? Shows what a clear conscience can do for you.' Faith hasn't changed much either. At 35, the features are still sharp, there is no Presleyan paunch, the clothes make no concessions to middle age. He has gone into all and none of slots traditionally occupied by the ex-pop star: movies, from inevitables like 'What a Whopper' through 'Never Let Go' with Peter Sellers, to his justifiably acclaimed performance in 'Stardust' (he wasn't acting the limp); television, with the Keith Waterhouse and Willis Hall series, 'Budgie'; management with Leo Sayer; and cabaret.

'Cabaret? Thank God I only had to do it for a couple of years. It was dishonest. All those puerile songs.' (A moment of nostalgia.) 'When there were two and a half thousand people screaming and there was me in my leather jacket with hair all over the place and wiggling, it meant something... I started audience participation at rock 'n' roll concerts: these po-faced idiots would put flowers round the stage and I'd rip them up and throw them at the kids and it would start a riot – and it was honest!'

Faith may have thrown flowers, but he never believed their mystical sixties significance. 'I had grown up by then. I started in the business when I was 19 and I grew up ten years every year.' He did. The night of his car accident he had to sack Leo Sayer's backing group. 'Leo was playing with Procul Harum at St Albans and while they were playing 'Whiter Shade of Pale' I was sacking his group. It was horrible; they wanted to be good, but they just weren't up to it.' ●

The muppet show

from 'Uppity muppets' in T.O. 348, by **Andrew Nickolds**

Twiggy was having difficulty coping with two three-foot Muppets and a cow. A A Milne's poem 'The King's Breakfast' was being rehearsed – 'the King asked the Queen and the Queen asked the Dairymaid (Twiggy): "Could we have some butter for the royal slice of bread?" The Queen asked the Dairymaid, the Dairymaid said "Hold on, the Queen's got her head caught".'

The trouble was that while Jim Henson and master puppeteer Frank Oz were actually inside the King and Queen – Henson kneeling on pads, Oz waist-high to the raised set – they couldn't see anything and therefore didn't know which camera to react to. Henson was also concerned in case moving his head meant losing his line, since the microphone was round his neck inside the muppet.

Finally it was all worked out:

'"Nobody," he whimpered, "could call me a fussy man; I only wanted a little bit of butter for my bread!" the Queen said "there there" and went to the Dairymaid. The Dairymaid said "I'm coming undone underneath... I've lost me bustle, I can feel it dropping".'

After two hours Henson was satisfied, the scene was recorded, the Queen goosed the Dairymaid and everyone broke for lunch.

Toots and the Maytals

from 'From Rasta with love' in T.O. 312, by **Giovanni Dadomo**

The interview was less than illuminating; the atmosphere thick and sweet, and the ubiquitous *Daily Mirror*-wrapped stash well plundered. A monologue for three voices followed.

'It come from de 'eart,' said Toots, defining his music.

'Yeah. From de 'eart,' confirmed Raleigh.

'Um, From de 'eart,' was Jerry's opinion.

'If you don' 'ave de 'eart, you can' play it,' Toots continued. Whereupon Raleigh enlarged with a 'dat's right, from de 'eart' – thereby sparking Jerry's profound 'Raight from de 'eart.'

After about 15 minutes of this brains trust I stopped declining the spliffs.

Tom Waits

A seventies storyteller with fifties beat style

from 'Waiting for the man' in T.O. 324, by **Mick Houghton**

'I was born at a very young age in the back seat of a yellow cab in Murphy Hospital parking lot. I had to pay a buck eighty five on the meter. I realised then you have to plan things out.'

So Tom Waits, songwriter and storyteller, mapped out his assault on the music world that has seen him rise from dishwashing and working in a maternity hospital to become the leading professional support act in the States. He's on the road most of the year and about to open at Ronnie Scott's. Naturally he's supporting.

Waits was in London recently. We sat in an Islington pub, Waits chain-smoking, rocking to and fro in his chair to the sound of old Animals and Them singles (his choice) on the jukebox, wearing the same battered black Burtons' style suit, loosely tied striped tie and grubby beat cap as on the cover of his current album 'Nighthawks At The Diner'.

Waits is a misfit, a refugee from the beat era of the fifties, but living and writing very much about the seventies. He's virtually impossible to categorise. He's not a jazz singer, though his phrasing is a hybrid spoken/sung scat that owes a strong debt to jazz and blues, though his musical accompaniment is a blend of Monk, Oscar Brown Jr, and Oscar Peterson.

He's not simply a poet either, though his longer story songs are streams of images laced with alliteration, punning and Lord Buckley-style hip talk. He'll list Dylan Thomas as an influence as readily as Kerouac or Corso. He's very fond of pouring out names: 'I just have a lot of very incongruous influences, George and Ira Gershwin, Cole Porter, Johnny Mercer, Irving Berlin, Clarence 'Frogman' Henry, James Brown, Martha and the Vandellas, Rev Gary Davis. Everything influences me – conversations, expressions, jokes, bus drivers, desk clerks, even the maid who made my bed this morning at seven while I was in it and emptied my ash tray before I had time to put a cigarette out. I'm an imagist, or a curator. I collect nocturnal emissions and inebriated travelogues.'

If Waits is a master wordsmith, his application of that craft is best revealed live. He's been six years on the road learning how, building pockets of followings throughout the States. He's big in LA, his home base, New York City, even Philadelphia – 'I played there for two weeks one weekend,' he croaks, adapting WC Fields. They share a common philosophy: 'I don't trust anybody who doesn't have a drink problem. My problem is that I can't always get a drink.'

'Nighthawks at the Diner' is recorded live, capturing inspired stories whose comic and tragic episodes crack like colliding pool balls. The tales grew from introductions to the songs on Waits' previous studio albums.

On the first, 'Closing Time', Waits was stifled by producer Jerry Yester's attempts to create a new Randy Newman, but enough of the genuine article peers through.

His second album 'The Heart of Saturday Night', fared better. Produced by Bones Howe, it introduced the beat-inspired vernacular poetry of songs like 'The Ghosts Of Saturday Night'. The next album, tentatively titled 'Pasties and a G-String', will be another shot at a studio album. He's aware of the need to make records and tolerate the 'pomp and circumcision' of the music business.

'The music business is too insulating. They shoot you full of confidence by telling you you're the biggest thing since the invention of the indoor toilet but what I'm concerned about is not compromising my integrity, and keeping one foot in the streets.

'Right now, what I'm doing is no longer what I do, it's what I am. Anyway, I've quit my day job so it's too late to go back.' ●

Genesis P. Orridge

from 'Dirty porridge' in T.O. 318

'I seek to send something very personal, a gift,' said Genesis P Orridge, a 26-year-old artist, to the magistrates at Highbury Corner Court last week. He was explaining his motives for sending five allegedly indecent postcards through the post in contravention of the 1953 Post Office Act. The sentencing magistrates sought to send him something less personal – a total fine of £100.

The trial was precedent-setting in that it established that a person can now be prosecuted for sending 'dirty' postcards even though they have offended no-one, and traditional in that the arguments eventually came down to one person's art being another person's porn.

Mr P Orridge (or Mr Porridge, as the Scottish magistrate, Mrs Colwell, felt more at home in calling him), is one of the leading practitioners of 'mail art'. (Again

there was confusion; the Post Office thought he was a 'male artist'.)

'I like to use an existing popular structure,' said Orridge, 'I want to be sure that anyone could do it.' But included in the designs of some of the postcards sent off last year were certain images – 'copulation', as the Post Office lawyer had it – that caught the GPO's investigative eye, and led to the case GPO v GPO.

The lines of battle were drawn. There was the defendant, P Orridge, resplendent in lurex suit, red socks, silver finger nails and with his hair just growing back on the crown of his head from where he had but recently shaved it. Facing him was the doughty magistrate, Mrs Colwell, in a twin-set that matched her blue eye shadow. The defence team consisted of David Offenbach and Geoffrey Robertson, whose campaign medals in the Obscenity Wars have included the defences of *Oz*, David Waterfield and John Lindsay.

'I think,' said Robertson during his speech, 'that we could say that the postcards were of a humorous nature, that they were sent tongue in cheek.'

'A rather unfortunate turn of phrase,' said the clerk, noting that one of the messages was an extract from a girlie magazine which ran 'to my delight I felt his tongue running up and down my slit.'

The magistrates were not to be moved. 'We think the postcards speak for themselves,' they said. And they seemed unwilling to accept the argument that the messages on Orridge's cards 'we bucked and heaved, our mingled juices soaking our groins,' – were as banal and inoffensive as the more common 'Wish you were here'. After a ten-minute recess, during which the clerk was able to peruse the *Club International* which had been flashed around as evidence, they returned a verdict of guilty on all five charges to a slightly stunned courtroom.

Tom Waits – Genesis P. Orridge

1977

Fat Elvis went to Hamburger Heaven and punk purged what musical dinosaurs were left. We all stole a guitar, learnt a chord and started a band. The National Front made their last shows of racist strength before starting their inevitable unsung decline. Meanwhile, we all had a flutter on Red Rum and bought a mug with the Queen on it.

January
In the US, convicted murderer Gary Gilmore is the first person executed for ten years.

March
After being dropped by their previous label EMI, Sex Pistols sign to A&M for £75,000. The deal lasts six days.

May
Liverpool wins European Cup, after beating Borussia Monchengladbach in Rome 3-1.

Sex Pistols sign with Virgin. Their debut single 'God Save The Queen' receives widespread bans.

June
Celebration of Queen's Silver Jubilee causes outbreak of street parties.

Sex Pistols organise boat party and perform 'Anarchy In The UK' outside the Houses of Parliament.

July
Mary Whitehouse brings a successful prosecution against *Gay News* for blasphemy.

August
Violence erupts in Lewisham as thousands gather to protest at National Front march.

Elvis Presley dies.

September
Maria Callas and Marc Bolan die.

Freddie Laker commences Skytrain service to New York.

October
Pelé retires from football after an exhibition match between former club Santos and New York Cosmos.

December
Charlie Chaplin dies.

Piccadilly Line extension to Heathrow is opened.

Star Wars
Nearly 50 years after it was conceived, pulp space fiction is here presented for the first time as a truly viable movie genre.

Saturday Night Fever
A disco movie for people who don't go to discos, this is really about Growing Up. Pity really, discos deserve better than to be represented as watering holes for arrested adolescents.

Annie Hall
The one-liners are razor-sharp, the observations of Manhattanite manners as keen as mustard, and some of the romantic stuff even quite touching.

Fleetwood Mac – Rumours (Warner Bros)
Fleetwood Mac's phenomenal American success is

hardly surprising, since they have the same 'safe' streak running through their music as Frampton and Boston.

The Clash – The Clash (CBS)
Exactly the kind of sounds a reincarnated Eddie Cochran would make in the Clash's shoes. If the Rastas are right and

this is Babylon, then the Clash has few rivals for its soundtrack.

Sex Pistols – Never Mind The Bollocks (Virgin)
An album that has simultaneously made number one and been involved in bannings, police raids and general 1984 havoc has to verge on the brilliant.

Arnold Schwarzenegger

Arnold Schwarzenegger
interviewed in T.O. 392,
by **Scott Meek**

Pumping Arnold

At one time, Arnold Schwarzenegger was in the running for the part of Superman in the forthcoming movie epic. There were two reasons why he didn't get the part. The first problem – his Austrian accent – could be overcome. The second couldn't: when they dressed Schwarzenegger in a lounge suit to play Superman's mild-mannered alter ego, reporter Clark Kent, he still looked like Superman.

Saying that Schwarzenegger is a bodybuilder is like saying that Mark Spitz swam a little or that Muhammad Ali is a boxer. Those who know about such things claim that he is not only the world's premier bodybuilder, but also the most perfectly developed male body of all time. Actually, he's more than that. He is the sort of personality who affects the public's idea of a sport so strongly that he radically changes the status of that sport. The proof lies in the fact that it is now possible to use the word 'sport' in connection with body-building.

For years, bodybuilding was no more than a freak's sideshow, run for profit by various outfits trying to sell fast ways to the perfect physique. Their advertising was garnished with images of a host of bodybuilders who all claimed the same titles: four Mr Americas, four Mr Universes. All of these titles were legitimate, except that they were awarded by different federations, each of which jealously refused to recognise the others.

The change in bodybuilding's status (to the extent that body-building competitions are now televised nationally in America on the 'World of Sport' programme) is largely due to Schwarzenegger's skill as an ambassador. But it's also attributable in part to the writer Charles Gaines. His subjective but undeniably powerful romanticisation of bodybuilding is a modern equivalent of Hemingway on bullfighting. Gaines wrote the novel 'Stay Hungry'; when Bob Rafelson filmed it, Schwarzenegger played the part of the lead bodybuilder Joe Santos, acting against Jeff Bridges and Sally Field. Gaines also wrote the book on which 'Pumping Iron' is based; it was ignored by literary reviewers, but it has already run to 15 reprints in the States, which suggests that someone is taking it seriously.

The movie 'Pumping Iron' appears to be a documentary about Schwarzenegger in training and competition, but the film was, in fact, scripted. Some of Schwarzenegger's direct-to-camera statements are true, and some are not: it isn't true, for instance, that he skipped a family funeral to avoid breaking his training routine. But audiences and film critics in America have taken the film as an 'authentic' glimpse of a hitherto 'closed' world; it has (along with 'Rocky') upset the legend that movies about sports never do well, and achieved a remarkable success for a low-budget, independent film.

Schwarzenegger has now retired from bodybuilding (the film includes his seventh and final 'Mr Universe' win) and freely admits that he's making a bid for movie stardom. He probably has the right mixture of charisma and business acumen to make it. His next project is a film of Robert E. Howard's 'Conan the Barbarian' to be written and directed by John Milius. Below, Arnold pumps up some opinions on acting, sex and success.

'I always thought about acting. I think that's why I chose bodybuilding, as a kind of means to that end. I knew that in the past some people made it into films because of their builds. The question was, how to do it again? It's not exactly the "in" time to make Hercules films, and anyway that wasn't what I had in mind. As time went on, I thought more and more about how to make the break. I learned about acting. I lost some of the body weight, so people won't cast cast me just for muscle parts.

'It's difficult for the ego to be the best in one field and then go into something else and be a beginner – that's very hard to take. But it's healthy to be brought down like that, because it levels you off at about the right place. Rafelson was very helpful: I hope I can do another film with him because he's really good at bringing out talents that you didn't know you had. He has the patience to work with you, rehearse, explain the character, and things that usually only an acting coach would do.

'For "Stay Hungry", I lost weight. I weighed around 240, and went down to around 210. One, because I had to act with Sally Field, who weighs only 100 pounds. Two, I didn't want to emphasise the body. Rafelson wanted my acting to come up more than the body, so I wore a lot of navy-blue shirts and black training outfits to look smaller. Plus, losing weight makes you much more agile, and this just looks more pleasing on the screen; 240 looks like 260 on the screen anyway.

'Jeff Bridges? He's a professional. He knows how to steal scenes from you. He knows what to do in front of the camera so that people will look at him rather than you. There are certain things you have to learn which are almost called dirty tricks. Like, I'd be occupied with getting my scene done and he'd be standing there alongside the shot fingering his nose, stealing the show. Everybody does it, actually. If you don't know about it, you learn fast. It's the same kind of thing you do in bodybuilding competition.

'When people ask if "Pumping Iron" is all real, we just say "no". Certain things are real, and certain things are made up.

'In sex, the supreme feeling is coming, that's what you have sex for; in bodybuilding, the supreme feeling is the pump.'

Accept it for whatever it is: it's documentary style, with a storyline, based on a book. It's sort of a new way of making a film. When you want to put a little story together, you want to create a little bit of suspense; if you put it across from the beginning that this guy is gonna win, there's no excitement.

'The way it's put together, it's rather sensationalistic. For instance, it made the pump sound like a sexual thing.' (The pump is when blood suddenly rushes to the muscles after a training session.)

'What I really meant was a comparison. In sex, the supreme feeling is coming, that's what you have sex for; in bodybuilding, the supreme feeling is the pump. You train and what you are really looking forward to is the pump because that means growth, and that's the ultimate you can achieve. Now, sex is something that hopefully everybody enjoys, and my comparison lets people think, "Wow, if he feels like that in a gym then body building is a great thing." Of course, a lot of weirdos ran

▶

to the gym training to get a pump and hoping to get a big cock or something like that... which you just can' t do.

'Right after I read the first Conan book, I felt that I would love to play this character. Milius feels that he was born to direct Conan: it's a big picture, a violent picture, fighting against thousands of skeletons in the desert and all those crazy things. It will be made as a serious type of science-fiction, as serious as "Star Wars". Milius wants to tone down the violence because it's supposed to be a film also for kids. So there won't be any close-ups of a guy's stomach failing out when it gets cut with a sword. Milius has a tendency of specialising in that, he loves violence.

'For Conan, I signed a five-picture contract with Paramount. That means, if the first picture is successful, they have an option on another four. But if it does turn into a series, I have a clause that lets me make other kinds of films between Conans.

'America is so money-oriented. (Thank God! It's always helped me!) But it has its disadvantages because the psychia-

Arnold Schwarzenegger

trists know that their business doesn't mean a thing if there are no sick people around, and so they make everyone feel guilty. You know, all New York City is running to a psychiatrist. All America thinks it has sexual hang-ups. Everybody's running to shrinks. Nixon was always being attacked sexually. It was always said that he was a fag and that he had no sexual relations with his wife for 15 years and that was why he liked power. And Hitler had only one ball, and that was why he wanted to conquer the world.

'But when you train and deal with your body, it doesn't mean that you are a homosexual. Straight guys can deal with their bodies, look in the mirror and say "I look like shit, and I want to do something about it". I try to be very careful when I talk about this. I don't want anybody to get the impression that I'm knocking homosexuality, I'm not. I don't give a shit. What I want to do is to make Americans aware that they're fucked-up when they equate everything a person does with some sexual trip. You know, if you hold a pencil in your hand, it's a phallic symbol and you really want to hold a cock in your hand. And a football coach doesn't really want to be a coach, he likes to slap football players' asses... he's a latent homosexual. And it goes on and on and on, all the fucking time.

'It's the same with bodybuilding. They think you really want to build your body because you have a short cock and you're ashamed of it. Can you imagine the effort... four hours of training a day for 15 years because you have a short cock? It's so absurd.

'I have wives sending me letters saying their husbands are in terrible shape and can I send some courses. The amazing thing is how many women write in for their boyfriends and husbands because the trend has changed so much now. The ideal male body is going from being slim to being muscular again. I think it has a lot to do with women's liberation. Women are fed up with being supposed to look great all the time, and they're turning the tables.

'America is still the country where you can do things. That's why everyone is going over there. People think it's bombed out, that the time for having a dream and making it come true is over. And it isn't so! If you put work and time into it... it's harder there, but it's the best place.

'You just go out there. That's how we did it. We Europeans went to the gym twice a day when the others went only once. We just had this drive. We had to make it or we might as well have stayed home, it's as simple as that. Any European gets to think like that. You see guys coming over. The guys that own the most real-estate in Los Angeles are Europeans. There are people coming over from Yugoslavia with hardly any money... a friend of mine came over from Czechoslovakia in '68, and he now owns four apartment buildings. Americans are still sitting on their asses waiting for it. Europeans are hungry because we don't have that much.

'You're over there and you see that a guy can have ten dollars one day, and 100,000 dollars five years later. That makes you hungry. You say "Gee, if I can do that, I'll put it in." The American doesn't put it in. It's harder, but it's the best place. They're open for anything. I mean, if they were open for me, I tell you...' ●

from 'Is your sword very sharp, Mummy?' in T.O. 402, by **Adrianne Blue**

Susannah York

Androgyny doesn't scare Susannah York. Except for the soft, red ballet shoes, she is dressed like a little boy, in jeans and a short-sleeved shirt. 'Peter Pan' is in rehearsal, and York is trying to ignore the cold that is making her achy, clumsy and a danger to Captain Hook, with whom she is duelling. The tip of her sword is barbed. His is covered with a wad of paper and sellotape.

Ron Moody, who made his name as Fagin in 'Oliver' (now reopening without him), plays the dual role of Hook/Darling. In his blue double-breasted blazer, khaki pants, and brown suede shoes, Moody resembles a suburban father, which he isn't. Is Moody, like the mean pirate/daddy he is playing for the fourth time, obsessed with castration? 'Well, I'm watching her all the time: "'Twas he cut off my hand".'

Ever since 'Peter Pan, or, The Boy Who Wouldn't Grow Up' opened to rave notices at the Duke of York's Theatre in 1904, at precisely the season when Christians ought to be pondering Virgin pregnancies, child theatregoers and their middle-class parents have been served up Peter's symbolic castration of villainous daddy and his/her symbolic ravishment of a surrogate Mum. This is a pagan, grown-up and very Freudian feast.

Peter, you'll remember, is always played by a woman. There is a glittery babe's gallery of actresses who have played the role: Maggie Smith, Hayley Mills, Glynis Johns, Dorothy Tutin, Anna Neagle. In America, Mary Martin constructed a career around Pan. But let's not over-react to this skewed sexuality. In English pantomime it's traditional for the Principal Boy to be acted by a woman. Madame Celeste started it in 1855, when she took the title role in 'Jack and the Beanstalk'.

Susannah York is no stranger to sexually adventurous roles. Remember the every-which-way triangle in 'Happy Birthday Wanda June' and the lesbian love scene in 'The Killing of Sister George' and the schizoid sexual fantasies York was prey to in 'Images'? But her acting history probably has as much to do with film directors' predilections as with her own. An able and versatile actress, at Cannes she won the Best Actress Award for 'Images'. She even writes children's books. It was York's son Orlando, four, greeting his tired mother at the train station in Cambridge one evening, who asked, 'Is your sword very sharp, Mummy?' Daughter Sasha, six, has other anxieties, 'You are playing Wendy, aren't you, Mummy?'

York herself is sanguine about the role's androgyny. 'A boy of a certain nature could equally well play Peter Pan. The person who plays it, whether he's a boy or a girl, a man or a woman, has got to be able to hold both sexes within herself. To some extent, I did that as Childie in "Sister George". Peter Pan is extremely a boy, but also spritelike and female.'

Isn't it odd though that in this psychologically-aware era, a woman should still play Peter, especially considering the play's rather obvious Freudian implications?

'The Oedipal analysis is a bit old and repetitious and rather boring,' York says hoarsely.

'The surrogate Wendy, that, of course, is very Freudian. But it won't occur to a child. Children always play at being grown-ups. I am constantly the baby when I play with my children. Orlando always wants to be the mummy and Sasha plays the daddy. Lately though, Orlando wants to play daddy.'

But the play is a denial of grown-uphood. 'It's a very, very sad play. Peter Pan's tragedy is that he can't throw off the carapace of childhood and he doesn't want to. That's a conflict that resides in all artists. I recognise it in myself!

Isn't it a dangerous conflict to foist on children? 'Odd children, when they think about it at night, might be bothered. When I saw Disney's "Snow White and the Seven Dwarfs" – I was about six – I do remember having awful nightmares. But children love being scared, and I agree with Ron Moody about Hook's incompetent evil.' ●

Elvis RIP

from T.O. 387, by **John Collis**

It is perhaps sad to realise that, had Elvis died in 1960, his musical reputation would remain intact. Those who claimed that such later recordings as 'Big Boss Man', 'Burning Love' or 'Promised Land' showed a revival of the youthful fire were prompted at best by desperate optimism, at worst by a defect of the ear. Such up-tempo numbers were in fact more distressing than the big ballads, because they emphasised so cruelly that as a rocker he was only a cabaret parody of his revolutionary self. Even the lauded TV special, while showing once again that he had an engaging and self-mocking personality, was at best only a slightly embarrassed recognition of his past.

But it is this past – what he did before the US Army gave Colonel Parker a heaven-sent opportunity to secure his own pension – that makes Elvis undeniably the King of rock'n'roll. Something would have happened without him, but only of Presley can we confidently say that, without him, it couldn't have been the same. He symbolised the moment when black music, white music, sex and the newly discovered 'teenager' were fused into a culture: the lingering racism of the time would have prevented a black artist doing this, and Haley just wasn't pretty enough.

Once Elvis had made the breakthrough with 'Heartbreak Hotel' in 1956, the way was open for such as Buddy Holly, Chuck Berry and Eddie Cochran to consolidate a youth culture. Presley's music was never concerned with highschools – but it made possible a music that was. And, since then, popular music has formed a constant back-drop for people as they grow up, influencing their lives to the extent that it is difficult for today's teenagers to realise that there was a time, before Elvis, when pop was aimed at the parental generation, and adolescents didn't exist.

Gulp!

In 1968, after drama school and six unsatisfying years in classy reps with such directors as Michael Blakemore, Frank Dunlop and David Scase, Steven Berkoff founded his London Theatre Group.

In 1974, after two productions of Kafka's 'Metamorphosis', further Kafka adaptions ('Life in a Penal Colony', 'The Trial'), versions of Aeschylus, Shakespeare, Poe and Strindberg, spots at the Place, Arts Lab, Oval House and Edinburgh, Berkoff was still worried about the state of English theatre.

Today he puts it bluntly: 'I do most of my worrying in the theatre.' Now, at the National Theatre's prestigious workshop, the Cottesloe, punters have the opportunity, for two weeks only, to worry about him. For the last nine years Berkoff has pursued a dream, an obsession, albeit not an original one, but a fixation which has made him, with Pip Simmons and Lindsay Kemp, one of the very few genuine and gifted *metteurs en scene* in English theatre. His goal is simple: to literally wrest the stage from the observational realism of mainstream drama, from the holy writ of the playwright, from the hierarchy in which the actor ('a human and mysterious entity') comes bottom, from directoral privilege and restricted performers. In its place he wants a liberated, multi-disciplined and ultra-disciplined explosion in which actors reveal rather than impersonate, and an audience identifies not on the plane of mundane recognition but on the level of its innermost fantasies and nightmares.

Interviewing Berkoff, one is conscious of his perpetual prepossession with 'the performance'. Resembling a hybrid of a Soviet dissident poet and a Billingsgate porter who spends his evenings boxing amateur bouts, his gestures are expansive, his voice a musical instrument, his manner at once apologetic and dauntingly powerful, his breathing gulped, his sentences striking for their hugging and repetition of key words.

Berkoff's influences in the early days were (obviously) Artaud, (less obviously) German expressionistic movies, the mime of Marcel Marceau (he studied mime for a year in Paris), the early writings of Jean-Louis Barrault and his own unemployment in straight theatre (one thing he shares with Kemp).

However, his interests were primarily non-theatrical at the outset: 'My earliest interest came through books and I couldn't become a writer (so I thought) but I also thought the nearest thing was through the theatre where I could be something practical, namely an actor. But I found that the theatre was so grossly inferior to novels, short stories, myths. Everything was working on the level of heavy realism, it didn't tap the unconscious, it didn't make you use your voice, your body, your mind.

'I thought we were clogged, that we were choked full of playwright's words, which were *(gulp)* choking us up, *(gulp)* and people couldn't move, there were just these ruptured vessels *(hands wave)* spewing out this garbage at each other. They couldn't move their arms, the actors, they'd come to me at auditions *(very fast now)* suffering from rep lag and their bodies these truncated things. So I thought: "Free the gesture", "Work on the body". At first we probably lost on the words, but now we're much more conscious of the words, mimetically and plastically. You've got to be like a *(pause)* whaler, you've got to harpoon the imagination of the audience and trap it and hold it. You have to limit yourself to a few shows a year, you have to push yourself to the limits and go beyond what the human energy can do, go on like the runner in 'Agamemnon' and, in doing so, escape the shyness and the reservation, the failures of communication which lead to the real cruelties among people.

'People say we're not political but the theatre of political observation is so limited to what's going on at present. It may inform a few people, it may illuminate a few facts but basically it becomes drab, locked in the scheme of the writer. Art belongs to itself; it's a selfish, grasping thing. Sometimes we try to give it a "message", as if its worth lay in how much message it has. But its worth can lie in the depths of psychology and in the imagination. In political theatre actors are often the most oppressed, going on about social justice while shivering in filthy dressing rooms on a pittance. Liberation lies within the human being. I mean I'm excited mainly about great performers, about Kean and Olivier, and I think we liberate the actor from the writer/director hierarchy, make him articulate inside his body, inside his imagination, make him capable of creating an object of fascination on the stage. *(Pause).* Does that make sense?'

It's not surprising that when Berkoff recently approached the American equivalent of Equity for a work permit he convinced them by making an impromptu speech. 'I expected a few people and was faced with this massive

Steven Berkoff
interviewed in T.O. 381,
by **Steve Grant**

1977

Steven Berkoff

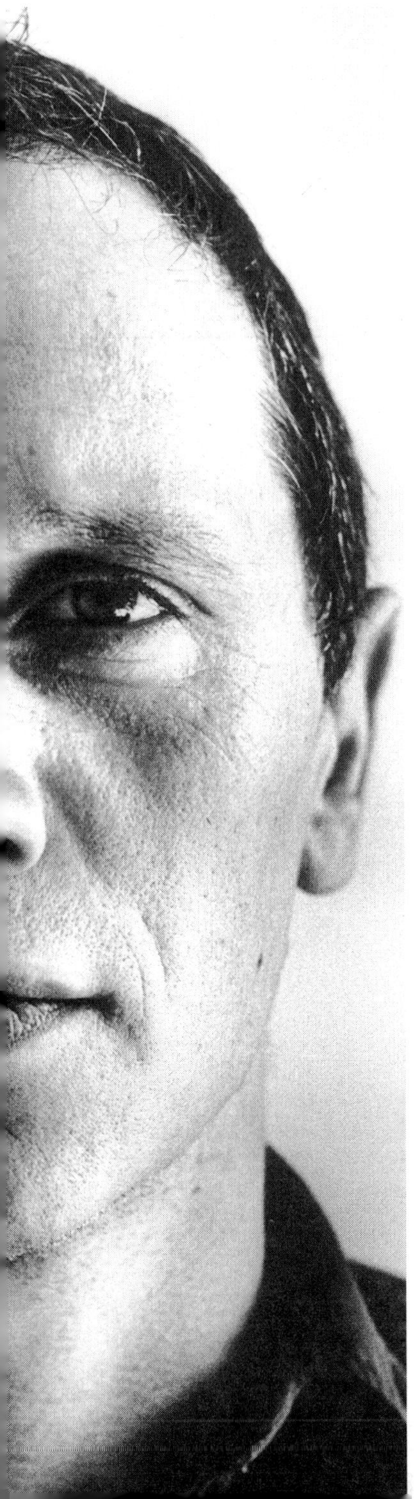

body, so I reacted as if the curtain was going up and I didn't have any lines – I did the Sicilian immigrant and they liked me.'

At the Cottesloe, Berkoff's London Theatre Group is offering his eight-years maturing version of Kafka's 'Metamorphosis' and his own 'East', a semi-autobiographical, episodic tone poem of the violent, sexually gross and clumsy lifestyle of the East End. In 'Metamorphosis' Berkoff has sought and found a unifying image – as he did with 'Miss Julie', (boot fetishism) and 'The Trial' (a series of labyrinthine screens). In 'Metamorphosis' a skeletal framework of steel scaffolding is stretched across the stage, serving as both the home and the shell of the slowly evolving insect which Kafka's victim Gregor Samsa becomes. Lighting is utilised to enhance the isolation, the family's horror at their breadwinner's predicament captured in formally choreographed gestures, frozen movements reminiscent of old Victorian prints.

'East' is Berkoff's s exorcism of an energetically wasted youth; a hilarious, sexist, joyously bawdy collage of cockney argot, Shakespearian imagery and Joycean stream of consciousness, a bizarre mixture of 'Romeo and Juliet', 'Ulysses' and 'Till Death Do Us Part'. A TV-sodden, imprisoned family unit with dad reminiscing about Mosley's good points and mum about her 'meeting' with Hemingway in the Brasserie Lip is counterpointed by the fuck-blood-and-motorbike obsessions of two adolescents and their love object Silv: 'He clocked the bird I happened to be fianced to, my darling Sylv (of legendary knockers), and I doth take it double strong that this long git in suede and rubber, pimples sprouting forth like buttercups on sunny days from off his greasy boat… so I said to him "fuck off thou discharge from thy mother's womb before with honed and sweetened razor, I do trouble to remove thy balls from thee".'

'I wanted to burn out my waste but I found that by distorting it I could make it more schizoid, paranoid, extreme, brutal, lyrical. "East" is filthy but the energy sanctions the act. When the writing and the acting are at full throttle you can hopefully turn into pure energy and the audience can identify, not on a "Oh yes, that's just like dad" level but with their most inner senses.

'The writers I use, Kafka in particular, work in a many-layered way. Kafka's search is my search for the right language in theatrical terms to break down the walls. *(Gulp, pause)*. Does that make sense?' ●

"1977"

"The profits are astronomical. Only the Mafia does better."
Steve Rubell on superclub Studio 54

"I § NY"
The legendary ad campaign kicks-off

"To say no to Concorde is like saying we should stay with sailing ships when steam came out."
John Dyson, NY Secretary of Commerce

"Extra-terrestrials. Researcher wants to meet people from other planets or spacetime continuum. Write with details. Confidentiality guaranteed."
Ad in the *Guardian*

"A wall is a rectangle with horizontal and vertical sides."
Department of Education and Science circular sent to local education authorities on picture-hanging

"No sex is better than bad sex."
Germaine Greer

"Don't knock masturbation. It's sex with someone you love."
Woody Allen, in 'Annie Hall'

"When the President does it, that means it is not illegal."
Richard Nixon to David Frost

"Whenever you accept our views, we shall be in full agreement with you."
Israeli General Moshe Dayan to US negotiator Cyrus Vance

"The most potent weapon in the hands of the aggressor is the mind of the oppressed."
Steve Biko, black South African leader, murdered by state police

"Turkeys don't vote for Christmas."
David Penhaligon, the Liberal MP, after being asked why they did not support a motion of no confidence in the government. They entered the Lib-Lab pact shortly after

"Let's do it."
The last words of Gary Gilmore, the first US prisoner to be executed for ten years

This Nigger's Crazy

1977

Richard Pryor

Rapping over tea at the Dorchester

Richard Pryor interviewed in T.O. 368, by **Brian Case**

There's nothing take-away about Richard Pryor. He doesn't tell gags and he won't sell himself in interviews. Like any improvising artist who runs on reflexes, head just ahead of overdrive, he knows enough to resist analysis.

'Where ya from? What was ya mother like? Huh, fucks ya shit up. People come to you and ask what it was that you did. It's hard, man. I'm a doer. I mean, I work live. Like, if I could articulate how I feel about what I do, I wouldn't be on stage.'

Like the Blues, his comedy comes from his roots and functions as therapy among black club audiences – wounds recognised, the same bind, artist and ghetto community on the same hook and hanging together.

His themes are the Blues themes, too: to mean mistreatin' women – 'OK, take the television but leave ya pussy'; injustice – 'Why are we holding our dicks? 'Cos ya took everything else, motherfucker.'

He works in little adrenalin playlets, fast, impatient, shaping the rap against the response. Sometimes the pain is out front. He blocks in a backdrop, low wages, the treadmill, the weekly release of a Saturday night on the town.

'Cops put a hurtin' on your ass, you know. Whites know them like, "Hello Officer Timson – going bowling tonight? My licence? Glad to be of help". Niggers don't know them like that. "I am reachin' in my pocket for my licence." "Get outa the car, take your pants down, spread your cheeks. There's been a robbery, nigger looked just like you". Just go home baby, beat ya kids. Take that shit out on somebody.'

The mirror he holds up may not be flattering, but it sure is clouded with life. Blacks – boastful, cowardly, vain, dicty and profane, jostle for position on the floor of America. Motherfuck! Git outa my face! The penny-ante pickings of prestige, where wino lays it across junkie like 'You dunno how to deal with the white man. I know how to deal with the white man. Tha's how I'm in the position I'm in today.'

He draws deadly parallels between the races in the sheets: no winners. 'Pass the potatoes,' Voice of Middle America, Jazz Hour, 'thank you, darling. Could I have a bit of that sauce? Think we'll be having sexual intercourse tonight?' Black Voice, thick in rut, 'bitch was so fine, I wanted to suck her daddy's dick!'

In the middle '60s, Richard Pryor had achieved considerable public acceptance as a stand-up comic, and featured on the Ed Sullivan and Johnny Carson shows. One night he walked out in the middle of a performance in Las Vegas. 'It stopped being fun, you know. I was doin' that safe kinda shit, and it was hollow. Good evening ladies 'n' gentlemen. I was only kidding hahaha. I'm putting my cock back in. No offence but wasn't it cute? You know that kinda thing. No matter what you did, you always had to clean up. I quit. I coulda went on to make that money you know, rich and famous – but I got lucky, man.'

Print that. His last two albums, 'This Nigger's Crazy' and 'Is It Something I Said' won Grammys without trimming for Mister Charlie. In 1974, he received the American Writers' Guild Award for his screenplay on Mel Brooks' 'Blazing Saddles'. He has acted in 'Lady Sings the Blues', 'Wattstax', 'Bingo Long And The Travellin' All Stars' and, most recently, 'Silver Streak'. All of which has moved him a long way from the ghetto in Peoria, Illinois.

'It's hard, man, the growth thing and the accolades thrown on you, and the money. On the other hand, you see how they treat other niggers. No, you say Shit! – that's me too. Showbusiness, it's like a whorey business – you sell yourself, give interviews. Some people thrive on this, they get sick. I don't wanna be sick. I really have a hard enough time talkin' to my old lady. Get to your own peace – that's the thing. It's hard to keep it though, man, because Shit! you gotta eat. I mean, that's how they gotcha. You gotta go out there and eat – that's the fuckin' trick. You can wake up feelin' great, but you're gonna say hello to those motherfuckers sometime during the day.'

Like a lot of funny men, he isn't privately a barrel of laffs. S J Perelman, goaded to perform on television, once retorted that he was 'a tower of resignation'. Pryor retreats behind courtesy, costive of his talents, unwilling to deal unless it's for real.

'When I was growing up, man, it was serious. We had a real affection. You didn't hafta say it. I once got busted for drugs and I came home to apologise for bringing shame on my family. It was in *Jet*, that's a black national magazine, everybody reads it every week – *Jet*, you go right to *Jet* – Where's *Jet*? So I said to my mother, "I'm sorry, I hope I didn't embarrass you" and my mother said, "Who the fuck you think you're talking to? You been in Hollywood too long, ain't you?" You understand what I'm saying?'

Childhood values, childhood characters. One that recurs time and again in his act, gratuitously advising, appallingly personal is Mudbone, eminence noir on the block. '"Say boy! Where ya goin'? Come here! Them your shoes?" There was a

lot of that around when I was a kid. Old man who didn't have nothin' else to do. Right for the jugular vein. "Was that your mother? One that looked like an elephant?"' A portrait emerges of the youthful Pryor tugged between the warnings and the sporting crowd, a hapless pinball in the stand-off between Parents and the Pimps and Players.

'"Whatever you do, don't you kiss no pussy!" I couldn't wait.'

The Afro-American is the only minority without its own language. Pryor uses a small vocabulary and a range of nuance so wide that meaning resides in the fall of accent and emphasis. Obscenity becomes a portmanteau category, and 'ass' the fundament of self. 'Death was quite a surprise to his ass.' Language and life are stripped to iron rations.

'I was thinking about "Dracula". See, if black people did movies, my premise is that movies would be much shorter, because they wouldn't waste the time with a lotta excess shit. Dracula, he wouldn't get far, man. I mean, who in the fuck'd be fool enough to fuck with some strange person like that? Motherfucker don't cast no shadow I'm through with you! Whyn't ya get the teeth fixed? You ain't suckin' nothin' here, junior! So how you gonna get close to me? I'm just blowing that kinda black logic. That's the way you had to be to survive.'

There is no room down here for the luxury of liberalism or the bijouterie of radical chic. Jews and Jesus: 'I said boy don't you go down there fuckin' with them Jews without no money.' Deep South crackers adopting Vietnamese orphans: 'Ain't your eyes ever gonna round out?' Meanwhile the entire black population remains unadopted.

'I'm doing what's true, what I feel. I say what's on my mind.' Pryor won't sit still for sociology or significance. A Spokesman for His Race? You need the crutch, baby… With Luther King gone, Malcolm gone, Cleaver going going gone,

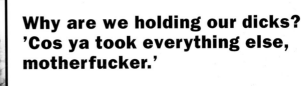

Why are we holding our dicks? 'Cos ya took everything else, motherfucker.'

and Black and Proud assimilated by the boutiques, the gig could be Pryor's. If he wanted it.

'It's like everybody's been paid off. I find this Outer Space. The world changes faster, it passed me, I missed it.' And takes refuge in solipsism. 'I don't know if I got my political thinking together. I got me together. I always thought like the truth or justice was the kinda thing where you wanted to see the motherfucker. Like Nixon – it'd be nice to see him pay, but justice don't work like that. I found out justice is as individual as everybody's fingerprints. You live with it and deal with it yourself. It's inside us – the heavens and hells and all that shit, man.'

'Justice?' says the black voice from the jail. 'Just-us'.

'I hope I'm funny.' ●

Skateboarding

A few 360s in search of the skateboarding bandwagon

from 'Sidewalk surfing' in T.O.381, by **Stan Hey**

A writer friend of mine was once approached by a bloke in a pub who suggested he do something about the craze. 'Which particular craze do you mean?' he asked. 'Roller-skating? Hula-hoops? That sort of thing?'

'Nah, nah', said the bloke. 'Not that sorta craze – the Krays, Ron and Reggie!' My friend made an excuse and left.

I was tempted to do exactly the same when the idea of a feature on the current skateboard craze was suggested. A natural distaste for Americana was compounded by a distinct feeling of being not so much on a bandwagon as a good hundred yards behind it.

So it was with ill-grace that I set-off for the Hammersmith Assembly Rooms on a dreary Monday evening for the inaugural meeting of the Pro-Am Skateboard Association of Great Britain at which, I had been assured, I would meet 'all the cats that matter'. Arriving outside the Hall, I saw over 100 of the 'cats' milling around on the forecourt. Some were paddling idly up and down on their boards, others exchanged info on the latest skating areas discovered. By far the majority however were huddled around what I initially suspected was the unfortunate victim of a mass mugging. It turned out he was a radio reporter with a tape recorder – suddenly the bandwagon put on a spurt and lurched out of sight.

By now, I'd also become uncomfortably aware that, at 25, I was at least ten years older than anybody else around me. An impulse to retreat to my own generation was arrested by the arrival of my contact, an American teenager named Trey Casimir. 'Hi, you must be Stan Hey, right?' 'How did you know?' I asked. 'Well', he said coolly, 'You're the only old guy around here, and you've got a briefcase.' I surveyed the mob with evident unease. Trey caught my look. 'We're a real bunch of hooligans, huh?' he said reassuringly.

Trey had advertised in *Time Out*'s Sportsboard section for 'empty, round-bottomed swimming pools, empty cemented reservoirs, or banks' where he and his fellow skateboarders could practise their sport. 'Get many calls?' I asked. 'Oh, er, one, to be exact.'

It's perhaps ironic that surfing should have spawned the ultimate urban sport, an activity that needs no fields, no water, just a strip of concrete or a tarmac slope. And yet despite its generally soulless context, the essence of the sport is very much improvisation. I guessed as much when on a visit to the South Bank, a clutch of skateboarders were busy forming a slalom run

with a dozen empty Coke cans.

I'd been told to ask for Tim the Australian who, in the prevailing argot, was deemed a 'hot' skater who talked 'straight shit'. Unfortunately Tim wasn't around. Nor was 'Crazy Simon'. 'He broke his board and went home,' I was informed. With my two intros blown, I decided it was best to sit back and watch.

The centre of the action appeared to be underneath a concourse to the left of the Royal Festival Hall. There, a large paved area sweeps up into a three-sided bank and a seemingly endless stream of kids were hurtling up to the bank, riding it, and turning back down and away. The favoured stunt seemed to be the kick-turn, swivelling the board round on the rear wheels just as it stalls at the top of the slope. One or two were trying spins (Hey, don't call 'em spins, they're 360s') while others were riding along the top edge of the bank, crouched down holding on to their boards ('carving').

It was an impressive display, particularly when I recalled my only trip on a skateboard, across the vast expanse of a friend's dining-room floor. Only the flashier skaters seemed to be wearing safety gear (helmets, gloves, knee and elbow pads). I spotted one kid wearing his mum's best sheepskin mittens; another sporting his dad's racy black-leather driving gloves.

The thinking about safety gear seems to be that once you've hurt yourself you'll bother to wear it. For one lad there, it had taken a broken arm to do the convincing.

Above this, on the next level, other kids skated around, over and sometimes through the variety of chrome phalluses and rusting hulks that pass for sculpture there. Many of the better skaters have been enlisted into teams by the various skateboard manufacturers. Given free boards and equipment they're required to skate demos for their masters as well as plugging their boards around the various runs. Rivalry has become intense with one team sabotaging another by throwing refuse under their wheels during a run.

In the main, however, it seems a friendly clan. When they're not riding they're talking boards or wheels, with a mystique that's almost masonic. Before long a G & S Fibreflex (an ace board) or a Bennett Truck (an ace axle) begin to sound like the Holy Grail.

The other big topic is, of course, places to skate. Often it's a car-park left empty at weekends or a quiet street with a tempting slope. Many even hitch it to Weymouth where there's a bona-fide skate-park. I asked a young American if he was disappointed with the lack of facilities. 'No, not really. I don't mind as long as I've got somewhere. This place has got plenty of curves, and it's fun.' ●

Robert Mitchum

From 'Beer and loafing' in T.O. 402, by **Chris Petit** and **Chris Wicking**

What's the strongest drink you've ever had?

'Carolina moonshine's pretty tight, you know. Gets up around 170, 180 proof. Pretty close to ether. Most lethal thing's poteen, Irish moonshine. Some pretty tough ones down in Mexico though. Some of that wild mescal!

'Then there's marc. Love that, oooh! Eau de vie de lie. Pure white gin. Marc. Double distilled residue of brandy. Unaged. Fruit alcohol. But they make that – framboises, poires for those eaux de vie. Framboise in particular is very expensive. Dunno how many acres of raspberries it takes to make one jar. After that first fiery initiation you kinda become adjusted. Find yourself whacking off the whole jug. All out. Suffused pleasant glow of raspberries, lovely! Pull up the sheets and… what is that stink??? Jesus! Gave some to Roddy Mann. Never has got over it. Mentions it every time he discusses me. Said I was drinking it. I gave him the bottle. Shows you. Pearls before swine, the sonuvabitch! Took the whole jug and lays it on me…

'There's a Chinese drink. Gives you the Iron Hat. Take a shot of that after everything else… BOOM! It's all over.

'But mescal. Gets pretty juicy, mescal with mescal in it, the way they still make it down in Oaxaca. Fifty cents a shot and everything comes out in Technicolor!

'Pulque is another cactus altogether. More like a beer. Only three days old. Drain the sap out of the cactus, let it be for a minute. Viscous. Limpid. Full of gnats. Take a litre of that down, walk outside and throw it up. Come back in and drink another. By this time things are beginning to go numb inside. Then it ferments in the warmth of the stomach. Stays with you a coupla days.

'Remember when I first went down to Mexico. Was with the President's bodyguard. Used to see people lying all over the place. Thought it was the plague. Saw one guy walk into the same metal lampstand over and over. BAM! Right into it. Backed off, circled round, got it wrong. BAM! Straight into it again. I thought it was because of the dark aperture, you know… Fission. Fissure. He hit it four, five times from different angles. BAM! Whoops! Decided there was no way round and hit the slab like all the other guys. I asked, what is that?! They shrugged, mescal, pulque. Very normal sight.

'You walk into a pulqueria and all osmosis ceases as they look around. They know you gotta be crazy. What's he doin' in here? He's not an Indian. Place smells like baby vomit. Not bad to drink though. The beer of peons. They endow it with all kinds of magical principles. Goes way back to the Aztecs. Makes your lips red. Killed Mario Lanza. He went on an almost exclusive diet of it. Finished him off…

'Sure, I try to keep a cellar at home. I have a large legit bar, but I wind up tending it all night. It's not easy… all my friends drink. Far more than I do.'

The Royal Jubilee

from 'A touch of ruling class' in T.O. 375,
by **Crispin Aubrey** and **Duncan Campbell**

The Queen is in the counting house
Counting all her money.
The souvenir touts in Oxford Street
Are eating bread and honey.
The rich men queue at County Hall
To join the honours roll.
And meanwhile 1,500,000* of us
Are starving on the dole!
(**not counting all the working women ineligible for benefits*)

It may be 25 years since the accession, but it's also 60 years since the first socialist revolution in Russia, and to many socialists the Jubilee is nothing less than an appalling affront to the working population in 1977. So while the Oxford Street bazaars ring up massive profits on china mugs and royalist trivia, an entirely other industry is moving into gear to produce a very different view. As one recently printed sticker puts it, the cost of keeping the Royal Family for a year (£5.5 million) is almost exactly that of building a new public hospital.

Already the Queen has not received quite the easy ride through her kingdom she might have expected in the '50s. Though the television cameras studiously ignored them, there were demonstrations at every major town she visited in Scotland. In Aberdeen, residents living along the route played the Internationale as the Queen went by. In Dundee, the route was spray-painted with 'Stuff the Jubilee' slogans. This week's London tour is expected to receive the same sort of barracking from people, angry that the year of a worsening economic crisis should be seen as a time for celebration.

The Socialist Workers Party, which is at the forefront of the anti-Jubilee campaign, says it feels it a duty to put two fingers up at the whole self-congratulatory performance. 'But we don't only want to get rid of the monarchy, we want to get rid of all those elements for which the Royal family is a symbol. Our main thrust is to build a socialist alternative, and we see the Queen and her entourage as a symbol of all the useless classes that clutter up the top end of society.'

The SWP has taken the fight against the Jubilee image more seriously than most of the left. The cover of this week's eight-page special supplement of the party's paper, *Socialist Worker*, reads: 'Stuff the Jubilee. Roll On the Red Republic'. Inside, there are more serious explanations of why the monarchy still holds sway in the land, how much they cost the British taxpayer, and why the real battle is against the social contract.

A series of stickers summarises the party's attitude. 'The world's richest pensioner got a 47% rise' says one, referring, in case you didn't realise, to the Queen Mother. The rest of the country's pensioners got a measly 7%.

Another contrasts the drop in living standards for most of the population with last year's pay rise for the Queen of £225,000. The response to this propaganda has been enormous – 100,000 stickers sold in three weeks plus thousands of posters and badges – an indication to the SWP of the strength of anti-monarchist feeling.

The International Marxist Group has been less active, concentrating on badges which show a leering Queen and the legend 'Abolish the Monarchy'. Its main push will be for an anti-Jubilee Festival in July, for which a special play is being written by Trevor Griffiths.

Meanwhile, the newly formed Movement Against a Monarchy ('Ma'am' – get it?) has been responsible for a particularly virulent series of stickers which includes the Queen in a dustbin and the slogan 'Rot All Rulers'.

1978

The first test tube baby smurf was born, christened Blondie. Jeremy Thorpe had a Close Encounter with the law, but he got off on charges of conspiring to kill his old boyfriend. New York did for Sid, we Rocked Against Racism, and none of us wanted to drink Reverend Jim Jones' Guyanese Kool-Aid.

January
Sid Vicious admitted to hospital in US with heroin overdose. The remaining Sex Pistols split up following day.

February
The Tom Robinson Band is 'Glad To Be Gay'. The BBC aren't: they ban it.

March
Oil tanker Amoco Cadiz runs aground off coast of Brittany causing biggest ecological disaster to date.

May
First ever May Day public holiday celebrated in UK.

June
New York's notorious 'Son of Sam' mass murderer, David Berkowitz, sentenced to a total of 315 years in jail.

'Evita' opens in West End.

July
World's first test tube baby, Louise Brown, born in Oldham.

September
Newspaper boy Carl Bridgewater is murdered.

Georgi Markov, a Bulgarian defector living in London, is murdered after being stabbed with a poisoned umbrella.

October
Daily Star launched under editorship of Derek Jameson.

Karol Wojtyla becomes the first non-Italian Pope for 450 years.

November
Nearly 1,000 people commit suicide in Guyana under the orders of cult leader Jim Jones.

Management suspends publication of the *Times* after angry disputes over manning and the introduction of new technology continue to blight the newspaper.

'PACMAN'

Superman
Given the publicity hoopla, it is easy to overlook how effectively Richard Donner visualised this revamping of the Depression-born defender of the weak and righter of wrongs.

Midnight Express
As a thriller, it makes some of the stereotypes as good as new, and panders to its audience's instincts magnificently.

The Deer Hunter
Moral imperatives replace historical analysis, social rituals become religious sacraments and the S/M of the love affair is icing on the cake. One of the films of the decade.

Various Artists - War Of The Worlds (CBS)
Jeff Wayne's production is a sincere recreation of Wells'

original theme of catastrophic death and powerful rebirth.

Billy Joel - 52nd Street (CBS)
Billy Joel's enormous success, in the face of so little substance, is easy to equate with the audience's need to feel they're experiencing a vicarious existence through a songwriter.

Siouxsie & The Banshees - The Scream (Polydor)
The group's songs are oblique, sparsely furnished cautions; Lillywhite's production is cleanly urgent. This is a compulsively fierce opening volley, and arguably the first native LP to successfully meet the Television-led New York axis head on.

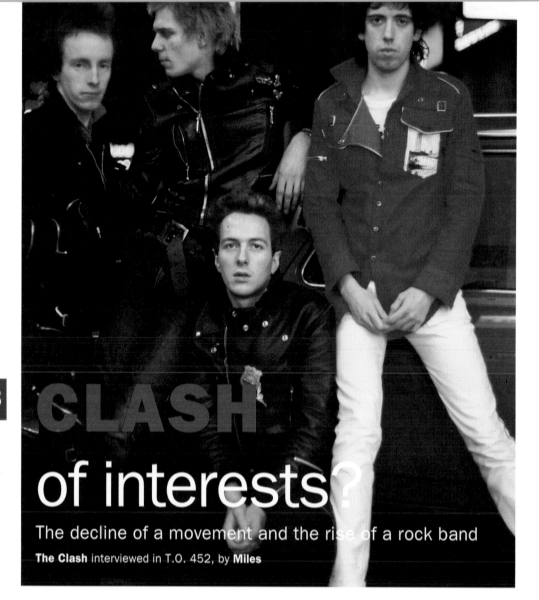

CLASH
of interests?
The decline of a movement and the rise of a rock band

The Clash interviewed in T.O. 452, by **Miles**

t's been a long time since anybody regarded The Who as a mod band, the Beatles as exponents of Merseybeat, or Bob Dylan as a folk-rocker. Musical movements enjoy even briefer life spans than the careers of the musicians that emerge from them, and bands that start life in the turmoil of a new departure either vanish when times change or find a direction of their own. This has already happened to the British punk movement, and a magnificent crop of new groups are now developing in very different ways: the Jam, the Stranglers, XTC, the Buzzcocks, Siouxsie and the Banshees, the Only Ones, Wire.

The Clash are the punk band who've stayed closest to their roots, and by being the most uncompromising, they have retained most of that original hard energy. Now they're poised at that difficult stage between local artistic success (which these days means Europe) and a place in the global rock industry. They have embraced the advanced technology of rock and risked the pressures of the market and yet managed to retain their integrity. With a second album produced by the heavily metallic Oyster Cultist Sandy Pearlman and recorded in London, New York and San Francisco, the Clash no longer can feel at home in the dole queue. But they're still broke. The new album, 'Give Em Enough Rope', entered the British charts at number two, the four punks stared balefully from the covers and centrefolds of the four rock weeklies, and even in New York City, *Soho Weekly News* headlined its front cover 'The Clash, Britain's Best New Band'. Yet as journalists rushed to deem them the Rolling Stones of the eighties, the band themselves closed ranks against a flurry of lawsuits from erstwhile manager Bernie Rhodes.

The day after the press reception for the new album, vocalist Joe Strummer and drummer Topper Headon were to be found selling clothes at a cold open air stall in Dingwalls Market in Camden Town. 'We're broke, man, so you just have to do what you can,' Strummer shrugged. 'Bernie's kicked us out of our rehearsal studio and changed the locks.' Not long ago the Clash filled the Rainbow Theatre three nights in a row and then had to take the bus home because they couldn't afford a cab. Once upon a time punk really was the music of the unemployed school-leaver living at home with his parents in a high-rise council block, numbed by TV, harassed by the police and funded by the dole. The supergroup stars living in tax exile might just as easily have been living on the moon. Johnny Rotten: 'We have to fight the entire superband system. Groups like the Stones are revolting. They have nothing to offer the kids any more…'

Punk energy was negative energy, pure nihilism. A response born of poverty instead of sixties affluence cancelled the kids' subscriptions to hippie hopes of a counter-culture and replaced them with… nothing. They suggested no alternative, they saw no future at all. Perhaps not surprisingly this turned out to be a more universal message than anyone suspected. In Jubilee week the Sex Pistols' 'God Save The Queen' made number one on the charts despite having no airplay and being banned by most large chain stores. Public school boys scenting doom in the dialectic pointed out that 'No Future' could mean even more to them than to the unemployed.

Lead guitarist Mick Jones recalls the community feeling that existed when punk first started. 'In them days it was definitely more of a movement in terms of people working together with one aim. It's only since the record companies came in that all

'Public school boys scenting doom in the dialectic pointed out that "No Future" could mean even more to them.'

the competition and bitchiness started. Before, it was like all other art movements, you know? Like art movements didn't mind having their photographs taken together and they all worked together like one group and it was the *one group.*

'All the people that used to be around were working for one aim. Some kind of change really, to do something more interesting and different from what we had at the time. Like, if you wanted to go out there was nothing for us to do…'

Joe Strummer used to go on stage with 'Hate & War' stencilled on his boiler suit. Not just because it was the opposite of the hippies' 'Love & Peace' dictum but because it was an honest statement of what is happening today in Britain with our personal Vietnam in Northern Ireland and ever growing racialism at home. 'Things will get tough,' Strummer says, 'I mean a fascist government. But people won't notice like you won't notice your hair is longer on Monday than Sunday… What I'm aimed against is all that fascist, racialist patriotism type of fanaticism.'

This he sees as the role of the Clash. 'There's so much corruption: councils, governments, industry, everywhere. It's got to be flushed out. Just because it's been going on for a long time doesn't mean that it shouldn't be stopped. It doesn't mean that it isn't time to change. This is what I'm about, and I'm in the Clash, so, of course, that's what the Clash is about. We ain't no urban guerrilla outfit. Our gunpower is strictly limited. All we want to achieve is an atmosphere where things can happen.

We want to keep the spirit of the free world. We want to keep out that safe, soapy, slush that comes out of the radio. People have this picture of us marching down the street with machine guns. We're not interested in that, because we haven't got any. All we've got is a few guitars, amps and drums. That's our weaponry.'

The band may not be packing any pieces, but they do have an armoury of ideas – and they weren't welcome on the airwaves:

All the power is in the hands
of people rich enough to buy it
While we walk the streets
too chicken to even try it.
(– 'White Riot', their first single)

The Clash began in May 1976 as a drummerless group, rehearsing in a small squat near Shepherds Bush Green. In the grand British rock tradition as laid down by John Lennon, Keith Richard, Jeff Beck, Jimmy Page, Ray Davies, Pete Townshend, Eric Clapton and David Bowie, they were all art school dropouts. When guitarist and lyricist Mick Jones formed the band he was still at Hammersmith Art School. He comes from Brixton. His father was a cab driver and Jones lived with his parents until they divorced when he was eight. His mother emigrated to America and his father moved out, leaving Jones to live with his grandmother. When he wrote 'London's Burning With Boredom' for the Clash he was still living at his grandmother's flat on the eighteenth floor of a tower block overlooking The Westway. 'I ain't never lived under five floors. I ain't never lived on the ground.'

Jones asked Paul Simonon to join his group. Simonon had been playing all of six weeks, just strumming at a guitar but now he 'found' a bass and began playing. Simonon was also born in Brixton. His parents had split up and he lived mostly with his father. 'I had a paper round at six in the morning. Then I'd come back and cook me dad his breakfast. Then I'd fuck off to school. Then I'd come back and cook me dad his dinner and do another paper round after school and then I'd cook me dad's tea…' He got a council scholarship to the Byam Shaw art school in Notting Hill. 'I used to draw blocks of flats and car dumps.' At the time of meeting Mick Jones the only live rock band he'd seen was the Sex Pistols.

Vocalist Joe Strummer was in an R&B pub band called the 101ers and had even made a single, 'Keys To Your Heart' (Chiswick Records), when he met Mick and Paul. The guitarist and bass player, together with Glen Matlock of the Sex Pistols, were just leaving the Ladbroke Grove social security office when Joe arrived on his bike. They had seen the 101ers play The Windsor Castle and recognised in Joe 'the right look'. 'I don't like your group,' said Mick, 'but we think you're great.'

'As soon as I saw these guys,' said Joe, 'I knew that that was what a group in my eyes was supposed to look like.' Almost immediately afterwards the Sex Pistols supported The 101ers at a gig and convinced Joe of what was happening. He broke up his group the next day. 'Yesterday I thought I was a crud, then I saw the Sex Pistols and I became a king and decided to move

▶

into the future. As soon as I saw them I knew that rhythm and blues was dead, that the future was here somehow. Every other group was riffing through the Black Sabbath catalogue but hearing the Pistols, I knew, I just knew!' Joe's art school was Central ('A lousy setup').

The first thing the band did was refurbish an abandoned warehouse in Camden Town, then, with Terry Chimes (nick-named Tory Crimes) sitting in on drums, they began rehearsals. They played their first gig in Sheffield in June 1976. Since places like the Marquee wouldn't book punk bands, they often had to create venues such as cinemas or playing The ICA.

The Clash signed with CBS Records, controlled from New York by the mighty Columbia Records Corp. The deal, for some-thing over £100,000, received a lot of press. But it wasn't, in fact, very good since it included no tour support and it is easy to lose £50,000 or £60,000 on a national tour promoting an album. The band remained on £25 a week, though times were better than in November '76, when they had returned to their cold warehouse after flyposting an ICA gig and desperately devoured what remained of the flour and water paste that they had used to put up the posters.

Then came the tour with the Pistols on their ill-fated 'Anarchy' dates and an album for CBS. They cut it in three weekends using their sound man as a producer. He'd never been in a studio before and the production was, not surprisingly, muddy. Despite this, the power of the music comes through and 'The Clash' remains one of the best punk albums ever made. It entered the charts at number 12 and sold over 100,000 copies in the UK. But Columbia refused to release it in the States because they thought the sound qual-ity would preclude airplay.

This was the period of punk violence. During one particularly unpleasant gig when the spit, bottles and cans were falling like rain, Terry Chimes watched as a wine bottle smashed into a million pieces on his hi-hat. He quit. Life on the road under such conditions took its toll on the others as well. Mick Jones remem-bers making the first album…

'Two years ago we did the band's first interview. On Janet Street Porter's "London Weekend Programme" it was, and me, being all young and naive, I blamed bands taking too many drugs for the great mid-'70s drought in rock. I recall saying it really well. And a year or so later, I found myself doing just as many drugs as them!

'Y'know, taking drugs as a way of life, to feel good in the morning, to get through the day. And it's still something I'm getting over right now. I was so into speed, I mean, I don't even recall making the first album.'

They auditioned 206 drummers and rejected them all. Number 207 was Nicky 'Topper' Headon, a friend who'd played briefly with them in the old days. Headon was born in Bromley. His father is a headmaster at a primary school and his mother is a teacher. 'I first played drums when I was 13. I was working at the butchers, cleaning up and I saved the money to buy a kit for £30.' After school he worked the Dover Ferries and then on the Channel Tunnel before moving to

London. With their lineup complete, the Clash began to tour Britain, always taking with them a number of other bands that they felt close to philosophically or musically: the Buzzcocks, Subway Sect, the Slits, Richard Hell & the Voidoids from NYC and the Lous, a French female punk band. The art-rock bands of the sixties took rock out of the dance hall and placed it, lit-erally, in the concert hall. The Clash took it back to the dance hall again – partly by necessity since their audiences have been known to pogo as many as 200 seats per concert into oblivion. With replacement costs at £20 a chair, the band began to insist on seatless venues.

Nonetheless their concerts were banned by local watch com-mittees, and the police continually busted the band for drugs and vandalism. They survived bomb threats in Sweden and found one of their most devoted audiences in Belfast, a town many English bands refuse to play. Everywhere they went dozens of fans were allowed backstage and their hotel rooms were always packed out with local punks crashing on the floor because they couldn't get home.

After a month-long tour of Europe the band returned to discover that their everyday movements had become prime fodder for the music press. Anything that could possibly be interpreted as 'selling out' was jumped upon. Since the punk stars had not been imposed on their audiences (in the way The Bay City Rollers were) but had risen from their ranks, to 'sell-out' was not a con-cern that the band would lose artistic integrity and produce overtly commercial records, it was a concern that they would sacrifice community to commerce. And it was true, the band was feeling more and more distanced from its audiences. It was a subtle change: the scene's originally negative, yet commu-nal, charge was unavoidably transformed into individual craft pride as the musicians became more professional. The very technology of rock, its expensive amplification equip-ment and studios, introduces the businessman into the musi-cians' lives. Playing becomes the band's work, performed while everyone else is at play. In 'The Sociology Of Rock', Simon Frith pinpointed the problem perfectly: 'Their work is everyone else's leisure, their way of life is everyone else's relaxation, escape and indulgence. They work in places of entertainment. What for them is routine is for their fans a spe-cial event. Musicians themselves are symbols of leisure and escape, their glamour supports their use as sex objects, as fantasies and briefly held dreams.'

The Clash are now a long way from the squat in Shepherds Bush. They remain on a level of intimacy with many of their fans, perhaps a little too intimate at times. (A few months ago Joe Strummer got hepatitis from a well aimed gob of spit which caught him in the mouth.) But as their fame grows, particular-ly with the release of their new album in the States, the only way they will be able to express their original ideals will be through their music. That is now their job.

Joe Strummer: 'I think people ought to know that we're anti-fas-cist, we're anti-violence, we're anti-racist and we're pro-creative. We're against ignorance.' And their music is real fine as well. ●

'We're anti-fascist, we're anti-violence, we're anti racist.'

Carl Perkins

from 'You can do anything but...' in T.O. 419, by **John Collis**

When he tells the story of his first meeting with Sun label owner Sam Phillips, the self-mocking humour in Carl Perkins' voice still, after 24 years, fails to mask the recollected awe of a country boy in the big city for the first time. Perkins had a band with his brothers Jay and Clayton, and when they first heard Elvis on the radio they realised that 'their' sound was being recorded. They stowed their instruments in an old car and made the pilgrimage to Memphis, only to be turned away by Phillips' secretary.

'We were sitting at the kerb, wondering what to do next, when this huge car rolls up. It was dark blue on top, light blue on the bottom. A Cadillac Coupe de Ville! Then this cat gets out, and he's dressed exactly like his car! Dark blue jacket, light blue slacks. I was out of the car and beside him before he had a chance to shut the door. He told us later that he only gave us a hearing because he could see how hungry and desperate we were. He was right; it was our last shot.'

Perkins began recording in his own version of Hank Williams' style, as a deliberate alternative to Presley, but in December 1955 Phillips let him rock. Originally the B-side to 'Honey Don't', 'Blue Suede Shoes' became the first song to top simultaneously the pop, R&B *and* country charts. Alongside Berry's 'Johnny B Goode', it has since become the most enduring of rock & roll anthems.

Perkins was the first rocker to be on national television, and the band set off for a weekend that was to include the Perry Como and Ed Sullivan shows. A car crash caused injuries of which Jay eventually died, and put Carl into hospital. By the time he came out, Presley had established himself as the top rocker... with a cover version of 'Blue Suede Shoes'. Debts, label-hopping and heavy drinking followed. Family tragedy came full circle a few Christmases ago, when Clayton Perkins committed suicide.

The most exciting concert I've ever attended was at Bristol's Colston Hall in 1964. On the bill were The Animals with 'Rising Sun' about to break, The Nashville Teens with 'Tobacco Road', and two idols: Chuck Berry, having recently completed the jail sentence he still denies, and an alcoholic has-been, Carl Perkins. Completely overwhelmed by the adulation,

Perkins ripped through a set which confirmed him in British ears as the greatest of the rockabilly creators.

He visited Britain again several times, before joining Johnny Cash for a two-day stint that lasted ten years. Then, with his two sons out of school and ready to play, he parted amicably with Cash and formed the C P Express, featuring sons Stan and Greg on drums and bass. Although Perkins has been billed on the Wembley country festival for the past four years, this time he embarks on a rock & roll tour with Bo Diddley, instead of returning immediately to America for another year.

A new contract with Jet Records, a heavily-promoted album 'Ol Blue Suede's Back', and the tour itself look like re-establishing Perkins here, although as his reputation at a recent lunch time gig proved, he's always been the living king among the rockabilly faithful.

One legend which has clung to Perkins for 20 years waits to be resolved. He was recording a Sun session, with Jerry Lee Lewis on piano and Johnny Cash also in the studio. Then Elvis paid one of his periodic visits to his home town, and a 90-minute jam session developed. The tape was left running, and the results have long been referred to as 'The Million Dollar Quartet'.

'It's held up in court now. It's me against Shelby Singleton (who bought up the rights to the Sun label). I say the tape belongs to me; I paid for the session. I heard rumours that Singleton wanted to get in session players and over-dub the tape. That's wrong; the tape stands for itself. The record will come out... in fact Singleton's got a warehouse full, ready for shipping! He's a multi-millionaire. Why should he make another million from something that's not his? Elvis can't speak for himself, but he wouldn't want that. I'd like to see, say, half the royalties do a bit of good; do something for kids.'

The geniuses of rock & roll were usually country boys... Perkins was a share-cropper's son whose first guitar, like those of all the rest, apparently, consisted of baling wire, nails and a cigar-box (there seem to have been as many cigar-box guitars as there were intended passengers for Buddy Holly's plane). They were ripe for exploitation, but at least one of them seems to have learnt from it. Perkins is enthusiastic about his new record contract, and has never in his life received the interest and support that he's now enjoying. But in a *Melody Maker* interview last May he said: 'I feel real good about my new deal. It appears they're really interested and are really going to push.' He was talking of his *previous* record deal – a nasty irony. ●

The infinite
spaces of *Disco*

in T.O. 416, by **Simon Frith**

In public I'm into punk like everybody else (saviour of rock 'n' roll's soul and all that) but privately I'm a junk rock junkie and the junkiest music of all is disco. Everybody hates it. Hippies hate it, progressives hate it, punks hate it, teds hate it, *NME* hates it, even Derek Jewell hates it. Disco is music for the disillusioned. It isn't art: no auteurs in disco, just calculated dessicating machines. It isn't folk: no disco subcultures, no disco kids seething with symbolic expression It isn't even much fun: no jokes, no irony, only a hard rhythmed purposefulness. Disco is the sound of consumption. It exists only in its dancing function: when the music stops all that's left is a pool of sweat on the floor. And disco's power is the power of consumption. The critics are right: disco is dehumanising – all those twitching limbs, glazed-eyed, mindless. The disco aesthetic excludes feeling, it offers a glimpse of a harsh sci-fi future. 'What's your name, what's your number?' sings Andrea True in my current favourite single, and it's not his telephone number she wants, but his position in the disco order of things. The problem of pogoing, I've found, is not that it's too energetic for anyone over 30 years and 11 stone, but that it requires too much thought.

Popular music has always been dance music; disco is nothing but dance music. It has no rock'n'roll connotations; off the dance floor it is utterly meaningless, lyrically, musically and aesthetically. Every disco sound is subordinate to its physical function; disco progress is technological progress. The end doesn't change but the means to that end, the ultimate beat, are refined and improved – hence drum machines, synthesisers, 12" pressings. And disco is dance music in the abstract, content determined by form. Popular dance music of the past, in the 1930s say, was a form determined by its content. The content was developed by dance hall instructors and sheet music salesmen and band leaders whose rules of partnership, decorum, uplift and grace, can still be followed in 'Come Dancing': the music is strictly subordinate to the conventions of flounce and simper. In contrast, when Boney M, German manufactured black American androgynes, sing for our dancing pleasure, 'Belfast', it means nothing at all. Any two syllables arranged and sounding just so would do and how we dance to them is, of course, entirely our own affair. There are no rules in disco, it's just that individual expression means nothing when there's nothing individual to express. I trace disco back to the twist, the first dance gimmick to be taken seriously and the first dance step to be without any redeeming social feature. I blame disco on Motown, the first company to realise that if the beat is right, soul power can be expressed without either the passion or emotion that made it soul power in the first place.

Disco is nothing like muzak. Muzak's effect is subliminal; its purpose is to encourage its hearers to do anything but listen to it. Disco's effect is material; its purpose is to encourage its hearers to do nothing but listen to it. Not even think.

Disco music is only disco music in discos. These days there are CP discos, women's discos, anti-fascist discos, students' discos, youth club discos, cricketers' discos, punk discos and reggae discos. The disco form can be used by anyone who's got a record player, records and a large enough room. But a proper disco exists only to be a disco and the records it plays exist only to be played by it. The Musicians' Union hates discos because they put live musicians out of work. I hate discos because they seem like such a soft way of making money: a DJ doesn't do anything except buy records and put the needle on them – I can do that too. The whole enterprise is parasitic: if there is such a thing as disco creativity it happened in secret studio places long before. The best discos are the best just to the extent to which nothing unexpected happens – feet never falter, taste is never threatened, offence is never taken because never given. If you want a surprise don't go to the disco.

Clubs with records as their only means of entertainment came to Britain from the continent in the early '60s. Before then DJs and records had been used in ballrooms (cf the pioneering career of Jimmy Saville) but not as alternatives to live music and, initially, discos simply served two sorts of incrowd: rock aristocrats seeking social exclusion and soul freaks seeking musical exclusion (as they still do in the Northern Soul clubs). The main British disco development occurred in the late '60s/early '70s as live rock became increasingly undanceable, expensive and in the wrong places (colleges and concert halls). British disco went teenage pop and, in a commercial sense, it mostly still is. The style of consumption involved is working class provincial. Bouncers, louts, uneasy sexual posturing; dance hall culture really, but cooler and smarter than in the '50s, and with flashing lights and much better music. Women do most of the dancing, men most of the drinking, and none of them take disco as seriously as, perhaps, they ought. Because meanwhile in America discos are the setting for adult chic consumption, part of the culture of singles rather than of teenage courtship, anonymously safe places for elaborate displays of apathy. Can't imagine drunks in Manhattan's spruce discos, bumping buttocks with Susan Sontag and Lennie Bernstein.

The European connection is that discos in Paris are more like they are in New York than they are like they are in Nottingham. And French and Italian teenagers are, anyway, chic-er than Britons of any age. But the, most wonderful Euro-discos of all are the ones in the holiday belts – Costa Brava, Riviera, Costa del Sol. Cellars which are open permanently in the summer months and in which earnest Northerners – Dutch, British, Swedes, Germans, develop their own singles culture, their own disco style. I can only explain it by noting that they dance to Donna Summer in their sandals. Ah disco! Ah Baccara!

As a rock writer, I've always been a frustrated DJ rather than musician. 'Hey you,' I've wanted to shout, 'Listen to this!' The model was John Peel, music lover and eclectic. I certainly didn't fancy the provincial disco DJs I knew – big, hearty philistines who knew nothing about the records they played but enjoyed the patter and had dreams, like Albert Finney in 'Gumshoe', of moving from master of ceremonies to master of a comic routine. But this was a doomed approach anyway, survival from dance hall days. Real disco DJs aren't entertainers at all, have nothing to with music. They're technologists, men (very few women) of the future: their job is to play the audience. It's a job I want again. By 1984 it'll probably be called 'consumption-coordinator'.

Discos are where people dance and dancing can be anything from the shuffle to a pre-rehearsed and elaborate routine to a straight display of cartwheels. What disco dancing isn't is a) musical interpretation and b) self-expression. The opposite of disco dancing is what Legs and Co. do on 'Top of the Pops' – ie choreographed responses to the 'meaning' of a song. What they do is so embarrassing that I usually turn the picture off, but I turn it back again for the rest of the show because, at an admittedly low level, it does reveal the difference between the Anglo-Collective disco style – all those dumpy little boys and girls looking nervously at each other – and the American-Individual style (on the clips from 'Soul Train') – all those intense boys and girls looking determinedly at their own feet. Most disco dancing has little to do with elegance, grace or agility, which is OK by me because if it did I wouldn't do it.

Rock music, dance music, has always been a form of sexual expression – girl meets boy physically. The social problem has then been the control of this expression – hence the moral about rock 'n' roll, Elvis's hips etc. Disco's greatest achievement has been to develop a form in which sexuality is expressed and controlled simultaneously. Critics have missed the point of the standard formula – machinery plus orgasmic sighs. The problem is not that the sighs are fake, but that it *wouldn't make any difference if they were real!* Disco isn't a frustrating music – preventing the climax from occurring – but a music of control – preventing the climax from being disruptive. It's a noisy form of some Eastern mystical discipline and the only puzzle to me is why disco is so important an aspect of gay culture. I'm not gay, so I can't say, except that it seems as if disco stylisation allows gays public displays that are sexual without apparently being offensive to the usual custodians of public morality.

The only thing to say about disco music as music is that it has given extraordinary opportunities to pop's previously second class citizens – its session singers, engineers, Bee Gees. The technicians, in other words, who always could produce any sound to order but used not to know what to do with them. They know now.

Previous popular music has only reflected the world, in various ways; the point of disco, however is to replace it. ●

"1978"

"Of course they have, or I wouldn't be sitting here talking to someone like you."
Dame Barbara Cartland, after being asked on BBC radio if class barriers were breaking down

"This is an act of revolutionary suicide."
Rev Jim Jones leaves a sick note after the deaths of his 1,000 followers in Guyana

"There Will Be An Interruption."
Times leader before one-year strike

"Where's my fucking leather jacket?"
Sid Vicious after being released on bail from Riker's Island

**"Poop poop Peru!
What're we going tae do to you?
Too true!"**
Poet Alan Bold predicts disaster for the South Americans against Scotland in the 1978 World Cup. Scotland lost

"You know what comes between me and my Calvins? Nothing."
Brooke Shields slips into something a little less comfortable

"Your experience will be a lesson to all of us men to be careful not to marry ladies in very high positions."
Idi Amin sends his condolences to Lord Snowdon on his divorce from Princess Margaret

"With Nixon in the White House, good health seemed to be in bad taste."
Jane Fonda in 'California Suite'

"If we had let the men shoot at looters at will, you would have had dead people littering the streets. A lot of dead people."
New York Police Commissioner Michael Codd after a power failure on the East Coast led to 3,800 people being arrested for looting

"Perhaps 17 November 1978 will be remembered as positively the last appearance on the public stage of this raddled and discredited prima donna."
Lord Jeremy Hutchison QC on the Official Secrets Act

A prodigy **zooms in**

A child cineaste who now makes movies and money with equal facility

Steven Spielberg interviewed in T.O. 414, by **Dave Pirie**

Film directors are not best known for their modesty or their tact. And to be signed by Universal Pictures to an exclusive seven year contract *before turning 21* would be enough to turn most of them into monsters of the first kind.

Nor do Steven Spielberg's accomplishments stop there. Only a couple of years later he made 'Duel', probably the most critically acclaimed made-for-TV movie in television history. And before he had quite turned 30 his name was on not one, but two, of Hollywood's all-time box office hits. On his last two films alone he was entrusted with around 25,000,000 dollars of other people's money.

The record is so formidable that it's hard to envisage the man behind it as anything less than a thoroughgoing egomaniac. And the prospect of a long hotel room interview shortly after he wrapped 'Close Encounters' seemed more likely to test our therapeutic than any critical ones.

But unfortunately life sometimes defies the bland character assumptions of the movies: Steven Spielberg turned out to be the most engaging and unassuming of film makers. His conversation is shy and thoughtful, warming especially to his first passion: movies. Spielberg made his earliest film at the age of 12 and you get the feeling that his child-like enthusiasm for the movies has – in complete contrast to someone like Bogdanovich – actually helped to isolate him from the usual neuroses of power.

Locked into the technical side of film from such an early age, he seems to enact his present eminence less like a superstar than a slightly absent-minded scientist – one so immersed in his own experiments that he is not too surprised to find more and more resources at his disposal. Unlike Orson Welles and other young prodigies who came to films via other media, Spielberg is essentially a pure film freak who has spent almost all his life absorbing popular movie culture. Consequently he needs no alibis.

But unlike so many other new American movie-makers Spielberg did not start off in film school. 'I began making a lot of films in high school. But I didn't go to film school, in fact I majored in English. At Long Beach State. I was actually just staying there so I wouldn't have to serve in Vietnam. If the draft had not been after me I probably wouldn't have gone to college at all. So over those four years I did almost nothing except movie-making. I was able to make enough money working in the cafeteria and doing odd jobs to be able to buy a roll of film, rent a camera from Burns & Sawyer and go out on weekends to shoot small experimental films...'

After raking together enough cash to make a short called 'Ambulance', Spielberg hawked it through Universal, where people knew him as a kid who was always hanging around.

'I had met a lot of people. None of them were willing to help me. Matter of fact I couldn't get a producer to sit down and look at anything. The toughest thing to do was to get someone to sit down and look at your work. But I knew some of the editors from hanging around the editing rooms and one day I met a man called Chuck Silvers in the hall. And I showed him a few of my films. He *did* take the time to see them. He was very nice to me. He got the film to the head of Universal Television. And eventually this man summoned me to his office. He was sitting there in his French provincial office overlooking Universal. Just like a scene out of "The Fountainhead". And he said "I'd like you to work here under contract. Start in the TV area, and then maybe branch out and do a feature." It was all very vague. So I signed a seven year contract without consulting an agent.'

Not yet 21, Spielberg was put to work straight away on the pilot for what would become the TV series 'Night Gallery': 'It was a very macabre story starring Joan Crawford. I read the script and I said. "Jesus, can't I do something about young people?" And he said: "I'd take this if I were you." I was so frightened that even now the whole period is a bit of of a blank. I was walking on eggs. I was told not to change one word of dialogue or they'd have me. They'd put sprocket-holes up and down my sides. And I had no idea I was telling a story. To me it was just a menu of shots. It was a memorandum of things

to do that day. It was only when I saw the show years later that I suddenly discovered the story I was telling.'

After this traumatic initiation, Spielberg was repaid by not being asked to do anything else for at least a year. His contract was suspended: 'I was regarded on the Universal lot as a folly, a novelty item, bric-a-brac for the mantlepiece. Something to joke about at parties. I even left Universal for a year. And then finally I got back into television on a series called "The Psychiatrist". I guess I was 22 then and they felt I was old enough to direct television. So the ice cracked and I got in. And I did "Marcus Welby" and "The Name of the Game" and "Colombo", and this and that until "Duel" came along.'

'Duel' was the remarkable made-for-TV movie based on a short story by Richard Matheson about a man fighting an anonymous truck. Released in Europe as a theatrical feature, it established Spielberg in many critics' eyes as a cool and brilliant handler of hardware, perhaps even an unconscious visual poet of the technological society. But Spielberg talks with unexpected penetration about the film's implications:

'The hero of "Duel" is typical of that lower middle-class American who's insulated by suburban modernisation. It begins on Sunday: you take your car to be washed. You have to drive it but it's only a block away. And, as the car's being washed, you go next door with the kids and you buy them ice-cream at the Dairy Queen and then you have lunch at the plastic McDonald's with seven zillion hamburgers sold. And then you go off to the games room and you play the quarter games: the Tank and the Pong and Flim-Flam. And by that time you go back and your car's all dry and ready to go and you get into the car and you drive to the Magic Mountain plastic amusement park and you spend the day there eating junk food. Afterwards you drive home, stopping at all the red lights, and the wife is waiting with dinner on. And you have instant potatoes and eggs without cholesterol, because they're artificial – and you sit down and you turn on the television set, which has become the reality as opposed to the fantasy this man has lived with that entire day. And you watch the primetime, which is pabulum and nothing more than watching a night-light. And you see the news at the end of that, which you don't want to listen to because it doesn't conform to the reality you've just been through primetime with. And at the end of all that you go to sleep and you dream about making enough money to support weekend America.

'This is the kind of man portrayed in "Duel". And a man like that never expects to be challenged by anything more than his television set breaking down and having to call the repair man.'

Spielberg admits that 'Duel' and 'Something Evil' – the astonishing occult thriller that climaxed his TV career – were among the last films he's actually enjoyed shooting. 'Jaws' in particular was a production nightmare: 'The problems were so enormous on "Jaws" that even after a week I forgot I was in the film business.

I thought I was working for the Oceanographic Institute. Which was just as well because it was in the first week that I learned my very first theatrical feature, "Sugarland Express", had died at the box office. "Jaws" was about four hours a day shooting, eight hours anchoring boats and trying to fight the ocean and get the shark to work. The shark didn't work so often that I was forced to cut it continually on about the fourth frame. If I didn't, you'd see what the shark was made of, how the eyes really looked and the air bubbles roaring out of the mouth.'

The huge success of 'Jaws' has partly served to obscure how much pure visual dexterity Spielberg brought to a relatively conventional story. He works from his own sketches, laboriously mapping out every shot in advance of production: 'On every movie I make, unless there's enough money for me to have a personal sketch artist, I sketch out all my shots in advance and then use them to edit the movie in my head. This really paid off on "Jaws" which was the most intricately sketched movie I've done. At the start of shooting "Duel" I did about four or five hundred individual sketches and stuck them to the walls of the motel in the desert where we were shooting. I can still see them wrapped around the living-room, wrapped around the bedroom, even wrapped around part of the bathroom. But the tough thing is somehow to get these conceptions on the screen. It's terrible because it preoccupies most of my REM [rapid eye movement, i.e. dreaming] hours at night. I'm thinking of lost film most of the time.'

One 'lost' film which Spielberg has now managed to reconstruct with the help of Columbia is the prototype of 'Close Encounters of the Third Kind'. Ironically, the new blockbuster is partly based on a two-hour film about UFOs called 'Firelight' which Spielberg made with 400 dollars borrowed from his father while he was still at school.

Spielberg appears to be so much at home both with the visual arts and electronic technology that he was the obvious person to make the first high-budget Hollywood feature about flying saucers. But 'Close Encounters' is quite different from either the popcorn munching kid's adventure tone of 'Star Wars' or the hysterical paranoia of the UFO exploitation features of the '50s.

It is less a mystery or even a science fiction story than a film about wonder. Its true progenitors are not Heinlein and Asimov but Disney and DeMille. In fact there are explicit references to both these film-makers in the film and, like their work, 'Close Encounters' is determinedly and intentionally naive. The bizarre thing is that, while moving into this almost-impossible-to-recapture territory, the film remains so effective.

The basic theme takes up a favourite hypothesis of every UFO enthusiast: namely that the US government has been covering up all UFO sightings while quietly preparing its own reception for the aliens. In fact in one superbly Spielbergian moment the top secret personnel set out for their mysterious rendezvous in a fleet of trucks masquerading as the icons of consumer America: Baskins-Robbins, Coca-Cola etc.But the difference between 'Close Encounters' and the earlier cinema of wonder is that while DeMille and Disney could make their audiences gasp with the tackiest special effects, Spielberg and 'Space Odyssey' maestro Douglas Trumbull have to go to much greater lengths. For one amazing sequence they hired a huge dirigible hangar in Mobile, Alabama, and set about creating an exterior night location inside it, including a night-sky studded with hundreds of arc-lights. ('A nightmare in lighting,' Spielberg says, 'at least 40 electricians had to be flown in to handle it.')

The result of all this may not be a masterpiece of intellectual sophistication. But it *is* the first film in years likely to give its audience a tingle of shocked emotion not based on fear, approaching, in fact, a child's first feeling in the cinema. And that is an emotion Steven Spielberg seems uniquely equipped to communicate. ●

The *Star* shines out of Derek Jameson's...

in T.O. 440, by **Duncan Campbell**

Derek Jameson, Editor of the *Daily Express*, asked Anna Ford how much she paid for her knickers. The point he wanted to make was that most people don't spend a great deal of money on their underpants and therefore it was silly of the *Daily Mirror* to run stories about Janet Reger and her £19 range of lingerie. And the point of all that is that Jameson wants to let people know that the *Daily Star*, due to be launched on October 16 by the Express Group under Jameson's editorial eye, will have the interests of its readers at heart – right down to the price they pay for their underpants.

The occasion for this elevating discussion was the launching of the *Star* for the benefit of the advertising world in a special 'extravaganza' (which means basically free drink and some women not wearing all their clothes) at the Mayfair Theatre, last Thursday.

The *Star* is aiming for a slice of the massive *Sun-Mirror* market – currently both papers are selling almost four million copies a day and raking in profits of around £1 million a month. The *Star*, with a similar tabloid, easy-to-read, tits-and-bums-and-racing approach wants to have three million of this market by 1980. More realistically, Jameson told *Time Out* in an interview this week that he hopes for a readership of around one and a quarter million by then.

The *Star*'s politics will be 'left of centre' says Jameson who is 'annoyed' by the right-wing stance of the *Sun* and Larry Lamb's 'love-affair with Margaret Thatcher', which weekly grows more embarrassing. Nor, he claims, will there

be any racist stories. Women, however, will be treated just the same as by the other tabloids: pin-ups, cutesy captions and 'birds' galore.

1979

January
Winter of Discontent continues as lorry drivers start one-month strike.

Pol Pot and Khmer Rouge are overthrown in Vietnam.

Shah of Iran forced into exile. One month later Ayatollah Khomeini returns from France.

February
Sid Vicious is found dead in Greenwich Village apartment.

March
Welsh and Scottish voters vote against devolution.

Labour Government loses vote of confidence by one vote. Parliament is dissolved.

Airey Neave, Tory spokesman on Northern Ireland, is killed by IRA.

Jubilee Line opens.

May
Conservatives win power as Margaret Thatcher becomes first woman Prime Minister.

June
Jeremy Thorpe is acquitted of attempted murder at Old Bailey.

John Wayne dies.

July
Bjorn Borg wins fourth successive Wimbledon Singles.

Sandanista comes to power in Nicaragua.

August
Earl Mountbatten killed when IRA blow up his boat.

November
Prime Minister names Anthony Blunt as 'fourth man'.

The Times is back on streets.

December
Soviet Union invades Afghanistan.

After the winter got us snowed in and Discontented, we all found ourselves working on Maggie's Farm. She quoted St Francis but primed the place for Thatcherite fundamentalism and snaking dole queues. Power shakes went down in Afghanistan (the Russkies) and Iran (the Ayatollah). We were post-punk now, so we traded bondage jackets for tonic suits and two-toned it into a mod revival.

Alien
The limited strengths of its staple sci-fi horrors always derives from either the offhand resonances of its design or the manipulative editing of its above-average shock quota.

Quadrophenia
Fine as long as it sticks to recreation of period and place, and stays with a simple enough plot. Good performances, too.

Apocalypse Now
This is a film of great effects and pretension. The casting of Brando is the acid test: brilliant as movie-making, but it turns Vietnam into a vast trip.

Rickie Lee Jones - Rickie Lee Jones (Warner Bros)
The infectious simplicity of Jones' tunes

Joy Division - Unknown Pleasures (Factory)
It's rare for an album to evoke such a consistent sound-and-landscape as does this. Ian Curtis' vocals slice through in knowing, resigned desperation. The best produced and pack-aged independent album you'll find in a good while.

is complemented by the loose-limbed understatement of the arrangements and playing.

Talking Heads - Fear Of Music (Sire)
Their flair for beautiful innovations of a discreet magnificence hasn't deserted Talking Heads. You can dance to this record all night.

Death and taxes

A Mormon murderer is shot by a Utah firing squad and Norman Mailer cops a cool quarter million.

Norman Mailer interviewed in T.O. 503, by **Adrianne Blue**

Confession is good for the bank account. Mailer got a quarter of a million dollars up front for 'The Executioner's Song'. Unfortunately to a man in Mailer's present state of financial bereavement, to a writer who commands enormous literary capital, that is fairly puny potatoes for two years' work.

'I didn't write it for money,' Mailer says softly. 'It got me deeper into debt. That's why I was ready to kill Burgess.' He is referring to Anthony Burgess' review in the *Observer*. 'I mean, that man's going in and stepping all over me with his smelly socks and he doesn't even know what he's talking about. He can hate my book. Fine. Then he writes a bad review. That's cool. But to attack my character – that makes me want to get my hands on him, caress him up a little.'

But isn't it a lot of money for one book, even a 'true life novel' by one of the half a dozen American writers who can lay claim to be the living greatest? 'I've got got nine children. I'm paying alimony to four wives,' Mailer says. There has been a protracted struggle with internal revenue, and last year in divorce proceedings Mailer lost a couple of rounds. 'So I lost my house in Provincetown and I lost my house in Stockbridge and I sold the house I had in Brooklyn Heights. Still, if 'The Executioner's Song' takes off...'

And then the 'quicky' he has written about Marilyn Monroe (his second book about the goddess) does well when it comes out next year, Mailer might just be able to pay his agent the $20,000 he owes him. And, oh yes, he might get around to finishing the novel he has been writing on and frequently off for seven years now, the Egyptian novel, which is set 1,100 years BC. 'Well, they've paid me $450,000 over the years on that book and I have 700 pages of manuscript done. And they're going to pay me some more. I may eventually get a million dollars from it, but it'll be a long book when it's done. It took plenty years. And, odd as it sounds, the rate, since I work very slowly on it, was not enough to pay for my expenses.'

So Scott Fitzgerald was close to right. The rich think they are different from you and me.

Frankly, I've been stalking Mailer for a long time now. In 1967, on his way home from the March on the Pentagon, the anti-Vietnam War protest which spawned 'The Armies of the Night' – a more personal and much more important book than his new one – I glimpsed him at a motorway café on the Washington-New York run. Mailer had been jailed at the historic demo, and he was surrounded by a retinue of admirers. He was dressed in what Saul Bellow, another contender for chief of the literary illuminati, used to refer to as the bourgeois disguise. In this case, it was haut-bourgeois. Mailer was wearing a dark three-piece suit, a pinstriped suit. He didn't look then like the sort of citizen who had once stabbed his wife; and certainly not one who would attempt to accrue interest from the dead.

Mailer was living in Brooklyn Heights, in the house with the fabled view of Manhattan. The Heights, just a 12-minute subway ride to Greenwich Village, is even closer to Wall Street – you see a lot of men in pinstriped suits. At the time, I had a flat around the corner from Mailer's house, a fifth-floor walk-up, and

although we never met, I would see him sometimes at 6.30am in the morning, unshaven, swaying down Pineapple Street.

'Yeah, I was probably finishing for the night,' Mailer says. 'Now if you see me at 6.30am, it's because I got up early and I'm out jogging. I love that neighbourhood,' he says. 'You notice little architectural details on the brownstones as you're running along. Once in a while, like once a week, I box,' Mailer says. 'You can't box without jogging. A little,' he says. 'We used to call it roadwork.'

Somehow, I can't help doubting the punching prowess of a man of his squat, baby-like proportions. But 'The Fight', his book on the Ali-Foreman match in Zaire, is world-class sportswriting, though it too was a 'quicky' interruption of his Egyptian novel – and though it, like most Mailer books, is prone to self-serving, ad hoc theories of human nature. I've always regarded Mailer as a nasty, dangerous romantic who can write like hell – so I was prepared for the vanity, but not for the personal charm.

It is three days into his pro-'Execution' blitz of Britain. Mailer is coughing way down deep in his barrel chest. He is coming down with an English cold. 'I threw my back out a little, and it's still coming around, so I'm gonna sit in the hard chair,' Mailer says. 'You sit wherever you want.

'I was boxing and threw my back out, he says. 'I got a son who is getting too tough. Gotta stomp him to the ground – or try to,' Mailer says. He pauses, considering: 'Look, are you comfortable sitting down there, and I'm up so high? Does that bother you?'

His chair, dining table height, towers over mine. He a short man, sensitive to the issue. I tell him I'm used to being smaller than everybody else.

'This much smaller?'

It's fine, I say. Does it bother him?

'What, a macho-sexist-pig like myself in a position of dominance, how can I be bothered by that?'

It is going to be hard not to like him. 'The Executioner's Song', a grim prose ballad in the plain style, displays a chorus of Mailer's baser obsessions: money, murder, female masochism. It is the story of Gary Gilmore, the killer who demanded that the state of Utah carry out the death sentence it had imposed on him for two murders he committed in a small Mormon town.

In *his* murder book Truman Capote says more or less directly that murderers are loose all over the place. You don't have to be Jay Sebring or Sharon Tate or an isolated Kansas Clutter to face dying 'In Cold Blood'. You can stumble into the sights of Son of Sam or the Yorkshire Ripper. Capote resuscitated a moribund career with his exquisitely crafted book of death. But it is now old news that random rage is abroad in the land.

John Cheever recently restaked his bet on placing in the literary sweepstakes with his prison novel 'The Falconer'. Mailer actually had been a prisoner. More than once. So Mailer, a crafty competitor, must have felt he had to write at the least a murder-cum-prison book.

Capote had already introduced the 'nonfiction novel'. Mailer himself had subtitled the account of the Pentagon battle, 'History as a novel, the novel as history'. The new book would be fact; a Dreiserian agglomeration of detail, assembled by the

'What, a macho-sexist-pig like myself in a position of dominance?'

1979

Norman Mailer

techniques of fiction. The term 'New Journalism', everybody seemed to be feeling, was debasing. Or maybe somebody knew that it would be impossible to fight Kissinger's memoirs to the top of the non-fiction bestseller list.

So Mailer decided to categorise the Gilmore book as a 'documentary novel'. Just before publication in America he insisted it be billed as a 'true life novel' and sold as fiction. 'If I had to do it over again,' Mailer says now, 'I'd call it a true crime novel. The corniness of the phrase appeals to me.'

Essentially, 'The Executioner's Song' is a casebook, an unusually stylish dossier. It is first of all the story of Gilmore and the Gilmore clan and how Gary came to shoot two men he had never met. There are snippets of interviews with Gilmore, his and Nicole's love letters, newspaper cuttings, official pronouncements, and Mailer's fairly muscular narrative for connective tissue.

'I've been looking for a panoramic novel all my life because there's something most agreeable about panoramic novels,' he says, citing as his example his first novel, 'The Naked and the Dead'. 'But unless you have a very good story,' Mailer says, 'a panoramic novel lies there like a pancake. And here I had a plot as great as "Les Miserables", as solid as Dickens.'

There's always been a degree of paranoia attached to Mailer's analysis of other people's analyses of him. If he had written a novel, changing the names, or a book about his personal response to Gilmore (all of the things he is defter at than what he has done here) – if he had written himself into it, he says, 'No one would believe it. If I had succeeded in transposing it into a novel at that point people would say, I don't believe this story. This is Mailer. Mailer invented these kind of murders. This is Mailer imagining himself as a criminal. So I thought, all right, I'm gonna stay away out of it completely. I'm not gonna allow anybody to say this is Norman Mailer romanticising his characters. I've got this material and I'm gonna obey it, I'm gonna respect it. I'm gonna stay away from it. I'm gonna just present it. I'm not gonna use my arts as a writer, I'm gonna use my skills.'

The Gilmore case had important civil liberties implications. Utah had not had an execution in ten years, and all over America prisoners sat on death row, sure that their sentences would not be carried out. Capital punishment in many states was still on the books; but there existed a de facto prohibition.

It was widely feared that if Gilmore, by refusing to appeal his sentence, forced the state of Utah to impose the death penalty, capital punishment would be reinvoked throughout the country. Gilmore, who never gave a damn about the quality of anyone else's life (or death), didn't give a damn about this issue. He won his death. Widespread judicial slaughter followed. From the evidence of Mailer's book, though Mailer himself draws a different conclusion, I think it is clear that Gilmore was a psychopath, that he had no sense of guilt. Knowing he had utter power over a highly-sexual, dull-witted woman, he asked her first to abstain from sex as long as he lived, then forever. Then he asked her to commit suicide with him. Perhaps in 18 years of prison, he had lost his conscience; perhaps he never had one. Certainly he was totally self-obsessed.

Macho one and beyond

The mannered man from Manhattan searches for the right stuff.

Tom Wolfe interviewed in T.O.500, by **Adrianne Blue**

Naturally there is a punching bag in Tom Wolfe's study. There is the requisite gargantuan plant in the sitting room, and in the study of his terraced house on Manhattan's haughty East Side, along with the fitted carpet and the gleaming typewriter, there is the requisite American hewriter's emblem of macho. 'Punching bags don't help you fight at all' Wolfe says in the soft Virginia gentleman's voice that matches his Dapper Dude apparel so perfectly. 'Punching bags just kind of give you something to do.' He demonstrates. One-two, one-two, one-two. Six fast punches. Educated punches.

Fifteen years after 'There Goes (Varoom! Varoom!) That Kandy Kolored, Tangerine-Flake Stream-line Baby' Wolfe is, at 48, t he grandest old man of New Journalism. A revivifier of comic book slang – 'varoom' – and a creator of catch phrases – 'radical chic' and 'the Me generation'.

'I wish I could get royalties off that phrase, the "Me-decade",' Wolfe says. 'The piece has been cited many, many times as a study of the ruinous nar-

That would have enthralled the part of Mailer who yearned for the rage to actually kill his wife. It would have enthralled the Mailer who is capable of answering a question about the morality of writing a book which glorifies a murderer in this fashion: 'I've got to confess, and this may be shocking to some people, that I worried about that to the greatest degree because I thought it would affect the fortunes of the book, you know, naturally, I want my books to do well.'

Mea culpa, he is saying, I was worried people would use their hard-earned cash to buy James Herriot instead. But he skitters away from the moral issues, as he has from the issue of capital punishment. He admits his view of capital punishment is not in

'...a little capital punishment, but, please, not too much.'

the book. 'My ideas on it are misty but I'm willing to get into it. I guess I think ultimately a man has a right to insist on his execution,' Mailer says now. It parallels a woman's right to abortion, he says or a terminal patient's right to have the tubes pulled out.

This too sidesteps the issue of capital punishment – the right of the state to murder, usually against the prisoner's will. 'It's very unpleasant when the state kills somebody,' Mailer says. 'Because most of the people who do it, don't know what they're doing. Anyone who has known attorney generals knows that they're no better and no worse than anybody else. They're not brighter than we are, they're not wiser, they're not deeper.' Like wardens and defence attorneys, 'they have no more knowledge of ultimate matters than doctors do. So, it's a bad system when the state starts taking original power and deciding,' he says.

'On the other hand, it seems to me, if no crime is ever punished by death, then we lose one of those faint threads we still have running back to primitive days. There's hardly a primitive society that doesn't have a deep feeling about the necessity of society to kill one of its own once in a while. There's something profoundly ritual about all that. Because it stirs up all sorts of emotions. And primitives have that wise notion of society, that it begins to deteriorate at a great rate – that awful things happen to it – unless you stir up the emotions of people from time to time.

'I mean I'd go as far as to say if we're gonna have capital punishment, we can have it on television. Let all those people who yell, "Kill the bastard," see that bastard be shot or hanged or what ever on TV. What I'm saying – and I know it's a ridiculous position in the middle – is a little capital punishment, but, please not too much. And when we do have it, make it very public; by all means accentuate the horror.'

Gilmore had actually been asked, 'If you had a choice, would your execution be on television?' He wrote his answer like a poem:
'No.
Too macabre.
Would you like your death televised?
At the same time, I really don't give a shit.'
That last line is, I think, the key to Gilmore. ●

• •

cissism of American life. I didn't mean it that way at all! This is the first time in history large numbers of people have been able to indulge themselves, so they are doing it. I don't see anything pernicious in it. The freedom is rather exhilarating. I may live to eat those words though,' he adds.

'The Right Stuff', his eighth book, published this week, has been sold to the movies for half a million dollars. In America, where the book has been out for two months, it is a big bestseller in hardcover, and the paperback rights have just been sold for another half a million.

Essentially, it's an anecdotal history of the first seven American astronauts, who sprang nearly full-grown from the winged protoplasm of military test pilotry. We get a jet jockey's view of the flying phallocracy – all brave men and true out to make it to the top. They may have been aiming at Mach One and beyond, at an orbit of the earth; but those were only prizes on the way to the top of the military pyramid. Alan Shepherd, the first American in space, John Glenn, the first in earth orbit, Gus Grissom, Scott Carpenter and the other Boys never really sought astropower, never cared much for politics or abstractions. Mostly, they feared 'being left behind' in the military status stakes. Careerism, Wolfe says, was the astronauts' prime mover.

Back in 1972, when Wolfe began researching this down-to-earth chronicle of the nativity of NASA's Project Mercury, he was not seeking any Great Abstractions. 'I was interested in who do you get to sit on top of these enormous rockets, on top of really enormous amounts of liquid oxygen. Highly volatile stuff. The Saturn 5, as I remember, was 36 storeys high. You just light a match and varoom! it goes up. My god, I wondered, how do they sit there?'

'I very quickly found out that there's nothing really very unique about the background of astronauts,' Wolfe says. Twenty of the first 23 astronauts happened to be first sons. But Wolfe, a first son himself, didn't put much stock in that factor. Like most of the astronauts, Wolfe was a White Anglo-Saxon Protestant whose early obsessions included baseball batting averages. But Wolfe never ever deluded himself – he was no candidate for the top of any rocket. Not even a small one.

Nearly all of the astronauts were test pilots. 'So there you go,' Wolfe says. 'The way to approach it was to find out what test pilots were like – and this led to the whole theory of "the right stuff".' Wolfe crisscrossed North America to talk to test pilots, ex-test pilots, former astronauts, failed astronauts – to the whole conscientious and highly conservative brotherhood. The right stuff, he discovered, was an amalgam of stamina, guts, fast neural synapses and old-fashioned hell-raising – military macho emboldened by the exigencies of the Cold War. Wolfe developed a hunch about the nature of bravery. 'I'm now convinced that physical bravery only happens in a social context. There has to be a sphere of people, a fraternity which sets standards and whose approval is all-important to you – and there has to be no honourable alternative to bravery,' he says. 'Otherwise you're just not going to have brave people.'

There has never been anything cosmic in Tom Wolfe's assessments of humankind. 'If I would do a story on the President of the `United States,' he says, 'I'd just be interested to know what the daily life of the plain man from Georgia is like. What the kicks are.' Thus, in 'The Right Stuff' it is the personal stories that interest him far more than speculating on the political or even the philosophical implications of manned orbital flight. The ensuing mission to the moon didn't really engage him, Wolfe says, because, well, even cool wars are sexier than space. 'God yes, war galvinises people like nothing else. The space race was war.' Space exploration really doesn't excite me in the slightest,' he says. And he means it. 'In science fiction books, wherever a spaceship lands, there's always some superior civilisation. If they're not superior morally and mentally, they have some extraordinary physical powers that earthlings can't deal with. Well, I have a feeling that the opposite is true – that there's really not much out there.' ●

The blind belletrist

Amidst a burst of recent publicity, the Argentinian writer celebrated his 80th birthday.

Jorge Luis Borges interviewed in T.O. 499, by **Peter Godfrey**

Perhaps I should have recognised the cynicism implicit in a blind man having a spy-hole in his front door.

Jorge Luis Borges, always pleased to see an English person and to indulge in the literary dance of an interview, ushered me into his flat high above the hooting cars of Buenos Aires. On the walls were sepia pictures of his ancestors and shelves full of English literature and Scandinavian sagas. In the half-light of his flat – the blinds were permanently drawn – the frail old author's aquiline features and long sideburns

took on an eerie look. He reminded me of one of his own protagonists, an inhabitant of a city of grey-faced immortals who dwell in the realm of speculation and pure thought, with all events in the universe, past and future, spread out before them. He had been discussing a line from Tennyson with some Uruguayan writers: 'God made himself an awful rose of dawn.'

'Did the poet mean that the morning sun was awesome', Borges asked, 'or terrible? The awful truth was that I didn't know.'

Talking of European literature Borges vol-

unteered to recite the Lord's Prayer in Anglo-Saxon – a party piece, which he declaimed with linguistic passion and a hint of sorrow for the vanished past. 'What a pity that we lost the Battle of Hastings.' His enthusiasm is fired by partly English descent – as a youthful anglophile he answered to the name of George.

'I have Andalusian and Portuguese blood on my grandfather's side, but my grandmother was from the Staffordshire Potteries,' he explained. 'She had old English family names: Haslam and Davis.'

Davis, I pointed out unthinkingly, can also be a Jewish name of East European origin, derived from David.

'No, I have no Jewish blood in me,' Borges said scornfully, dissociating himself from the notion.

'My family name is Davis – they came over from Eastern Europe,' I said,

'Well, perhaps I have some Jewish blood too – who knows?' he was quick to rejoin. 'We were all Jews once.'

So this was Borges, inventor of fantastical beings and learned metaphysical schemes in which the seeker after truth who follows one path is confronted by a multitude of diverging ones; the person who consults the library of the universe encounters languages composed entirely of adjectives or impersonal verbs and millions of permutations beyond human comprehension.

Libraries are an even more familiar landscape of Borges' life than of his work. With boyish enthusiasm he showed me some of his treasured books – he knew each volume by touch: 'Beowulf' ('rather dry reading'), a copy of an Icelandic saga inscribed to the King of Denmark, and a first edition of 'Kim'. He had spent much of his childhood,

---

Not a step beyond tomorrow

A sci-fi writer who prefers today's technological totems to future galactic gadgetry. **JG Ballard** interviewed in T.O. 498, by **Giovanni Dadomo**

JG Ballard is still described – and he makes no move to refuse the cloak – as a writer of science-fiction. But the fact is that Ballard has rarely taken a step beyond tomorrow. Which is why the image of a wrecked motor-car has a far stronger rate of recurrence in his work than anything intended for upward and outward travel; even his aircraft are of the low-flying variety.

His reaction to the bombardment of the century's busiest decade was to evolve the compacted, multilateral style of the stories later collected as 'The Atrocity Exhibition' (1969),

which included some of the most durable and exciting prose to emerge from the entire era.

What humour there is in 'The Atrocity Exhibition' is very grim indeed. Witness the uneasy laughter produced by 'The Assassination Of President Kennedy Considered As A Downhill Motor Race'.

'Oswald was the starter... From his window above the track he opened the race by firing the starting gun. It is believed that the first shot was not properly heard by all the drivers. In the following confusion Oswald fired the gun two more

times, but the race was already under way.

'Kennedy got off to a bad start.'

Kennedy and Monroe, Malcolm X and Ronald Reagan, radiation burns and Vietnam newsreels are the key images here, linked by the fragmented relation of a psychologist's route to nervous breakdown and its recurrent motif of the relationship between sex and violent death, both set in that deadliest new toy, the motorcar. Ballard's new brothers were the pop artists (Warhol in particular, with his silk-screens of autosmashes, electric chairs, etc)

he said, immersed in study of the King James Bible. 'My education was my father's library,' he said. 'I was brought up on Swinburne, Keats and Shelley.' His literary knowledge still enables him to make mock-esoteric references in his stories from a dazzling array of sources. 'Literature has been my way of life. My mind is full of verses in so many languages.'

He pointed to one of the sepia portraits on the wall. 'Over there is my great-grandfather – a handsome man, don't you think? He fell in Peru at the cavalry charge of Junin, aged 27. All my people were soldiers, but soldiers who fought. Since 1880 there has been no fighting.' I thought I heard a note of regret in his voice.

Borges' atavism stretches to fatalistic acceptance, even pride, in his family's congenital blindness. He went virtually blind in 1955, but it did not prevent him becoming director of the Argentine national library in the same year. 'I found myself ringed in by 900,000 volumes and remembered a phrase of Kipling's: "abounding in loud self-pity" – I endeavoured to avoid it.'

He sent in his resignation on the day Peron returned to Argentina in 1973. 'I was looted, degraded by Peronism,' Borges said bitterly. 'My mother and sister were imprisoned, and I was attacked personally. I suffered a great deal.' The sufferings of many thousands of others under the subsequent Videla military regime, however, seemed to have made little impression on him. 'I think Argentina has the best possible government at present. Perhaps it is not very efficient, but at least we are governed by gentlemen and not by pimps.'

Borges enjoys the laureate mantle which Videla has conferred on him in an effort to give some cultural respectability to the regime. 'We'll muddle through somehow,' Borges said, 'that's enough.' He pondered. 'I wonder if we are worthy of liberty?'

I asked him his views on religion. 'There is something I dislike about Catholicism,' Borges said, remembering another great-grandfather who was a Methodist minister. 'Maybe I could be a Protestant. but I am not sure I can believe in a personal God.' He wiped his mouth with a handkerchief and sat back. 'I hope there is no individual immortality.'

Undercurrents of elemental forces run through his work. Borges recalled that, as a child, he would ride bareback ('I was quite a good horseman') in the suburbs of Buenos Aires on occasional sorties from his father's library. 'You looked for a bulge inside a man's shirt and a knife was nearly always there, almost with a life of its own.' The universality of such symbols appealed to him. 'The knife is perfidious, yet it stands for personal courage. There is something intimate about it.'

Some of his later stories, I commented, seem to inhabit the earthy world of gauchos, tango singers and low quarters from which he had been sheltered as a child and distanced as a writer, although like his earlier stories they are characterised by chance occurrences and the bibliophile's attention to detail.

'My old stories are too decorative and self-conscious, don't you think? Bounded in purple patches, like Sir Thomas Browne. I am not trying to be Browne, I am trying to be Kipling. Now if I were Stevenson…' Borges has sought a folk-loric tone in his 'fictions', drawing heavily on the English literary device of understatement. 'I hope there is something uncanny in my stories. I try to write them in an ambiguous way – Henry James taught me that trick.'

At Borges' request, I read him one of Chesterton's 'Father Brown' stories from his bookshelves, stopping while he savoured some turn of phrase or ingenuity of plot. Ingenuity – tricks – play a large part in his own work – literary virtuosity for its own sake. Although his stories have become shorter and less baroque, they still take a delight (as he does) in the ring of his phrases, his cryptic aphorisms, and are imbued with the same library fatalism as well as a fascination for violence.

'If I could I'd live in Europe … Borges said as I guided him along the street to tea. 'I am so attached to Buenos Aires that I don't have to live here – I carry it around with me. Argentina's in a pretty bad way, but at least it is the only Latin American country which is all white.'

He confided that he would like to emulate Shaw and Kipling, his literary mentors, by winning the Nobel Prize, but felt it was unlikely on political grounds 'I am not a pacifist, for example. They want a Latin American author to be a communist or a friend of the Indians. I am not. I am not Latin American enough.'

He was sceptical anyway of whether great literature was being written anywhere in the world. 'When I think of great men I think of dead men. We know the past, we don't know the present – time selects.' There was a disillusionment in his voice as striking as the atmosphere of solitude in his flat. ●

and William Burroughs. Ballard recalls reading 'Naked Lunch' and literally jumping for joy. The appreciation was returned in Burroughs' introduction to the US edition of 'Atrocity Exhibition', retitled 'Love & Napalm: Export USA'. Burroughs calls it 'a profound and disquieting book. The nonsexual roots of sexuality are explored with a surgeon's precision. An auto-crash can be more sexually stimulating than a pornographic picture.'

And as offensive. In 1969, Ballard arranged an exhibition of wrecked cars at the New Arts Lab. André Breton would have been delighted by the results: the cars were defaced and smashed even further; a topless dancer hired for the opening was almost raped in the back seat of a ruined Pontiac.

Spurred on by this extremity of response, Ballard began work on 'Crash' (1973). An ugly, frightening, deliberately provocative book, it could well turn out to be the key British novel of the decade. And although its focus (sex, cars, violent death) is perhaps narrower, it's one of a handful of books this country's produced that can comfortably stand alongside Burroughs at his best. Ballard's never refuted accusations of being a pornographer in this instance, and admits being horrified when he reread the book at the proof stage.

'My first reaction was that the man who wrote this book is mad! I was in no doubt about it. I'm still not sure if that isn't true. But I wanted to be honest, I wanted to be true to the impulse I felt. I wanted to be true to my own imagination ... what I was trying to do was to uncover totally ambiguous feelings about violence and death. More important, what it's really about ... is the way in which modern technology plays right into the hands of what are potentially – what seem to be – our worst motives. But in fact; it may be that it's leading us to a different kind of realm where a different set of values is going to operate.

'And to some extent that's already happened. The death of effect that I was talking about in "The Atrocity Exhibition", that anaesthetising of human emotions has already taken place; we're all much less tolerant of other people's pain and unhappiness than we used to be, I think.'

Ballard's newest book, 'The Unlimited Dream Company' is his most optimistic book in several years, and contains some of his strongest, most vivid prose. 'A lot of what I've written is pure imaginative fiction, and I think "The Unlimited Dream Company" belongs in that category.' It's also a book about the power of the imagination, Ballard emphasises. 'To the external world, Shepperton's just the sleepy town it always was.

'And what I'm hinting at, I suppose, is that these processes may be going on all the time. We're not aware of it. We look at people on the street and we have no idea whatever of the powerful imaginations burning inside them, deep inside their minds. Inside each person's head is an Unlimited Dream Company.

'In a way the book is a sort of plea for the imagination against the forces of reason. Reason rationalises reality for us and presents us with a more and more conventional world. In a sense reason is the death of the spirit. And the book is really about the unlimited imaginative power that we've all got capable of transforming anything – the most humdrum little room, or little town, or what have you.' ●

from T.O. 491, by **Steve Bell**

Maggie's Farm–Chrissie Hynde

Rock against racism

from the rising of the neon star' in T.O. 469, by **David Widgery**

From a letter to the music press to a national organisation and a radical culture roadshow in 2½ years isn't bad going. So Red Saunders – tour toaster, socialist impressario and co-author of the famous letter that founded Rock Against Racism in August '76 – could be forgiven his scorn at the pet-rified, Heinekened, baggy-flared steward screaming 'You've got to stop them' as the Bradford gig reached yet another climax of crashing speaker towers, abducted singers, skins dancing on their heads and militant mayhem. 'Stop them? Why?' Red asks, ever the honest Ted. 'It's like this every night, Guv.' He returns, dirty raincoat, dimple and brilliantined DA to conduct further choral anthems of 'Mash the Nazis', 'Punk Lives' and 'Wipe out the Racists with our Culture'.

For though the political aim of the tour is deadly serious – to confront the National Front's bid for youth support – the method is fun. Riot and rhythms: the politics of free emotions and musical unity against the racialist Big Fear. Castro Brown, UK Reggae big wheel, has never seen anything like it. 'There's an election coming up,' he says. 'You lot could win it easy.'

Geoff Dene of the Leyton Buzzards, who has changed the words of their evocation of a misspent London youth to 'Saturday Night Underneath the Painted Rhino', thinks RAR are lovely people. 'I mean, without them, there'd be nuffin'.' As the Buzzards jam away with the Barry Forde Band, their bass player is in tears with emotion. The kids feel it too. They don't talk of Good Vibes anymore. Just 'Really good feeling tonight. All together like.'

Chrissie Hynde

from 'The Golden Hynde' in T.O. 484, by **Steve Taylor**

'I'd been saving some bread, drawing coats of arms for some quack mail order firm and I thought "I'm getting out of here." I called the airport, said I was going to London. What day do you want to go? Thursday. All right, you've got yourself a reservation. I went to work the next day and said goodbye to everybody. Boy, am I glad, I'd have stayed there and I'd have been in a mental hospital by now.'

That's Chrissie Hynde on Akron, Ohio and her sudden departure that initiated several years of transatlantic hopping from Akron to London, Paris, back to Ohio, Paris again and finally London and the Pretenders, a band that incorporates Chrissie's writing, singing and rhythm guitar into a set that can display a more thorough understanding of what makes rock 'n' roll immediately viscerally exciting than most of your current circuit-bashers'll ever dream of having.

That she's finally ensconced in a working band on a national headlining tour with one top 30 taster – Ray Davies' 'Stop Your Sobbing' – behind her and possibly bigger pickings with the current single, her own 'Kid', is a result of stretching childhood ambition over a daunting rack of frustrated attempts at realisation:

'When I was about 14 I went to an amusement park where one of the local radio stations, WHOL, had an annual appreciation day with Mitch Ryder and The Detroit Wheels playing. Jimmy McCartney, who was playing guitar, just blew out the rest of my mind. I thought, "Fuck me!" They faked a fist fight on stage – I didn't know it was phoney so I stayed for the next show and… same fight, oops! From then my fate was sealed.'

Sitting dressed in tight black and white and pork pie hat, opening a letter with a red Swiss penknife that hangs from her belt, Chrissie insists that her Akron upbringing didn't contain the least germ of idiosyncrasy, it was 'very, very straight. Bud and Dec Hynde from Akron, Ohio – they play bridge, my dad golfs and they belong to the bowling league. I would never discuss anything like sex in front of them, swear, I would never even dream of going to the dinner table without my shoes on…'

But: 'I never went on dates and all that number. It wasn't that I didn't like guys; I just wasn't interested in having one for myself, didn't want to be hanging round with some poxy guy all night ... when I could be out seeing a band.' She began playing guitar at high school, singing in a band called Satsun Mat with Mark Mothersbaugh, who later looned into the limelight as Devo's synthesiser player. She recalls being so shy that she sang in the adjoining laundry room when the band had basement rehearsals.

Stints in bands in London, Paris and Cleveland followed – and a few months freelancing for NME, poacher turned gamekeeper – but it never quite gelled. During the English punk brouhaha she became friendly with Vivienne Westwood and Malcolm McLaren, who hatched fleeting ideas of dressing her as a man to join New York anomie-monger Richard Hell. She flirted with the embryonic Pistols, Damned and Clash but the nearest she got to tasting the 15-minute fame that was readily available was to unwittingly take part in a photo session for a bunch christened the Moors Murderers. The subsequent abuse of her good name led her to call up the NME to inform them that 'You guys are full of shit', although she now dismisses that period as 'almost irrelevant'.

What finally set the ball rolling was the growth of her songwriting and guitar playing, to the point where it inspired faith and more importantly for the impecunious wanderer, investment firstly from Steeleye Span manager Tony Secunda and then crucially from Dave Hill, who'd just left Anchor to set up the fledgling Real label. Hill took over the lapsed rent on Chrissie's Covent Garden rehearsal room and gave her the financial freedom to go through the ruthless motions of recruiting sympathetic musos.

'Because the songs were not exactly your ordinary 12-bar 4/4, a lot of blokes were really wary, especially taking orders from a chick. If you say "Now look, on this song you just keep it very simple and at this point you go onto the tom-toms and really beef it up like Sandy Nelson"… a lot of guys'd be out the door by that time.'

As they'd worked on Hill and his backers, Hynde's songs won over the musicians who eventually became the Pretenders – James Honeyman Scott on vocals, guitar and keyboards, Pete Farndon on bass and Martin Chambers on drums – three Hereford lads who Chrissie is anxious are seen with her as four equal members of the band. But it's going to be hard to take the focus off her, whatever she says. ●

"Labour isn't working."
Tory Party advert

"The day after you don't bother to vote will be the first day of a Tory government."
Labour Party advert

"Where there is despair, may we bring hope…"
Margaret Thatcher, paraphrasing St Francis of Assisi. The quote machine begins.

"Mind, I've been here through the bad times, too. One year we came second."
Bob Paisley, Liverpool FC manager

"Our only chance would've been to sandbag the 18-yard line and pick them off one by one with rifles."
Michael Robinson, Manchester City footballer after losing 4-0 to Liverpool

"It may be costing me a lot of fans. Maybe I'll have to start singing on street corners. Still, I'll give all the praise and glory be to God."
Bob Dylan finds the Lord

"I love the smell of napalm in the morning."
Robert Duvall finds an alternative to coffee in 'Apocalypse Now'

"I should very much like to take a vacation."
The Shah of Iran goes into exile, never to return

"In the name of the Prophet I call upon American Muslims to take this acolyte of Satan from his bed and dismember him."
Ayatollah Khalkhali offers alternative therapy for the Shah after he enters a New York hospital for the removal of a gall bladder

"No More Iranian Students Will Be Permitted On These Premises Until The Hostages Are Removed."
Sign outside a licensed brothel in Nevada

"Any woman who understands the problems of running a home will be nearer to understanding the problems of running a country."
Prime Minister Margaret Thatcher

Maggie's Farm–Rock against racism–Chrissie Hynde

The barred of Salford

John Cooper Clarke interviewed in T.O. 453, by **Ian Walker**

They said, 'Nudge, nudge,' as we goroff the bus,
Extra-terrestrial, not like us.
It's bad enough with another race,
But fuck me, a monster from outa space.

The first outlet for the poetry of John Cooper Clarke was a Roneo'd sheet circulating the Manchester subterrain a few times a week. When he wasn't indulging his main leisure-time pursuit of rooting through rubbish on the derelict estates near his Salford home, he recited his poems in boozers and clubs around the Manchester megalopolis. Now he has finally reaped the rewards of a turbulent generation's worth of poetic endeavour: poetry in which an exquisite fusion of street-wise raunchiness and old-world erudition cuts a terrorist's swathe through the values and objects which clutter advanced capitalism. He is 29.

Where do you really come from?
Germany – originally.

Born in Germany?
Yeah. Not far from Hamburg but you would have never 'eard of it.

So you are, in fact, a German?
No. I couldn't in all honesty say I was German. I couldn't put me hand on me 'eart and say I was a German – that wouldn't be fair 'cos I was sent away from Germany at an early age.

I see. Your mum and dad weren't German?
Well, me father was a German lard mogul but me mother wasn't. So I was mailed off… when it all went off you know, when me father committed suicide two weeks before I was born.

Did he?
Me mother died of multiple stab wounds – the victim of a Mau Mau hit squad. Some kind person mailed me to a friend in Canada.

Is this true?
Yes. But I was erroneously delivered to Eros Luxury Club, which was a converted charabanc in the bowels of the Manchester subterrain. After that things get rather… more exciting, but this will appear in my biography – an autobiography in fact – called 'Ten Years in Open Necked Shirts'… perhaps. Or 'Tadpoles – the Poor Man's Caviar'! Not sure what to call it. But those and other details will be referred to at more length like the fact that I was adopted by a pair of alsatians who lived in an art deco cocktail cabinet on a Whalley Range bomb site.

Interesting stuff. How old are you?
45.

He wears it well. OK. How did you earn your living before?
A number of jobs: window cleaner. It's also been erroneously pointed out in other publications that I was a grave digger. I wasn't a grave digger. However, I did work at a mortuary. But there wasn't much life in it. Actually, when I did an interview with the *Daily Star* and they brought this bloody photographer and they were real hacks, you know. Like the pop columnist was this geezer called Ron Bile – nice fella, nice enough bloke – but like his only concession to the pop world was this very loud check jacket. He brought this photographer who had this too-big safari suit on, with a little moustache, and a shirt with veteran cars over it. But that's all right, he's a photographer and they're a peculiar breed as you know. He was about 70.

What did they ask you?
'Is it true you used to be a grave digger? I read it somewhere.' And I says no, but I did work in a mortuary. At which point the cameraman cracked up and says, 'Oh fuckinell, we had it all planned out – we were gonna take you to a graveyard, stick a shovel over yer shoulder and put a witty caption underneath. Oh well, we'll 'ave to think of something else.' Obviously threw his whole week out…they won't let you take photographs in a morgue. They'd offend sensibilities like by showing it: posing in front of a team of stiffs, you know.

Was the feature abandoned by the *Star*?
No, no. They put it in but it was very short. It was a picture that they got in a hurry from CBS. They didn't use any other pictures. We had some belters took actually in Piccadilly Gardens in Manchester where there's a huge statue of Queen Victoria and I sat on her knee and grabbed her tits… Not amused and neither was the reporter. Neither was the photographer.

So you had lots of different jobs. You were always a bard …
Always barred.

Why have you got a band behind you now?

Well I've been in a few groups meself. I'm no stranger to the elongated name: Rocky Morocco and his Rococo Guitar. I was a bass guitarist in most of the groups I was in. The Phoenix were the last group who employed my capacities on a bass guitar. Just used to do reggae instrumental hooks. In '75. Didn't get anywhere of course.

So then you turned your back on bass guitar and became lead poet.
Yeah, well I used to write songs …

That's how you started writing poetry is it – by writing songs? Poetry is a horrible word isn't it?
Not many poets were wet. It's a hangover from the Victorian attitude to all sorts of art – painting and poetry, anything like that. the idea that it's a wet pursuit, a poncey thing to do, comes from the Pre-Raphaelites you know, people with purple faces that were gonna cop it any minute. Probably impotent.

Obviously benders.
Corkscrews. To a man… question mark. No, let's not get sexist about it. A lot of it isn't just the Pre-Raphaelite idea but the whole Victorian attitude to art with a Gothic Capital A. Before… immediately before that, there hadn't been anything of the kind. Poetry is really one method of recording something that you think is worth recording. I think poetry in the twentieth century has got more and more journalistic you know. Probably as a backlash against the fripperies of Victorian high art, which was I admit, a load of crap. You could show a nude figure in a painting providing it was dead or looked Greek. The amount of huge pictures in the Victorian era that featured statuesque female corpses in some great plague – oceans of dead flesh, the only way anybody could get away with anything erotic. Very necrophiliac period was the Victorian era. ●

In 'Just Above My Head', James Baldwin returns to the theme that has dominated his life and his writing as much as his sexual orientation and the colour of his skin: the black church. At 14, Baldwin was a preacher himself. For three years he bore witness in front of a Harlem congregation, and in his new novel one of the main characters, blessed with the Holy Ghost at the age of 12, also takes to the teenage pulpit. Children are still preaching today, he says, 'although it may not be quite as spectacular as it was when I was young'. Baldwin's memory of his blazing witness is always with him, and every page of the new book rings with the language of the church.

'The black American church comes from the auction block,' says Baldwin. 'There was a kind of survival technique used. The creation of the church was also the creation of black language and the forging, in America, of black identity in an utterly hostile and lonely place. Everything, therefore, comes out of the church and refers to it in one way or another, from Ray Charles to Malcolm X. Blues, the music, everything. We did with the church what white people had never done, except in prehistoric or pagan times.' He smiled '–if you see what I mean.' Even today, says Baldwin, when its very existence might seem an anachronism, the church remains a vital force in the black community on both sides of the Atlantic. 'It's still the conduit, everything does still come out of it. It's not exactly the frame of reference, but it's a certain kind of touchstone. The energy of a whole people flows through that creation.'

Baldwin's writing is full of the pent-up emotion that comes from centuries of oppression of both the external and internal kind. In his latest novel, 'Just Above My Head' some of the most profound passages occur when the characters discuss survival strategies and air their political ideas. 'There's a lot of politics in the novel – a little obliquely perhaps – but the situation in which we live is political,' he says. 'It may still be a white world in terms of power, but the situation of black and white today is double-edged because you're aware that the kingdom is about to fall, but in a sense I'm much less frightened than you are. I've got much less to be frightened of because I've been through it, I've been through what you're going to have to go through. In England, for example, you never saw your slaves till lately. You didn't know their names, then you gave them English names and now here they are. And you don't know how to deal with your former slaves as free men.'

From time to time, Baldwin's writing explodes with uncontrollable, 'crazy' laughter of blacks forced to hide their feelings in the presence of whites. In his own life as an isolated intellectual, he is surrounded by white people who enjoy that explosion as long as they remain unharmed by it. And his essentially white readership has thrived off his passion and rage for years, even, as entrepreneurs, making money from it. It's an uncomfortable situation for anyone to be in, and one that has led to him being attacked by blacks who see him as being out of touch with black realities.

None was more scathing than Black Panther Eldridge Cleaver who, inhabiting the machismo image that characterised black militancy in the '60s, slammed into Baldwin for being gay. But Baldwin was revolutionary precisely because he wrote about sexual liberation at a time before, as David Widgery says, 'those two words had been placed together.' His pub-

'You never saw your slaves till lately'

James Baldwin interviewed in T.O. 500, by **Val Wilmer**

lishers rejected 'Giovanni's Room' initially because he treated homosexuality in a radical way. They did it, they said, for his own good, a story of love between two men being supposedly bad for the image of a promising black writer.

Sadly, though, Baldwin's attitude towards homosexuality remains non-political: 'everyone's bisexual, anyway.' In her book 'Black Macho', Michele Wallace accused him of abandoning his formerly sympathetic attitude towards women to take a macho stance in answering Cleaver. Baldwin replies, 'Contrary to my legend, I dig women very much. And I'm not macho because I know there's a lot of woman in me and a lot of woman in every man.'

Wallace's book created a storm among blacks as well as many socialist feminists who opposed her premise that the black man, in liberating himself and benefiting from the legend of his sexual superiority, has left the black woman far behind as a revenge for historical humiliation. Admitting that he had not read the book, Baldwin could say, nevertheless, 'I think she's as wrong as two left shoes. It's much more complex than that. What she is saying could, in principle, drive a wedge between black men and black women and that possibility is extremely dangerous in compounding an already accelerating disaster. Black women know a great deal about black men – they have to. No matter how stormy our relationships have been – and are – the black woman knows much more than that. She has to understand her son, her lover, her brother, her father. The situation of black men in white society is not entirely the black man's fault, after all. And without that understanding, I don't think there'd be any black people at all.

Today, Baldwin divides his time between America and France, which he visited first in 1948. He has a home near Nice where he goes to relax, catch his breath and write. He misses the idea of church when he's away from New York, although he no longer belongs to any specific one. 'I believe in something I perhaps can't name – or refuse to name, probably both. I don't believe in safety, I believe we're responsible for everything, including God – who needs to be corrected from time to time.' Above all, he misses the street life of Harlem, the barbershops and Saturday nights – 'Well, I suppose in a way I miss my youth.'

At the beginning of next year Baldwin embarks on a fact-finding mission for the *New Yorker*, to see how the South has changed since the Supreme Court decision on integration, a prospect he views with more than a little fear and cynicism concerning what superficial changes mean. Until then, he has little energy left for writing. 'It gets harder as you get older because you try to grow. The world becomes more complex and therefore more difficult to tell.

'Anyone who's really trying to be a writer is almost certain to be a disturber of the peace. You can only write in two ways – you can write to affirm everything everybody thinks, to comfort the sleeper, or you can try to wake him up. When you try to wake him up, you're controversial. But, you know, there's a certain sense of uselessness, too. Really, you don't know what writing is about, what you are doing it for. It doesn't save anybody, it doesn't do anything. So it becomes an act of faith, an act of faith and love to try to bear witness.' ●

The m⊙d revival

A touch of *déjà vu* in Wardour Street.

from 'Remodelling' in T.O. 487, by **Phil Shaw**

When I was an aspiring mod in the mid '60s I had a mate called Chris. I remember we were sitting in his Mini one night – he'd ditched his Lambretta – when Petula Clark came on the radio. Chris turned the volume up. 'You don't like this, do you?' I asked him. 'Yeah, it's good,' came the reply, and he meant it.

Hope I die before I get old? My naïve ideas about mod-as-eternal-youth were punctured at a stroke. Sure enough, we all drifted apart within a couple of years: some turned hippie and a few ended up in the nick, but most just settled down and faded away.

Standing in Wardour Street in the summer of '79, I can't help wondering what my generation would make of this lot. In groups of four or five, the new mods, nearly all white males between the ages of 15 and 19, are descending on the Marquee Club.

If they lack some of the flamboyance of their antecedents – I don't see any red leather maxi-coats – there's still a strong sensation of reincarnation. Their cropped hair is neatly parted; most wear sta-prests or Levis and Fred Perry tennis shirts. There's a few pork-pie hats and the occasional mohair suit with only the top button of the jacket fastened, the trousers hitched up just enough to reveal the statutory white socks and hush-puppies. Despite the muggy evening and the Marquee's sauna atmosphere there's an abundance of parka coats, replete with union jacks and the legends 'Small Faces'and 'The Who' emblazoned across their backs. For a second or two, it's as if the last 15 years haven't happened. No Wilson government, no Watergate or Woodstock, no Women's Liberation, no National Front...

The illusion is soon shattered. Out of a building across the street steps Billy Idol and the rest of the punk group Generation X. 'Flash wanker,'mut-ters a queuing mod. 'Poofs', says another. In those days it was the mods who revelled in being 'flash', the mods who were slagged off for effeminacy by the rockers.

Inside, too, badges and fanzines, icons of the punk era, are everywhere. And the group they've come to see is not the Who, who stopped playing venues like this before most of tonight's audience could walk, but the Chords, one of the bands now playing specifically mod dates around London.

One band's place in the 'mod revival' should not be understated. In late '76 the Jam emerged from Woking fitted out in mohair and two-tone shoes to play the punk shrine that was the Roxy. Weller's sarcastic opening remarks there in spring '77 ('Good to see so many mods here tonight') were greeted with dumbfounded looks, the customary shower of saliva and shouts of 'boring'. The Jam stuck to their guns and their unashamed plundering of the dynamics of The Who circa 'Can't Explain' began to draw a younger, working-class following, many of whom couldn't identify with Kings Road bondage chic and what they saw as its nihilism and its scruffiness.

While most punk bands heaped scorn on the 'boring old farts' of the '60s and screamed about sewers and high-rise flats – a veritable 'revolt into style' – the Jam presented an alternative. Songs like 'The Modern World', 'Here Comes The Weekend', 'Carnaby Street' and 'All Around The World' harped back to the mythical world of the mid-'60s mod, the latter being packed with 'positive' words like 'action', 'reaction', 'new direction' and 'youth explosion'; all very 'Ready, Steady Go!', but new and exciting to a fresh generation of adolescents seeking an identity. ●

We are proud to present arguably the most important person of our times: self-confessed houseperson, superstar, visionary and philosopher queen...

The neue sachlichkeit Edna

Dame Edna Everage and **Sir Les Patterson** interviewed in T.O. 453, by **Diana Simmonds**

In an elegant semi-penthouse office high above the camper vans surrounding Australia House in the Strand, Sir Les Patterson, Cultural Attache to Britain, administers his highly respected and influential programme of artistic and cultural education.

How do you view the great cultural changes that have been wrought by Dame Edna?

Well... Dame Edna... and you've caught me on the hop here... Dame Edna represents the spearhead, the tip of the iceberg-vis à vis the Australian cultural revolution. For a considerable period of time we have been leading the world, pretty unobtrusively, in the major ongoing cultural renaissance... and this woman... is merely a kind of spokeswoman for a groundswell. A groundswell of cultural ferment which is pretty well universally acknowledged to be shit hot in terms of the the world culture spectrum. That's about it on that topic.

And what about Barry Humphries?

Humphries is a knocker. K-n-o-c-k-e-r. Humphries is one of those typical Australian so-called pseudointellectuals who makes a nice living thank-you-very-much *rubbishing* Australia. Pouring *shit* all over our wide brown land. They come over here, they make a bit of a splash on the TV, or the wireless or some rag like *Time Out*, they decide it's smart to tip the can on their homeland – to kick their heritage in the balls. That type to me is Lower than the Basic Wage. That type is as Low as a Snake's Armpits.

There's this image of Australians as a rough, beerswilling mob – the Barry Mackenzie syndrome started by Humphries in bloody *Private Eye*. Making us out to be a nation of Piss Artists. You know. Spewing all over the place, parking the tiger at cocktail parties. Talking on the big white telephone. Of course, we all *do* it, but you don't *talk* about it. This image is almost entirely due to the Unstinting Negativism of fucking Barry Humphries. *That's* off the record and you can print it. People say the little bastard's on the avant garde side. I don't think so, on the other hand, I think he's a Reactionary. He's a french letter on the prick of progress, and you can quote me.

I'd like to ask you about your Knighthood – it came as a bit of a surprise to some people...

Not to me dear, not to me. I know, there are plenty of types who've been slaying their arses off for years for a gong. Brown-nosing away round Buck House, but as far as I'm concerned a lifetime of service has been rewarded. Of course Betty Windsor's call was a bit of a bolt from the blue but there it is. Mind you, it can have its disadvantages, certain disadvantages – any knight who reads *Time Out* (and I think it's pretty likely that they do) will agree with me wholeheartedly I'm sure.

Can you give us any pointers towards a deeper appreciation of the show?

Well I'm fucked if I know. Dame Edna just breezes in, has a chat with the audience and pisses off. The tickets aren't particularly expensive, either, even for Poms.

Then it was onwards from the statuesque portals and convenient washing facilities of Australia House to the heart of the West End, where the cream of cultural ferment was resting in her Denman Street dressing room.

Dame Edna, how much of your Superstar status do you owe to Barry Humphries?

Many moons ago when Barry Humphries invited me to help him in his one-man entertainments, I *thought* I was there to lend a little glamour to the occasion . Arguably (I think that's one of *Time Out's* favourite words, so I use it a lot), arguably, Barry Humphries is a nonentity to most people – though not to me of course, I owe him a lot. After all, it was he who first plucked me from a passion play in Melbourne in which I was appearing as Mary Magdalene. But as I said, I thought I was there to lend a little glamour so that when he did his send-ups of the Australian way of life, I would reassure the audience that there were some nice natural, warmhearted, approachable and, to use another modern word, *accessible* people in Australia. I am above all, accessible, by the way.

But I'll tell you what I am darling, I'm a housewife basically (and I hope I still am, despite my Superstardom). It's nothing to be ashamed of, it's not like being a leper or a pariah to be a housewife. It's an honourable thing; Houseperson, I think I should call it.

Could you tell us about your theatrical ambitions?

I'd love to do a Brechtian evening: 'Edna Und Brecht'. I was thinking of adapting 'Mother Courage' for Australian audiences and calling it 'Edna Courage' or the 'The Good Housewife of Szechuan' – or even 'The Australian Chalk Circle'. Then of course I'm a Plath and Woolf freak. An absolute Fitzrovian. I feel in a way that I was there. I'm probably a reincarnation of Katherine Mansfield (who was a Kiwi by the way, just like my bridesmaid Madge. It's funny to think that Katherine Mansfield *could* have been my bridesmaid – if she hadn't been born hundreds of years ago). However, I feel that I'm part of that Bloomsbury *thing*.

As well as my interest in the Art Deco People – Scott and Zelda Joplin – I was going to play the part of Zelda. My favourite little couple, they burnt themselves out of course. She in more ways than one, poor darling. However, I do have that sort of *empathy*. It's the way I dress too – the *neue Sachlichkeit*. I'm a neue Sachlichkeit *buff* really.

Could you tell us about your children. How have you coped with them and Superstardom?

Fundamentally, the first thing is not to overawe your kiddies. Now look at Lana Turner's – went berserk. And what else do they get up to – shoplifting, vandalism, giving themselves little jabs. It's Terrible. Show me a Superstar and I'll show you a Raving Ratbag Kiddy (to use an Aboriginal expression – 'Ratbag': an Abo word for deeply disturbed,

'I *think* I can safely say I'm an unobtrusively normal, loving mother.'

troubled, disadvantaged. *Mentally* disadvantaged).

I, on the other hand, have kept my kiddies out of the limelight *and* I've never really gone professional (here's another Exclusive for *Time Out* readers). Although I'm a member of Equity on a global scale, I've never really turned professional. I don't demand huge fees, I'm a contented unspoiled sort of woman.

However, I *must* admit that I often wish my relationship with my daughter Valmai was closer. The doctor *did* say it might have helped us find out why she was the way she was. Of course, I never thought the drop of sherry before breakfast was a good idea. She's a lot better though. I think there's an early menopause for a lot of women, Valmai had it at about 17. I *think* I can safely say I'm an unobtrusively normal, loving mother.

You met Prince Charles recently at the Royal Gala, did he seem nervous?

Of course Charles' niceness is largely due to his Australian education. He went to Timbertop, near Melbourne – did you know that? My son Kenny went to Timbertop. For a week. I wanted him to share something of the Royal background as I mentioned to Charles. He seemed quite taken aback, lost for word's in fact, but nevertheless a Charmer.

You seem to have a special rapport with the gay community. Could you tell us about this affinity?

Well, there's a lot of silly talk about what they get up to and I don't believe it for a second. Actually when I spoke to the little laddy from *Gay News* the other week I must have shocked him because I said something to him that he didn't print! Isn't that *sweet*! I said to this lad, we *all* come from the same place, Keith, exactly the same place. We all *sprang* from the same part of our mother's anatomy, it's just that some of us can't bear to look on that spot *ever* again.

Whereas women on the other hand – well, you can't help but glance down from time to time can you? I mean there's nothing shameful about our bodies or most people's anyway, though I wish I could say the same about Madge's because I see more of that one than any other. Mind you, I can tell you it's No Joy for Me. I give her a little cuddle, because I'm a warmhearted woman, but there isn't a great deal of pleasure involved in sharing accommodation with a woman as prickly as Madge Allsopp, and I don't refer to her temperament either. But I suppose it's only fair that Madge should have the same access to me as is enjoyed by the British Public. Doctors prescribe me, did you know that? Harley Street types have said – well there's nothing I can do for you dear, it's just *off* to the Piccadilly!

Finally, Dame Edna, have you any personal message for your British public?

Of course darling! Come and see me possums, I'm at the Piccadilly Theatre and don't take *any* notice of the Filth, Smut and Depravity that abounds in the West End. If you can't do that there's always my new record 'The Sound of Edna' available from good record shops everywhere to go with 'The Coffee Table Book' which will make some lucky little person a really lovely Chrissie pressie! ●

1980

Jump right. We'd had a whole year of Thatcher and then America elected Reagan. As a flirty gesture, Mags invited him to park his Cruise on Airstrip One. Punk and disco seemed over; rap and the New Romantics were bubbling into being. *Fame* put us in legwarmers and the Rubik's cube had us in knots. We knew who shot John Lennon, but what about JR?

The Shining
If you go to this adaptation of Stephen King's novel expecting to see a horror movie, you'll be disappointed.

Raging Bull
With breathtaking accuracy, Raging Bull ventures still further into the territory Scorsese has mapped in all his films – men and male values.

Ordinary People
Any movie starring Mary Tyler Moore as a neurotic mother papering over the cracks as her husband and son go to pieces, should get full marks.

John Martyn - Grace And Danger (Island)
Grace And Danger is both a disappoint- ment and a delight. One to bring out

the aficionado's warm smile, but convert few.

Michael Jackson - Off The Wall (Epic)
The LP consolidates rather than innovates, working some of the most effective ploys of modern disco into exuberant settings for the man who is now the most influential singer in black music.

Dexy's Midnight Runners - Searching For The Young Soul Rebels (Parlophone)
Whilst the Runners' horn section have availed themselves of the Stax/Volt catalogue, their 'soul' is infused with a vitality which would not have been poss- ible before punk. So you see, soul can be for pleasure, too.

HEAVY METAL

1980

from 'Old iron/new wave' in T.O. 540, by **Gerry Kelly**

'These kids in the audience, they'd all like to play like Iommi. WHAM. WHAM. WHAM. And they could. Or at least they think they could.'

July 31 1980. Tonight the Anvil Heavy Metal disco opens at Camden's Electric Ballroom. On the dance floor, beneath a banner advertising rollerdisco (another night, another song), 100 or so kids are headbanging to records by Black Sabbath, Deep Purple and AC/DC.

Ian, alias Superloon, raves about the dance floor, his head flopping about like a doll with its neck broken. He wears a schoolboy's uniform, complete with short trousers and satchel, in imitation of Angus Young, lead guitarist with AC/DC.

'He's my hero,' he confides, 'the ultimate headbanger'.

Records by newer bands like Sledgehammer and Iron Maiden – part of the spearhead of the New Wave of British Heavy Metal

Space invaders

from 'Valley of the ultramoths' in T.O. 547, by **Malcolm Hay**

Cosmic Alien. Astro Fighter. Space Chaser, Lunar Rescue. Balloon Bomber. Super Earth Invasion. First Encounter. No Man's Land. The names rear up from the pages of Coin Slot International like a threat, a warning of things to come. Video games: the bright new future for Britain's leisure industry. Or is the space bubble about to burst?

The fever started, of course, with Space Invaders 18 months ago. (In this world, I'm told, 'three months is a generation'.) Brainchild of the Taito Corporation in Japan. A revolutionary concept in simulated aggression that immediately took the world by storm. Already part of our general consciousness, while cognoscenti wait eagerly for the next revelation –

'Before long they will talk to you. Work you up a bit. Tell you how brilliant the last player was. Get the old adrenalin and competitive juices flowing...'

My quest for the electronic grail took in some unlikely places. I had this vision of finding a video wizard: he would destroy wave upon wave of asteroids and UFOs with a flick of the wrist and dab of one finger. I might pick up a few tips and astonish

my friends. Should I confess that I'm a novice, a mere beginner? Four or five times in my life, at the local pub, throwing away 10ps as if there were no tomorrow...

'There's only one way. You learn by experience. I can tell you the moves, but then you have to make them. It can be an expensive business while you're learning the game.'

A phone phone call to Taito Electronics Ltd, UK offspring of the aforesaid Oriental giant. The replies were guarded, particularly when I asked about the future. 'We don't like to talk about it.'

'This is a very tight industry. Any indication of our thinking, however general, would be telling our competition far too much. Anyway all the development takes place in Japan.' Always the optimist, I made my final pitch: 'Could I try out a few of your games?' No problem. Two days later I was at their Alperton showroom, matching my sluggish reflexes and limited skills against a mean machine called Stratovox.

Dennis Rawlings, sales manager of Taito UK, said that the future will lie in sounds. (To back him up, one of the dozen or more video games in the adjoining room chipped in with a few quick bars of (henceforth NWOBHM) – are also playing. Heavy Metal (HM), that loud aggressive rock music of the late '60s and early '70s, is currently experiencing a massive and unexpected revival.

The week after the Anvil's opening, AC/DC have crashed into the album chart from nowhere to number one. A compilation of old Deep Purple hits holds second place. NWOBHM outfits like Saxon, Samson and Girlschool are riding high alongside Black Sabbath and Hawkwind. WEA has issued a HM singles pack. Heavy Metal is again big business.

It never really went away. Bands like Black Sabbath have always had a market, especially for albums. It is rock music played at deafening volume and based on crashing chords and screaming guitar solos. You don't so much hear it as get assaulted by it.

At American guitar hero Ted Nugent's recent London concerts there certainly is a lot of movement. In a packed Hammersmith Odeon, seething waves of heads flow to the music of a man whose slogan is 'if it's too loud, you're too old'.

The headbanging stops only for the customary burst of triplets, played at blinding speed, which provides the finale to each Nugent number. At this crucial point the lights are on Nugent alone. The rest of the band fades into darkness while the guitar hero takes his rightful place, alone in the white glare of the spotlight, before the ranks of his followers. The heads are still. Hands formed into peace signs or horns reach towards the ceiling of the theatre as Nugent's sweat-dripping fingers

wrestle with his wild beast of a guitar. And so on to the end.

The cult of the guitar hero was supposedly killed by punk. But it was never buried. Some NWOBHM fans have now taken it to lengths that are almost absurd. A majority are content to strum invisible guitars, but some want something more tangible. On Sunday night at the Bandwagon, a long-running HM disco in Kingsbury, one kid stands for the whole of the session in front of a speaker. Soaking up the blast from the 2,000 watt sound system, he expertly mimes every record on a homemade cardboard cutout of a guitar. 'They could drop the bomb and I'd hardly notice,' says Paul, a Nugent fan from South Harrow. It seems to have a limit. A cardboard fantasy is real enough. As HM star Ian Gillan points out, 'the fantasy is only good enough if the object is just too far out of reach.'

Despite this apparent separation between artist and audience, there is still a bond of identity to which both sides adhere. An identification which works both ways. Would Ian Gillan, were he not a musician, be watching a band like his? 'Oh yes, absolutely… and Gillan would be top of the list!'

Whether it is viewed with horror by those who greeted the relief columns of Punk in 1977, or welcomed with glee by those who saw the old new wave as an annoying diversion from rock 'n' roll, the NWOBHM is providing some sort of boost, however temporary, to an ailing British record industry.

Some fans suggest that the wave has already subsided. But what else in the current rock music market place has a following to compare with this? 'Heavy metal is so much about hero-worship,' says doyen of HM rock criticism Geoff Barton (of *Sounds*, a paper which has defected in the last year from punk to HM). 'They don't want to emulate their idols, they just want to adore. They just want to have their eyes open and their ears blasted.' ●

'The Yellow Rose of Texas'.) And before long all the familiar noises – the shots and explosions, the whistle of missiles traversing the screen – will be nothing without the latest ingredient: next in line is the game equipped with a humanoid voice.

The prototype is already upon us. Stratovox. Alias Space Echo. Alias Speak and Rescue. The player fights off attacks from flying saucers. Nothing unusual in that. The catch is that the enemy is constantly manœuvering to kidnap your astronauts. If they get one, as he's dragged away over the edge of the screen and into oblivion, a tiny, electronic voice pipes out 'Help me!' Not a heart-rending appeal, you understand, since the tones are reminiscent of Tweety Pie. If the enemy spaceships are forced to withdraw, there's a menacing croak of 'We'll be back!'

Mr Rawlings invited me to try my luck. Clutching hard at the joy stick I tried to look cool. I checked the instructions and gathered my resources. 'Use joy stick to control your aim and shoot flying saucers.' First time round my defences were wiped out in 23 seconds. Ten astronauts lost. 'Game over': the cold words of the standard printout. Second attempt: over a minute! Flushed with success, I was ready to tackle anything.

I never found the video king I hoped to find. Instead I found Shahzad Ali, in the Crystal Room Arcade in Leicester Square. He was knocking up 66,690 on Space Invader Kamikaze. Well short of his all-time best (99,000) but well ahead of the previous best score of the day. 'Up to a few months ago I never came in here. I'd never played a video game before. Thought it was a waste of money. It took me six weeks, coming every evening, to get up to 99,000.' He still drops in now and again to keep his hand and eye in, before starting work at 9pm at his father's mini-cab firm in Cranbourn Street. 'But I need someone I can challenge. It's no good trying to top your own score. You don't bother enough. I play best when there's a challenge. Come and watch me when someone else gets 150,000.' A week later I looked in to check the highest score of the day. It stood at 105,000. I phoned Shahzad and he said he was going in later to beat it.

Video games at best are high-grade kitsch. Moral scruples have no part in their carefully programmed dream world. Consider Missile Command: a nuclear war rages until all the player's cities and missile bases have been destroyed. Cut to garish flashes and the image of a mushroom cloud spreading across the screen. Then, superimposed in colour, for all the world like the death throes of a Cecil B De Mille extravaganza in letters several inches high…

'THE END' ●

Contradictory
champion

Martina Navratilova interviewed in T.O. 532, by **Mandy Merck**

Half-past five on a typical afternoon at Eastbourne. The air is cool, the wind is high and the Centre Court umpire is having trouble with the name of the Number One Seed:

'Game to Miss Kloss and Miss Novrotrolova.'

'Sorry, Miss Nav-ra-tro-la.'

'Miss Na-ro-to-lee-va.'

'Nav-ro-tro-lie-va…'

She may be, in Wimbledon parlance, the 'holder' and the first woman with a chance at winning the Championships thrice consecutively since Billie-Jean King did it in '66-'68, but Martina Navratilova is still something of a stranger to the world of British tennis.

She's probably best known to the public as the Czech defector who was tearfully reunited with her mother at last year's Wimbledon, and finally with the rest of her family this December when the authorities allowed them to join her in the United States. But the Czech tennis scene isn't the Kirov Ballet, as the international successes of non-exiles like Tomanova and Marsikova, and lately the conspicuously talented young Hana Mandlikova, attest. Perhaps it is more accurate to say that Martina, who first journeyed to the States in 1973, became an accomplished Americanophile and went to live where she wanted to.

Indeed it may be the American qualities in her style which put the British off. After her defection, a month before her 19th birthday in 1975, these were crudely characterised as a penchant for junk food and jewellery. And the longeurs of her acclimatisation did include extra poundage, as well as an emotional rawness that manifested itself in tantrums and tears. Navratilova's on-court collapse after losing to Janet Newberry in the first round of the '76 US Open simply stunned her opponent.

But Martina is a quick learner, and once under the wing of Sandra Haynie, the Texan ex-golf pro who became her manager and close friend, she not only sorted out her tennis, but also achieved an unusual expertise in Americana. Five years after her defection, the aspirant US citizen and WTA champion at 'Boggle' (a sort of quick Scrabble in which you construct the maximum number of words out of randomly chosen letters) laughs at the US immigration forms: 'One of the questions they ask is, can you write your name in English!'

Like Billie-Jean King before her, Martina is a tomboy, which is a fine thing to be in America, where both the culture and the Women's Movement support such options – but impossible in Britain, where little girls grow up to become Virginia Wade. America, which once deemed Billie-Jean one of the world's ten most influential women, admires female athletes. The British like games captains who put on their cardies to shake the Princess's hand – a decency which Martina omitted when she raised the Wimbledon plate aloft with her bare muscled arms the first time she won it.

She wanted, she said later, to show how strong she was, a strength that has distinguished her style of play from the outset. 'When I first watched

her down here years ago,' said my Eastbourne taxi driver, 'I knew she'd become a champion.' On her day (which is often these days) the Champion almost matches Cawley's agility, Austin's placement and Evert Lloyd's will to win. Most importantly, she exceeds the athleticism of King at her finest.

With the best serve in the women's game and a volley behind it that looks unnaturally natural for a player raised on European clay, Martina tends to bring her service points to rapid conclusions – picking off vulnerable returns with an authoritative volley, forcing stronger opponents into similar straits with a single approach shot. At Eastbourne she rushed Tanya Harford's return of service, which is a bit like rushing a bulldog when it's approaching at speed – the sturdy South African is a very useful grass player with a string of scalps to prove it.

It takes muscle and touch to kill the impetus of a strong drive with a half-volleyed drop-shot; but Martina dished those out with abandon when she played 'almost a perfect match', on her own and everybody else's estimate, against Tracy Austin in January. No longer the little girl of legend, the 17-year-old US Open Champion arrived in Eastbourne last week with her deltoids bulging out of her pinafore. Her ponytails still fly behind her as she flails away with that two-fisted backhand, but the results are lethal – ground strokes which seem programmed to skim over the lowest part of the net and clip the tramlines on whichever side is least convenient to her opponent. Just the sort of shots with which to pass a volleyer, and in late March Austin knocked her rival out of the top rank with a three sets win in New York, dispatching her with a final backhand cross-court.

Martina regained her pre-eminence by defeating Tracy in May, but the rivalry is bound to continue. Offensive tennis depends on a rhythmic, fluid relation of the volley to a good first serve – a complex action vulnerable to its own inconsistency and the steady pounding of the baseliner. Achieving that rhythm depends on a contradictory combination of match fitness and appetite for the game which Martina finds difficult to keep in phase.

Never an ardent practicer, she diversifies her days with other sports, presiding over the Women's Tennis Association and, recently, a determined assault on media celebrity. Spots on game shows, walk-ons on her favourite soap operas, and the usual TV commercials have been successfully sought for her by the William Morris Agency and PRs Rogers and Cowan. And this spring Martina finally left Dallas and Haynie's management to join the Mark McCormack empire, where she will presumably enlarge the over £1 million fortune she's already amassed.

Meanwhile, the player's campaign for tennis honours has been somewhat more subdued. Despite brave words in January about going for the Grand Slam, Martina told the Eastbourne press corps, 'I haven't played the French Open since '75 and that suits me just fine.' Nor has she played the new 'separate but equal' European season set up to avoid subordination to the men's events. Clay may be the Czech's native surface, but she's undoubtedly happier on the faster carpets of the American indoor circuits and British grass. It's a preference not lost on her critics, who've raised questions both about her playing range and her participation in unofficial events at the expense of WTA tournaments.

When Martina didn't play at Roland Garros this year, or even drop by

"1980"

"There is no easy popularity...
I believe people accept that there
is no alternative."
Margaret Thatcher offers an alternative

"She is the Enid Blyton of politics.
Nothing must be allowed to spoil her
simple plots."
Richard Holme at the Liberal Party
assembly on Margaret Thatcher

"She is clearly the best man
among them."
Barbara Castle on Margaret Thatcher

"To those waiting with bated breath
for that favourite media catch-phrase,
the U-turn, I have only one thing to
say: you turn if you want to. The
lady's not for turning."
Margaret Thatcher in full manœuvre

"The soil of our country is destined to
be the scene of the fiercest fight and
the sharpest struggles to rid our
continent of the last vestiges of
white minority rule."
Nelson Mandela's message from
prison after power transferred in
Zimbabwe

"My ambition is to be remembered as
the greatest player of all time. I guess
you could say I have come close."
Bjorn Borg, after winning a fifth straight
Wimbledon Men's title

"We are now co-masters of this land."
Lech Walesa, after the rise of
Solidarity in Poland

"When we first moved here, I'd be
walking around tense, waiting for
somebody to jump on me. It took me
years to unwind. I can go right out
this door now. You know how great
that is? I mean, people ask for
autographs or say 'Hi', but they
don't bug you."
John Lennon

"Life is what happens to you while
you're making other plans."
John Lennon, lyric to 'Beautiful Boy'.
He was assassinated in December.

"No-one would have remembered
the Good Samaritan if he'd only
had good intentions. He had money
as well."
Prime Minister Margaret Thatcher
explains the Good Book

in her official capacity to pick up the gold ball which the International Tennis Federation awards annually to number one players, the Paris papers, no doubt short of stories on the Royal Family, explained the snub by announcing her marriage to 'self-described lesbian' novelist ('Rubyfruit Jungle') Rita Mae Brown!

With one eye on her endorsements and another on her citizenship application, Martina declared it 'offensive and ridiculous that anyone should think that I am gay'. But for the *People*, the *Star* and their ilk, even her denials were news. Fleet Street may have harboured hunches about dykes in whites for years, but nobody had any evidence. When Martina purchased her Virginia plantation with Rita Mae, nobody had a shred more, but at last a player's name had got tangled up with a 'gay rights leader'. On the first day of Eastbourne, Martina turned up defiantly in scarlet Tacchini togs and played some awful tennis to eventually defeat the low-ranked Betty Ann Dent.

Afterwards, she claimed that the headlines just 'made me more eager: it's all so laughable.' She'd stayed in Virginia for the previous three weeks to practise on her grass 'every day, which is a lot for me' and reckoned her chances for another Wimbledon title were good. 'The grass would suit me the best of all the players, except Evonne and Billie-Jean. I don't think I'll cave in mentally.'

On the next day she raised her game to beat Harford and play a relaxed round of doubles with her friend Ilana Kloss, only to have her Wimbledon warm-up brought to an abrupt halt on Wednesday by Betty Stove.

Which brings us to the final contradiction faced by champions. The higher they fly, the more their opponents (and at Devonshire Park that Wednesday, the crowd) want to bring them down. In the words of one sportswriter, the 30-year-old Dutch doubles specialist 'played out of her brains' to knock Martina out of the singles, 6-3, 3-6, 7-5. That left the holder with five days to prepare to open the defense of her title on Wimbledon's Centre Court – and prospects as uncertain as any in her career. ●

[*Evonne Cawley took the 1980 Wimbledon title*]

Social sculptor

Joseph Beuys interviewed in T.O. 541, by **Sarah Kent**

Parallel with conservative government and economic recession, the 1980s are seeing a retreat in the visual arts from the avant-garde positions of the 1970s into a new conservatism. Artists are packing away the weaponry of cameras, tape recorders and video cassettes and taking up the brush and palette of peacetime.

The 'classical values' of painting have been resurrected along with anti-modernists like Derain who abandoned his Fauvist style 'to rediscover lost values' through academic painting, declaring that 'modern art had been a detour'. More and more young British artists share this view.

In this climate Joseph Beuys stands out as an artist of the politically active 1970s. For him painting is not a valuable activity, its boundaries are too narrow and its sphere of influence too restricted. 'Everyone is an Artist' was the title of one of his pamphlets, though 'artists' are still needed to develop this potential by acting as teachers and catalysts, not by making objects.

Originally a sculptor, Beuys has worked during the last 15 years in performance, using live action followed by discussion as a means to engage and influence his audience.

The process is an interesting one. His materials refer back to World War II experiences as a Luftwaffe pilot. Shot down over the Crimea in the deep snow of winter, his life was saved by the Tartars, who covered his numbed body with fat and rolled it in felt to insulate him against the intense cold. Felt and fat have now figured in Beuys' work for over 20 years, gradually accumulating layers of symbolic meaning. Felt is seen as a protective insulator that stores the mental and physical energy needed to trigger evolutionary change, while also retaining both physical warmth and the 'soul or brotherhood warmth' produced through the creative interaction of the revolutionary process.

Fat of all kinds – margarine, lard, dripping, butter or tallow – alludes to bodily fat and the metabolic processes which regulate our body temperature. The presence of fat, often in large quantities, stimulates disgust mingled with curiosity, which provokes fierce discussion amongst spectators.

A strong element of ritual pervades these performances. Beuys, his scarred head protected by a felt Homberg, assumes the role of a shaman or Druid priest. An image dredged up from the past which deals with other levels of consciousness or 'inner reality' and enables him to contact his audience on a subliminal level. He is 'radically opposed to materialistic understanding of thinking in which the brain is declared to be the centre of consciousness. Old cultures knew that the process of consciousness is not specialised in this bowl under my hat. Thinking is a bodily process, every part of the body is a kind of receiver... I think with my knees!'

After the spectators are tuned in, discussion turns to contemporary political issues. Beuys outlines his plan 'to end capitalism within seven years' and to establish a society based on equality, with the existing parliamentary system replaced by 'Direct Democracy through Referendum', all major decisions being taken at grass roots level. Irrespective of achievement, everyone would receive a basic income: 'It is not a duty to work. It is already a problem to find enough work to employ people.' Fewer people would be employed in the production of goods and more would concern themselves with 'mental growth or production in the area of knowledge, creativity and morals. The most important places of production, the schools and universities, are in the hands of the state, so the establishment determines how people are to be educated. Decentralisation is essential to allow people to decide their own method of education.'

Revolution, he explains, must be brought about by 'non-violent transformation. The only revolution that leads to real change in the social order is one which changes the inner structure of thinking. Violence must take place within people in terms of changes in consciousness. Only art – by which I mean the wider understanding of art, not the traditional constellation of artists, dealers, museums, art schools etc – only art is able to build the human character to the point at which every mind can work in freedom, not through the traditional means of painting, music, dance and yoga, although these have their place. By the word "art" one must understand a comprehensive enterprise with an anthropological dimension – a science of freedom.'

Beuys' first brush with authority came in 1967, when he lifted the entry restrictions to his class at the Dusseldorf Academy where he was Professor of Monumental Sculpture. As a result 50 students enrolled and the numbers later mushroomed to 142. Repeated clashes with the authorities over the next five years led to student occupations, the formation of the German Student Party, and finally to Beuys' dismissal from the academy in 1972, a move countered with a hunger strike by his students and subsequently fought in the courts for six years. Beuys won the case and now uses his room in the Academy as an office to promote the Organisation for Direct Democracy.

Probably because of their provocative and ambiguous character, which sits uneasily in between art and political action, Beuys' actions have repeatedly aroused fierce antagonism from both left and right. During a performance in Aachen in 1964, right-wing students stormed the stage and attacked Beuys, killing the action but sparking off the first of the heated political discussions which were to become such an important feature of his work. Five years later a 'concert' in Berlin was broken up by left-wing students with fire extinguishers and water hoses in disgust at the 'spiritual, mythological and irrational content' of the performance.

Beuys' preference for 'provocative ideas over pragmatic action' has caused many to dismiss him as a Utopian dreamer. Yet, before his death, Rudi Dutschke, former leader of the student movement, joined forces with him under the umbrella of the Green Party, 'a non-violent evolutionary-revolutionary movement, which is not a political party so much as a stream of different arguments coming from different historical backgrounds, but equally dedicated to changing the system. We have to leave behind all prejudices, forget division, and work towards something completely new.'

Throughout his career Beuys' activities have attracted continuous media coverage. He refused offers to exhibit until he was already 43: 'I am glad I avoided the whole circus until then.' Now, each performance produces a residue of objects, like the blackboards on which he makes explanatory diagrams and notations. Afterwards these are set up in galleries and are sold, along with his spindly pencil drawings and potent early sculptures, for extremely high prices. Beuys sees no conflict: 'I have a duty to use my present position to help people, and the income from sales of my work is very important in the struggle.'

Beuys is standing for election to the Green Party in the German elections this October. If he succeeds, his parliamentary activities will still be thought of as 'art'. He will use them as a platform for the dissemination of his ideas for the future 'Social Sculpture', an organically evolving society conceived of as a Total Art Work. 'Evolution without coercion and without arbitrary use of power.' ●

Signing off

Four days before his untimely death in a traffic accident, critic, academic and bon viveur Roland Barthes spoke to *Time Out*.

Roland Barthes interviewed in T.O. 521, by **Philip Brooks**

Roland Barthes once had an operation to cut out some tubercular tissue from his lungs. He kept the 'spongy knob-like matter' and, instead of throwing it in the rubbish bin or displaying it in a glass-jar on the mantlepiece, he one day cast it out of his window into the street below.

A flamboyant sort of a gesture, and an anti-social one, from the man hailed as the founder of the science of signs: semiology. Semiologists study the elaborate correlation between words, images and concepts to analyse the significance of a building's design, a

photo, an ad, a literary text – any representation. If Barthes' work had only one effect, it was to demonstrate the mythology in such representations. 'Semiology', he wrote, 'has taught us that myth has the task of giving an historical intention a natural justification and making contingency appear eternal. Now this process is exactly that of bourgeois ideology.'

Barthes was a mythical figure among French intellectuals. More in the tradition of Proust than of intellectual activists like Sartre or Foucault, he frequented Paris' fashion and design world and had been recently named a 'nightclubber of the year' by the weekly *Paris Hebdo*. It may be hard to imagine a corpulent, silver-haired and very correct French professor at Le Place, Paris' top discotheque – often surrounded by an admiring circle of young men. But Barthes was fascinated by the *mondaine* world, finding it 'a perfect eyeglass for observing changing fashions, and, there is also of course the eternal game of seduction.' Surprisingly, Barthes regarded fashion as the enemy of myth. 'Myths need to take root and styles change too fast for that.'

Barthes was a prolific essayist – he preferred the short form to avoid boring others or himself – but he is perhaps best known in the Anglo-Saxon world for 'Mythologies', written 25 years ago. It was and remains possibly the most popular semiotic text. 'Semiotics started off for me as a political idea,' he declared. 'It was a way of making sense out of social symbols and ideological tricks.'

The myths that Barthes found, he tried to explode. 'Even though they have a basis in reality,' he argued 'they are not something good and should not be perpetuated.'

When Barthes wrote 'Mythologies' he took his subject matter from cuttings out of papers like

Paris Match, women's magazines, from ads and popular cinema. At the time he wrote that 'myth comes almost exclusively from the right.' But at the end of his life he admitted that if he had rewritten 'Mythologies' – a reason he said why he didn't – he would have had to criticise left-wing myths. The growth of the left and the counter-culture over the past 20 years has not been devoid of its own mythology. Bourgeois myths still maintain the power structure, he believed, but left-wing myths also perpetuate stereotyped ideology. 'Even the new left has its myths,' he complained, citing the David-and-Goliath moralisms of its views of police violence and ecology.

The militant language of activists in groups on the right and left turned Barthes cold. 'My sphere is language,' he said between puffs of cigar smoke, 'and the role of the intellectual should be to continually budge and move and attack discourses every time they begin to become fossilised and stereotyped.'

Today French intellectuals are suffering an identity crisis. The dominant doctrines of the last 20 years, Marxism, psychoanalysis and structuralism, are no longer fashionable and these last few years, for the first time, there is no one current dominating the French intellectual scene. Barthes worried about the anti-intellectualism gaining ground in France, and pointed an accusing finger at the mass media, which he said, often 'throw in sly sideways comments, which make fun of, or attack, the behaviour of people who think.'

Dubious about the power of intellectuals to directly attack the power structure, Barthes had become a champion of a purposeful individualism. 'I don't mean individualism in a petit-bourgeois form', he said, 'but of an absolute

interiority of the subject.' 'It is,' he added, 'the only marginality that is at all consequent. Protest by withdrawal is something that established powers can never tolerate or assimilate.'

Such a personal idea of protest would horrify many of Barthes' disciples, who used his relentless analysis of society's symbols as weapons against bourgeois ideology. And Barthes himself admitted that a radical individual was virtually a contradiction in terms: 'You have to survive by tricks, by being non-arrogant, non-dogmatic and non-philosophic. A problematic lifestyle in today's society.' He quoted Tolstoy: 'By escaping from evil I take no part in evil, but I participate in another evil as long as I don't struggle against evil.'

Yet Barthes was frightened by what he saw as a trend toward conformity among marginal groups today 'I would probably be considered to have a right-wing position in liberationist thinking,' he laughed, 'but the sexual revolution of the '60s and '70s, which was meant to have broken down taboos, only seems to have led to a lack of desire.' Pessimistically Barthes believed that the malady of modem civilisation is a lack of desire among the young. 'People do things today without much pleasure and when a man is struck by a lack of desire, it is almost a sickness, not in the moral but in the physical sense.'

Barthes once wrote that 'language is neither reactionary nor progressive, it is simply just fascist; because fascism is not stopping one saying something, it is obliging one to say it.' One French writer exclaimed that 'it is Barthes' dogmatism that makes him fascinating.' Other intellectuals accused him of attacking structures of power, while at the same time creating them. Not perhaps a difficult trap for such a man to fall into, considering that his lectures became unmissable on chic Parisian social calendars.

'If I had lived 100 years ago,' said Barthes. 'I would have loved to have been a psychologist, because what interests me is the game with the Other.' Instead, he played that game in his writing. 'A creation,' he called it, 'and a process of giving birth. A way of struggling against annihilation, of dominating death. Not that we think we'll be eternal as a writer, but when you write you scatter seeds and thus become part of the general circulation of seeds in the world.' ●

Knitty gritty

from T.O. 516

Last month three women were asked to leave the Mother Red Cap pub in Camden apparently because they took part in a 'knit-in' at the pub. They were asked to cast off by the landlord and the police were called. 'All right girls,' said the police, 'out you go.'

'We're not girls, we're women,' replied the knitters. 'All right, women, out you go,' said the police. Mother Red Cap was reticent about the issue. A barman said it was about not wanting punks rather than knitters, but was woolly on further details.

Superstud

from T.O. 514

Disturbing news from Pinewood Studios where shooting progresses on 'Superman 2'. It seems that Supe and Lois Lane are to have what is known as a 'bedroom scene'. Comic experts can find no evidence of such activity ever taking place, but our etymology department says, 'This could throw new light on the expression "go take a flying fuck".'

1981

Don't riot, get on your bike and find a job. Or watch the nice Princess get hitched to Prince Chuck. Such advice was just the thing to fan the flames of Brixton, Toxteth and several other riotous inner-cities. Egypt's President Sadat, The Pope and Ronald Reagan all offered themselves up for target practice, and Bobby Sands died hungry. London's Blitz kids made night buses beautiful.

Diva
Marvellous amalgam of sadistic thriller and fairy-tale romance, drawing on a wild diversity of genres from film noir to Feuillade serial.

Chariots Of Fire
This is an overblown piece of self-congratulatory emotional manipulation perfectly suited for Thatcherite liberals.

Raiders Of The Lost Ark
Whether you swallow it or not, see it for the handful of totally unexpected visual jokes, worth the price of admission.

Human League - Dare (Virgin)
The revised line-up have gone straight for the jugular: deliciously infectious

hooks, irresistible melodies and insistent dance rhythms.

Phil Collins - Face Value (Virgin)
Nice irony: where hosts of mascara'd boys have bombed out, the balding drummer in an unfashionable supergroup cleans up.

Adam And The Ants - Kings Of The Wild Frontier (CBS)
The Ants' incredible tenacity over the last couple of lean years has justly been vindicated by this first album for CBS, a dramatic improvement over past form. Song for song, not so much a concept album, more a way of life.

Amazing Grace

Grace Jones interviewed in T.O. 580, by **Michael Roberts**

Grace Jones is Black. Deep Blue Black. On stage, punctuated by the whites of her eyes and the slash of her fuschia lipstick, she is a stark silhouette capering in front of a bright pink backdrop. Bash Crash. In a scarlet hat, she attacks the cymbals. Bang Clang. Looking svelte in a pelt she beats the drums. Now dolled in drag like an old *Vogue* poster she semaphores chicly in a Spic-style suit.

In close up, Grace Jones, disco diva, is not so much the fashion plate. More the Missing Link. Darkly primitive with lopsided cheekbones and a massive domed forehead. Her natural hairline is monkeylike – 'You see, I'm a very hairy person' – and starts somewhere near her eyebrows, but this has been shaved back. The same electric razor has also mowed across the back of her skull leaving a two-inch tuft of hair perched neatly on her crown. The effect is pretty only to those with a fine appreciation of Post Frontal Lobotomy Chic. In New York's fashionable clubs they have such an appreciation. She is, they whisper, the Ultimate Shriek.

As an androgynous disco diva with a passion for fashion, Grace Jones comes equipped with all the essential accoutrements appropriate to her trade – a talent for wearing male drag, a voice as deep and dark as a walk-in wardrobe and a smart line in sexual ambiguity. It would not be giving anything away to say that her appeal is on the whole – how can one put it? – Camp. Not that she's Judy Garland in black face serenading wistful window dressers in the front row stalls. No. When Grace Jones becomes overexcited, she leaps from the stage, grabs a fan and makes a graphic show of sodomising him over the footlights. Timid window dressers have learned by now to choose the dress circle. 'Hmm, I think the sodomy has to go,' tuts her mentor, Jean Paul Goude.

We are backstage in Amsterdam on the initial leg of Grace Jones's first European tour. Out front, ululating Dutch youths high on Edam cheese and Grace Jones costumes have just showered the star with red roses and begged for an encore. But Goude, a finicky little perfectionist, is not happy. The show wasn't Goude enough. For Jean Paul, nothing is Goude enough. Even he is not Goude enough. This is why he is wearing shoulder-pads in his T-shirt to bring him out to THERE and stack-heeled footwear to bring him up to HERE. Curtain calls over, enter the star looking a trifle weary on her ankle-strap sandals. Goude proceeds to conduct a rapid post-mortem. 'The show is his concept,' explains a man from the record company while Jean Paul clip-clops earnestly by, armed with notebooks bulging with doodles of Grace Jones wearing his fashionable brainwaves. 'You see this,' says Goude indicating an inscrutable scribble, 'in this scene Grace could wear a long green nose.' Quite.

And next season they'll ALL be wearing them.

For Goude, ex-art editor of *Esquire* magazine, illustrator, false nose couturier, Grace Jones's longtime companion and father of her child (Paulo, two), the Grace Jones Show affords the perfect opportunity to display his idiosyncratic notions for visual melodrama. Each song is staged in intricately mapped out 'Tableaux' (rather like old *Vogue* fashion photos) with the abstract-looking Grace placed just so to complete the composition. In other words, we are now talking about Art. Unfortunately, when it was previewed a few weeks ago in Manhattan, the *New York Times* thought the show spoke less about Art and more about Fashion with unsubtle S&M overtones. 'They're just racist,' grumps Goude, 'it's not about fashion. That's middle class. It's Style. And they resent Style when it's associated with negroes. Critics want the negro entertainer to be rootsy and sweaty – like James Brown. They said it was wrong to use a catwalk in a rock concert. But why? It's a great theatrical device.'

Of course, it might be that the critics were simply not taken with her choice of Paris-style headgear, her masculine drag. Or that fetchingly ethnic gorilla suit she lumbers around in to open her act. Goude laughs: 'That's a parody of how people used to see her when she was a model – a grinning black monkey.' It is also how people saw Marlene Dietrich, in 'Blonde Venus', Paramount, 1932. 'An *hommage*,' explains Goude airily as Grace Jones begins pottering about restlessly. The star doesn't appear to care whether it's *hommage* or fromage. She just wants to party.

In the early hours of the morning Grace Jones makes her dramatic entrance at the most fashionable discotheque in Amsterdam. And it's empty. Almost. From the shadows flit two desultory youths in silver lamé clown costumes to flutter about Grace Jones. Goude groans. 'That's exactly what I don't want the show to be associated with,' he sighs, visions of High Art creativity being wasted on Low Camp sensibilities dancing before his eyes. Unperturbed, Grace Jones merrily signs autographs. What did they say? 'They wanted to know if I was really the same as I am on stage,' she smiles, flexing her shoulder-pads. The short answer is No. She's shorter. And not quite so interesting.

Grace Jones grew up in Jamaica, one of seven brothers and sisters in a strictly religious family. Her father – a former boxing champion – is a minister in the Pentecostal Church, one brother is a preacher and her uncle was a bishop. Thus Grace spent her childhood being told that playing games is devil's work and went to church two nights a week and twice on Sunday. At school she was not allowed to show her knees and was always covered from neck to wrist. Naturally, not being particularly interested in any religions – 'They're all the same to me' – Grace was a little peeved by these sartorial restrictions. 'I suppose that's why I rebelled,' she muses. As a tomboyish teen, Grace related best to her twin brother, Christian, a flamboyant youth much obsessed with dressing up and *maquillage*. When he left home to move to America, Grace soon followed, attending college in Syracuse, a picturesque New York suburb, where she studied languages and planned to become an interpreter. But somehow, she always felt apart from the other girls: 'I felt so much older. In Jamaica at 13 you're no longer a child, at 15 you're ready for marriage and if you're not married by 17, you're considered an old maid.'

Grace was 15, not ready for marriage, not about to be seen as an old maid and far more interested in nightclubs, wearing make-up – 'It made me look 30' – and, after appearing in a college play, Showbiz. So after appearing in a few more plays, she decided to improve her acting technique by 'experiencing things'. She became a bar girl, a go go dancer and indulged in a spot of private enterprise – flashing the odd breast at any patron of the arts willing to pay 50 dollars a peek.

Grace Jones decided to experience a spot of modelling. Armed with a portfolio of artistic studies, she powered about New York on her 500cc motorbike – 'I was never very feminine' – stomped the agencies, eventually signing up with one that specialised in ethnic mannequins, Black Beauties. Alas it was not an auspicious debut. 'Nobody wanted me for commercial work. They didn't understand my face at all,' says Grace, who had also added fuel to the fire by lopping her hair off to skinhead length so that several clients thought she was a drag queen. 'The agency thought so too,' says Grace, 'they screamed at me "You'll never get any work here looking like that" and told me to go abroad.'

With enough dollars for a cheap plane ticket, Grace flew to Luxembourg and hitch-hiked to Paris. Another would-be model, an alarmingly tall Texan farmgirl called Jerry Hall, had also arrived to seek fame and fortune and cover girl status. Together the eccentric-looking duo made the rounds of the agencies, eventually signing up with, Elite, run by a Spanish smoothie named Johnny Casablancas. Within three days Grace rowed with Casablancas, was thrown out and signed up elsewhere.

In Paris, there are fashions in models as there are fashions in clothes. Simply because bizzare-looking models were in heavy demand that season, Grace Jones finally took off. One magazine put her on three covers in a row; *Vogue* followed suit; and one of the most celebrated fashion photographers, Hans Feurer, became so besotted by Grace he booked her for almost any assignment that came along – even when clients asked specifically for a blue-eyed blonde.

At model crowd shindigs, her favourite party turn when was to sing along to records in a rich basso profundo tempered by years of hymn singing at the Pentecostal Church in Jamaica and Martini-drinking in Manhattan. A model's boyfriend, working in the record business, mentioned that he had been requested to seek out 'unusual' new talent. Grace Jones was ready. She cut a demo.

Encouraged by the response to her effort, Grace Jones sat down with a couple of friends and a songwriter and, at the height of the disco craze, penned a little ditty which they eventually called 'I Need A Man'. It was recorded (badly) on the Orpheus label and tinny and tacky as it was, became an underground hit in Paris discos – particularly in those discos (surprise, surprise) where men seek out other men. Fired by this limited success, Grace then took herself to England, to record with 'more professional people' and at the height of the disco boom, came up with a doublesided hit, 'Sorry' and 'That's The Trouble'. Released in America, it quickly climbed to Number Seven. With shrewd timing, 'I Need A Man' was then remixed and rereleased and in two weeks shot to Number One.

Back in Paris, Grace Jones's phone was ablaze with transatlantic calls urging personal appearances. And so, the jet-black model with the uncommercial face finally returned to New York to be greeted by hysterical hordes of gay disco-goers. She did not disappoint. Blessed with a talent for kitsch exhibitionism, she turned herself into the quintessential image of a drag queen. Clad in gold lurex and Egyptian snake bangles, she parted the dancefloor at downtown dives borne aloft on a stretcher marshalled by musclebound slaves wearing jockstraps. Draped in a black cape and a balaclava helmet, she brandished a bullwhip, and mimed 'I Need A Man' in Greenwich Village leather bars.

> **'I felt so much older. In Jamaica at 13 you're no longer a child, at 15 you're ready for marriage and if you're not married by 17, you're considered an old maid.'**

' It was blatant homosexual exploitation,' shudders Jean Paul Goude, who remembers seeing her giving a particularly cheap performance surrounded by a dozen glittering, scantily-clad boys at the opening of Studio 54. 'Fag Fantasy. All her newness and originality had gone.' And so, crying 'Don't do it, come with me', the short, balding artist who calls himself a 'heterosexual sissy' took the wild black disco queen who 'feels like a woman, and looks like a man' in hand. A sort of black Pygmalion? Not quite. 'She's still an animal,' admits Goude. 'She'll let you pet her and she'll snooze with you. Then she'll turn right round and scratch you in the eye.' ●

1981

Divine

The Divine Mr M

The actor with the most makeup, the highest heels, the biggest hairdo and the tightest dress

Divine interviewed in T.O. 591, by **Ian Birch** and **Cynthia Rose**

Divine: I started with John Waters in 1962 with the first film, 'Roman Candles', which was 8mm with three projectors, each a shot above the other. The films have all been made in the Baltimore area. We all grew up there; that's why John always called me 'the girl next door almost'. We didn't really get along when we were growing up – he had a very strong Catholic upbringing and I was Protestant. He was always the first one to call me fat.

T.O.: *Had you previously done any acting at all?*

No, I'd never really done much. I played a beaver once and somebody ripped my tail off and I had to hold it on the whole time because I had to flap it. I was so upset they ripped my tail off – it made a lasting impression on my mind.

Then the following year we made 'Eat Your Makeup', which is about a couple that kidnap fashion models and make them model themselves to death and I'm one of their friends and I have a Jackie Kennedy fetish. Kennedy had just been killed about four months before we made the movie, in '63. And in it I have a dream sequence where I'm in drag and I'm reading Jackie Kennedy books ... I've got a pink suit and a pill-box hat and JFK gets shot and I leap out of the back. And try to get out of the car, which is what she was doing. She claims she was trying to pull somebody in the car. Which you can't blame the girl for.

I was the first person to portray Jackie Kennedy on the screen.

Then the next film was ....

'Mondo Trasho'. I think you should see them in their order, too. Cos in the beginning we were just kids fooling around. No one had any idea anything would happen – but my dream was to be a movie star; I idolised Elizabeth Taylor all my life. But when you're a kid in Baltimore, Maryland, and you want to be a movie star you think, 'Well, what hope is there?'

And now you've recently finished John Waters' latest opus, 'Polyester'?

Yes. I play a frumpy suburban housewife; the look is completely different. It got to the point where I was being typecast and my plays, 'Women Behind Bars' and 'Neon Women', were very much like the movies because the movies were so popular. In 'Neon Woman' I play Flash Starr, who's a retired stripper. I have a daughter in school in Paris who thinks I'm just this wealthy woman. She leaves school because one of her male teachers makes advances towards her and she comes home to find me in the arms of a black man, who takes care of the strippers but he's my boyfriend. And, she flips out and realises that nothing is like she really thought it was.

I have no patience with her because I think well here it is, this is what it is, there's no way to hide it. And she meets the strippers one by one and eventually becomes one of them. Then she's on heroin and then she's a nymphomaniac. Then – what do you call people who make love to dead people?

Necrophiliac.

Yeah. It's very funny. She suffers a lot through this.

And the next thing is another stage play?

Yes; it's called 'The Thorn'; it's a take-off on 'The Rose'. I figured if Bette can use my name, I can use her movie. It's about a rock star of the highest magnitude and the lowest morals, this woman who'll stop at nothing. It starts off like 'All About Eve', then it goes back and tells the whole story; it's 'All About Eve', 'The Coal-Miner's Daughter' and 'The Rose,' all wrapped up in one.

How would you describe your achievements as an actor?

I've created my own character to the point where it's so strong I think people actually assume that's the way I am. And I've had trouble with that too, living that down in the press. They never know how to say 'What do you do?' I say, well what do you call people that walk onto a stage in costumes? They're actors? Well, if they're actors, then I must be too.

That's one reason I got this script for 'Polyester': I'm a frumpy suburban housewife who's so good it's just like Jesus walking around in drag. I'm so good everyone takes advantage of me; even the dog that I feed hates me. My kids hate me, my husband runs around with his secretary. Then I meet this man after I'm divorced – who is Tab Hunter!

It's very realistic, the whole thing. That's why I really wanted to play it. I'd never played a dowdy character before. I was always the aggressive one with the most makeup on and the highest heels and the biggest hairdo and the tightest dress. And in this one I have the lowest heels, the ugliest dress and the flattest hairdo. I refer to it as my 'Mildred Pierce' because Joan Crawford was always the aggressor in all her films.

The one film where she was the nice person she got her Oscar for. I kept that in mind all the time. These movies were written to be vulgar, to be shocking, to be outrageous, and to make people laugh. But this one doesn't have one dirty word in it. Not even the word 'hell'. Because all that has become so easy now – there isn't a movie or even television you don't watch where they're cussing at each other. When we made 'Pink Flamingoes' there wasn't another movie like it – but now it could be on TV.

John Waters' casting seems like a perversion of the old star system?

Well, John does work very much like the old movie star system, and he was the one that helped me build my whole career up. We worked together on it; you wash my back and I'll wash yours. That's how it worked. And now I am treated like a star or whatever. I love all that, I can't sit and say that I don't love it. I love going special places and meeting special people, and being treated in a special way. But sometimes I think that in some of the movies we actually went too far. Where I didn't think there was any need for it, but once again it was John's movie.

What have been your main aims?

I've always tried to put in some glamour because I think it's very important. That's why I used to like Elizabeth Taylor. No matter what, I could always count on her to look real good – you'd always know there was a movie star up there. And Davis and Crawford and Stanwyck, they were all bitches in the movies, they always had guns and they were mean to everybody. People love that aggressive woman. So my character was loosely based on all of them. My main objective is to make people laugh – and have a good time and try to forget all the horrible things that are happen-

ing for that hour and-a-half or two hours. I don't want final say and I don't ever ask for that. John is the producer and director of the films. He of course has final say and everything – but we all work together.

Is there any one inspiration you've all shared?

Jayne Mansfield always inspired us. She was more or less the icing on the cake. To be like Jayne Mansfield, but to be blown out of proportion... Because when people think of a blonde bombshell, they think of what Diana Dors was, or Jayne Mansfield, or Marilyn Monroe. A platinum blonde, wasp-waisted woman in a very tight dress. I thought we'll take it a step further, and have a 300lb blonde bombshell in a tight dress with a bare midriff, which I think gave some fat women hope. Just because you're fat you don't want to have to wear navy blue polka dots. I've seen some fat women that are so beautiful, but they're so so uptight about being fat.

I remember when I'd wear a raincoat at all times, when I was a teenager. I thought it covered me up. It was hideous, I would never go to parties or anything and I got beaten up every day by a gang of boys because I wasn't athletic. I was very artistic and musically inclined. But I wasn't in dresses or anything. I had girlfriends and went out on dates and did all of that.

Finally, has your cult popularity created any problems for you?

Well, I am an actor. That's the main problem I have in America – convincing people that I'm an actor, not a transvestite. A transvestite is a man that lives in drag, or gets off sexually in drag. And I don't do either of those. I'd ruin all my costumes, number one – it costs too much money to clean and that never really comes out. ●

"He didn't riot. He got on his bike and looked for work and he kept looking until he found it."
Norman Tebbitt on his father

"Maggie Thatcher, are you listening, Maggie Thatcher? Your boys have taken a hell of a beating tonight!"
Norwegian football commentator after Norway's 2-1 win over England

"At upper class tables, people wonder what will happen to Lady Tryon and Camilla Parker-Bowles, Charles's two blonde, married ladyfriends."
New York commentator Marie Brenner asks, after hearing of the impending marriage of Lady Diana Spencer to Prince Charles

"Yes... Whatever that may mean."
Prince Charles, clarifying whether he is in love with Diana

"A triumph of the embalmer's art."
Gore Vidal on Ronald Reagan

"You must arrest him. He's the worst umpire I've ever seen."
John McEnroe to a policeman at Wimbledon

"My problems are all behind me."
Ken Brett, Kansas City baseball star, on his piles

"American [art] collectors would rather have Van Gogh's ear than a Van Gogh."
Robert Hughes

"If there's any emergence of a fourth party in this country, the task of the Liberal Party is to strangle it at birth."
Cyril Smith MP reacting to the launch of the SDP

"I have always said about Tony that he immatures with age."
Harold Wilson on Tony Benn

"During my seven years in office, I was in love with seventeen million French women... I know this comment will inspire irony and that English language readers will find it very French."
Valéry Giscard D'Estaing, following his defeat in the Presidential elections

1981

Divine–New romantics

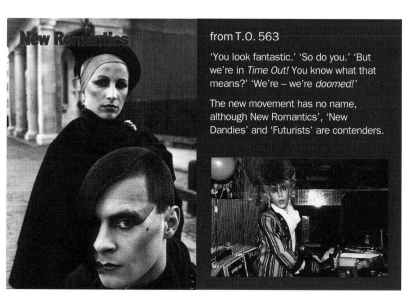

New Romantics

from T.O. 563

'You look fantastic.' 'So do you.' 'But we're in *Time Out!* You know what that means?' 'We're – we're *doomed!*'

The new movement has no name, although New Romantics', 'New Dandies' and 'Futurists' are contenders.

from T.O. 574, by **Colin McGhee**

Eye Witness

As Brixton exploded, Colin McGhee was probably the only reporter to have gone through the cordons and seen both sides of the conflict

Mayall and Railton Roads were places of choking smoke and of youths collecting and hurling missiles at the police. It wasn't a place for dialogue. There was one note of unanimity. 'Make sure you tell the truth,' they said. The youth of Mayall Road wasted little time explaining why they were there. 'We hate the police, they arrest us for nothing.' The police had beaten their friends. The police insulted them on the streets. If the police caught anyone now they would beat them half to death...

The heat from the burning building was intense. The light from a blazing plumber's shop just yards away made the police easy targets for the barrage of half bricks and broken paving stones coming from both ends of Railton Road. At the junction with Effra Parade, Chaucer Road and Leeson Road the rioters pressed a relentless attack, making a mockery of an inspector's exhortation to 'hold the line.'

The police could hardly spare men to deal with the wounded. The limp and bloody forms of officers, some of them half conscious from head and face wounds, lay in Chaucer Road and Effra Parade.

'We need more bloody shields!' yelled one. 'Has anybody here got a radio? Get that man back out of the line – if they get in here they'll kill him.'

Two buildings were totally gutted by fire and as the rioters came on, petrol bombs claimed more property. Burning vehicles pulled across the road formed shelter first for police, then rioters. Masonry from burning buildings crashed into the street and you had to shout above the crackle of flames. But when police reinforcements arrived there were few immediate arrests – the rioters melted away into the smoke.

Police fury by this time had reached boiling point. They vented their frustration on any black youth they could find. I saw one youth – I do not know if he was a rioter or not – severely beaten. Not more than 14 years of age he was being dragged behind a fire engine by a constable who had him in a headlock. Before he arrived at the police vans I saw a group of about ten policemen converge on him. The youth, totally subdued, moaned and cried as batons, boots, fists and knees thudded into every part of his body accompanied by curses and racist invective.

On Coldharbour Lane a *Time Out* photographer and I saw a young black man standing alone doing nothing. He was seized by a police snatch-squad. They beat him with truncheons and kicked him, dragging him away. A social worker had been taking notes of the incident. She approached an inspector who had been seen to order the snatch and asked the reason for this unprovoked violence. 'I didn't see it,' explained the inspector.

A young policeman born and brought up in Brixton told me – visibly upset – 'I never thought it would come to this, but I feel it's only the beginning.' He was one of a minority of officers who by Sunday afternoon were actually talking to blacks in Railton Road. But the opinion of the local community was ominously similar. ●

The virgin Queen

As the Royal stallion is led to stud, a feminist studies the form

in T.O. 568, by **Frankie Rickford**

A young woman teacher with a nice flat and plenty of friends decides to chuck the lot and move in with an 80-year-old widow. Five months later she marries her landlady's grandson – 13 years older than she is and her first boyfriend – to spend the rest of her life as his official shadow and the first decade of it in obligatory childbearing.

As you may know by now, Lady Diana Spencer is the perfect bride for our heir to the throne. HRH has vetted her pedigree with the skill that only a horseman of his experience could command. Her previous owner, the eighth Earl Spencer, commends his daughter as a fine physical specimen; and her uncle, Lord Fermoy, has publicly guaranteed that the merchandise will be delivered to the Royal punter in virgin condition.

Lady Diana enjoys – or so we are led to believe – the virtues of total passivity. She's 19, three years out of school with six months in a Swiss finishing school, and has recently worked part-time in a private nursery in Pimlico, a suitably trivial occupation according to conventional standards.

Introduced as 'Shy Di' she's been celebrated as 'sweet' (despite her objections to the word), 'retiring', 'coy', 'demure', 'giggly' and 'domesticated', with a distinguished record for having almost nothing to say for herself – so endearing in a woman.

She's pictured, with or without an armful of well-bred toddler, gazing across the inside pages at her intrepid Prince as soldier, ship's captain, parachutist or deep sea diver.

Three papers carried 'Action Man' headlines on their Prince Charles profiles and some ran astrological guides to the two as a precaution against anyone missing the sexual stereotypes all Perfect Couples should embody.

According to IPC's glossy 30 page Special Royal Engagement Souvenir (off the presses and onto the bookstalls within 24 hours of the announcement) Scorpio Charles was born 'energetic, determined, self-contained, pleasure loving and sexy with enormous courage and love of danger'. Meanwhile Diana, a typical Cancerian, tends to be (you guessed it) 'strong on the intuitive and emotional side of things', 'sensitive', with plenty of 'charm and quiet persistence'.

All the papers examined her worthy ancestry, enthusing about the various historic genes she'll bequeath her Royal offspring in terms very similar to those recently employed in a well known dairy farming weekly to report the servicing of a pedigree Friesian cow by a distinguished breeding bull in Ayrshire.

'The girl with a history but no past' was the headline to the *Daily Mail's* souvenir pull-out, a double page spread juxtaposing an account of Lady Diana's blushing innocence with an illustrated catalogue of 'The Girls He Left Behind'.

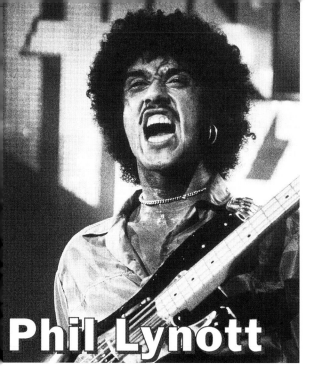

Phil Lynott

from 'Black and white and rock and roll'
in T.O. 587, by **Ilene Melish**

Thin Lizzy is a rock and roll band. Rock and roll bands are white, and Phil Lynott knows it.

Musical forms are the products of social conditions, not genetics, and whatever Lynott might otherwise suspect, he was born to the same sounds and visions that produced other Irishmen. When he delivers 'Still in Love with You', it is Van Morrison soul more than US black 1960s balladry. Growing up in Ireland was a battle of class, not colour. And for whatever barriers the music crosses, despite the eloquent fusion of its birth 25 years ago (and it was that fusion of black and white which was the original – conscious – defiance, not sex or sideburns), audiences still divide by colour. It wasn't until Lynott got to England in the early 1970s, roomed with a Nigerian in London and was bottled off the stage in Liverpool, that he began tentatively to explore the social meaning of colour. In his early work there was pungent commentary on black reality, virtually never remarked upon, long before Lynott's 1981 'Ode to a Black Man' on his 'Solo in Soho' LP.

Lynott sometimes talks of being a black Irishman, sometimes an Irish blackman. Significantly, his lingering personal identification is neither black nor white, but 'half-caste of any denomination'. Sometimes the black world comes out in Lizzy music as it would for any Irishman: the exclusivity of blackness, a mysterious romantic allure – '*Hoodoo rhythm devil and voodoo news; down skid row where only black men can go*'. But defiance and irony are never far away, and over the years they built up to what Lynott now calls 'outrage'.

'I was, to a certain extent, protected by living in Ireland from blatant racialism. If there were insults I couldn't deal with, I had to go home and rethink it. I put an end to an awful lot of it simply because I could handle myself. I was a real little hard nutter.

'I could have got a nine to five job, which never, never was my idea of the way I wanted to live, And the only other things that were really open to me was like showbiz, athletics – you know, boxing. I was from a poor area anyway, so I would have just regarded it as class. It never would have entered into me head that it could have been because of colour.

'It was only when I came to England in the early '70s I realised how deep it could get.'

Within months, Lynott was bottled off the stage of the Liverpool Empire to shouts of 'Black Bastard'.

'We did a tour supporting Slade. Then they put Suzi Quatro on the bill, but it was just announced, "Slade plus Support". At that time, Slade was like a skinhead band. Suzi Quatro comes on, they put up with her. Then they were all thinking Slade were gonna come on. And out walks Thin Lizzy.

'That was the only time we ever cut our set short because of fear. There was guys throwing cans and they weren't trying to hit the other two guys. They were trying to hit me and they were going; "Go on, get that black bastard," Lynott laughs.

'I've often met black guys and they've sort of went, "how come you don't play any reggae, or any funk or soul?" And the point is, if I could, honestly, if I could play with feel – I just feel there's better people that can do it than me. And if I could play it, I would play it. But the thing I play best is rock music.'

Heavy metal has become the arena of mythological fantasies which blend in with 'Celtic revivals' and similar manifestations elsewhere, and quickly bring to mind every social current Wagner was blamed for. Lizzy, and Lynott solo, have, of course, never simply been a heavy metal band and Lynott's mythology is a direct and personal one. He came upon romanticism as a private discovery.

'Words like — *How can I leave the town that brings me down, that has no jobs, is blessed by God, and makes me cry, Dublin?*' – that was the feeling I felt as I left my home town. I didn't want to leave I learned around '76 I could never really go back as such. For that period I drew very heavily on Irish myths and legends, where this had happened to men far greater than I.

'All Irish, all the Irish writers I've been through. I mean, that's just a period you go through in Ireland. You have 'Dubliners' by Joyce, and you have all his early works. You try to understand 'Ulysses'. And then there's Frank O'Connor, there's Yeats, Oscar Wilde, Bernard Shaw, Samuel Beckett, they just go on. And they're in all idioms, they're not just a period piece.

'I draw a lot of strength from my Irish heritage. When I lived in London, I lived with a guy who was from Nigeria and he played African sounds all the time. One of the things I noticed was the scales in African music and the tempos were very like traditional Irish music. The chant was also there. So I tried to link Irish music and black music, through the "Sitamoia" chants. "Sitamoia" – that was a bastardisation of Irish. The real Irish in the song means "for the money". The idea was, it's shit if you do it for the money.'

The question remains of how much the vagabond-gypsy-wanderer-stray theme – 'all male descendants of the fatherless child' – so pervasive in Thin Lizzy's music, is rooted in the impact on Lynott of the western world's belief that 'race' is a meaningful concept.

'I always felt like, in the 1960s and early '70s, there was an awful lot of black people saying it for black people. Whereas I regarded myself as a half-caste kid from Ireland. I try more to relate to – for example, in Rod Stewart's band there's Philip Chen who's a Jamaican Chinese guy, and with Ian Dury, there's Norman, an Indian-English guy. I'm an Irish black man. I relate more to the half-caste kid, like the black Scottish kid – the guy that's got two cultures.

'It's only in the last couple of years that I've begun to stand up and be counted. The first one I did right up front was "Ode to a Black Man" on the solo album. I mention Haile Selassie, Jomo Kenyatta, Robert Mugabe. *"If you hear Stevie Wonder, tell him I see: I don't want songs for plants, I want songs for me."* At the time, there was nobody saying it and he was about the only guy that could say it.

'The more I learn about black history, the more I feel the sense of outrage. *Then* I look for the strengths, like to get from slavery to the state of the majority of westerners. It's a fickle sort of equality, but it is an equality of sorts. I can see the strength in that; what is really playing on my mind is what's going on in Eastern Africa — starvation. *That* is the greatest racialism of all.' ●

The style is
the man

Martin Amis interviewed in T.O. 571, by **Richard Ra**

Martin Amis

Feminism, optimism, ideas, politics, they all get a hammering in the writings of Martin Amis.

The thing that strikes you first about Martin Amis is a near-neurotic concern to safeguard his own image. At four o'clock on a Friday afternoon the TV set in his flat was on, scenes from a B-feature flickering above a gleaming IBM typewriter on the floor. Amis quickly turned the set off. 'It was for the cleaning lady's kids,' he explained. 'I wouldn't like you to think I spend all day watching crappy Westerns.'

He was, he said, worried about taping the interview. 'It might be best if you give me the questions and I prepare written answers. I don't want to misrepresent myself. I did a taped interview a few months ago and they printed everything. Even the ums and ers. Made me look a real jerk.' One remembers that Amis's literary hero, Vladimir Nabokov, treated his questioners with disdain, scrawling carefully worded replies on the back of index cards. But Amis is not so well established, not yet, nor would he wish to appear so solemn. After all, his public character is that of showman. 'In 200 years,' he has stated, 'I want them to be talking about Dante, Shakespeare and Martin Amis.' So he decided to let the tape run. Image maketh Martin.

'Actually I have no consistent self view. Only people with a total lack of imagination do. Like most of us, I swing from thinking I'm wonderful to thinking I'm absolutely abhorrent about 100 times a day.'

'But most people don't think that way,' I suggested.

'Don't they? Oh Christ.' He sighed. 'I hope you're wrong about that. I think even quite brusque people are very wobbly inside about how they're going down. I know I am.'

Eight years after the publication of his first novel 'The Rachel Papers' Amis is, at 31, London's most publicised and most notorious literary figure. After leaving Oxford with a first in English he started work on the editorial staff of the *Times Literary Supplement*, where it is unlikely that the name of his father actively hindered his chances. Four novels, three screenplays (only one actually making it to the screen – the dire 'Saturn 3'), innumerable articles, and the prestigious literary editorship of the *New Statesman* have followed in less than a decade. During this time Amis learnt a lot about marketing his product: people expect him to be mordant, flashy, controversial, and it is precisely this gossip column persona that he cultivates.

This conscious presentation of himself as the trendiest, most cynical penman in town, the Writer-As-Celebrity, has made Amis familiar to a wide audience while alienating many potential readers, with the result that his fiction is more talked about than read, more often

the subject of unthinking approval or dismissal than analysis. While his novels have generally been well received in the press, he has provoked widespread popular criticism on the grounds that: he's arrogant and complacent; he's misogynistic; his writing is repulsive, at best merely clever; he'd walk a million miles for one of his own smiles and a million more to see that smile portrayed in the *Observer*.

Amis's attitude to this dubious celebrity he has created is ambiguous: he is delighted about being controversial and sought-after, yet anxious to promote his more serious literary credentials: 'I've been accused of not taking my work seriously enough,' he says. 'Of course my writing is serious. It's much too serious to talk seriously about it.'

In fact his four novels – 'The Rachel Papers', 'Dead Babies', 'Success', and 'Other People: A Mystery Story' – establish him as one of the

'In Queensway you can walk around at any time and hear ten people screaming.'

most provocative and consistently daring writers of fiction around, in marked contrast to his journalism, which has such a smug, self-serving air about it. His expressed intention is to sweeten the pill of modernism, annexing complex narrative structures with a certain commitment to the populist techniques of realism. At best his books are both penetrating and funny, meticulously contrived comedy counterpointing the almost surreal quality of the environments he describes. Amis chronicles various urban neuroses, particularly those of contemporary London.

'Psychosis is the normal answer to urban life. Perhaps the inevitable result of the city idea is to push people to extremes – concentrated lifestyles, emphasis on speed, complete subservience to money. In Queensway you can walk around at any time and hear ten people screaming a mad commentary on life. The streets sing.'

'Other People: A Mystery Story' is easily his most controlled and assured novel to date, less uneven, less extravagant and self-indulgent than its predecessors. It opens with an eerie, memorable description of a woman waking up in a mental hospital. She is an almost total amnesiac, having forgotten not only who she is but also the nature of 'everyday' reality.

Of course there is a problem, as it seems there must always be with Amis. For all its qualities (wit, haunting imagery, measured construction),

'Other People' still remains open to the charge that Amis' fiction parades violence, despair, and particularly sexism in a wilfully gloating, even sadistic fashion. In all of his novels there are characters who are dismissive and contemptuous of women. Amis admits that the most consistent criticism of his work is sexism but doesn't regard it as a matter worth losing his cool about.

'I really think that it's just fashion criticising me. My stuff will still be the same when feminist criticism moves away from it and on to something different. If you want to talk in those terms then my fiction isn't anti-women, it's anti-people. Everyone has a bad time in it.' He points out that in 'Success' the twin first-person narratives work as parodies of gloating male sexual attitudes, the parodies appearing as recommendations only if the irony is missed. 'People assume that these characters express my attitudes. That just isn't so – my books are satires.'

While it is true that Amis effectively removes his own voice from the surface of his fiction through the use of unreliable narrators, it is perhaps too simple to equate the sexism, violence etc with their prejudices, call it all satire, and leave it at that. The relationship between Amis and his narrators suggests that their presence operates only as an element in an artistic game, rather than to make any moral or intellectual point. 'The idea that the novelist punishes bad characters and rewards good ones doesn't bear up any more. Of course the nastiness is an element in my stuff. I write about that because it's more interesting. Everyone's more interested in the bad news. Only one writer has ever written convincingly about happiness and that's Tolstoy. Nobody else seems to be able to make it swing on the page.'

Amis has written that ideas are 'the novelist's fatal disease' and perhaps regards all politics as irrelevant to literature. It seems difficult not to conclude that his novels are merely experiments with different patterns of expression, all surface and no depth, and that he believes style to be the critical factor in fiction, not ideas and content.

'I think that expresses a half truth. The structures of my books come on a bit like that. But I see things as being more chaotic. It's true that I'm not particularly interested in politics. I'm more interested in rival versions of sanity – one person saying to another "My sanity is saner than yours". Nonetheless I'd calculate my imagination to be of the Left. I'm more obsessed by down and outs and the griefs of ordinary people than in life at the top end of the scale. It's not the novelist's business to worry about social causations. All he must be alive to is the effects they have.' ●

Black flash

Rollerskating is, for many young blacks, less a sport than a matter of pride.

It was during those unexpectedly warm, New York-like weeks of late summer that it happened: all of a sudden, the sheer weight of their numbers on the capital's roads thrust the anarchic warriors of 1980s leisure technology that are London's black rollerskaters upwards into a contemporary sub-cultural league of their very own. In these almost too tribal times, it seemed that finally there was a youth grouping quite literally making contact with and utilising that much-abused concept of The Street.

In those hot days, the rollerskaters seemed everywhere: a rush-hour knot of Knightsbridge pedestrians would loosen with a nervous shake, and out of its midst would silently dart a lone, heroic figure, flashing by and vanishing seconds later in a high-speed dance to the eternally fast-forward funk rhythms into which he was wired via his Sony Walkman. Or maybe at two in the morning you'd be driving down one of South London's near-deserted main thoroughfares when up ahead you'd make out a handful of figures scuffling and sliding from side to side of the road, sticks held low to the ground, as a late-night journey back from a roller disco north of the river was turned into a casual hockey match.

Again, you might be walking down Oxford Street – a favourite route for roller-skating scene makers – when some cool cat would roll effortlessly by on the road, one hand tucked deliberately casually into a trouser pocket, the other equally loosely gripping a rear rail on the truck or bus by which he was being towed. A faint grin would be the only evidence of the self-satisfaction the rollerskater was experiencing from the fury surging in the hearts of so many passers-by at the sight of such blatantly heretical contempt for British highway traditions.

In fact, rollerskating as practised by the soul-heads who lapped up the possibilities for sharp-styled mobility preferred by the advanced rollerskate designs that emerged in the late 1970s is a positive expression of youthful Black Pride. After all, you literally stand tall on a pair of rollerskates.

Those who have been impressed by roller-skaters travelling backwards at high speeds down steep hills will perhaps be disappointed to learn that the reason they ride down slopes in such a manner is because it is the only safe way to do so. Raymond Stevens remembers when, as a novice skater, he first went down the long hill

'I just went straight out like a flag.'

to Arsenal tube station. Suddenly he was moving at a ridiculous rate, close to losing control: 'At the top of the escalator, I tried to go into a powerskid – I thought if I didn't make it I might end up on the tracks. As I was doing it, I grabbed hold of a railing – I just went straight out like a flag, at a 90 degree angle.'

Mind you, a particularly macho mate of the Stevens brothers called Carter would probably have had few qualms about continuing at such a headlong tilt right down into the very heart of the station itself; Carter's favourite trick is ski-stopping as near as he possibly can to the edge of the platform and, therefore, the electrified line itself. Carter's even been known to jump, wearing his skates, onto the road from the platforms of moving buses.

As with any similar sub-culture, the rollerskating scene is dotted with near-mythological heroes. These legendary figures are adepts at such advanced skating abilities as barrelrolls or tea-pots – skating on your haunches with one leg thrust out in front – or spread-eagles, a skating high art for which Electric Ballroom regular Andrew Gray, an expert at two-wheeled spreadeagles, is famous.

However, is rollerskating simply a passing fad, the last couple of years' equivalent of the hula-hoop or of streaking? The consensus view among rollerskaters seems to be that a sizeable number of rollerskating faint-hearts will fall by the wayside before next summer. It is also agreed, though, that many have invested so much time and money in skating that they won't feel they can afford to regard it as just another seasonal whim. The dedicated and the mean will still be skating next summer.

'People assume because they don't see the glitter and the satin shorts and the headphones that rollerskating is dying out,' says Alpine Sports' Rory Farrell. 'But it's entering a new phase, it's going to be maturing over the next few months.

'It's not just in London either. Turnover is so fast at our Glasgow shop that it's just had to acquire its own warehouse – they need so much stock that it's no longer cost effective to make deliveries to them in our own vans.'

Whatever, it seems that rollerskating is certainly going to stay with us for a while. After all, to many of Britain's young blacks it means a lot more than just a set of wheels at the end of their feet. ●

1982

We are at war (sshh, it's not official). Our much-loved Iron Lady and Argentina's brass-buttoned General boosted their flagging approval ratings by throwing a little bash down the South Atlantic. Meanwhile, Poland's Solidarity started twitching the iron curtain, Jacko gave us a Thriller and ET phoned home, but we were all busy signing on.

February
Laker Airways collapses with debts totalling nearly £300m.

March
Barbican Arts Centre opened.

April
Argentina invades the Falkland Islands. Britain declares an exclusion zone of 220 miles around Falklands.

May
General Belgrano is sunk by British submarine outside of exclusion zone. 368 are killed.

British soldiers recapture Goose Green and Port Darwin.

Argentinian footballer Diego Maradona is transferred from Boca Juniors to Barcelona in Spain for a record £5m.

June
Official surrender of Argentina.

Princess Diana gives birth to Prince William.

July
Italy beats West Germany in Madrid to win the World Cup.

August
Unemployment reaches 3,292,702: one in seven of the 'working' population.

Princess Grace of Monaco killed in car crash.

October
Lindy Chamberlain jailed for life in Australia for the murder of her baby, who she claims was eaten by a dingo.

Poland's Solidarity is banned.

November
Channel 4 begins broadcasting.

Soviet leader Leonid Brezhnev dies and is succeeded two days later by hardliner Yuri Andropov.

Blade Runner
The script has some superb scenes, but something has gone wrong with the dramatic structure. The android villains are neither menacing nor sympathetic.

E.T. The Extra-Terrestrial
Speilberg takes the story and invests it with exactly the same kind of fierce magic that pushed Disney's masterpieces into a central place in 20th C. popular culture.

Tootsie
The tone is quick-witted and appealing, with some of the smartest dialogue this side of Billy Wilder. Tootsie is one of the most polished situation comedies in recent years.

Marvin Gaye - Midnight Love (CBS)
The music is mostly fast, crisp dance come-ons with intricate, humanising layers of vocals and sharp horns to offset the electronic funk base.

Michael Jackson - Thriller (Epic)
Michael's songs, while strong on grooves, lyrically suggest mounting paranoia. Is he truly becoming the Howard Hughes of black pop?

Kid Creole & The Coconuts - Tropical Gangsters (Ze/Island)
It's their most populist statement to date, so expect to hear it on every box and through every open window this summer. Don't resist.

The gnarled, ravaged figure of Ian 'Lemmy' Kilminster is a familiar sight on the streets of West London. Resembling the archetypal villainous Portobello Road dealer in his grime encrusted jeans, battered black leather jacket, cowboy boots and matted shoulder-length hair, he looks the kind of person who'd sell you a lump of black rubber shoe heel as hash. Pausing only in the odd hostelry to partake of a refreshing glass of Special Brew or to engage in conversation with a member of the female sex, this ageing Knight of Notting Hill displays an odd restlessness that seems to demand he incessantly wander London's highways and by-ways.

This strange love of movement is almost certainly due to the vast quantities of amphetamine surging through Lemmy's system – and the personal Holy Grail for which he appears to be questing is most likely to be a large bag of sulphate. But the hedonistic Lemmy is no ordinary 36-year-old drunken speedfreak: he is also the singer and bassist of Motorhead, the power trio whose last LP, the appositely titled live recording 'No Sleep Til Hammersmith',

Heavy Metal Hero
The Life And Times Of Motörhead's Lemmy

Lemmy interviewed in T.O 600 by **Chris Salewicz**

went straight into the album charts at number one last summer – just like a Police album. Lemmy, in fact, is the Anti-Sting.

In both Britain and Europe the Motorhead team of Lemmy, guitarist Fast Eddie Clarke and drummer Phil(thy Animal) Taylor are the undisputed gods of Heavy Metal music – though Lemmy himself prefers, more correctly perhaps, to classify them as A Beat Group.

That there is a strong macho element in Heavy Metal cannot be denied. However, in the best of the music there is always that deflating comic quality – a constant, deliberate teetering on the verge of self parody – that is part of all great rock 'n' roll. Such conscious humour is certainly in Motorhead, both in Lemmy's lyrics and in the attitude with which all three members go about their chosen vocation: their Born To Lose diehard rock 'n' roll outlaw image is as vital to the group's importance and popularity as the hippie lifestyle that supposedly characterised the music of Hawkwind, the previous group with whom Lemmy sang and played bass.

At 36 Lemmy's bedraggled figure may seem an unlikely candidate for the post of number one heavy metal hero, a position he has held for two years, since Motorhead's popularity reached its current peak. However, his very age is one of his main qualifications: for though he is as old, if not older than the fathers of many – he even has a 15-year-old son himself – Lemmy most certainly is not A Grown-Up. In many ways he is the ultimate bad schoolboy, William Brown two and a half decades after Richmal Crompton stopped writing about him: he smells because he rarely washes and doesn't clean his teeth; he lives on Marmite sandwiches and chips; he stays up all night most nights and does everything he's told not to; and he is often in trouble with teacher, in the form of the police.

He is, in fact, the leader of the gang, with a godfather-like attitude towards its members. 'If you can give the kids a good time then that's what it's for,' Lemmy will insist in the guttural Northern growl that still lingers about his catarrh-encrusted vocal chords. 'Forget Art and all that – it's bullshit. If you can send that shiver down a kid's back, then that's what it's all about.

'That's what rock 'n' roll was for in the first place and, as far as I'm concerned, that's what it's still all about. I'm trying to give them that feeling I felt the first time I heard "All Shook Up" or "Good Golly Miss Molly". I just want to send that shiver up their back because it's the best thing I ever felt. It's even better than screwing.'

Lemmy is the personification of the rock 'n' roll romantic.

He was born in Stoke-on-Trent – itself often considered the very heart of Heavy Metal land – at the end of 1945. He was, accordingly, a teenager when the media first discovered the word to describe the new breed of youth whose lives were dominated by a popular culture that consisted of Elvis Presley dressed as a cowboy, John Wayne movies at the cinema, and nightly TV westerns: 'We're all sashaying into town looking for the fastest gun, aren't we? Of course it's the cowboy thing: I used to come home from the caff to see "Maverick". It's been all cop shows on TV since the mid-1970s: I hope that doesn't mean that all the kids today are going to grow up to be security guards.'

Like Maverick, Lemmy is a

compulsive gambling man. Indeed, his dedicated ingestion of all manner of intoxicants suggests he is gambling as much with his life as his cash. On a Saturday evening spent with him roaming the pubs of West London— an expedition which ends predictably in his long time roost of the Princess Alexandra in Portobello Road – a good portion of my time is spent propping up one-armed bandits as Lemmy rapidly loses all the money he has on him.

Lemmy is also a Space Invaders addict, the machines in his favourite haunts inevitably bearing his initials as top scorer. In fact, Lemmy's love of such machines is logical: speed freaks often need something to do with their hands to keep them occupied. The other two group members groan as they recount tales of Lemmy at the end of week-long speed binges coming home and taking apart household appliances in order to 'mend' them.

As we sit on stools at the bar of a nondescript Irish pub in Shepherds Bush, Lemmy recalls the wild Swinging Sixties parties the Rockin' Vicars would throw at their house outside Manchester.

Following his spell with the Vicars, Lemmy moved to London and found himself sharing a flat with Noel Redding, who subsequently became bassist with the Jimi Hendrix Experience. As a result of this acquaintance-ship, he became a roadie on one of the last great package tours of the 1960s, a legendary affair that included Hendrix, Pink Floyd, the Move, the Nice, and Amen Corner. Lemmy's chief memories of those dates are of the handfuls of Owsley's White Lightning acid he was dropping.

At the beginning of the 1970s, Lemmy was living in a squat in Gloucester Road. One night a girl who also lived there turned up with a certain Dik Mik whom she had met in a pub down the road. Dik Mik was the electronics wizard in Hawkwind. He had left the group, intending to go to India, 'but he only got as far as Gloucester Road, which from Ladbroke Grove is the wrong direction anyway.'

Lemmy and Dik Mik discovered 'a mutual interest in how long the human body can be made to jump about without stopping.' When Dik Mik duly rejoined Hawkwind, he immediately set about campaigning to get Lemmy into the group as guitarist (the band's original guitar player had taken a cereal-bowl full of acid at the Isle of Wight festival, gone for a walk and never come back). The addition of Lemmy was discouraged by the other members, however, on the grounds that he was a friend of Dik Mik's.

'Finally, in August of '71 Hawkwind were playing a free open-air gig in Powis Square – how apt! – and I'd gone along for the ride. The bass-player hadn't turned up, but his bass had. The cry went up, "Who

►

plays bass?" "I do," I said, never having played a bass in my entire life. So they hung a Rickenbacker on me and Dave Brock said, "Ah, you must be Lemmy: this is in E.'"

In fact, it was precisely because Lemmy did play the bass like a rhythm guitar that he fulfilled a vital function in Hawkwind's sound. He sang on the group's million-selling early 1970s hit, 'Silver Machine', and became established as its most charismatic member.

By 1974, however, the differences between the various band members had become too great.

A number of individuals in Hawkwind's large line-up – at various times there were up to nine musicians in the group – began to feel uncomfortable about Lemmy's conspicuous consumption. After he'd been awake on speed for ten days at a stretch, his deranged babbling became impossible for some of them to bear – he'd even been known to crash out from exhaustion and sleep with his eyes open, a sight his fellow musicians found somewhat disconcerting.

In May of 1975, a stash of white powder was uncovered on Lemmy's person by Canadian customs officials as Hawkwind were crossing the

The stench of his feet is legendary

US/Canada border. The nabbed substance was not cocaine, however, but amphetamine sulphate, at that time luckily categorised under Canadian law as a Pure Food. Lemmy was released from custody scot-free. But by the time he caught up with Hawkwind for their next date in Toronto, he discovered a group decision

had been taken that he should be sacked.

And so Motorhead came into being, with the current line-up being finalised in March of 1976.

Notwithstanding Lemmy's initial, astutely self-publicising claims that the group would be so horrible 'that when we move in next door the grass on your lawn will die,' it was near-impossible for Motorhead to secure live work. United Artists refused to release the LP they had paid for the band to record – it was later put out to achieve considerable sales after the group had left UA and were enjoying the first fruits of their success on the Bronze label.

Ultimately, it was because of this rejection by the rock establishment that the group rose on a groundswell of grassroots support to their current status.

Sitting on the sofa of the Battersea house the group are currently renting, Phil(thy Animal) wriggles uncomfortably as a result of a recent operation for the removal of anal warts. 'You hear a lot of good things and a lot of bad things about Lemmy,' he says, 'and most of then, are true, He is a cunt, he is a bastard, he does knock other people's chicks off. But he's also incredibly funny; every time you go out with him it's a memorable experience. He taught me a lot – knocked a lot of naivety out of me.

'Yet he does borrow money off people, and rip them off,' he continues, reminding me that the origin of Lemmy's name lay in his incessant requests to 'Lemme a fiver'. 'In the days when he used to sell speed, you could guarantee if he sold you a gram it was probably half a grain. He's very good at making you feel guilty. He's definitely got the gift of the gab on

his side.'

Such glib verbal dexterity is representative of Lemmy The Street Animal: it's applicable mainly as a means of survival, and occasionally self indulgence – a definitive loner, Lemmy can be prone to manipulative self-justification.

However, paradoxically, he makes no attempt to justify his disapproval of drug-taking in others much younger than himself. In fact, Lemmy adopts an extremely moral stance on the manner in which large sections of British youth now self destruct all too willingly on stimulants; his utter loathing of heroin consumption is rooted in a girlfriend having OD'd on the drug and died in his arms.

'I think the drug thing has got totally out of control,' he says shaking his head disbelievingly as we wander through the streets of west Kensington on our way to another pub. 'People are trying everything far too early. They have access to a lot of drugs which are going to bend their minds completely out of shape before they've even got an identity to fall back on if anything gets nasty.

'I was 21 before I took any sort of drug or even really started drinking. But by then my personality was pretty well formed.

'Mind you, I don't advise anyone to take speed. I'm definitely an exception. I've seen no end of people go straight over the top on it. They do it for about a month and then they're gone. Locked up.'

Much as he hates politicians, Lemmy reserves an even greater hatred for organised religion – even if he is a firm believer in reincarnation. This abhorrence of the Church has understandable roots which make his surname of Kilminster seem seem darkly

bizarre: when he was three months old his father, an RAF pastor, left his mother – something for which he was subsequently defrocked.

When his mother eventually remarried some ten years later, Lemmy found himself living with his step-father, step-brother and step-sister on a farm several hundred feet up a Welsh mountain some miles away from Anglesey. By then he was already a confirmed loner, and most of of his spare time was passed in wandering the mountainside fields or in reading. He is still a voracious reader, and spends many of the long hours and days he is awake immersed in books, reading and rereading them with a speedfreak's compulsion.

There is practised hatred in the utter contempt he expresses for his father: 'He's the most grovelling piece of scum on this earth. A weasel of a man with glasses and a bald spot, about a foot shorter than I am.

'I've met him twice: the last time he said, "What can I do to repay the damage I've done to you? I feel so guilty." I said, "Give me a grand then just forget it – I need some new equipment."'

Instead, Lemmy's father offered to get him a job as a trainee sales rep. 'The reason he said that was because he himself was a brilliant pianist, but he didn't have the nerve to try for it on a professional level Lemmy adds, revealing also the harsh irony that his musical abilities probably are inherited from a man he despises.

But there had been another, equally cataclysmic experience in Lemmy's life. At the age of four, he had ten teeth removed without any anaesthetic: 'It was 1950 and for some reason there was no anaesthetic you could give to a kid that young. So what they used to do was take you to the infirmary, hold you down and rip your teeth out.'

This must have had a very formative effect.

'It had a very informative effect… You never believed there was that much pain, did you? Well, there you are!'

His association with London's Hell's Angels chapter resulted in Lemmy's disgusting dental state deteriorating still further. Essentially, he has

'The biggest buzz I've ever got is screwing'

only good to say of the Angels, who obviously recognise kindred spirit in the stringent ethical code by which Lemmy lives his anarchic life: 'It's a very rigidly organised set-up. Sure, it can be negative in some ways, but it can be very positive in others.

'They're good lads. I get on with all of them. As an alternative to disco-dancing you must admit it has its merits.'

However, there was one Angel with whom Lemmy didn't get on, a certain Big Vinnie from the New York chapter who was over in England for a few weeks at the end of 1975, a year that certainly marked the nadir of Lemmy's fortunes.

At the time, he was living with a couple of London Angels in a squat in Stadium Street near Worlds End. From incorrect information he had received, Big Vinnie inferred that Lemmy had badly maligned the integrity of the English club. Big Vinnie went round to the Stadium Street squat. Unfortunately, none of Lemmy's squatmates were present to serve as character witnesses, and the net result of this Angelic visitation was that the Motorhead leader received

'a fuckin' awful beating – he knocked me all around my room for about three-quarters of an hour.' One of Lemmy's bottom front teeth was knocked straight out; another was cracked by the root.

Lemmy didn't fight back: he is basically a pacifist. But it is because the cracked bottom tooth is finally working itself free of his mouth that he has decided he must take up the £5,000 estimate that a Harley Street dentist gave him for a complete set of new teeth. And Lemmy is apparently quite serious when he claims to be considering having his front replacement fangs in stainless steel.

In fact, Lemmy has a reputation for being financially tight, though he can also be very generous and will, for example, insist that most of the group's money be ploughed back into lavish stage shows and financially disastrous touring.

'All the money goes back into the pockets of the people from whom it was stolen originally,' he says, giving a dry chuckle as he loses another fiver's worth of change in a Nudge machine.

'The biggest buzz I've ever got,' he adds, 'is not with a roll of banknotes or a pocket calculator. The biggest buzz I've ever got is screwing and going onstage, in varying orders, depending on what I'm going to do next.

'You can always make money. You can dig graves or paint skyscrapers. But you can't always make music and please people.

'It's not really based on love, more a sort of contemptuous admiration,' he laughs again.

Late the next afternoon, I visit Lemmy at the Motorhead Battersea residence.

Whereas the other two members of the group have relatively sumptuous rooms filled with colour TVs, VCRs and kingsize beds, Lemmy's basement front room contains little but a battered mattress.

In the upstairs bathroom I notice a bidet, and wonder if it is the reason the group chose to rent the place; the stench of Lemmy's feet is legendary. Fast Eddie claims its cause lies within the chaos wreaked on Lemmy's metabolism by his vast speed and alcohol intake: by some arcane combined law of biology and physics, Eddie claims, it sinks down through his whole body until it reaches his feet, where it is excreted in the form of sweat.

Indeed, though Lemmy doubtless unwittingly consumes a large amount of vitamin C powder nasally, it is still surprising that the years and years of excess have not completely ruined his health. 'I think I have the constitution of an old iron tank,' he admits. 'The occasional bout of flu might lay me up for a couple of days, but I always believe that if you lie down germs have more chance of attacking you: keep moving and it confuses them.

'Mind you,' he confesses, 'I'm probably nearer to being alcoholic than I've ever been. I sometimes wake up in the morning and lean across to the bedside table and pour myself a vodka and orange. Of course, from that point on, the day does tend to slope downwards a bit...'

And as the rain pours down into the basement outside he leans across and pours us both giant tumblers of vodka and orange.

'You know, you can't talk about me as being anything out of the ordinary,' he decides after a few seconds' reflection, 'because all I am is persistent. I think I'm persistence personi-

fied – I wouldn't give them the satisfaction of giving up.

'I'm on the street. I like the street and I live there. I love grotty old boozers with blousy old women and beautiful girls. It may sound just like an attempt to be really poetic, but it works. Because if I once believed I was above all that now and I didn't want to go there anymore and found it a bit difficult talking to the old friends and felt that I'd better stick around where it's a bit cleaner and a bit nicer and a bit less of a hustle and a bit easier… well, I don't care how easy it is as long as I don't get hit too much or kicked in the mouth, because my teeth are really in a bad way.

'I'm a slag and I'm 36 years old… I've always been a slag – it's a long time to be a slag, 36 years… But I've had a great time doing it, and I can recommend it to anyone if they can stand the pace... I've been lucky, I can. I'm 36 years old, and I've realised almost every ambition I've ever had.' But, Lemmy, don't you think it's time you grew out of all this now?

'It's time I grew back into it, more like. It's time everyone grew back into it.

'If people listened to more rock 'n' roll and less Margaret Thatcher or Michael Foot or Roy Jenkins… In fact, if the bits of their brains that wanted to be politicians could be exterminated, and the bit that would've liked rock 'n' roll somehow could be artificially enlarged, wouldn't it be more fun to be around them?

'I don't see how you can get sick of enjoying yourself – I haven't so far, and I'm damn sure I resent anyone who tells me I should.

'Just have a good time and don't hurt anyone else doing it' ●

1982

Lemmy

Jam session

from 'Heroes and junkies' in T.O 603, by **Pete Townshend**

The Jam are a great rock band in the old tradition. They have listened to the music that created the roots of the great bands of the 1960s and kept clear of the evolutionary demise of those groups. Weller's love of early Who stuff has never, for example, been affected by my own disenchantment with the 1960s.

Weller's writing is so full of pent-up energy. He rarely uses controlled metre and never bothers to rhyme a line. The words of his songs laid out in naked print appear art school self conscious but are actually far from it. Weller is a slasher. He cuts and mauls. He drags you from complacency. He buttonholes you so you feel an urge to defend yourself, then you are opened up and weakened. Then the attack touches your heart and you realise that the purpose of the Jam is Revolution. Both Weller and Buckler sing with the vengence of men cornered. Their threat is that if you approach you will feel the full force of their anger: stay at a distance and you will hear their venomous condemnation of your cowardice. There is a fully fledged taunt in 'Eton Rifles'. A totally sweeping derision in 'In The Street Today'. In both cases there is also the thread of merciless self-analysis; so typically British. The Jam are so fucking British. Paul Weller is a Hero, a British Hero.

Jam fans are thinkers and musical reactionists, who tend to reject all politicians pretty much out of hand. They choose to dress in the rather sober style of the mid-1960s rather than adopt the peacock styles of the avant garde and they listen very earnestly to the words written by their spokesman. There is no bitterness in Weller's writing that isn't fully shared by his fans. God is not in his heaven, and if he is then he isn't doing a very good job of handling the population explosion, political corruption and global disintegration.

The Jam represent an antidote to London's volatile Art-Rock scene. The Jam appeal to British youth on a national level. They encourage kids to stop worrying about the global wobble and start dealing with affairs at home.

While the 'lucky' few snort cocaine, kids in Toxteth and Brixton are struggling to scrape together the money to buy glue. Yet both groups of people are fighting boredom and futility in their own way. Weller quite consciously tries to represent a kind of being that manages to be aloof and proud in the midst of ennui. He is also very aware that he is under a microscope. I have never come across any other artist or writer so afraid of appearing hypocritical; he is genuinely concerned that anyone who identifies with his feelings should not be let down.

Weller takes on the whole of British society without a blink. The Jam are a small army dedicated to the awakening of a sleeping nation. It sounds a bit pretentious to say this, but I think it's true, The Jam actually do give a shit about the downtrodden soul bereft of spirit and direction, whether they are on the dole or living on handouts from decaying country estates.

Their stance is not a show of 'stiff-upper-lip', it's an almost spiritual surrender to the inevitable. On their first album they ask: 'Where is the Great Empire?' The question is asked with cynicism but it's asked nonetheless. It's almost as though they are saying: 'Your badly run society fucks us up but it hasn't made the leader's lives any better either.' The Jam are a new kind of blues band. ●

Pete Townshend

from 'True confessions' in T.O 615, by **Chris Salewicz**

He recalls ruefully his own springtime in the 1960s, a supposedly vibrant, liberated time whose increasingly visible human and spiritual wreckage indicates much of the cause of the current sickness and confusion: 'Was it not similar to a load of ostriches going around with their heads in the sand? Or a load of people doing what I did last year, walking around drunk, having a lot of fun, supposedly enjoying life when really everything was terrible behind the scenes, or at least on the route to going wrong?'

The absolute nadir of 1960s youth culture is for Pete Townshend represented by the Woodstock festival, at which the Who played. 'All those hippies wandering about thinking the world was going to be different from that day. As a cynical English arsehole I walked through it all and felt like spitting on the lot of them, and shaking them and trying to make them realise that nothing had changed and nothing was going to change. Not only that, what they thought was an alternative society was basically a field full of deep mud laced with LSD. If that was the world they wanted to live in, then fuck the lot of them. That self-deception lasted a long time.'

A decade of heresy

Germaine Greer interviewed in T.O 598, by **Penny Allen**

Anyone who has a stereotyped image of a feminist (and who hasn't?) might find 'Art of The Ad', Germaine Greer's upcoming 'South Bank Show', unsettling. Ignoring the wider implications of advertising itself, turning a blind eye to the manufacturers and consumers, and a partially sighted one to the depiction of women in adverts, Germaine has selected a handful out of 200 ads to praise for their good taste and dinky storylines. Surely this is not proper behaviour for a feminist? But Greer's strength is unpredictability and originality. She may have helped inspire a mass movement but she was never to be spotted slouching anonymously among the crowds at women's conferences. She is an independent, a risk taker. 'The Female Eunuch', published in 1970, had no guaranteed readership but its anger, energy, rebelliousness and joy caught the mood and fanned a spark into a blaze.

Orthodox feminism is not a view of the world generally promoted by the media. Though Greer says, 'I am just an intellectual, profoundly irrelevant,' she is more than that. She is a performer, unapologetically provocative and bold – and that is why the media loves her. She has the knack of making men as a species seem naturally smaller than women. Unlike so many feminists who now speak only to women about women, Germaine still has lots to say to and about men. And men, who are so

Orthodox feminism is not a view of the world generally promoted by the media.

rarely publicly described by women, have a thirst to hear her. What does she think of rape sentencing, they ask.

'It's ridiculous to call it rape,' she says. 'That girl hitchhiker was slashed across the face with a razor. It is Grievous Bodily Harm and should be treated as such. Dicks don't hurt; razors do. I'd rather be raped than have my nose cut off. Wouldn't you?' She turns to me for support. I give it, recalling that in an article on rape a few years back she mentioned that the Nazis cut off their victims' noses after raping them. 'Rape is not about sex. In group rapes most of the kids don't even have a hard-on. They do it because their mates are.' She has removed her fur coat. She is no longer posturing but sincere and angry.

Greer has always been a more convincing writer than broadcaster. There is a hint in her appearance of the Shirley Williams stance – 'I defy you to comment on my looks when I am trying to make a serious point.' But it is hard to believe that both this and her impassioned plea for us to show the quality advertisers 'that we now know the difference and care' are not just posturing.

'My father sold advertising space,' she explains as we walk to a café for tea. 'I used to tell him we were making a living from selling lies. He didn't answer. When the "South Bank Show" approached me, I think they expected me to make a pious denunciation of advertising. But advertising is a necessary part of our culture and it might as well be good. That does not mean I am not opposed to a free market economy. But advertising is by no means the principal culprit. The change I want is so total it is not to be achieved by simply replacing state capitalism with state monopoly. Television advertising is often much better than television programmes. Advertisements are much more aware of the fine arts than documentary or drama are. I hope my programme will make people watch television in a more critical way.'

Ms Greer has never been hot on revolutionary theory. Her notorious personal plan for a radical lifestyle outlined in the 'The Female Eunuch' was to bring up children in an Italian farmhouse with other women, children and, occasionally, men. The plan was inspired by the desire to destroy the family as we know it yet the house and garden were to be 'worked by a local family who lived in the house'.

Her concern has always been to inspire and celebrate individual creativity. So how can someone who worships creativity bear to see it tamed and harnessed to selling consumer items? 'Everything,' she says, 'is an advertisement.' So there is no distinction between advertising and art? No, she says. Advertising is art and 'fine art is the advertisement of the ruling class.'

We agree that to order another pot of tea would be unnecessarily consumerist. Germaine goes to get the pot topped up. Suddenly she snorts in the direction of an Andy Warhol poster – a picture of a man's behind entitled 'Torsos'. 'Torsos indeed! More like bums!'

'What's that advertising?' I ask.

'Homosexuality. And Andy Warhol.' The man who made his name selling soup advertisements as art perfectly illustrates her point. And he is also the man once violently attacked by a feminist as a symbol of the male art elite. Germaine agrees the ruling class is male. 'Women,' she says, 'have never really belonged to that class. They have belonged to a primitive society of their own.'

A 30-second television commercial may cost, the programme informs us, 'a great deal more' than a 30-minute programme and £100,000 is mentioned as the cost of shooting an advertisement. Television commercials are clearly the preserve of the ruling class. And, to judge from the composition of her interviewees, a male preserve. 'We had to stretch,' Germaine admits, 'to get our one woman in.' Commercials, at least the ones chosen

> ## 'Though I have been accused of it, I have never been starry-eyed.'

for this programme, advertise the values of male supremacy. Germaine has selected two car ads: one for Fiat renowned for their slogan, 'If this car were a lady she'd have her bottom pinched' and its classic riposte, 'If this lady were a car she'd run you down'; and the other for Renault who once advertised a car as The Seductress and have now commissioned an ad with the brief 'to make a connection between the beauty of the car and the beauty of women'.

The women in the advertisement, explains its creator, 'are stylish rather than sexy. I am making sure people who look at my film know they are not real situations.' If the women were sexy, they might at least have some humanity. As it is, they are veiled and elegant, a chorus line of anonymity and, like the car, vehicles of fantasy, objects to enhance a man's status.

Germaine Greer's study of women painters, 'The Obstacle Race', was published in 1979. In it she succinctly demonstrated how women, even if they managed to break out of the role of muse and subject to the artist and create their own art, were still criticised as Things of Beauty themselves. So, in a week in which the theorem Car = Woman = Male Possession reached its logical conclusion in the virtual acquittal of the attacker of a hitchhiker, it was disturbing to see such an ad praised by a feminist. That same week I also saw the logical extension of the fad for drivers' and passengers' names on car windscreens: ME... IT. And the It in question was still meekly sitting there.

Doesn't the stereotyping of women bother Ms Greer?

'I don't go along with this post-feminist piety,' she says. 'It is useless for me as a feminist to say advertisements should do my job for me. I don't expect them to show men washing up. I don't like the piety involved in pretending things have changed when they haven't. Why show a man in

---

Falklands

from 'All the news that wasn't fit to print' in T.O 613, by **Paul Charman**

Task Force journalists, unwanted by the military from Day One and constantly harrassed by MoD censors – both on board ship and back at Whitehall – are saving their best stories for their letters home. *Time Out* – by kind permission of relatives and friends – publishes exclusive uncensored extracts.

A journalist aboard one of the Royal Navy's aircraft carriers writes to his wife:

April 11: 'You may think that the reports being filed are pretty colourless. This is because they are being censored by a Ministry of Defence censor (press officer).

'You're assigned one particular spot for action stations which sounds at any time of day or night, and believe me, you daren't linger because the compartments are closed with watertight doors within minutes. The worst part is having to wear anti-flash hoods, made of asbestos, and similar gloves, which are pretty hot and sticky, and we've also got gas masks.

'If there is action it won't be too good because my action station is right next to the main magazine where an the explosives and missiles are stored, so I won't be unduly worried about the mortgage.

'However, I believe that there will, within the next few days, be a deal made with the Argentines, and we shall turn around at Ascension. Otherwise the future looks uncertain as we will have to remain off the Falklands for some considerable time. I don't really think that this will happen... Filing is becoming a bit difficult as we only have access to overnight signals, meaning we have to file in advance of each day. It's by no means the best situation, and we might have to go in to complete silence as we near the Falklands.

'There's a great deal of rumour around the ship – it really is a complete floating community and one of these rumours says we will be kept down in the Falklands until June. There is nevertheless a great deal of opinion that a diplomatic solution is the best way, but this is not shared by the fighter pilots who have been training up.

'Of course they haven't seen action; I think there's only a few of us who have, and I don't relish that sort of thing much.' ●

an apron with a dry-up towel? I am aimed at destroying the apron and the dry-up towel, not encouraging men to do it.'

But surely the woman in an apron is as much a fantasy as the Renault chorus line of women in veils?

Germaine's response could have been her father's: 'I don't think it's fair to make people live without a colour television and a car. They want these things because they desire them, not because they have been wickedly persuaded to have them.' She pauses. 'Everything has a cash nexus in our society. If a thing doesn't have a cash nexus it doesn't exist. Cash is our blood. We may dream of a cashless economy, but I've lived in a few and they dream of joining ours.'

So does she object to any advertising? Yes, she objects to ads that use chimpanzees because 'it's unfair to chimps.' She objects to advertising directed at children 'because children are obviously much more vulnerable and advertisements incite desire.' And she objects to advertising in the Third World, where 'we try to impose our lifestyle and values, which are totally materialistic, on people who don't have the same values. All traditional societies are under pressure from the vitality of ours. People outside consumerist societies are more dignified. However illiterate they are, they are more poetic and their response to experience is much more complex.'

This curiously paternalistic attitude is familiar from 'The Female Eunuch.' But such gentlemanly behaviour towards the 'innocent' seems paradoxical from one who has displayed on behalf of her sex little more than contempt for the chivalry that has kept it subservient. Does Greer suffer from romanticism?

'Like all revolutionaries, I am nostalgic for a golden age that might never have existed. I would prefer a society not built on money but I don't mean to say that traditional societies are paradise. The wastage is enormous; there is huge human suffering. Though I have been accused of it, I have never been starry-eyed.' ●

Sergio Leone

from 'A fistful of spaghetti' in 620, by **Christopher Frayling**

'When they tell me that I am the father of the Spaghetti Western, I have to say, "How many sons of bitches do you think I've spawned...?"'

Sergio Leone bellows with laughter, grabs a fistful of cashew nuts, and drags on his Havana cigar. He's in London to discuss his new film 'Once upon a Time in America' and he wants to talk about my book 'Spaghetti Westerns'.

'The newspaper critics have always accused me of trying to copy the American Western. But that's not the point at all. There's a culture behind me which I can't just wish away. We live and breathe Roman Catholicism, even if we don't believe it all. So perhaps this comes through in my films, as you say in your book. I also have my own things to say, when I make a Western. At the time I was making "A Fistful of Dollars", I really felt like William Shakespeare. Why? Because Shakespeare wrote the best Italian romances without ever having been to Italy – far better than the Italians. Apart from the fact that a few people claim that Shakespeare was an Italian... but that's another story.'

"1982"

"I'm flying high and couldn't be more confident about the future."
Freddie Laker. Three days later, Laker Airways collapsed

"New Orleans lost 14 games in a row when freebasing became a popular pastime in the NFL. Players snorted coke in the locker room before games and again at half-time, and stayed up all hours of the night roaming the streets to get more stuff. I know. I was one of them."
Don Reese, NFL footballer

"The British are coming!"
David Puttnam after winning the Oscar for Chariots of Fire

"The British won't fight."
General Galtieri offers his view of the Falklands conflict

"STICK IT UP YOUR JUNTA!"
The *Sun* offer theirs

"We did not tell a lie – but we did not tell the whole truth."
Sir Frank Cooper on the Falklands invasion

"GOTCHA!"
Sun headline after the sinking of the Belgrano

"We had to do what we had to do. Great Britain is great again."
Margaret Thatcher

"For the past few months she has been charging around like some bargain-basement Boadicea."
Denis Healey on Thatcher

"The battle for women's rights has largely been won."
Margaret Thatcher

"God is punishing me for being gay."
A patient in a New York hospital with what comes to be known as AIDS

"I don't think we lost control. We never had it in the first place."
San Franciscan policeman after the celebrations that followed the 49ers Superbowl victory

"Pennies do not come from heaven. They have to be earned here on earth."
Margaret Thatcher clears up a misunderstanding

1982

Sergio Leone

Fast frames, slow draw

William Burroughs interviewed in T.O 631, by **Duncan Fallowell**

It is a very hot day. 'Did you read this? A professor at Gainesville, Florida, murdered by three gay boys. They had a smother party. *The head of the 41-year-old bachelor was wrapped in canvas, with sheets, a pillow, and a bag of ice tied over his face so there was no chance he could breathe.* Dumb jerks! I hate criminals, they're stupid. One of the three, a very good-looking boy, he's going to get his arse fucked off in prison, then beaten up, then fucked, then beaten –'

'Excuse me.' Wayne, the plumber, props himself in the doorway in paint-spattered denim. 'Will that be all, Bill?'

'I guess so, Wayne,' says Burroughs, twitching wildly about the mouth. 'Are you going out to John's? I've got to go there and fetch my .45 automatic.'

'No, I'm going to take a shower and get back to you guys and talk about getting this place secure before you go to England, get some locks.'

'Yeah, some big ones.'

William Burroughs – junkie, subvert, cat-lover, America's greatest living writer – is moving house. He's been here three days but the hot water doesn't work. The flat in New York, which was the shower and locker room floor of a converted YMCA building with

latrines intact, has been turned over to a friend. Burroughs then moved to a stone farmhouse a few miles outside Lawrence – 'Very convenient for shooting, I blasted my sculptures there, shotguns blasting sheets of plywood which produces very innaresting splitting. Then I sign 'em.'

Now into a tiny one-floor, weatherboard house on the edge of town. Last night he was woken up by a possum eating the cat's food on the back porch: 'I may have to shoot it with my air rifle. Did you know that in the old days air guns had to be pumped up by an assistant before they could be used? I say, Carruthers, some ruffians are approaching – where is my pump boy?'

'Have you met your neighbours?'

Burroughs convulses violently – is it laughter or a cry for help? 'Not really,' he says, jabbing an electric cattle prod in the air. 'I spoke to the woman next door over the fence. I asked her if there'd been any burglars round here. And she said no. And I said good, let's keep it that way, I'm getting some real locks, anyone could pick these little things with a fucking paperclip – I haven't seen her since then.'

He speaks in a slow drawl which is at first incomprehensible but which reveals very elegant characteristics when you tune in. It comes out of a long lugubrious mask of a face, criss-crossed round the eyes like a clown in a fundamental expression of infinite disappointment. He grew up in St Louis. He and Judy Garland are the only people to have put it on the map. The country here is very similar – it's almost coming home after long absences in Central and South America, North Africa and Europe. 'But I've never been further east than Athens – I was married first time in the American consulate in Athens.'

What about father? 'He was very distant. He knew about my addictions – his brother was a morphine addict. It was one of the few things that ran in the family About the homosexual stuff – sex in any shape or form embarrassed him acutely,' and Burroughs starts furiously to polish the table with a dirty rag.

'Contrary to a rumour put out by Kerouac, I was never rich. My parents gave me an allowance of $200 a month. I couldn't have written my books without it. All this about millions from the Burroughs Adding Machine is nonsense. It never came my way. Now half my income comes from these public readings. You don't just pick up any old thing and start reading it. I rehearse, usually I concentrate on the comedy like where the captain of the sinking ship gets up in women's clothes and rushes into the first lifeboat. You mustn't go on too long. At that poetry festival out on the beach near Rome – this 81-year-old poet got sand thrown at him by 10,000 people and well, I said, that's not going to happen to me and we did three minutes.'

Burroughs is happy to be out of New York. 'It isn't true that I spent my time going to parties with Andy Warhol. I hate parties, I hardly know Mick Jagger, I don't know those pop people – well, I know Chris Stein and Blondie – they visited me out here and we had a very pleasant afternoon shooting guns and fooling around – he's into guns and knives and stuff.'

But why Lawrence of all places? 'My assistant James Grauerholz lives here, I have a doc-

tor here, someone to look after the cat when I'm gone, very little crime – although James had some things stolen out of his car the other day, some tear gas cartridges and the like. And I hear the Indian college down the road can be dangerous. I must look into that. They have a bad reaction to alcohol.'

You didn't think of moving to California?'

'Hell no, everything is wrong with California. They have the most ridiculous gun and weapon laws in the country.' He is twitching up against one of the walls at the moment, then slowly zigzags across to an ancient air-conditioning device in the middle of a bare wall and turns it on, almost drowning out the conversation. 'It's a misde-

In 1951 Burroughs accidentally killed his wife. But it didn't put him off.

meanour to carry a gun but a felony if you carry a knife and you have to go on a course before you can carry a tear gas gun, which is ridiculous.'

In 1951 Burroughs accidentally killed his second wife with a gun in Mexico City, but it didn't put him off. 'It isn't a question of the gun,' he says, piling sugar into a cup of tea, 'it's a question of carelessness.' They were looning around playing William Tell with a glass on her head and he missed. 'We were together about five years, she was very intuitive, one of the more intelligent people I've known.'

'Well, not that intuitive – how is your son by the way?'

'He's dead. He was 35, he had cirrhosis of the liver and had a liver transplant and lived about five years with it. After a transplant the anti-rejection drugs they give you have very bad side effects. It makes people self-righteous. You are dealing with the whole immunity mechanism – if you reduce the body's ability to reject, you get a paranoid reaction. The person feels himself vulnerable, will react with self-righteousness or terrible rigidity of character.'

'His book about amphetamines was very popular.'

'I hate speed, I hate anything that makes me chew the carpet.' He walks round the room in ever-decreasing circles and eventually reaches a point of introspection.

'…this is a really English cup of tea.'

'Glad you like it. Well, I lived in London for ten years, behind Fortnum and Mason. I was never more glad to get out of a town in my entire life.'

'Did you use the Piccadilly boys?'

'Certainly. I notice circumcision is on the wane in Europe. Is this wise? Most American boys are still circumcised. Virtually all the uncircumcised boys in Lawrence High School are Roman Catholics. I'm circumcised myself. Then everything got so expensive in London and went

downhill fast. When I got to New York everything was a helluva lot cheaper. In New York there's this violence problem which I rather like. It kinda tones you up to sort through your weapons before you go out visiting friends. I carry the lot there – except a gun of course.'

'Guns are illegal in New York?'

'Good God, are they ever! And they always were,' he adds, picking a crust of dubious origin off his green nylon trousers. His body is painfully thin and agitated. 'A mandatory jail sentence of a year if you're caught with one. My dear, incarceration in an overcrowded zoo, in New York they're absolute... animals. I don't like prison and always get myself bailed out.'

There is no furniture in the house yet. The only American home with no TV. 'There is an old black and white out the back, I occasionally flick it on, it might produce some synchronicity for me.' A few magazines lie on the bare wooden floor – Gun, Guns & Arms, Warriors, Science Digest. And a few paperbacks, 'The Mask of Apollo', 'The Silva Mind Control Method'. 'I read a lot of horror,' he says, opening yet another packet of Player's Navy Cut – he chain smokes them and they've stained his teeth a canary yellow. 'I especially like medical horror.' After Harvard, Burroughs studied medicine for a year at Vienna. 'Have you read "Brain"? It's by the guy that wrote "Coma". Titles are very important. I like those ones in the Reader's Digest – "Thank God For My Heart Attack". And "My Eyes Have A Cold Nose" by some writer who went blind,' he collapses into choked laughter like a muzzled hyena.

'They don't give you nightmares?'

'There's a recurring one where I'm attacked by a giant centipede, sometimes a cross between a centipede and a scorpion. In the typical centipede nightmare it suddenly rushes me and fastens onto my leg. Then I wake up kicking the bedclothes off – ugh! Centipedes – I have to kill 'em.'

'Have you worked out this phobia's origin?'

'It's not a phobia! I can't think of anybody who would have a good word to say for centipedes. Generally I don't have nightmares but dreams. I keep a notepad handy. Maybe 40 per cent of my material comes from dreams – sets and characters. There is no line between the dream world and the actual world – of course if you get to the point where you find it difficult to cross the road then you should see a doctor. That's a fly! I can't stand a fly that alights anywhere near me – wait a minute.'

'Do you have a spray?'

'Sure I got sprays but this isn't a spray case.' Burroughs shuffles and hops out to the kitchen, scratching his thin gray arms like two broken pencils, and returns grinning with a large orange plastic swat.

'Where was I?' he says, sitting down again, swat erect. 'Yes, from the evolutionary point of view dreams are very important. Man is an artefact designed for space conditions – and I don't mean going up in as it were an aqualung which is all we've done so far. The evolution from land to space is equivalent to the evolution from water onto land and will involve biologic alterations quite as drastic.' Thwack!!

'From where you are sitting, what do you think it'll be like?'

The gristle-green, needlepoint eyes scan the environment with a measure of fatigue tinged with disgust. 'I'm sitting in time. The transition to space is the escape from time, immortality even – because my definition of time is that which runs out. You got water creatures looking up at the land – can they conceive what it's like to live up there? Hardly. The fear of failing means nothing to a fish.' Thwack!!! 'The key to what space is like is to be found in dreams.'

'Interesting.'

'Gore Vidal said he never heard me say anything interesting. But I have no interest in being interesting. It's what you say to those writers who send you unreadable stuff – very innaresting".'

'Have you ever heard Gore Vidal say anything interesting?'

'He was asked if he believed in corporal punishment and he said yes, between consenting adults. Dreams are a biological necessity. If animals are deprived of REM sleep they eventually die. This is the clue. One of the the big barriers to getting into space is weight. But we have at hand the model of a much lighter body, the dream or astral body which is almost, probably not completely, weightless. Of course very little research is going in this direction at the present time. You see, man is designed for a purpose. This is the flaw in all utopias – no purpose. How dull it is to rust unburnished, not to shine in use. You know where that's from? "Ulysses".'

'I didn't know Joyce –'

'By Tennyson.' Thwack! ... 'Got him.'

'You're pretty expert at this now.'

'Oh, my dear, I've been in training ever since I was old enough to pick up a fly swatter. Would you care for a drink? I can only drink Coca Cola and vodka but I always drink them simultaneously.'

'Are you alone with the dream theory?'

'Maybe Governor Jerry Brown will be up there. He believes the future of the race is in space. That's the only thing I agree with him on – he's a gun controller person.'

'You're pretty gun crazy.'

'I don't think crazy is quite the word. I just like a gun. Some people like butterflies, some people like... knife collections are very popular you know. I don't like centipedes and I don't like flies. Flies are dangerous, they can lay eggs in your ear, then the larvae hatch out and eat into the brain and kill people. If you are ever in the South Seas and see a tiny blue octopus on the beach, don't pick it up – they bite and every-

one who's been bitten by the blue ring octopus has been dead within the hour. There's no antidote. I'm going to do a book of things you mustn't do, if it's 16 below zero and there's a slight wind, say 30mph, that makes it the equivalent of 60 below. Several people. round here in the winter popped out to collect their mail and a little wind came up and they were killed like that.' But now the temperature is in the 80s in the heart of America and the crickets whirr like a Lancashire mill. Burroughs is slowly dancing along the perimeter of his property, waving the long pink-handled cattle prod. 'It packs 5,000 volts. Enough to make the trespasser apologise. It works best if there's a little water around – perhaps you should spit on 'em first.'

'Are you healthy? I mean physically.'

'I am. I used to do judo but this bit of jumping up six feet into the air and kicking your opponent in the back of the head, my arthritis gets in the way. I go walking round Lawrence.'

Burroughs is happy to be out of New York. 'It isn't true that I spent my time going to parties with Andy Warhol.'

Burroughs is really beginning to participate in local life. He has written a song for the local punk group which includes the District Attorney's 17-year-old son. It goes 'Old Mrs Sloane, chewing the bone, chewing the bone, of her dead child...'

OK, let's lighten the approach. 'Have you ever wanted to commit suicide?' Sorry, but the atmosphere's contagious, Burroughs is a real charmer.

'Never! I can't see that suicide is bettering one's position at all.'

'That means...'

'Sure, I never doubted the possibility of an afterlife, nor the existence of gods –'

'But surely an afterlife presupposes –'

'Hold on – wait a minute – I'm quoting from— "The Place of Dead Roads", my new book. Kevin never doubted the possibility of an afterlife, nor the existence of gods. He thought that immortality was the only goal worth striving for and he knew it was not something you just automatically get from believing some rubbish or other like Christianity or Islam. It was something you had to work and fight for like everything else in this life or another. I do rather feel that Christianity is the most virulent spiritual poison ever administered to a disaster-prone planet. It is parasitic, fastens onto people, and the essence of evil is parasitism.'

'So what is your function as a writer?'

'The function of all art,' he shouts from the other side of the garden crawling round a tree on all fours after the cat, 'and by that I include creative scientific thought, is to make people

aware of what they know and know that they know, 'cos you can't tell anybody anything they don't know already on some level.'

'Bill, do you cry very easily?'

'Not easily – but I do. I cried not so long ago.'

He continues to talk in this fashion for hours, then on through the next day, always responding unexpectedly to the commonplace idea. In the limited space available it has seemed best to convey something of what the conversation with William Burroughs is like, rather than give it all the critic-as-artist treatment. Also, when you fly 5,000 miles just for the weekend, you can't waste time making smart alec remarks about why Kansas is a dry state, why Lawrence is called the Paris of the Plains, what a boy has to do to get his vice round here, what actually is 'the Plains sensibility' – 'Good God! These aren't the Plains, they're 300 miles west of here, the most goddam desolate country I've ever seen, not a tree in any direction – the Plains sensibility must be whatever lunacy causes people to carry on living there.'

James Grauerholz arrives in goldrimmed spectacles to take us to dinner. Burroughs produces a big shopping bag and starts filling it with weaponry. His books are full of weird sexual events and strange worlds: in them the prophet of doom collides with the master of high camp in bursts of outrageous comedy, gruesome mixes and probes. 'You must get a lot of people just turning up on the doorstep making horrible suggestions.'

'It's not something I encourage, but I'm prepared,' he says, clanking the shopping bag. 'Some people call it paranoia. Was Pasolini paranoid? That kid murdered him from behind with a plank with nails sticking out of it. The nails penetrated his skull. I have heard from various people who should know that this kid was hired by a right-wing group.'

It's getting dark outside. Magnificent sheets of shocking pink lightning light up patches of the sky and tornadoes are forecast over the next few days. 'Look at this. Beautiful eh? My favourite, my Charter Arms 2" Barrel Undercover .38 Special – I'd like to see some dumb fucker with a bag of ice get past that! And look at this,' he says, pulling on a jacket of blue-based tartan in some plastic material. 'I got it from the Thrift Shop. They're the Salvation Army places. Eight dollars – pretty good eh? I enjoy a bargain.' And donning the famously unalluring spectacles, plonking a pork pie hat on his head, he selects a stout walking stick, picks up the shopping bag, and moves eagerly into the outside world. ●

1983

Facing off the hi-gloss, Crayola multicolourings of Boy George, Madonna and Wham!, we slapped on the pancake, charcoaled our eyes-lips-hair and invented goth. We worried about the bomb (as well as jobs), thanks to the plucky Greenham wimmin and hackers playing Missile Command on Pentagon computers. The Hitler diaries weren't, but Maggie was… again! If you could afford a car, it was clamped.

January
Police shoot Stephen Ward in London after he is mistaken for escaped prisoner David Martin.

February
Racehorse Shergar is kidnapped and a £2m ransom demanded.

Alliance wins by-election in Bermondsey after homophobic campaign is conducted against Labour candidate Peter Tatchell.

March
Writer Arthur Koestler and wife are found dead in London after carrying out a suicide pact.

May
Hitler 'diaries' first published in *Stern*, then in *Sunday Times*, are exposed as a fake.

June
Conservatives win second term in office with 144 seat majority, against Michael Foot's Labour Party.

August
Opposition leader Benigno Aquino assassinated in Philippines.

September
Soviet Union 'accidentally' shoots down South Korean Boeing 747 in Soviet airspace.

October
Neil Kinnock elected as new leader of Labour Party.

USA invades Grenada.

November
Dennis Nilsen is sentenced to 25 years in jail after being convicted of six murders.

Cruise missiles arrive at Greenham Common.

December
Harrods bomb injures 90 people and kills six.

The Big Chill
The script avoids the pitfalls of solemnity or sentimentality which threaten such a scenario; instead it's perceptive, affectionate and often very funny.

This Is Spinal Tap
Reiner's brilliantly inventive script and smart visuals avoid all the obvious pitfalls. One of the funniest films about the music business.

Trading Places
It's a great vehicle for Eddie Murphy, who fulfils with outrageous confidence all he promised in 48 Hrs.

Wham! - Fantastic (Innervision)
Michael seems to have lost that acute lyrical edge which made 'Wham Rap' and 'Young Guns' essential purchases.

Culture Club - Colour By Numbers (Virgin)
That the rest of this LP is just as wonderful as the two stunning singles should leave little doubt they are the most important British band since the Beatles. Culture Club have produced a classic album and quite worth all the fuss.

New Order - Power, Corruption And Lies (Factory)
Although still miles off of being larf-a-minute stuff, this is a fine, powerful and well-balanced contem-porary pop record. An album of vigorous, engaged, heroic and quite beautiful music. Its importance towers over their seeming fatalism.

Svengali steps out

Into a pop climate of ethnic exotica comes another glossy product: Malcolm McLaren's new LP 'Duck Rock'. It continues the themes begun by McLaren's last two releases: the huge hit 'Buffalo Gals', which, by introducing scratching to the UK, threw down a musical gauntlet which has not since been taken up, and 'Soweto', which, although backed up by the best promotional film of the year, failed to do as well. But McLaren isn't deterred: after years of other projects – from Teddy fashion to the New York Dolls, the Sex Pistols, Adam and the Ants, Bow Wow Wow and Boy George – the project is finally himself.

McLaren is best known as some demented Dickensian figure – the Fagin, dressed in leather, who foisted those foul-mouthed yobs the Sex Pistols on the nation while making them speak his lines. Or as the child-molesting puppet manipulator of Bow Wow Wow. But this trouble-making is only the logical, although to some surprising, outcome of his background in '60s radical politics. What is interesting is not that he has retained those politics – a personal mixture of various anarchic, libertarian and situationist elements – but that he has been prepared, like few of his generation, to adapt them to the times. For a generation that is schooled on ideas of 'authenticity', this is scandalous: and McLaren has never been afraid to home in on the first pop law – whatever society's greatest fear is at the time, mash it up, ram it down people's throats and turn it into trash and, in one of his best slogans, Cash from Chaos.

Perhaps his greatest problem since the Sex Pistols has been that of diminuendo: that was such a powerful coup that every-

thing else must have seemed stale, for a while. The Sex Pistols, and the clothes for 'Sex' and 'Seditionaries' which his then-partner Vivienne Westwood designed, were a perfect, practical expression of his own contradictions: in Fred Vermorel's words, 'the vision of an artist, the heart of an anarchist, and the imagination of the spiv'. But later projects like the Ronnie Biggs Sex Pistols, Bow Wow Wow and mid-period Adam and the Ants seemed half-cocked: good ideas ruined by bad timing or application, with the spiv taking over at the expense of anything else. He's recently solved that problem by simply doing it himself. His latest incarnation as travelling pop star and pied piper is both surprising – very few pop managers ever cross that divide – and effective as it seems to have given him a new lease of life.

Each fresh McLaren project comes with a separate theory, and this one is no exception: one central idea on 'Duck Rock' is that by presenting music from around the world in a fresh context, you can stimulate interest in travel and tourism, and thus the exchange of information. It is this belief in content, however much you may disagree with the nuts and bolts of it, that differentiates McLaren from other pop hustlers; behind every apparently cynical stroke has been a firm belief in the idea of getting information across: content in culture. And thus, while many will criticise the new record as another example of cultural imperialism – just more exotica soma for 'Top Of The Pops', I don't find this approach very interesting. What I do, though, is that McLaren, in a profoundly tawdry and amusing medium, isn't concerned with authenticity, but with research, polemic and effect.

This combination of huckster and visionary – McLaren is one of the few pop theorists (although he'd hate that term) or social motivators to celebrate the tension between art and commerce in pop – has already succeeded in tapping the nation's subconscious several times. And one key to the way McLaren works comes from the way he talks: he is concerned with the links between things, both temporal and physical – like the links between Dickens and the Sex Pistols – and those links are expressed in bursts of talk that appear like flights of fancy but, when examined, have a logic of their own. People have always worried about being conned by McLaren, but that's only because he's so blatant: it's never worried me, and I'm quite content to hear the latest stories he has to tell.

'The Zulus liked the idea of the Sex Pistols not being able to play but being able to steal all the money off the record companies. They used to roll up in fits of laughter. Each Zulu guy, when I saw him the following day, would go, "Eh man, tell my friend the story of the Sex Pistol, man." That's all they wanted to know, they thought it was just hilarious. They love the joke of someone being conned. They loved the trickery of it all. And when I finally recorded that song "Punk It Up", that was the only song they were ultimately interested in. It was their favourite, because it was something that was bringing in a whole new story to their lifestyle.'

McLaren's latest batch of stories on 'Duck Rock' is, initially, a bewildering mixture of Zulu, rap and Cuban music among others. I wondered whether a common thread had emerged.

'I think it made sense in that everything could be termed anti-Christian. I thought there was a common parallel between the square-dance caller in Tennessee who is still living out his European culture and the rapper in the South Bronx and the Zulu chief who banged the drum, who called the announcement of the dance, and the Peruvian Indians in the hills of Lima. I found that in all cases it was all about things that go bump in the night. It's all about your magic. Dance suddenly becoming pantomiming of animals, and all the things that are very magical about this. I felt that related very much to, I suppose, the excitement felt when somebody saw Elvis doing his dance on stage in the '50s. We live in a Christian society concerned with order: rock 'n' roll was always concerned with disorder. Punk rock promoted blatantly the word chaos. Cash from Chaos.'

He chuckles at a successful slogan, and throws a question back: 'Do you think that pop music is very pagan in its outlook?'

I mumble some agreement, and this sets him off on another story: 'Do you know, the origin of the square-dance is traced back to ancient Rome? It's just about the old round dance and someone finding a partner for the night, in a society where marriage wasn't the ordained thing. And I was interested when I talked to this old cattle man in Tennessee. He said to me: "You know what? I used to come into town and we'd go into a barn dance, sometimes called a beehive." And I thought right, it reminds me of the old song: "I'm a king bee, baby, buzzing round your heart." He said, "The local parson would always try to ban the barn dance or the square-dance because in a square-dance you get to dance with everybody, and he was afraid we'd get his daughter. And we used to hold these girls real tight and when the caller said 'Swing 'em up', we would swing 'em up and they would squeal and we would pull 'em up and brush our bodies against theirs. We used to love the square-dance," he said, "and the fiddle player would play this real high note and the local parson and the church would call the fiddle the instrument of Satan." And I thought that well, there was an absolute common parallel with those

irate fathers in those clichéd movies of rock 'n' roll in the '50s when they called the electric guitar the same thing. But it was all about the same thing: they disliked the pagan attitude. They disliked the disorder. They disliked the idea that you could exchange partners. It was the classlessness of the square-dance that was the problem.

'Well, that was the beginning for me of this album. When I found that out, I thought for the first time I'd found something that I could actually say was European in concept. It wasn't borrowing from some black tradition. It was European, and had as much rock 'n' roll in it as anything else I was likely to hear later on in my travels.'

Pop's other master plunderer, David Bowie, has also turned to ethnocentricity for inspiration, albeit in a different spirit. The 'Let's Dance' and 'Soweto' videos caught brilliantly this latest pop fancy. I ask Malcolm about what many – perhaps more prosaic – souls see as a lack of constancy, a dilettantism which is part of the way he makes pop music work for him. Is this ability to change his ideas fast necessary to stay alive in this medium?

'Depends on how strong your original idea is. I don't know whether you have to change your ideas very fast. It appears that's what David Bowie does. I think to me, I'm a punk rocker – it's just evolution really.'

In a different way, and not with as much power, McLaren's latest record subverts the current pop norm. It exhibits a wit, in the collating and editing, and joy, in the performance, which exists rarely in today's calculatedly fizzy pop. But he's up to his old tricks: taking the conditions of the moment – in using the producer (Trevor Horn) as superstar archetype, and in packaging this glossily exotic product in a typically fizzy sleeve – like he did with Bow Wow Wow or, more forcefully, with the Sex Pistols. If it's difficult to conceive of anything that he could do that would match that power, it's remarkable that he's still functioning, and still on the ball.

'Well, I think if you didn't accept those conditions the game would be up, you see. And you have a problem in convincing people. I suppose that's all. You're playing the game.'

Does he agree to bide by the rules?

'To a certain extent, yes. But the rules are very tiny. At the end of the day they aren't the things that govern your ideals or your ideas. They should only be used, I suppose, as a selling point. They give you the framework on which to operate. They also make it – oh, I suppose that if you live in a room with finely coloured walls, you wish everything around it to relate to it. If it doesn't relate to it, you're not too sure whether you should have had your walls finely coloured or not. If you're a hobo on the road, you don't need those highly coloured walls and you probably don't need the gloss. You just need the content.'

> 'The Zulus liked the idea of the Sex Pistols not being able to play but being able to steal all the money off the record companies.'

1983

Malcolm McLaren

I protest that he could hardly be called a hobo, but this sets off another train of thought.

'No, but I dream of being one, and I think that spirit is probably the most noble and the most modern spirit going. There's not really much point you see, in staying in one place. There's a great deal of point in moving from place to place. I got very inspired by an American, Harry K Mcintyre, who was better known as Haywire Mac. He was probably the first Communist in the United States of America. He was the inventor of the American folk tradition; he wrote the song 'Big Candy Mountain', which is nothing to do with the Burl Ives version, but was far more vehement and far more to do with the idea of the hobo, you see. It's a bit like Fagin and the Artful Dodger, and he had to invent a song in which those young kids would be solicited or seduced by the Lemonade Spring and the Big Rock Candy Mountain.'

Dickens has been a recurring theme in McLaren's iconography, from the view out of Glitterbest's grimy windows to the poster he concocted for the Sex Pistols' Christmas Day appearance in 1977. Why was he so fascinating?

'Because I think myself that his most famous character Fagin, and the Artful Dodger was such a potent classless and powerful political force in England at the time that it gave great freedom to a lot of people; the thought that to go out of your way to grab hold of what you need by hustling was something totally opposite to all the class structure. It was a very subversive idea and Fagin and the Artful Dodger became such colourful characters because people loved them. Dickens therefore summed up everybody's noble dreams in England.'

And didn't he cut into the nation's consciousness in a way which most modern novelists don't?

'Well, weren't the Sex Pistols great storytellers? They gave journalism such a new lease of life because for the first time they could write pages and pages about these storytellers. The music was irrelevant. They gave these terrific ideas every five minutes – you know, 'God Save The Queen', 'Anarchy in the UK'.'

He snaps his fingers. 'I think the biggest problem with the Sex Pistols is that people tried to make you believe they were working class. The fact of the matter was that they were fairly classless. The Sex Pistols became to my mind more important when they had the money, because money is the critique, you see. It was really then that I noticed a vast change with the Sex Pistols: when they were able to have money behind them, they were really important and the more money we could house behind us, the more we flaunted that idea.'

It's now six years, a generation, and a cultural and political world away from punk rock. Does McLaren have a perspective?

'I think it had an enormous influence internationally. I think punk rock is more alive in Harlem, in some respects, than it is in Bracknell. I think you'll find in probably a year from now, punk rock will be something that has been seized upon by the black culture in Harlem and the South Bronx and you'll be hearing a lot of punk-rock-type lyrics with all the funk and the New York rhythms. I think there's a song actually coming out in two weeks' time called 'Punk Rap Attack'. They loved the word. They'd heard of the Sex Pistols. It was extraordinary: I was in the Bronx, and I saw a boy and a girl hand in hand, two black kids from the South Bronx, and they were walking down the street and they were both wearing 'Never Mind the Bollocks' T-shirts.'

He laughs. 'Great! That's what's extraordinary. In 1982. That's what's amazing. Now they may not have even known of the Sex Pistols. They liked the look of it. They homed in on it. They saw something. They liked the words.'

In November 1977, a record shop owner was prosecuted for displaying that slogan on record sleeves in his window; now it's on T-shirts throughout the world. An interesting contra-

Kathy Acker

from 'Hot Type' in T.O.689, by
Steve Grant

'My cunt used to be a men's toilet' – 'Blood and Guts in High School'

Born of a comfortable upper middle-class East Coast WASP family, and harbouring literary aspirations from an early age, at 20 Kathy Acker transformed into a wild sicko punk, running with street gangs, ingesting bucketfuls of speed, turning to crime, fucking anything in sight, working in sex joints and porn shops, sharing jail cells with junkies and prostitutes, and becoming so inured to casual abortion that next time she might go DIY with a twisted clothes hanger. Disowned by her family for marrying a Jew and subsequently driven by the expense of a debilitating illness to working behind the counter in sex shops and simulating sex in live shows, the utilisation of a simple typewriter turned the outsider Acker into a powerful aggressive commentator – a feminist Hubert Selby for the '80s – whose notoriety in the book world and beyond is spreading fast.

While her work is not autobiography, Acker is writing from personal experience and observation. She writes as a free agent, bounced out of the middle class as part of the society of punk marginals, numb, apolitical, disenfranchised, listless, futureless – The No Wave. She doesn't mean to offend people or, as has happened at public readings, make them puke. 'It just seems that that's what happens. I'm not terribly aware of that when I write.' When writing, she never considers how a work will affect her audience and says it just comes out, almost like automatic diction. The whole English idea of pop culture is one McLaren still has fondness for since, despite seeing London from abroad as a 'muddy hole', he thinks it can still run counter to the existing power structures.

'We never seem to know where our roots are, what our origins are, who the hell we are. We tend to borrow from hither and thither, we have a tradition of being the greatest pirates, the greatest plunderers, the best presenters of other people's ideas. If that's the case, then we can use that notion. Then they should engineer the situation of allowing kids to go out and explore other cultures internationally and bring them back to England, to give a whole new feeling towards tourism in England, and pursuing the idea of England being a cultural centre.

'There's a whole new class building up of unemployed that really genuinely desire to get out and experiment and create a new lifestyle for themselves. But in order to do that, they've got to travel. They have to pick up and exchange views. I think if England had that potential, that would create jobs in the worldwide industry of tourism. But that idea isn't allowed to generate itself simply because people aren't allowed to feel that international about anything.

'We are always told what is right and, I suppose, basically, the suppressed part of our class structure has always agreed that the King and Country and the ruling class know best. After all, they are gentlemen, and that tradition is something that people have prospered by in this country and suppressed the whole idea of a classless viewpoint in our culture. I think that people like Adam Ant and Boy George and all those other characters that have cropped up from time to time in pop culture are important because basically, they are classless. And that's why the

'I think punk rock is more alive in Harlem, in some respects, than it is in Bracknell.'

whole notion of style and dress and fashion is exciting in England: because it demonstrates a classlessness.'

Isn't this new record a much better realisation of what he was trying to do with Bow Wow Wow and even Adam?

'Well, in those cases I was acting as a mercenary and I suppose that after a while, a mercenary has to finish. Being a mercenary in the form of a manager was...'

Boring?

'Not even just boring, it centred me in a position which I didn't want any part of. I preferred, in the end, to opt out. So I took it upon myself to be controlled by some record company to make this album because it was a way of resolving what my thoughts were in the past few years. My own inspiration, I couldn't secure that in Boy George or Bow Wow Wow. Maybe I never had the confidence at the time. Maybe I never saw myself as a presenter in terms of being the artist.'

In the end, it's only logical: instead of telling Johnny Rotten what to say or, more accurately, guiding him in what to say, say it yourself and cut out the middleman. If a Svengali is to be honest, he'll do it himself. But very few do.

So what's next, Malcolm?

'I've just discovered Opera. And I'm working on something with Puccini. I'd like to use that and put it in the context of the street and maybe even introduce it to the South Bronx.'

I'll leave *that* to your imagination.

In the end, McLaren is obsessed by England in the widest sense – in its politics, class structure, outward appearance, and in its own peculiar product, pop culture; his latest guise as world traveller is fulfilling yet another quintessentially English dream, but the perspective it has given him still makes him one of our most acute and exciting commentators. ●

writing. Her audiences might like to know it also has a similar effect on her.

'I've had what I guess you'd call nervous breakdowns after I've finished a book. It not only frightens me, I have immense physical reactions to it. And sometimes I do things that just *appal* me.' Which might make her sound diabolical and mischevious, but she adds, 'I never want to cause anyone real harm. I'm absolutely appalled at violence. But you know, a word isn't a knife. The effect I want on an audience is shock, yes. There's a great deal of anger in me that comes out. I don't censor outside me or inside me. And I *have* had a hard life. Just being a female is rough.'

Acker didn't really find her own society until the Pistols stepped off the Jumbo at JFK. It was only with the eruption of the American punk scene that Acker was able to publish. 'I never felt before that I could talk with anyone. I felt

like a freak. That was the first time I didn't have to explain everything all the time.

'There was this very big split in the art world, between the formalist artists, people like Laurie (Anderson), and the people who were sick of this nice little culture, which was basically for the upper middle classes and rich people. They were living on the street, not actually on the street, but lives like mine, very very, poverty stricken lives.

'That was a wonderful period, where everyone was broke and on the edge, not knowing what they're doing but for the first time they could talk to people, and they were together. Watching a whole bunch of people working together in this city is just *lovely*.'

But this golden time was not to last; 'I think with Sid Vicious's death everyone saw how absolutely nihilistic it was, except for those people who became junkies and just *went out*. It was

too death-oriented, and just wasn't interesting any more. Now there's an attempt at what you might call positivism, to not be miserable all the time, and there are a lot of other reasons, like everyone's getting into rap, the graffiti artists and that stuff. But it's very hard.'

It may seem at times that Acker's voice is that of the little rich girl who got lost while out walking with daddy in the big city, but with her real dad missing and step-pop not answering the doorbell any more, it's not unreasonable for her to want to find love and affection.

'Like, yeah,' she laughs, 'that's the problem with my life! What can I say? I DON'T WANT THE WORLD TO BE HORRIBLE! It just keeps on being horrible. Despite it all, she still thinks she'll find love in the ruins. 'I *hope* so. If one can't, and if I can't, it's gonna be a fast death. For me and everyone else.' ●

Wit and Walters

Julie Walters interviewed in T.O.658, by **Steve Grant**

J ulie Walters is what you might call a Fun Person. She laughs loudly, talks at breakneck speed in a half-croaky Midlands accent, commits the occasional conversational faux pas which outrages her Irish mum and reveals that she doesn't much like Joe Allen's restaurant because of past trouble with the waiters. 'Mind you, I've usually been pissed at the time.'

At 33 she is, along with Maureen Lipman and her cohort, friend and collaborator Victoria Wood, one of the funniest and most gifted actresses on the British scene. Though she's stuck with the tag of 'comedy, regional, working-class character acting', her recent performance as Chrissie's wife Angie in Alan Bleasdale's 'Boys From the Blackstuff' was a notable extension of her repertoire of hard-pressed, hilarious Northern roles. And when Lewis Gilbert's film of 'Educating Rita' opens in May, she is likely to find herself a star (even though she nearly lost the part to Dolly Parton). Whatever one's reservations about the picture, there are none about her own performance, opposite Michael Caine, as a working-class Liverpudlian housewife who ditches babies and husband for an adult education in order to 'sing a better song'.

Walters comes from Smethwick near Birmingham and a working-class background, although such a tag drives her mother into paroxysms of rage. She went to the local grammar school but was such a terror that by the end of the Lower Sixth she had been 'asked to leave'. She took an office job, 'watching the traffic going up and down the Hadley Road, thinking this was freedom', and then studied to be a nurse. But after 18 months of nursing she decided that acting had bitten her for real.

'I didn't come from a theatrical family at all but I started off by imitating people on the telly when I was very young. I've always been a very speedy person, a bit extrovert. My dad, who was in the building trade, gave me his support, but my mum was a bit more hostile – I think she was worried about me giving up the security of nursing, you see. I didn't know what to do anyway, didn't know who to apply to. I wrote to the British Drama League for Christ's sake, and they wrote back and said, "Well, my dear, you should think about going to university". I only had four bloody O-levels.' Finally, she joined her sociology student boyfriend at Manchester Polytechnic and, after a three-

Alan Bleasdale

from 'Yosser's Election' in T.O 667, by **Steve Grant**

Ten thirty am, Shaftesbury Avenue. A 19 bus pauses as it rounds Piccadilly Circus. Two ten-year-olds leap off into the traffic. 'Gizza job!' they shout, giggling their way down Windmill Street. A wall in a street in Hackney: 'Yosser is Innocent'; another in a Yorkshire mining village: 'Yosser turned this job down'. Anfield: Liverpool v Watford. Graeme Souness connects with a cross from Dalglish and whacks it high over the bar and into the Kop End. 'I can do that, I can do that,' the massed ranks exclaim.

Everybody has their own 'Boys From The Blackstuff' story. Alan Bleasdale knows most of them. They came to him over the phone; anguished, laced with booze in the early hours, as his wife and kids slept in their Liverpool home. They came through the post, sometimes splattered with tears, notes written by the light of the telly screen as the unfolding tale of Yosser, Chrissie, Dixie, George and Leggo halted, and the

images passed on to other things. Letters from Cornwall, from the Midlands, from Scotland, the South; surprisingly few from his native city where the man can be reached over a pint in the pub, or in the phone book – until, that is, the much-harassed and heart-torn AB became a reluctant member of the ex-directory club.

One Liverpool phone call did particularly cheer him. It came from a middle-class woman, a psychiatrist in a big local hospital whose main function was to treat people suffering from disorders brought about by the effects of long-term unemployment. During the transmission of 'Blackstuff', said the woman, the morale of her patients had changed dramatically. No longer did they think it was all their fault. 'I had been in tears reading letters from people who were in tears when they wrote to me. But that call meant more to me than ten BAFTA awards,' says Bleasdale.

year stint, she was lucky enough, in her own words, to go straight to the Liverpool Everyman in its greatest days under director Alan Dossor. There she met Willie Russell and Alan Bleasdale and first worked professionally with Bernard 'Yosser' Hill and Anthony Sher, Matthew 'Game For A Laugh' Kelly and Peter Postlethwaite. The audition was taken by actor Jonathan Pryce who was standing in as director at the time.

When I asked her about her early life at the theatre she replied: 'I can't remember much. I was always pissed.' Her initiation consisted of a lot of pub tours around Liverpool which in retrospect were the happiest days of her career. 'We used to play these really rough places and you didn't know what was gonna happen because they were pubs and they didn't always want the show in the first place. One night we were doing Alan Bleasdale's 'Scully' and one bloke in the audience tried to kill Peter Postlethwaite who was playing the title part. He'd been in Walton jail for about ten years and he'd been listening to it on the radio every other night. He was shouting: "I've promised my mate that when I get out I'm gonna fucking kill youse..." Everybody was calming him down, being dead sympathetic. But we had a real rough lot in the company then. They could give as good as they got...'

In 1976, after playing in Mike Stott's 'Funny Peculiar' for 18 months in London, she moved there permanently – missing the North for the people but glad of the anonymity of the capital. Mind you, anonymity wasn't easy in Greek Street, Soho, where she lived for some time opposite the famous Actresses Hostel. 'God, it was murder. Every time I took the dog for a walk I got ten propositions. Everyone thought I was on the game and the ladies from the hostel used to do running commentary on my daily routine. They'd all be sitting at the window shouting to each other: "I bet she hasn't fed that dog in days."'

Her next big stepping stone was a meeting with Victoria Wood while the two were appearing in revue. 'We got on really great from the start. Victoria always makes me laugh more than anyone I know and we used to take a piss out of the director something rotten. All in good fun of course.' Wood is still her greatest and funniest fan, sending her a continual stream of Henry Root-style missives such as the one which followed 'Blackstuff': 'Dear Julie, I came in a bit late and I haven't got all the plot, but I take it that hubby was unemployed...'

Julie prefers books and a good film to a night at the theatre. She loves soul, jazz and swimming and has given up coffee because it makes her heart beat too fast. She's also passionate about the Campaign For Press Freedom, having recently taken part in an 'Open Door' programme on the ASLEF strike. She couldn't ever vote Tory but admits that her earlier sense of class bitterness has been denuded by success and time, and anyway she hates labels as much as she hates Thatcher.

With 'Educating Rita', Rita White à la Julie Walters could well be a hit in the USA – Americans in London loved the stage show. And if the film succeeds, our Julie could even be among the Oscar nominees. 'I love comedy,' she says, lighting up a Marlboro, her first of the day, 'but I hate it when it's the poor relation. Comedy is hard work – and a sense of humour is so fucking important, isn't it?' ●

"1983"

"Victorian values – those were the values when our country became great, not only internationally but at home."
Margaret Thatcher. Who else?

"The longest suicide note in history."
Gerald Kaufman MP on the Labour Party manifesto for the '83 Election

"History buffs noted the reunion at a Washington party a few weeks ago of three ex-Presidents, Carter, Ford and Nixon: See No Evil, Hear No Evil, and Evil."
Senator Bob Dole

"This right is not given us by the State. It is a right given by the Creator."
Pope John Paul II explains the Lord's view on free trade unions

"This so-called Solidarity lot aren't a trade union. They're an anti-Socialist organ who desire to see the overthrow of a Socialist state."
Arthur Scargill at the NUM conference

"I know a lot of people think I see a demonic plot, but I've reached this conclusion after a great deal of research: digital stinks. It's the emperor's new clothes."
Editor of The Absolute Sound, on CDs

"The armed struggle must go on until the last British soldier has left Ireland.
Gerry Adams MP, recently elected leader of Sinn Fein

"I think it will go down in history as one of New York's great buildings."
Trump Tower architect Der Scutt blows his own trump(et)

"This must be the first time a rat has come to the aid of a sinking ship."
Anonymous employee at the BBC on Roland Rat's addition to the ailing TV-Am roster

"Yes, I haven't had enough sex."
John Betjeman on being asked if he had any regrets in life

"Don't blame me. I didn't vote for her."
Bumper sticker after Thatcher won the election

King porn

'I've been eating pussy for 24 years, which means that even if I were not enthralled with the act of lapping the labia, the mere repetition of the experience would make me better at it. But the truth is that I'm a confirmed cunnilinguist, and I'm good at eating pussy because I genuinely enjoy it.'

Al Goldstein, pornographer, journalist, cigarist, gadget freak and editor of *Screw* (founded 1968, circ 160,000 copies weekly) is in town. He greets me in the foyer of the Dorchester Hotel, a smallish, fattish, bearded New York jogger dressed in tracksuit bottoms, sneakers and a garish, striped jumper. He is in town to organise the mooted November launch of the London equivalent to *Screw*, his New York sex information sheet-cum-satire rag, which along with his cable TV chat show 'Midnight Blue' has made him into 'a thinking millionaire'.

It's unlikely the London equivalent (which will go out under another name) will match the all-out ferocity and filthiness of its predecessor: a crude, often revolting mix of hooker ads, massage parlour reviews, porno pics and drawings, and occasionally deft but more often gross attempts at political satire. A brief glance at the headlines in the back issues will give an idea: 'The G-Spot Fraud'; 'Twat Art'; 'Feminist Sluts Who Kill For Fun'; 'Reagan's Faggot Past?' and 'Growing Up Obscene'.

Dirk Bogarde

from 'Rank Outsider' in T.O.664 May 1983, by **Richard Rayner**

Dirk Bogarde is not ageing with grace. 'I hope I never grow up,' he announces petulantly. 'Who the fuck wants to? Not me, I'll tell you that.' At 62 he is still youthful, a Peter Pan figure with a full head of (too?) black hair, a neat blue blazer, flannel trousers and a silk tie. His face is lined and pale, but his eyes are sharp and he is still unmistakeably a fine looking man. In conversation he is alert and arrogant, pouncing with pedantic glee on mistakes of grammar or diction. His manner is scrupulously polite and yet bitchy. As far as age is concerned, he's not raging against the dying of the light. He's spitting at it.

I meet him in the Connaught Hotel in Mayfair, one of his favourite haunts, a tiny fraction of England that remains about 30 years behind the times, with its decrepit lifts, hushed atmosphere and rather seedy glamour. He always stays here when he comes to London. He enjoys watching the waiters age and explains with approval how actors were once not allowed in the hotel. 'They just made too much trouble. They weren't banned, they were just sort of omitted, as some are omitted still,' he says.

Confirming the cliché that performers never forget a bad review, it transpires that he has a score to settle with *Time Out*. 'I'm very aware of your paper,' he says. 'They reviewed my last movie and said – "Who gives a shit about Dirk Bogarde?" Fair enough. They said I was old and gaunt and haggard. Criticism doesn't bother me in the least, my dear. But I'm not used to having illiterate press. I was supposed to look old, gaunt and haggard. It was a fucking part in a fucking movie. Maybe it was a bad day for the boy. I thought: well, Dirk, that's what you've got in England, so it's much better to be where you are and who you are.'

All of which is the cue for Bogarde to offer his reflections on contemporary England. And, let me tell you, it isn't good news. Dirk thinks we've gone downhill. Dirk thinks it's all a shame. Dirk thinks Things Are In A Dire State. This is the first time in a decade that he's paid an extended visit to his native land and he speaks of it with tetchy and eloquent intolerance.

Al used to stutter; he got beaten up a lot on the streets of his Williamsburg youth; he was very fat (305lbs). He couldn't get laid; he was very, very worried about the size of his 'schlong'. One thing Al always knew, however, was 'love' was lust and 'doing it' beat talking about it. 'When I was an adolescent I used to have this test. If I thought I loved a girl I would jack off. If I wanted to phone her afterwards I'd know I was in love. I never called nobody.'

'I've been eating pussy for 24 years. I'm a confirmed cunnilinguist, because I genuinely enjoy it.'

In 1968, Al founded *Screw* with a friend, $300 cash and the promise of hassles to come – eight arrests in the first year, eleven in toto and a now-famous trial in Kansas for 'sending obscene material through the post' which could have netted him a life sentence.

'My friends talked about sex in a different way than the media represented it. Words like "fellatio" and "cunnilingus" would occasionally appear, but my friends and I didn't use those words. We used words like "fuck" and "cunt" and "tits" and "ass". At that time Playboy not only didn't use that kind of language but they would airbrush pubic hair. There

was a reality out there, a reality that consisted of married men paying for sex, masturbation, homosexuality, and none of that was represented. So I started *Screw* to fit a vacuum – to reflect sexual reality.

I've democratised sex. *Screw* is the real thing. Our women have stretch marks, pimples, some of them are uglier than our readers' wives. You'll meet them on the street – you'll never meet a centrefold.'

Feminists? Al does not like feminists. He now employs two bodyguards, armed with shotguns, and receives regular death threats 'from religious nuts mainly. Feminists would kill me but they don't have the brains. My second wife was a feminist; she was a Pan Am steward who got fired for writing a feminist article in a magazine. I have feminist friends – they love it as much as anyone else.' He puffs contentedly on an Al Goldstein-inscribed Havana cigar.

Hookers? 'Okay, some of them get oppressed, the poor ones in Harlem, but the ones I know are earning up to $1,000 a day. How can you talk about exploitation? The average *Screw* hooker is a model, actress, airline stewardess, college-educated, fun to be with. They're performers, they like acting.'

Herpes? 'A minor ailment. Jesus, I know a doctor in London who says it's one case in a thousand, and it's minor,

Steve, very minor. It's not the Bubonic Plague. And if guys aren't fucking, well it's plenty more for Uncle Al.'

Goldstein is something of a leper – his own terms. 'I'm hated by everyone: the Right, the Left, Reagan, the Commies, the Ku Klux Klan, the Jewish Defence League.' The Jewish Defence League??? 'Sure, they're as bad as the Nazis. God, I hate boring people, boring journalism. At least Hitler made good speeches. I'd rather have one Adolf Hitler speech than eight Jimmy Carter speeches.'

'It's only the zealots who hate me, the blue noses, the screwballs. What's the name of your chief blue nose, Steve?' Mary Whitehouse? 'That's her. Needs a good fuck.'

Goldstein's latest visit has not been without incident. 'I tell you what, the British customs raided me again.' Cue belly laugh. 'They ripped up the magazine. If they do it again I'm gonna move here permanently. How would that affect your neighbourhood? Boy, you thought the Indians were bad, wait until a Jewish pornographer turns up. I'll probably start a cartoon strip with Margaret Thatcher and Reagan fucking. Wow!'

Al moves onto his other fave topics: cigars (he brings in re-wrapped Cuban cigars and runs a regular newsletter for addicts), electronic gadgets (another newsletter), clothes, food and death. 'We're all gonna die one day. The only thing is to have good pussy, nice things to eat and fine cigars.' ●

London: 'It's sloppy and nothing surprises me. It's dirty and I can't even read the newspaper it's so full of mistakes.' Lavatories: 'You simply dare not risk the lavatories, my dear.' Cinemas: 'How the fuck can you go? I went to see 'ET'. I was sitting next to Mr and Mrs Joe Bloggs with their sweet papers and their popcorn. They had a McDonalds. She said "I don't like the onion" so she threw it under my seat. We just don't do it that way in France. We go, not with reverence, but at least with some sense of event.'

The '60s: 'It was the menopause. The whole English world was changing. Morals, standards, everything. Young people seemed sweet and jolly. Then they got trapped in the shoals of the '70s. Up until then we were perfectly happy to be English and British. Now we're not. You have a great time in your generation. All the changes have been made for you.'

The gay scene: 'Don't know anything about it. It's obviously important for lots of young people.'

Bogarde is vain. Of course. He is cruel and arrogant. Naturally. But it is this sense of a rather vulnerable, but still intensely felt, individuality which gives him this appeal. In 1947 the now defunct *Sketch* magazine singled out four young men to watch. Two are now forgotten. One was a certain Harold Wilson, while the fourth was Bogarde. He remains, despite exile and now infrequent screen appearances, one of the most attractive, even magnetic actors of his generation. He smiles when the photographer notes he has a winning way of looking into the camera. 'Of course, darling. What do you think I've been doing all these years? But if you've got one of those wide-angled lenses with all the pores showing I'll fucking kill you.' ●

American
gothic

Stephen King interviewed in T.O.666, by **Richard Rayner**

The first thing you notice about Stephen King is his stature. He's almost as tall as the stories he tells. 'You've been talking about me haven't you? Talking about me behind my back.' He emits a paranoid whine. 'People talk about me all the time. They think I don't hear, but I do. I hear plenty. I'll take care of them later. And I'll take care of you as well. You'll all pay.' He cackles and a mock leer spreads across his features.

Now 35 and married with three kids, the world's most successful exponent of horror fiction still has an adolescent sense of humour. He sits down and whoops: 'Welcome to the Bates Motel, folks. Heh-heh-heh.' We settle down and tea arrives. King grasps a sandwich in a hamlike fist and inspects it with suspicion. 'Oh Jesus. Fishpaste. Ugh.' He throws it back on the pile and picks another. 'Oh my, you English.' He throws back his head and laughs. 'Yessir, Sticksville USA is my home. Thank God I'm a country boy.'

King lives in a quiet town in Maine, where he owns a large American gothic mansion which is guarded by high gates with wrought iron bats on top. When away from home, the role of rural hick at a loss in the big city is one he enjoys playing. And why not? For he's a man who owes his fortune, some $35 million to date, to the writing of plain fiction for, well, plain folks, the literary equivalent of a Big Mac and fries to go. 'Yeah, that's right,' he says. 'But who wants to write books which will only be read by bright academics who drive old Saabs?'

But what type of person wants to earn his living by terrifying people? King quickly deflates one theory, that writing horror is a way of working out unresolved childhood trauma. 'Nah. Isaac Asimov's wife, a psychiatrist, tried to give me that psychological stuff when I told her about seeing a friend hit by a train when I was a kid. But I don't go for it. I think people write what they like to read. Me, I've always loved horror. I read comics when I was six.' He relishes the idea of frightening people and talks about the horror writer's ultimate buzz: to scare someone to death. 'Well, it'd certainly be a shame. But part of me would be saying, "Wow, that really worked." And I think I know how it can be done… I know the scene.' He cackles and refuses to reveal it.

'Sometimes both writing and reading horror fiction is a little like knocking on wood. Or making the sign of the evil eye. Anticipate the worst and it might not happen. That kind of thing. And right now we've got plenty to worry about. A lot of people retreat into horror and fantasy because the world is such a gruesome place. But it's not so simple as that. You'll find that horror fiction works on a subtextual level and all those things are discussed. It's real tough to say what makes things popular.'

For King success came abruptly. In 1974 he was struggling to make a living. His first novel 'Carrie' had been accepted, somewhat grudgingly, for hardcover publication. And then the day after he completed his second, 'Salem's Lot', the paperback rights for 'Carrie' sold for $440,000.

'Yeah. I got a call from this guy saying you're rich. You don't have to work any more. Kinda strange. It's made a difference obviously, but I can't honestly say it's changed my life. The money is just figures on a bank balance. Someday I'd like to get the advance for a novel in one and five dollar bills and stick the whole lot in a tub and just roll around in it.'

King's 11 books have sold in excess of 40,000,000 copies and he can reckon to earn around $3.5m a book once the inevitable movie sale is taken into account. He describes the advance he took for his latest, 'Christine', as nominal. But for King 'nominal' means $1m.

Sophisticates may sneer at King but for millions he's required reading. What he's done is to take the gory gothic and transpose it to modern suburban America. He wholeheartedly embraces American popular culture and writes in a down-to-earth style which is accessible and literate without becoming literary.

At his best King is a marvellous writer by any standard. 'The Shining', a complex variation on the haunted house theme, is his scariest book, mainly because it touches most closely on his personal anxieties: alcoholism,

the possibility of failure as a writer and more important, his paranoia about the possibility of hurting his children. As he says, 'It sounds morbid and it is morbid and I'm still a prisoner of it. Each night at midnight I go in and check my kids are still breathing. The worst thing I can imagine is finding one of them dead. Actually, that's not true. The very worst thing would be to know I'd killed one of them myself.'

King says he tries harder with some books than others. 'The Shining', 'The Dead Zone' and 'The Stand' were serious efforts, 'Christine' is more of an 'entertainment' book. 'It's one of those books where I walk up to the reader, touch him on the shoulder and say, "Hey, I got this great story. Wanna hear it?"' The central character is Arnie Cunningham but the book's dominant personality is Christine, a red 1958 Plymouth Fury which Arnie buys. And which then takes over his personality (haw, haw, haw).

'Actually I was more interested in the car as a sexual object. For a lot of American kids, cars are associated with sex in a real close way.' He admits, 'Yup. I'm a totally American kid in that way as well. I lost

> **'Each night at midnight I go in and check my kids are still breathing.'**

my virginity in the back of a car at a drive-in. A Corinthian white 1960 Ford Galaxy. You pop that bastard into second gear and your head'd come off. Man, it ate up the road and left fossil tyre impressions behind. It was really something.'

Modest and likeable, King is a regular guy who spends less than $200 a week, prefers beer to champagne and confesses to only one extravagance: cars. Yet he remains worried about success. It's got nothing to do with the money. It's how to better the last bestseller.

King was irritated that Le Carré's 'The Little Drummer Girl' is keeping 'Christine' out of the top spot in the US. 'I've had four successive number ones,' he says. 'And I wanted this to be my fifth. So I thought I'd better come and beard the old bastard in his lair.' ●

1984

Frankie said Relax, but Big Brother *was* watching us, only he was a she. The Iron Lady survived the Brighton bomb and strode onwards, facing off against the miners, privatising everything in sight and emasculating local government. Decadent London turned up the music and we all became either 'gender-benders' or 'yuppies'.

Paris, Texas
If Wenders' previous film was on the very limits of possibility, this one pushes the frontier three steps forward into new and sublime territory.

Ghostbusters
Reitman shows greater flair at controlling the anarchic flair of the Saturday Night Live crowd than most, and the effects are truly astonishing.

The Terminator
The pacing and action in Terminator are terrific; even the future visions of a wasted LA are well mounted.

Madonna - Like A Virgin (Sire)
Madonna's penchant for exotic lingerie far outweighs her ability for spotting an original tune. At the

end of the day, surely it's just sanitised dance music for the Habitat set.

Everything But The Girl - Eden (Blanco y Negro)
Eden emerges as a triumph of great musical variety and sharp lyrical intelligence. It's fresh and frequently up-

lifting and it has a candour and grace all of its own.

Blue Nile - A Walk Across The Rooftops (Linn)
The overwhelming impression is that these lads have spent a number of evenings listening to the collected works of Brian Eno. It's only art school rock'n'roll; but I like it.

Grin and bear it

Jack Nicholson interviewed in T.O. 708, by **Chris Peachment** and **Chris Petit**

T
he door swings open to reveal… the EVIL GRIN. You have seen it often enough before to obviate description; but the GRIN has many functions, all of them socially useful. 'Ah HAH. Come in, my MEN!' is the greeting we receive, followed by a slightly softer shout into the depths of the hotel room, 'And goodbye, my WOMEN.' As one striking, dark woman (Angelica Huston, for it is surely she) and a younger fair woman leave us to our devices, the dark one receives a pat on the behind to speed her on her way, with a 'see ya later, LEGS' followed by the EVIL GRIN. This is known in the 'Book Of Etiquette' (Sir William Segar, 1590) as the Grin Courteous. There is also the Grin Modest, the Grin Churlish, the Grin Valiant, the Grin Quarrelsome and the Grin Direct. We will receive them all at one time or other throughout the interview. The Grin Modest may cover an outrageous piece of self-promotion. The Grin Quarrelsome might be used to soften some particularly scathing insult. But there's no question it's a vital weapon in his armoury. And very disarming.

The briefing from our circulation-conscious editors had been to loosen our normally vice-like grip on the professional details of the quarry's film career and try to delve a little into the profundities of his personal life. 'Ask him what his favourite cocktail is, stuff like that.' After we have arrived and the female population of the hotel room have been decorously shunted on, he relaxes into his armchair and says: 'I'm pleased to talk to *Time Out* again. You seem to take film seriously and don't just ask me dumb questions about the size of my belly, which all the other pressmen seem to have done today' ('Jack THE LAD' shriek the tabloids. 'HAPPY JACK' shrieks the *Time Out* cover. Sorry, Jack.) So that knocks our briefing on the head in one swift movement. Followed by the Grin Direct.

We begin by explaining that we had just had lunch together to determine what sort of questions to ask, but had both come to the realisation that he had not been very evident on the screen since his last film as director, 'Goin' South'. 'Well, I'm taking some time off, and I mean really off. By that I mean that I get a little peevish when people say "Are you working?" when all they mean is "Are you shooting a film?" I regard what I'm doing now, talking to you, as working. Have you ever talked to a lawyer for two weeks on the phone? I tell you: that's work. It consumes all your time. I remember I once asked Richard Burton if he had taken a break lately. He had started acting at 15 and he was now in his fifties. He thought for a while over his 35 odd years of acting and said, "Yes, I've had three weeks holiday since I started. That was all I needed".'

So how does he fill his time when he's not working? 'What I call Random Living. (The Grin Suggestive.) I make a point of no lunches, no travel dates. You take your name off the telephone answering service, so that takes care of all the calls, and I prohibit talk about the movies in my presence. And then I might take off and bum around in the South of France, which is kinda like New Jersey with a foreign language going on. Had the place wired in two days, rest of the time I just did what I wanted. I don't remember a damn thing about it. Spent two winters skiing in Aspen, Colorado too.'

There is suddenly a long drawn silence while one interrogator waits for the other to speak and the other stares at the ceiling waiting for the first one to step in. 'Well, gentlemen…' this backed up with a particularly ferocious Evil Grin, 'it must have been a kind of short lunch you had…' Collapse of stout interviewers. 'Well, that's all right. I can talk away without questions.'

Was all this Random Living a reaction to the strenuous demands made by the shooting of Stanley Kubrick's 'The Shining', which involved a reputed 11-month shooting schedule? 'Well, I sorta like it. I'd as soon be doing 40 or 50 takes in order to get a scene right as be trying to hide from make-up in my dressing room. But Stanley is very efficient. He's the best producer I know for allocating money and buying time.

'Now with Stanley, he'll make you do 98 takes and stand around all day, and yet you love him. He turns in a fucking great movie too. There was only one place where I had serious disagreements with him and that was in the hotel bar-room scenes which I thought were just too stylistically broad, while I was doing them. Usually I'm right about things like that. But they are the scenes that everyone likes. I was completely wrong and he was completely right.' Followed by the Grin Modest.

Nicholson was originally slated to play 'Fitzcarraldo' in Werner Herzog's modest attempt to annex the whole of the Matto Grosso and subjugate it to his will. 'Well, I first picked up on German cinema when I was travelling through that country and I was very taken with it. Fassbinder, Wenders, Herzog, they seemed to be the most vital film cell going on at that moment. But you develop suspicions about directors. I honestly came to believe that people would die on this movie. I have had that experience before and there is simply no movie in the world that is worth it.

'And if there is such a thing as a death on a movie being justified by the excellence of the finished product… well, I don't think that "Fitzcarraldo" is that movie. Werner is… some directors are just too attached to the adventure of making a movie. And it always worries me. I'm not afraid… but if you want adventures, have adventures and leave the camera at home. People get injured a lot on movies, and I wouldn't want to be encouraging that.

'Now, old Jim Brooks, now his new film ("Terms Of Endearment") has 11 nominations for Oscars, now he's a horse of a different colour.' The Evil Grin starts up very slightly here, and its meaning is a little uncertain. After the first few minutes of spiel about 'Terms of Endearment', however, we realise that we are getting Jack The Consummate Professional. He is in this country to promote the film after all, and by God that's what he is going to do. Even if the Evil Grin does suggest a little irony – a case of 'well, you know, and I know, and I know that you know, but hell it's what I'm here for.'

We confess that we haven't actually read the Larry McMurtry novel from which the film is extracted. Aware of the tape recorder, Nicholson mouths silently but very obviously 'Neither have I' at us and then expounds: 'My character is not actually in the novel. I took the part on because I thought it would be a cake-walk. I told Jim: "Look, I've been studying acting all these years now so I've earned my rights as far as acting goes, so. There's only so many kinds of human behaviour. So I'm going to play this guy in the same way that an Impressionist painter doesn't paint a tree green every time, know what I mean? I may play the scene where he's 50 by looking a lot younger than the scene where he's 40."

'And that worked out just fine. What was really good though was… I'm getting offered a lot of mid-life parts these days, and this was the first part I'd read in which the guy wasn't impotent. You'd think that these days America was populated with 50-year-old guys who can't get it up anymore. Actually, I just think it's the screenwriters who can't… you know. They think: "Well I'm not the guy I used to be… and I'd be dishonest if I didn't…" Da, de, da. I know that in reality – well, people imagine I'm some kind of Lothario or something, but I… well, hell I know lots of guys of my age and… (Evil Grin again) very few are impotent.'

We lighten the tone a little by asking what was his least favourite line in a movie. 'One of the areas that I know I'm below average in my acting stakes is if I get a line I know is a cruncher. I often can't pull it off. I just coast through and do it, but it drives me nuts. I wasn't a professional at the time, I was still working as an office boy at MGM and they asked me if I wanted to be an actor and I said sure so they gave me a screen test. So I go in there and it's a scene from a detective story and my second line I have to say out loud is "Be my sensible Susan". Now you try saying that aloud. I'm standing there with my face going blood red, trying to look at my knees or something. But that always was a hallmark of all these Roger Corman pictures, there are probably thousands of other lines I could think of.'

Suddenly the phone rings. It is Jerzy Skolimowski for Nicholson. He wanders up to the phone with the Evil Grin already spreading: 'Yes. POLAND! You beauty… yes, my radio show was brilliant, it was Wildesque and Cowardly as well… Yes… You going to Martin's tonight? It will be just a frivolous party and the best damn time you'll ever have… Yes, it's at 48 (address), you'll see me out front collecting the money… Right, turn up then, that should be around speed time… But you have to do me one favour – you CAN'T talk about the movies… Yes, you can talk about Poland… no movies.' He hangs up.

'That guy! I have had a writer's block about four years now. Can't even write a letter. Suddenly I wake up in the middle of the night in Berlin and I write about 55 poems. The next day someone asked me what I did last night and so I show them the poems and the next thing I know it's published in 15 countries. Now Skolimowski has been a prize fighter, jazz drummer, film-maker and a poet… So I tell him some of them and he's very impressed, so he's going to help me with them…

'Jesus, what am I doing? I have enough problems with the image I've got, if I've now got to be poetic on top of it, I'm finished. It's the Irish in me. Anyway, I hate poetry so it doesn't matter. I'll probably be in Poland next week at some meeting, reciting this poem about East Germany just because some Polish film-maker liked it. How do you get around it as an occupation? I mean what do you call yourself? People say to you "What do you do?" and you reply"Oh, I'm a poet".' Modest Grin again.

'Do you know they have no sense of irony in Japan? A propos this movie "Terms of Endearment", I made a great hit to the press there, because Jim thinks it's a comedy, but over there they are selling the movie as a tragedy. And I open with the accusation that they don't have a sense of humour. Great, I find it a little hard to believe because I watched a little television out there and everyone on TV has a chicken on their head when they are talking. Or else they're being pursued by a three-legged bear, biting on a banana, or… God, who knows what they got, it's crazy, even the news guy looks like a comedian… So I got in there to the press conference… and I get zero laughs. That was it as far as I was concerned. I was going samurai from here on in. It's "Oshima, Kurosawa, Ah so, boom" and OUT.' ●

> **'I might bum around the South of France, which is kinda like New Jersey with a foreign language going on.'**

1984

Roman Polanski

Roman Polanski interviewed in T.O. 700, by **Martyn Auty** and **Richard Rayner**

The most public film-maker in the world launches his new production: 'Roman by Polanski'.

Roman

'Look,' says Roman Polanski. 'Let's get one thing clear before we start. I want to straighten something out. I am not an asshole. OK?' His restless eyes swivel around the living room of the Avenue Montaigne flat in Paris, just a few doors down from Marlene Dietrich, which has been his home since he fled the US. He's lived here permanently since 1978, but it looks as though he's just moved in and the interior designers have just moved out. The room is chic but impersonal: glass tables, an enormous suede-covered sofa and a black leather chair with the appearance and proportions of a tugboat. Gold statuettes are tucked neatly on a bookshelf, the rewards for 25 years of movie making. On the walls hang original paintings by the surrealist Erro, who blends icons from communism, capitalism and catholicism with a cool wit. There's an enormous TV screen in one corner of the room and enough electronic equipment to gratify someone who has invested heavily in Sony or Bang & Olufsen. A shell for a jet-set hermit crab, the room has style and about as much warmth as an icebox. Polanski does not want to be photographed here.

'I'm not being difficult,' he says. 'We can take pictures anywhere else. But not here, you know. Lots of photographers try to take pictures of me in my home but I don't let them. You were waiting outside, I let you up here 'cos it's cold. I'm not being an asshole. I just don't want it. OK?'

Polanski is not planning to debate the matter. He does not give interviews, he gives performances. This one is part of the promotion for his latest production, the autobiography 'Roman by Polanski'. At last a rebuttal of all the gruesome media portrayals? The true story of the Krakow ghetto, the Sharon Tate murders, Nastassja Kinski and the Los Angeles rape case, straight from the horse's mouth? Well, yes and no. With Polanski the truth is rarely easy to establish.

It's not surprising. He is the world's most public film director and his life is a legend, created by a combination of extraordinary circumstance, adept self-promotion, and lurid media fantasy. But in recent years Polanski has found he no longer controls the fiction of his public self. In part he has only his own antics to blame. Now an increasingly hostile and mocking press tends to characterise him as a vicious monster: rapist, pervert, child seducer, and callous exploiter of his own tragedies.

Polanski was born in 1933, not in Poland but in Paris where his father, a Jewish entrepreneur, was working. Three years later Ryszard Polanski took his family back to Krakow. With hindsight, it was scarcely a wise career move. The Germans invaded Poland during the exceptionally hot summer of 1939 and the Polanskis found themselves literally walled into one of the newly designated 'Jewish areas': the Krakow ghetto. In the following year, both

Scandals

his parents were taken to concentration camps. His father survived but his mother died in Auschwitz. Polanski, then nicknamed 'Romek', escaped from the ghetto to the countryside and lived with a Catholic family in the primitive rural conditions which he would later portray in 'Tess'.

'It was easy to get out of the ghetto, but difficult to survive,' he says. 'One day I was picking blackberries in a lane. I heard a whistling sound followed by a sharp crack. A couple of hundred yards away I saw two German soldiers. One had taken a pot shot at me for no apparent reason.'

This was the first time anyone tried to kill Polanski. Subsequently he was nearly killed by a bomb blast and, after the war, he was lucky to survive a murder attempt when he was battered on the head by a thief. Polanski describes the aftermath in 'Roman': 'It was still raining. Looking down, I saw that the front of my shirt was sodden with blood. A woman in a beige trench-coat caught sight of me. She came closer, emitting little bird calls of distress. She turned nasty when I thrust her aside and she saw the bloody imprint left by my palm.'

In 1953 he entered the Polish national film school. 'I'd been obsessed with movies for a long time before the war. I'd sneak out of the ghetto to watch newsreels. Post-war, he had enjoyed success as a child actor on radio and had been introduced to the Polish film industry by his performances in the early Wajda movies.

This gave Polanski exactly what he wanted: a ticket to the West. He left Poland in 1962, together with his first wife Barbara Kwiatowska, and lived in Paris, hoping that the critical success of his early film-school shorts, together with his coruscating first feature 'Knife in the Water', would be enough to encourage Western producers to give him work. In fact he had to wait three years before he would direct 'Repulsion'. By that time his wife had divorced him, and he had moved to London.

London in the 1960s was the age of innocence which Polanski never enjoyed as a child. Parties, work, money and, of course, women were abundantly available. 'It was the time of my life,' he says ruefully. To cap it all he married the actress Sharon Tate, the epitome of the 1960s dream girl and probably the only woman he has ever treated as an equal. He was invited to Hollywood to direct 'Rosemary's Baby' and while wholly faithful to Ira Levin's novel, Polanski succeeded in infusing the movie with his own highly personal style and sense of danger, and still came up with a massive commercial success. Polanski was in the idyllic period of his second marriage and secure in his chosen profession.

It all changed on the night of Friday, August 8 in the Polanski house on Cielo Drive. 'The murder of Sharon Tate and several close friends is the central event in Polanski's life. He evidently still feels pain and anguish at the memory. To sit opposite him and watch his face as he recalls those events and their aftermath is in itself a moving experience. 'The toughest part of the book were things like anything concerned with Sharon's death. I'd just got it out of my life. I thought it was all there but I realised there were gaps. Parts of my memory which I had deliberately dimmed. Until Sharon's death the future had seemed like some never-ending road full of surprises. After it I came to realise that life was not eternal and that happiness was only transitory.'

Polanski says that afterward he felt guilty whenever he was enjoying himself, and since that time he has not been able to live on a permanent basis with any woman. He writes: 'Even after so many years I find myself unable to watch a spectacular sunset, or visit a lovely old house, or experience visual pleasure of any kind without instinctively telling myself how she would have loved it all. In these ways I shall remain faithful to her till the day I die.'

In 'Roman' the passages dealing with the event of Sharon's death seem curiously muted. What he writes instead is a cinematic account of how he assumed the role of investigator into his own wife's death. 'I bought bugs to be left in people's homes,' he recounts. He tested friends' cars for bloodstains.

It's hard to resist the conclusion that his sleuthing was the intuitive reflex of a character always more in control of fiction than reality. Playing investigator was perhaps his only way of coping with the tragedy, but it led him to suspect many close acquaintances: Bruce Lee, who'd been an occasional visitor to the house and who let slip he'd recently lost his spectacles (a pair was found near the scene of the murder); John Phillips of the Mamas & The Papas; and even novelist Jerzy Kosinski, an acquaintance of Polanski's since his time in Poland.

As if the Manson murders weren't enough to daub him in lurid publicity, there followed in March 1977 the business at Jack Nicholson's house with the 13-year-old girl he calls 'Sandra'. When his arrest on six counts of sex and drugs-related offences hit the front pages, no reporter missed the opportunity to exhume the Manson murders story and to draw specious parallels with his 'films of sex and violence'. Polanski found himself up against the

As if the Manson murders weren't enough, there followed in March 1977 the business at Jack Nicholson's house with the 13-year-old girl he calls 'Sandra'.

stark reality of the law in a town whose major industry was make-believe. In a country where movie stars become presidents, where real life and fantasy fused and clashed, the contradictions were too much for him to handle.

First, he blurted out his account of the aftermath at Nicholson's house. Then he heard the girl's (and her mother's) story. Later he was offered alternative scenarios which would help in the plea bargaining. It was like a Hollywood script conference: lines were changed, scenes were re-written. Small wonder the truth remains ▶

so elusive, especially since the case never came to full trial. Polanski's account in 'Roman' has it both ways. A conviction that the girl was sexually experienced and willing ('She spread herself and I entered her. She wasn't unresponsive...') and an admission of guilt ('Overnight I'd crossed the line between decent folk and scum... now, because of a moment's unthinking lust, I had jeopardised my freedom').

When we broached the question over lunch, towards the end of the interview, it was clear Polanski had been waiting for us to ask about 'Sandra'. He had the upper hand. Did he actually feel guilty? 'That's what they kept asking me at the time and in prison. I knew that I had to answer "yes", but I didn't really. I didn't. Let me explain. I feel I've done something wrong if I harm someone or cause grief. I didn't feel I'd caused grief here. Or any harm, mental or physical. I don't think there really was a victim in the incident.' Except perhaps himself, the ensuing silence suggests.

Interpretations of the event hinge on the girl's prior sexual knowledge, her mother's motivation in bringing the charges and, crucially, whether you accept Polanski's account or the girl's, or something between the two. Polanski has continued to state, undiplomatically, that he 'likes young girls'.

Polanski admits the sexual encounter and, by omission, denies the other counts that included 'furnishing a controlled substance to a minor', 'perversion' and 'sodomy'. He served 42 days under psychiatric observation before his release into yet another 'script conference'. This time the scenario for his sentencing was being redrafted: the villain, it seemed, would have to serve more time inside than originally scripted. In desperation Polanski did something he'd never done before in his career. He walked off the picture, catching a flight from Los Angeles to London.

Overnight, he moved on to France, from where he knew he would not be extradited. That's how the situation stands. If Polanski returned to the US he would be sentenced. If he comes to England he faces possible extradition.

'I will go back to clear it up. I don't miss America. How could I miss a place where I had so many misfortunes? But I would go back, just to clear up this mess, and then come back to Europe.' He has issued the same assurance, over three years ago in Cannes. What would it take to make him return to the US? 'State of mind,' he says, somewhat mysteriously.

Polanski's autobiography is almost devoid of self-analysis. It's not a habit which he indulges in. He argues that you don't know about your ego, or your talent, until someone tells you about it. 'Listen,' he says. 'As a child learning to walk, you don't think "I have a talent for walking", you just do it. Later on I became aware that I had a talent for drawing, for writing and for fucking. People ask me – "Why do you do so much exercise?", "Why do you screw so many women?" and it's just because I like it. Anyone who has plenty of sex or does a lot of sport knows the pleasure and satisfaction it gives. But sex is no substitute for exercise: it's not physically demanding enough.' He then proceeds to describe with relish his recent physical endeavours, trekking in the Himalayas. 'It's only in the last few years that I've really discovered a life outside movies.' And that, increasingly, involves pushing himself to the limits of endurance, to revive a jaded appetite for adventure.

What does Roman Polanski want from life?

He shrugs. 'I don't know.'

It's late afternoon by the time we leave the restaurant. Shoulders hunched beneath a Marlowe-style raincoat, Polanski is jigging around on the pavement, as if playing a solitary game of hop-

• •

Paul McCartney

from 'Do you still need me (now it's '84)' in T.O. 738, by **Steve Grant**

I turn to a subject near to the McCartney heart-strings: his upcoming possible purchase of Northern Songs, the Lennon and McCartney publishing company sold for a song in the early days of Beatlemania. It is a matter of understandable bitterness that McCartney has to ask permission to record 'Yesterday'.

'The news is that they're apparently willing to sell,' he says, 'and we're certainly interested. It's just a bit galling and absurd having to buy back, for millions, songs that John and I tossed off in an afternoon. When we came down to London we were kids, we didn't know that you could own things like songs. It was like somebody owning the air.

'Same with the Sotheby's business. Bizarre. I actually tried to buy back a postcard that I'd sent to John – and somebody out-bid me. It's apalling to have to buy back your own used toilet paper. Ringo's started signing himself "Ringo 'Sotheby's' Starr".'

McCartney makes no secret of his contempt for those who have exploited their proximity to the Fab Four to produce a series of lucrative, tell-all memoirs. 'Trash merchants, who'll have to live with themselves,' he says. He was particularly unhelpful to Philip Norman, who approached him when writing his book 'Shout!' What does he think about Norman's asser-

tion that Lennon was three-quarters of the Beatles?

'Fair enough. He's a John fan. I'm a John fan. If you asked me who my favourite Beatle was, I'd say John as well. He was the guy's Beatle. He had the edge in conversation, repartee. I got lumbered as the pretty one. On an intellectual level, though, we were equals.

'I know I've lost my edge. I like edgy stuff actually – it was me who decided that the house should burn down in 'Norwegian Wood', not that that's any big deal, but I need a kind of outside injection, stimulus, and it's not there any more. And remember, the edge came from all the Beatles. If Ringo or George didn't like anything, it was out. My stuff has got more poppy without that outside stimulus, but then I've always been more at home with love songs and anthems.'

How does he feel now about Lennon's death?

He pauses. 'There's just a big hole. I still get a shudder when I talk about him in the past tense. I've never been able to put it into words. I've certainly never faced up to it. I still go around thinking he's still alive, someone who lives in New York, who I don't see too much of these days. Which was the case. Like a lot of people who die – I just wish I'd said a few more things to him...' ●

scotch. 'Just look at it,' he says. 'Shit. It's everywhere. Know how many dogs there are in Paris? I tell you. Five hundred thousand. And they all shit on the pavement.'

But dogshit is evidently the only aspect of Parisian life for which Polanski reserves any particular venom. 'I like it here,' he says. 'Remember, I lived here right after I left Poland and made most of my friendships here. I never liked Los Angeles. I felt good there because I had a great wife and good friends. But I never stayed for more than two or three months at a stretch and I missed Europe all the time I was there.'

Paris is the traditional haven of the refugee, with a population swelled by thousands of exiles and fugitives. To Polanski, it's home. Paris is just about the only place left for a man who holds the unusual distinction of having fled first from the East and then from the West.

Kenneth Tynan, who co-scripted 'Macbeth' with him, noted that Polanski divides the world into Lenin's categories of 'Who' and 'Whom' – those who do and those to whom it is done. The curious thing about Polanski is not just that he belongs to both these categories but that he does so in such extreme fashion. He has been both victim and victimiser, a manipulator of extraordinary determination who has retained a childlike gullibility.

His autobiography is the work of a consummate storyteller and role player, and from it one deduces that if Roman Polanski is to continue to shock and startle the world he will have to return to America. Paris, for all its attractions, seems like a trap for him. He has the nerve and the guts to make that trip; the question is whether he still has the ambition. 'I'm still a dreamer, but I want to be able to control my own fate,' he says. 'The problem is that one is seldom able to distinguish between courage and foolishness.' ●

● ●

"1984"

"There were so many candidates on the platform that there were not enough promises to go round."
President Reagan on the Democrats during the New Hampshire primary

"As far as I'm concerned I have the backing of my members."
Arthur Scargill calling the miners' strike without a ballot

"We had to fight the enemy without in the Falklands. We have always been aware of the enemy within which is more difficult to fight and more dangerous to liberty."
Margaret Thatcher

"It's the sort of police state you might expect to see in Chile, but not here."
Arthur Scargill, after pitched battles at the Orgreave coking plant

"Today we were unlucky, but remember – we have only to be lucky once."
IRA statement after the Brighton bombing

"This was the day I was meant not to see."
Margaret Thatcher, the day after the Brighton bombing

"Advice to black immigrants – run fast and look pretty."
Graffito in Brixton after Zola Budd had been made a UK citizen in record time

"One nanny said, 'Feed a cold'; she was a neo-Keynsian. Another nanny said, 'Starve a cold'; she was a monetarist."
The Earl of Stockton's (Harold Macmillan's) maiden speech in the House of Lords

"Where's the beef?"
Wendy Hamburgers slogan appropriated by Walter Mondale to taunt Gary Hart on his lack of policies

"This is not the end of anything, this is the beginning of everything."
Ronald Reagan's victory speech after re-election

"Everybody's sucking fat. It's hot!"
Dr Julius Newman, founder of the American Society of Liposuction surgery, drums up business

The least effort for the
Greatest Return

Robert Mitchum is a big man from an era of big men. He stands sufficiently above six feet to make shaking hands a matter of reaching upwards. His shoulders are not much wider than the axle of a beer truck. There is a realisation about him that people still find hard to make. And that is that he is the best actor that cinema has yet produced. It has nothing to do with histrionics; how could it, when the man barely moves? His success depends more on the exact knowledge of the depth to which an emotion should be buried. Director Richard Fleischer once kept doing take after take in close-up, in order to get Mitchum to react to something (against all the actor's protestations that he was reacting). Only when Fleischer ran the rushes did he see that Mitchum was right. The camera can discover what life too often disguises.

The Writer

After a number of jobs in his teens, including being a boxer, and winding up on a chain-gang in Georgia, Mitchum auditioned for Long Beach Civic Theatre and stayed as an actor, stage-hand and author of one-act plays. He also used to write comic turns and songs for his elder sister Julie's night club act, and in 1939 even wrote an oratorio which was directed by Orson Welles at the Hollywood Bowl.

I was what they call a junior writer at a studio. Another writer in the Pool told me to get a hat. I said, 'Why? No body wears a hat in California except a cowboy.' He said, 'Well, you can hang it up, and when they come looking for you, they'll all say, "Well, he must be here somewhere because there's his hat." 'I'd be on the beach.'

Do you regret not pursuing writing?
Hell no, this is much easier.
You also write poetry.
I do yeah. Not much future in that.

Horse Soldier

His first break in the movies came with seven Hopalong Cassidy Westerns in which he was the disposable villain. He got $100 a week 'and all the horse manure I could take home', and puts down his quiet deep voice and laconic nature to having talked to horses too much. He was renowned for punching in the mouth one horse

which threw him, and horses continued to dog his working life, particularly on 'The Lusty Men' for Nicholas Ray, a tale of the rootlessness of rodeo life.

Yeah. Nick Ray was a fine man. He was a drinking fellow, you know. Very intense.
Did you have much knowledge of the rodeo circuit?
Not much. I got close to some of the rodeo riders. Casey Tibbs and Jim Shoulder. Tough men. One of them was killed in a plane crash. Another one died of 'pneumonia' in a jail in Arizona. You know, they beat the bejasus out of you, and then turn a cold hose on you, and throw you unconscious in the jail. And then say that you died of 'pneumonia'. One of them, he was at Madison Square Gardens, and he started to cross the street and a cop shoved him back and he took issue with that. And the cop reached for his pistol, and he took the pistol away from him and shot him dead. Pleaded self-defence and beat the rap too. He did the same thing later at the Boston Gardens rodeo. A coupla rough boys.
Was it tough riding the horses?
Pretty physical. All those guys on their broncs, they just look like they're on rocking chairs. And I get on a horse and they all say, 'It's OK, he's just a retired old bronc' and this thing is turned loose… and I can't get off him. Bloody horse, they'd go in to try and pick me off and my horse would turn around and kick the pick-up horse. He's heading for the fence and I just can't fall off him. I'm bleeding from my hair by this time. They blew whistles and fired guns and everything. I got the rough one.

Howard Hawks

Sadly, Mitchum only ever worked once with Howard Hawks and John Wayne, in 'El Dorado', and he was great, playing a drunken sheriff with a hole in his leg whom Wayne wrenches back into shape.

Westerns. They are always good, cheap, outdoor fun even if they do get a little physical. When Howard called me, I said, 'What's the story?' and he said, 'No story, just characters' and that's the way it was. Did one scene, put it away, did another, put that away. Carried on. At one scene we had five guys sitting around a table, and I look up and point out that one of the

guys has already been killed in the film. Howard says, 'What the hell, I wanna use him again."n I asked the script girl about some move I make to a wagon and I said, 'Is this the same night as the last scene?' and she says, 'if you're talking about continuity, forget it. I gave that up last October.' That was the way Hawks made pictures.

I was shot in the leg. The right leg, so they insisted I carry my crutch under my left arm. I said no, the crutch is supposed to substitute for the injured member, and Duke says, 'Goddammit I know what I'm talking about, I used to break my leg every Saturday afternoon.' And then Howard says, 'Besides, you've got to have your gun hand free.' So, OK, I put the crutch under my left arm and go hopping around. Then we got to shoot some interiors, and the guy playing the Doc is actually a doctor from Canada, and he says no, the crutch has to go under the right arm if you're shot in the right leg. So I do all the interiors with the crutch under my right arm. Producer has a look at the rushes. Oh God! 'Every time you make an entrance or an exit from an interior to an exterior the crutch goes from one arm to the other!' Howard says, 'Nobody'll notice.' Finally it ends up about half and half throughout the picture.

Leading Ladies

How did you find working with Lillian Gish. She has this reputation for being a very pure person, and you…
We hadn't investigated each other's reputations. I don't think she reads those fan mags… and I don't.
Jane Russell?
(Mitchum gestures with his hands in front of his chest, palms turned inward, a rounded sort of motion.)
Well, you had to maintain your distance. But she's a really pleasant… lady. In the kissing scenes she'd pop her chewing gum up your nose. Very romantic.

The Movies

I never see anything really.
You don't go to the movies?
Can't find anywhere to park.
Did you ever watch your own films?
No.

Oh, Henry

He worked for Henry Hathaway on 'White Witch Doctor' and 'The Snows of Kilimanjaro'. Mitchum would wind Hathaway up, by appearing on the set and asking what he was supposed to say. Someone would gingerly hand him a script, he'd glance through it, then Hathaway would shout, 'OK, you smart Sonofabitch, Action.' Whereupon Mitchum would recite six pages of dialogue without mistake.

Hathaway used to scream and holler at people too. He'd fire everyone on the set. Stupid son of a bitch. He had Dale Robertson on his set once. Dale had just come to 20th Century Fox and Hathaway was one of the big directors at Fox, big stockholder too. And Henry comes over and takes the big cigar out of his face and says, 'Listen, I'm gonna call you a stupid Okie son of a bitch sometimes, but don't pay any attention to me. I get a little nervous directing, and five minutes later I will have forgotten all about it.' Dale says, 'That's perfectly all right, Mr Hathaway, I was in the army for four years, and I'm a little goofy myself. Please feel free to say anything you wish. And if I should happen to step across and lay you flat on your ass don't think a thing about it because five minutes later I will have forgotten the whole thing.' Henry never said another word to him.

In Bogey's Shoes

Mitchum played Philip Marlowe twice, first in Dick Richard's 1975 retrostyle 'Farewell my Lovely', and later when English director Michael Winner attempted a remake of 'The Big Sleep', set inexplicably in the Home Counties.

Michael gives a great performance. Set fire to a corpse from a morgue once. He was walking round eating a ham sandwich, didn't like the way the body looked on fire, so he asks the guy if they've got another stiff. Sure, he says, so they bring on another and fire it up. Michael denies the whole thing. He set fire to Munich zoo, too. Leaves a trail of destruction behind him. Disaster, hysteria. That's his joy.

I found five young Arabs around the set one day so I told them that Winner had demanded 10 per cent of our salaries to be donated to the Zionist movement. Gave them his address and told them they'd recognise the house by the effigy of Arafat hanging in the garden.

South Of The Border

One of his greatest roles, in 'Out Of The Past' (Jacques Tourneur, 1947), took him down to Mexico. The country seems to have set its stamp on him.

I have a particular affection for it. Last stronghold of individual independence. I don't know if it's a statute, but it's called 'Falsificado'. If you accuse someone of something, you'd better be able to prove it, otherwise they kill you. It goes that far. Dishonouring someone is a far greater crime than murder.

Confidential magazine published one issue down there and they took to task some young man about town in Mexico City. He was sitting in a bar, and he read it. So he jumps into his Maserati, drives down town, goes in the office, and says to the hack, 'Are you the man responsible for this?' and he says, 'I am', and so the guy pulls out his .38, blows his head off, walks out, gets in his Maserati, drives back to the bar and finishes his Martini.

Great friend of John Huston's is Indo Fernandez. He's shot about eight people. He was working down in Acapulco and he lost patience with one of his actors so Indo shot him. Then he calls up Central Casting and says, 'Send me another actor, this one leaks.'

John Huston

For John Huston, he was in 'Heaven Knows, Mr Alison' (1957), playing a hefty but polite Marine stranded on a Pacific island alone with Deborah Kerr as a nun.

I was in Ireland once and went round to see him. He was wanking this monkey. I said, 'What are you doing?' He said, 'Well, he likes it, kid.' He had this script by Arthur Miller for 'The Misfits' he wanted me to do. I read it and it didn't make no sense at all. I just went and hid. Said, 'If Huston calls, tell him I'm dead.' He told me that he had Gable lined up for the part. I said, 'You'll kill him.' He said, 'You think so?' I said, 'Look he's uninsurable, when he gets up to that altitude, fighting those wild horses, he's going to pop an artery.' I like Houston, though. Great fun.

Atlantic City

While he has worked with many English directors, the new generation of European directors seemed to have passed him by.

Only time, I can remember offhand, I got a call from Louis Malle. Wanted me for 'Atlantic City'. Trouble was I'd just been swimming down in the Caribbean, all tanned and healthy. He said, 'You look far too young and active.' So I said, 'In that case, you'd better look up Burt Lancaster, he looks like Methuselah.' So that's what he did. Good script that. I'm sure he was very good too. It's like my mother used to say, 'You can't buy diamonds in a five and dime.' It's difficult to be good in a very bad part.

What do you look for in a script?

My inflexible and inviolable rule: the least effort for the greatest return.

A Glass Of Urine

When Robert Bolt called Mitchum and asked what he was doing in the immediate future, Mitchum said not much except that he was about to commit suicide. Bolt asked him to wait 11 months so that he could be in David Lean's 'Ryan's Daughter'. By all accounts the first option would have been less painful.

Went on for 11 months that shoot. Sorta pleasant. Used to have weeks without working. Used to come to London, stay at the Dorchester, they'd call me up, say I was wanted, I'd go back and wait for 23 days for my first shot. You get used to it, but you have to stay near a phone. Saw Sarah Miles the other day. Looks very young. She puts that down to the practice of ingesting her own urine. I don't know how she gets at it. Carries a cup around maybe, goes into contortions, I don't know. She returned from Katmandu, said she's given up everything, found peace. I asked how she spelled that, peace? '

Cary Grant

What Cary Grant is to good conversation, Mitchum is to silence – its most perfect interpreter. Not surprisingly, their pairing in 'The Grass Is Greener' (Stanley Donen, 1960) is less than successful.

Very charming. But no sense of humour. I mean, he's very light and pleasant, but his humour is sort of old music-hall jokes. 'What's that noise down there? They're holding an Elephant's ball. Well, I wish they'd let go of it, I'm trying to get some sleep.' I guess that was when he was coming off his LSD treatment. He was a little weird. Had a of of trouble just saying 'Hello' in front of the camera. Whenever the camera turned off me and onto him, I'd go for a drive.

He did a clever thing. All the films he ever made reverted to him after seven years. Shrewd businessman, believe it. Never parted with a kopek. We had lunch one day and Deborah Kerr leans over to me and whispers, 'Eat all you can.' I said, 'I'm not hungry.' She said, 'I don't care, eat it all.' I said, 'Why?' She says, 'Cary's paying.' She did tell me that in that acid treatment he'd regressed to 15 years old or something and he didn't like it at all. But he was a very pleasant fellow.

Marlon Brando

He has never acted with Marlon Brando.

I saw him last at Jimmy Durante's funeral. Very strange that. He looked well. He's on that routine of going up to 250 pounds then coming back down again. Lives on an island. Raises mosquitoes big as camels. I think he's dedicated to putting every motion picture studio out of business. Did pretty well for Metro. Sank that enterprise.

I believe Cannon paid Sly Stallone $12 million for his next picture. Broke his father's heart. Father sent him to Europe to get an education, fancy education in England. Can't make a living out of that, so now he talks like 'Ugh… hey…You…', you know.

You've never wanted to go for those high fees?

Whatever the traffic will bear… ●

An America

Al Pacino interviewed in T.O. 733, by **Chris Peachment**

O rdinary people are not like this. After some 20 minutes of talking about the genesis of David Mamet's 'American Buffalo' in his house in Bayswater, Pacino suddenly says: 'Well, we are going to go into the country for a couple of hours, to relax before the show tonight, would you care to come along?' 'Going into the country', turns out to be not quite what I expected. 'Going' means having someone drive you in a limo, with five other people in attendance. 'The country' turns out to be a very large country house with swimming pool and tennis court belonging to a very large movie producer who doesn't seem to be in evidence, although his wife and children are very welcoming.

Pacino plays a little tennis with the children of the house. 'No one ever taught me how to play. I never learnt anywhere. Part of it is that I can mimic things. But then suddenly I can play tennis. I feel that someone gave me this gift.' He doesn't care to go swimming, but two men from his entourage take a dip. 'Tell him what Lee Strasburg said about swimming once, Al.' Pacino obliges: 'Lee was looking at the ocean one day and someone said, "Why don't you go swimming?" and he said, "I love the ocean, but I wouldn't want to get involved."'

Pacino's cook brings some food, steak and a salad, beautifully arranged. There is, however, no dressing on the salad. 'Is there any oil for the salad?' Within seconds there is oil. 'I believe Marlon is here today,' says one of the entourage. My ears go like radar dishes. 'What is he doing here?', 'Oh, I think he's being wooed, for the producer's next film'. 'No,' says Pacino, 'he and the producer are old friends. He's just here for tea, maybe. Marlon doesn't need to be wooed.'

The talk ranges over old theatre gossip. The early days of the Living Theatre, of the off-off-Broadway café theatres where Pacino used to appear in one-act plays while people drank coffee; what Larry did when he played Richard III; how he managed to play both Oedipus and Sheridan in one night. As I said, ordinary people are not like this.

But then there is a crucial difference between this court and the form of 'king and retinue' which usually attends upon stars who have dwelt too long in the gardens of Babylon. For Pacino does not surround himself with the murmuring starlets, nor the sycophants, nor the pig-eyed minders that usually accrue to men of wealth and no discrimination. Two of the men here by the pool are trusted friends of long acquaintance, one of whom runs a Rep Theatre outside of New York, the other going right back to the earliest days of Pacino's acting career when he gave him lessons. Their humour is gentle, their conversation with Pacino quiet and easy with the assurance of old friendship. Pacino grew up an only child (surely the best training for anyone with any artistic aspirations) and while the expression 'extended family' has become debased lately, it wouldn't be stretching credibility very hard to see that this is roughly what he has created here. It is perhaps ironic that the first time he came to notice in the movies, he was also playing the head of a family.

It may have been De Niro and Brando who picked up awards for 'The Godfather' films (the one for imitating the other, the other for imitating himself), but to see the two parts in tandem is to realise just how much Pacino is the lynch-pin for the whole terrible dynasty. 'It was very daunting,' he admits. 'I never expected to be offered a role like that. And that was really down to Francis (Coppola) who had seen me on stage and put his faith in me. The studio didn't want an unknown at all, but Francis insisted. Nowadays, you know, I have to be certain about whether a director really wants me for a part or whether he just wants me to get backing for his picture. But Francis knew exactly what he wanted. It was very reassuring.

'Someone once asked my bodyguard whether I was in the Mafia,' he says, anticipating a question I would be far too polite to ask. '"No" says my bodyguard. "Well, they say, Frank Sinatra has a bodyguard and he's in the Mafia." "Yeah," says my bodyguard "and the Queen of England has a bodyguard, does that mean she's in the Mafia?"'

Pacino's face took a beating in 'The Godfather'. Like so many Method actors, there is a hint of masochism in what they allow happen to themselves in their roles. In 'Serpico', which came between the, two 'Godfathers', Pacino gets a bullet through the face, thus giving full reign to the gritted Method mumble.

'Serpico' is memorable for the volcanic eruptions of violence which punctuated Pacino's otherwise placid hippie cop. 'Someone once said that actors are "emotional athletes" and it's true. You work hard with your body and your voice and then the emotion comes up and out. It's exercised and exorcised.' He seems pleased with the pun.

buffalo in London

'That's why you often find your expressions carrying over into real life. That used to happen with Edmund Kean. I read about him. He drank a lot.' Pacino himself doesn't indulge. 'People are always wanting to get away, you know, have a holiday. Drink and drugs is just a way of "getting away" without leaving your armchair. I do that by my work.'

The mention of Kean is intriguing, for Pacino is very interested in the man: a great actor who found it increasingly hard to tell the difference between lying and acting, and impossible to differentiate between acting and 'ordinary' life. Method actors just love all that stuff.

The actors' craft is one which does not admit of rational analysis, nor even requires intelligence on their part. Emotion and intuition are their strong suits (which is why they are intolerable to live among, except to their own kind). 'The closest I get to an explanation,' Pacino says, visibly trying hard, 'is, it's like breaking into a sweat when you're exercising. You keep running and running, and suddenly you break into a sweat, and it's great.' Clearly the 'emotional athlete' wasn't a chance remark.

'The Method is great though for filming, because it enables you to maintain the mood of what you are doing over long periods of time.' However it has become associated in people's minds with a certain manner, not to say mannered form of acting. 'Oh yeah, every so often up on the stage there, I give myself a little scratch, just to remind them that they are watching the Method,' he says, not entirely seriously.

Just a little scratch! Any night you can see him down at the Duke of York's all but chewing the carpet in a performance which has perhaps three seconds of stillness in it and none of them consecutive. The man just will not trust in quiet. There are moments when the other two actors are talking between themselves, and all eyes are on Pacino who is busy adjusting his fly, running his fingers through his hair or bouncing off the walls.

Whatever else the Method does for you, it certainly invades your life. While playing a lawyer in 'And Justice For All', Pacino was travelling in a car and someone was moaning about a raw legal deal they had been given, and Pacino turned around and snatched the contract from their hands with a 'Let me see that', before he even realised that he wouldn't know which way up to look at a legal document. Similarly when he was playing Serpico he used to flash his badge from the back of his car at recalcitrant taxi drivers and tell them to pull over, before he was fully in his senses. 'Fortunately, they usually took off the minute they saw the badge.' The spectre of Kean is hovering once more over the anecdotes. Can he really not tell the difference? 'Oh yeah, I knew I wasn't a cop. But it felt great.'

And the theatre, of course, that makes him feel great too? 'I was doing "Richard III" in Boston once, in the round, which is tremendous for getting audience energy – you get a great sense of feedback. And I was winging it on the wooing of Lady Anne, you know: "Was ever woman in this manner wooed, was ever woman in this manner won!" and I looked down and there getting up froom the front row and charging the stage was this little old lady

with a stick and a hunchback, and I thought, "Jesus, yes, we are flying tonight, aren't we? We are right over Hoboken now."'

Does it always work, this sucking of energy from the audience? 'Yeah, the best thing that ever happened was during one performance when I could feel a pair of eyes on me all the time. They just never let me go, it was incredible; I played for three hours to those eyes, and I gave it my all. It had never happened before to me so when the curtain call came I was determined to seek out this person who was giving me so much charge. And as I took the curtain call, I looked out into the audience, and there they were. It was a seeing eye dog, sat there with its master. All the front rows were full of blind people, and it had been this dog following me around all evening. So you never know where you are going to get your inspiration from.'

On the way back to town in the limo, the subject of the Cannes film festival comes up. Pacino has never been. 'Well it's very hard for someone like me you know. You can enjoy it all, because you're not very visible. You can see what's going on. With me, everywhere I go I get the lights shining in my eyes. I can't see what's going on. That's why I avoid doing all those things, you know, events and interviews. It's not out of disdain, it's because when I'm here the event becomes different. It's not an event I can watch, because I am the event. In New York, I am recognised everywhere I go. If I want to study people I have to go out in the back of the car and watch them while I'm cruising around.'

Sure enough, right on cue the limo comes to a halt at some traffic lights and a cabbie leans across the open window. 'Orlight mate are yer…' accompanied with much leering and thumbs up signals. Pacino treats it with the accustomed weary good humour. 'Fine thank you… and you?'

The car rolls on, down St Martin's Lane to the theatre. There on the pavement is Pacino's bodyguard, keeping at bay some of the less fortunate autograph hunters. They swell

'Every so often up on the stage there, I give myself a little scratch, just to remind them that they are watching the Method.'

toward the car in a great wave. 'I love work.' It is Pacino's parting shot; maybe he had saved it up all day as a curtain line, but it doesn't really matter because one of the indisputable facts about the man up on the stage is that he loves what he is doing. He is fighting his way to the stage-door alley now, scribbling at the tendered programmes and envelope backs, smiling a lot and talking out of the side of his mouth to his impassive, vast bodyguard.

As I said, ordinary people are not like this. ●

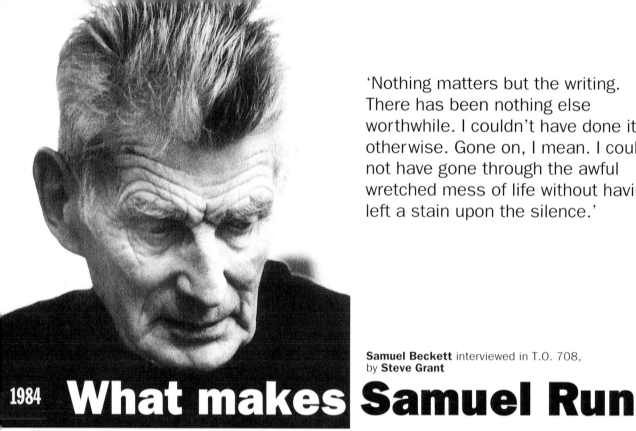

'Nothing matters but the writing. There has been nothing else worthwhile. I couldn't have done it otherwise. Gone on, I mean. I could not have gone through the awful wretched mess of life without having left a stain upon the silence.'

Samuel Beckett interviewed in T.O. 708, by **Steve Grant**

1984

What makes Samuel Run

Samuel Beckett

A 77-year-old man sits in the foyer of the Riverside Studios all but ignored in the lunchtime buzz of rattling plates and conversation. He seems tired, occasionally rubbing his eyes, sipping at the half of Guinness in front of him on the scrubbed wooden bench. He's painfully thin, the quarter-miler's wiry face having succumbed to stiffness in the last few years; the hair, neat and silvery, is stroked up from the lined forehead in a self-supporting ridge. His voice is soft, almost a whisper, a Dublin voice, lilting, musical, despite the bearer's long residence in Paris, despite the artist's adoption, long ago, as World Citizen.

'This isn't an interview, is it?' says Samuel Beckett. 'I never give interviews.' Friends and colleagues everywhere attest to Beckett's great kindness and generosity. His modesty is legendary. When he was awarded the Croix De Guerre for his work with the Resistance in wartime France he told none of his friends for almost 30 years, despite his obvious pride in the award and its accompanying citation from De Gaulle. His unpretentiousness is equally famous. A friend of mine once left a note pinned to the door of Beckett's Paris residence many years ago. 'I am a research student and I would like to meet you to discuss modern European literature.' On his return he was greeted by Beckett: 'I know absolutely nothing about European literature but come in and have a drink.' But Beckett is now an older, wearier man. How many more visitors, well-wishers, students, old friends, visiting professors, agents, acolytes have pecked at him, eroded his firm resolve to be left in peace, not to be questioned.

Samuel Beckett, winner of the Nobel Prize for Literature in 1969, is in London briefly to attend and advise on final rehearsals of the latest production of his most famous play, 'Waiting for Godot' by Rick Cluchy's San Quentin Theatre Workshop. It's a chore, but one which Beckett performs with a tired duty – both to himself as an artist (he has always attempted to influence productions which he can and ignore those which he can't) and as a friend to a man whose life he has transformed in a way which almost seems grotesque, were it not one of life and the theatre's best Happy Endings.

Rick Cluchy, an affable, accomplished actor and writer, was in 1954 awaiting execution on death row. Cluchy was a young punk, a bank robber, in his words 'not a very successful one' who once made the mistake of taking a bank security guard as a hostage after a particularly ill-starred armed escapade, thus incurring a mandatory death sentence. Cluchy was 21 years old. The sentence was not carried out. Instead Cluchy, a poor white from Chicago, served 12 years in California's notorious San Quentin prison on a diet of knife fights, rapes, boredom, survival. During that time, in 1960, Alan Mandel's San Francisco Theatre Workshop staged a performance of 'Godot' for the inmates and Cluchy experienced something akin to Paul's conversion on the road to Damascus; parts were touched which Johnny Cash obviously couldn't reach.

Thirty years on, Cluchy is still propounding the Beckett gospel: his company, now featuring professional actors and internationally if not too financially successful, devote themselves almost entirely to 'Godot', 'Endgame' and 'Krapp's Last Tape'. Cluchy's son, Louis Beckett Cluchy, is playing the Boy in this production, a nine-year-old who cuddles his uncle Sam at every opportunity. For Cluchy, the idea of Beckett as a dry artist, a skull beneath the skin, as a propagator of obscure fables of disembodied voices and old men in barren rooms, is sacrilege. 'For us, Beckett is a political writer. Sam has told us that he regards each of his plays as a completely closed system, that nothing about one can be assumed from any of the others. But we see the plays very much in that context.'

No doubt Beckett would run a mile from any 'political' label but that doesn't prevent him taking a more than polite interest in the rehearsals. For him, the plays are akin to music, require very precise articulation and stress, careful orchestration during which he even paces out precise numbers of steps that the actors should take in any given direction.

Sitting in the front row, Beckett's frame sometimes contorts in time to the words of his most famous text. He raises himself, walking on stage to demonstrate his 'step-by-step' approach by which he looks for unity through repetition – of words but also of movements, precise, step-by-step patterns to accompany and amplify the spoken words. In one sequence when Cluchy as Pozzo is addressing Estragon and Vladimir, Beckett pulls Cluchy back to emphasise a word: 'It shouldn't be "Even when the likeness is an imperfect one…" It's "Even when the (pause) likeness is an imperfect one." Pause on "the" and look him in the eye with your glasses…' ●

1985

January
Kim Cotton becomes the UK's first commercial surrogate mother.

House of Lords televised for first time.

March
Millwall fans riot after cup-tie with Luton Town. Thatcher calls for tougher sentences for hooligans.

Mikhail Gorbachev becomes leader of Soviet Union.

April
Princess Michael declares herself shocked at the revelation that her father was a member of Hitler's SS.

May
A fire at Bradford City results in 52 deaths during a game with Lincoln City.

38 Juventus fans die when a wall collapses during fighting at the Liverpool-Juventus European Cup Final. UEFA announces indefinite ban on English clubs in Europe.

July
Live Aid raises over £40m for charity. Bob Geldof is temporarily elevated to God status.

State of Emergency declared in South Africa.

September
Rioting breaks out in Brixton when Mrs Cherry Groce is shot by police during a search for her son.

October
PC Keith Blakelock is murdered during riots on the Broadwater Farm Estate after Cynthia Jarrett dies during a police raid.

December
Canadian businessman Conrad Black buys *Daily Telegraph*.

'Send us the fock'n money,' said Saint Bob and the world's richest pop stars fell over each other to give up their entire savings and personally deliver food to the starving in Ethiopia. We marched for jobs and watched the mining industry get switched off after the strike. Football was in pain at Heysel and Bradford, the French sank the *Rainbow Warrior* and the ozone hole was definitely there. But they brought back *Classic* Coke.

9½ Weeks
The film has evidently gone through innumerable revisions, and little remains that is truly daring for the jaded '80s.

Desperately Seeking Susan
The female characters are offbeat, off-the-wall, out-to-lunch and thoroughly engaging: Céline and Julie let loose in a Big Apple sub-culture.

Jagged Edge
This shows that a contemporary whodunnit can still rivet sophisticated modern audiences without retreating into horror or camp.

Prefab Sprout - Steve McQueen (Kitchenware)
The Sprouts' second album profits from the presence of

Thomas Dolby who has brought a new dimension to their sound.

Kate Bush - Hounds Of Love (EMI)
The care and attention and hours of work that have obviously gone into the production are almost enough to make you go out and buy a new hi-fi.

Run DMC - King of Rock (Profile)
This LP takes the art of beatbox brutality and riotous rapping to a previously uncharted state. Their scorn is tempered with humour but really it is their fluency that is most notable. Run DMC's bottom-line is poise and precision. Truly, one of the greatest Rock LPs.

Tina's Turneround

Tina Turner interviewed in T.O. 760,
by **Geoff Brown**

1985

Tina Turner

Whenever I hear that line in Stevie Wonder's 'Livin' For The City' about the pretty black-skinned girl whose 'skirt is short but Lord her legs are sturdy', my thoughts turn unerringly to Tina Turner. How could Stevie *know*? The young man is blind! Then I think of that other, older blues lyric insisting that the most handsome of women do make the blind man see – and I think of Tina, fundamental, long-legged, soul-singing Earth Mother, some more.

Watching her perform, one cannot help but feel… um… *renewed.* Hers is a physical presence of extreme proportions, an animal magic expressing itself exuberantly through music and dance. It is something singularly undiminished by 46 years on God's Earth, 16 of them spent in a marriage monstrously appalling even by show business standards, and by over 2½ decades of touring and recording almost constantly.

Now, after a phenomenally successful last 18 months, Tina Turner has promised herself the whole of 1986 off. I reckoned she wouldn't know what to do with herself. 'Oh yes I will,' she affirms – '*Nothing*! Abso-loootly!'

The reason for her proposed 12-month vacation is the success of 'Private Dancer', the pop-rock album recorded predominantly in England that has given her the big hit singles her career had lacked since divorcing Ike in 1976. The album has even won her three Grammies, including Record Of The Year for 'What's Love Got To Do With It'.

This sudden upsurge started a few years back. She had been working the clubs and cabaret watering holes in Las Vegas and Lake Tahoe, paying off the enormous debts which resulted from the break-up of her marriage. (Broadly speaking, after one last beating at the hands of Ike Turner, one during which she finally struck back, she left him snoring on a Dallas motel bed, walked out with the clothes she stood in and some loose change, let him have the house, recording royalties, the lot, and claimed no alimony, anything to be free. Trouble was, they were in the middle of a tour which had to be cancelled and she fell liable for damages claimed by many promoters.)

Realising that if she was ever to escape her debts she would need a strong boost to her career, a few years ago she changed management. 'It's the difference between young and aggressive guys and an older secure man that's not really hungry for it anymore,' she explains. 'And I just couldn't wait. I didn't have time.'

The result was a series of collaborations with Heaven 17's Martyn Ware and Greg Walsh. She contributed the vocal to BEF's version of 'Ball Of Confusion' on their 'Music Of Distinction & Quality' album and went on to cover another venerated R&B song, Al Green's 'Let's Stay Together', which proved a massive hit. Hearing her voice in a new electronic setting was certainly an ear-opener. It reminded her, she now says, of working in 1966 with Phil Spector on 'River Deep, Mountain High'. 'That's what I felt, it was similar to a Wall Of Sound. That's why I took it. I still enjoy doing some R&B but you need a change in your life and I needed a change musically. It's not like dropping the old habits, the old style, it's like I just want to get away from it for a while in order to be able to get back to and enjoy it.' Besides, she says, 'I was never really a fan of R&B. It was basically how Ike produced. But it wasn't my true taste in music, so when I left I just went totally into covers, I did very little of my own music.'

Yet at one time she had become a quite prolific composer, spurred on at Bolic Sound (Ike Turner's studio, the apartment annex of which he called The Whorehouse) by her husband's indifference. 'Ike was a great writer but he'd write, let's say, two lines of the first verse and then would blow with the rest. So I started correcting it. I thought, "Well, phooey, I can do it, I just might as well start myself." But then all I had to write about was my own experiences, about women, about reincarnation, things that I was just learning about, and that wasn't fun. But now I'm so busy and you have to stop to write. I think the first real breather I get, the songs'll start coming.'

As well as picking up the threads of her rock career – 'It was no plan to say "Let's get music out for pop or rock people", it's just – "Let's get some good songs". It just happened that way' – Tina's also reactivated a film career. Adding to previous outings in concert-based films like 'Gimme Shelter' and a cameo role as nightmarish hooker 'The Acid Queen' in Ken Russell's 'Tommy', she's recently finished filming a major role in the third Mad Max movie, 'Beyond Thunderdome'. 'The character is a strong woman,' says Tina, 'a real queen. She doesn't have a beautiful city but she built it. She really is a foundation there.' Overjoyed at getting the part, she didn't however find acting all that easy; there was no singing or dancing to use as a crutch for her interpretation of the role.

'It's the stillness. I'm so physical on stage but for the camera you have to be still and let the camera do it. That was the hard part, making everything look smaller. There is a thin line between acting and singing and the thinnest of all is just being still and letting it happen instead of doing it. I gotta tell ya that is not easy for a physical singer. I got it with biting the fingernails and going "Oh Christ!"'

Turned around and defiantly in the ascendant, Tina Turner's career now seems limitless, especially if the reports are right about the quality of her acting in 'Mad Max III'. 'Not that I want to jump out of singing,' she interjects, 'but I've been doing it a long time and I think it's a way to bow out gracefully and slowly, to travel less and continue to record, and then to do movies.'

If Hollywood's film moguls were ever at a loss for script ideas, they could do worse than base one on Tina's True Life Story: what could be more dramatic than her self-deliverance from artistic and marital subjugation into personal triumph. Her success today is looked on as an example to many. Is she aware of just how highly she's regarded by the women's movement?

'Yeah,' she says, 'but you know – and not to let the girls down because I think they've done a really great job – it seems that I live a woman's liberated life but I was not aware of it because I'm not into movements. I was just surviving. That is the kind of woman I am.' ●

AIDS
in T.O. 758, by **John Gill**

'We came out of the cinema and kissed each other goodnight to prove to each other that we didn't have AIDS' – a friend.

The 52 Britons who have died from AIDS are not the disease's only casualties. Gutter press homophobia, government inaction and sheer ignorance have all conspired to victimise thousands, whose privacy, welfare and jobs are now at risk.

Until recently, no one could have imagined a world without kissing, a world without affection. Since the arrival of Acquired Immune Deficiency Syndrome (AIDS), millions have had to contemplate it. Thousands now inhabit it, their sexuality restricted to mutual masturbation, 'dry' kissing and body rubbing (and there are even cases where that is discouraged). Some of them have AIDS, some of them do not. Some have been found 'positive' in the blood test for Human T-Cell Leukaemia Virus 3 which carries AIDS, some of them have not. Some of them are gay. Some of them are heterosexual. Ignorance, government inaction and FSBS (Fleet Street Bingo Syndrome) have made them all potential fatalities. Fear of the disease, fanned by the current climate, has reached alarming proportions. Gay Switchboard, which reports that AIDS related calls have quadrupled to the point where 'it's getting out of hand', have had calls from healthy, unaffected men so frightened they have become celibate.

Ecstasy
from 'Drugs: an A-Z of usage and abusage' in T.O 787, by **Andrew Tyler**

Ecstasy: Also known as Adam, or more formally as MDMA. Originally a psychiatric tool used on warring marriage partners, it has reached the rec set these past three years and developed a fabulous reputation. Said to enhance colour, sound, feelings of empathy, provide a speed rush, trigger hallucinations, rounding off with sedation and sleep. A new strain also makes the tea and puts out the cat. The drug is modelled molecularly on MDA, a member of the phenylethylamine family. Little seen in the UK except by readers of *The Face*, who must pay £20-£25 per hit.

Geldof's gospel

Inscribed in Gothic lettering above the dining-room doors of Davington Priory is the following motto: 'May Health, Peace and Grace abyde in this place.' The current occupants, however, are Bob, Paula and Fifi Trixibell – the Geldof-Yateses – who, while not quite the future tenants the Benedictine nuns perhaps envisaged when they founded the place back in 1153, nevertheless abyde in an atmosphere of ecclesiastical tranquillity that Billy Graham would give his organ stops for.

In the room the mistress of the house uses as an office there is a stone channel set into the floor which once served as a monastic lavatory. 'The nuns crapped in my fireplace,' confides Paula. 'I thought it would have a good effect on my writing.' A flight of stone stairs adjoining the master bedroom leads to a tiny, bare cell with a single, shuttered window; open the shutter and you're looking directly into the nave of Davington Church, down on to the heads of the choir. 'I had "Jerusalem" in bed this morning,' whispers Paula. Outside, the cloisters gleam a rich red – 'Gothic Red,' she says. 'You have to use human blood to get the right colour. The previous owner bought a pint from the blood bank.' All in all, Davington Priory would appear the perfect retreat for a man who has been elevated to the un-holy heights of pop sainthood. Much, it must be added, against his wishes.

'What do they want?' wails Bob, running both hands through his tangled shock of dark hair. 'What do people *want*? I mean, they come up to me and they *cry*, they hold *on* to me… it's preposterous! What the *fuck* do they think is going on?'

'If you're in a band, your knobbing ratio goes up a thousand per cent.'

We are sitting in the Flock and Formica Bar of the Cliff Pavilion, Westcliff-On-Sea. The Cliffs, a production-line 'entertainments complex' overlooking Canvey Island's liquid gas terminal, is the 32nd stop on a gruelling 43-gig tour to promote the Boomtown Rats' latest album, 'In The Long Grass'. Geldof and fellow Rats have just driven halfway across the country after the previous night's concert in Bristol and, with a streaming cold, another sound check and the prospect of 11 more gigs left to play, the pressure he's under would test even a saint. Which, unhappily, in the wake of the mammoth success of Geldof's Band Aid project to feed the starving millions in Ethiopia, is how the public is treating him.

'Like, some guy from the *Sunday Mirror* rang up about "Number One" [A new film, released this week, in which Geldof portrays a weasly snooker player] and said: "Don't you think it's unfortunate that it's coming out at this time?" I said: "Why? Summer? Is it a lousy time for films?" And he said: "No, you know… your charity work." I didn't get it at all, what he was saying. I thought perhaps he's thinking I won't have time to promote the film, maybe. "No, no," he says. "It's just that there's a lot of *cursing* in the film." *Cursing*. I said: "I don't give a bollocks what people fucking think of cursing!" Believe me, it's a weird situation.' Geldof wearily strokes his perennial five o'clock shadow. 'Y'know, I bet if I walked up the pier there I'd come back with 20 quid. People would just come over and stick it in me pockets, without saying a word. Or in the pub, they just come over and hand you a fiver. I mean, the amount of *trust* implicit in that… I bet if it happened to you you'd think it was pretty weird.'

As if to illustrate his point, the young waitress who arrives with the band's belated lunch is definitely under the impression she's serving Mother Theresa. 'Oh!' she exclaims, recoiling in surprise as Geldof forks a drumstick on to his plate, 'I thought you were a vegetarian.' 'Nah,' growls Bob, not one to pass up the chance of evening the score with an enemy, 'yer confusing me with Morrissey. Meat might be murder, but veg is *torture*.'

For a man with such a saintly image, Geldof is beset by an unholy number of enemies; as he always has been. In fact, it has been chic in a number of circles to dislike Bob almost from the moment he first arrived from Ireland a decade ago, a mouthy upstart in a mohair pullover, and announced to the world that all he wanted to do was to get rich, get famous and get laid. And when he teamed up with Paula Yates, an equally brash 'face' whose rapid climb up the TV tube appeared to be propelled by nothing more than champagne bubbles, they became Pop's Most Un-Loved Couple. The Smiths' Morrissey, pop's current heartthrob, is only the latest in a long line to bury the hatchet between Bob's shoulder blades, viz last month's *Time Out*: 'I'm not afraid to say that I think Band Aid was diabolical. Or to say that I think Bob Geldof is a nauseating character.'

'I think they're just an *awful* band,' replies Bob. 'A classic example of people who've nothing to say and plenty of money to say it with. I dislike ineffectual, effete people. I'm not effete and I've never been ineffectual. I hate anything ineffectual.'

For the moment at least, Geldof seems more at home before the TV cameras – standing in his carpet slippers in Addis Ababa haranguing the Ethiopian Foreign Minister, berating Mrs Thatcher for not doing more to move the butter mountain south – than he ever did in *NME*'s centre pages. So what is it like along the corridors of power?

'Look, in their eyes I'm a pop singer and that's precisely right. I'm a pop singer, she's the Prime Minister, and it must be seen in that perspective. Like, when I saw her there were things I would have been very interested to talk to her about – I think she has a *formidable* intellect – but it was my one opportunity, being the person most closely associated with Band Aid, to suggest that if you can speak with Chernenko, Gromyko, Mitterand and Reagan about the theoretical death of millions through nuclear destruction, why isn't it just as easy to talk about the actual death of just as many millions that's happening now?

interviewed in T.O. 765, by **Don Atyeo**

She said (mimics): "It's *not* that *simple*, Mr Geldof." I said: "No, nothing is as simple as death – one minute you exist, the next minute you don't." And I also got the X-ray glare when I contradicted her about the butter.

'But that doesn't bother me because I don't have any constituency other than myself. Basically, everybody just thinks either I'm a smart-arse, or that I'm trying to do something for myself or whatever. Which is irritating personally, but allows you to work very well because you're not beholden to anyone. When I talk to these guys I hear them clinking up the votes; now, I'm lucky, I don't have to attract votes, so I can argue with Mrs Thatcher, shout at the guy from Ethiopia, I can say and do exactly what I like. And it's quite evident that I'm speaking for no one but myself and I'm speaking absolutely honestly, because I've never had a fear of looking like an idiot or saying things that might appear idiotic. I don't *mind* being the world's clown, if I'm allowed to do things that are effective.

'There's plenty of things that bother me, and if I'm in a position to change them I will and I'm not afraid to. Like in Dublin last week I said things on television about Northern Ireland that resulted in a death threat and we had to be put under protection. I don't want to repeat it because I said it where it was most effective, but nationalism in any guise is dangerous, I think, and so-called freedom fighters to me are nothing but murdering fascists. But I think if you are in a position where people poke a camera at you, you must say these things regardless of the consequences. And if in doing so I offend a minority of people, that's okay because although that minority maybe won't accept what I say, they might at least argue the toss.'

Death threats notwithstanding, the minority most offended by Geldof's attempts to – in his words – 'seize the time' is not the IRA but the Jewish community, the result of an impassioned off-the-cuff speech at the British Record Industry Awards. Attempting to convey the magnitude of the Ethiopian disaster, he produced a rash of headlines along the lines of GELDOF IN HOLOCAUST TEA PARTY SHOCK.

'I did not call the Holocaust a tea party, which I keep reading now and which irritates me beyond belief!' explodes Bob, thumping the table and making the potatoes jump. 'I said that if we can compare at the end of this century the scope of these disasters, then one would seem like a ghastly and perverted tea party. Which in scope of numbers and in scope of what we're allowing to continue to happen, I still feel is the case. You mean to say, with a hundred million people dying, I can't talk about genocide? What else do you call allowing a hundred million people to die? When they look back on this century they'll say how the fuck did people allow this to happen? Why were there such surpluses. That's wilful murder!'

So, no regrets? 'You know, a guy from the television rang up and said he was going to chop it out of the replay. I said I would prefer it if he didn't, but he cut it anyway. Which I think was a shame.

'Still, it was all very healthy for me because the halo was getting very heavy. You've never seen a halo rust so fast in all your life. The next day I thought, "Thank God I've gotten rid of that thing!"

'People are constantly saying, "In 1976 you said you wanted to get rich, get famous and get laid." Absolutely! I mean, here was a guy who'd never had money, who felt he didn't want to be part of the anonymous crowd. Working in a factory or going to the pub or a football match, that wasn't part of me. I had to get known. That's the way I could operate. Fame is not liberty, but fame expands you greatly.

'And as for getting laid, for some reason, if you're in a band your knobbing ratio goes up a thousand per cent, like even from your first gig. I dunno why, I can't explain it at all.

'So I think all those things are perfectly valid aspirations. And when guys do get that, their yachts, their boats, their beautiful girls as per Duran Duran, I actually like watching them do it. I think it's fun for them. Because in two years or whatever it changes back. We never had that because we were never that successful. But really that isn't what I wanted, the yachts and the boats. I still don't have a car. I wasn't bothered about that stuff.

'There are three things that are important to me, and that is Paula and the baby, the band and the Band Aid thing. The band is what I do. The Band Aid thing is certainly the most important thing I've ever done, I think, in that the result is that millions might stay alive, which is an awesome thing. And obviously my family are hugely important to me because they're ultimately what I care about most. Paula I love very much. We get on really well, better than most people I know. We're very lucky. I'm an extremely lucky person in a lot of ways. Which is probably why I get so much stick.' ●

Ken Livingstone

from 'Knight of the long knives' in T.O. 771, by **David Rose**

Partly it's the change in the quality of his voice: less resonant, with a funny deep-down crack in it like someone just out of bed with a hangover when the phone rings too early on a Sunday morning. Then there is his weight: up two stone, a sprawling, bulging tum that probably wouldn't remotely fit into the trim safari suit that was the hallmark of his early days in power. But the most telling signs of permanent change are in the skin tone, which

> '*Last week the fate of the GLC was finally sealed when Royal Assent was given to the Government's Abolition Bill. Which means that in 248 days, after an uninterrupted period of 96 years, London will cease to have a single directly elected authority.*'
> – GLC poster

imperceptibly has crossed the divide between youth and middle age. On Ken Livingstone's forehead, the wrinkles are deep furrows now, and his lively sallowness has been replaced by

a leathery flush, its texture slow to spring back into shape when he moulds his cheeks to ponder a question. He is *wunderkind* no more.

What then, asks the deadly serious interviewer, have been the effects of leading the Greater London Council on your health and physique, Mr Livingstone?

The exact right length of pause. 'There's been the most *enormous* swelling of my genitalia…' ●

Cher bounces back

Cher interviewed in T.O. 774, by **John Preston**

Once, Cher was simply the other half of a '60s singing duo which looked like it had just been eaten by a grizzly bear. Now she's flying high in Hollywood.

This had all the makings of a minor scoop. Perhaps an entire new chapter in my forthcoming treatise, 'Stars: Their Baggage, Their Retinues'. Cher, I was confidently informed by the PR girl in the hotel lobby, had arrived the night before with 23 suitcases. And *three* trampolines. Now the trampoline has long been regarded by seasoned celebrity baggage watchers as an essential accessory to the star wardrobe. But three? This was something else entirely, prompting vast spirals of speculation. Was she planning an aerial display? The systematic divebombing of those critics who had been just a little too, well, critical. Information please. As it transpired, however, I had been soaking up disinformation. Certainly there were 23 suitcases plus the three trampolines, as well as rumours of an unspecified number of food blenders. But Cher was travelling with two companions. Divide therefore by three, making a modest, indeed a positively unglamorous total of seven and a bit suitcases and one trampoline each.

Up in the suite there are more bunches of flowers than in an undertaker's office. (Cher has just picked up the Best Actress award at Cannes.) There too, leaning against the wall by the door is what looks like… yes, the first trampoline has been run to ground. Cher herself is wearing an

immaculately cut trouser suit which, having by lucky birthright the eagle eye of the true *haut couturier*, I immediately recognise as a very expensive number indeed. ('Yeah', she says later, fingering the lapel, 'not bad for 60 bucks. I got it in a sale'). On the inside of her left forearm she has a little tattoo.

'A friend of mine in LA designed it'.

'What is it?'

'It's a kind of symbol'.

At one point in our conversation she asks, 'How do you think people in this country see me?' This is a tricky one to answer. Until six years ago those keepers of the Cher flame on this side of the Atlantic mainly still wore bearskins and crooned 'I Got You Babe' to one another at annual get-togethers. Some modernists had graduated onto 'Bang Bang' but after around 1974 the screens went blank and information came in fitful gobbets, garnered

from old copies of *Time* and *Newsweek* in doctors' waiting-rooms. Divorce from Sonny. Marriage to and subsequent divorce from Greg Allman (of the Allman Bros southern boogie-ists) and somewhere down the line two children graced with names that even a Hollywood birth registrar would blanche at: a daughter called Chastity and a son called Elijah. But while her star may have gone into partial eclipse over here, in America it was still firmly locked in the ascendant: sell-out shows at Caesar's Palace in Vegas, her own TV show and enough money to cushion her happily until the Last Trump. 'I got fed up with it though. I got very frustrated and decided that I wanted to try and act before it was too late. I was 35 at the time and clearly if I was going to make it I couldn't afford to wait too long. Everyone in Hollywood told me not to bother and so I went off to New York to do lessons. One day my mother tried to call me and ended up getting Robert Altman instead.'

Within six months she was starring in 'Come Back to the Five and Dime Jimmy Dean, Jimmy Dean'. Four years and two more movies ('Silkwood' and 'Mask') later, she could probably get backing for 'Heaven's Gate II' if she agreed to be in it. In hotel she may talk earnestly about the integrity of the artiste but onscreen she gives the impression of wielding a large and fearsome bullshit detector.

In fact, she says, she'd always wanted to be an actress, but Sonny wasn't too keen on the idea. Bono said no. But there was compensation

on the way because Sonny and Cher soon found themselves being hailed as the hippest couple to come out of a cave since Fred and Wilma Flintstone. 'I met Sonny when I was 16 and we started living together. He was working for Phil Spector at the time and I became a backing singer. The first song I did for Spector was "Be My Baby" by the Ronettes and the last was "You've Lost that Loving Feeling" by the Righteous Brothers. Then Sonny and I started out on our own'. The songs may not have been anything special but their stage gear prompted a flurry of raised eyebrows and incredulous guffaws. 'I have to tell you that when we dressed up in all that stuff we thought we looked fabulous. As a matter of fact when we started out we would wear bearskins to the gig and then change into more conventional clothes to go on stage. It wasn't until one night when we lost our suitcases and went on in our regular stuff that the whole thing started. And you know the funny thing, everyone thought we were English. Because only English people dressed outrageously. When the Rolling Stones first came to America they were so excited to meet us because no one else in America looked anything like them. We went on their Southern Californian trip with them because I guess they were kinda lonely'.

This sounds like a very novel theory. But while the Stones were ravaged by homesickness, dreaming of Dartford and points west, Sonny and Cher prospered and consolidated a useful reputation for being outrageous without ever doing anything that could ever possibly offend people. In her library cuttings Cher is painted as some kind of mega-harpie taking on richer and deeper scarlet hues as the years go by. But examine the evidence and you'll find that just about

the only time she ever caught a whiff of scandal was when she bared her belly button on national TV. 'I've never really thought of myself as being that outrageous. It's not that I wouldn't mind being like that. I admire people who are different. But I just don't think it's me.'

Cher, may describe herself as a combination of the 'very gutsy and the very immature' but she knows Hollywood better than most, having successfully kept her head above water there for 20 years. 'You have to pretend to be tough to begin with and after a while you find that you've become quite tough. It's a real easy business to be in for two or three years. To be in it for 20 years is really difficult.'

'You once remarked that men develop character as they grow older whereas women just grow old.'

'Yeah, I still think that's true.'

'You're now 40.'

'No, 39.'

'Really?'

'Yeah, I've just turned 39. Give me that year, I need it. There's no doubt that the older you get the harder it becomes. I just have to make the best of that. But I don't think there are many women who have completely changed their careers at 35. If I think what the rule of thumb really is, it's a lot more scary than what I've been able to make it.'

It's time to go. Cher has to go and be photographed by David Bailey. On the way out I spot the trampoline again. The temptation is too much to resist. I quietly climb up on top of the wardrobe, prepare to launch myself at the circle of rubberised canvas and reflect that for the first time in my life I will be able to finish an article with the words: And with one mighty bounce I was free. ●

"1985"

"The petrol engine will be seen as a thing of the past by the end of the century."
Clive Sinclair launches the C5

"You should all stop being moaning minnies."
Margaret Thatcher reacts to reporters' questions about high unemployment

"You campaign in poetry. You govern in prose."
Governor Mario Cuomo

"We are not going to tolerate these attacks from outlaw states run by the strangest collection of misfits, Looney Tunes and squalid criminals since the advent of the Third Reich."
Ronald Reagan gets tough

"I have the good fortune to be the first Liberal leader for over half a century who is able to say to you at the end of our annual assembly: Go back to your constituencies, and prepare for government."
David Steel MP gets a tad too confident

"I think historically, the term 'Thatcherism' will be seen as a compliment."
Margaret Thatcher

"As far as I am concerned I have not been defeated and neither have the working class communities of Britain."
Arthur Scargill as the NUM calls off the year-long strike

"People are now discovering the price of insubordination. And boy! Are we going to make it stick."
Ian McGregor on the sackings that followed the end of the miners' strike

"A government is not legitimate merely because it exists."
Jeanne Kirkpatrick, on the Sandanista government

"A gentle invitation to insight."
Dr Lester Grinspoon of Harvard University says of Ecstasy. To no avail. It's banned by the DEA in the US

Issey Miyake

from 'The art of clothing'
in T.O. 758, by **Steve Grant**

To describe Issey Miyake as a designer of clothes is rather like saying that Picasso painted pictures or that Miles Davis plays the trumpet. It was Davis who once paid Miyake the following huge compliment. 'Issey,' said Miles, 'designs like I think.' Not a bad tribute.

What did Davis actually mean? I ask Miyake as we sit in the office of his design studio in downtown Tokyo, a building shared with the Singer Sewing Machine company. Miyake's extraordinarily handsome features break into a grin. He was once described as the only Japanese to 'look good in a tuxedo'. 'Ah Miles. Well, we both like women very much. And we both like to be free. He plays like a bird. I design for myself.'

Miles Davis isn't the only superstar to don Miyakewear. Boy George and Marilyn swear by him; both recently plundered the stock of Plantation, Miyake's Brompton Road shop. Both took several weeks to settle their accounts. Apart from very occasional commissions for stage tours or because he is very taken with the individual in question, Miyake doesn't design to order. 'Too many European designers become rich and famous because the rich and famous wear their clothes. I'm more interested in a fusion between me, the designer, and the wearer, who creates a third personality by putting my clothes on. I was very excited and thrilled by the news that Boy George and Duran Duran were wearing them, but George and Simon Le Bon could bring something of their own to bear. Create something new for themselves out of me.'

Grace Jones, a former Miyake model, markets her own sensual brand of feline aggression in his other notable creations: not the loose, beautifully coloured robes that are rooted in the Japanese traditions of kimono. Rather, Grace Jones is the queen of the gridiron, those war-like chest-plates and looping hard-hats that look like a melting together of the Kendo player and the American footballer. Or those red plastic *bustiers* which he describes as 'second skins', armorial wrap-arounds that seem to hint at a designer's split personality. 'No, not really,' says Miyake, 'it's more humorous than that. I like to have fun in my designs. There is a great deal of deliberate parody: of martial arts, of those big American football stars. We are not so tall here! A lot of people have read things into my designs but ultimately I am interested in the body, in the beauty of the human form and how clothes should be more than a function, more than a way to keep you warm or in the right job. They should enhance the human potential. But most of all they should be… fun!' ●

Alexei Sayle

Great Bus Journeys of the World, from T.O. 793
No 28. Golders Green to Wandsworth via West Hampstead

Bus journeys can be a great adventure. Unlike cycling or driving you are free to look around you at the outside world and at your fellow travellers. Hey! If you see me on a bus why not produce a copy of *Time Out*, approach me and say, 'You are Alexei Sayle, this is my copy of *Time Out* and I claim my free futon.' And I'd tell you to fuck off.

10.30am, Golders Green Bus Terminus: One of the things – I mused – that has always annoyed me about other travel writers is that they always pretend to know immediately the proper name for everything; for example: 'As I looked over the side of the Arabian Dhow I espied a Yoruba chieftain sitting under a mango tree holding a bunch of Polyanthus Calivorus chatting to a lesser necked Andover duck.'

As I sat on the empty 28 bus waiting for the crew to arrive I stared blankly and unknowingly at many varieties of animal and plant life. If I was going to be a proper travel writer, maybe I should make up some names.

11am, Golders Green: 'Out of the window of the empty bus I looked past the tupperware bushes and three nobby stiles trees. I saw some pork pie birds, a lionel blair gull and some tigers.'

After a few minutes I got off the bus and wandered into Golders Green Tube station. Inside, my heart leapt – I saw one of the most exciting and neglected features in London termini – a Photo-Me-Booth. I am the world authority on Photo-Me-Booths and an author of the standard text on the subject, 'Les Photo-Me-Booths de Cherbourg'. There are many exciting and unknown facts about Photo-Me-Booths. For instance, did you know that these booths are not just a big wonky Polaroid but are gateways to another parallel dimension which closely mirrors our own. Sadly, life there is much harder than here and that is why when you get your photos they are always of a dispirited stranger who stares pleadingly at you through the glass. It also rains a lot in this other dimension which is why your photos are always wet.

I wandered outside the Tube station. Over the road I spotted one of those round blue plaques which tell you that someone you've never heard of lived in that building. This one told me that this was one of the 947 buildings in London which had been occupied by the great Albanian poet and writer KlepkeKlepke. Immediately I recalled a passage from his famous autobiography and classic of Albanian literature, 'Man of Soup':

'Later, much later, I went to the café. The one we called "Novae" joined us at this time. One of Novae's drawbacks was that he entirely lacked imagination. He once wrote a book called "One Thing To Do With A Dead Cat".

'Shortly before he died he was working on a new book, or rather a series of stories, called "Roget's Adventures of Tin-Tin": "Captain Haddock the mariner, sailor, sea-dog, seaman, seafarer, salt, shellback, tar looked, beheld, spied upon, observed, caught sight of, glimpsed at, viewed, witnessed, watched, gazed upon, stared at, peered at, noticed, scrutinised, inspected, contemplated, rubbernecked at Tin-Tin. 'Blistering excrescence-filled, noded, emphysemic, carbuncled, warty, vesicled, pustulent barnacles, whelks, crustacea, razor-sheds, winkles, mussels, cockles, cephalods, lobsters, crabs, crayfish, langoustines, oysters, clams, whelks,' he said."'

When I got outside the bus had gone, so I called a taxi and went home.

1986

January
Space shuttle Challenger explodes 90 seconds after take-off, killing all seven crew.

February
President Marcos escapes with the help of the US, as Mrs Cory Aquino comes to power.

March
Eddie Shah launches *Today*.

The GLC finally ceases to exist.

April
The US bombs Tripoli in attempts to wipe out military bases.

Major leak occurs at Chernobyl nuclear power station near Kiev. Radiation levels soar all over Europe.

Clint Eastwood is elected as mayor of Carmel, California.

June
Argentina defeats West Germany 3-2 in World Cup final.

July
Prince Andrew and Sarah Ferguson marry in Westminster Abbey.

Estate agent Suzy Lamplugh disappears after meeting a 'Mr Kipper' at a West London house.

September
Prince Charles admits on TV that he talks to plants.

October
Jeffrey Archer resigns as chairman of the Conservatives after (subsequently disproved) allegations that he was involved with a prostitute.

The *Independent* is launched.

November
Mike Tyson becomes the youngest world heavyweight champion in history at 20 years old.

December
Derek Hatton resigns from Liverpool City Council.

An explosive year. First the space shuttle Challenger lit up the sky, then Chernobyl made our sheep glow in the dark, bombs over Libya kept things booming and it was all rounded off with the Big Bang in the City. 'Spycatcher' was banned, The Singing Detective was told 'it won't get better if you pick it,' and at Wapping, Murdoch told the print unions pretty much the same thing. On TV, anti-AIDS advice was to avoid icebergs.

Withnail & I
Robinson's debut as writer/director is that rare thing: an intelligent, beautifully acted and gloriously funny British comedy.

Jean de Florette
It is Depardieu who supplies the heart and soul of the film with a towering strength and heartbreaking pathos.

Something Wild
Jonathan Demme observes the human eccentricity that underlies the corner-store banalities of Middle America with warmth; while faultless performances from Daniels *et al* ensure pleasures galore.

The Smiths - The Queen Is Dead (Rough Trade)
We're still waiting for the unflawed Smiths album. But this new

comic melodrama is still vastly superior to the work of 90% of their competitors.

Anita Baker - Rapture (Elektra)
Baker has ensured stylistic continuity by selecting eight slow, sensual declarations of emotional or physical intent. 'Rapture' sets standards few can hope to match.

Paul Simon - Graceland (Warner Bros)
Inspired by a mounting interest, in South African music, there's an occasional touristy note but the music is just too good to nitpick. It's not only the first he's done in some time but a considerable achiev-ement even by his own giant standards.

1986

Madonna

Bad girl

Madonna interviewed in T.O. 841,
by **Harry Dean Stanton**

Harry Dean Stanton: *Talk about your view of the world
as a child.*
Madonna: When I was a child I always thought that the world
was mine, that it was a stomping ground for me, full of opportunities. I always had the attitude that I was going to go out into the
world and do all the things I wanted to do, whatever that was.

*I read that you liked the song 'These boots are made
for walking – I'm gonna walk all over you.'*

That attitude wasn't it – not like I'm going to go in and terrorise
anybody or walk all over anyone or conquer – but just that I was
going to get out there and take a bite of the big forest. And I think
I did that. And now I'm a woman, I'm still doing that. But as big
as I am and as much as I know, I still have that same wide-eyed
feeling that there's still a forest for me to go out in.

You're still a virgin.

(laughs): Yeah.

Did you have a best friend?

Yeah, there was one girl. We were pretty good friends and I
think we laughed at the world together for a while, but we grew
apart. We did a really funny thing once. We thought we were better than anybody else, and our main point of interest was boys,
obviously, and we decided that we were going to dress up as ten-
cent floozies.

And that's where it all started.

I remember one summer I went away and hung out with my
uncles. They were very young, a couple years older than my

brother, and I thought they were the coolest people in the world.
They had a rock band. I'd visit my grandmother, up north in
Bay City, Michigan. She wasn't an extreme disciplinarian like
my parents, so I loved going there. We could have two desserts
at grandma's and stay out past ten and go out with beers and
drink boys. But I remember that summer I was watching my
uncles' rock 'n' roll band – wearing tight jeans for the first time
in my life. I smoked a cigarette, not too successfully, I started
plucking my eyebrows and I started feeling like, 'Yeah, this is
it, I'm cool.' I remember I got back and my stepmother told me
I looked like a floozy and I was really smashed.

*This was before you had taken dance or music or
anything?*

I was studying dance in high school, but this was before I was
really committing myself to it every day. At that time, I was going
to dance classes but they were fun. It was really a release for me,
just so I wouldn't beat up my brothers and sisters. I knew that I
was really good at it. They were jazz classes, so they weren't as
strict as, say, a ballet class. I'm talking like eighth grade, the summer between eighth and ninth grade I went to my grandmother's
house and did all this. So then I came back and after that summer
I felt like I had really grown up – only to find out that I was a floozy
(laughs). Then it was a private joke between my girlfriend and
me, that we were floozies, because she used to get it from her mother all the time, too. If we did one little thing, like wear a little lip
gloss or try to wear opaque pantyhose, not nylon stockings that
you could see through, not sheer, just tights.

So somewhere you did the floozy look.

Only because we knew our parents didn't like it. We thought it
was fun. We got dressed to the nines. We got bras and stuffed
them so our breasts were over-large and wore really tight sweaters
– we were sweater-girl floozies. We wore tons of lipstick and really badly applied makeup and huge beauty marks and did our hair
up like Tammy Wynette. She's got the pictures actually, I don't,
of us laying in the bed. We both took turns, lounging on the bed
with our hands behind our heads. We took pictures of each other
and we developed them and these were our ten-cent floozy pictures. We were going to keep them so we could look back at them
and laugh, because we knew how ridiculous it was.

Do you still have them?

I don't, but when I went home last spring I saw that girl and she
showed them to me and it made me laugh hysterically.

Maybe you could get them back so we could use them.

No way. I've had enough blasphemous photographs.
Everybody knows I'm a bad girl.

What about reading – what authors do you like?

Books are my next favourite thing, after kissing my husband.
I love to gobble books. You want to know who I gobble up?.

Like boys and beer?

I don't drink books, I gobble books. I gobble books and I read
my husband, okay?

*In one of your interviews you said you're basically a
very sweet person, a very good person – a very healthy
person and you like your body.*

I am. I know that I've incited a lot of bad feeling with the Moral
Majority or Parents and Children. There's this big scandal about
banning music with sexually explicit lyrics, but I think ultimately

children, more than anybody, sense the realness of somebody and the goodness of somebody. I don't think they would have attached themselves to a person or believed in them or looked up to them if there wasn't some innate goodness or sweetness to them. You let go of that trust and innocence and that intuitive psychic ability to see that in people as you grow older. I think it's these kids' parents who don't understand it and they're fearful of it.

Do you think it will have a positive effect on all these little girls, the 'wannabes'?

I do, because I have a positive attitude about life, and I think they see that. What they see more than anything is that I was a little girl from Michigan and I had a dream and I worked really hard and my dream came true. I believed in myself and now especially, more than ever, children really need to have those kind of people to look up to, people with positive life-messages People who believe in dreams and magic and things that are happy. Everything is so real and grim. Children in school today are thinking about their life being over soon because of nuclear holocaust or… All I'm trying to say is that it just seems that more and more negative things are happening around the world, whether it's incurable diseases or famine or the threat of the atomic bomb. What kind of thing is it for children to grow up with that fear? I think it's really important for them to have an image or something to inspire them and take them out of that. Not so they don't even think about it, but to realise that there are also some positive things going on. It's not just 'What's there to look forward to in life?'

This friend of mind told me that men see women from the outside in – in other words they've got to look great and have a great body, and then after you pass all those tests they'll talk to you. A woman looks at the inside of a man first. They look in his eyes or at his attitude – from the inside out, is that true?

I'm sure there are exceptions on both sides, but generally I would agree with that.

You know who said that?

Who?

Sean, your husband.

Isn't he the smartest!

Madonna, what inspires you in your music?

Gee willikers – I think the things that inspire me to make music are the things that arouse my curiosity and make me happy in life, whether that be romantic love, the love I feel for my husband, for instance, or the love I feel for my friends.

Have you felt differently since you've been in love with Sean?

Totally. I feel calmer now than I ever have before. What that means is that I can really concentrate on the important things. It's funny, now that I'm in love, all the songs I write I feel like I do it all for him. I do it for myself, but I do it for him. I'm writing the lyrics or doing the music, or something that's creative, I think, "Would he like it?" I do.

What are your feelings to the press? Do they abuse their privilege?

'Sean asked me to marry him but he didn't say it out loud, I read his mind. So I read his mind back to him.'

The thing that annoys me more than anything about paparazzi is that they really feel that they have put you where you are. They really think that because you're a celebrity, you owe them all the pictures they can get. I think it's completely unfair. I think it's one thing to want to be there at social functions like premiéres and parties and gala events, to want to be there to chronicle those events. I know people are interested in reading about that, but I don't want to get my picture taken every time I walk out of Jane Fonda, and I do. It's not even the taking of the pictures that bothers me, it's the element of surprise I always encounter every time they jump out of the bushes or jump from behind a corner. It's like a teeny heart attack every time it happens. Every time I go running in Central Park around the reservoir, and they're waiting… I'm gliding along listening to music and all of a sudden they jump from behind a tree. They're always scaring me, so I have to deal with that constant fear. And every time they jump out to take a picture, the way they take them – it's like they're raping me. I feel like they just might as well have taken a gun out and shot me, because it takes me at least an hour to come down from that shock every time that happens. It's a very traumatising situation for me.

It also isn't right to have six helicopters hovering over a marriage ceremony.

No, but America is a really life-negative society. People want to know all the underneath stuff – all the inside stuff, your dirty laundry. Which isn't to say all the stuff the press has been getting on me is negative or dirty or whatever, but there's always a hope, for them, that they'll uncover something really scandalous. So papparazzi hover above you like helicopters; they're vultures. If they truly understood what they're trying to capture in a photograph, they wouldn't want to do it. I want to be able to go through the day – go to my exercise classes, get married – without the whole world watching. I've given enough to the public through my music and videos and one movie that I've done, and I plan to keep on giving it. I don't see why they have to keep on trying to take more from me. That's all I have to say about it.

What about the Playboy spread?

When they were taken seven or eight years ago they weren't meant for publication in any magazine. At the time I wasn't a known person and it didn't really occur to me that I was setting myself up for scandal for years to come. When I first moved to New York, I modelled for a lot of art schools for the drawing and painting classes. I was a dancer at the time. I was in really good shape and I was slightly underweight so you could see my muscle definition and my skeleton. I was one of their favourite models because I was easy to draw. So I sort of made the rounds. I got paid very well for that, versus having to work eight hours in a restaurant. I could work in a school for three hours, and take dance classes all day, then do my show at night, if I was performing. And then a lot of people wanted me to start modelling privately for them. They had little get-togethers on the weekends, say three people in the class, so I got to know these people in a friendly kind of way. They became like surrogate mothers and fathers for me, they took care of me. Then, what would happen is, they'd say they knew a great photographer and he's doing an exhibit on nudes and he'd like to do some pictures.

▶

So I'd get involved with photographers that way. Then he would turn me on to somebody else, and for the photography sessions I'd be paid a lot more than for drawing. I consider the nude a work of art. I don't see pornography in Michelangelo, and I likened what I was doing to that. It was a good way to make money. As it turns out, I became very successful and famous and America, the media and the press, geared the way it is…

…Trying to make something smutty out of it.

Of course, a life-negative society. Besides, that's sort of the course of events when anyone gets successful, to go back and try to find all the deep, dirty, dark hidden secrets and expose them. Well I don't have any, because I'm not ashamed of anything that I did. I would have preferred that those photos weren't printed, because obviously the way they were promoted wasn't very flattering to me, but, when people actually saw them they thought,

'What's the big deal here?'

The press has written that your rise has been like a meteor but that you're going to burn out; they also quote you as saying in 20 years you think you'll be a great actress.

As far as acting goes, I'm not sure it will take me 20 years to be a great actress. I think what I said was that I hope to be acting 20 years from now, when I know I won't be making pop videos for MTV any more. I ultimately think my career as an actress will outlive all my other careers. I don't think my success would be sustained as it is now if my career were only based on my physical appearance. It just shows that looks mean a lot and image means a lot. But you have to back it up. People didn't really have any preconceived notions of me until they started seeing my image – my face, the way I moved, putting the voice with the face.

Rogue male

Oliver Reed interviewed in T.O. 841, by **Chris Peachment**

You can discover which Home Counties farmhouse belongs to Oliver Reed quite easily. It's the one with a life-size stuffed rhino guarding the gate. If the *National Geographic* is to be believed, the rhino is a fearsome beast. Shortsighted, thick-skinned, a real heavyweight with a frightening turn of speed, it will apparently attack anything it feels like attacking just for the hell of it. In short, it's something of a bully.

Clanking away on the ship's bell, which serves as the house's summoning call, produces no sign of life. The house is as dark and quiet as one of the Hammer sets in which Reed started his career as an actor. Threading my way gingerly around the garden path, I knock on the back door, to be confronted by a man with a bruiser's face and truculent stare. 'I'm here to speak to Oliver Reed.' This is answered by an exaggerated 'Who?' accompanied by a neverheard-of-him look. After much explanation that I am neither the tax man, nor the local magistrate, the lady of the house appears and explains that Ollie is down the local pub.

Reed is indeed at the village pub, sinking gin and tonics at 11 in the morning,

and looking a little sheepish as he does the introductions. 'Sorry you have to meet me here, but I am evading the police.' I commiserate and ask what the trouble is. 'They want me for assault,' he says. 'Who did you assault?' I ask. The sheepish look disappears and one fierce eye surveys me like a menu. 'A journalist,' comes the reply. From somewhere at the back of my throat I can hear a strangulated voice asking what the man had done to warrant getting a bent nose. 'He was rude about my wife,' says Reed without further elaboration. I don't actually fall to my knees and promise that I will never, ever mention the good lady in his presence, but I make an indelible mental note to that effect.

For Reed is still a very big man, with a barrel chest like the Guardsmen one remembers from childhood, and a pair of fists like hambones. He also wears glasses with coke-bottle lenses in them, which only serve to accentuate that bulging stare. I doubt if anyone has ever asked him to remove his glasses before stepping outside. I doubt if anyone sane has ever asked him to step outside.

In fact he is looking remarkably trim these days. He has shed a good couple of stones for his new role in Nic Roeg's film of 'Castaway', in which he plays Gerald Kingsland, the man who placed a personal ad in the back of this very organ for a lady to accompany him for a year on a desert island. As everyone knows, she, Lucy Irvine, went off the poor fellow and refused him any fun during the long dark nights on the island. I say that this sounds like a rather sad tale. 'Well, I hope we can make it with a twinkle in the eye. I mean we're not doing "The Blue Lagoon", are we?' No we certainly are not. If Nic Roeg is making the film, that must be a racing certainty.

'It's actually all very funny. If you read Lucy Irvine's book and then you read Gerald's version of the events. Obviously neither of them are telling lies. It's just that they see things from their different points of view. He is saying, "Look, I haven't changed since you knew me. I haven't gone bald or fat, so you're the one who's welshed on the bed." And then he goes spare when she won't come across. That is pretty funny. Some Aussies arrive on the island and take up with the sheila, and then they find poor old Gerald, going spare, living in a hole in the ground, with a tiny dick.

'Can you manage that last bit?' I ask, chancing my arm. 'That's exactly why they cast me,' Reed says benignly. 'Also that's why I've gone on the diet. I mean, when you've got a big gut, then your winkle looks very

You're one of a handful of musicians – and I'm including Michael Jackson, the Beatles, Elvis – who have had to compete with themselves on the charts. To get another hit you would have to knock yourself off.

Gee, I can't complain, the more the merrier. I like the fact that all my songs are doing well, who wouldn't?

Tell me your goals. What do you want to do?

I think in the back of my mind, no matter what I was learning to do, I've always had the deepest desire to pursue acting as a career. I guess I'm sort of getting to it in a roundabout way.

You mentioned earlier that a lot of your work now is for Sean. He inspires you tremendously, you feel more together, connected, being in love, so let's just cut the bullshit, Madonna – did he ask you to marry him or did you ask him? How did it happen?

Sean asked me to marry him but he didn't say it out loud, I read his mind. So I read his mind back to him.

Where were you?

In Tennessee, at the Something Inn. We were out in the middle of nowhere, and 7-Eleven was the high point of interest there. It was a Sunday morning and I was jumping up and down on the bed, performing one of my morning rituals, and all of a sudden he got this look in his eye and I felt like I just knew what he was thinking. I said, 'Go ahead and say it, I know what you're thinking.' No! What I said was 'Whatever you're thinking, I'll say yes to.' That was his chance. So he popped it.

Did you say yes immediately?

Of course I did. I'm a woman of my word. Then we went to the 7-Eleven and bought a whole bunch of jawbreakers and celebrated. Sean is my hero and my best friend. ●

⬤ ⬤

small. I can't change the size of my winkle, but I can change the size of my gut. So I'm going on a diet so I can hold my head up high in the stalls.'

There is also the major problem of a tattoo which he is reputed to have had engraved on that very organ. There were reports in the tabloids some time ago that he was not so ashamed of it that he could not bare it for the assembled company one heavy night in a Madrid restaurant. One wonders if perhaps it will be likewise on view in the forthcoming film, but I do not ask this, because I am suddenly mindful of the last journalist who crossed Mr Reed, and besides, I wouldn't want to spoil the movie for you all.

Lee Marvin has a good story about Reed which has never made the tabs. They were drinking in some dusty cantina down in Mexico while on the set of some long-forgotten Western and, as the evening wore on, Marvin noticed that a group of Mexicans at a nearby table were taking exception to some of Reed's louder expressions of distaste about this and that in Mexico. Marvin noticed that they were easing their pistols in their holsters and generally giving the pair the evil eye, so he told Reed to quieten down a bit and, whatever else, not to look in their direction. Apparently Reed ignored both instructions, and the bandidos began firing their guns into the air. Reed then gets up, walks over to them, and pastes them with a perfect tirade about Mexico, which rises to a crescendo, with 'And furthermore, we beat your fucking Armada!' (a little geographical confusion here, no doubt due to the local mescal). The Mexicans lapse into a dumbfounded silence. 'And what's more, I'll bet you can't do this,' says Reed, who promptly does a handstand on the arms of his chair. 'Or even this,' he cries, small change clattering to the floor. He removes one hand and tries a single-handed stand on one arm of the chair. Alas the chair is not well balanced. Reed crashes to the floor and dislocates his shoulder, laughing like a drain. Quite how the Mexicans responded I cannot recall. And if you want to know if it's true, you'll have to ask Lee Marvin.

Reed might have been invented purely to keep tabloid gossip columnists happy. But while there are endless stories in their pages about his recent marriage to his 'child bride', his three-day-long stag party in which, clad solely in a kilt, he made his way through his favourite tipple – an ice bucket filled with every available drink in the bar – his imprisonment in Guernsey, his exploits with a soda siphon, there never seem to be any pieces in the upmarket papers about his strengths as an actor. And as Paul Mayersberg's film 'Captive' reveals, he can be very good indeed.

That bullish intensity, so marked in his early films like 'The Devils' and 'Women In Love', is still plainly in view; if the dialogue becomes a shade heated, his neck always looks like it is going to burst his collar. But middle age also seems to be bringing to the fore a certain sensitivity which in fact was always there but rather swamped in his youth. His scenes with his daughter, played by Irina Brook (daughter of Peter) in the film, are memorable for a rather touching, semi-incestuous, custodial sort of love from him. It is clear why she has to break away from his influence if she is ever to achieve adulthood; nonetheless, the emotion is genuine. And, in spite of being in very few scenes, Reed is an object lesson in screen acting to the rest of the cast in that troubled film.

'I can't change the size of my winkle, but I can change the size of my gut.'

Unlike many British actors, especially the heavyweight drinkers such as O'Toole, Richard Harris and Richard Burton with whom one usually brackets Oliver Reed (although he is something of an exception, not being a Celt), middle age has improved him. The face is marked by experience, the ardour cooled to a bearable temperature. And if it seems a surprise, that is because it has come upon us with so little warning. Unlike Michael Caine, who elected to go to LA to keep working, Oliver Reed decided to stay. The British Film Industry is not only erratic in its highs and lows of production, it is also very small. There simply are not enough films to go around; most especially if your face has fallen out of favour for a while. So Ollie fetched up in Canadian co-productions, and films about killer snakes called 'Venom'. 'I like being a father figure now. There's nothing worse than a man hanging on to his youth. Either he starts pumping iron and looks ridiculous. Or he goes the other way and eats a lot of spotted dick.'

The morning wears on. His cronies in the pub come and go. I am not counting, but that must be at least the seventh gin before lunch. Suddenly, the rhino charges. 'I don't speak to journalists any more because they piss me off. There aren't any critics any more. They are all just film reviewers. And there's a very hostile reaction to them from all the businessmen behind films, whose business you depend on. And you'll be out of a fucking job. I don't know what else you can do. How dare you call yourselves critics. I was always panned by critics, but the public made up its own mind and came anyway.' Since there isn't a tree nearby which I might climb, the only option is to brazen it out; an option made easier by the fact that the tirade seems curiously impersonal. It's not exactly directed at me; more like some vague malignant force, somewhere, *out there*. The rhino is a shortsighted beast (with a bloody great horn).

So it's, 'Yes, Oliver, no Oliver, up to a point Oliver, I can't agree with you there, Oliver, no you're wrong about that, Oliver, life is more complicated and besides you should be above all that really.' And, do you know, he found himself agreeing. Either way, it is very good to have him back. Let us hope that the British film industry feels the same way. ●

from worse to
baad

James Brown interviewed in T.O. 817,
by **Timothy White**

'**S**ometime, you like to let the hair do the talking!'
booms the massive burnt-umber visage in the gild-
ed mirror; stubby hands briskly smooth out the
sparkling surface of his highly teased bouffant with a savage
styling comb the size of a shark fin. Up close, one recognises
the matte finish of his complexion as well-rendered pancake,
the keen edge to his gaze as a thick application of eyeliner. This
is his street face.

The puggish, broad-chested man steps back from the looking glass in the Barron Room South of New York's Waldorf
Astoria. He savours the sight of his Luster Silk-soaked mane
and buffed countenance, as his hairdresser of some three
decades scrutinises each meticulously layered lock of conked
tonsorial confection.

'Ummmmm,' Henry Stallings purrs, ringed fingers weaving
pinpoints of light into a cut-rate halo above his cousin's
chunky head. Stallings is careful not to touch his latest James
Brown 'do.

'I look good, huh?' Brown offers to no one in particular as he
contentedly strokes the lapels of his plaid twill suit. 'Henry
Stallings is my kin, you know. This is a man that never have
said, "I don't think that looks good on you." He would say,
"What you want? Do you want to roll it? Do you want a bush?
Or a 'fro?" Right now he's only freelancing and doing a few
things 'cause he's with me on the road. But we're getting ready
to build a shop around the country and we're gonna call it
Groom Me. Groom Me, sir! Groom ME! GROOM ME!'

Mr Brown, the Godhead of Get-Down, has been haunting
the corridors of Gotham's grande dame of a hotel for a solid
week. He joined Ray Charles, Fats Domino, the Everly
Brothers and other surviving architects of
the pop pantheon in the main ballroom
downstairs at the glittering January 23
inaugural induction dinner for the Rock
and Roll Hall of Fame. At the ceremony he
worked the summit conference of rock
stars and record industry bigwigs like the
dancing street pug he'd once been as he touted his scrappy
hit single from the 'Rocky IV' soundtrack, 'Living in
America'. It was Brown's first ascension into the upper
reaches of the pop charts since 'Get On The Good Foot' lin-
gered briefly at number 18 in *Billboard* in the autumn of
1972, and it was an unsentimental journey of epic proportions for a man marking the thirtieth anniversary of his
recording career.

James Brown was four when his parents' marriage crumbled; six when he could buck dance to the accompaniment of a mouth organ; seven when he was living with Aunt Handsome 'Honey' Stevenson and becoming proficient at rolling dice and picking out tunes on the household's rickety pump organ when he should have been in school.

'He would stay out of school two and three days a week, but when he came to class, he would still do more than the other children,' Laura Garvin, his seventh grade teacher, recalls. 'We used to have little performances in class. We would charge ten cents to see James Brown and the children would just pile in, so we had to rule out the classroom shows. Sometimes we would move the show into the library. There was a piano there, and James Brown would play it or dance or sing. That was the real beginning.'

He dropped out of the seventh grade before the end of the school year and went to live with his paternal grandmother. He earned board by pumping gas alongside his dad, dancing for tips beside the troop trains snaking out of Fort Gordon, and shoplifting. At 16 Brown found himself in Richmond County Jail on Fourth Street in Augusta, after breaking into four cars in a single night. Following several months in the local lockup, Brown was sentenced to eight to 16 years hard labour in a state prison; he served only four in a reformatory before having his time commuted for good behaviour

After his release from reform school he took a job as a janitor at Toccoa, Georgia High School and married Velma Warren Brown in June 1953; the licence carried the cooked data that he was born June 17, 1928 in Pulaski, Tennessee. (Joe Brown registered the birth of his son as May 3, 1933 in Augusta, Georgia.) After two years of evening rehearsals with the Famous Flames, Brown quit his day job and made for Macon, crediting his self-confidence to 'white people in Toccoa who believed' in him.

'God got me in on the ground floor of every kind of music,' Brown exults backstage at Radio City Music Hall. 'He put me into the game before Prince and Sly and Rick James and the Funkadelics. When –'

Instantly Brown cancels the thought and explodes with a torrential verbal outburst: 'SEXMACHINEGOODFOOTTHINK DOINGITTODEATHICAN'TSTANDMYSELFWHENYOU TOUCHMESUPERBADCOLDSWEATFUNKYCHICKEN INEEDYOURLOVESOBADBABYBABYBABY!'

He pauses, grinning ferociously, and spews it out again. The feat of precisely merged enunciation is doubly impressive on the second pass, the humming whole too specific to be psychobabble or doggerel filler, and yet not exactly a boast either. It's more of an involuntary mantra disclosure.

'Down in DC they talking the go-go but I had them kids out in the streets while they were still babies, doing the popcorn with the Original Disco Man. Funk I invented back in the '50s. The rap thing I had down on my "Brother Rapp (Part I)" and you can check that. I enjoyed my thing with Afrika Bambaataa on "Unity" but I did it more for the message than for the music. Michael Jackson, he used to watch me from the wings and got his moon walk from my camel walk – he'll tell you that if you ask. Same way, I was slippin' and slidin' before Prince was out

of his crib; that's why Alan Leeds, who used to work for my organisation, is on his management team, tipping and hipping him. I ain't jealous, I'm zealous. I ain't teased, I'm *pleased*. Who's gonna do James Brown better'n *James Brown*? Think!'

He halts with a wheezy gasp, his nostrils flaring dangerously and the upper lip quivering on the brink of another mantra stampede. But it misfires: 'SEXMACHINEGOODFOOT (*cough cough-cough*) – aheheheheh – yes suh! Show business!!' One more pair of these hot-dogging larynx wipe-outs and he'll be phoning in this evening's programme from an oxygen tent.

'This is a family operation,' Brown says, referring to his third wife as he idly unbuttons his silk burgundy shirt and unclips the waistband on his matching slacks. In late 1984 he wed Adrianne Modell Rodriguez, who sometimes appears on the soap operas 'The Young and the Restless' and 'Days of Our Lives'. 'Mrs Brown, she's an actress, a beautician and a personality in her own right and that am quite a combination. She do my production co-ordination, sees I'm ready for the people anytime, anywhere 'cause they can want me with no notice. I can draw 50,000 people in Arkansas like *that*, or 10,000 in Chicago on a rumour I might be there. Last summer Vice President Bush sent me a letter saying thank you for not forgetting the unemployed.

'I been friends with Presidents! Johnson, Kennedy, Mr President Habib Bourguiba of Tunisia – you know where that is? I'm trying to get the dignitaries to send me over to Moscow to get the static outta the Hot Line and start everybody talking about love. Senator Strom Thurmond, he belongs to my church, and he's somebody who's been there in the background for me for years.'

How's his financial picture these days?

'Looks good, pretty good. I got me a Scotti Bros contract since the "Rocky" movie, and Polydor and I are working on reissuing a bunch of things. Don't have all that ranch land anymore, but my wife and I still got some nice property to fall back on to. I ran into taxman troubles and had to sell my jets, had to sell my radio stations. I was the only black man in America to own three radio stations but I travelled and left it up to accountants and they messed it every kinda way, but I'm coming back from it. I got a lotta new ideas, I wanna do a keyboard record, I wanna produce some of the young talent, find another Michael Jackson like I did before.

'I'm not afraid to be the boss, see? That's how James Brown music came to be. Back when everybody was listening to soap-suds songs and jingles, I emphasised the beat, not the melody, unnerstand? Heat the beat and the rest'll turn sweet. I heard the percussion in everything – even the rhythm guitar sound like a drum to me. My guitarist, Jimmy Nolen, God rest his soul he's gone to his reward (the originator of the hugely influential signature 'chicken-scratch' riff died of a heart attack December 16, 1983) – Jimmy knew how to get the guitar to hit like a snare for me, 'cause I wanted a band that would punch back when I swung at 'em.

'It was a new attitude, better than the Marines, better than boot camp. I wanted the band onstage to be like soldiers, with me being the general, calling out the battle plan.'

And how is troop morale?

'We gettin' on, gettin' along. Sometimes I got to lay down the law, but everybody know the rules at this point. I useta be *hard*, right,' he concedes, a grin growing on his lips, 'but I'm mellow now, I slowed down and lightened a little bit. I got enough veterans to take care of the vet. We funky enough to take on any takers.'

Maceo Parker, an old campaigner who sparked or witnessed his share of melées and mutinies in the Brown camp, agrees. 'Problem was, it used to always be kinda stressed, pretty tight quarters for all of us, in the studio and on the road. The material was worked out on the road, in the time before each night's show, with James letting us in on the grooves he'd been developing and almost giving us assignments. Everything was set up to keep you in line and sharp. Thing is, there's a right way and a wrong way to do anything, and then there was James Brown's way, which always had to be considered righter than right.'

Parker says he lost patience with the $50 fines and the insensitivity to *esprit de corps* they exemplified. Most grown men don't need to be told when to drink, swear or shine their shoes, but it was Brown's fierce anti-drug stance that rubbed many a sideman raw in the late '60s and early '70s.

'Everybody would be sneaking reefer and other shit on James,' Bootsy Collins recalls. 'He was always storming into the dressing room to ask what the funny smell was and throw a shitfit. So a lot of us headed up the other direction just to get a leg up. It was acid that eventually made things extra crazy, same as with P-Funk, which I joined after leaving James's band. One night with James, I thought the neck of my bass guitar turned into a snake. I didn't want no part of it and went back

to the dressing room in the middle of the show. That pretty much cooled my deal with the Godfather.'

The last straw for others on the squad was less cerebral. During a 1974 concert trip to Zaire that was carrying BB King, the Spinners, the Crusaders and Lloyd Price, the plane almost failed to clear the runway because it was so severely overloaded with Brown's personal effects. The luggage of others had to be removed in order to make liftoff just barely possible, and several of the passengers described the stunt as potentially life-threatening. By the end of the protracted tour the following year, Parker and other key members of the troupe had tendered their resignations.

'Last really good time I had with the whole James gang was on a bus coming back from LA in 1975,' Parker says. 'We were drinking, joking, doing the dozens and carrying on great. It was the *heck* with the fucking rules, thank God.'

Did James enjoy himself as well?

'James? On that bus with us? James Brown was not on that bus, my friend. No, no, no, no.'

For the time being, Parker says he's 'content – print that – content' with the situation, although he feels bad he and the rest of the present line-up did not play on 'Living In America'.

'When the hit is on the radio, you like hearing your contribution,' he muses. 'If you playing with James Brown, hearing that contribution is what you definitely come to count on. I can promise you that.'

Sad to say, despite the best efforts of Parker and the rest of

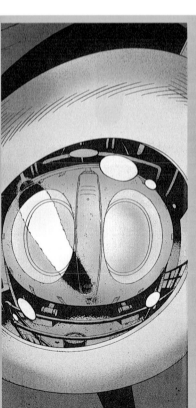

Comics explosion

in To 839, by **Neil Gaiman**

'Watchmen' is a phenomenon. Issue four of this 12-part comic series has only just appeared, but 'Watchmen' already sells over 200,000 copies an issue, the film rights have been snapped up by director Walter Hill and the critical response is the best that American publishers DC Comics, the outfit responsible for 'Superman' and 'Batman', have ever had. It tells the story of an alternative earth, a world in which the balance of power is even more messed up than it is now, where Richard Nixon is serving his fifth term as US President, the Russians are complaining about the American presence in Afghanistan, Vietnam is the fifty-third American state and insane vigilantes stalk a society on the brink of nuclear armageddon.

SF critic and novelist John Clute says, '"Watchmen" is the first comic to take the material of the superheroes, the fantasies that have built up around them, and make them a part of legitimate fictional discourse about America. It's the first time a novel – and make no mistake, "Watchmen" is a legitimate novel – has been written which assimilates those grotesque childhood fantasies into an adult model of the state of the US and its future.'

Fans have gone wild about 'Watchmen's' plot and look. That's not surprising, given that it's the first series in nearly 30 years to assume that comic reading doesn't stop with the advent of adolescence. What is surprising is that 'Watchmen' is created entirely in England by writer Alan Moore and artist Dave Gibbons, and that London has become the centre of a comics explosion. The artistic potential of the comic form is at last being exploited.

Writer Alan Moore says, 'It is as if the first films had come out and people said, "Yes it's a very good medium for children." You would have never had "Citizen Kane" or anything adult or anything worthwhile. So 'Watchmen' as well as proving a phenomenal success, is helping to re-write the history if comics.

Brown's 25-piece orchestra, the first half of the Radio City show is less than an epiphany. Al Sharpton's pallid invocation gives way to excruciating treatments of the 'Entertainment Tonight' theme, 'There's No Business Like Show Business' and 'Take Me Out To The Ball Game'. The exotically pell-mell pageant doesn't catch fire until the finale, which builds from simmering versions of 'Sex Machine', 'Super Bad' and 'Get That Feeling' to a six-minute 'Living In America'. A hornscreech-*cum*-rim-shot signals the start. Dead on the reverberant *bop!* Brown drops into a full split, grabbing the throat of the mike stand as he sinks and then whipping it out to cord-length as he leaps up again. With the slack wire hooked around his pinky, he executes a double spin and snaps the mike down to within four inches of the floor, catching it in his cradled palms – *this man is 53 years old* – as he swiftly genuflects to growl, 'I live in America – say it!!' Time alone will tell if 'Living In America' co-writer and producer Dan Hartman can draw out of the mid-'80s model the brand of visionary output that once kept Brown a decade ahead of his most savvy emulators.

The secret seems to be in the degree of musical autonomy that can be provided, while steering the man away from the pointless score-settling, quirky self-parody and paranoia that have snapped and distracted his muse in the recent past. The voice is still intact, the moves as deft as always when left to their intuitive grace, all or most critical quibblings short-circuited by the lasting grandeur of an America original still triumphantly immersed in his own spirit. ●

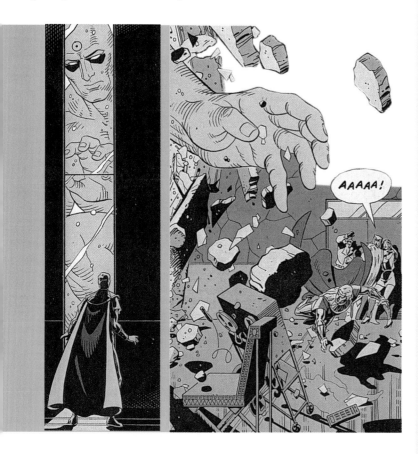

"1986"

"Loadsamoney!"
Harry Enfield launches the phrase that adorns a thousand East End T-shirts

"A billion dollar tragedy with a 50¢ cause."
A journalist's view of the space shuttle Challenger explosion

"Preparing for suicide is not a very intelligent means of defence."
Bruce Kent, chairman of CND

"They said there is definitely a distinction between real life and the movies, despite the fact that President Reagan once mentioned as an example of inspiring patriotism a heroic act that turned out to have been from a World War II bomber movie starring Dana Andrews."
Journalist Calvin Trillin

"No-one can kill Americans and brag about it. No-one."
President Reagan's response to the bombing of a disco in West Berlin

"I never said I had no idea about most of the things you said I had no idea about."
White House staff member Elliot Abrams, giving evidence at the Iran-Contra hearings

"First of all the Georgian silver goes, and then all that nice furniture that used to be in the saloon. Then the Canalettos go."
The Earl of Stockton attacks the Tories privatisation programme

"Greed is all right. Greed is healthy. You can be greedy and still feel good about yourself."
Wall Street financier Ivan Boesky

"Everywhere I go, I see increasing evidence of people swirling around in a human cesspit of their own making."
Manchester police chief James Anderton, referring to AIDS sufferers

"If freedom were not so economically efficient it certainly wouldn't stand a chance."
Milton Friedman, economist

"Tell Sid."
Annoying British Gas share issue slogan

1986

James Brown – 'Watchmen'

1986

Marvin

Son of a gun

Lee Marvin interviewed in T.O. 814, by **Chris Peachment**

When they come to write the history of violence in the American cinema, Lee Marvin will be the protagonist. In film after film of his early career you can see him, his slack lower lip hanging open with green swamp moss dangling off it, as he turns to insensate violence. In 'The Big Heat' he throws scalding coffee in Gloria Grahame's face, permanently disfiguring her. In 'The Man Who Shot Liberty Valance', he just keeps whipping that lawman from out East, way past the moment when the point has been made. As the business-suited assassin in 'The Killers', he opens the film by terrorising a blind woman in such a way that he hardly has to do anything more in the film, because the memory of that keeps you in fear.

The real Marvin served his time as a Marine, fighting his way across the Pacific, through the Marianas before buying it at Saipan. Two hundred and forty seven men hit the beach and ran into Japanese crossfire at point-blank range. After a 15-minute fire-fight, there were just six men left alive from 'I' Company, Third Battalion, 24th Marines. Marvin hit the deck. 'There are just two prominent parts of your body in view to the enemy when you flatten out – your head and your ass. If you present one, you get killed. If you raise the other, you get shot in the ass. I got shot in the ass.' This might sound very droll, but in fact it was a nine-by-three wound at the base of the spine which earned him 13 months of surgery on a severed sciatic nerve, a Purple Heart, and a disability pen-

sion of $40 a week which is still running.

'My father had a Colt .45 Automatic, serial number C 9688. He bought it at Abercrombie & Fitch in the '20s, so it was the civilian model which is rather better finished than the standard government issue. He gave it to me when I went off to fight in the Pacific, but I lent it to my best friend and he got shot. Even to the end my father used to say, "You lost my pistol," and I used to say, "It wasn't a pistol, it was an automatic." But he knew that.

'He was the US Smallbore Champion in 1936 in New York. He was working for Kodak at the time, and he made a 16mm film of himself, he stripped to the waist, firing that gun. It was to improve general shooting technique, but it also helped me to shoot that gun properly, because it's a big weapon and hard to handle. To watch it in slow motion: the ripple from the gun going off travels up and down the arm three times, before the hand moves with the recoil. And then the hand moves up and to the left (because of the cartridge ejecting to the right) and it goes bob, bob, bob like that.

'A Magnum has a much bigger kick, but it goes straight back. The .45 is much harder to fire. No one can fire it straight, but my father taught me how. (At this point Marvin demonstrates with his .45.) Now, if you just hold the butt in your fist in the normal way, then your hand can move around in all directions because of the wrist's mobility. It's like you can write your name with the gun barrel. However, if you bend all your fingers at right angles to the palm, so they are pointing left, then you point the gun to the left and place the butt in your fingers, forefinger on the trigger, back of the butt nestling in your right angle of your hand. Then you turn your hand back at the wrist, so the gun is pointing in line with your arm, but there's a dog leg at your wrist. This greatly restricts the movement of the wrist, for when the gun fires. There's still a certain amount of lateral movement, but not much up and down.

'But the .45 is a real coke-burner. It's not an attacking weapon, more of a defensive one. I wouldn't use it unless the target is going to get powder burns on him. It's strictly short range. But the slug is big, very heavy. When he gets hit, he stays hit.

'One time in the Pacific, after we'd hit the beach, I'm crawling around, and look up and there's this wrapee right in front of me. (The Japs were called 'wrapees' because of the wrappings they wore around their legs, like puttees.) So I pull the .45 out from under my arm, and I've got it primed and with the safety off just as it's coming up, and I get him right in the chest and that's that. Later on I realise I've hit him with my old man's gun, so I crawl back to get some kind of memento. And the guy's got lots of gold in his teeth. So I get out my knife and use the handle to knock a few of the teeth out to take back. Unfortunately they fall back into the guy's throat. By this stage, rigor mortis has set in, so I can't force the guy's jaw open. I go away and think about this, then come back later only to find someone else had beaten me to it. Cut the guy's throat wide open, and taken the teeth for himself.

'I was making 'Point Blank' with John Boorman, and we were in Alcatraz for that sequence. And I said to John that I never did like the small sound that most movies have for gunshots, and he agreed. So I pull out my .44 Magnum, which I just happened to have on me with some live rounds, and we are standing on 'Broadway', which is the main hallway with the cells on either side. And I say, 'Why don't we send everyone home, except the sound man?' And I start firing down the hall at this steel door, which has a two inch armoured glass window in it. So I start blazing away, shooting out the glass, with a full Magnum load, and let the sound echo and die away. And there's all this paint flaking off the ceiling and falling down like a snow storm; that's how powerful the Magnum is. We used that in the film, when my ex-buddy shoots me in the cell, all this paint comes falling down. It gives a better impression of the power of that gun, than me taking the hit. (He keeps the .45 up on a high shelf just to the right of the kitchen door.) If some guy comes in the door with a gun and says, 'Hands up,' well, I just put my hands up, and there it is, ready to hand. ●

1987

Capitalism crashed momentously on Black Monday, but they fixed it quickly enough to carry on making money out of us. Oliver North said he knew he had broken the law but didn't know that breaking the law was illegal. Chief Constable James Anderton, with his hotline to God, told us that gay folk should be flogged. His daughter then became a lesbian.

January
Gorbachev announces widespread democratic reforms for Soviet Union.

February
Robert Maxwell launches *London Daily News.*

March
Herald of Free Enterprise capsizes shortly after leaving Zeebrugge.

Winston Silcott and two others are jailed for killing PC Keith Blakelock on Broadwater Farm.

May
Iraqi Exocets accidentally sink US frigate Stark.

June
Conservatives win third term in office with majority of 102.

July
London Daily News closes.

August
David Owen resigns as leader of the SDP.

Rudolf Hess found hanged in his cell at Spandau.

Michael Ryan goes on the rampage in Hungerford, killing fifteen and wounding sixteen. He then kills himself.

October
South-east England is hit by a hurricane which kills 18 people and 15m trees.

Shares in BP go on sale.

Lester Piggott is jailed for three years for tax fraud.

November
IRA bomb kills 11 and injures over 60 at a Remembrance Day parade at Enniskillen.

Kings Cross fire kills 31 people.

December
Manchester Chief of Police James Anderton calls for the outlawing of homosexuality and flogging of criminals.

Dirty Dancing
After so many movies trading in the traumas of male adolescence, here's one that looks at a young girl's sexual adventures in a serious and self-effacing manner.

Fatal Attraction
A predictable dog's dinner of Pavlovian thriller clichés, this will appeal strongly to those who think women should be kept on a short lead.

Raising Arizona
What makes this hectic farce so fresh and funny is the sheer fertility of the writing. The film leaps into dark and uncharted territory to soar like a comet.

Guns'N'Roses - Appetite For Destruction (Geffen)
Guns'N'Roses affect to construct a code

of violation, a stabbing list of teen torpor. It doesn't sound exciting and it isn't.

George Michael - Faith (Epic)
'Faith' will go like a rocket for many months, and can be considered classic and mature adult pop. But there's really a lot better at the moment.

Prince - Sign O' The Times (Paisley Park)
Not afraid to take one step back to take two forward, Prince has returned to the DIY recording of his earlier albums while continuing to display the ability to encompass a quite breathtaking range. Pretty soon you'll be drawn into his weave of styles.

Angels over America

U2 interviewed in T.O. 874, by **Simon Garfield**

In Las Vegas, word is out that Frank Sinatra wants to meet U2. The band show up at one of his Golden Nugget charity shows to find they don't quite fit in with the middle-aged clientele 'dripping with diamonds'. Midway through a set that U2's vocalist Bono describes as 'still awesome', Frank stops his band and points the spotlight on the Dublin four-piece. The audience, tonight including Gregory Peck, gets up and cheers. This has not been a bad week for the band. This is the week they're on the cover of *Time*; the week the album is at number one in the States and goes double-platinum in the UK; the week they have their best-selling American single thus far; the week they're really warming up on stage in the first month of their 18-month world tour, every date a sell-out in a matter of hours.

America has several biggest bands in the world, but this is the one, right now. Here are the real signs: there's a limo-jam of six assorted chauffeured Lincolns and Cadillacs as the band prepare to leave their $200-a-night hotel for the short drive to tonight's New Jersey arena, there are champagne corks shooting through the moon-roof of their manager's hired car as he speeds from the gig back into Manhattan, there are seven different sorts of backstage and security pass, the lowliest one letting you talk to the drummer's empty snare cases; there are drug pushers at the venue gates, and ticket 'scalpers' charging $300 a pair; there are the influental backstage guests – Island chief Chris Blackwell and America's largest and wealthiest tour agent Frank Barsalona (rumours too that Brucie will stop by); there is a small planeload of Irish journalists flown over just for the one New Jersey show at the record company's expense; there are $16 T-shirts and $10 tour programmes, and by the end of the show thousands of fans will have bought both.

U2, as ever, are religiously untainted by the circus – in many ways they are less affected by the rock myth today than they were when they played their early shows to ten people at West Hampstead's Moonlight Club. They remain studiously serious and often alarmingly boring. I mean really: a rock band for 11 years, and still no mescaline habit. Making a fortune for the last three years, and still Bono drives an early '60s Humber, still

guitarist/keyboard player Edge a Volvo. They live in modest homes in or near Dublin, two of them quietly with wives and kids. Many would contend that this gives rock a bad name.

Often the only evidence of pop life is the silliness of their names – not least drummer Larry Mullen Jr, an addition designed to put an end to his dad receiving massive tax demands.

The U2 business

Bono and Edge speak with an unswerving, unsettling intensity of purpose, and it appears they think of their music and musical responsibilities to the exclusion of all else. This is not a band with hobbies; like their manager Paul McGuinness, the band are not in the music business or even the band business, but in the U2 business. It's an empire all right and one still in its formative years, but it's an empire without the gaudy spoils. It may be a super Christian pose, but I doubt it.

That's rock contradiction number one, the first of many. 'People tend to tie U2 up in ribbons and bows,' says Bono, 'but even I don't understand all the ingredients. For a lot of people we're either a spiritual band, or a political band, or just a rock band, or a band of "dem liddle people who give de world hope". And for some people I'm just the guy with the white flag who jumps off the stage. But the real truth about U2 lies in the complications. Don't you think we're an interesting group? It won't look good in print but I really believe that we are more interesting than most other bands. You just can't sum it up, though.'

There may also be words to sum up the live U2 experience, but 'passion' 'commitment' or 'honesty' will not do at all. All the fans I spoke to in the 20,000-seat Meadowlands arena talk of an affiliation with the band that runs far deeper than a kick for the odd good guitar hook or snappy Bono lyric. Though U2's first three studio albums are not in the major league of their 1984 release 'The Unforgettable Fire' or their current chart monster 'The Joshua Tree', they too are strung through with something which, at the risk of pseuding it, most fans would describe as an intimate bond with the band.

One 15-year-old from Brooklyn tugging at my jacket and begging to be taken backstage says she feels she knows the band 'really well already – now I just want to meet them.' It's not a sexual thing at all, she says, it's more a sister's devotion to her elder brothers.

Her favourite brother tonight is Bono, and she's unlikely to agree with my impression that much of his performance tonight is still rather embarrassing heat-of-the-moment bravado – not macho or aggressive, just plain OTT fan-fire as evidenced in his desperate Live Aid attempts to dance with a woman who really didn't care to foxtrot with anyone. (The band felt that that incident may have blown their whole performance, and Bono became profoundly depressed. He says his actions were rather dubiously inspired because they hit the stage just after 'Linda McCartney 'kissed me'. The rest of the band now demand nightly promises that he will not fall into the audience in similar fashion again.)

Yet the non-schoolboy bulk of Bono's show rates swayingly and dangerously high on the demagogue scale. The band are increasingly aware that saviour-style garment-tugging is the big order of the day. In this respect alone, Irish rock has found four more Geldofs. 'Yes of course we're aware we can be used,' says guitarist Edge over afternoon tea in his hotel. 'We do have a power of a kind, and it's definitely been acknowledged by politicians in this country. In fact we've had a couple of Democrats make contact with us. But I've often felt that there's a real conflict between expressing political feelings in our lyrics and writing great rock 'n' roll songs. You limit a song if you become too direct – great rock 'n' roll has a timeless quality… I don't want to write songs that date.'

Powers of influence

The band's powers of influence have so far been put to high-profile support for Amnesty International – their last US 'Conspiracy Of Hope' mini-tour with Peter Gabriel and the Police saw all proceeds going to the cause, clearly with positive results. Out of their 'adopted' six prisoners of conscience, more than half have been released, and one wrote directly to the band acknowledging their vital assistance. Significantly, most banners at their current New Jersey shows are not for U2, but for Amnesty. Bono has said frequently that 'the biggest compliment anyone can pay U2 is to go out and do something themselves.' Adds Edge: 'Instead of following the band like lemmings and picking up on every word we say, people are doing something for Amnesty themselves. That's what' s exciting – acting as a catalyst.'

Rather less publicised was Bono and his wife's post-Band Aid trip to Ethiopia in 1985 to spend several weeks working in a relief camp. He says he was fortunate to be able to 'afford to go – a lot of people would give their right arms to go and help out.' Bono's personal crusade continued last year with a trip to Central America. This year though, and most of next, he'll see only hotels and backstage corridors. Backstage tonight he meets with U2's lawyer Owen Epstein, a person who could easily be

taken for an exceptionally cerebral garbage man. Like all major acts, U2 are occasionally bothered by people who claim to have written one or all of their songs, the most recent case being being an artist who sent a tape to the band's own Mother Records project and later claimed that his tune inspired 'With Or Without You', the song that last week went Number One in the States.

These claims, however, are only minor irritants. Thanks largely to their long period of contract-free musical gestation, the band have avoided most of the major industry pitfalls, and both their financial and creative independence is the envy of almost every chart band. Both Island and Atlantic Records (their US distributor) appear to exist essentially as tools in the U2 worldplan.

Much responsibility for this lies with their manager Paul McGuinness. McGuinness, a stout and effusive mid-thirties Trinity College Dublin graduate, has been with the band virtually from the beginning, the days when 'they could barely play'. There were some small, very early, business mistakes, he says, but nothing that's a hindrance to the band now. Indeed, three years ago he renegotiated the band's Island contract into what is the most generous deal the label has ever agreed to.

McGuinness is a studiously diplomatic man, and gets narked when quizzed too firmly about money: 'In no other business in the world would anyone dare to ask how much money you're making. I'll only talk money with those I do business with.'

Consequently he has 3am after-gig discussions in the hotel bar with two young promoters, one Australian, one Dutch, who have flown in specially to iron out details of U2's future shows. The Australian dates are pencilled in for February 1988, the Dutch ones, already sold out, are in a matter of weeks. 'I've got two dates packed solid,' says the Dutch promoter, 'and I want to add a third, but Paul and the band won't do it. With anyone else I'd say, "Want another half million dollars?" and they'd say "Great!" and take the money and run. Not with these guys.'

Earthquake force

Despite the prominence of Bono and Edge, the band remains very much a four-piece. And they have that crucial arena ingredient: loudness. Bassist Adam Clayton's foot gizmos once shook a Brussels hall to such a degree that when the boys from the seismic lab came in to examine their equipment they found that according to their Richter data, the city had experienced an earthquake the force of the one that flattened Mexico City.

U2's current bollocking live set comprises most of the new album, much from 'Unforgettable Fire', and the singles and great anthemic faves – 'Sunday Bloody Sunday', 'I Will Follow', 'Gloria', 'October', 'New Year's Day' and '40', the song that's closed almost every gig for the last four years. At its best it's a classic arena show, full of moral passion, guitar swirl and grand gesture, and really no one does it better. 'The Joshua Tree' tracks are unquestionably the band's most mature collection to date,

▶

rich in a blues and country feel that had previously escaped much of their '76 Television and Patti Smith guitar blast. Yet the bulk is still thunder rock – some of the loosest, grimiest and most dashing they've yet produced in the studio. Tortuous U2 idealism? Yes, there's that too, dripping with biblical, Christian and desert imagery. Lyrics, ever obtuse though increasingly political, embrace heroin addiction, US arms build-ups and other Stateside and Central American maladies, the miners' strike, and anything else you'd like to read into them.

'People are seeing all sorts of things in the songs which weren't intended directly,' says Bono, 'which is OK by me. Eno (the album's co-producer) always says, "Why tie things up? Why write a song just about America when you can write about ten other things as well?"' 'Personally, right now I'd like to get away from U2 just releasing mega LPs every few years and do some great non-LP rock 'n' roll singles. Our songs are now being played on radio, and we must use our position to subvert the Top 40. There are songs I really must write. I must get America out of my system because I want to look again at what's happening at home. There's the biggest exodus out of Ireland since the '50s – both the brain drain and the people quite unable to see any future anymore. As a direct contradiction, U2 are enjoying this huge success…'

Dublin the leveller

Dublin remains a crucial leveller and inspiration for the band, and they speak as if to leave it would be to cut off their life force. And whereas Geldof and the Rats have long deserted, U2, true to perverse form, refuse to follow them. As ex-Millwall footballer and current U2 chronicler Eamon Dunphy told the *LA Times* last month, 'This is one of the first times anyone has shared their success with Ireland. People have left for the stimulation, the money, whatever. Not just rock musicians but everyone… Beckett, Shaw, Wilde… even all the great race-horses were shipped off – yes, even horses get out of Ireland.'

Anyway, listen: Bono is now off, the man who probably bit the Blarney Stone is away with a rim of non-sequiturs, *bons mots*, assorted philosophical rambles. 'I missed pop music – I was listening to Jimi Hendrix when I was ten, not pop. But I remember being turned on by Marc Bolan, the sexuality of it, but essentially I missed it. I thought David Bowie and 'Hunky Dory' was a duo. We began writing our own songs originally only because our cover versions were so bad. This is a group that could not get 'Paint It Black' together. I don't think I'm anything like an archetypal popstar. Maybe it was an error.'

One cannot summarise snappily with a band like U2, one can only rather pretentiously close up on their dreams. 'I'll tell you this: the best is yet to come,' says Bono. 'Really what we want to do is do everything,' says Edge. 'We want to be a country band, a soul band, a blues band, a traditional Irish band and a great rock 'n' roll band, all at the same time.'

Still only in their mid-twenties, all four are heavily into longevity. Some old words from manager Paul McGuinness seem appropriate. 'Quite honestly,' he said in 1984, 'nothing would surprise me less than to see them, as 50-year-old men, making some kind of album. I mean, what do you do when you're an ex-member of a rock 'n' roll band… ?' ●

Best Bette

Bette Midler interviewed in T.O. 890, by **Brian Case**

Oh, Baby Divine, what an Entrance –
As Demure as the Fourth of July!
Mr and Mrs Divine didn't know
If they ought to Rejoice or to Cry.

You can imagine their Terrible Shock
When they lay down their Babe in her bed
And found she'd arrived with High Heels on her feet
And a Sprig of Red Hair on her head.

But the Heels and the Hair-do were only the Prologue –
Another Great Shock lay in store
For their Baby had already mastered a word
And the word she had mastered was "MORE!"
('The Saga Of Baby Divine' by Bette Midler)

'Autobiographical, Miss Midler?' I enquire, leafing through the glossily illustrated doggerel. It is her book for kids. This Baby Divine hops the hutch for vaudeville, lights up the night sky like a comet, and wins the parental love at last. 'Yes.'

Gad! What archery! She hefts her head up and down in assent, very slow and shmo-like because it was a very slow shmo question, but the way she does it is nice and you can't help laughing along.

Bette Midler in person bears no relation to the Red Hot Momma in the Miss Community Chest sash, the mermaid in the wheelchair, nor to the grandstanding gobshite in the frankfurter costume. She calls to mind those well-heeled Jewish matrons who spend their afternoons shopping – 'Shall we deliver or will Modom shlep it herself?' – at Fortnums. The famous bazooms are an irreproachable bolster in her highnecked blouse, her peewit feet are elegantly crossed Charles Jourdan nibs, and she looks as if she smells of gloves.

Torch songs

Mel Brooks, I tell her, wrote somewhere that he went into showbiz to make a noise, to pronounce himself.

'Mel didn't write that! I wrote that!' she surfs, without disturbing the poise. 'When I was a little girl back in Hawaii I always thought I was gonna turn out to be Wallis Simpson. I never doubted it.'

Bette rose in the steam of New York's Continental Baths in the late '60s with Barry Manilow at the piano. 'Friday and Saturday the place was packed because there wasn't anything for these gay fellas to do, except the usual thing 2,000 gays do on these nights, so the owner put me in as cabaret. It was a chance for me to do anything that I could think of, and they were a very generous audience, they loved everything. They wanted me to be funny, but I'd never done stand-up before. I turned up with three songs because I'd been used to opening for a comic out-of-town. I had 20 minutes of torch songs. Well, I got really free in that atmosphere, coming up with new stuff, and I stayed three years and built up a following.'

of a performance,' wrote the *New Yorker*'s Pauline Kael, echoing a consensus that Bette, given the right vehicle, could be the American Anna Magnani. Whatever Bette felt, she accepted 'Jinxed'.

'It was the aftermath of 'Heaven's Gate', and it was death around United Artists. Everybody walking around and worrying about when the axe was gonna fall. It was a mess. They had half a script and they were so desperate they were grabbing at any suggestion anyone made. I wanted to be a star all my life, but after 'Jinxed' I didn't want to be a star anymore.'

'Jinxed', made under the shadow of Michael Cimino's financial haemorrhage, was not a happy ship. Director Don Siegel hasn't said much, but Ken Wahl, Bette's co-star, has dished plenty armpit. 'In one scene I have to hit her in the face,' the gentleman told the press, 'and I thought we could save some money on sound effects here.' And talked about trying to recollect his dog to help him over the clinches…

Was it a Streisand scenario? What Bette said then was this. 'I wanted to make the best movie I could, but not everybody else involved felt that way, and they resented me because I did.' Who knows? In interview, she comes across as that complicated but not unprecedented phenomenon, the hausfrau astride a warhead. 'Karel Reisz! That's the director I wanna work with'. 'Isadora'. He did 'The French Lieutenant's Woman', one of the great Historical Romantic whatevers. I couldn't believe he didn't think of me for Patsy Cline for 'Sweet Dreams'. I could sing that shit! Achh – I couldn't watch it.' And the watchful eyes, gauging the trajectory of her remarks, report back to the brain, uh-huh – and switch to a parody of ambition. 'I always thought I'd have made a WUNNERFUL Mrs Macbeth because I understand her motivation which is the key to her character and all that good stuff. And I could do it Yiddish. So, out det spot.' Whatever, she took some damage to the helium tanks over 'Jinxed'. 'Yes,' she shrugs, 'I had bad luck with that movie and had to start all over again from ground level.'

Anxiety entered her life
'The Figure was Fearful and Dismal and Huge
And wrapped in a Sulfurous Fog.
It had snakes round its ankles and moss round its heart
And its voice was as hoarse as a Frog's.'

Actress for hire

She had a breakdown and didn't work on another movie for three years. She fields those rough questions that interviewers save till last with rare candour. 'Ruthless People', 'Down and Out in Beverly Hills' and her latest, 'Outrageous Fortune', feature one-dimensional Bette Midler turns. And took a fortune. 'That's the gig. A job is a job. That's my new credo. The nice thing about these scripts is they don't live or die on me. I was just part of the puzzle. I'm no longer forward and pushy about what I think is right and wrong. I no longer feel that way. I *don't* know everything. I'm an actress for hire. Disney were the only people who came to me and offered me a job, and they've stood by me and I owe them loyalty. People say to me – "Bette Midler with Walt Disney! That's funny!" I'm laughing all the way to the bank!'

But the parts that you're playing, I persist – these would furnish you with two minutes in your stage act.

She nods. She consults her watch. It's coming up to feeding time for baby Sophie who has earthed and grounded much of the Wallis Simpson in Bette. 'I know my part and that's really all I'm paid to do. Directors want to perceive actors as being co-operative and not wasting their time. A lot of suggestions that come from actors are good and valid, but if they're not asked for, you can get yourself into a lot of hot water. I prefer to make my contribution and stand back.'

So what changed you?

Her timing is terrific. The voice is perfectly puzzled and plaintive. 'Well,' she says, and I'm laughing and liking her already, 'I think, not working.' That'll do it every time. ●

She taps up a cigarette and advances that faintly pelican chin towards a light. 'Oh, thank you. Late '60s – and it was New York. That whole time, that revolution was very exciting. You felt that anything could happen, day or night. Physically, I'm a terrific improviser, but no, I'm not a great wit. I've stolen from the dead, the nearly dead, the lame, the halt. I wish I could give credit to all the people who've influenced me. Many Americans, especially young ones, don't listen to everybody. You know, what's going on is all that ever went on. I've always been interested in historical perspective in pop music. Always! Ruth Etting, Helen Morgan, Ethel Waters, Dinah Washington – I was so in love with the idea of popular music I listened to them all. I even listened to 'Salty Songs For Underwater Lovers'. Yes, it exists, I have it, there's a mermaid on the cover, one of my earlier inspirations.'

She puts a great din together, and, like all comics, her eyes remain separate from the motor-mouth below. Her last line has sashayed, bridled, and dallied with the cache-sexe of modesty, but she doesn't laugh until I do.

And the Last of the Red Hot Mommas, Sophie Tucker, I ask?

'I saw her once. Big! She didn't move much. She wore a pale blue floor-length gown with a sweetheart neckline, coupla strings of pearls, white hair and little turd curls across the bang. I'd heard about her all my life, and a drummer friend of mine took me to see her, and I have to say I didn't quite get it. By that time the fashion in performing had moved on to something more violent and she was sorta sedate and nowhere near as vulgar as I've made her out to be, ever.'

Rock 'n' roll kamikaze

Bette's progress towards divinity took her beyond her stage show, the Grammy and the Emmy, to an Academy Award nomination for her rock 'n' roll kamikaze performance in 'The Rose'. 'A paroxysm

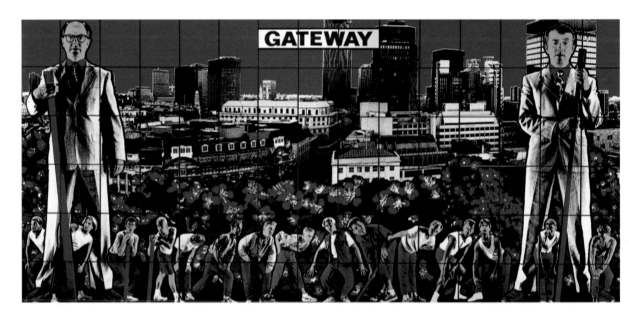

1987

Missionary positions

Gilbert and George interviewed in T.O. 881, by **Sarah Kent**

Gilbert and George must be the most famous British artists alive. 150,000 people poured in to see their show of huge, brightly coloured photo-pieces on its year-long tour of Bordeaux, Basel, Brussels, Madrid and Munich, breaking attendance records at every venue. But while their popularity abroad increases, back home their name is linked with nasty right-wing tendencies.

There was a time, back in the 1970s, when Gilbert and George were the darlings of the artworld. They appeared at openings, two distant young men in ill-fitting suits, old before their time. Their hands and faces painted, they became 'living sculptures'.

They printed postcards and pamphlets which they sent to all the right people. 'A Message from the Sculptors Gilbert and George' was like a wedding invitation which contained photos of the duo, samples of their make-up, tobacco, hair, clothing and breakfast and an ad for their services: 'Gilbert and George have a wide range of sculptures for you – singing sculpture, interview sculpture, dancing sculpture, meal sculpture, nerve sculpture, and philosophy sculpture... So do contact us.'

People did and G&G rapidly rose to fame, performing and exhibiting installations of paintings and drawings showing the two artists out in nature 'frozen into a gazing for you, Art'. In 1971 they began to make photo-pieces showing themselves in the wildernesses of nature or the East End, contemplating the bare rooms of their Fournier Street home, staring listlessly out of the window or getting paralytically drunk. They began to drink socially too and as their formal, 'living sculpture' presentation eased, so rumours of their unpleasant politics began to circulate and to colour the interpretation of their work.

A series of swastika-shaped drinking pictures of 1974, titled 'Human Bondage', were seen as sure signs of neo-Nazism rather than, as intended, a comment on the wastefulness of addiction and self-destruction. But it was their Whitechapel show of five years ago that finally tipped the scales. Gilbert and George had been out with their cameras photographing local graffiti. Words like 'Suck', 'Cunt', 'Scum', 'Wanker' and 'Smash the Reds' were juxtaposed in the new work with images of riot police, soldiers, blacks, alcoholics and skinheads to create an atmosphere of despairing rage and aggression, while titles such as 'Paki', 'British' and 'Patriots' fanned the flames of critical displeasure.

But since then their work has continued to develop. The recent pieces are larger, colours brighter to resemble stained glass, and the mood much lighter and more optimistic. Their subjects have multiplied to include life, death, morality, fear, hope, religion and sex. The role of Gilbert and George has also changed – from being the main subject they became dispassionate observers and, more recently, messianic 'speakers' who, staff in hand, lead London's youth on to a bright new future. Humour has also leapt in with startling graphic images of cocks with spiky balls that appear near open mouths or are repeated in cruciform patterns. With explicit titles like 'Tongue Fuck Cocks' and 'Buggery Faith', these are more likely to offend the Moral Majority than the Liberal Left.

From this new perspective Gilbert and George seem like courageous, outrageous loners, determined to pass on their message no matter how unpalatable, unfashionable or bizarre and regardless of whom they offend. Over a 'working tea', I found them in fine, missionary fettle.

The mission

George: 'We don't believe in art – we don't want to have anything to do with it. We want to change life. We don't want to reflect society, we want to form it. We want people to go into the gallery and come out different – thinking, dreaming, hoping, fearing, behaving differently.'

Gilbert: 'The museum is the best platform – everyone is welcome. Art is there to stimulate thought – the speaking artist preaching, stimulating the idea of life. Our work is like someone making graffiti – an advertising campaign of pure thought, just as the church used painters to campaign for religion. Except that we are more free – the language that we use is ours completely.'

George: 'We're speaking louder, it's a louder invitation – don't you think there are enough museums and galleries in the world with bland works of art that people glide past? We've had incredible responses from people of all ages, races and classes. Most artists make work for posh people involved with the art profession – pictures which would mean nothing if you took them outside that elitist group. The cleaning lady doesn't like them. Where we exhibit they always remark, "It's very strange, the cleaning staff never look at the shows, but with your work they're crazy about it." We're amongst the few artists who give dignity to the viewer – we allow the viewer's life in front of the picture. There are no franker, more explicit artists than ourselves – we're never ambiguous.'

Suffering

Gilbert: 'We are putting up our views and our unhappiness for them to see – we are depressed and unhappy people.'

George: 'We never met anyone more miserable than ourselves. It's better, more serious. There's never been a greater accessibility of pleasure in the whole history of mankind. Never did so many people have so much fun as now.'

Gilbert: 'Every good artist is unhappy, that's the driving force.'

George: 'We're anti-pleasure seeking, completely. All the happy people are dead without having done a thing – happiness is to take, to contribute is to give. The history of civilisation's advancement is written in misery, blood, personal sacrifice and controversy, even Jesus Christ was controversial. That was the Christian message on which Western civilisation is based. Every school, every university, art gallery, museum, policeman, hospital is based on the one inspiration – of misery.'

Religion

Gilbert: 'We accept and would like to honour Christian power – we're happily in debt to the Christian tradition. We do not say we're sophisticated atheists, let the peasants go to church, which is what all people of intelligence said this century. They had a classist attitude towards religion. We don't even know where we stand exactly, we're trying to work it out – our religious pieces are pro- and anti-religion.'

George: 'When we first did our Jesus pieces in 1980 some of our admirers thought we were cuckoo. Now everybody talks about religiosity, morality or politics in art. We are interested in the power of the individual and the freedom of the artist. In the past they were either serving the church or the toffs – they either did Christian pictures or pictures of the toff's house, his family or their animals. There was very little in the way of serving people. We are at last free and we have a sense of service, of purpose – we want to give in exchange for the gift of life. We don't do it to please ourselves – we're just these miserable chaps trying very hard to give. No joke.'

Gilbert: 'We work as many hours as we can, day and night, until we're exhausted.'

Racism

Gilbert: 'We are the only honest artists. We want to be free to speak – to have a view of the world through art. We are not campaigning for any parties, but we are political. Secret socialists – that's how we described ourselves. We are the only artists that are able to accept black people and white people in our work completely on the same level. For 50 years you haven't been able to put a black person in an artwork.'

George: 'We have enormous support from people of all backgrounds and walks of life because of that. In Milwaukee a young black person came up to us and said, "I know all about art and I know all about artists and it's always looking down its nose at me, but you guys are different – you speak with the heart."'

Homosexuality

George: 'A white boy – he couldn't have been more than 13 or 14 – his eyes filled with tears said, "I would like to tell you how comfortable I feel standing in front of 'Naked Love'." It meant something to his life. We would say that the acceptance of sexuality is important. Sex is sex – I don't want to decide what a person does with their hands and their sexual organs. We are freedom fighters in that way. The narrow-mindedness of educated people on those subjects is appalling.'

Gilbert: 'We use the male because the image is not so used up. A woman is immediately seen as sex symbol. We are the first artists to tip the balance.'

George: 'The image of woman has been used largely to terrorise men – have you never thought of that? It's very simple, people order more drinks in a topless bar. We are opposed to the bigotry of people who say that the people in our pieces are "nasty boys" or yobboes. They're being classist. We say they are people. If you pick some flowers for the table, you won't choose a bunch of rotten droopy ones, you'll pick the teenagers. They represent life, before they've been wrecked by the system. They are there, like extensions of ourselves.'

Gilbert: 'We believe they are our roots.'

Isolation

George: 'We never decide how to do a piece. How we are is how the work is – we trust that entirely. So if in the early work we looked lost, sad, naïve and old-fashioned that's because we were – we are – lower class, uneducated country people.'

Gilbert: 'We want to have our ideas, put them up and that's it. We don't want to discuss it, we would never agree anyway.'

George: 'The discussion is between the viewer and the picture. We want our effect to be cultural not social, otherwise we'd have to go to every damn silly dinner party. This is a working tea, after all – we're not personal friends.' ●

Spit
and polish

Alkarim Jivani in T.O. 897, on **Spitting Image**

While it is notoriously difficult to measure the effectiveness of satire, one criterion is whether the show is biting enough to become required watching for the people it lampoons and if, after watching it, the targets are influenced by its message. Measured against that yardstick, 'Spitting Image' is a resounding success.

'I heard that the Liberals did some research during the election,' says Geoffrey Perkins, the programme's producer, 'which showed that the way we portrayed David Steel being bullied by Owen had done Steel a lot of damage. They even suggested that in order to get away from this image of himself, Steel forced the merger issue so that he would appear a tougher politician. In fact it's a complete accident that the puppet is small. We had built a lot of small puppets and big puppets and the two were never supposed to meet Then one week we needed a David Steel puppet and the only one we had was small. It felt right so we kept it there, which means Steel complaining quite a lot and pointing out that he is taller than Neil Kinnock.'

Margaret Tebbit is reported to have said that her husband longed for a black leather jacket until 'Spitting Image' made it impossible for him to wear one in public. Leon Brittan collared former producer John Lloyd at a party given by David Frost and complained that he wasn't as much

of a glutton as they made him out to be. Mrs Brittan, when asked by Roger Law and Peter Fluck – the poisonous puppets' progenitors – for any criticisms, said, 'Not enough spots'. Clare Rayner is said to have videoed her transmogrification but couldn't bear to watch it and the story goes that when one of the puppeteers came across Rayner's daughter at a party, he couldn't resist introducing himself as 'the guy who operates your mother's bosoms.' Michael Heseltine has repeatedly tried to buy his puppet from the programme-makers. They always fended him off by insisting that the price would be a contribution to Labour Party funds. When he resigned from the cabinet, Perkins and co thought they might relent and have the puppet sent around – in a hearse. But the idea was vetoed on the grounds of bad taste. (They can tell the difference.)

But if the reaction of those politicians immortalised in rubber by Fluck and Law is an eye-opener, what is even more astonishing is the response of those people who haven't been paid this compliment. Jeffrey Archer, for instance, bombarded the team with tapes and photographs until his features were cast in foam. 'Our first inclination was not to do the little bastard,' says Roger Law. A booming laugh creases his Old Testament-prophet features and reveals a gold tooth to match the gleam in his eyes. 'Then of course he was all over the news and we had no

Trouble shooter

Don McCullin interviewed in T.O. 887, by **Brian Case**

Don McCullin opened the front door and grimaced in the sunlight. 'It's like Vietnam in Belgravia,' he remarked. 'You can't get to sleep for burglar alarms and sirens going off. I hate London these days.' Like Vietnam? I looked down the crescent but all I could see were a couple of incoming trouts in blue rinses and an exclusive shopfront featuring an Etruscan pisspot on a pedestal and no price tag. I followed the photographer into the house. It wasn't his place, and the only personal item in evidence was a vase of peonies which he'd brought up from his three-acre spread in Hertfordshire. These days, he raises flowers and photographs them, photographs the landscape and the cloud formations too, but his Walden Pond idyll never lasts long.

War photography is a rap he can't beat and his feelings on the subject are deeply ambiguous. He's been covering the world's trouble-spots – Cyprus, the Congo, Vietnam, Lebanon, Northern Ireland – for over 20 years, working in close to the carnage and it shows. You wouldn't want his dreams.

'McCullin has seen it all. The worst,' Steve Weber told me, one of the young soldiers in John Irvin's 'Hamburger Hill', the movie where McCullin was Special Assignment Photographer. 'McCullin's whole profession is people's expressions, so he was a great help to us actors. He'd been in enough battles to know how soldiers react. I had one scene where a buddy dies in my arms and I asked him how I should play it. He told me it wasn't a big griev-

choice because we are meant to be a topical show. But that kind of pushy individual, like Edwina Currie and Archer, couldn't wait to be on the bloody show.'

The kindest interpretation is that politicians have such thick skins that the savagery spills off them like water off a snake's back, but at Westminster, an appearance on 'Spitting Image' is considered a sure indication that a politician has arrived. Apparently Thatcher doesn't watch the show. She has been told not to because she may find it too hurtful, and that's the God's own truth. ●

● ●

ing scene, it should be puzzlement, just staring and taking it all in. Almost curiosity. Almost how a dog is puzzled when it hears a high-pitched whistle.'

McCullin laughed shortly when I reported the actor's comments. 'Yes, there's not a lot of time in war to feel emotion. Things happen painfully slowly or wickedly fast. You go into yourself. Fear dehydrates the body so you drink a lot of water. The thing you're most afraid of is losing concentration because if you want to stay alive you have to concentrate. Robert Capa, who was the best chronicler of war and the photographer I was weaned on, lost concentration and stood on a mine when he was taking a pee in Indo-China.'

McCullin's war photographs are among the most anguishing documents of our time, both for the images and for the implications of addiction one reads into that unflinching eye. 'I used to be a war-a-year man, but now it's not enough,' he said in 1967. 'When it gets to three or four a year, then I will get worried.' A decade later, even after being wounded in Cambodia, he was still high on war. 'At the end of the day, you have lived more in one day than some people would live in their whole lives.' Vietnam was a bonanza for war photographers, with little censorship to con-

tend with and a media market hungry for images back home. 'Jesus, take the glamour out of war?' Tim Page had said. 'How the hell can you do that? You can't take the glamour out of a tank burning or a helicopter blowing up. It's like trying to take the glamour out of sex. War is good for you… war has always been glamorous.'

McCullin, Page, Larry Burrows, Philip Jones Griffiths – Vietnam was Edge City for a new breed of photo-journalist and if it made reputations it also entered the bloodstream and scrambled minds. PRAY FOR WAR, read the helmets of the grunts, which went double for the press corps, the whores of war with Bao Chi sewn on their fatigues.

'War?' said McCullin. His face worked silently before the words came out. 'I've lost so many friends, you know. Constantly losing companions. I shouldn't be here. I was supposed to be doing a story for the *New York Times* with Charlie Glass in Beirut but they sent him on ahead and he's been kidnapped. Nobody knows where he is.'

Emphatically, he is not a comfortable man to be around, out of his element here in a house in Belgravia. I was reminded of Weegee, who, asked if he would like a day in the suburbs away from the city's killing floor, replied, 'No. There'll be trees.' ●

"1987"

"I want to have more kids."
Bill Wyman predicts his future relationship with Mandy Smith

"She only went to Venice because somebody told her she could walk down the middle of the street."
Neil Kinnock on Margaret Thatcher's departure to Italy for a EC meeting

"He's a semi-detached member of the Cabinet."
Bernard Ingham offers his opinion on John Biffen

"I don't mind how much my ministers talk, as long as they do what I say."
Margaret Thatcher on John Biffen and his fellow 'Wets'

"People think we do not understand our black and coloured countrymen. But there is a special relationship between us."
SA President PW Botha's wife Elize clears thing up

"You can rest assured there isn't going to be a hurricane."
Michael Fish responds to a viewer's query the night before one of the biggest hurricanes in UK history

"That's cricket, Harry. That kind of thing can happen in boxing."
Frank Bruno

"There is no such thing as Society. There are individual men and women, and there are families."
Margaret Thatcher. She was later heard to regret this comment

"You have to give this much to the Luftwaffe – when it knocked down our buildings it didn't replace them with anything more offensive than rubble. We did that."
Prince of Wales on British architecture

"At least I left shoes in my closets and not skeletons. And besides, I didn't have 3,000 pairs of shoes. I had 1,060."
Imelda Marcos confesses all

"Losing my virginity was a career move."
Madonna

"If you're a groovy fucker, watch the Tube."
Jools Holland

1987

LL Cool J

Rap race

When the subject is himself, even offstage, rap's mightiest mouth never shuts up.

LL Cool J interviewed in T.O. 896, by **Richard Guilliatt**

L L Cool J is striding back from lunch, six-foot plus of 19-year-old muscle looking like a million dollars, which is probably what he'll be worth after the Def Jam label's lawyers tote up his royalty cheques. He's got the red Kangol cap, the sneakers-jeans-training suit combination, the gold watch, the gold chain swinging like a knotted rope around his neck, a diamond ring wider than a quarter on his left hand… and just as we walk past his gleaming red Audi sports car with the tinted windows and car-phone, this bum staggers out of a doorway, begging for quarters.

Since this is New York's Lower East Side, we ignore his outstretched hand and just keep walking, but the bum checks out LL's gleaming B-Boy presence and breaks into a comic 'it's like a jungle sometimes', mock-rapping the chorus to 'The Message' with a grin and a wagging finger. 'I know all about that, man,' he calls out to Cool J's departing back.

Even the bums in New York have an attitude: you might sing about this jungle but I'm in it. LL Cool J would agree. Rap's mightiest mouth is a suburban boy, not a product of the Bronx or Bedford Stuyvesant, and on his new album 'Bigger and Deffer' you won't find a rhyme or lie about slum life, black power or racism. Its vision is confined largely to one thing: the irrefutable, incredible, all-enveloping greatness of LL Cool J.

The President woke and he called the Pope/the Pope went to heaven on a golden rope/he asked the Lord to raise/from the dead/so he could make a fresh painting of my head…

I mean, how far can boasting go after this? In the video of 'I'm Bad' he comes across like Son of Shaft on a mission to bust the Mafia, and on stage he prowls around like a caged animal shaking his fist at the boys and his

nuts at the girls. He's fond of Muhammad Ali analogies and he's got the mouth to match. On just one LP he takes on the entire New York Police Department, trashes every sucker MC from Hollis to Bed Stuy, travels to the centre of the earth, scares off the Russians, brags about his jewellery, his sexual prowess and his annual income, and finally closes the LP with a gleeful, cackling message: 'Don't touch that needle. Yo, this is LL again. You didn't think I could do it again, did ya? (Muffled laughter). Another album ... the joke's on you, jack!'

The closing message, he said over lunch, 'is dedicated to all the people who thought my second album wouldn't be as good, or thought that the first album was a fluke. And it's not knowhumsayin'? It's God bein' on my side, and talent and that's what it takes.'

Interviewing LL Cool J is like listening to his records: he's got a relentless line in self-boosterism and almost no politics. His manager has to patiently explain to him why *Essence* magazine is down on him, why the black middle-class resents rap's aggression and reputation for violence, as LL nods silently like the schoolkid he was not so long ago. The politics of black publishing and radio-programming hold no interest for him. Rap's rep for sexism and violence gets short shrift. And as for hip-hop's musical limitations, he won't even admit there are any.

If he's got a message for black kids it's this: you could be as rich as I am, sucker, if you got your act together. He's the superstar who's too young to drink. He's got thousands of dollars' worth of gold hanging off him, but at lunch he ordered a cheeseburger and two Cokes. He's just sold 2m. LPs but he still lives with his grandmother in St Albans, Queens.

So, LL, what are you doing with all your money?

'Savin'. Chillin' it.'

Isn't there something you bought with your first royalty cheque?

'Nah it's not like I'm some big excited kid. I was never deprived as a kid, knowhumsayin'? It's not like all of a sudden I got money. My grandmother and grandfather and mother treated me fine and gave me bikes and every toy you could ask for. I bought my mother a car and myself a car, a few things, nothin' major.'

So how is fame affecting your life in Queens?

It's like… I can't walk around. I don't walk around, never. It's like this, I'll tell you what happens: your fake friends become your enemies, your enemies become your friends and your real friends stay your friends. You just handle it from there. You keep things in their proper perspective. You never let nothin' go to your head and you take everythin' everyone says with a grain of salt. You just gotta keep in your mind what's goin' on and watch the surroundings.'

But who do you trust these days? Who are your confidants?

He looks puzzled. 'Well that's a funny question, knowhumsayin'? That's an odd question. You know, you gotta trust someone in life but as far as me gettin' by you gotta rely on yourself to get you by. Yourself is the only person you can rely on. My family, my grandmother, my girl. Everythin' is cool. I know what you're talkin' about: confidin'. I don't do too much of that 'cuz I ain't got nothin' to confide about. I keep myself on the ground by being level-headed and keepin' everythin' in its proper perspective.'

LL flashes the two-inch-wide gold bracelet around his wrist. Soon it will be embedded with diamonds that say 'Thank You, Father.'

Outside Madison Square Garden there are white protesters handing out pamphlets about Steve Biko to young blacks from the outer boroughs who look bemused, the whites patiently explaining to the blacks who Biko was in a comical example of consciousness-raising going nowhere. But the homeboys and flygirls couldn't give a shit about Biko; they're here to party.

On just one LP he takes on the entire New York Police Department, trashes every sucker MC.

There's 20,000 people here tonight to see Def Jam's 1987 tour, a bill that has rolled around the country for months thanks largely to the crossover double-whammy of LL Cool J's album and his single 'I'm In Love'.

There's a symbolic significance to playing Madison Square Garden, given the complete reluctance even by many black radio stations to support hip-hop. It's a homeboy homecoming that proves just how much bullshit is spoken about hip-hop's 'cult' audience.

The stories about rap's relationship with violence, however, are much closer to the truth. There are metal detectors at all entrances and a small army of cops, a reminder that the trouble at last year's New York City Fresh Festival tour hasn't been forgotten. And space has been made on the bill for the South Bronx rapper KRS 1, whose partner Scott La Rock was shot dead just the week before in an apparent neighbourhood dispute.

There's a spirit of conciliation involved in putting KRS 1 on the bill, considering the tongue-lashings he has dealt out to his Queens rivals on raps like 'South Bronx' and 'The Bridge Is Over' during the past year. Roaming the stage with a poster of the tragically murdered La Rock behind the turntables, his set should have been the ultimate message to the crowd: shoot off your mouth instead of your stupid guns or the pointless black-against-black ghetto violence that claimed La Rock's life will never end.

But it's not a point that gets through to the gangs of homeboys roaming the upper wings of the Garden, snatching jewellery and making lightning assaults throughout the night. The first fight breaks out just before nine o'clock, a flurry of fists and elbows up there in the dark as someone is silently stomped during Public Enemy's set. At one point, as the cops try to arrest a black woman, about 20 kids bound down through the crowd to confront them, a momentarily chilling confrontation in which the cops stand with their batons drawn and 20,000 eyes look down, horrified.

It's stupid. It wipes out the memory of a peaceful Run DMC/Beastie Boys gig here only two weeks previously, and it doesn't take long for the word to spread. The director of Long Island's Westbury Music Fair hears about the violence, and when a fan is shot dead at a small rap gig in a Queens park only days later, that seals it. He cancels the Def Jam bill's scheduled appearance. 'We had the Fat Boys and Salt'n'Pepa here in the summer,' he said. 'We had car fires, muggings… I don't need to spend $5,000 repairing seats that are ripped up with knives. It's just getting progressively worse.'

Fights aside, the Def Jam tour delivers hip-hop's strengths and weaknesses in equally strong doses. Rap is the only American pop music left that has anything new to say about adolescent rebellion and anger, and if you can sit through three hours of it, the concert's a treat. But as stadium music it's a mixed proposition. The stage sets look fine but the sonic

subtleties of scratching sound better up-close, and there comes a point where breast-beating boasts, faggot jokes, underpants-flashing, skeezer-insulting, testicle-rubbing and all the ladies in the house saying 'arrgghh-argh' reach saturation point.

Public Enemy, the only remotely political act on the bill, reduce the lyrical punch of their 'Yo! Bum Rush The Show' LP to a cartoon by brandishing plastic Uzi sub-machine guns and sporting urban-guerilla-chic jumpsuits. At the Garden they opened with an absurd blast of rhetoric ('The US Government is the most wicked and deceitful government in the world') and then claimed the Klan were trying to stop the show (apparently that's just part of the act because they did exactly the same thing in New Orleans). They closed by yelling 'Peace!' and marching off in their military uniforms, black-gloved fists raised high and fake Uzis in the air. Some vision of peace. At least they didn't play 'Sophisticated Bitch', one of the most hateful songs about a woman that rap has ever spewed forth.

Eric B and Rakim's set is, by contrast, effective because it's so underplayed. 'I know You Got Soul' marked this duo as the big find of 1987, and while the stadium stage is not the perfect venue for Rakim's insinuative poetry, his raps are the most subtle and intricately judged of the show.

LL Cool J co-headlines with Whodini, but there isn't much doubt about where the audience's preference lies. Whodini put on a flashy show that's all dance routines and jokes and flash clothes. LL makes his entrance via the world's biggest beatbox, which drops from the ceiling in front of a replica of his old neighbourhood school while flashing lights blaze his

initials at the crowd and the LA Posse – in silver, light-bedecked podiums – scratch up a storm. His act is pure bombast. It's ego taken to an art form. He stalks around, waving his fist at the floor, and even the plaintive 'I Need Love' is transformed into sheer smut as he simulates sex on a velvet sofa. As Cool J's butt grinds up and down before their startled eyes, for once all the girls in the house are going 'arrgghh-arg!!!' without prompting.

Like his records, however, LL is better on the knockout punches than he is over 12 rounds. There are monstrously good moments – 'Rock The Bells', 'I'm Bad', 'Get Down' – but coming at the end of a long night of boasting, the effect is dissipated despite his undeniable stage presence. Even this hometown crowd seemed to be flagging by night's end.

So we're sitting at lunch at the Noho Star restaurant and the actress Lauren Hutton suddenly walks up to the table and fixes a bright smile in LL's direction. 'Hi,' she says, 'my name's Lauren Hutton and I think we did an I Love New York commercial together. Aren't you Run DMC?'

'No, that ain't me,' he replies, looking baffled that she'd mistake him for the Kings of Rock. This kind of thing can really rankle when you spend most of your career bragging about how you're the baddest motherfucking rapper on planet Earth.

One suspects that there is a pussycat behind Cool J's snarling badass pose. On the road, he reportedly keeps to himself and steers clear of the groupies. He doesn't drink, and if there's much real rivalry between the MCs who slag each other off every night, he doesn't let on. 'I don't care about the next man, knowhumsayin'? I wish 'em luck 'cuz I'm doin' what I gotta do. What they eat don't make me shit, knowhumsayin'?'

'That attitude, like people callin' rap music egotistical and all that, that attitude comes from the origin. When we were playin' the parks and clubs, everybody wanted to make a name for themselves, and to make a name for yourself you gotta do somethin' outlandish or say somethin' outlandish. And it's like that, it's just makin' a name for yourself. And once you got a name for yourself it seems like you're being egotistical, but what it is is you're not leavin' your roots. You still got the same hunger. When I stop mentionin' my name in my records and stop braggin' about myself, that means I'm not hungry no more.'

Was he disappointed with the violence at Madison Square Garden? 'No,' he shoots back immediately. 'I was totally satisfied. I don't have anythin' to do with that, knowhumsayin'? Those are personal situations, isolated incidents. I'm there to entertain. They got security guards to handle that, police. I gotta do what I gotta do. I'm not gonna stop my show because they act stupid. There's too many people wantin' to see it for me to let a few knuckleheads ruin it. If they was gonna cool out, they would. What makes you think they gonna listen to me?'

Because they admire you, they came to see you.

'It's like you got 20,000 people in the house and 300 didn't come to see LL, 300 came to see who was wearin' what and what they was gonna get. And second of all I don't really see a lot of those incidents goin' on. Those be happenin' out in the middle of the crowd. I feel bad about it afterwards, y'know, it concerns me. But what can I do? The tour has been a success, there haven't been many incidents, and if there were they were minor. It's like a car, y'know, it has a few knocks but basically it runs good.'

So to use your boxing analogy, LL, how long can you stay on top, keep up the energy level to be the best rapper around? Isn't there a limited lifespan to this game?

'I know what you're talkin'about, it's like Ali got old. Me, all right, if it's a boxin' match let's just say I'm gonna keep knockin 'em out until my jab ain't poppin' no more and my right hook just ain't as hard and then I'm gonna bow out graceful. In other words, I'm gonna do this the right way. I'm not gonna go out like a sucker, knowhumsayin'?'

And have you thought about what you'd do after that?

'Yeah.' A broad smile. 'Relax.' ●

The Beastie Boys

from 'Naughty but nice' in T.O. 873, by **Simon Garfield**

I was at this party the other night and this man went on and on about how the Beatles had ruined Western Civilisation,' said Hester Diamond, the mother of a Beastie Boy, to the *LA Times* in February. 'I listened for a while and finally said, "If you had problems with them, you ought to hear my son's band"'.

There are only three Beastie Boys, average age 20; but they've spent the last four months terrorising America with a colossal caricature of teenage rebellion. A lot of people have taken it seriously. Not, presumably, the 2 million teens who bought their Number One album, but the parents and the ministers. Never mind the Sex Pistols, they say, here's the Beasties, and they've come for our tinies. Look! say the mums, they hold their crotches on stage – if I would have known this going to happen, I wouldn't have been so tough on Iron Maiden. They've been so naughty that Tory MP Peter Bruinvels has called for a ban on 'these disgraceful, sick records being launched on an innocent public. This kind of thing shouldn't be allowed in Britain.'

So here we go: a catalogue of wickedness. They got banned from all Holiday Inns for turning the furniture in one room to wood shavings. They left another hotel with a large hole in the floor because they didn't get the adjacent rooms they asked for. In LA they flooded their suite after their famous 'shower trick' exploded. (About $25,000 of damage. 'Yeah,' says Beastie MCA, 'but we probably make that much in a week.')

They got banned from their parent-label CBS for allegedly stealing a video camera 'because they didn't like the way it was looking at them.' Their own video for their 'Fight For Your Right (To Party)' hit was banned by the Beeb because, in the words of the *Sun*, it contained: PASSIONATE groping and kissing; SEX-CRAZED women dragging a young boy into a bathroom; BEATEN-UP party guests. They were also banned from a US TV show because a 15-minute interview carried an excellent 216 obscenities. This is one every four seconds.

The current Beasties stage show is also a touch rude. The highlight is a whopping great hydraulic phallus that leaps out of a black box at a crucial moment; the *Star* says the phallus is 20ft but *Today* has it at 21ft. The show also features topless women in a cage. 'Actually we're not misogynist' says Beastie MCA. 'I like any girls so long as they've got great big tits.' Stage right you also get a giant Budweiser can, a monument that's recently inspired a writ from the Bud manufacturers for giving their beer a bad name. The Beasties in fact involve themselves in a lot of writs, not all of them detrimental. A while back they sued British Airways for using an obscure B-side in one of their adverts without permission. The Beasties won, and got $40,000 and 100 pairs of gratis airline slippers.

'In America last week armed state troopers were on standby to stop the show,' said Mary Whitehouse, 'and I hope that can be done here.' ●

1988

ACIEEEEEED! Returning from Ibiza, a clutch of London DJs promote the combined benefits of house music and Ecstasy, thus committing us to a chemically altered future. Misguided by the name 'Acid House', the tabloids get it all as wrong as possible. The capital's 'cool' club scene is blown as smiles and smileys become endemic. The Olympics is filled with girls with long fingernails.

January
The Liberal Party votes for merger with SDP at its Blackpool conference.

March
Three unarmed members of the IRA are shot in Gibraltar by the SAS.

The divine Divine dies.

During the funeral of the three men killed in Gibraltar, a man throws grenades into the crowd and opens fire on them, killing three and injuring 50.

April
Kenneth Williams stops messin' about for the final time.

Alan Shearer, at 17 years old, becomes the youngest player to score a hat-trick in the First Division as Southampton beats Arsenal 4-2.

May
Kim Philby dies.

Wimbledon's 'Crazy Gang' unexpectedly beats Liverpool to win the FA Cup.

Soviet forces begin withdrawal from Afghanistan.

Local Authorities Bill (including the notorious Clause 28) officially becomes law.

July
US shoots down civilian Airbus in the Gulf, killing everyone on board.

167 people die in Piper Alpha disaster in North Sea.

August
Iran-Iraq war ends.

November
George Bush elected as President of the USA.

December
A Pan-Am jet is blown up over Scottish town of Lockerbie, killing 276 people.

Three trains collide at Clapham Junction resulting in 36 deaths.

Cinema Paradiso
Warmly nostalgic without falling foul of Fellini-esque caricature, the film is too emotionally manipulative for its own good.

The Accused
Though it does make a clear stand on vital social and legal questions, one is left feeling distinctly uneasy at the inclusion of the gang-rape scene.

The Last Temptation Of Christ
Neither blasphemous nor offensive, this faithful adaptation of Nikos Kazantzaki's book sees Christ torn between destiny and an all too human awareness of pain and sexuality.

Pixies - Surfer Rosa (4AD)
The music often matches, and

sometimes even surpasses, the expectations raised by the beautifully packaged artwork – which is really saying something.

Eric B & Rakim - Follow The Leader (MCA)
Rakim is allowed the space to pursue the logic of his philosophy by Eric, who treats each rhythm track as

a fluid counterpoint to the text as well as a dancefloor drone in its own right.

REM - Green (WEA)
Peter Buck's guitar-playing ploughs through rock clichés with growing confidence and style, as does Stipe's rusty growl. Thrill to 'Green' and be totally astounded if REM don't get to Heaven.

Starstruck and Hutch

The INXS lead singer with a stadium-sized voice and a peculiar use for condoms.

Michael Hutchence interviewed in T.O. 950, by **Paula Yates**

One would not, at first glance, guess that the man standing waving a palm frond about weakly in a Fifth Avenue church on Palm Sunday was potentially the hugest mega-star of 1988 (according to *Rolling Stone*). Not that too many fellow worshippers were wearing the regulation off-duty-sex-symbol, custom-fitted black leather suit or the post-Morrison glory of falling curls. With the exception of the palm frond, which could possibly be a late '80s addition to the rock armoury of poses – a sort of compulsory 'new man' sensitivity totem – Michael Hutchence looks like the logical conclusion of 30 years of pop star attitude. A sort of rock star composite. A compendium of attitude and sexuality in a way that is dangerous,

'I just love churches,' he croons, 'and art galleries. I've cried in every major art gallery in the world.'

appealing and admirable. Something that, no matter how hard they may or may not desire it, bands like the Pet Shop Boys, Hazel Dean and all these girls who haven't had their periods yet could never be. A proper pop star.

Michael Hutchence is seductive. He has none of the winsome appeal of English pop stars who look like they couldn't threaten a jam roll, and spend their spare time at home with their mums writing thank you letters to fans for purple furry gonks. Michael is seriously alluring, in an old-fashioned, louche and loose-limbed way. His sex appeal is careless and seemingly lacking in narcissism. There's an odd dichotomy between the visual, which is a heady cross of Dolores del Rio and dream boy, and the man who speaks, who is shy, sensitive and probably writes poems on the back of laundry lists.

It all makes me nervous in church. I'm standing there waiting to be struck down by a large bolt of lightning.

'Look how lovely the ceiling is,' I say.

'I just love churches,' he croons, 'and art galleries, they make me cry. I've cried in every major art gallery in the world.'

My shopping weekend was now off schedule. My friend Sue, who accompanied me, came not only for the shopping, but also to visit the land of her ancestors. She's from Chertsey, but her ancestry stretches back in an unfaltering line through Boadicea, who she in fact was, to various woad-daubing people.

Having exhausted herself reverting to some deep-seated folk memory, we went back to the hotel to wait for Michael. Hutchence is now 20 minutes late, and the anticipation is palpable. Sue has done the I Ching twice to decide what to wear and the thermostat has broken. I douse myself in Jungle Gardenia and practise looking like a soignée older woman wearing mink-trimmed underwear.

In the end we decide, without consulting the cards, that he's fallen asleep so I call him. He says, 'Sorry mate, I'm just feeling up Virginia. I'll be down in a minute.' Sue and I collapse on to the spindly sofa together, clutching her crystal for 'inner peace'. We had dreamed of a long-haired Australian version of Rossano Brazzi, but he'd just told me he was late because he was feeling up a six-foot blonde in his bedroom.

'They'll send a load of black girls in hot pants up now,' says Michael, strolling in.

'Have we met in a past life?' says Sue.

Michael's having asparagus for lunch. He's displaying a talent hitherto only demonstrated by Daniel Day Lewis in 'The Bounty' – the ability to chew and suck one's cheeks in at the same time. He looks pretty happy.

In the past five years INXS's unique blend of unstoppable funk, extreme Australian loudness and the kind of stadium rock where you can shout 'Are you out there, Philadelphia?' at the end of every song and not look silly, has been massive in America. And everywhere else except for England, half imagining INXS to be a pub rock band with wobble boards. However, since the release of their sixth album, 'Kick', it appears that even England cannot resist.

attitude of the bands that sit around on the sidelines, saying "we're too good for that, we're too good to be popular, it's too good to be successful. It's art." It's a load of shit. "If only 500 people see it it must be great." It's a load of wank. Get out there and change pop, give it some respect. Pop has no respect. It's like England's a complete fuck-up. It's all Spanish drinking songs and Gothic death music.'

The harpist is playing send in the fucking clowns for the eleventh time.

In Australia the myth of Hutchence has become so potent that his life has taken on that horrific fish-bowl quality. He has become the sort of sexual/musical equivalent of the Sydney Opera House. He seems at once restless, now without a girl-friend for the first time in eight years, and homeless, although he lives in Hong Kong. He is very 'global' in that way Australians are, willing to go 400 miles to buy a bucket.

'I live in Hong Kong. It's totally removed from everything. It's 'Blade Runner'-ish. I live in a little apartment

'This album has a lot more bubbling underneath; the last album was very white guitar music, and this is funkier. I hate, more than anything, sexless music. The more we indulge ourselves, the more successful we get, we're very lucky that way. We indulge ourselves in a positive way, our first albums are very naïve – horrible. We've done six and they're like half brilliant and half naff. We just do whatever we want, we don't do anything for anybody else, and I'm enjoying that.

'If it feels good, do it. I'm not precious about it. My philosophy to music comes very much from a black attitude. I'm not interested in pulling it apart and putting it back, carrying the world on my shoulders like U2, my causes change every week, every month, every year. I'm enjoying myself and I'd like others to enjoy it with me, that's what the band is about.

'I like pop music, I like turning on the radio and listening to good pop music. Half the reason a lot of pop is crap, is the

and you have to go up six flights of 20 steps to get to it and it's all covered in moss and dirt. Australia's great. I tour there. I rehearse there. I've got a Harley there. I love to ride my bike. I go out to the bush and watch the bull riders. You can't ride a bike in Hong Kong like that, but in Hong Kong I have really varied friends. Chinese friends who live in squats and smoke opium, and other friends who are filthy rich capitalist pigs, make millions of dollars and go out in the biggest boats you've ever seen and have little guys in hats and uniforms to pick you up. It's the other side of life, the old jet set.

'I like Australians. I really like them, they're straightforward, dry, laconic. Also, it's the end of the hippie trail, so there's a whole generation like that, a whole stratum of Australian society that's devoutly liberal. We're so lucky to have a country at such a raw stage. If we get it right now we won't fuck it up in the future. Look at America, it's hideous, and England too.

▶

'Anyway, in Hong Kong no one knows who I am.'

Leaning over the glass counter in Chanel, he's just not sure if he prefers bows or camellias. He's a Chanel aficionado, which comes as a surprise because you'd sort of imagine he only hangs out with seven-foot women entirely upholstered in quilted spandex. 'I love girls in Chanel.'

The assistant, who had been painting her false nails and reading a paper with details of a diet aliens gave Elizabeth Taylor last time they were in LA, starts to watch him. He's lolling against a row of gilt-buttoned suits, his long legs stretched out. His suit would easily fit a fat bouncer from Batley Variety Club, and he's wearing Chelsea boots with a silver toe-cap missing.

Bands need at least one person who is good at conducting business and talking money. In the finely balanced mix of creativity and commercial sense which constitutes the sensibility of most pop people, Michael Hutchence may be considered wildly successful despite his furious denials.

He has an astute business brain that marries his idealism and nationalism by investing in Australia (well, art and 'Crocodile Dundee', actually). But the obvious pleasure he derives from business seems to derive simply from a desire to take a punt.

'I really don't buy anything,' he says, 'I bought my Harley. I buy art. I just bought a John Lennon poem. A big beautiful poem he wrote to Yoko, 'the alphabet of love'. There were also some erotic drawings of Yoko giving him head, so I went for the poem.'

We get out of the taxi at Bloomingdale's and I notice that every single dummy in every single window is wearing the same thing that I'm wearing. I mention that I have a Saturday job as a dummy there. We get on the up-escalator.

Being on an up-escalator with Hutchence is a deeply moving experience because of the stress of having to hold everything up and in and speak at the same time.

We get off in the pan department.

> ## 'I'd like a baby, but not just one woman, maybe five, I guess you'd have to have an arrangement.'

A big blonde with an egg poacher whimpers loudly when she sees him, drops her poacher and rushes over for an autograph. 'I LURVE YOUR MUSIC,' she breathes, before rushing off to check out the liquidisers.

His father is an importer and exporter, 'who lived in China. He's a firm believer in China, a capitalist pig. He went back to Oz and went bankrupt a million times so the dynasty's had its ups and downs.'

With a mother who worked as a make-up artist on movies, what's to rebel against?

'How rosy it all was.'

Michael's hair is falling out of its red ribbon. Some very little girls are staring covertly at him. In the baby-wear department he's flicking restlessly through racks of pink flowery dresses for chicks three foot and under.

'I'd like a baby,' he says.

'I'd like a baby, but not just one woman.' He pauses next to a blue and white gingham pinafore like the one Dorothy Gale wears. 'Maybe five women. I guess you'd have to have some kind of arrangement…'

'It'll never work,' I mutter darkly.

It's cold in the street. Michael's only wearing a thin white T-shirt. He stamps his feet and pulls his jacket around himself. A man on the corner starts to play 'Send In The Clowns' on a trumpet. That song's like torture now. We get a taxi.

'The thing about Australian politics is they're like a tacky, trivial version of English politics, everyone craps on each other. Labour is much more liberal than our last Liberal government. And there are a couple of guys who run Australia, legally or otherwise. But Hawke basically understands that to get a country going, he doesn't want to indulge the unions, because Australia doesn't want the same problems England's got. All the cockney union leaders came out on holiday and stayed so every Christmas we have our postal strikes, our

Harry Enfield

from 'The trouble with Harry' in T.O. 923, by **Don Perretta**

The strength of Loadsamoney is that, in the same way as Yosser and 'Gissajob' neatly summed up a period when unemployment characterised by a depressed Merseyside was a national obsession, 'Loadsamoney' is the rallying call for a new age of acquisition and self-interest.

'He's a complete Thatcherite,' says the character's creator Harry Enfield. 'His politics can be summed up in one line – "she's done a lot of good for the country but I wouldn't want to be married to her". But I don't want it to be used as Thatcher propaganda, as a role model for success stories under Thatcher's Britain. Every interview I do I make it clear that I think he's a complete wanker and what he stands for is hateful, "I've got money and a big car and fuck you". He is British culture and the way it's going.'

petrol station strikes. He wants to keep it working, which is why he appears very right-wing.'

Despite Hutchence's obvious brains and concerns, the sole and unfortunate manifestation of his political consciousness (with the exception of the usual benefits) came with the now famous condom-throwing incident in Queensland. It was an almost perfectly Dadaist gesture in that most unreal of places,

For this, let's face it, hardly revolutionary act, he went straight to the top of the political credometer. He became a political exile. In the prime-ministerial days of the bizarre right-wing populist Joh Bjelke-Peterson, Queensland introduced and maintained a series of laws designed to keep this vast and beautiful land in '40s aspic. This was God and Man and Developer country. It is a matter of some concern to native Queenslanders that their state is now regarded as little more than a colony of Japan. The Japanese consider it their idyllic honeymoon spot, to which they flock in their millions, buying up the land on the way.

Hutchence likes to view Queensland as Australia's own little fascist state. While the rest of the world was throwing its homosexual-related criminal law in the dustbin, Bjelke-Peterson was insisting there were no 'pansies' in his state, and therefore concluded in a characteristically conceptual leap of brain, that there was no need to sell condoms.

As the rubber police removed the vending machines from pub and club, in strode the black-leathered, rubber-toting rock star. Incensed by this defiance, and not being much of a believer in the concept of punishment fitting the crime, the Prime Minister issued federal warrants for Hutchence's arrest. Hutchence & Co legged it and were subsequently allowed back upon 'ol' Joh's' recent – and much celebrated – forced removal and demise.

As I said, pure surrealism.

Michael would like to be in films. He says he always wanted to be an actor, he was brought up on film sets. His acting debut is in the fim 'Dogs in Space', which opens in London in June. It is directed by Richard Lowenstein, who also directed most of the INXS videos. In ten years he wants to 'maybe be sailing around the world – not like Simon Le Bon, I don't want to over-stretch myself like him, but I like boats and I love the sea. I don't like being on the road. I like being on stage, but not the road, sitting in a hotel room watching 40 channels at once.'

He doesn't drink any more, he doesn't throw his TV out of the window – he watches it and reads books. 'Yeah, maybe I'd like to go to space and see the world. I want to be my own man, I don't want to he constantly compared to people who are dead, like Morrison. I saw my second video of Jim Morrison, in my life, last week. I hate the fucking Doors.

'I didn't decide to be this. I just am what I am. There's a lot of self-made sex symbols out there, and it's really not conscious. I'm either hamming it up, or it's humorous, and people don't get that, either.

'I hate looking at myself in the mirror. I have to in the shower, it's my neurosis. I don't look at myself a lot. Only occasionally do I go "Yeah, I'm okay" which is terrible – it's your weapon, I should feel better about it.'

It's very hot. Michael is standing by the window, leaning on the frame watching the cars passing below. His hair is hanging in long damp curls. Every few minutes a neon sign that says SALAMI drenches the room a suitably Chandler-esque red. Sue is panting gently on the sofa reading Carlos Castaneda. He's lit a cigarette and the smoke just hangs listlessly in the air. 'I was dancing on that rooftop at four this morning,' he says.

A few minutes later, I get a phone call. Coincidentally, it's from an Australian friend. I tell him I'm interviewing Michael. 'Effeminate Sydney poof,' he informs me. 'They're not fucking like that in the rest of Australia.'

I wandered back into the other room. By the light of the shivering neon, Michael Hutchence looks a real heart-breaker. A proper pop star. ●

Jerry 'Gobshite' Sadowitz
from T.O.910

When was the last time you went to Regent's Park Zoo? It's a great day out and real value for money. For £2.60 you're guaranteed a shit, a piss, a wank and intercourse all in the one cage!! What a bargain!! You try finding that at Camden Lock Market. Bootleg tapes cost more money! Why settle for the Pet Shop Boys when you can see the real things hard at it in Regent's Park? I can personally recommend the Farmyard Animal section and any of the water creatures, but for fuck's sake avoid the pandas: they do fuck all. In fact, they should be shot. They sit there doing nothing till my back's turned then they tear a little boy apart and I miss the whole thing. Bastards. The other thing to avoid in Regent's Park Zoo is the monkey section. They don't swing about and go mental like they used to. Quit holding back on the drugs, ya cunts! I can remember the good old days when the baboons used to press their swollen red arses against the window. Nowadays you have to wait for budget day to get a glimpse of Nigel Lawson. Another thing – the bird cage is shite and all. I don't go to the fucking zoo to see fuckin' birds crap. I can see that anytime. And I don't like to see empty cages with fuck all in them and a sign that says 'LIONS VERY DANGEROUS – DO NOT FEED' when they're never ever fucking there. Just a pile of fucking rocks. It's the same with reptiles. They're never there either. And anyway, a reptile isn't an animal, is a snake.

And I don't like cages that profess to hold 'RARE ANIMALS' either because they're boring – that's why they're rare, ya dozy bastards. And anyway, if they're so rare what are they doing in Regent's Park? That goes for your elephant too. It's shite. In fact, I've seen it before and its the same one, ya thieving cunts. Plus, I don't like the giraffe. It's got a rubbishy expression. Avoid the giraffe. Anyone can stand about chewing grass, its easy. I don't pay good money to go to the zoo to see fuckin' giraffes and elephants, right? And don't give us your fucking zebras, we all know. I don't go to the zoo to see fucking animals.

Boy's own story

Boy George interviewed in T.O. 947, by **Simon Garfield**

Acid was never one of George's big drugs, nor was Ecstasy. This may explain why he gets insulted when he visits the Acid House clubs. It may explain why at Spectrum recently a girl came up and said 'You're really ugly in real life' and why he got into a feud with some guys in the toilets. Or why he got called a fucking queer outside the Wag. Or why his accompanying friend Fat Tony got head-butted at the Future. But it doesn't explain why, after a Michael Jackson Wembley show, George is locked into a car alone being screamed at again. 'Bloody poof! You fucking queer bastard!'

A quiet life this man leads. Up in Hampstead, where he still lives in his turreted Gothic pile, you can see him walking his dog alone in the early evenings. A lot of days there are still fans sitting on the bench opposite his house, no longer surrounded by tabloid journalists, still in their Boy baseball caps, ever hoping for a chat. Why do they hang around? They couldn't tell you. Last week an Australian girl followed George up the High Street to ask for £10, but that's rare. George thinks they're there for the social life and to come out as gay close to a figure they can relate to. It's like a small all-weather club, and it looks to be getting smaller all the time.

People are growing up. The clubbers have lost their style, says George. The music has changed. Too old at 27 maybe, George is occasionally asked to relive his past for the press – witty, confessional, vein-opening interviews that roll into clubland, hit parades, world tours, drugs, drag, and a twilight London world that touches people called Paranoid Pete and Sex-Change Marie. A fabulous upbringing. You can get quite cheesey about his last decade and quote 'Citizen Kane': 'All of these years he covered – many of these years he was.' The London Party Novel? A walking talking five volumes. It was like Lou Reed said: his week beat your year.

Today there are slight reservations in the re-telling. 'My comments have hung me so many times,' he says. 'Followed me around the world. Everyone thinks that I'm a camp fool. It's very difficult for me to want to be taken seriously because people just see me as a joke.'

He says the whole press thing 'baffles' him. Before the heroin downfall he was friendly with many journalists, particularly one who we can refer to as Mr X (though his real name is Jonathan Ashby, a writer on the *People*). George used to go to his house for tea. Kind of naïve, but rather too much a part of his nature. When the drugs story broke, Mr X was 'evil as fuck'.

'I was so shocked. But it doesn't change me because I'm not going to go around thinking everyone's a cunt. I just can't do it. I just won't survive. God, I'm from Woolwich, I'm not living in Beverly Hills. The thing I realise is that most great pop careers are built on illusion, and I'm not very good at illusions.'

Woolwich. A moderately unhappy Catholic childhood. George will tell me where he's from three times in the next two hours. His great rise and fall, 'From Luxury To Heartache' as Culture Club called their last album, maybe it's a little clearer now. 'When you come from suburbia… suddenly we were eating at expensive restaurants and getting fat and being asked about things we probably wouldn't even have thought about. One day I'd wake up and think, I don't want to do this. This is fucking bollocks. I never go out, I never enjoy myself, I haven't got any friends. And I didn't have any friends. When Culture Club became successful I stayed in my little flat in St John's Wood. I never went out. One of the reasons was because I remember going out one night to the Camden Palace, because I always used to go there for years, and somebody then wrote this piece saying that Boy George was out trying to get noticed. *Noticed.* Like going out was seen as a career move…'

Going out, dressing strange: it was his early life, of course. Before his band, before his drugs, there was a place in the West End which would be forever home – the mirrored nightclub washroom. They tell him to fuck off now, but 11 years ago, aged 16, he got into his first gay club on the Charing Cross Road and Woolwich didn't seem such a party anymore.

'I was going out with a girl called Laura and we came up to the West End and we couldn't get into the Lyceum because we had holes in our clothes and spikey hair. This queen behind us said, "Come with us to Bangs if you like." I was like, "What's that then?" I was from Woolwich. I used to come up on the train. He said, "It's a gay club. We'll get you in, we're members." And I remember going into Bangs and seeing (Pistols groupie) Catwoman. I met Phillip Salon. He was wearing this velvet skirt and two horns and he had black lipstick on. My girlfriend goes, "Look at him, he's brilliant, isn't he?" and I said, "Yeah, go and speak to him." She goes, "What will I say?" I go, "Ask to borrow his lipstick." So we got friendly with Philip, and I said to him, "Are you gay?" And he said, "Why? Are you interested?"'

You can see those early club years as snapshots now, selling in Japan for plenty yen. George at Madame Louise's. George at the Camden Palace. George at Planets with Kirk Brandon. George as the hat-check at Blitz. George with Marilyn everywhere. George has been writing some of his seedy-made-glitzy memoirs for a possible book. One passage tells of how a friend of his first met Marilyn in the high street in Borehamwood and later called round to his mum's place. He found Marilyn in gold stilettos with a piece of lamé wrapped around him, hoovering the house. 'Just thinking about that picture is so funny.'

George's own home was as startling. At four in the morning at the turn of the '80s two squats in Warren Street and Carburton Street reeked of vile crashed bodies, but they were the bodies that would shape young Soho style for the coming years. Nothing much to see now, of course, but you can still smell the rooms and hear the squeals. George lived in Carburton Street. 'It was unbelievable. In the back of that house there was the biggest heroin dealer in London. They were selling drugs all the time. We lived in it, we never became part of it, but people died there. I remember Mitsu, she's the girl that Iggy wrote that song about, 'China Girl', she died there.

'It was a weird house. This guy Barry chained Molly Parkin's daughter Sofa up… one day these guys with gas masks and sledge hammers broke into the house… there was loads of people… Stephen Jones, Kim Bowen, Andy Polaris, Jeremy Healey, Sex-change Marie, Paranoid Pete, Melissa Kaplan. Spandau Ballet came around all the time. Everyone hated them and used to be really horrible to them. Marilyn moved in as well, which was like the downfall of the squat… the only things I used to eat was fish and chips and bread rolls… Kim would dress up as Mary Queen of Scots and we'd go into the local shops and she'd start screaming at the top of her voice, and we'd start stuffing things into her bag and go up the road.

'I used to be the biggest handbag thief in London. Perfume, books, clothes. Everyone used to do it actually, and I was really bad at it, got a bit of a reputation for it. So many of those people have done well now… big clothes businesses in Japan.'

Culture Club, by most reckonings a perfect new pop creation, formed in 1981. The decade's first and most accomplished escapist dreamplan, the band dressed ethnic-clubland but played hi-tech soulful chart pop. Its drummer, Jon Moss, was an alumnus of various punk bands, but his new group suggested strands of a sweeter rebellion. Make-up, dyes, robes – if it had any antecedents they lay in early '70s glam.

'I think I wanted it to be like Marc Bolan,' says George. 'I want-

When George got offered heroin in a Paris club in 1985, he could reason that somehow his band and his fame 'wasn't enough'.

ed to write really good songs and I wanted to create the same kind of feeling that Bowie created in me. I don't care what anyone says, Bowie has done some brilliant things and he's part of my childhood and I was inspired by his music. I still listen to his records – I buy all the CDs I can get on him and all the Bolan records. The only thing I had in my house when I was really young was Sinatra and stuff like that. My dad was a builder and he used to find records in houses when he cleared them out. Also, my brother was very into early Rod Stewart and Bowie and I'd listen to them on headphones in his room and get beaten up when I got caught.'

At Culture Club's peak – the ten million-selling 'Colour By Numbers' album of 1983 – George was unshakeable. Still the hit of the clubs, ever a Fleet Street headline, seldom off the TV, cosily outrageous and all drug free. And when it collapsed, and George got offered heroin in a Paris club in 1985, he could reason that somehow his band and his fame 'wasn't enough'. Looking back now, he sees more.

'I think Culture Club were important for lots of reasons. Musically we did a lot of good things, but a lot of it went over people's heads because of the way I looked. But I think we definitely opened the door. I see that people now respect you for being a good idea. You don't have to be talented any more, and I'm sorry, but when I started in Culture Club I did think that you had to be able to sing. And I thought you had to be able to write songs. Now with Bros and these new bands, I just think that they've now kind of perfected the marketing technique. I suppose we were like the prototype.

'And God, it was fun. You can forget that.

▶

'I don't want to sound big-headed, but we were talented and I think that I can sing. I'd always wanted to be famous, but I wanted to be famous for doing something… But then it all got taken out of my hands. Suddenly it was all about schedules.'

He didn't want to talk much about drugs, but then it was like it all got taken out of his hands. In the TV room at Willesden's Powerplant studios, life is once again about schedules; he's got a new solo album due at the end of the month, his second, called 'Tense Nervous Headache'. It's not a sugared commercial album, but there certainly are some snappy titles. One track is called 'You Are My Heroin'. This is not about Hollywood.

'What it's about is, well, when I was a junkie I made it a career. If you take drugs, you make it into a lifestyle. It's about being an addictive person. I was completely addicted to Culture Club. I worked, I did interviews, it was exactly like a drug. And then Jon was such a major part of my life. It was one of the reasons I stayed in the band, because I wanted to leave a long time before I did. Like a drug… I mean I did terrible things when I went out with Jon. Like when he split with me I bricked his girlfriend's window up.'

The tabloid onslaught hit in June 1986, some 15 months after the heroin gripped. In a story given, not sold, to the *Sun*, George's brother David made public what George's friends had known for months, that the Boy was in trouble. The tabloids that had made George now hustled to destroy him. The theory was that if George saw the story – an embellished 'Junkie George Has Eight Weeks To Live' – and if he felt at least some of the high-octane hysteria that accompanied it, then maybe he'd be jolted into some sort of reality. In practice the jolt took six months more, and the death of Mark Golding, one of his closest friends.

'There's something about being really young,' says George now. 'You think you're indestructible and you want to find out just how indestructible you are. Again, it's about making drugs your career. A lot of the people who run clubs in London, their talent is how much they can party. And that isn't my talent. I'm useless at it because I just fuck up with things like that. I couldn't do anything at all. You hear about people taking drugs and writing the great songs. I couldn't do anything like that.

'And also with heroin, it was a trap. It hits you so hard and you don't have a chance. All those tragedies (George survived the death of another close friend Michael Rudetski and clubbing partner Trojan)… I thought, "My God, I've got to stop." And it's scary stopping. It's so scary because you don't know what to do. I always used to think, "I'm just going to die." I'm telling you, some of the people I was mixing with, I'm not saying how beneath me they were, it was just that I couldn't believe it. I had nothing in common with them apart from the fact that I was getting out of it. Drugs don't make you relate to other people – they just give you a similar problem.'

George says he gave up his last drug, sleeping pills, last Christmas; this was 'harder than stopping heroin'. His public drug this afternoon is cigarettes, so many that they've badly stained his fingers. He does meditation and hypnosis. He goes to counsellors to speak of things he'd 'never say to anyone'. He's got a close boyfriend. He believes he's still overweight, but in jogging pants and poncho-style top he's probably as fit as he's been for three years. The test they say is in the eyes, the pupils,

Ecstatic reviews

from T.O. 939, by **Dave Swindells**

It's not hard to imagine the angle the tabloid press will choose if they 'report' on the Acid House scene. Its supposedly symbiotic relationship with psychedelic drugs will make banner headlines of shock-horror proportions, along the lines of 'London Gripped By Ecstasy', 'Drug-Crazed New Hippies In Street Riot' or 'Yuppies On Acid!' The clubs will be portrayed only as 'drug dens', the music will be 'mind-numbing' and the clubbers 'hooligans'. Should it actually happen, the negative publicity could harm what has been an incredible summer of clubbing in London.

Time Out first mentioned Acid House in January and covered the Balearic Beat club the Future in March. Since then we've kept a close eye on the rapid development of this scene. It hasn't been a media circus and in many ways is still an underground movement with some of the best nights run like regular warehouse parties. There have been exceptions. When the Shoom Club shifted to the West End at the end of May they invited the major monthly magazines and the Sunday papers but none turned up. Recently, Jenny and Danny Rampling, who run the club, turned away a BBC camera crew who arrived unannounced. They knew that their club would be misunderstood or misinterpreted. Radio London has boldly asked club-runners if Ecstasy is easily obtainable on their nights. What do they expect them to say? 'Oh yes! Come on down, see for yourself, and bring the Drug Squad while you're at it!'

There is no denying that psychedelic drugs are a part of the scene. The use of the designer drug Ecstasy has been closely linked to Acid House clubs, but in fact it is frequently too expensive (£20-£30 per tablet) for clubbers who resort to the cheaper acid tabs costing around £3. Ecstasy itself is certainly a dodgy concoction, for all the sensual, uninhibited highs it offers. In its pure MDMA form it is not known to be physically addictive, but it is sometimes cut with heroin and if taken too often can lead to feelings of extreme anxiety, confusion and depression. Long term use may even damage the nervous system. However, experienced users say that the reaction really depends upon their state of mind and the environment it is used in. It's too easy to over-stress the significance of stimulants. Without drugs the scene would not have developed so quickly or so radically, but its continued expansion depends on the dance music. Acid House does not automatically mean Acidheads but House music, which is what so many punters are packing the clubs to hear. This is particularly true as the popularity of Acid House beats takes it outside London.

Surf-Disco Pirates

Drugs or not, it has been a sensational summer. Never have there been so many young people going out to nightclubs, nor from such but with George it's in the mouth, the manipulative lash, the fact that he's bitchingly, coherently funny again. 'Same old George,' people say.

'I think the most shocking thing about being off is the normality of it,' says George himself. 'Everything is really up close. And normality is so scary. Does that sound like a weird thing to say?'

Normality since Christmas has meant writing and cutting his new album, promoting his new single – the militant 'No Clause 28' – and venturing out into the Acid House scene. Except for brief periods at the height of his music and drugs fame, George never really stopped going to clubs. He still gets abused, but he still has to go. In most eyes his clubbing days should be over; they see a man out of time, last season's face, a hanger on. George isn't as keen on the music as his close clubbing-friend Jeremy Healey, but still. He goes. Why does he go? To belong? To enjoy himself? To sup the lager?

'The first time I went to Spectrum there were about 20 people there. What's happened now is like the punk thing. When punk happened loads of people found out that being a punk was jumping up and down and spitting and fighting with each other. With Acid House, the money's there now and people are making a fortune from it. I went to this thing on Saturday and the only thing that the people there had in common with each other was that they were on Ecstasy. Ecstasy's massive, I'm telling you. Everyone, everywhere you go. You can always tell because you go to clubs

George wears no make-up for our meeting. 'I'm not very good at illusions,' he says.

and people go (fast and aggressive) "HI! HOWAREYOU?" I go, "Have you taken drugs?" and they go, "No, not drugs, E-C-S-T-A-S-Y." I just worry that something awful is going to happen. Someone's going to fucking die or something.

'I just don't want to go out and dance with football hooligans. It's so heavy now, and I'm sorry, but I just feel uneasy about people like that. You know, someone got stabbed at Spectrum two months ago. That's what you're dealing with, that kind of bull-terrier mentality. If you look at someone the wrong way you might get a black eye, or worse. They'll all probably be back on the terraces next season.

'I think there's an incredible lack of style now. In the punk days, even with the New Romantic thing, you could tell if someone had got it right. You could tell where someone was from by the way they looked. I know it's really snobby, but with the Acid House thing, everyone's wearing white T-shirts and you can't tell who's got style. The only places where people dress up are gay clubs. Leigh Bowery is still holding the torch up for everyone in London. Leigh always says to me whenever I wear make-up, "Oh I do so like to see you with your face on." He says, "I do love this Acid House, but you do have to keep up the appearance."'

George wears no make-up for our meeting, but the foundation and the blusher and the liner and the lipstick are there for the photos. They take three hours to apply, a long time for a professional. 'I'm not very good at illusions,' George said. ●

1988

Boy George – Acid House

● ●

widely differing social backgrounds. Everybody from hardcore Millwall fans to wealthy Sloanes to Boy George and Fat Tony have joined in the trance dancing. All human life is here, spouting a philosophy of happy hedonism and love, while dressing down in New Age hippy chic (kaftans, ethnic prints, Converse baseball boots and headbands with flowers stuck in) or as Surf-disco Pirates (Dayglo shorts, Converse baseball boots, bandanas, baggy T-shirts and fluoro-zinc body paint). At clubs like the Trip, Spectrum, the Shoom and Love they've queued in their hundreds or thousands, often starting over three hours before a club opens.

Usually it's far too sweaty to dress up for and in the haze of strobe-light-and-smoke, distinctions of status cut no dry-ice. It's the freedom to freak out, the pure physical energy and a positive spirit that's been important. On the dancefloor the drug-happy few stimulate the intense atmosphere so that clubbers feel a 'contact high'. Once hooked they've sought their dancefloor fix as often as possible; there are now Acid House/Balearic Beat clubs every night at a time when traditionally it's the tourists who fill the venues. The August lull in nightlife activity hasn't happened this year.

However, veterans of the Acid House scene now see a split developing between the sheep-like punters who gaily wave their arms around to the tunes (while actually concentrating on getting out-of-their-brains) and the clubbers who appreciate the music and the original 'matey' spirit. Away from the dancefloor it can be awfully boring in some venues, where people wouldn't know a conversation if it walked up and spoke to them. They are commonly called Acid Teds by their enemies, who love to repeat the maxim 'Better Dead than An Acid Ted!' and lament the way things are moving.

Second Summer of Love

Inevitably the scene has become more commercialised as the clubs get bigger and the music is pushed toward chart success. The emphasis on the dancefloor is likely to shift away from Acid in the coming weeks towards more soulful and deep House sounds which have a wider, more lasting appeal. The popularity of records like Mory Kante's 'Ye Ke Ye Ke' or the Gipsy Kings' 'Bambooléyo' have opened people's ears to World Beats for a more mainstream audience, and of course there are Balearic Beats, too.

These have been hyped as the new 'underground' grooves, which they plainly are not. Nonetheless, its existence has enabled DJs to play the kind of pop-rock, indie faves and Eurodisco classics that might otherwise have been spurned by London's dancers. As one DJ commented recently: 'You can play anything with a beat and it goes down a treat!

The reputation of the scene is spreading beyond the clubs. Young clubbers have gone home and told their eager, inquisitive parents what they're up to, and the so-called second Summer of Love has become a dinner party topic. The scale, ubiquity and characteristics of the phenomenon have drawn frequent comparison with the punk era and/or the original hippie movement. What does seem surprising is that some parents love the idea that their kids are now having wild times and experiencing the kind of highs and lows that they went through before they gave up being hippies and started making money. More strangely still, they evidently look back at those lost years with some lingering affection. Now they want a piece of the action, demanding of our hapless Editor at a recent gathering 'How do we get into these clubs?' and 'Which ones could we go to?'. The answer is probably none of them. Unfortunately the age range of London clubbers is very narrow, usually 17-30, so unless they encounter a broadminded doorperson their chances are slim. It begs the question of whether they would have let their parents in to some hippie happening in 1971 to see them freaking out with their friends? ●

Bird song

'I'm like the guy who paints for himself and doesn't think about the art collector.'

Clint Eastwood interviewed in T.O. 950, by **Brian Case**

If Clint Eastwood is superstitious it sure doesn't show. He's elected to take one of the biggest risks of his movie-making career with his thirteenth film, 'Bird' –a film which tells the story of Charlie Parker, a black jazzman and heroin addict, uses virtual unknowns, concentrates on an inter-racial love story and ends unhappily, 'And I'm not even in the film,' he cracks. $10 million is riding on the project, and all of his love. 'This project felt good from the beginning. I had the same feeling going in that I had when I first saw Charlie Parker play. I've done all my movies for myself, and sometimes I've been right. Jazz is about musicians playing for themselves, not for the money. I'm like the guy who paints for himself and doesn't think about the art collector.'

He strolls about the set at Burbank with that slowpoke walk, casual in a yellow Slazenger sports shirt, unflappable and endlessly available. Unlike many directors, he eats with the crew and insists on quality catering. There's a comfortable sense of camaraderie about Malpaso productions, a refreshing absence of bitching, and interfering Warner Bros executives are not in evidence. As the laconic director once remarked, 'They know Clint Eastwood's not hunching around or shooting up. They're still putting in faith that I'll make the best picture I can.' In fact his films have grossed $1.5 billion dollars and he accounts for about 18 per cent of Warner Bros revenues, shoots fast and invariably comes in on or under budget.

'Print that, thank you.' After a successful take on the Three Deuces nightclub set, Clint snaps into a spot-on John Wayne imitation 'Dukey, ya did a helluva job!' – and everybody cracks up, 'Thank you, gents,' he tells the applauding extras in the audience, 'good stuff' and to the actors on the bandstand faking like men possessed, every uptempo fingering exact, 'You guys were… adequate.' He seats himself at the piano and digs into a blues. 'One

of those things you always wish you'd stayed with,' he tells a couple of musicians. 'You think, what would I be doing today? Would I be playing decently today if I'd stayed with it all that time? I'd probably be sitting in some saloon today – could ya lend me a buck, mister? – and playing "Melancholy Baby" one more time.'

Michael Zelniker, who plays trumpeter Red Rodney, puts his horn back in the case. Clint hums 'Now's The Time', and reflects that Parker's tune was lifted whole for the R&B hit, 'The Hucklebuck'. 'You get hot by the time the picture is finished, you'll be sitting on the road with the hot players. Your lip will be twice as strong.'

Zelniker laughs. 'It's already happening. That's what my girlfriend says.'

'Oh, yeah?' says Clint. He flutters his fingers over imaginary valves. Well, once you start doing a lot of that real fast – 'he laughs and dummies up – 'oh, I won't get into that. She may notice a lotta things. Trumpet players are very popular.'

The jazz life has been notoriously difficult to put on screen. In recent times, it has eluded both Scorsese and Coppola, though not as laughably as it eluded Michael Curtiz way back in 1950 with his Bix biopic, 'Young Man With A Horn'. It has become a jazz joke. Kirk Douglas, playing the self-destructive genius, or nearest offer, is dying in the paupers' hospital when he hears the wail of an ambulance – it's that note! – raises himself on an elbow and recovers. That was one of the Hollywood travesties that got in among Clint in a big way, and made him determined to cut through the hagiography and tell it true. 'He didn't want to glorify anything, and he didn't want to leave much out,' commented Bird's last lady, Chan Parker, now 63, after he approached her. She was impressed enough to give him access to her unpublished manuscript 'Life in E-Flat'. His Bird, like the real one, capsizes employability somewhere between the put-on and the let-down and the shoot-up, cracks his wig on the Coast, dies of pretty much everything, and leaves in his music the most revealing portrait of our times. The 58-year-old director is a jazz fan, and he trusts the music. 'When I was in Paris,' says Clint, 'Chan Parker played a tape where he went into one of those booths like they used to have years ago, put in 50 cents or something, you cut a little disc. I remember making one when I was a kid. Bird must've been around 17, 18. It's real scratchy and seedy, but, boy, you'd still tell he had something special. He was headed someplace special.

The cast swear by him. 'He wants an uninhibited response,' says Diane Venora who plays Chan. 'His theory of not rehearsing is to create that off-balance thing for the actor. You say, "You want that?" He'll say, "Uh-huh." And that makes us laugh at ourselves and not be too precious. Clint doesn't do a lot of takes because most actors make one choice and stick with it. The great dramatic scenes, he really steps away from that and lets the actor go. I find on this set people are very sensitive to the work in hand, crew and everyone alike, and they support the actor who has to go through that tunnel or over that mountain in that scene.'

And it's extraordinary the depths of experience that Venora has dredged up for the part of Charlie Parker's long-suffering lady. You can still see women like Chan when the veteran bebop survivors hit town, women who've put up with most things and can't divorce the eternally newborn music from the originator with the old excuses. She's giving the sort of performance you'd expect from Gena Rowlands in a John Cassavetes film – and she's doing it in a Clint Eastwood movie. Well, when you think of 'Tightrope' and 'Play Misty for Me', that's not so extraordinary. The old macho labels have been peeling off for years. 'As far as the tormented masculinity goes,' he told journalist Carrie Rickey, 'maybe I'm interested in it because it's an obsolete thing. Masculinity, I mean. There's very few things men are required for, except maybe siring.'

He avoids preaching on the drugs issue. 'I won't say I'm making an anti-drugs film, but if it turns out that way it won't break my heart.' It's hard to go up against Bird's words on the habit to pianist Walter Bishop. 'Bish, you know there's quite a number of things wrong with me. I go to this heart specialist, give him $100 for the relief of my heart. He treats me, don't do no good; my heart is still messed up. I go to this ulcer man, give him $75 to cool my ulcers out; it don't do no good. There's a little cat in a dark alley round the corner. I give him $5 for a bag of shit; my ulcers gone; my heart trouble gone, everything gone, all my ailments gone.'

On set – a meticulous reconstruction of New York's 52nd Street – Forrest Whitaker emerges from behind a clutch of vintage automobiles, Diane Venora wrapped around his waist, riding on a white horse. Bird has just swept Chan off her feet. 'Forrest. Will you come here for a second. Ride him over,' Clint calls. 'C'mon, pony, go! Come here, Thunder! Whoaah. Just pull right in.' The precariously perched actor and the director confer. 'Say what? Okay. Say all that… "I got a way about me too"… and you go off in the sunset.' He waves a lazy hand.

'Just give us one more minute, okay.'

'Sure', says Clint in that spoke-shave whisper, smoothing the way, turning aside to bite into a salsa burrito, an artist all the way down in his cool. ●

Hunter S Thompson

from T.O. 946, originally published in 'Generation of Swine' (Picador)

I was sitting at the bar in the Woody Creek Tavern last week, sipping my normal huge flagon of whiskey and getting cranked up to the right level of alcoholic frenzy for an afternoon of fast driving on the local highways, back roads and maybe even a few residential districts, when a man from Miami came in and said he had a fast motorcycle to sell, for $5,000 cash.

It was a café racer, he said – a fancy little hot rod with a silver engine the size of a football and hand-tooled Italian leather seats... And he had it just outside in the parking lot, strapped down with pink bungee cords on the back of what looked like a flat-bed Peterbilt truck.

Nobody paid any attention to him. There was a film on TV about a team of French scientists trying to load a polar bear onto the fantail of what looked like a Caribbean tourist yacht. The beast was howling and thrashing, but they had it wrapped up in steel mesh-net – and then a woman wearing a topless bikini came out and shot it in the back with a tranquilliser gun.

It was the middle of a slow afternoon on a cold day in the Rockies, and there were only a few paying customers at the bar, all of them deeply engrossed in their own business... They were locals, cowboys and gamblers, and the last thing any one of them needed was a high-speed Italian motorcycle.

The stranger took a long look at the place, then he slumped on a bench near the window and ordered a sloe gin sling. 'Who gives a damn about polar bears?' he muttered. 'They're dumber than dogs and they'll turn on you for no reason at all.'

I saw Cromwell shudder on his stool at the far end of the bar, where he had been nursing a Moosehead all morning and brooding helplessly on the 9-point spread for the Celtics-Rockets game... He had bet heavily on the Rockets and given 16-1 against four straight and now he was feeling deep in the hole.

Electrical Implants

The day was already queasy. The morning had bloomed warm and bright, but by noon it was raining fitfully and the sky was turning black. By 2.30 we were getting thunder and lightning, the first spring storm of the season.

The polar bear film was still rolling. The brutes were being taken off to some zoo on the outskirts of Paris, where they would be loaded with electrical implants in their bodies and then turned loose on the slopes of Mount Ararat

The reasons would never be explained. It was one of those top-secret international security gigs that only the French can do properly. Meanwhile, on the other side of the world 8,000 feet up in the Rockies in a roadhouse on the low-rent side of the river, some little fruitbag from Miami was trying to peddle a slick Italian motorcycle

Cromwell eyed him for a moment, then he stood up and pulled a pair of ribbed leather gloves out of his hip pocket. 'OK,' he said. 'You've come to the right place. Let's have a look at the bugger.'

'What? You want to buy it?'

'Not yet,' said Cromwell. 'But I *will*, if it's fast. I just got back from Vegas and I have a lot of money.'

There was a hoot of dumb laughter from somewhere back in the kitchen, but I kept a straight face.

The price was $10,000, said the stranger, but he was new in the neighbourhood so he would let it go for five... The only other one of these things ever built he said, was sold to Steve McQueen for something like $40,000.

'Which one of us should ride it?' Cromwell said. 'I want to run it against my jeep for about a mile down the road – to the gravel pit.'

We went outside and unloaded the slick little speedster off the truck.

Cromwell pulled on his motocross gloves. 'If it's faster than my jeep,' he said, 'I'll give you ten grand – if it's not, you give it to me for *nothing*.'

The stranger stared at him, and nobody else said a word. 'Are you nuts?' he said finally. 'You want me to race my Ducati against a goddamn Jeep? For $10,000?'

'Why not?' said Cromwell. 'Let's go do it before the storm hits.'

We all agreed. It was winner-take-all. Cromwell backed his rotten-looking, mud-covered Jeep out of a corner of the parking lot and aimed it down the road, while the man from Miami got his bike tuned up. I drifted around Cromwell's machine and pulled a Parnelli Jones-Baja bumper sticker off the rear end; the thing was a monster, so fast and strong that he was afraid to even drive it on the roads in Colorado. The engine was a 600hp turbocharged Ford-Cosworth.

Money changed hands. There was serious talk about 'honest dollars' and escrow. A man called Tex stepped forward and agreed to hold the cash without prejudice

Knocked Stupid

We were all involved in this thing, more or less, but nobody really cared... and it was just about then that the whole world exploded with a boom and a flash that blew us all sideways. Cromwell's Jeep turned blue like a gas bomb, and then fell on top of the motorcycle, sending up a cloud of nasty electrical smoke.

We were all knocked stupid. The next sound I remember hearing was a woman screeching, 'Please, Tex – don't die.' And then I felt myself being dragged across the road by people I didn't recognise. There was a smell of burning hair all around us, and I heard voices talking about 'oxygen' and 'heart failure' and 'burned like a human cinder.'

No money changed hands that day, and we never saw the man from Miami again. Several days later I went back to the tavern and heard more or less what happened. We were whacked by a huge blue ball of lightning that bounced once in the parking lot and then rolled down the road about 200 feet before it exploded in the creek

Tex lived, but his heart was like a small lump of charcoal and his face shriveled up like a raisin. A doctor in Phoenix said his body was about 400 years old, and if he ever bumped up against anything solid he would probably break like cheap glass.

I never saw him again. His family put him in a rural hotel somewhere in Arizona, where he remained helpless for whatever was left of his life.

There is still a big crater in the parking lot across the road from the Woody Creek Tavern, with a crust of black ash on its edges and a pool of stagnant water at the bottom... I have not been back there since I quit work and moved north, for professional reasons. ●

1989

And the Wall came a-tumblin' down. It all looked so rosy. Eager to see the back of the mean and avaricious '80s, we all rejoiced for the caring, sharing '90s a year early. The cold war was officially defrosted, rave-culture blossomed and we drove all night round the newly-finished M25 in search of a muddy field full of smiles.

When Harry Met Sally
Nora Ephron's slightly sentimental script includes enough funny one-liners to hold the attention of all but the most jaded viewer.

Drugstore Cowboy
Van Sant's movie takes a contemplative and comic look at US drug culture and manages for the most part to dispense with easy moralising.

sex, lies and videotape
Working from Soderbergh's funny, perceptive dialogue, the actors ensure that the film stimulates both intellectually and emotionally.

Soul II Soul - Club Classics Vol. 1 (Ten)
Lacking nothing in 'front', the first substantial outpouring

from Jazzie B is subtly adventurous. Club Classics proves the promise of Soul II Soul soulmates.

Lenny Kravitz - Let Love Rule (Virgin)
At no point in this odd bundle of received ideas do you feel that Lenny Kravitz amounts to very much more than a record collection on legs.

Madonna - Like A Prayer (Sire)
We all know, Madonna – pop is a genre, but never in our born days did we realise it could be like this. It's the way the tunes turn corners, the way the voice is netted like a porpoise, the very fact that this record will not need its video-echo to make you love its every second.

Daniel Day Lewis
interviewed in T.O. 987,
by **John Morrish**

Disparate Dan

Johnny, a belligerent south London yob and sometime racist snogs in a car with his Asian boyfriend. Cecil, a thin-lipped black-suited Edwardian suitor, confesses his chilly passion for his doll-like fiancée. Henderson Dores, the archetypal Englishman abroad, falls out of a Red Indian kayak into the ornamental pool of a giant Atlanta hotel, several times; the young Franz Kafka struggles within the giant and oppressive bureaucracy of his insurance company; the glacial surgeon and philanderer Tomas instructs a series of women to take off their clothes; Hamlet throws himself around the stage of the National Theatre, raving and self-destructive. And now, Christy Brown, writer and painter, wheelchair-bound, unshaven, rages against the frustrations of his cerebral palsy.

Daniel Day Lewis has been all of them. More than any other young English actor, he's made himself by becoming other people, lots of other people, and the more varied the better. Even so, his latest role, in 'My Left Foot', a translation to screen of Christy Brown's painstakingly tapped-out autobiography, represents a new level of immersion in a role, and of submersion, too. Submersion, that is, of the famous good looks, the high forehead, the sharp cheek bones, the heavy brows, the deep-set brooding eyes of a Mills & Boon hero into the twitching, contorted agonies of a young man struggling with an appalling congenital disorder. Mimicry, at the highest level: but fine acting too.

One of the 'secrets' of the chameleon tendency is research. For the role of the surgeon Tomas in 'The Unbearable Lightness of Being', Day Lewis attended an operation and had to steel himself against passing out. But on 'My Left Foot' things were taken to extremes. The production notes issued by the film's distributors speak of the actor spending eight weeks at a cerebral palsy clinic in Dublin, learning to paint and type with his foot and studying the effects of the disorder in detail. But it didn't stop there: for the six weeks of filming, he spent his entire working day in Brown's wheelchair. More, members of the cast would have to feed and wash him while he twisted in the chair, speaking all the while in Brown's own hard-won voice. The relentless small humiliations he endured brought out real anger, as did the awful experience of being treated like a moron just because your muscle control is not all it might be.

Actors don't like talking about their private lives – that's fair enough, neither do I. But Daniel Day Lewis stops a very long way short of that. While interviewed he sits like something out of a commercial for a headache cure, the famous long forehead furrowed from top to bottom with a series of creases (as a forehead it would make a good toast rack) and his eyes sink under his brows as he proceeds to explain, in paragraph-long sentences, why he doesn't want to talk about these things.

Nevertheless, under torture, the slow drip-drip-drip of the repeated question and the rolling tape, he admits that the wheelchair story is true. 'Yes, it was part of the work, part of life.' But why? 'It wasn't really a question of why. It never entered my head that there was another way of working.

'The way films should be made is that pre-production should be to do with people growing into the life that's necessary to make that film possible. The whole life: it's a very complicated thing, the fabrication of the whole life.'

As it happened, the weeks of pre-production rehearsal time were happy and successful ones. 'I always do try and find that time because for me a great proportion of the pleasure that I get from working is in the time I spend before I arrive in the theatre, before I arrive on the film set. The thing about films, which everyone knows now (except that for some reason they don't know it at the same time), is that it's very boring, potentially, and that there are these long periods of time when machinery and equipment is moved around and aeroplanes are waited for and food is waited for and all that kind of nonsense. The whole campaign grinds to a halt, regularly.

'And the great danger is that if you haven't found for yourself a sufficiently rich life before you encounter all that you're going to be side-tracked by all those things and the periods spent between one shot and the next are going to be periods of waiting, which they should never be.

'It's much easier to use that time if you've had a sufficient period of time beforehand in which to understand what it is that you're looking for and what it is that you need.

'I'm talking in ridiculously abstract terms: none of it means anything at all…'

Well, yes and no. He avoids specifics, that's for sure. His worry is that he doesn't want to sound like what Richard Harris calls 'the bank clerk generation of actors.' 'We all talk about our preparation,' he admits. 'But regardless of how seriously I take the work I try and alleviate the burden by not talking about it. It's true that nothing you can say is going to make the film better, but I do believe that there are some things you can say that in people's prejudgement of it will make it substantially worse.'

Of course, all this reticence is part of his character. There's a little bit of mystery, a little bit of 'I want to be alone'. He doesn't even do the interviewing act, the confidences designed for publication, the careful indiscretions, the safe bitching. But there's more to this taciturnity than that. People interviewing him after 'The Unbearable Lightness' found him still in Tomas's solemn mood and struggling to shake it off. He's not being Christy Brown now: belligerent, passionate, obnoxious. But that doesn't mean he's quite done with the Irishman. Something about the part keeps on hanging on. It was a delicate subject, he says.

'I felt it was terribly important that we didn't begin the film by trying to define Christy Brown through his disability. Because that wasn't the manner in which I read the script, although of course the two things are bound up together to such an extent that you can't differentiate between the artist and the impulse, where the impulse came from.

'Maybe the fury derived directly from his disability: I'd say the fury derived much more from people's inability to cope with his disability and so on. But of course those two things are bound up. It's not the story of a disabled man, although that man is disabled. And secondly it is not the story of an able-bodied actor, supposedly able-bodied actor, learning how to play a disabled man. It's terribly complicated, but all those things have to be gone through to arrive at a point where you can actually begin to reveal the story of Christy Brown who was an extraordinary man and a great writer, full stop.'

He's thought about it all right: but then, if you'd spent weeks in a wheelchair pretending, on and off set, that you were a person with cerebral palsy, to the extent of making yourself helpless, wouldn't you want to make sure you were doing it for all the right reasons? Dedication, authenticity, seriousness spring to mind. Still, it's odd behaviour. You can't imagine Mel Gibson doing it. Tell us Dan, how do you turn yourself into someone else?

'I'm suspicious of all rigidly applied methods, but at the same time I know that the system by which I work has its own particular structure. Each actor has his own way, regardless of whether they've spent three years in the same way, listening to the same theories, reading the same books. De Niro without a doubt is a supreme exponent of The Method but I don't think of him as being The Method Actor, because that to me is nonsense. If he studied The Method, then fine, but it's what he's made of that. It's his method, not The Method.

'I do think the truth is that you have to be a very acute observer on two levels: you have to be an acute observer of other people and you have to be a very acute observer of yourself. I think you can only begin to work with other people's lives if you can understand how to work with your own. The two things are absolutely necessary.

'And of course you work with yourself. I think for me the protection of creating for myself the illusion that I'm moving some distance towards another life allows me the freedom to work more closely with my own: to feel less protective of my own.'

But doesn't that get to you after a while? Doesn't everything in your life become just 'material'? Do you have any life left?

'It's a terrifying question, that one,' says Day Lewis, warming up now. 'A lot of people have described the sensation of watching themselves reacting in very extreme situations, people who have nothing to do with this business whatsoever. Very often in very extreme situations you find yourself reacting at one remove, so to speak. I remember one of my teachers, a very good teacher, always said to us, "You have to watch yourselves. It'll drive you mad, but you have to do it."

'I kind of despise that bondage, in a way, and of course it's not something that applies all the time. Thank God: it would drive me mad! It would be the thing that would really accelerate my desire to have nothing to do with my acting profession, if I felt it was constantly forcing me to observe rather than to participate.'

But what else would he do? The man's a career actor: school, Bristol Old Vic theatre school ('I loved Bristol,' he tells me, spotting my accent), the West End, the National, TV, movies, and nothing that wasn't worthwhile, serious, sensible, at least on paper. Look at the film career, the double of 'My Beautiful Laundrette' and 'A Room With A View': 'the cultural history of this country in two films', he says, and you can see what he means. With the barricades up between gritty Thatcher's Britain reality and glorious Thatcher's Britain escapism, Day Lewis managed to stand on both sides almost simultaneously. It doesn't say much for my political commitment, does it? Or I think it does, but that's another story…' The two films opened on the same day in New York.

'It'll drive you mad, but you have to observe yourself.'

His casting in 'My Beautiful Laundrette' as Johnny, racist thug turned tender homosexual lover, has always been the subject of humorous anecdote, mainly advanced by director Stephen Frears, who tells two stories. In one, he meets the rockabilly-quiffed Dan at a casting session and says, 'You're the poet laureate's son, why have you got a cockney accent?' 'It never happened,' says Day Lewis, though he recalls, 'He did a sort of 360-degree tour around me, shuffling around in his plimsolls, eyeing me up and down like an ostrich in a zoo.' In the other, Frears claims not even to have realised who Daniel Day Lewis was until he saw him in 'A Room With A View', coping with Cecil's upper-crust accent as if it were natural to him: to a large extent it was.

Much was made at the time of the young Day Lewis's 'street-cred', despite the obvious facts of his background. He's ever-so-slightly embarrassed about it now. In one breath, he claims, 'It was very much part of my life. That was my life. All my friends during that time were people who, in different ways, led the kind of life that Johnny led. I did understand that way of life very well. If I'd not gone to boarding school I would probably have gone that way myself.' In the next breath he changes his mind: 'I have to say about this business of drawing on the street-cred, all that is nonsense. I was a puny little fucker. I wasn't in the running… I got on well with people after I'd been battered a couple of times. Perhaps it's just now, I'm fulfilling my fantasies of leading the F-troop. That was my team and everything, those were the people I mixed with and was very keen on them.

'I was eight or nine when I first heard the word "posh" and began to understand there were different things going on. These friends of mine used to come back to my place and they must have been absolutely astonished by the place where I lived; but it never occurred to me in my innocence at that time. Those differences were just things we didn't really think about.'

'Confusing actors with characters is a telling mistake.'

The ability to swim up and down the precipitous gradient of the class system is not to be sniffed at in an actor who wants to stay in work, and good work. 'It was good fortune at that time because you had to count your blessings to work on a film. You still do, but not quite to the same extent. More films are made now,' he adds, in clarification of this burst of apparent immodesty. 'But to make one film and then another was kind of bizarre. I didn't really know what was happening. I'd met James Ivory (director of 'A Room With A View') and got on with him. He asked me which character I saw myself as, George or Cecil – he hadn't cast either part at the time and I said "No one in their right minds will admit to seeing themselves as Cecil but that's the character that I love."'

Madonna

'Do something, Lou,' Madonna Louise Ciccone said, leaning forward on the seat. Lou, a beefy-shouldered, balding bodyguard with a tendency to sweat, turned from where he sat in the front seat beside the driver and regarded her pleasantly.

Stretch limousines were out by the hundreds – drunken dream fish, silver and schooling there in the late afternoon light in front of Trump Plaza Hotel and Casino in Atlantic City, where Mike Tyson and Michael Spinks were about to go against other in the convention centre for the pleasure of Madonna and Sean Penn and me and 20,000 other souls, plus untold millions around the world via satellite.

'Goddamit, do something,' Madonna said again.

What Lou was supposed to do was not entirely clear. We were in stretch-limo gridlock. That fact did not seem to occur to Madonna. *She* had arrived, goddamit. She knew where she wanted to go, what she wanted to do, and she was not prepared to wait on anybody or anything.

Madonna left Rochester, Michigan, for New York at the age of 18 with nothing but a suitcase and a heart scalded by ambition to be somebody. She came with a million nobodies in the annual pilgrimage to the brutally indifferent, dirty, savage shrine of power that is Manhattan. A decade later she was married to a handsome, hot-at-the-box-office, totally unpredictable actor named Sean Penn, had more money than she could ever count, a house in Malibu and an apartment on Central Park. She also still had a heart scalded by ambition, a heart unsated and insatiable that will be lusting for action when the first shovelful of dirt drops on her coffin.

We are approaching the ballroom of the convention centre now, where we are invited to a private party given by Donald Trump. A crush of people pressing down on the walk leading to the building. As the car pulls to a stop and Madonna becomes visible through the window, a great roar bursts from the collective throat of the crowd.

'My fucking *fans*,' Madonna said, and the word fans was a greater obscenity in her mouth than the adjective modifying it.

For the first time I noticed the incredible number of men and women with cameras of one kind or another slung from their necks and shoulders. As if on a signal all the cameras raised and popped in a great flash of light as Madonna stepped from the car to take Sean's arm.

Once inside, it went from hair, teeth and hysteria all the way to nightmare as the howling mob of photographers broke through Trump Security and came in with us. Madonna's bodyguard was in the lead and we followed. But Lou did not know where to go to get away from the sea of popping flashbulbs. Finally we ducked out a back door and into an elevator and went down one floor where we stayed inside the lift with Lou positioned in the open door. Somewhere along the way we had picked up a woman who was a Trump Casino employee. Madonna was beside herself with anger, really major-league pissed off.

'Why were those fucking people allowed in where the guests are?' she demanded.

'They weren't supposed to be, but…'

'Where am I supposed to go? What am I supposed to do? I can't believe Donald Trump. This is outrageous.'

The woman was full of apologies: 'There isn't a room in the hotel. But I've got a conference room you can sit in.'

As we were leaving, Warren Beatty and Jack Nicholson – Nicholson with a bottle of beer in his hand and wearing his trademark dark glasses – started into the elevator.

'Man, you can't go up there,' Sean said.

'The hell I can't,' said Nicholson.

'It's a madhouse,' Sean said. 'They've let photographers in.'

'Come on,' said Nicholson. 'Let's go to the party.'

Instead of the party, we went down back corridors and back stairwells and sat in a little conference room where Madonna munched on popcorn until fight time.

Of all the celebrities at ringside – and everybody I'd ever heard of seemed to be there,

It was a sly, gently comic performance that did nothing to prepare anyone for his next big break, which saw him on the receiving end of a lot of tabloid treatment. For 'The Unbearable Lightness of Being', Day Lewis had to play a Czech surgeon with a prodigious and unfashionable appetite for casual sex. Whereas Milan Kundera's masterly book circumscribes every act with long passages of philosophical/psychological justification, Phil Kaufmann's film goes straight for the bare bones. 'Don't Call Me Dirty Dan', screamed the tabloids, but if Day Lewis saw it he's not going to worry about it now.

'The confusion between character and actor is an irritation, of course. It always worries me when describing what happens to the characters in the course of a review, they use the names of the actors. It's quite a telling misapprehension.

'People want to know you very much. They want to know of you very much. There's a sort of insatiable appetite.' And against that, Day Lewis builds up barricades to protect his privacy. 'I want it that way. It would only take me to put one foot wrong. It would only need me to get caught shoplifting or something and that's it, end of story. That's it for the rest of your life then, condemned. So I'd better not get caught.' It's a joke, but he won't let it go at that.

'I wouldn't mind being condemned for that, that would be okay. It's the fascination with people's sexual proclivities that I find so appalling, I really do. I find that absolutely disgusting. I'm kind of puritanical about all that.'

Indeed, but he chose to do the film, no one else. Surely the dangers were always there? 'Well, I didn't do the film because I wanted to be seen to fuck for three-and-a-half hours on the screen. I did it for other reasons.'

As for being a screen heart-throb, he sweeps back the luxurious black locks from the florid eyebrows, the unfeasibly high forehead, the elegant roman nose, and denies it. 'I don't think I am. I'm not trying to be coy about it. I wasn't aware of that aspect of "Unbearable Lightness of Being".'

Ask him what he's doing next and he claims to have no idea: 'I never make plans.'

Whatever it is, though, it's likely to be a serious piece, in prospect at least. Other people can do meretricious rubbish and harmless trivia, but not Dan. He won't be doing James Bond, in all probability ('Never say never,' he jokes), and he won't be going to Hollywood. 'I don't mind seeing those kind of things but I have no particular inclination to do them. I'm very selfish about this. I don't have any responsiblities other than to do work which most interests me. I'm always amazed that people think Hollywood might be a lure for anyone.

'I do feel that I have limited resources of whatever it is, however you describe the impulse. I don't know whether it keeps me alive or whether it kills me, you never find out, you just die and then you find out it's killed you, a second before you go. But at the moment it is something I believe which is very important to me, that impulse, and so I try to be gentle with it.' ●

---

including Jesse Jackson and Richard Pryor – Madonna's picture was the one on the 'wanted' poster. And she was not enjoying it.

Suddenly Donald Trump appeared, hustling between the seats toward Madonna.

'I've better seats for you,' Trump said.

'We can't go,' Madonna said, 'I have a guest.'

'Go ahead,' I said – 'This is a great seat. I'll be fine.'

Still Madonna refused. 'We can't. He's my guest.'

Trump touched my shoulder. 'Come on. It's all right.'

So the three of us, with Trump leading the way, went down to the aisle situated directly on the ring. Trump waved his hand and a gofer in a tuxedo appeared with two chairs. Trump said I could sit two rows behind them, but Sean and Madonna were having none of that either. Sean took Madonna on his lap, and Madonna motioned for me to take the chair beside them.

Later I told her it would have been fine to have left me where I had been sitting initially.

'Would you have left me if I had been your guest?' she asked.

'Well, no, but…'

'I don't leave my guests either.'

When Spinks went down, we went out, led by the indefatigable Lou. To wait for the car and escape, we were forced to take refuge in a kitchen. When the steel doors slammed behind us, the sudden silence was like going under water.

And out of the dim recesses of the kitchen came six or seven young men, all black or Hispanic, wearing garbage-spattered aprons and walked-over shoes.

'Could I have your autograph?' one of them asked, holding a napkin and a well-chewed pencil out to Madonna.

She stood there, harassed, tired, regarding the napkin for a moment and then said, 'Sure. Of course.'

They were the first and last autographs she gave that evening. Later, I asked her why.

'These guys that work back in the kitchen don't see a hell of a lot. They're just back there doing a bad job. They sure as hell didn't see the fight did they? And they weren't like most people wanting an autograph, coming up to you and demanding it. It's that impertinence that bothers you more than anything else. And I didn't get that feeling from them, not at all.'

On the three-hour ride back to Manhattan, Madonna put on a tape and dozed with her head in her husband's lap. At the Parker Meridien Hotel I thanked them and said good night.

'You're coming to the play tomorrow night' she said.

'I'll be there.'

'I'll send someone to get you.'

'That isn't necessary.'

'I'll send someone anyway,' she said.

'In that case,' I said, 'thank you!'. ●

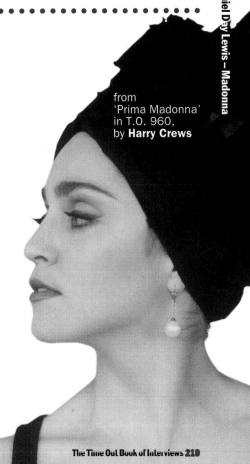

from 'Prima Madonna' in T.O. 960, by **Harry Crews**

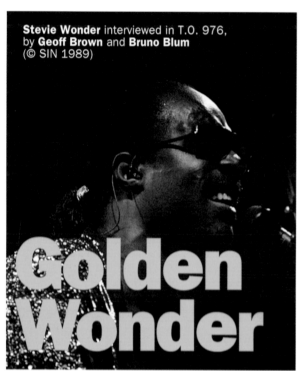

Stevie Wonder interviewed in T.O. 976,
by **Geoff Brown** and **Bruno Blum**
(© SIN 1989)

Golden Wonder

They were magical performances, joyful and serious and, in the end, almost tearful in their painful honesty. In August 1973, Stevie Wonder, at the peak of his creative powers after releasing 'Music Of My Mind', 'Talking Book' and 'Innervisions' in quick succession, was nearly killed when the car in which he was travelling collided with a logging truck. He was in a coma for four days. By the end of January 1974 he was on-stage at the Rainbow Theatre in London with a brand new band, a new show and a new song, 'Contusion', which he'd composed in memory, as it were, of the near-fatal brain injury he'd sustained. Wonder tentatively eased his way into the set and although he had not fully recovered from the accident – he got tired quickly – by the end of the show he was burning up the place. Things had gone so well that he stayed on for an extra week and booked more dates for the following weekend. He'd over-reached himself.

The second weekend was an anticlimax and I will never forget the sight of Stevie Wonder, drained of energy at the end of a lacklustre set which time and again he'd tried to crank into gear, standing near the lip of the stage not knowing what else to do. So he gently took off the dark glasses which permanently shaded his blind eyes and lobbed them into the audience.

In cold print Wonder's gesture possibly reads like an unbelievably corny act of symbolism, but no one in the audience could mistake the powerful sincerity and artist's honest desire for explanation and revelation. In his concert work, Wonder simply does not short-change an audience. These days some of those who worked at Motown with him play 30-minute sets; an hour is normal. The half-dozen or more Wonder sets I've seen

since 1974 have lasted at least two hours, often three. They pass like seconds because you are bound up in the breathtaking Wonder songbook – new twists given to '60s material, the vibrant versions of his more mature works, the completion onstage of a new song he's working on. His recordings have been patchy but 'Songs In The Key Of Life', 'Hotter Than July' and a substantial proportion of his most recent album, '87's 'Characters', stand comparison with the best of his work.

Instead of writing about social and political issues as he did in the early '70s, he's become just about the most active supporter of causes among contemporary music artists – from pressurising the American Government into making 'Martin Luther King Day' an annual public holiday in the USA to appearing at last year's Welcome Home benefit concert in Washington for Vietnam veterans. He will move into politics for real in 1993 when he hopes to be elected Mayor of Detroit. He also keeps an alert ear cocked to new sounds on the radio, most of which he hopes are being played by KJLH, the Los Angeles station in Compton, California which he owns. The initials stand for Kindness, Joy, Love & Happiness. Now, *that's* as corny as 'I Just Called To Say I Love You'. But Stevie Wonder means it.

What are your feelings towards Jesse Jackson?

I like him a lot. I have a lot of confidence and faith in him.

What do you feel has a greater impact. A song or a politician's message?

It's just another form of expression. It depends. Jesse has his own way of saying things. A singer has a way of spreading a worry or a belief too. But I think he's a very nice person. I think he's a good politician.

Should singers should take part in the 'Satanic Verses' conflict or should they just create songs?

I think singers should have the right to do whatever they feel. There's songs that praise the creator, songs that praise women or songs that praise men in their own way. If I say I like something or I don't like something, it's my opinion. I'm not the centre of everything, nor is any artist or any person. The only all with anything is the creator. I think none of us have the right to create conflict, negative conflict. I don't believe in negative conflict. I think constructive criticism is always good.

You were the first to have a huge hit with reggae ('Master Blaster'). Do you plan to record more reggae or African beats or something different from mainstream American music?

Obviously, the rhythms of Africa are in the African-American people as well. And there's no way that we can get away from the rhythms of what is our history. I have a great love for all kinds of music. I love reggae music, one of my favourite albums right now is the one by Ziggy Marley, and there's a couple of things that I wrote that possibly will be on his next album.

I have basically been waiting to see what feels right. But I am not ever going to limit myself to any one kind of anything. I love rap music very much. A lot. At the moment my

'To be with instruments
makes me feel comfortable.'

favourite song in that is "Self Destruction". It's the kind of song that deals with anti-crime and the whole attitude about rap being not positive.

Do you think rap is the future of black music?

Well, it is happening right now, definitely a new black form of expression. But rap has been around for a long time in different ways. I would say that the different dub mixes that reggae artists did was a form of rap. But the rap now that exists is a new black art form for a lot of people to learn from. I think it will be great for schools to use. I made a recommendation at my children's school that they maybe start a programme where they use the different rap songs, and actually take the lyric, that the kids are actually able to… recite and then they should be able to spell all those words that they can sing. It's no different than music that happened in the '70s where teachers would take various songs and the kids would sing them and learn the words. Well, here's another form that's happening, going into the '90s, that is just as exciting to me as the beginning of Motown.

You were one of the first musicians to record alone, Do you prefer to work without a group?

I like doing both. The point is you can't forever be yourself and do everything by yourself. But I think that if you can imagine an artist who paints, who uses different shapes to make the total expression, the computers and synthesizers has enabled a person like myself – and not based on me being visually handicapped – to go into my mind, into actually taking something that I have inside, and play it, and get the feel that I want.

Today you have what most people would like to get out of life: success, a family, but still you don't have the use of your eyes. Do you feel resentment?

I don't feel resentment. I feel that all things happen for some reason or whatever. It was a medical error and it happened because of that. The thing about it is I look forward to a time when technology will make it possible for me to see. And technology is helping me, digital technology, no question about it. It's all based on numbers, series of numbers, the same as braille.

Travelling in Africa, do you feel something special ?

The one thing I feel is that it is where the beginning of the history of black people started. It is the motherland, and it's a combination of a spiritual feeling. Senegal is a very favourite country of mine in Africa. I've also been to the coast, in Nigeria, but there's nowhere like Senegal. It seems very exciting and spiritual. I wrote a song about Senegal, and I'll be presenting it in the coming month.

How important is your family to you? What's your life like on daily basis? I hear you have your instruments ready everywhere you go…

Well, my family is fine. If I could see them every day it would not be enough. Every time I leave my daughter I tell her "You're the captain of this house. You've got to make sure your mother and your sister are fine." And that happens. And as long as they understand, that's all that matters to me. However anybody else thinks or feels, I'm not really concerned or impressed. As to music, I love music very much, and as much as I can do it, I will. Sometimes I'm tired at night… but I love writing songs. And to be with the instruments makes me feel comfortable, so I make sure they're around most of the time. ●

"1989"

"The author of the 'Satanic Verses' book, which is against Islam, the Prophet and the Koran, and all those who were aware of its content, are sentenced to death. I ask all Muslims to execute them wherever they find them."
Ayatollah Khomeini offers the olive branch of friendship

"It's just called 'The Bible' now. We dropped the word 'Holy' to give it more mass-market appeal."
Editorial spokesman, Hodder & Stoughton

"We have become a grandmother."
Margaret Thatcher announces an addition to the family to Mikhail Gorbachev

"There was no tragedy in Tiananmen; there was no bloodbath. There is no change in China's basic policy. The open door remains open."
Prime Minister Li Peng of China, shortly after slaughtering hundreds of students and executing others who aided them.

"I am taking my orders from television."
East German guard patrolling the Berlin Wall as thousands without visas poured through

"If these are all students, then the whole nation is a university faculty."
Worker in Prague's Wenceslas Square

"I am not a great communicator but I communicated great things."
Ronald Reagan's farewell

"It was like a Chieftain tank going over a Metro. It didn't stand a chance."
Ken Dwan, owner of the Marchioness pleasure boat

"From now on, I'll do my best to be a tidier man."
Ken Dodd, after being cleared of tax evasion

"In America there are 30 channels, amazing documentaries, excellent serials. When I arrive here all I find late at night is snooker."
Rupert Murdoch replaces snooker on Sky with the non-stop excitement of American Football

Denholm Elliott – Alan Parker

Denholm Elliott interviewed in T.O. 1001, by **Brian Case**

talking about, "Oh, is it Ascot next week already?" No, you mustn't allow them anywhere to get in.' Once shriven on Sunday, one kept one's eyes averted until one got indoors, he advised, in the reasonable tones of a family practitioner. It was as if the gremlins that downed his Lancaster in the war – 'The Night My Number Came Up' – were still around.

'Salt,' he said, and got up to get some. I wondered if he was on the point of some precautionary rite, but he merely sprinkled it on his meal. It isn't hard to see why Denholm Elliott has been in such demand – over 90 films – in the cinema. Emotions billow across his face, every mood-swing clear as a print-out. He's been the only good thing in scores of Brit stinkers over the years. 'I haven't seen "Killing Dad" yet. I was told' – he tuned his voice to clubman confiding a blackballing – *'it wasn't very good'*. Was there any point in being good in, for instance, 'Percy', a coarse comedy about a penis transplant?

'None. I played the surgeon who sewed the dick on. Some jobs you do for the money. My agent, who's a genius, struggles with me *like a tigress*, when I try to do something just for the money. She puts up *such* an argument. "You can't *really* be that broke."'

On her advice, he turned down an offer to play the butler – Gielgud had already refused it – in 'Trading Places'. If he accepted their terms, she said, they'd despise him. Back came the offer, doubled – 'Double everything *and* Concorde!' Denholm laughed uproariously. Eddie Murphy, however, had been less amusing. 'I hardly talked to him and he hardly talked to me. He did praise my mobility of expression. I tried to get a much closer relationship with him, first of all because I like blacks, get on with blacks very well, and I was playing his butler, but he regarded that as being absolutely not on. "I'm not an Uncle Tom. I'm an aggressive black!" White was the worst thing you could be. I tried to play it as sensitively as I could in spite of that. I got offered a lot of butlers over there after that. One of them on television has been running for four years so thank God I didn't do it!'

He has a very low boredom threshold, and a taste for the surreal, for Lewis Carroll and Luis Buñuel, those disturbers of the spirit's slumber. 'I got a nice role in "A Room With A View" though. I saw Mr Emerson as a Walt Whitman

Denholm genes

When you go into the professional world, at a stock theatre somewhere, backstage, you will meet an older actor – someone who has been around a while. He will tell you tales and anecdotes about life in the theatre. He will speak to you about your performance and the performances of others, and he will generalise to you, based on his experience and his intuitions, about the laws of the stage. Ignore this man.

(– Sanford Meisner, quoted in David Mamet's 'Writing in Restaurants')

It has taken a plum role in David Mamet's two-hander, 'A Life in the Theatre', to lure Denholm Elliott back to the boards after a decade away. 'I tried to get out of it several times. Do I really want to be involved in the theatre when I've got a film career going?' – He reached over to the pub table to rap – 'Knock wood! Then I thought, oh God, you've got to go back to your grass roots. Oh, dinner! How lovely! Absolutely gorgeous!' And he tucked into his chicken and chips.

Bill Bryden, Mamet's director at the National, had been rehearsing him and Sam West all morning in a newly written scene. Denholm's character, Robert, an old repertory actor, has taken it upon himself to instruct the young rising star in backstage protocol. 'Robert is entrenched in the theatre including all the fucking superstition,' explained the Scottish director. 'It's a private club. "Did I hear you whistling?" We don't do that!' He's so theatrical that he seems to bring out the dead bat in Denholm. 'Hmm,' he says, and chews his thumb. Blazer, beige trousers, brown suedes, hair raffish about the ears, a plastic bag, he lacks only a run-down British Warm to be the complete Rattigan player, but in fact this character fits like a glove. Peevish, insecure and vapidly apostrophizing – 'Greasepaint! What is it?' – Robert's is the bruised ego of the stalled career.

Did he believe all those theatre superstitions, I asked him on the way to lunch? Did he ever! 'Yes! Forces of Evil surround us on our little grain of sand as we tumble round the sun, and we pretend they're not there by

character, someone with one skin less than other people, a man to whom a tree wasn't just a tree – it was an astonishing phenomenon. I've often said to people that if you lived on a planet which was completely round and smooth like a billiard ball, and one day you went for a walk and came across a tree, you'd be terrified by this great hairy witch standing there. People have a skin over their eyes, like a cataract. You want to *make* them see things fresh. It has always been one of my ambitions to pull up all the trees in London at four in the morning and plant them upside-down. Everybody'd say, "Christ! What's that!" – but within a few weeks the council would be saying: Please Don't Put Your Laundry On The Upside-Down Trees Because It's Unsightly.'

He treasures those moments of divine inspiration. *Duende* had descended twice like a hot coal upon his brow. 'Yes. Dress rehearsal for "A Sleep of Prisoners" at three in the morning. Oxford was asleep, the sun had gone down and the artificial lights had come up, and we were in this twelfth-century church and every movement you made cast a giant shadow on the Norman ceiling, or whatever it was. I was sort of... *taken!* It was terrifying! First the silence of the church and the silence of the city and the full moon coming through the window and we were playing these four prisoners locked up in the church. Christopher Fry said, "God! Can you ever do this again?" and I said no, I don't think so. And I never did. The second time I experienced it I was in a play called "Traveller Without Luggage", but I couldn't hold it. I felt my ego was in the way. I felt it was all up to me to sustain this rattling silence which had enveloped the audience. When you get on to this level with them, it's almost nothing to do with you. It's a state that you're in. I couldn't sustain it. I wanted to do something vulgar to break it, to give them a chance to breathe again. It happened both times, I'm convinced, when there was a high barometric pressure. I'm a great believer in people's spirits being lifted or depressed by high or low pressure. I don't think you can get these moments of catalytic inspiration, the spirit that comes through you and you're taken, unless there's this barometric situation. When the clouds are heavy and low, everybody's spirits are down, down, down.'

He pushed away his plate, and lit a fag. 'I'm a big fan of Jack Nicholson's. I love the thing he said the other day. "Don't tell me I'm over the top. You can *push* the top. You can *push* the borders if your imagination contains the possibility of this performance. As far as I'm concerned, *my* imagination doesn't stop there. *I'm* going further because if I can make it real for me, I can make it real for everybody else too." I love his courage, his outrageousness.'

He blew a smoke ring. 'I learnt to dilate my pupils artificially,' he confided suddenly, and then, almost shyly, 'I'll do it for you if you like.' His eyes bored forth like a lunatic's. Christ! 'I pump blood into them from behind, contract the ciliary muscles or something. I just sort of… *push* all round. It's like those people who can move their scalps, but I can't do that. Quite a useful thing if you're playing an emotional scene with a hangover. You think, thank God for that trick!'

'Actually, I don't believe in analysing acting very much myself. To me the essential thing is, well, it's like when a tomato is growing on a vine in the summer, and before you pick it, you touch it and a sort of dust comes off on your hand which is the *essence* of the tomato. When you read a play for the first time, you get an essential atmosphere. That's the bit to cling on to. If you pick the tomato and put it on the kitchen table, three days later it's something you buy in a shop. If you work on a thing too much you get bogged down on what sort of shoes your character should be wearing. I act like children act. It's an immediate total involvement. Cardboard sword, slippers and a wig. It's play. Once I've played them, I leave 'em on the train.'

What a train-load, Denholm's cast-offs! Duffel-coated snotties and cashiered captains, backstreet abortionists, bent prebendaries and an entire Pullman of stained Old Colonials. When he isn't working, he shunts off to his home in Ibiza. 'Garden a lot. Daydream a lot. I talk hardly at all. Bits to my wife, bits to my daughter, pass the time of day with the neighbours – *hardly talk at all*. Well, generally speaking, what is there to talk about? It's something which is incredibly boring to me. People ask me the same bloody stupid questions. My daughter's boyfriend came up last night and asked me a lot of questions and round about the seventh question I said, "*That's* the last question. I'm very tired and I'm going to bed." I could've been there for an hour, you know! You're in your own home, you've got your beans on toast and your *Evening Standard* propped up against a cup of tea, and the last thing in the world you want to do is talk.

'I loved doing "Indiana Jones", this one and that one with the spiders, loved Spielberg, but the times I've been stopped and looked at since then has gone up two or three times. It's now really horrendous!' I quoted Jerry Reed's riposte to fans pestering him in restaurants. 'You made me a star? Well, y'all didn't do it when I was eating.' Denholm surged in with asperity. '*And* you didn't do it when I needed you! Those ten years when I was in the wilderness. I think my hard work and my talent made me a star, and where were you, may I ask, in the hard times when I needed you. Bullshit! Bullshit! When the kitchen sink came in with John Osborne and Kenneth Haig, I was "Tennis, anyone?" I think I was sort of despised. Passed over. Middle-class actor, or something. I knew what the kitchen sink was, but I didn't particularly want to get involved with it. You really had to be able to scratch your arse and, you know, crabs and that, and I didn't have any of those so I was – Hahaha! – *out* when all those angry people were around.' ●

Southern
discomfort

Alan Parker interviewed in T.O. 971. by **Brian Case**

Blocky and foresquare in preposterously baggy trousers and shirt and leather braces with belt buckles, Alan Parker looks a bit like early Soviet inspirational sculpture. He'd vote for the idea of being a workman, an artisan in the film foundry, rather than anything as effete as an *auteur*.

Parker's latest film 'Mississippi Burning', has run into a shit-storm of abuse from the National Association for the Advancement of Colored People and old radicals who took part in the Civil Rights marches in the '60s. Most of the criticism has centred on the film's white FBI heroes and the general passivity of the Mississippi blacks during the investigation into the Ku Klux Klan killing of three Civil Rights activists in Meridian in 1964. Parker is viewed as the intruder in the dust.

'I was warned that the Civil Rights movement was a quagmire and that I'd never ever *ever* please everybody,' he says. 'Advice from a lot of people was ▶

that it was a very precious part of American black history. It's Holy Writ. It was their struggle. You must not tamper with it.' The warnings were correct. Parker defends himself vigorously. The film is a fiction based on facts; it stars whites because it is intended as popular mainstream cinema; he had tried to give a balanced view of black involvement, but his story was set in a rural backwater where the blacks were afraid; these weren't the assertive people of Birmingham or Atlanta.

To compound the offence, Parker's insertion of a socialist viewpoint has got up American noses.

'To blame anything on economics is not an American way of looking at problems,' he explains. 'Down South, white trash was manipulated to hate by middle-class businessmen, that's for sure. They won't see that because it's a criticism of the system, of the American Dream. The American Dream is everyone can advance through society and benefit economically by hard work, and anybody can have their chance. And it's true – except if you're black. One group cannot get off the bottom end.'

Against advice, he insisted on filming in Mississippi. Wouldn't this be, as they say at The Grand Ole Opry, like Daniel walking into the lion's den with pork chop pants on? 'Alan thought it would be a cop-out not to,' Gene Hackman told *American Film*, 'and he kept an edge on the project that was very valuable.' Along the dusty backroads, he found an old barbershop that probably still had magazines with cover-stories about US marines going native on Timor. He found an old courthouse Faulkner's Gavin Stevens might've defended in, sharecroppers' shacks, sanctified churches, an old movie house. They hit the wrong season for cotton and they, white men, had to labour in the fields putting the cotton back. He found a black-owned shoe repair shop in a little town in Alabama, and used that as the work place of one of the Klansmen. 'No one could ever dress a set like that. In the ground are embedded nails from many, many years. I wrote the whole scene there because of finding the place.'

He interviewed hundreds of locals and used some of their testimony in the film. 'It's not documentary. I asked them

what they thought, let them speak, but I knew what I was going to get. One of them said, "Down South we don't care how close the negro gets as long as they don't get too big. Up North they don't care how big they get as long as they don't get too close. Up North, the liberal attitude is that everybody should be equal, but they don't really want to live next-door to them." We found a guy fishing, old guy, sad, who said, "We've got to eat with them, live with them, and that's very difficult for us." He was a simple man and a bigot only because all his life he'd been taught one thing, and didn't understand anything. People tell me my picture of Southern attitudes is too far-fetched, and how it's all changed today, but David Duke, the former Grand Wizard of the Ku Klux Klan, has just been returned to the Louisiana State Legislature.'

Mississippi has the highest illiteracy count and the worst record for lynchings in America. Here, the humidity lands like a warm wet flannel, and that curious Deep South ivy, kudzu, drapes everywhere like a dustsheet over furniture. Indianola, Clarksdale, Fayette, Tupelo – each township boasts its statue to the Confederate soldier and a score of used bedstead sales. The past is everywhere here. Whatever they say about the New South – and, fair play, they have stuck the word 'alleged' on the bottles of Money Drawing Oil and Success Incense in the general stores – for sheer truck-patch, dirt-poor privation, Mississippi takes some beating.

Faces are very important to Parker. Walker Evans's and Dorothea Lange's Depression photos of America's poor, the Dustbowl and the Delta faces with their stories of daily humiliation, numbing economies and impotent figuring, fixtures on his office pinboard were joined by the famous *Life* magazine news Photo of the Mississippi Sheriff and his Deputy at their arraignment for the murders.

'At press conferences they ask me why I show all these people to be caricatures. I ask them if they've ever seen that photograph. You look at *that*, and my people are mild by comparison. It's not just that they're ugly human beings, it's the contempt that comes across. No one's going to touch us here in Mississippi! They're sitting there laughing at the court. The Deputy happened to be stuffing his mouth with Red Man chewing tobacco, and from then on he kept on getting given free boxes of Red Man by the manufacturers to keep doing the same thing. This is the other side of American capitalism.'

Oscars apart, and the film has been nominated for five, lots of interests are hounding Parker on 'Mississippi Burning'. He looks tired. His guilts resurface. 'I read this poignant thing about a journalist talking to a social worker about white racism in Mississippi. "I'm sick of all that, sick of you lot worrying about the KKK," said the social worker. "I spend my entire working day in Mississippi worrying about poverty, about crack addiction, unmarried mothers who gave birth at 15 because they never had a father of their own, the entire breakdown of the family and colossal unemployment." See, I can have my liberal thoughts, but in the end I'm white and I run away from it all when I finish the film. That guy, he's there now, working.' ●

1990

A riot of our own: the South African Embassy on fire, burning cars in Charing Cross Road, Regent Street's posh shops in ruins – no, we didn't want the Poll Tax. Madchester and indie dance widened our seams and T-shirts grew sleeves. In fact, we just wanted to get loaded. Nelson tasted freedom, we ditched the Thatch, and the Wall came tumbling down.

February

Nelson Mandela is finally released from jail in South Africa.

'Buster' Douglas shocks the world (and probably himself) by knocking out Mike Tyson.

April

Rioting breaks out in Trafalgar Square after protests against the Poll Tax get out of hand.

May

Boris Yeltsin is elected as President of the Russian Federation.

July

Martina Navratilova wins the Wimbledon Women's Singles for a record 9th time.

West Germany defeat Argentina in Rome to win the World Cup.

August

Hostage Brian Keenan is released in Beirut.

Iraqi forces invade Kuwait.

September

Soviet troops begin withdrawal in Eastern Europe.

October

Germany is reunified.

November

Margaret Thatcher resigns. A nation celebrates. John Major replaces her. A nation yawns.

Roald Dahl, author and chocolate aficionado, dies.

December

Lech Walesa is elected as President of Poland; Slobodan Milosevic becomes Serbian President.

USA sends troops to Saudi Arabia and issues a notice to quit for Saddam Hussein's troops in Kuwait.

Silence Of The Lambs

Much has been made of Hopkins' hypnotic Lecter, but the laurels must go to Levine's killer, and to Foster, who evokes a vulnerable, pragmatic intelligence.

GoodFellas

This excites the senses in a way few filmmakers dream of; its epic sweep and energetic film language rest on effortlessly expert performances.

Ghost

The credit for turning this into one of the most enjoyable movies of the year rests on an excellent script by Bruce Joel Rubin, and the sure direction of Jerry Zucker.

Happy Mondays - Pills 'n' Thrills And Bellyaches (Factory)

They give the nation's social workers grief, preaching the drugs-'n' ladies, good-time message of black '70s soul with a '90s council estate tweak.

Digital Underground - Sex Packets (BCM)

DU celebrate the advantages of Sex Packets with pranks, comic-strip lyrics and excursions into Clinton and Bootsy.

Public Enemy - Fear Of A Black Planet (Def Jam)

This is destined to be a future measure of excellence, not only for the rap industry, but for all recording artists with any pretension to protest and effect. If you only have room in your life for one rap album, make it this one.

Mama Mia

Mia Farrow interviewed in T.O. 1039, by **Glenn Plaskin**

On a typical New York weekend, pizza-delivery men scurry up to Mia Farrow's Central Park West apartment with great speed, for her hungry brood of nine children are each given an allowance of three playmates. 'And that,' Farrow explains, 'means 27 kids, 54 slices of pizza, plus the ice-cream.'

This does not even include the Wheaton terrier mutt Mary, the Yorkshire terrier puppy, the parakeet, the canary, the guinea pig, the rabbit, the three hamsters, the two cats, the four frogs, the tropical fish and the box turtle. Or, for that matter, Woody Allen, quietly practising the clarinet. Or attempting to.

'When it all becomes too much for him,' Farrow laughs, 'he goes home.'

That's the sprawling penthouse he keeps on Fifth Avenue. That's his place.

This spacious, three-bedroomed, well-worn apartment, with burnt orange walls, oriental carpets and a piano heaped with sheet music – this is her place. This entirely satisfactory arrangement is the secret of the couple's very happy ten years together.

'Living together would be too disruptive,' Farrow says. 'I like the idea of seeing one another in our prime time. When we want to. Particularly as I get older (Farrow is 43), I appreciate that freedom. If I want to hang a picture, I hang it. It's my house. It sounds petty, but it's great. All my life, it seems, I lived with a man and it was always his house.'

She reflects upon the two marriages, the hotly impulsive one to Frank Sinatra, the heartier one to André Previn. Another marriage is not contemplated at this time, she says. 'Woody is an obsessive worker and uses his day with utter discipline. He comes over in the morning to be here when the children wake up, he goes off to work at ten to edit one movie and write, cast and produce the next, he comes back at the end of the day, stays until they go to bed – then we go out for a quick bite to eat. I like the arrangement. I'm married in the sense that Woody and I are together in a committed way, happily so for many years. We have a good life.'

Farrow laughs again. And knocks on a wooden table.

Never before, in fact, has she known such rock-solid support. Allen functions as surrogate dad to The Nine – 'though André is definitely the older six children's father' – and Allen has, more-

over, engineered for Farrow a renaissance, pulling her career from the doldrums of the 1970s back on track. This month, she is celebrating their ten years together with 'Crimes and Misdemeanors', her tenth Woody Allen film. 'A nice, even number,' she says.

All the roles were custom-designed for her by Allen, from the dizzy dolly in 'A Midsummer Night's Sex Comedy' and the brainy psychiatrist in 'Zelig' to the suicidal patient in 'Another Woman' and the WASP fiancée in 'New York Stories'.

'I've been the luckiest actress alive,' she says of her films for Allen. 'Where else could I enjoy that kind of variety?'

And how else could she work and raise her children? 'It is,' she agrees, 'perfect for me. Most actress-mothers are tormented – agonised over whether to leave their children behind for a good part or tear apart their kids' lives to take them along. I would never do that. Woody's movies are made in New York, the children stay in New York schools around the clock, they're welcome on the set, and my dressing room is a nursery for the babies. That's what I call integration without too much stress.'

'Mia,' Allen confides, 'has a talent for mothering the way some people have green fingers for gardening or an ear for music, or a talent for medicine. It's no chore for her.'

Unlike stressed-out Hollywood starlets, reclusive Farrow leads a determinedly normal life: no parties, no make-up, no Mia Farrow Loungewear, no nonsense. 'Forget it. I like being home,' she says. The sensibility extends to her career as well: 'I like being a character actress. Being leading woman, in the usual sense, doesn't mean anything to me. Glamour is tedious. I get paid to change clothes eight times a day and I'm not keen to do it in real life.'

No sir. Today, she is dressed like a camper in faded jeans, oversized military T-shirt and sensible brogues. Today, she is picking at a finger crusted in Super Glue, having repaired a child's toy. Today, she is entirely ordinary. She is radiantly lovely.

This is a rare interview, her first in four years, and the children have been sent to Central Park to play. Farrow, soft-spoken and reticent, projects steel nonetheless. 'I've never thought of myself as a wispy creature, I've always been strong. But before I met Woody, I was very lonely.' She had returned to New York in 1979 as a single mother raising seven children. 'I don't feel lonely any more.'

Small wonder. Twins Matthew and Sacha are 19 now, studying at Yale and Drew University respectively; they visit most weekends, sharing a room with 15-year-old Fletcher. These are the Previn boys, who welcomed –'with total love and incredible patience,' she says – the adopted Vietnamese girls, Soon-Yi, 17, and Lark, 16, and the Korean children, Daisy, 15, and Moses, 11.

'The girls were foundling children, abandoned,' Farrow says. 'One has to assume that their parents were killed. They came to us very physically ill. When Daisy was airlifted out of Vietnam, she couldn't hold her head up.'

Moses, adopted at age two, had been born with cerebral palsy on his right side. Farrow had specifically requested a handicapped child. 'That was the project. His learning to walk and talk was a family accomplishment.'

Moses wears a leg brace, but he is quite mobile, after two operations and the unswerving support of his brothers and sisters. 'He's a "cool" kid,' Farrow says. 'Woody is absolutely besotted with them all – a friend to the older children, the father to the youngest three.' He worried, Farrow says, when she decided four years ago to augment the family again by adopting another daughter, Dylan. 'Woody told me he had no idea how he would feel about Dylan, maybe nothing. So I said, fair enough, participate to the extent that you want to. He wasn't prepared for the commitment and love that came rushing in on him.' Nor was he prepared when Farrow bore their son, Satchel, 18 months ago: 'He had never been a father and he had no desire to become one,' she confides.

Fatherhood, Farrow says, has 'deepened him. It was very painful and scary for him at first. He's more pessimistic than I.'

Maria de Lourdes Villers Farrow was born in high style on February 9, 1946, with a silver spoon stamped 'Hollywood' in her mouth. Her godmother was gossip queen Louella Parsons. Her best friend was Judy Garland's kid, Liza. Mistress-of-the-household Maureen O'Sullivan had given up a shining career – 'David Copperfield', 'Anna Karenina', 'Pride and Prejudice' – to raise her brood of seven. The golden-haired, third-eldest Maria, schooled in London and Madrid, knew from very early on what sort of destiny she had.

One Hollywood friend recalls: 'Her life had been Hollywood crazy from the beginning. Her parents had shipped her off to a convent school, then in her teens she became a total libertine, hitting the scene in New York at 16 as a wild child.'

After appearing off-Broadway in 'The Importance of Being Earnest', the 98-pound actress – she had beaten polio at age nine and been nicknamed 'Mouse' – was chosen, in 1965, to play the frail, naive Allison MacKenzie in the hit 'Peyton Place' TV series. Offscreen, the not-so-naïve lass shrewdly reeled in her big man – Frank Sinatra, whom she made a point of meeting while wearing a transparent gown she had borrowed from the 20th Century Fox wardrobe department. She was 19, he almost 50.

A year later, Allison was written out of the series and Farrow married Sinatra – plunging headlong into a calamitous 16-month union that was rarely out of the headlines. 'This one don't talk, she don't eat, what's she do?' Sinatra's mother moaned. 'It won't last long, so I guess it's a good thing they weren't married in the church.'

'Oh, I don't know what I was looking for,' Farrow reflects now. 'I had a touch of Zelda Fitzgerald in me. Possibly, it had something to do with looking for a father. There are worse things to look for.' (Her own father was the director John Farrow, and Mia had adored him.) Sinatra, meanwhile, bitterly opposed his young wife's career ambitions at every turn. The marriage, Farrow agrees, 'wasn't an experience I would want to repeat.

'I was too immature to handle that situation, and I became very withdrawn and tried to find other values in life.' She tried tiger hunting. She tried the Maharishi Mahesh Yogi. In 1968, Sinatra sued her for divorce.

'I met Mia shortly after she had been divorced from Sinatra,' recalls one actress friend. 'She was a real sad little girl – the walking wounded. She'd had a miscarriage, and she was very lonely.'

A year later, Farrow found happier times with conductor André Previn. Their twin sons were born several months before Previn could divorce wife Dory and marry Mia in 1970.

Thereafter, Farrow semi-retired to a 20-acre farm in Surrey to raise her children, the accolades from 'Rosemary's Baby' and 'The Great Gatsby' fading as she found herself making films like 'Hurricane' and 'Death on the Nile'.

'Most of them are best forgotten. I did them for very bad reasons. André had negative feelings about Hollywood and didn't want me working, and he was always gone... I found myself very lonely, sitting at home in the drizzling rain of England without my friends or family.'

By 1979, she'd had enough, and by the time she celebrated New Year's Eve 1980 with Woody Allen, Farrow had, at last found a partner who could be 'a gentle supportive pal, the perfect remedy. He wasn't classically handsome, but I thought he was neat-looking – immensely appealing.'

Though Allen continues to tell Farrow they have nothing in common – 'except a movie and dinner and walks', Farrow says – their compatibility is apparently quite complete. 'We have enormous differences. I love spending summers at my house in Connecticut; Woody doesn't, though he endures it. He still won't put a fingernail into the lake because fish are living there. He doesn't even take off his shoes.'

None of this bothers Mia Farrow even remotely. 'God, no. He's the sweetest man I've ever known.'

'André,' she adds, 'hadn't wanted me around the movies, because he believed they were all bad. I'm around good ones now and I don't have to feel ashamed.'

And so, towards the end of a long afternoon, with seven of The Nine piling back into their rooms, Mia Farrow gets up with Mary the terrier, kisses Fletcher, then tends to Satchel and Dylan. 'My older girls are so proud when they take the babies to the park,' she smiles.

'That gives me immense pleasure, more than anything. I'm happier than I've ever been. I don't believe in reincarnation,' she says. 'But I do think my life has had three acts, definitely.'

Early stardom and Sinatra, the cottage years with Previn. And now Woody Allen, and Super Glue on her fingers in New York City. ●

'I've been the luckiest actress alive'

Two part harmony

Elvis Costello and **Tom Waits** in conversation, in
T.O. 1009 (© SIN 1989)

Just a short bus-ride west of downtown Los Angeles there's
a Chinese restaurant called the Red Eight. Inside, the walls
are painted a horrible shade of mental-institution yellow.
Nobody goes there. That's what Tom Waits likes about it.

Waits, who lives in the neighbourhood, is hanging around
town while devoting his nights to 'Demon Wine', a play that he's
appearing in. Today he's got a lunch date with a musician colleague who's in LA for a round of interviews at his new record
company. They've crossed paths on a number of occasions and
swapped musicians for their tours and recording dates, cultivating a friendship built on common interests and mutual
respect. His friend's name is Declan, but everyone calls him Elvis.

Elvis Costello, sporting pointy sideburns, his trademark shades
and black leather car-coat, finds his way to the Red Eight first.
He's with his wife, Cait O'Riordan. It's an unseasonally warm
day, but the Red Eight is cool inside. Soon Kathleen Brennan
turns up with her husband Tom in tow. Waits is casually eccentric in a too-small suit, his hair coloured red for the play. It's
growing out and the roots show strands of grey.
There's a round of hugs and smiles and
greetings, and Kathleen disappears
towards home, inviting Cait
along. A couple of other
hangers-on vanish, and
then there's nobody
in the Red Eight
but a waitress,
Elvis Costello
and Tom
Waits.

The Nature of the Music

Elvis: I always seem to be watching these nature programmes whenever I speak to you.

Tom: I love those nature programmes. I would love to do
some music for one. It's unfortunate that the nature programmes
themselves ultimately may be perhaps the only record of nature
itself. It's like if the camera shifts a little bit to the left, you'll
pick up the condo [apartment block] right next to the condor on
the beach.

Elvis: And the nice little wrapper that's been left there by the
previous film crew, probably a Kodak wrapper. I did actually see
one where they said, 'So the polar bears don't have any natural
predators. This far north, there are no hunters up here. In fact,
the only thing that interrupts them in their natural idyllic habitat is they're possibly harassed by nature film crews [laughs].

I saw this one thing about the sense that animals have. They
showed altered pictures of what insects and birds see, and they
showed flowers – really, daisies are not yellow and white,
they're purple and orange or something. Once you start taking
that into account in music, you realise that some people can't
physically hear things. A kid that listens to Metallica or something can't hear that because he's filled himself up with this
stuff – he physically can't hear a banjo or a harp or something.

Tom: Well, men and women have a different range of sounds
that they are sensitive to.

Elvis: And rhythm. Women hear rhythm different from men.
Do you think there's any kind of biological reason why so many
girls play bass?

Tom: I don't know. I always go for the low end. Kathleen's
always trying to kick my ass up the scale a little bit because I
find that if I'm left to my own devices I will discover various
shades of brown. And I'm seeing them of course as red and yellow next to each other. She says, 'What you've really just created here is sludge, dirty water.' So I kind of have to be reminded
of that. I'm also colour-blind, which is kind of interesting. I don't
see the world in black and white, but I'll never make the Air Force.

Elvis: I see it definitely in colour. The last record I made
before 'Spike' it was in red and brown, it was blood and chocolate. That was an actual picture of a room in my head all the way
through it, and most of the songs took place in it. But really the
only thing holding a lot of records together is the personality of
the singer, and the will to write all of these different things.

Tom: If you can put them all together on the same disc, though, you can perceive them as a collection, that they ultimately will develop a logic, even if you hadn't endowed them with that. It's like when you make tapes just for your own pleasure – you put Pakistan music and Bobby Blue Bland next to each other, you do have some type of logic about it. But I can't listen to so much music at the same time. I think you really have to have a diet. You're just processing too much, there's no place to put it. If you go a long time without hearing music, then you hear music that nobody else hears.

Elvis: I read an article about Jean Sibelius. He couldn't have the window open when he was composing 'cos if he did he would hear birds in the trees and they'd get into the composition. So his family used to have to go and chase the birds (laughs). Well, there's that other guy, that guy who's still alive, he's 80 – Oliver Messiaen. He's actually an ornithologist and a composer. And he goes out and records real birdsong and then transcribes it into composition.

Tom: Wow. Steve Allen used to take the telephone line, and then when different birds would sit at different places on the wire, he would write it out with the telephone lines as a staff and he would put where the birds were as notes – and then he would play it. On a TV show...

Ant Farms & Mellotrons

Elvis: Can you write scores?

Tom: No. I've developed my memory in order to compensate for my inability to... you end up with your own languages.

Elvis: Little hieroglyphics and set of hand symbols. And humming. I find humming is very useful.

Tom: You always lose a few things, but you also open yourself up to some other things.

Elvis: If you can divide everything up using a computer, like these machines now that will divide the beat up for you and will even...What about these drum machines which can programme in the human factor? I mean, how human? (Laughs) I know plenty of drummers that aren't that human, you know.

Tom: I love that thing the Mellotron so much. I just used one yesterday. Its owner guards it with his life because it's such an exotic bird, it's a complete dinosaur, and every time you play it it diminishes. It gets old and eventually will die, which makes it actually more human, you're working with a musician that is

very old, he's only got a couple more sessions left. It increases the excitement of it. And that great trombone sound.

Elvis: I used to go to church with my father, and right next door to the church was this big house that Dickens used to live in, apparently. The guy who lived there, he wasn't a musician, he was an executive from the company that made Mellotron originally. He used to lie in wait outside of the church for everybody to come out, and sort of capture them on Sunday morning and try and sell 'em Mellotron. One morning, I must've only been about 11 or 12, we were dragged into this big sitting room of this big old house, and he had this Mellotron that was like Dr Fife's organ, it was a huge thing, a big wooden contraption. It had foot pedals, as I recall.

Tom: Those Mellotrons, the first time I actually played one, it really thrilled me. It's like you touched somebody on the shoulder, everytime I touch you on the shoulder I want you to play a note. It was that real.

Elvis: But this thing did seem big, and I remember my father sat down to play, and he was pushing these buttons on it and engaging different tapes, and saying, 'Just listen to that! It's a real trumpet, you know, it's not an imitation like an organ, it's a real trumpet.' But the thing about it was, they hadn't really got the mechanism down at that time. It's a prototype we had. The way you hit the key, it engaged like almost a quarter a beat late. Within three years of that, they were absolutely the rage and the revolution. People thought that music was coming to an end.

Tom: Yeah, the industrial revolution. Hollywood used to have enormous string sessions for films, and now scores are done at home with two fingers. It's essentially done irreparable damage to the whole economics of sessions, of big session players.

Elvis: You know those cartoons they used to have of people running inside the head? Some of those synthesisers sound like there's a lot of effort. They wheeze almost in a human way, there's an awful lot of effort (laughs). There's a lot of microchips all going at once to create a rather insubstantial sound.

Tom: It's an ant farm. There's some activity inside of it...

Elvis: You know that sampling business where they put those records together, I always think: what a great idea. It's just that somebody hasn't found the right context for it yet. They can only think as far as sampling the best-sounding record that you can think of, or the coolest one, and then juxtapose things that by their very juxtaposition diminish them. Like they'll get James Brown's cool snare sound and they'll juxtapose it with a huge rap bass drum, which makes the snare drum sound silly. Not to mention there's often no logical musical relationship between the samples when they actually sample musical phrases.

Tom: I actually like it. I know that it's controversial in terms of publishing and copyrights and all that, but like you say, they always pick the clichés of things that we're all aware of.

The Creative Process

Elvis: Sometimes I write notes that I have difficulty in singing. I write them – and when you sing them at home, you're singing them not to try and wake up the neighbours or the kids or something – and you might be, "Oh I know I can get to that note", and when it comes to it and it actually puts you out of breath or something like that... well, maybe it's wrong because

►

I'm gasping for the next line. And you start talking yourself out of the bold melody and start wanting to arrange it in another key or something.

Tom: It's like translation. Anything that has to travel all the way down from your cerebellum to your fingertips, there's a lot of things that can happen on the journey. Sometimes I'll listen to my records, my own stuff, and I think, God, the original idea for this was so much better than the mutation we arrived at. What I'm trying to do now is get what comes and keep it alive. It's like carrying water in your hands. I want to keep it all, and sometimes by the time you get to the studio you have nothing.

Elvis: That carrying the water thing is a good description, because when you've got a song and you kind of know how it is, and then you work with certain players. I worked with the same band for ten years – the versatility is different, because of the ability to change it before you've fixed it. I think that's why some bands thrive on the idea of changing instruments. When they're off their real instrument, the ability to go very far from the original idea is reduced. And what if some completely incompetent bands make brilliant records?

Tom: With your own band it's music by agreement, to a degree. You look forward to the brilliant mistakes. Most changes in music, most exciting things that happen in music, occur through a miscommunication between people – 'I thought you said this'. Poetry comes out of that too. It's like song lyrics. Kathleen always thought that Creedence Clearwater song 'Bad Moon Rising', that line 'there's a bad moon on the rise' was 'there's a bathroom on the right'. That's outside, a song about that, because that happens all the time – you go to a club and 'there's a bathroom on the right'. But I love those mistakes. I salute them and encourage them.

The Global Village

Elvis: You worked with some of the same people all along, but I suppose when you actually have a group, which I have, you don't sort of notice (your own musical) development Somebody brings along a record they like, and it all becomes a fairly natural growth for a while, particularly when you're working at such a pace that time goes by and you go on little journeys and you go on detours around places.

Particularly when you're travelling, you get a tourist kind of… you know that shit that you buy when you're on holiday, you get home and you look in the mirror and go, 'God, did I ever wear that?' You have music like that, I think. I used to buy tapes of music which I was convinced was the greatest thing ever, and it would even have some effect on me. And then I'd get it home and listen to it in a different atmosphere.

Tom: I think it's like when you listen to opera in Texas, it's a very different world. In Rome you almost ignore it. I've done the same thing, gone out and bought music from Pakistan, Balinese stuff, Nigerian folk songs and all this, and I find that if I bring it with me to unusual places, the place itself is as much a part of the music. Because the music itself was born and nurtured in a particular environment. It's the same thing with fashion or anything else.

Elvis: Is there a fallacy in this notion of world music? Is that just a trend, you think? I mean, it would be very sad to be people who developed and refined and nurtured this beautiful thing, and they're invited to display it. You know that Bulgarian group, Balkana? They came and gave a talk. It's the way I imagined when they had Livingstone come back [from Africa], I imagine it was a bit like the talk he gave. It was that alien, slightly stilted, and more than a little embarrassing. Not so much for them, because I think

Roseanne Barr

from 'My life as a Jewish Mormon' in T.O. 1024, by **Roseanne Barr**
originally published in 'My Life as a Woman' (HarperCollins)

When I was three or four, I fell on the leg of the kitchen dinette and my face froze in a manner that resembled an older person who had had a stroke. When it did not return to normal the next day, Mother called the rabbi, who said a prayer for me, and nothing happened. The next day, in escalating panic, Mother called the Mormon priests, because she feared that my face would mar my chances of acquiring a meal ticket at a later age. Anyway, the day after the Mormons prayed, I was miraculously 'healed'.

Why, you may ask (as I did at a later age), was a doctor or a health professional not contacted? Well, the only rational answer to that is that we lived in Utah, where all illness, disease and mild upset is assessed to be a SIGN.

Even though we were not Mormon but Jewish, the mystique of the 'new Zion' had also enveloped us and Mother feared the wrath of the god of the gentiles.

When my face became healed, Mother (never having lived anywhere on earth but Salt Lake City) accepted it as a sign from God that the Mormon faith was the one true religion on the face of the earth, and that she and I should join it.

But she was afraid of the wrath of her own mother, and so there was a compromise. Friday, Saturday and Sunday morning I was a Jew; Sunday afternoon, Tuesday afternoon and Wednesday afternoon we were Mormons. So, after I learned about my people being murdered in every country but America I could then learn about my new forbears being persecuted in Illinois, New York and Utah. This

made for a complete and well-rounded feeling of paranoia.

At the church's behest, Mother travelled all over the holy city of salt proclaiming and testifying to the miracle that the priest had visited upon her daughter… Mother was a great public speaker, and in a way a good PR person for Jews everywhere, as those Mormons could see with their own two eyes that Mother did not possess horns, or humps, or a hammer and sickle, or the numbers 666 embedded on her forehead. In fact nothing was odd about Mother,

– well, they might have been a little amused by it.

But I felt there was a sense of embarrassment, because [fans] have moved on to something else they've been told to like, and leave these people who are from a real tradition high and dry, without anything. It's like inviting somebody to your house and then moving.

Tom: It almost seems like what is happening in terms of the industrial pop machinery that it, like any business, ultimately feels compelled to go out into the field. It's the Marco Polo effect, it brings home the spices and incorporates them into their own world.

Elvis Costello, TV Personality

Tom: The pre-play music for this 'Demon Wine' is all Tony Bennett music. It's really nice. It serves as a kind of a music for the main title of the play. Then out of nowhere I got a call from Tony Bennett, who's doing an album. He wants a song. His son called. I thought, that was great. I've always loved Tony Bennett.

Elvis: He has the chops still, that he could do whatever record he wants. I did that show with him, which is basically buried in the vaults of NBC.

Tom: With Count Basie?

Elvis: Yeah. He was the guy I had to sing with. I'd done three rock'n'roll shows and had no voice. I was down to that extent and had to go in, and I croaked my way through a ballad, which is fine until the bridge, till it gets into the solo, I was doing fine until I got to that. It was about six months before Count Basie died. He said to me, just at the point when I was about to admit that not only could I not do it even in full voice, I certainly couldn't do it in no voice. And he said, 'Listen, son, I'm 75 years old and I can't get my arm above here. And you can do it.' He just hexed me into doing it. I had to stand about three feet away from him when we went into the finale and I watch him take a solo from as close as I am from you, and then guess what happened next? The TV people said, sorry, the cameras weren't rolling, we'll have to take it again. It was actually physically painful for him to play. But that's all in a vault somewhere.

I think that is just a question of self-confidence. I don't believe anybody hasn't got a voice, for instance – I just think they haven't found it yet. I believe everybody can write songs in the same way.

I went on this television show in Italy. I looked at the audience and I thought, this is very strange – they're incredibly glamorous. They had these girls with manes of hair and long legs and short skirts, very elegant fellows in suede jackets, striking all kinds of attractive poses. And they go wildly happy the minute I come out. And then Buckwheat Zydeco is the next thing on there. There's Buckwheat and his band completely horrified because the audience is digging them so much, and they can't understand why they haven't come to live in Italy before. 'Cos they've never seen girls like this at their shows. Then I said, what's the scene of this, that all these young people in Italy dig R&B and Zydeco and music like I play, whatever that's called? And they said no, they pay them £25 a day each to be on this show. Really genius. He's presenting R&B and jazz. They go wild [rants in excited pidgin Italian] and you think they're going to introduce the new George Michael video, and you know what it was? A clip of Ben Webster [giggles].

Tom: That's the beauty of showbusiness. It's the only business you can have a career in when you're dead. ●

●●

other than the dark hair and eyes and skin, which I'm sure was frightening anyway to those fine Mormon folk, to whom Jell-O and cheese whiz are mouth-watering delights.

Then, when I was about eight, Mother stayed home and I began to speak in the Mormon church. I would always give the speeches for the youth, and later for the adults, saying 'I thank God for helping my mother to find the true church, and even though all of my ancestors were murdered recently, I still know that this is the true religion of God on earth.

I was the darling of the Mormon hour, as everyone was just so very excited by the 'blessing of a member of the House of Judah not going to have to spend all of eternity in hell'. I was quite pleased about it myself, feeling extremely superior to those other 'lost' people of Jewish, Catholic, Protestant, Buddhist, Islamic, Muslim, socialist and Sikh belief systems who were all, unfortunately and most certainly, doomed.

I still 'loved' them, though, that's what we were taught, to have Christian charity in our hearts, and still love the sinners, as they were going to be very lost for a very, very long time – and we did love them, unless there was a chance that they would acquire any political clout or power, thus making them enemies of our God.

I was very useful and also very popular in

'We lived in Utah, where all illness, disease and mild upset is... a SIGN.'

this very small circle. I was President of the Youth Group, and I also led the choir. People would say, 'Look at our little Jeweeeesh girl, not even a member, really, and what an example she is to our own young people.' I also considered it my duty to notify parents and other authority figures if I feared that any of the other young people had strayed or sinned – that is how we helped each other. I remember one boy I fancied quite a bit, Eddie, who was very cute, and had very cute hair. I told him that I felt he was smoking pot, I had heard the rumour and I was going to get 'help' for him from his mother and father... he called me a bitch, but I forgave him, of course.

I remember at the age of 16 I was at school, skimming through a medical journal, another of my 'hobbies'. Miraculously, the book just opened at the page of Bell's Palsy, which was the name of the disease which had led me into what turned out to be ten years of Mormon lifestyle. The information in the journal stated that Bell's Palsy was a temporary paralysis, usually lasting only 48 hours.

I only remember that I went just a wee bit mad, and started laughing and screaming at the same time. That very afternoon, I drank beer, smoked two cigarettes, tried to purchase drugs, and begged Eddie to go with me down a ravine and fuck my brains out. As a member of the church he declined, in a manner rather like blind panic, probably thinking that I was possessed by Satan himself... then later that evening, he called me at home, to inquire if I was okay, and could we still do it. I told him, as I have told them all, 'Honey, you never gets a second chance.' ●

Nigel Benn

from 'Glove story' in T.O.1056, by
Andrew Shields

Ah, the fight. Back from Miami, Benn must spend the final two weeks before the contest maintaining the peak of fitness which he's clearly reached. As well as physical preparation, he must also get his head in order, for the build-up to this fight has been one of hype, gripe and a notorious threatened swipe.

At a press conference to announce the match, a seriously worked-up Benn challenged Eubank to 'sort it out there and then' in an upstairs room. Eubank condemned Benn as 'unprofessional'; Benn was rather more forthright: 'I want to give Eubank a good hiding. Fighting people like Barkley and De Witt was an ambition, but I want to humiliate Eubank because I detest him. He is a loudmouth who cannot fight and he has made a good living by criticising me.'

Eubank responded immediately: 'Benn is a nobody and has not fought anybody except Michael Watson, who beat him. It is not the title I want because the objective will be to overcome the man and prove that he is a fraud.'

Benn: ' I want to shut Eubank's mouth forever. I really do detest him. I hope to shut him up with my fists.'

Eubank: 'Benn is a fairy liquid fighter and one day the bubble will burst. There is nothing genuine about the man.' And so on. Pages of it. A drawn round.

'Who's Fooling Who?' is the slogan atop the big fight posters, above photos of a snarling Benn and composed, almost smug-looking Eubank. Needless to say, Nigel Benn has no doubts about the answer to that question: 'He will be looking for a fire extinguisher. It will be so hot in there you'd better take out fire insurance. In the same way that Michael Watson taught me a lesson, I will teach Eubank one.' ●

Paul Gascoigne

from 'Perfect pitch' in T.O. 1052, by **Denis Campbell**

Paul Gascoigne happily admits he's still a big kid. After all, returning from the World Cup to greet thousands of well-wishers from an open-topped bus wearing clip-on plastic boobs and beer belly isn't everyone's idea of affirming your new-found status as England's Greatest Living Footballer. But Gazza did it anyway, smiling all the way from Luton Airport to the front pages of the tabloids, where he's been in residence ever since.

So bringing the boy a couple of presents, carefully selected from the joke shop, seemed like a good way of helping overcome his notorious mistrust of the media. A dutiful handshake, avoiding eye-contact, confirmed the mutual apprehension. The battery-operated seal which performs tricks with a football went down well, producing a big grin: one great dribbler's respect for another. Better received, though, was the red inflatable guitar. 'Cheers, mate. Brilliant. Thanks very much.' A second handshake, enthusiastic this time. The ice was broken.

The gifts were intended, of course, as something to help with each of Gazza's careers. His new career, almost inevitably, is pop music: his first vocal expedition, 'Fog On The Tyne (Revisited)', is out later this month, recorded with fellow Geordies Lindisfarne. A Jive Bunny-style singalong album, called 'Let's Have A Party' and credited to Gazza and Friends, follows in mid-November.

Inspiration for making a record appears to have come from Gazza's proud ownership of a portable karaoke machine, bought after one lonely night too many in the London hotel where he spent nine months after his £2 million transfer to Tottenham from Newcastle United in July 1988. 'I used to go to bed, pick up the karaoke and have a sing-song. It's like a little amplifier, and you put cassettes in. You get these things called backing tracks, Motown songs say. You put the Motown in, put the mike in, you've got a little echo and everything, you press "play" and you've got the words in front of you. I have it in the house when we have parties. It's fantastic (starts singing) "You do the Locomotion…"' He laughs.

Time Out understands, however, that Paul Gascoigne has at present no plans to give up his day job.

Richard Harris

from 'Richard Lionheart' in T.O. 1028, by **Brian Case**

'Irish, Welsh and Scottish – I'm hit for the whole thing. Don't blame me for my temper'. Hellraising Harris was a legend. 'When I got drunk or O'Toole got drunk it was a marvellous light-hearted madness, and we were out for sheer devilment. We had exorcised the devil within our soul. We were free spirits and we got into great fockin' trouble.' He hoists his nightshirt, hauls on his underpants and flings himself in a full-length tackle at the couch.

'One night we were wondering what to do and I told him let's go back to this girl's place in Warwick Avenue. Now O'Toole fancied her too, so we tossed to see who'd go up the drainpipe first, and O'Toole won. O'Toole goes up the drain-

pipe and I'm yelling, don't touch her now! Let her make her choice! I knew he didn't stand a chance, but the fockin' drainpipe comes away from the wall and I'm stuck halfway. O'Toole looks down from her balcony. "Are you stuck?" I am, Peter, says I. He goes inside, rings the police, tells them he's a householder and he can see a burglar across the street, and this fockin' squad car arrives in two seconds. The last I saw of O'Toole was me being arrested, cuffed, thrown in the back of the car, looking back and he's got his arm round the girl and smiling all over his face.'

The mention of football, Gazza's other career, sees him visibly relax. John Gascoigne gets the blame for instilling the football bug in his son: a ball as a Christmas present when he was just seven did the trick. Gazza's footballing philosophy is fresh and simple: good football means good entertainment. 'I aim to become the best player and greatest entertainer in English football,' he told the *Sun* in one of his exclusive chats. He said he wanted 'to put a smile back on the face of soccer'.

Asking Gazza why the game has become so serious produces this impassioned outburst: 'A lot of it's got to do with the press. The English press treat football like a joke. All they do is look for bad bits; every week, bad bits. You never see the good side of it. They've been writing great about me but people should realise that I had nearly two years of shit off them, you know. Nearly two years of absolute crap, [being] slaughtered by them. I'd love to see some of them come into the local pub I go to in Newcastle and see how brave they are then.'

The papers have got so bad that he stopped reading them about a month ago. He singles out 'girl scandal' stories as the worst: 'Girls I wasn't seeing but they put them in the paper, a girl I was supposed to be having an affair with, which was untrue. Some girls go in the paper and say, I've been with Paul Gascoigne. I mean, it's all right for me, she could be a good-looking girl so the lads are like – "cor!" even though I don't like it. What does this girl feel like? She must feel like a right tart.'

The unwelcome attention from Fleet Street's finest has plagued Gazza since his days at Newcastle. Crying after England's defeat in the semi-final of the World Cup, coupled with a series of brilliant performances, made it worse. His Hertfordshire home is now regularly besieged by hacks. 'They camp out at the end of the drive in cars, like little kids. I mean those people have got to go back to their families. Imagine one of them going home and his wife saying, "How did your day go?" "Great, I sat outside Gascoigne's house all day and all night waiting for him to come out." His wife must say, "What do you want to do that for, you prick?"

'I've had that treatment from the press since I moved to London,' Gazza says. 'Some of the stuff they wrote was quite hurtful, like that my mum and dad were splitting up. I've got a shotgun. I'd love to use it.' ●

James Ellroy

from 'Life Sentences' in T.O. 1048, by **Brian Case**

James Ellroy's world is a Gothic one. Its chronicler – six-foot-four of wired weirdness – is an amphetamine self-publicist. At his wedding last year he came down the aisle howling like a wolf. On the podium at the International Crime Fiction Festival, sneakers jigging, face working, raising his eyebrows at the ceiling, muttering at the floor, he resembles a huge pre-adolescent waiting in the Principal's office. 'Yeah, James is 41 going on 12,' agrees his publisher.

'The Big Nowhere', the second volume of Ellroy's LA quartet which started with 'The Black Dahlia', features a wealth of '50s detail about Howard Hughes and his RKO contracts with busty starlets, the McCarthy era, and... the worst murder yet. 'Blood on the walls. Huge, unmistakable streaks, exemplary textbook spit marks, the killer expelling big mouthfuls, spritzing the red out through his teeth, drawing little patterns on cheap floral wallpaper.' The body's torso has been bitten until the entrails extrude, the eyes have been removed and sperm deposited in the sockets.

How can he live with this stuff? 'Upset? Nah. Not really. I love this, it's what I do. I'm a happy man in my personal life. It doesn't get to me. Sure, my wife reads my books. She knows who I am. I had a shitty first 30 years so I'm grateful and so forth.'

Just how shitty his first three decades were is hinted at in his dedications. 'It was written that I should be loyal to the nightmare of my choice,' goes the Conrad quote in 'The Big Nowhere'. 'The Black Dahlia' spells it out in clear. 'To Geneva Hilliker Ellroy 1915-58. Mother: Twenty-nine Years Later, This Valediction in Blood.'

'About my mother's death? It doesn't upset me in the least to talk about it. It ties in directly to the Black Dahlia murder case. Guy found her in a bar, picked her up – I think she wouldn't go to bed with him – strangled her, didn't rape her, stripped her, wrapped her in an overcoat and dumped her body in the bushes outside a local high school. She was found in the morning by some boy scouts coming back from a field trip. I was ten. My parents were divorced.'

You can't help wondering how deeply that trauma lodged. 'I used to walk all around LA, steal outta markets, sell steaks to black pimps on Western Avenue. I was a big skinny kid and I always had a gap in the waistband of my trousers, I'd steal steaks and put 'em in there, pull my shirt out over. I'd go into drug stores and steal Benzedrex cotton inhaler wads and swallow 'em with Coca Cola and go on speed trips, and all I wanted to do on speed trips was masturbate. I'd get copies of *Playboy* and *Penthouse* and go into the bushes in the park and seclude myself because I had no place to stay, and look at these pictures and whack off for 18 hours. I used to flog my dog bloody. My sex drive almost killed me. I hadn't been with a woman in years, I used to break into houses and steal women's panties. I did this on and off from 1968-77, from 20 to 29. I'd do anything to get high on speed and flog my dog.

'I got sober in '77 – total, no booze, no drugs. I figured I'd die if I kept it up.' ●

Martin Scorsese

from 'Partners in Crime' in T.O.1051, by **Sarah Gristwood**

I grew up in an Italian-American neighbourhood which had no influences from the outside, none. This was the East Side – on the West Side, downtown, you have Greenwich Village, bohemians in black turtlenecks, but the East Side was Sicilians, Neapolitans, Calabrese. The West Side was only six blocks away, but I never went there until I enrolled in NYCU.

I was eight years old when I first became aware of this group within our community. From eight to 22 I met them. It's a cultural thing. I was in bars, and men were talking privately in corners. I don't know what they were talking about but I can tell you, it wasn't legal.

That's where I come from. That's who I am. My father would say, be very careful – don't go with that person, do go with that one. Being tight in a community like that everybody's aware. It doesn't mean that you are part of it but it does mean you have to have a way of dealing with it. A certain amount of respect.

I saw people who were just so powerful it radiated from them. People walking by would walk differently in front of them. I really learned how people behave differently in front of people with power, how people with power use it. Look at Francesco Rosi's film on Lucky Luciano. Gian Maria Volonte is quiet, so quiet. He doesn't have to yell. He doesn't have to move.

The toughest ones – as I later found out they were – were the nicest. The ones who were loud were lower echelon. They liked me. I had bad asthma. I couldn't fight, but I remember some kids punching me. I didn't cry, didn't tell anyone – afterwards they said 'He's okay, he can take it.' Afterwards I used whatever brains I had left to talk my way out of things.

There's a very delicate period, 13 to 17, when some boys shift very easily into the lifestyle, running numbers for the wiseguys, getting into fights. Others would go another way. I went the other way – but I had friends of both kinds. ●

1991

January
Gulf War begins.

Iraq launches Scud missile attacks on Israel.

February
Winnie Mandela's trial begins. She is accused of kidnap and murder.

The IRA launches a mortar attack on Downing Street from a van.

March
The Birmingham Six are released.

Napoli and Argentina star Diego Maradona tests positive for cocaine and is banned.

May
US troops withdraw from Kuwait.

June
Croatia declares independence from Yugoslavia. Civil war begins.

July
Paul Gascoigne finally moves to Lazio for £5.5m.

August
Hostage John McCarthy is released.

Mikhail Gorbachev quits as First Secretary of the Communist Party.

Mike Powell wins gold at the Tokyo Olympics and breaks Bob Beamon's 20-year-old long jump record.

September
Jazz legend Miles Davis dies. As does the Soviet Union: Estonia, Latvia, Azerbaijan and Armenia are all granted independence.

November
Queen singer Freddie Mercury dies of an AIDS-related illness.

Robert Maxwell forgets to take his water-wings with him as he falls from his luxury boat in the Canaries.

Terry Waite, the final British hostage in Lebanon, released.

It was a war about oil... I mean freedom – the inalienable freedom to sell cheap oil to America. The Gulf War killed thousands of young men; CNN showed us clips from video games. Maxwell went belly up, as did Yugoslavia and Freddie Mercury. Satanic child abuse was almost compulsory, and farmers gave up cultivating wheat and started growing circles.

Reservoir Dogs
Tarantino's powerful homage to the heist-gone-wrong thriller is probably the final word on the subject. It's violent, intelligent, well written and acted.

Thelma & Louise
The simplistic script reduces the men to stereotypes, while the women gain strength less through self-knowledge than through US gun laws.

The Fisher King
A partly fantastic study in loneliness, lunacy, despair and violence, it's also spectacularly visual. This modern fairytale is surprisingly enchanting.

Primal Scream - Screamadelica (Creation)
This new found talent for street soul did not automatically

mean they would be able to sustain a double album of the same, and they haven't.

Red Hot Chili Peppers - Blood Sugar Sex Magik (Warner Bros.)
They've got 'Physical Graffiti' and 'There's a Riot Going On' down there. Primal, sappy, foolish. In places quite brilliant.

Massive Attack - Blue Lines (Circa)
Stream-of-consciousness rhymes dust their surface and the overall effect is a sultry groove. Now that ambience has gone out of fashion the trick is to stem the unending wash of sound with space and rhythm – a craft at which Massive Attack are masters.

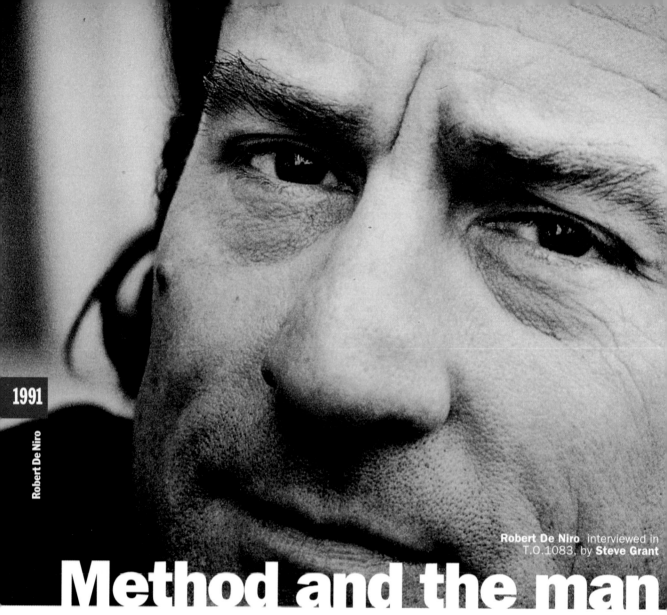

Robert De Niro interviewed in T.O.1083, by **Steve Grant**

Method and the man

Though Marlon Brando came first, Jack Nicholson makes more money and Paul Newman has the resilience, I would suggest that the greatest living film actor, certainly of the last two decades, is Robert De Niro. Obsessive, reclusive, but also very unselfish as an actor, De Niro is a virtuoso whose films leave room for others to shine. Something you could hardly say about Dustin Hoffman, the only other serious contender.

If one were pushed, or crafting a headstone, De Niro's best work could be summed up in three words from John Keats: 'truth is beauty'. He has what Sam Goldwyn once described as a 'muddy face', far removed from the expressive rippling cornfield that is Nicholson's mug; but the actor is the great master of rage and silence, the protean animal whose capacity for change perfectly mirrors the rootlessness of the modern world.

For 'Raging Bull', his greatest performance, he got dangerously fat and also became such an adept fighter that his doppelgänger Jake LaMotta told him he really could have been a contender. During 'The Mission' he became an accomplished swordsman; for 'New York, New York' he drove veteran

jazzman Georgie Auld nuts in his successful attempt to play saxophone like a swing-era pro. For 'The Deer Hunter' he lived in Pennsylvania and even took out a local gun licence, and insisted, along with John Savage, on not using stunt doubles when their characters hung upside down out of a speeding helicopter. Most remarkably, his Sicilian accent in 'Godfather II' was so uncannily authentic that many Italian speakers thought he hailed from there. He doesn't: his birthplace was Greenwich Village, New York; his parents were painters and poets who split up when he was young; his background was Italian-Irish with a touch of Dutch.

The nearest I ever came to meeting him was in a hotel garage on Sunset Boulevard where someone pointed out his car. But now it's eat-your-heart-out-Bananarama time. Robert De Niro is in London and he's waiting for, among other things, me.

Like Clint Eastwood, De Niro has become more accessible as his once explosive career has shifted into its mature phase, and the need to keep working in order to finance his own projects has given him more pegs to hang his chats upon. This is after all a man who used not to give out his phone number even to close friends, who were told to make appointments with his assistants. A man whom the aforementioned Georgie Auld described as being 'as much fun as the clap'. A man so hard to track down that some Italian lensmen set him up for arrest as a suspected terrorist just to get a good picture!

De Niro, at 47, is busy on both the business and performing fronts. There is his TriBeCa Centre, a transformed coffee warehouse in downtown Manhattan which has been turned into 60,000 square feet of office space, including a top-floor suite for De Niro's entourage, several screening rooms, headquarters for such outfits as Miramax, and a successful restaurant upon which Mama Corleone herself would shower benedictions.

His newest movie is 'Guilty By Suspicion', about the anti-communist witch-hunts of the early cold-war '50s. He plays David Merrill, a Hollywood hot-shot director. Merrill is not a communist but a fellow-traveller who had been present at a few of the meetings attended in the '30s and '40s by anyone to the left of Adolf Hitler. He returns from Europe into the middle of a crisis: lefties are burning their books and naming their friends. With two big movies ready to go, his lawyer advises that he clears himself with the committee, which means 'come clean, rat on your friends, name names, or say goodbye to the career which has meant more than even your marriage.' Writer/director Irwin Winkler says that Merrill is the nearest that De Niro has come to playing the kind of man he is in private, which suggests he is probably more Henry Fonda than Travis Bickle.

Meeting De Niro is a mixture of apprehension and overwhelming excitement. His rare interviews are notorious for their perils; recently he walked out on Barry Norman simply because Bazza asked him if Tom Hanks had beaten him to the central role in 'Big', as was rumoured. As it was he turned up 20 minutes late, but he looked fit and well, and smiled a lot. He won't replace Peter Ustinov as an after-dinner speaker and it's wise not to ask him about would-be Reagan assassin and 'Taxi Driver' fan John Hinckley, his last days with his buddy John Belushi, or his thoughts on Whitney Houston or Naomi Campbell. But he stayed and he spoke. Read on.

For 'Guilty By Suspicion' you're dealing with a highly charged subject. Some of the people in the film were actually blacklisted: Lionel Stander who wouldn't co-operate with the committee, and with Elia Kazan, who did. Were the ethical questions kicked around a lot?

> ## 'A grunt can do more than two paragraphs, or just even a look.'

Oh yeah. A lot. I read material, looked at documentaries, spoke to people who were involved in that period; Sam Wanamaker who plays my attorney in the film, he was blacklisted in absentia I think. And I worked with Lionel; I guess he was the first person I really met who had been directly affected by that period. In fact, I think 'The Gang That Couldn't Shoot Straight', which we did in '71, was the first movie he'd done in the States since he'd been blacklisted. I know that world, that lifestyle, and Irwin knows it well; there's an incredible rhythm to the way he's written it which really suits me, probably because we worked together for 20 years off and on.

As for Elia, it was really a no-win situation and I feel sorry for people no matter what position they took. It was terrible for Kazan that he had to do what he did; I know him, he's a friend and I have a great respect for him. And I know others who didn't co-operate and whose lives were ruined, so people's lives were changed by the witch-hunts no matter what position they took. It was a terrible thing, and I hope that in my lifetime I never have to face those kind of choices; but you never know. The old things resurface with new faces.

How is the TriBeCa project working out?

Oh you know, it's coming slowly. You have ten projects and one works out. It takes years. 'Bronx Tales' I'm directing; its been held back about a year but it's going. I can't wait. I wanna direct. It's the natural progression for many actors and I've wanted to do it for a long time, it makes me use my mind in a different way. On 'Guilty' we've got a producer writing and directing, Sam and Marty are acting in it, so things must be getting pretty fluid.

You've just completed a remake of 'Cape Fear'. Was that another case of immersion?

Yeah, I did a lot of research into revenge vendettas and I had another guy, Alan Greenberg, go around these different prisons in the South videotaping violent criminals, rapists and such, and giving them scenes from the script to look at and say how they would react. Because the whole thing again is about rage and hate and basically how a man terrorises a community to get his own back.

Your best movies have often been very violent but they always set out the limitations of violence, always point to positive impulses being perverted into negative ones. How do you feel about this newer, nastier attitude to violence that emerges from a popular hit like 'The Silence of the Lambs'?

▶

I am making a film with John McNaughton who directed 'Henry: Portrait of a Serial Killer', which is another violent movie but a very savage, compassionate one. Scorsese's producing, Richard Price wrote the screenplay; it's called 'Mad Dog and Glory'. I don't know though, I think that violence has always been accepted too easily. You see it every day, people getting killed for nothing, in America and in other countries, for a just or unjust reason. But then I find it funny that people are always worried about gangs in New York, guns, territory – and yet governments do the same thing, except it's legal. It's the same psychology, the same dynamic going on, so how do they expect individuals to be any different?

You seem more content to be away from New York; this film is set in lots of famous LA locations. I even heard you were a fan of the Lakers...

Whooah, who told you that? No, I'm just a big fan of Magic Johnson's. I don't mind LA, it's necessary to me, I depend on it, I can happily live and work there. But I always prefer to live in New York; it's where I grew up, it's more real, has an edge to it. I don't know, maybe it's guilt, but I don't like to drive around all the time.

Do you still play the saxophone? When you did 'New York, New York' Liza Minnelli raved about your playing.

No, I don't. I wish I did because I took a lot of time with that too, and it's a lovely instrument. Maybe I'll pick it up again one day because I love jazz, although at heart I'm an old rock 'n' roll fan.

One of your great skills as an actor is that you can provide a window into a character's soul just by a look or by a minimum amount of gesture. But how do you know when you've created that kind of effect; do you ever rehearse in front of the mirror?

It's a thing. Some things I don't have control over; you're just trying to get the character right. You don't need words to express feeling: a grunt can do more than two paragraphs, or just even a look; you just mustn't be afraid to express the character in that way.

So many people tell me you're their favourite actor – and obviously there are now so many younger American actors that are heavily indebted to you. Does that become a burden?

I don't mind. I'm glad they don't use me as an example of what not to do. (Guffaws.) In future I may be doing less movies as an actor. Or I might act, direct, produce, in one movie. Like 'Bronx Tales', I'm directing and I'll play the father. This is a story about a boy growing up, and there are two influences in his life: one is the father who is a bus-driver and very straight, the other is a gangster, and though the father resents him in many ways the gangster is more moral and less hypocritical, and so the kid learns some basic truths from both.

Jimmy Conway, whom you play in 'GoodFellas', is based on a real hood called Jimmy Burke. He sounds a nasty piece of work. Did you meet him?

No. I would have wanted to, but it would have been too complicated. He's known as Jimmy the Gent, he's a kind of criminal's criminal and he's trying to get out of the can now, although he's doing life for murder. But he knew a lot of people I used. He was a steely character.

Martin tells it from the streets, he knows that world, he knows how much garbage there is in the streets, whereas Francis (Coppola) is more epic, operatic, he's trying to make a different kind of picture – and both approaches are valid. When I played in the 'Godfather' sequel, I spent a lot of time studying Marlon's performance in the first film, trying to show the development of the character into someone who could have become that kind

from 'Pleased to eat you' in T.O.1081, by **Maria Lexton**

'Hannibal Lecter sprang into my mind surrounded by light. And I saw him as a kind of creature from the dark lagoon, a monster. But an attractive monster. Monsters are strangely compelling, and they are fascinating creatures to play. It's the power that attracts us. Watching Saddam Hussein, or any powerful figure go into action is awesome. I remember watching Olivier, and he was a pretty mighty personality – they have a way of just making you sort of disappear; they don't really look at you, they make everyone else seem invisible. It's power. You go to them; they don't come to you. It's strange... I don't think they are even conscious of it because they have no doubts, only certainty. Lecter has no doubt, no uncertainty – maybe that's why they're nuts, though he's probably very sane.

'It's to do with that dark, forbidden area that we don't like to acknowledge and we see it on screen and on stage or in literature and it twangs a chord inside. It speaks all the unspeakable that of man. He was a very noble guy. The scene where he shoots the Mustache, Pete, and he wraps the towel around the weapon – that was a beautiful touch and it was a kind of a killing done at arm's length; here was a guy getting into crime in order to protect his family from criminals.

Why did you turn down the part of Jesus in 'The Last Temptation of Christ'?

Well, I didn't think it was right for me. It was partly physical; I'd just done 'Once Upon a Time in America' and my head was shaved, so I took off my hat and said 'Marty, does this look like Jesus to you?' I always told him I'd be there for him if he really needed me; but Jesus is like Hamlet. I kept thinking: What can I do with it, where can I go with it?' I knew Marty wanted

'I always prefer to live in New york; it's where I grew up, it's more real, has an edge to it.'

to make him a person and all that, but I still saw him as a guy with long hair and a beard.

But you didn't mind playing the Devil?

(Chuckle) Yeah, but 'Angel Heart' was different. I didn't have to carry the movie, which kinda appealed to me at that time; it was what you'd call a cameo. But then it took me a lot of time to agree to that too, because I told Alan Parker that I thought there were a lot of things wrong with the script. He wanted me to do the main part, but I didn't think it could be made to work. Then when it came to Lou Cyphre I found that interesting, but even though it was beautifully done, had a lot of depth and character to it, it didn't work as a story. But it wasn't the lead part.

In 'The Untouchables', playing Al Capone was more like that because of all the weight gain I had to do because of Capone's image as a big guy, something of a monster in Brian's [De Palma's] hands. I used a bodysuit that fitted round my face very exactly in proportion to the rest so I got that roundness to my face within the time schedule I had.

Do you still see Jake LaMotta?

No, I don't really. I know he's still around and alive and well. Somebody told me they'd seen him in France and he was in good shape.

Is it true that you fought some bouts professionally under another name?

No. Jake said I could have been a professional, he thought I had it in me. I could I guess, but it doesn't just take skill, it takes determination and a willingness to be punished. I understand that, I had a taste for it during the film; I would have been okay. But that's all.

In 'Raging Bull' you did something rich and beautiful with his life, but I know what he saw in the film also horrified him. Does the power which you possess to so transform another human being, warts and all, fill you with any terror?

No, but I'm not aware of that; it's something that somebody would say, but not me. I'm doing just what I think is right to stay in character in any situation. Nothing is done for effect or gimmickry; it's done for a concrete objective which is to create a reality, a truthful picture. I identify a lot with the pain; when we did 'Raging Bull' I talked a lot to Jake, tried to get into his mind, but you can only go so far with people. Like I can only go so far with you here; there are things I can't tell you, I can't consciously or unconsciously give them up; sooner or later you have to make it your own. ●

we daren't speak. Lecter and Clarice, yes – it's very strange isn't it? It's almost Beauty and the Beast. It's a romance between them in a strange way. King Kong and Fay Wray. There's something about a man being caged up and locked up; something, I suppose, quite erotic about that.

'Consider Ted Bundy, the mass killer in America: women flocked to the court to see him; women sent him proposals of marriage, requests for his autograph, it's all very odd. Both he and the Yorkshire Ripper make fascinating psychological studies. Yet it's so dangerous when people generalise. We all generalise about human nature and talk about the good guys and the bad guys, yet it's difficult to sort out condemnation when people are just following a leader.

'Erich Fromm is very interesting in a book called "Escape from Freedom" in which he talks about our peculiar need to be actually overwhelmed, to be whipped. He talks about nations who surrender themselves or abandon them-

selves to a ruler – it's really a sexual thing in a way. That's what makes leaders charismatic – they have no doubts and they get things done, they get the economy moving, everything is looking rosy – it's that peculiar power of certainty, isn't it?

'My wife said to me not that long ago, "Maybe you're always going to be melancholy." When I asked what she meant, she said, "Well, you're Welsh, and you're always going to have a dark, melancholy side." She didn't really mean it, but I took it to heart. I don't mind being Welsh but I don't like being melancholy. A lot of actors believe that to be talented you have to be miserable all the time and I've decided the only way to live is to act as if you are the opposite of yourself – and the funny thing is that you then become what you believe you are.

'I used to put on my make-up in the theatre and expect nothing of anyone and if you don't expect gratitude or anything from anyone, life is such a wonderful bundle of surprises. Of

course if life kicks you up the arse you get upset but life is a tough place and it's always a choice whether you go under or rise above it.'

'I'm probably rather simplistic in my approach. I just learn the lines and I go over and over and over the scenes a hundred times and it literally goes into a magic memory in my mind; it's like a kind of ritual and I enjoy it. I enjoy the feeling that I'm accomplishing something. There's someone I can hear, which is me, I suppose, but it's a different shade and that's what I could hear when I thought about Lecter; and I'm able to become a character and even change the shape of my body. And I'm quite physically big, you know broad, while Lecter is a very slight man and very contained and once you get that image inside you – photograph it, I suppose, on the inside of your mind or inner screen – then you become it. On the set of "The Silence of the Lambs" I'd scare everyone by creeping up and whispering, "Are you having pleasant dreams?"' ●

A knight to remember

Sir John Gielgud, interviewed in TO 1095, by **Brian Case**

There's a theatrical anecdote about Sir John Gielgud finding himself involved in a rehearsal at which the actors were encouraged to exorcise their complexes. The cast threw itself about, reliving birth traumas and screaming primally. When it came Gielgud's turn, he dutifully sank a mine shaft into his deepest fears. He, ran up and down. 'The play opens in a week! The play opens in a week!' he cried.

'Oh, yes,' laughs Gielgud now. Peter Brook's dress rehearsal of the Seneca "Oedipus". We were all in despair. Irene Worth had to immolate herself on a spike at the end and she shouted out, "Oh, Peter, I can't! They've moved my plinth," and I said, "Do you mean Plinth Philip or Plinth Charles?" And after that we all felt much better!'

We are sitting in a snug-little room which is redolent of his Tibetan terriers – 'very spoilt, very affectionate, one must have animals about' – in the home he bought from historian Sir Arthur Bryant. Built in 1685 as a coach pavilion, the house and gardens echo the formal symmetries of a setting in 'The Draughtsman's Contract'.

Perhaps, that is one reason why the actor loves Peter Greenaway's work, and approached him to direct a version of 'The Tempest'. Over the years, Gielgud hoped to interest Kurosawa or Ingmar Bergman in the project, and discussed the music with Benjamin Britten. 'Prospero's Books' has seen the dream realised, and Gielgud is thrilled with it.

> ## 'I was so afraid I'd die before it was finished.'

'You can imagine, it was a great experiment. All Peter's pictures have mysterious moments. I don't understand always, but he's a great trickster, and he does it jolly well. I wanted to leave something behind as a record of my Shakespeare work and it's the only part I'm the right age for now. I hope it's all right.'

Actually, at 87, Gielgud dominates 'Prospero's Books', doing, thanks to sound editor Chris Wyatt, all the voices. 'When Peter said I had to play all the parts, I fainted!' As a feat of stamina, long hours, long takes, heavy robes, it is unequalled. 'Prepare myself? I didn't do anything except spout it out. I was really staggered when Peter said, "Take all your clothes off and be naked in the bath" and there were all these girls and fat women in the nude, but after a day or two one had completely forgotten. I don't think it offends one in the least, though Peter says in Japan they'll have to take out all the genitals.' Decades ago, he had joked about doing an all-nude 'A Midsummer Night's Dream', and retitling it 'Bottom'.

'We are such stuff as dreams are made on; and our little life is rounded with a sleep.' Shakespeare's valedictory speech is delivered to the camera against a background of theatre curtains, and it ends with Gielgud closing his eyes as the empty stage grows dark. Mark Rylance, who plays Ferdinand, had

been mightily moved. 'Sir John gives a lot of himself. It was amazing to hear him give that speech. A curtain fell dividing us from him and the camera – and obviously we were conscious of him very near the end of his life.'

'I'm awfully thrilled it will be released in time for me to see it,' says Gielgud. 'Peter showed me an hour of clips last year because I was so afraid I'd die before it was finished. One's getting on. It preoccupies one a bit, you know. All my friends are going. It's an awful feeling to be left. Peggy Ashcroft was such a sad loss. When Ralph Richardson died I was terribly upset, and at nine o'clock car-loads of press came down, and I heard one of the journalists say, "I wonder which of them is going to be next?" It wasn't quite the line to speak.'

He gets up and leads the way into his main room with its lofty ceiling, cherubs, statues of horses and gods, gilt Italianate mirrors and paintings of Victorian actors. 'Yes, it is pretty. I'm awfully happy here, except all my friends are dying. I watch the seasons come and go here. I adored London all my life until I was 70, but I think it is absolutely ruined now. I hear people are sleeping in the Strand.' He lights another cigarette. 'Give

me the old days where you saw two big features in a West End cinema for 4/6 and you could smoke all through it. It's so boring saying one mustn't smoke, one mustn't eat eggs, one must wear a seat belt. There is almost nothing left except fucking, and I'm too old for that unfortunately.'

The darkly brooding Slav side to his nature, inherited from his Lithuanian father, is in the ascendant, but he cheers up when one reminds him of his celebrated gaffes. These he puts down to impetuosity. Dining with a boring playwright, Edward Knoblock, who adapted 'The Good Companions' for the stage, another bore passes their table. 'Thank God he didn't stop, he's a bigger bore than Eddie Knoblock,' said Gielgud. Interviewed on American TV, he was asked about early influences. Claude Rains, he replied. 'I don't know what happened to him. I think he failed, and went to America.' Laughing now, he retells the story about going backstage at the Old Vic to take Richard Burton to supper. He hadn't liked Burton's 'Hamlet', and shouted into the crowded dressing room, 'I'll go ahead, Richard. Come when you're better. I mean when you're ready.'

Born in 1904, Gielgud was stage-struck early. Ellen Terry, ▶

Henry Irving's leading lady, was his great-aunt. He made his debut in 'Henry V' – 'Here is the number of the slaughter'd French' – as a herald at the Old Vic in 1921 at the age of 17, and, a young man in flannels in the wings clutching the book, understudied Noel Coward in 'The Vortex' in 1924. Ten years later 'Richard of Bordeaux' made him a star. His 'Hamlet' spearheaded a revival of the Bard, and ran for 155 performances to packed houses. He was the first young Hamlet; his predecessors in the role were usually in their forties. In 1936, he packed his cabin trunks aboard the *Normandie* and took the play to New York, where Lilian Gish garlanded him with an Hawaiian lei for luck on opening night.

'Did you meet Micheal MacLiammoir?' interrupts the old knight. 'Extraordinary character. Full make-up in the daytime, wig and rouge and everything. I thought he must be arrested the first time he came round to see me. He went to Scandinavia with Peggy Ashcroft in "Hedda Gabler" and his make-up box was lost en route. There was a most terrible song and dance. Everything he lived for was concealed in this box. He acted for me in New York in "Much Ado", but he had no idea really of team acting. I caught him waving a great stick around his head taking all the audience attention away from my duel scene, and I was very cross.'

Gielgud was instrumental in encouraging Laurence Olivier to play Shakespeare, alternating Romeos with him opposite Peggy Ashcroft's Juliet. Olivier was virile and dashing, Gielgud euphonious and reflective; it was a Gene Kelly-Fred Astaire standoff. 'It's obvious, isn't it? I'm Macready, and Larry's Edmund Kean.' Generous, uncompetitive, he gave Olivier the sword Kean had worn as 'Richard III', a treasured present from his mother, in tribute to his performance in the play. Besides Shakespeare, he brought Chekhov, Wilde and Congreve to the West End. As a drama school judge, he awarded the teenage Alec Guinness a volume of Shakespeare; in 1975 he tackled Pinter's 'No Man's Land'. His 70-year stage career ended with 'The Best Of Friends', which I watched him rehearse, mesmerised by the way he carried himself, upright as a bouquet, the cigarette in his mouth somehow suggesting a graceful accomplishment. Sir John Gielgud is the history of British theatre, spanning the century.

He hadn't, however, been quick to embrace films. It wasn't that he shared the young Olivier's attitude – 'this anaemic little medium which could not stand great acting' – but diffidence rather, and a dislike of early rising. He was horrified by his mannerisms in his first three films, 'Who is the Man?', 'The Clue of the New Pin' and 'Insult', yet fascinated too, 'because seeing one's own back and profile is an experience usually limited to one's visits to the tailor.' Acting, he felt, should be ephemeral. 'People tell me I should make films, just as they tell me I should tour Australia. I think it's superfluous,' he had commented then.

Hitchcock coaxed him to get into films, offering him 'Secret Agent'. 'He said it was another kind of Hamlet, but it wasn't. He wasn't very interested in actors, he liked pretty women. He used us. He was an awfully clever man, very coarse, awful jokes all the time. I said to him once, all you want to do is film a script that allows you to be in Westminster Abbey one day, and on the Alps the next, and San Francisco the next, and he laughed. Peter Lorre used to upstage one and put in things that weren't in the script to put one off. He was very wicked. He was a morphinomaniac and he used to go up and hide on the roof of Lime Grove and take a shot, or get his hair curled, but he was also rather fascinating.' It had been an exhausting experience, filming by day and on stage at night.

Orson Welles had played Moriarty to his Sherlock Holmes for the BBC – 'I had a cockney accent for Holmes disguised as a coalman, and it was so bad that it's played at parties as a joke against me' – and offered him ten days' work as Henry IV in 'Chimes at Midnight'. It was shot in testing November temperatures in a castle outside Barcelona. 'We were shivering. I had nothing on but tights and a dressing gown, and Orson sent out for brandy and we'd sit huddled over this gas fire trying to keep warm. Orson wasn't well. He had eczema and couldn't wash his hands, he was beset by writs, mistresses, bills, and he was trying to finish "Don Quixote" in one part of Spain and "Treasure Island" in another. How he managed to keep his concentration I don't know. We couldn't stay in the main hotel because they'd banned actors after Frank Sinatra and Ava Gardner had beaten up the whole place, and there were no conveniences in the castle. Hundreds of very ill-tempered Spanish extras were walking around screaming for their money and had nowhere to relieve themselves so one walked into piles of shit on every corner. Orson was very good on Shakespeare, but the film was very amateurishly put together because he had no money.'

He had taken over Orson Welles's Paul Masson Californian wines commercial. 'I stole it from Orson I felt so beastly! I was so fond of him but they were a bit sick of him, and offered it to me. It's humiliating, making commercials, but I resisted English butlers. Olivier made one too, for cameras, and I'm told – Ha Ha! – the camera was a flop.' Even more shockingly, perhaps, than doing commercials, he had finally accepted the role of butler in 'Arthur', with Dudley Moore and Liza Minnelli, and won an Oscar for it. 'I turned it down three times and each time they put the money up, so naturally I became reconciled. I thought it was rather vulgar when I read it. I was enchanted when it was so acclaimed.'

He has done lots of cameos in all-star productions like 'Around the World in Eighty Days', 'Oh What a Lovely War' and 'Murder on the Orient Express'. Until 'Prospero's Books', his favourite screen part had been that of the dying novelist, drinking chilled Chablis and inserting rectal suppositories, in Alain Resnais's 'Providence'. Wrote Pauline Kael: 'God, how this old knight loves to act, loves the sound of his great sing-song.' Alexander Walker warned that 'Gielgud steals the film, but then to put Gielgud in a film, any film, is rather like asking a kleptomaniac to tea.' Gielgud's favourite review is an early one, criticising his appearance in tights: 'He has the most meaningless legs imaginable.'

'There is almost nothing left except fucking, and I'm too old for that.'

In old age, he has learned how to cope with the longueurs of the shooting schedule. He discovered crossword puzzles. He indulges in formal reveries. 'I would sit there and think of all the masters at my prep school, the location of the buildings and the casts of the school plays I had been in – very good exercise for the memory.' He chuckles remembering an old Ellen Terry as the nurse in Romeo and Juliet' in 1919, incapable of remembering a word, her fellow players shouting her lines to her. His memory is phenomenal.

At 87, his voice hasn't, *pace* Shakespeare, turned again toward a childish treble, piping and whistling. With its thrilling vibrato it remains a chamber orchestra of woodwind and cello. His recording of the 'Ages of Man' is the study piece for today's classical actors. 'I play it every time I'm doing Shakespeare because there is so much to learn from it,' Ian McKellen told me. 'The rapidity with which he delivers the lines, the agility with which the poet's mind and the character's mind are revealed. There is no need for pauses while he gets himself into the emotion, which, in turn, is absolutely in accord with the words. The words are the cello and he can just play.'

Gielgud is a considerate host. 'Would you like a glass of wine? Would you like to use the loo?' punctuate the afternoon, and he insists on waving me off at the gate. Shakespeare has accompanied his life, and almost the last thing he says suggests how much he turns to the Bard for solace. 'In a way "The Tempest" has this serenity and the young people's romance has a kind of hope in it. Those last plays of Shakespeare had that wonderfully, don't you think?' ●

Victor Lewis-Smith

in the fast lane, from T.O. 1107

Regular readers of my column know by now that I live my life in the fast lane; number 32 Fast Lane, NW1 to be precise. My adoring public demands to see me driving fast cars and dining in exclusive restaurants, but some atavistic Protestant work ethic means that I can only justify such extravagances to myself if I've saved for them.

Luckily I've discovered an extremely rapid method of saving, requiring merely the time it takes to drive from Birmingham to London. How? Simple. I just bomb along at 180mph all the way down the M1 and, if I'm not stopped en route by Her Majesty's filth, I reckon that I've saved myself a £400 fine, enough for a slap-up dinner at the Ivy, with a bottle of '61 Petrus. If I fancy a month's holiday for two in Bali then I make sure I'm 20 times over the limit before I set out, and go at 160mph on the wrong side of the road. That's worth £5,000 and 30 days inside, easy.

I'm planning the big one next month; a hit-and-run, up the kerb, ploughing into a bus stop queue of schoolchildren and pregnant mothers, no insurance, wearing a kilo of cocaine on my bonce while committing a sexual offence at a motorway café, followed by a city centre ramming, and parking on a double yellow line. If I'm not nicked, I should have saved enough to retire to a villa in Antibes.

"Rising unemployment and the recession have been the price we've had to pay to get inflation down: that is a price well worth paying."
Norman Lamont, Chancellor of the Exchequer

"This is a ridiculous country. It can't do anything properly, not even carry out a coup."
Igor Zakharov, Russian journalist

"Democracy is now more secure in the Soviet Union. Stability and prosperity are not."
Neil Kinnock urging John Major to provide aid to Russia

"There were so many people who hated him. He had many threats. Many people would have been delighted to bump him off."
Robert Maxwell's widow shortly after his mysterious death

"Labour is the music of Dire Straits. The Tories are the music of Simple Minds. But we are the New Kids on the Block."
Liberal Democrat President Charles Kennedy

"I wear the pants in my house. You can see them under my apron."
Les Dawson on New Men

"It's not so much a marriage made in heaven as one pieced together in the Betty Ford Clinic."
Friend of Liz Taylor on her impending marriage to Larry Fortensky

"How nice; I see you've used my colour."
John Major, on discovering that the Sainsbury Wing of the National Gallery was painted grey

"Everyone is capable of writing one bad novel: Jeffrey Archer being the exception."
Julian Critchley

"I'm free. I'm free. Now I can really speak my mind."
Margaret Thatcher

"It's like hearing that Mary Poppins sweats."
Cilla Black revealing on Wogan that she tried drugs during the '60s

Carrie on scribbling

Carrie Fisher, writing in TO 1063

1991

Carrie Fisher

Albert Brooks does this great bit. You know how they say, 'Life is not a rehearsal'? Well, Albert says, 'What if it is?' That's how I like to think of life – as a really long, arduous rehearsal for some long, arduous show. At least it doesn't count. It can't possibly.

I knew as a little girl that my parents led an observed life. Of course it's humiliating to think that you're modifying your behaviour to satisfy some onlooker. But in Hollywood everybody does that to a certain extent. It's unavoidable. The result is that you wind up acting schizophrenic. You do stuff that's for them and you do stuff that's for yourself.

Mine was always a really interesting life.

I once asked a girlfriend how her mother died, and she replied, 'Well, you know the thing was, she was murdered by my father.' I couldn't get over the wonderfully nonchalant way in which she said this – the great way she backed off and let the information carry the situation.

I certainly didn't experience anything as extreme as my father shooting my mother. But stuff kept happening. It was French farce – complete with the maids, though without the outfits. By the time I was an adolescent – which is the point at which I think a child is trying to determine where its anchors are – my father was long gone and my mother was in big trouble. So for me there weren't any anchors. I had to rely on my own wits.

Now, that also happens to be the age when kids first tend to become disillusioned with their families. You think, 'These people, they're fallible. This could all blow up tomorrow.' Well, because my disillusionment coincided with everything falling apart, it was gigantic. As a result, I became this nonchalant, seemingly tough kid. I was going to handle it. I was going to put my head down and get through it as quickly as possible and get out.

Basically, I learned to say, 'Uh-huh.' As in:
THEM: Darling, we have no more money and you're having a breakdown.
ME: Uh-huh, so what's for dinner?
It was around then that I started writing.

I used to fill up these journals. Some of them were good and some of them were awful. Mostly they were weird. Lines like: 'My nose runs, my mind follows.' By the time I was 15, I wanted to be Dorothy Parker, and I began writing this terrible poetry. Writing became my escape – at least until I found dope, at 21.

I always felt as if I were looking out of this enormous melon-shaped head at a world that I couldn't manage. But whether or not I could manage the world, I could describe it. I could comment on it. I might not be able to escape from reality, but I certainly had something to say

about it. I remember writing in my journal when I was working on 'Star Wars'– I was 19 at the time – 'I narrate a life I am reluctant to live.' I've always felt that way.

My writing was scream of consciousness. It was verbal vomiting. I would feel possessed by these prose runs. My experience was extremely intense and writing was a way of siphoning off at least the top. In 1985, Simon and Schuster signed me up to do a collection of non-fiction articles about my take on the culture. But when I sat down to write them, what came out were these drugs monologues, which eventually became 'Postcards from the Edge'.

For me, there really is no distance between writer and subject. I am a spy in the house of me. Maybe it's presumptuous to think that my experience is universal, but I do. As a female, as an alcoholic, as a daughter, as a sister, as whatever it is that I am, I feel I'm part of a common experience that we all share, that connects us. And it's all stupid and it's all insane: the relationship of females to males, the relationship to work, to our biological clocks – all that stuff.

'That's how I see the difference. Fiction is the gun and nonfiction is the camera.'

The point is, if I'm going to place myself in the front lines of this struggle we're all in – and that's where I want to be – then I would rather be there with a gun than with a camera. That's how I see the difference: fiction is the gun and nonfiction is the camera.

Of course, I'm not exactly everyone's idea of who ought to be writing serious novels. Some of the reviews of 'Postcards' pretty much said that since I was a movie star's kid and since I'd been in 'Star Wars' I should shut the fuck up and sit in the closet. The attitude was, 'Oh, Christ, do we have to listen to the indulgent, pretentious ravings of this spoiled, privileged girl?' Because of my background and my other profession – namely, that of movie actress – they felt that my point of view was instantly invalidated. Not only was it totally without value, but it couldn't possibly be interesting.

Now keep in mind that I didn't write about my background in 'Postcards'. I was writing about drugs and obsession. But you can't get people to separate you from their preconceived notions about actors and show business.

As it happens, I never wanted to be an actor. What attracted me to the business had nothing to do with acting. What attracted me was the wonderful camaraderie I saw on movie sets – the camaraderie of a group of people who all shared the same inside jokes, who all had the same goal. As a small girl, a movie set seemed to me to be a little party, a little ant farm, a happy circus of

people who seemed fun to be around. And that's still what I like best about it – the sense of community. Eating lunch together. Talking to the people in the prop truck.

I remember visiting my mother on the set of 'The Second Time Around', when I was three or four. No one told me what was going to happen. All I knew was that she looked beautiful as she stood off to the side, all dressed up, waiting for the scene to begin. Then the director called 'Action!' She walked on to the set, said her lines – and fell face down in the mud. I was shocked. I thought she had committed some horrible error. But then the director yelled 'Cut!' and everyone howled with laughter. 'Yeah,' I thought. 'Now that's a job.'

I'd always had this feeling of being just outside life's door listening to all the laughter from inside. I wanted inside, and a movie set seemed as inside as you could manage. It was like a playground, but one populated by grown-ups who were somehow actually getting something accomplished.

I've always been fascinated by the man-woman thing. Everywhere I go I find people constantly talking about the nature of being a man or a woman or the nature of human relationships. Lately I've been thinking a lot about how the qualities that would make me attractive to someone as a girlfriend would probably drive them away if they were looking for a mate. That's because I may be vivid and charming and all that, but I am not restful. And I think a lot of people view a permanent relationship as a place to rest.

I think if you're looking to be stimulated in a relationship, you're looking to date, not to settle down with someone. That's because a relationship that's always stimulating can be very stressful and who wants to be stressed-out all the time?

At one point in my life, I thought I wanted to be stimulated. Right now, I'm looking to rest. Of course, what would be ideal would be if you could be stimulated by someone with whom you could also rest. But I don't think you can find someone who's both. I hope I'm wrong, but I think one should perhaps look to friends for stimulation.

Anyway, my hobby these days is naming perfumes. I think 'Empathy' would be a good name for a perfume. 'Empathy – feel like them, smell like you.' I'm also fond of 'Proximity', as in 'Proximity – for when you're too close for comfort.' And then there's 'Ambivalence'. I have such an extreme case of ambivalence about everything that it's an act of courage for me to get dressed in the morning. But it's a lovely fragrance. 'Ambivalence – the scent of confusion. For the man who doesn't know what the fuck he wants, and the woman who's following him.' ●

Great
Boers of today

1991

from TO 1076, by **Elaine Paterson**

I arrived in Ventersdorp, Transvaal headquarters of South Africa's neo-nazi Afrikaner Resistance Movement (AWB), three hours late. The motorway turn-off signs had been confusing. They'd say Armadale and then underneath 'SLEGS ONLY'; or Kimberley – 'SLEGS ONLY'. I knew for sure 'Slegs' wasn't on my way, so I orbited Johannesburg's skyscrapers on the expressway for a couple of hours. 'Slegs', it turned out, means 'only' in Afrikaans.

Hard-line Afrikaners don't get much press these days, but that tiny 10 per cent of the South African population are used to a lot more privileges than their own road signs. Where I was headed, reformers like De Klerk are considered 'white kaffirs'; the bottle-shop still has segregated entrances; Afrikaans is, defiantly, the first language and the 'new South Africa' doesn't mean so much as a piss on a tree.

Film-maker Nick Broomfield was there already with his assistant Rita Oord and cameraman Barry Ackroyd. 'Ventersdorp,' he said, as we drove along dull, deserted, characterless streets peppered with churches, 'is like the American Deep South in the '50s.' That was last October, two weeks before De Klerk abolished the Public Amenities Act, and the town council was contemplating draining the swimming pool rather than open it to blacks. Broomfield's film, 'The Leader, His Driver and the Driver's Wife', attempts to tap into this weird psyche.

'The Leader' is Ventersdorp's most celebrated resident; Eugene Terre'blanche, the AWB's whipcracking figurehead. Terre'blanche's driver is JP Meyer, who lives next door, and Anita is 'the driver's wife'; a munchkin-like matron with a tweetie-pie voice who roams the town-

ships in her little car – 'my ladybird' dispensing condoms by the bucket-load: 'Ja, they do it five times a day.'

Broomfield was ostensibly in Ventersdorp to film an interview with the Leader, but hadn't yet done so. When the film crew turned up late for the fourth arranged audience, Terre'blanche had left in a fury. Broomfield laughed: 'It's so funny, every time I see JP he shakes his head and says: "You've really done it now."'

'You're going to be very surprised by the situation here,' Broomfield cautioned as we made for the Meyers' modest bungalow next door to Terre'blanche's. That first night I supped on 'kaffir' (oxtail) stew courtesy of JP's wife Anita;

'Basically, women like hairy men with guns.'

petted the Meyers' black cat, Kaffir, and lit Rita's cigarette with a lighter that was 'like a kaffir' because, according to JP 'it doesn't want to work.' Eugene Terre'blanche drew up outside in his white BMW with 777 numberplate – the three sevens form the AWB's swastika-like emblem.

In the next couple of days I heard a lot about what would happen 'when the fertiliser hit the fan', as one town councillor quaintly put it, although opinions differed on when that would be. 'When they try to take away our guns,' said Keith Conroy, Terre'blanche's security officer. 'When they let black children into our schools,' said JP. 'When they let the blacks into parliament,' said another AWB hanger-on. 'When they try to take our land away from us,' said Terre'blanche. Since then blacks have appeared in white schools and De Klerk is

making moves to abolish the Land Act; the AWB still have their guns, but there's no sign of a white revolution.

I got used to the racist onslaught, to having all my carefully nurtured liberal arguments rendered useless by bone-headed bigotry. As the Kruger Day rally approached, more and more AWB 'commandos' turned up in Ventersdorp to drink and spout invective. They all looked like barrel-bellied, jolly Bavarian apple-growers in Action Man outfits. And their beloved Afrikaans sounded like tapdancing. Even the guns they carried in their belts didn't make them intimidating. Terre'blanche remained an enigmatic figure in his white BMW, and Nick pointed out that the Leader wears built-up shoes. I was beginning to wonder if there was anything behind the yobbish bravado.

'Basically, women like hairy men with guns,' Terre'blanche's Zapata-moustachioed chief security officer, Keith Conroy, assured me. 'It's inherent in every woman to have a male who will protect her, in this country anyway. They're attracted to our forcefulness because they're sick and tired of looking around at a bunch of pot-bellied wimps.'

The day turned into a sightseeing trip. They took me to the Boer monument in Pretoria out of sheer nationalistic pride. It looked like a water tower and had friezes inside depicting the voortrekkers in what could have been scenes from 'Little House on the Prairie' meets 'Roots'. They posed for a snap with automatic rifles taken from a cache in the boot. We went shopping for commando gear. We ate in Wimpey's in Johannesburg's Hillbrow area, where you can buy anything, said Rosy-cheeks, 'from a prostitute to a dead policeman'.

I asked Broomfield if he thought the AWB were really dangerous: 'I don't know, I don't know,' he mused. 'Nobody knows how much power they have in the security police and in the military.' Everyone I asked said the same thing.

Turnout at the Kruger's Day Rally was poor. Terre'banche was expecting 1,000 'commandos' and 5,000 spectators. Around 400 commandos marched around the Vaal Showground, their wives and children watching indulgently from the stands. The buzz of the day was that 'General' de Wet, the AWB's military commander, had spent the night at the home of the local police chief and that Terre'blanche, who had vowed to sleep with his horse, spent the night at the local Holiday Inn.

Broomfield got his showdown after a death-defying car chase in which he broke up Terre'blanche's security convoy to get a passing shot of the leader. Terre'blanche subsequently arrived at the venue alone. The security convoy got lost – Keith Conroy doesn't speak Afrikaans; he probably went to 'Slegs'. ●

1992

Jason was most definitely not gay. The rest of us were not only gay, we were perky, pinky and deliriously happy, since the nation was, as *The Star* informed us, 'IN THE GRIP OF E'. Most of the rest of the world was less happy, since civil war was its new drug, with addicts including Los Angeles, Somalia and Sarajevo. The queen had a horrible annus.

February
Boxer Mike Tyson is convicted of raping Desiree Washington and sentenced to six years in jail.

Kurt Cobain and Courtney Love are married in Hawaii.

Jeffrey Dahmer is sentenced to life imprisonment in Wisconsin after murdering 15 boys and men.

April
Jason Donovan is awarded £250,000 libel damages against the *Face* magazine.

Rioting occurs in Los Angeles after police caught on camera beating Rodney King are acquitted.

Benny Hill, Britain's most popular comedian abroad, dies.

The Tories are re-elected for a fourth term of office, with John Major as Prime Minister.

June
Denmark runs out surprise winners of the European Championship.

July
John Smith becomes the latest Labour leader, replacing Neil Kinnock.

Scandal envelops Woody Allen after he confesses to an affair with his step-daughter Soon-Yi.

Gianluigi Lentini becomes the most expensive footballer in the world when he is transferred to Milan from Torino for £13m.

August
The Football Association's much-vaunted and criticised Premier League kicks off.

November
Windsor Castle burns down.

Bill Clinton is elected as President of the USA.

December
John Major announces that Prince Charles and Princess Diana are separating.

MIND
IF I BRING A
COUPLE
OF FRIENDS?

Basic Instinct
The depiction of several bisexual women with murky pasts does illustrate that sensitivity is not always the strong suit of Verhoeven or scriptwriter Joe Eszterhas.

Unforgiven
Refuting conventional cowboy heroics, Eastwood's film achieves a magnificent intensity.

Glengarry Glen Ross
Mamet's play about the dealings of real-estate salesmen gets dedicated playing from a splendid cast, but gains nothing from transfer from stage to screen.

REM - Automatic For The People (Warner Bros)
Michael Stipe, who has always revelled in

the obscure and abstruse, has never before been so openly reflective and deeply affecting.

Manic Street Preachers - Generation Terrorists (Columbia)
'Generation Terrorists' is a cleanly produced rock album that twists their punk into slightly agitated heavy metal.

Arrested Development - 3 Years, 5 Months And 2 Days In The Life Of (Cooltempo)
Couple their eloquent oratory with a patch of samples and hip hop beats and you've got a killer. Underproduced rather than overblown with studio technology: easily the best rap album of the year.

1992

Michael Caine

Return of the native

Michael Caine interviewed in T.O.1152, by **Brian Case**

Harry's Jazz Club would be the jumpingest joint around, if it existed. On the stand is a wailing sextet, miming to a record. The walls are hung with Gottlieb photos of Bird and Diz, and there are tingling blue neon arcs over the bar. Everybody's smoking up a storm to promote atmosphere, and one extra in a beret is studying the menu which features Harry's Seaside Delight, a selection of today's shellfish marinated in a wine sauce on a bed of rice at £7.95. The interior of Harry's is in Ealing Studios, the outside is the Bass Clef in Shoreditch; the movie is 'Blue Ice'.

Make-up sprays imitation sweat at the Charlie Watts combo, and Michael Caine OBE, playing Harry, a former MI6 operative, starts his proprietorial stroll through the clientele, a word here, a pat there, a little touch of Harry in the nightclub. He coasts through the moves. Paul Newman once said of director Sidney Lumet that he was so fast he could double park outside a brothel. Caine too.

There's an example of the star's alchemy in the next scene. Caine is in amiable conversation with a customer on the subject of jazz. 'You know your music, Mr Stevens,' he says, but there's something cryptic and ominous in the man's response. Caine smells a rat. A stillness settles over him. His eyes assume the famous cobra look. Harry is about to be dragged back into

the world of espionage and the corpses will pile up. Cut. Perfect. Caine lights a cigar, and heads for his caravan.

Director Russell Mulcahy has worked with both Caine and Connery, our international stars, both with their accents defiantly intact. 'They're quite similar. One or two takes will suffice. Michael is particularly fascinating because his technique is so precise. You can see on film when he's listening, that he's thinking about what people have said. It's all in his face.' Caine handles himself like an old-time studio contract actor, and accepts almost anything. The strategy is famous: 'I'll make so many films that I'll be a star before they find out I can't act.' In the last decade, however, critics woke up to the fact that he can, and gave him an Oscar for 'Hannah and her Sisters'. His technique is invisible, and decades of duff directors have made him self-sufficient. His 'Master Class' on TV was a model of practical common sense. 'Be like a duck, my mother used to tell me. Remain calm on the surface and paddle like hell underneath.'

In the lunch break, the star agrees to an interview. Caine's regular stand-in, Reg, looks very much like him, except his brows are as inflexibly hoisted as Henry Cooper's. Slightly shorter, he wears lifts, and a patch of wig over his bald spot. 'Lead with "The Man Who Would Be King",' he advises. 'Michael loves that one.' But the thing everyone's been denying is that this Harry is the Harry from 'The Ipcress File', 30 years on.

'Nah, nothing to do with Harry Palmer.' The star denies it too. 'This guy's more like Dirty Harry. Very hard, very tough, lethal, professional. Harry Palmer was a gifted amateur.' And the jazz club setting? 'I've always liked jazz. Nicol Williamson used to take me round to the correct places because I never knew where to go. He was a big jazz fan. My era was the MJQ and Stan Getz and Gerry Mulligan, but I've never kept up with it. But I liked it enough to want to have it back in the picture, and it makes Harry so much more sympathetic. Anybody who owns a gambling casino or a strip club is only there to make money. Guys who own jazz clubs are crusaders in a funny kinda way.'

Crowding 60, he looks great. He's finally shed the weight he put on for 'Educating Rita', thanks to an exercise treadmill and no dairy products. We trot through directors. 'Old John was The Man. I always think if you ever heard God talking he'd sound like John Huston. Sean and John and me were three extremely different types of men on "The Man Who Would Be King", but with a common thread. More than that – a steel wire.' Huston's only direction had been to encourage him to speak faster because he was playing an honest man. 'Yeah. I pulled him on it one day, you never give me any direction, and he said, "That's because I cast it right. If you see a director giving directions every day he's screwed up the casting."'

Ouazazate, the Moroccan location where it had been filmed, remained in his memory – and mine – as Diarrhoea City. 'Oh fuck, yes, terrible place. You don't even have to eat anything for that. It's the dust from the camel shit. Once it dries it's carried on the air and you breath in the germs from it. I had a sinus condition there the like of which you wouldn't believe. I'd had the jab for typhoid but I got a mild bout – dunno wot the real typhoid is like, but fucking hell! Everything was reeling. I was right by the dustbins in the hotel and the hyenas was fucking grabbing the stuff out of them at night. One of the worst places I've ever been.' Another arduous stint involved months – 'that was a bastard!' –

in the jungle for Aldrich's 'Too Late the Hero'. His most heartfelt line, spoken from under an army beret worn at the dumb insolence angle, was, 'Why don't we all just bugger off home?'

He's cheerful about his flops. 'Yeah, I've done my share of crap,' he laughs. 'You've just gotta get to the end of it, and be responsible for giving your best possible performance. What happens with people like Jack Nicholson is there's always enough money to fix it. Once you've got Jack and you've paid him how many zillion dollars, you can't let the investment go in the toilet so if it's not right you fix it. Whereas if I make a picture and it's a turkey, they just throw it away. "Ashanti" was the worst, but I've been in bad films like "The Marseilles Contract", where I had the best bloody time in my life. We started off in Nice, went to Cannes, St Tropez, then to Marseilles and wound up in Paris. It was just after my daughter was born, and to get her out of London in the winter into the south of France was wonderful. I never even read the script. I said, "I'll fucking do this! I'm out of here!"'

John MacKenzie directed him twice, and had been amused by his pragmatism. 'Michael always dresses for the last shot. He always asks you what your shots are going to be, and he's hoping they're going to go long shot, medium shot, close-up. "You're sure you'll keep it in that order?" I said yeah. I get into the medium shot and he's changed into his going-home trousers, and he'd actually got his going-home shirt on for the close-up, and he's out the door like that.'

No, not overmuch mysticism in Caine's approach to the job. On 'Sleuth', Laurence Olivier had been amazed that he demanded a TV in his dressing room and watched Wimbledon rather than go over his lines. Improbably, they became friends. 'I told him to stay in movies and make a packet. I said, "All you've got out of it all is a Lordship. I've got several million dollars." I planted the seeds of avarice in him.' In a good year in Hollywood, after Denis Healey's 1976 budget drove him into a nine-year exile, Caine was getting $3 million, and his calls returned. 'You know wot Michael Caine's first ever words were to me on the set of "The Honorary Consul"?' Bob Hoskins remembered. "Come 'ere, my son. You're gonner earn a lotter money and you've gotter learn 'ow to look after your money. Come to yer Uncle Michael and I'll tell yer".' And there's a Caine dictum attached to this too. 'At 20 I was told money would never make me happy. They were wrong.'

He uses his loaf, an outlook derived from his background. He was born Maurice Micklewhite, son of a Billingsgate fishporter, and brought up in a prefab at the Elephant and Castle. In his youth he was a dish-washer, pie maker, pneumatic drill operator and – the stage name came from 'The Caine Mutiny' – an every-night moviegoer. He was also a Teddy Boy. 'Yeah. When I went in the army I had the full DA haircut, the long sideboards, brothel creepers, always had to be gaberdine suits otherwise you were out. I didn't have the velvet collars and all that – I didn't go that far. I was never an extremist in anything. I toned it down a bit, basically because I lived at the Elephant and Castle and if you went down the wrong street and you were a Teddy Boy you got the shit kicked out of you. I didn't wanna make a commitment to any cause – especially Teddy Boyism which was not paying me any money.

'The Elephant's a different place now. Around the Georgian part of Kennington you've got a lot of yuppies, then you've got a lot of students around Camberwell Art School, and then you've got a lot of immigrants, so nothing's the same. We

> **'All you've got out of it all is a Lordship. I've got several million dollars.'**

never had rich people, never had immigrants, never had students. We were just London working class. I knew all those back streets behind the Old Vic and right down the docks to Rotherhithe – I mean, you couldn't walk down there. That was the worst slums in London. I feel no nostalgia for it at all, no regret. I've cut myself off from that entirely. "You Can't Go Home Again" by Thomas Wolfe. I read that novel when I was a very young boy.'

But he had gone home again after success, hoping to make sense of it all – and bumped into Chaplin doing the same thing. 'I talked to him both times, but he didn't know who I was. I was more of a nuisance than anything, but I was less of a nuisance the second time because he remembered me from the time before. Eventually I went back and stood there and watched them demolish where he was born near the Kennington Regal. I thought – what a bloody thing to do.'

But old cockney London had formed him. 'Well, this is it. You know how hard I work. My character was formed by where I came from, and it was formed in stone so wherever I move it moves with me. What happened with me was by the time I was 14. I was better educated and more intelligent than my parents, and I'd read all of Dickens by the time I was 18. See, I read books, and I realised there was a better life than this – and that's all I was ever after. I became my own man then, and stayed that way. I had the morality that comes from there – it's very Victorian in some respects, and very free and liberal in others.' Loyalty to family and mates is part of it. He agreed to play the villain in 'Mona Lisa' for a small fee and smaller billing to support Hoskins. "'I bet you never thought I'd do it, you cunt,'" Hoskins says he said. Fair play is another. 'Otto Preminger was nice to me on "Hurry Sundown" but I didn't like how nasty he was to everyone else. He was particularly nasty to Faye Dunaway and I pulled him on it. My attitude was if he says anything to me I'll fucking deck him.'

Homesickness finally drove him back. He has a sixteenth-century rectory amid ten acres in Oxfordshire where he grows organic vegetables, cooks, and supports the local swan sanctuary. 'I was evacuated to Norfolk throughout the war. A little village outside King's Lynn. My mother was a cook for a squire and I used to drink little drops of great Bordeaux, throw up trying to finish off a cigar, take a leg of pheasant somebody had left.

'They were elderly people so they didn't eat everything. The woman of the house took a shine to me, you know, the cook's kid. She took me into the front room and told me if I didn't win the scholarship they'd pay for my education. I was looking round the room and it was very different from ours, and I thought, that's what I want.' He grinned with delight. 'And that's what I have. 'I have a scheming mind. I don't go for the obvious. I go – ▶

wait a minute, let's hold back here, see where this is going. If I'm driving I'm always driving 50 yards ahead about what's coming up. Figure it out before I get there, you know, and that's how I've done my life. It's not a quality I admire in other people, but I am quite devious about my own survival or wellbeing. Quite ruthless I suppose, though I think that's been brought about by this business. Ruthless with myself I think I mean. From myself, I take no excuses. I push on.' He still has Kipling's 'If' on his wall, that ode to striving. 'I've always had Kipling in my philosophy. There are things in that that I live by. It's like a mini-religious sorta thing.' Caine's values are very much on display in his forthright autobiography.

For over a decade before 'The Ipcress File' and 'Alfie'

rocketed him to stardom, he had shuffled about in uncredited walk-ons and provincial reps. He'd even done Merton Park quota quickies. 'Jack Greenwood, Edgar Wallace, the Danzigers. I'm guilty of all three. Well, they were very quick, in and out, you got seven guineas. I played a policeman until they sent the uniform to the cleaners and it shrunk and they got a smaller policeman. That was the casting criterion. I mean, I was like a fucking skeleton, I didn't have enough money to gain weight, but they found a thinner and smaller guy. Ronnie Curtis had a casting agency and we used to sit there all day, take sandwiches because you'd miss a job if you went to the toilet. He was cross-eyed and he used to come out and say, "You" – and like three people would stand up. He'd

Madonna's 'Sex'

from 'Virgin on the ridiculous' in T.O.1157, by **Sarah Kent**

Madonna's 'Sex' comes condom-wrapped to protect it from casual encounters. The material girl's face is printed on the rape-resistant Mylar in a blue swoon – head thrown back, eyes closed, mouth open. Classic Hollywood ecstatic: blonde and beautiful, a distant object of desire. But Madonna, dubbed by Martin Amis 'the most postmodern person on the planet', refuses to be merely a dreamy screen on to which people can project their wishes. She has to be in control, shaping any freefloating fantasies. We are her subjects, not vice versa.

Her book was proclaimed 'flagrantly pornographic', even before it was seen. French customs seized it and the Japanese censored it. Several printers refused to handle it, before a Mid-West firm agreed – on condition that it remain anonymous.

I suspect it's not the content that people find objectionable – it is relatively mild, anyway – but the fact that a woman is on top. Steven Meisel may have held the camera, but it is obvious who called the shots: 'These are fantasies I have dreamed up,' affirms Madonna.

Dubbed the 'dirtiest coffee table book ever', 'Sex' is actually more like a designer fanzine – searching after street rather than sitting-room or art-crowd cred. The book is best when at its most relaxed and humorous, least convincing when Madonna strives for crack-alley cred as a tourist in Manhattan's downtown dives: sex clubs such as the Toilet and the Vault and a burlesque theatre called the Gaiety. She play-acts S&M in basements and backyards, whipping a well-covered rump, being tied up by lesbian skinheads who threaten her with teeth and blade. 'There's something comforting about being tied up, like when you were a baby and your mother strapped you in the car seat.' But the atmosphere is wrong, the threat is unreal and the narrative without dynamic. The pictures are like fashion plates – for rubber goods and swimwear – without serious dread. A genuinely disconcerting shot shows a man in evening dress riding a pack of naked slaves, but then it gets ludicrous as he and Madonna, in a full-length sequined sheath, luxuriate amid the bulging beefcake.

Madonna is at her high-spirited best when pondering her solo obsessions. She simulates innocence better than wickedness – a large chunk of her is still a child. And innuendo is sexier than overkill. 'I love my pussy,' she proclaims, 'it is the summation of

my life. My pussy is the temple of learning. Sometimes I sit at the edge of the bed and stare into the mirror... Sometimes I stick my finger in my pussy and wiggle it around the dark wetness and feel what a cock or a tongue must feel when I'm sitting on it. I pull my finger out and I always taste it and smell it... It smells like a baby to me, fresh and full of life.'

We're in the realm of girl-talk, teen confessions for the post-feminist generation, who grew up unashamed of their bodies. Twenty-five years ago women crept to consciousness-raising groups clutching hand mirrors with which to examine their genitals, ridding themselves of shame and ignorance and discovering that their private parts were also for their pleasure, not just the possession of men.

One of the most inspired images, printed a soft violet, shows Madonna suspended naked from a gantry as though she had just been lifted from the sea – the modern equivalent of Botticelli's Venus, blown ashore on a shell: newly born but fully formed. The wackiest picture is of her tiptoeing naked across a lawn clutching a handbag and water bottle, like some daffy housewife escaping for the day. She hitches starkers beside the freeway and munches pizza naked in a parlour. The most telling fantasy in 'Sex' finds her in schoolgirl knickers and socks sitting on the lap of a father figure, smoking, as he adoringly fondles her breast – she is said to be driven by the need for her father's love and approval.

Madonna sees herself as a liberator: 'avenger of the libido dead, a sister of mercy or lady of head'. But I see her as a prisoner, occasionally breaking the bonds of fame by leaping naked into the light of day and photographing the brief moment of release, before beating a hasty retreat to the safety of a dark windowed limo.

The most memorable picture in the book shows Madonna in vest and boots perched on a radiator, peeping through the blinds – exposing herself to the world and monitoring the reactions. It's an image of loneliness and longing of a kid who can't go out to play; of someone tough yet vulnerable, exhibitionist yet reclusive, needing the crowd yet cut off from the street. The summation of a life spent struggling for fame, then learning how, on earth, to deal with it.

say, "Who's got a 38" chest? Who's got a short haircut? Right. You're the policeman then."' He laughed. 'See, those things for us, they were essential because they were rent money. Those films kept a lot of people in the business.'

He still cares about the British film industry. 'This picture costs nothing. Steven Spielberg isn't gonna be standing there in fear and trembling, but it brings a movie back to England, know what I mean? British bankers won't back a British film. Someone said to me the other day, "Why weren't you at the BAFTA Awards?" I said, because I was making a British movie.' Back on set, he removes his cigar to address the unit. 'And remember my motto: the flogging will continue until the mood of the crew improves.' ●

● ●

Sharon Stone

from 'Sex crimes' in T.O. 1131, by
Alex Mcgregor

At times it is difficult to work out where 34-year-old Sharon Stone ends and her character in 'Basic Instinct', Catherine Tramell, starts. They both have a self-confidence and a candour that borders on the brazen. It almost comes as a surprise to discover there are things she won't talk about, like her family. But this is just about the only thing she won't talk about.

She is the first to agree that 'Basic Instinct' is a murderous male wet dream and, like Catherine in the film, she laughs at Nick's hyperbolic description of her being 'the fuck of the century'.

'How can it be "the fuck of the century" when a woman has to pretend to have three orgasms in four minutes from anatomically incorrect positions? I mean that's a total male fantasy. But that's what the script called for, so that's cool.'

The part of the tough-talking, hard-fucking Catherine is, Stone thinks, a nice reversal of the traditional female film roles. 'It is almost exemplary of what has been considered an acceptable way for men to behave. I think it is good in the interrogation scene to have the men hear the talk-back and see the discomfort it causes.'

For Stone it was her character's strength which attracted her to the role.

'It felt right for me to play Catherine. She not only embodies a male fantasy but she also knows what she is doing. So she is not a victim of a male fantasy, it is her decision to do that to gain power.'

The root of Catherine's power is her sexuality and as she shows, she is quite happy to use it. Stone herself is phlegmatic about the film's graphic sex scenes, and even dispensed with the crotch patch many actors prefer to wear while filming them. 'Michael Douglas and I went as far as anyone could go,' she told one interviewer.

'I think sex is scary in real life,' she says now. 'The things that make it scary are the intimacy and the way it reveals you as a person. When you are another character and you are on a movie set, there isn't real intimacy and it isn't revealing you. So the things that are scary are a little bit different. There is the thing about being self-conscious and figuring out how you are supposed to feel because no one tells you how you are supposed to feel being nude in a room during a scene, and I found that I felt okay about it. And then I thought that you're probably not supposed to feel okay about it, I should pretend to feel scared.'

'Basic Instinct' is Stone's second film with director Paul Verhoeven and both readily admit that it was just as stormy as their experience together in 'Total Recall'. As to whether she would work with him again remains to be seen.

'I don't know yet. We have a working dynamic, we have a certain kind of magic that happens when we work together, even though we fight like cats and dogs. We love each other and hate each other but we make something that works. So I don't know if I'll work with him again, it might depend on whether or not I kill him first.'

While Stone seems to be lapping up the attention, she expresses surprise at the fuss that the film has provoked.

'I keep telling people that this is not profound, not important. Everybody wants me to say all these things about the deep psychological effects of this movie. This movie is a thriller! You know, I do these interviews, answer all these questions and try to be really thoughtful, and I go home at the end of the day thinking: "What is the big deal?"' ●

"1992"

"Keep your rosaries out of our ovaries!"
Slogan by Women's Action Committee against anti-abortionists

"My great-grandmother was your great-great grandfather's mistress. So how about it?"
Camilla Parker Bowles to Prince Charles

"In the next life I'd like to come back as your trousers."
Prince Charles, quoted in the 'Camillagate' tapes

"It'll be good to have a dope smoker in the White House. Better than just a dope."
Ian Hislop on Bill Clinton's election win

"Maybe it's because I'm a wog."
Secretary General Boutros Boutros-Ghali suggests reasons for criticism aimed at him

"That's only fair – it is, after all, their turn."
Paddy Ashdown reacting to the news that David Owen will support the Tories at the election

"If Labour Wins Today Will The Last Person To Leave Britain Please Put The Lights Out."
Sun headline on polling day

"They're all the same. They're short, they're fat, they're slimy and they're fundamentally corrupt."
Rod Richards, Tory MP on his feelings for Labour councillors. He later resigned after it was revealed he had had a long-running affair

"I'd like to thank the press from the heart of my bottom."
Nick Faldo, on winning the British Open, hits back at critics

"You need all kinds of players in this game – dour professionals and players with real flair, like me."
Geoff Boycott, on losing his batting record to David Gower

"A bullet, nearly."
PC Ray Hall, who was shot in the head preventing an IRA bomb plot, on what went through his mind when he was shot

The Player King

Robert Altman interviewed in T.O.
1137, by **Geoff Andrew**

In his latest movie, the maverick director not only
demolished Hollywood, he got its brightest stars
to help him do it.

obert Altman is in unusually ebullient mood.
Conspicuously delighted by the very enthusiastic reception for 'The Player' at Cannes, he embarks upon a rant
about one of his past producers (who, for legal reasons, must
here unfortunately remain nameless). 'He won't pay me a cent
for the movie I made. He says, "Fuck you! Sue me!" And now,
after the success of "The Player", he's going around saying, "Oh,
I produced an Altman film." But this man stole from me, he lied
to me, he's a despicable person. And the only way I can combat
that is to tell the truth about him. And if he says I'm telling lies
about him, then he should sue me for slander!'

If any film-maker was the perfect choice to direct the movie
adaptation of Michael Tolkin's novel – in which a high-ranking
Hollywood studio executive is driven to murder after receiving
anonymous death-threat postcards from a scriptwriter whose
calls he has failed to answer – it was surely Robert Altman. Few
major American directors have had such a troubled, up-and-
down relationship with the studio establishment in recent years.

His openness is not, as one might expect, the embittered out-
pourings of an artist belatedly welcomed back into the fold after
years in the wilderness. Indeed, Altman – who during the '70s
was widely acknowledged as the most adventurous and interesting film-maker working in Hollywood – is long resigned to
his fate ('I can't do what they want and they don't want what I
do') and seems far from bitter.

He's understandably wary of 'The Player' being seen as a
'comeback' movie. Admittedly, during the '80s his output was
far less conspicuous and included the clumsy 'OC and Stiggs'.
At the same time, however, most of his work – marvellous theatrical adaptations like 'Come Back to the Five and Dime, Jimmy
Dean, Jimmy Dean' and 'The Caine Mutiny Court Martial', and
the ground-breaking television series 'Tanner '88' – was unfairly neglected, and one can't help feeling that his low profile was
rather less to do with the quality of his work than with problems of marketability. Happily, the new film – a dazzling
comedy-cum-thriller and almost certainly the most honest, accurate and complex movie ever made about Hollywood – looks
set to change all that, even if only for a while. He must be pleased
with the way the film's been received: 'Let's say I'm enjoying
the absence of pain,' he admits. 'Someday I'll have to pay for all

this, but it's very nice while it's happening.'

Where Michael Tolkin's original novel was a straightforward
psychological thriller about a man threatening to crack up after
receiving anonymous vengeful postcards, the film uses Tolkin's
basic plot as the starting motor for a far funnier satire on the
greed, philistinism and rampant egotism of Hollywood, a town
where relationships, morality and even the movies themselves
are all subservient to the pursuit of power. Menaced studio executive Griffin Mill (Tim Robbins) seems worried less for his physical safety than about how much his career might suffer should
the postcard writer publicly reveal a faux pas Mill can't even
remember. In this paranoid world, the ability to pitch a good story
and firm up a good deal is everything.

'I made the film,' says a cheery Altman, 'not to take revenge on
or chastise Hollywood, nor to become the manipulator in a town
that likes to manipulate. True, Hollywood is a place I know a lot
about, so Michael's script was an opportunity to show a lot of the
truth – which is what art is. My real motive in doing it was artistic; I just saw a chance to make something that was interesting,
especially in terms of its structure, which is something most people don't discuss. If you could draw a graph of how the film works,
you'd see it has a very unusual structure – though I didn't know
if that would work until I'd finished the film.'

What Altman appears to be referring to is not only the way we
are continually led to reconsider our feelings about Griffin Mill,
but the fact that 'The Player' is a film-within-a-film. It opens on
a painting of a movie-lot, in front of which a clapperboard is
snapped shut (to the sound of Altman's own off-screen voice
ordering quiet on set) so that the action, itself set on a movie-lot,
can begin; and it ends with the story we've just seen being
'pitched' for a movie that Mill may one day produce… to be entitled, of course, 'The Player'. Within this circular framework are
endless in-jokes, allusions, parodies and star-cameos that not only
lend Altman's film an unprecedented authenticity but also help
it to operate successfully on two levels – as a piece of fiction and
as an attempt to document the state of the movie business today.

'The stuff about the clapperboard and the ending weren't there
in Michael's original script,' explains the director. 'The script and
the book are in the film, they're its nucleus, but they're not the
same as the film. In a way, the film is about itself; it's a film about

films about films, like a series of spinning mirrors. Similarly, the film is of Hollywood, but it's not really just about Hollywood. Hollywood is a metaphor for our society, which is based on greed – take, take, take, and don't give anything back to the system; lie and cheat. So though the film is about the stupidity of Hollywood, it's also about the moral problems of our society at large.

'The problem with Hollywood now is that the artists have lost a lot of their power. But that can only go on so long; eventually the public will just go away. Because when the artists are not there directly, what the studios make are just copies, and eventually the copies get so thin they can't be sold. So then the studios say, "We'd better find another artist and we'll get something else to copy!" And the artists are always there; they get their heads cut off, and another one comes up. There's a lot of us.'

Interestingly, back in '76, Altman pointed out that, for him, 'Nashville' was not only about the country-and-western capital and America in the wider sense, but a metaphor for Hollywood during the '40s, a time when he himself was dreaming of making it into the movie business: 'It's a place where people get off the bus,' he said. 'The money is generated, and there's a crudeness to the culture.' But where 'Nashville' dealt with both the successful stars, agents and entrepreneurs, and the no-hopers – the fans, session musicians and ordinary folk hoping that a little of the Grand Ole Opry glamour might rub off on them – 'The Player' focuses most of its attention on the moneyed movers and shakers. But not, noticeably, the agents.

'Why leave out the agents? How can you do a parody of what's already a parody?' laughs Altman. 'As for showing that executives can be human and that writers can be vain and vacuous, well, that's the way we are! To do a satire successfully, the satire basically has to be upon myself. I have to know that all of those things I laugh at in the characters also exist in me. While there is no single character I identify with, I do understand them.

'I don't have any perception of myself as being either in or out of Hollywood; I'm not, as people have said, "a maverick" or someone who went off into exile. To me, Hollywood is a state of mind. I'm in Hollywood, I work in the business, in the system, but I'm also out of it. I'm not a major player, I don't sit at the table. You know, people don't like to talk to me because if you say something to me, I'll tell somebody else. I don't have a good memory and I found out that the best way to deal with that is just to say the truth the way I feel it at the time; and then I don't have to remember what I said!

'And similarly, I didn't base the characters on specific real Hollywood people. The truth is, I don't even know the names or the faces of that level of Hollywood executive; I haven't dealt with them. I know and admire Alan Ladd Jr [who, as head of production at Fox, gave the green light to the risky 'Three Women'], and he's certainly not represented in the film, but I really don't know anybody else like that.'

What Altman does know, however, is actors. For every star who may have found some of his more outspoken pronouncements irksome, there are countless others who have found his generously supportive, semi-improvisational approach rewardingly liberating. That, presumably, is why he was able to assemble such an unprecedentedly starry cast for 'The Player', with dozens of name talents – from Julia Roberts and Bruce Willis to Burt Reynolds, Nick Nolte, Jack Lemmon and Susan Sarandon – contributing a day's work for next to nothing, to appear as often as not in wordless cameos or even, in about 25 instances, to end up on the cutting room floor. Karen Black, Cher, Louise Fletcher, Scot Glenn, Jeff Goldblum, Elliott Gould, Sally Kellerman, Lily Tomlin had worked with the director before, some of them making their first noticeable impact under his tutelage, and so may have felt they owed him a favour; others, perhaps, simply didn't want to be left out. Whatever, Altman insists that casting the movie was no problem at all.

'I just called them up, and they said yes. I think for all those people it was like signing a petition, making a political statement against the greed. And there was nobody turned us down that I know of, though there were people who wanted to be in it and couldn't because their schedules didn't fit ours. When I started the film I had very few people committed – Tim, of course, and Julia and Bruce, who had parts we needed to settle at the very beginning – but it sort of built up. It wasn't very planned; whoever turned up, I'd tell to go eat at that table, and they'd ask, "What should I do?" And I'd say, 'I can't tell you! You're not one of my characters, you're playing yourself, so do anything you want to do.

'Of course, one reason for casting them was part of the game: it's fun to identify all those faces. But mainly, it's because when I made "Tanner '88", where we mixed fictional characters with real people, it was very successful. And I thought I'm doing a film about Hollywood, so why wouldn't there be faces you recognise at the restaurants and so on?

'But the whole film is a game. Like the opening, nine-minute tracking shot [where characters pitch ridiculous scripts like 'Graduate 2' and allude to lengthy tracking shots in Welles's 'Touch of Evil' and Hitchcock's 'Rope'] which is so pretentious, and tells you you're watching a movie about movies. Or like Griffin's recipe for the elements to sell in a film – suspense, laughter, love, hope, sex, nudity, violence, a happy ending; we do all that, so in a way ours is a bad movie, too! Or like we don't say who the postcard writer is, but you can work it out from when you hear him use a phrase on the phone at the end of the film which is a phrase you've heard before. You didn't get it?' Altman laughs. 'You'll have to go see the film again!'

Though currently riding the crest of a wave, Altman is all too aware of the irony in the motto 'Movies, Now More Than Ever' – billboarded above Griffin Mill's company office. 'That's a paraphrase of an old Nixon campaign slogan! It is ironic in that in recent years I've got most of my financing from sources other than the studios. But there is a future for cinema, and I think it'll get very good in the '90s; we'll see big changes.

'I've always had trouble finding finance, and I still am. It should be a little easier now for a short while, because those guys are not very smart; they can only follow the crowd, so I have to take advantage of that. In fact, it looks at last like my plans to do a film of Raymond Carver stories, called "Shortcuts", will come off. But you're only as good as the perception of your last film. Still, I've done very well really, right through the '80s, and all my life. I can't think of one person who's had a better career than I have. So when people ask if "The Player" is vengeful, I tell them I've had it great. I'm a very lucky man.' ●

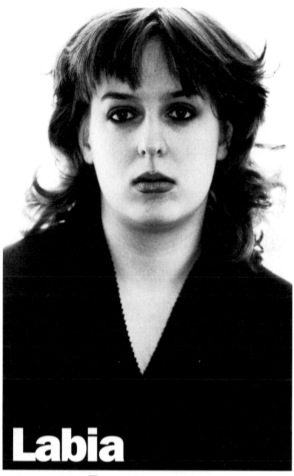

1992

Julie Burchill

Labia exchange

from T.O. 1153, by **Julie Burchill**

Every girl's mother – unless she is an irredeemably libertine sicko – brings her daughter up with one main message re life: DON'T EVER HAVE SEX WITH A MAN.

The perfect teens that only 14-year-olds can ever really be – eyes not yet bloodshot from too many bullshots and bullshit, no stretch marks on our minds or bodies – toss their heads and sneer. Evil old crone (all of 34). She's just jealous.

But no, she is not jealous. What she is is wise beyond your limited comprehension. Because our mothers know that if we have sex with a man, sooner or later we will write about it. And make complete and utter prannets of ourselves.

Much of my new book 'Sex and Sensibility' is not a celebration of sex but a narky, sarky do-I-have-to-Mum? critique of the sensibility which has surrounded it over the past decade. From the nerds who told us that penis size wasn't important (not if your name's Rothschild, it isn't) to the voidoids who told us that, for women, cuddling was more pleasurable than being fucked senseless (if you want to cuddle, buy a cat), the '80s and '90s have seen a concerted attempt on the part of the legions of muddle-browed, muddle-class media-ocrities to detonate the sex bomb, stripping it of darkness and despair and pushing it on video as just another form of indoor exercise, like aerobics with Mad Lizzie and Joggy Bear. (Kinky!)

As the critic Suzanne Moore recently wrote, women have been turned from mere sexual objects to sexual subjects; but rather as jobs for married women meant that they now had to work both inside and outside the home, the alleged 'reclaiming' of sex by women has simply made them more, not less, exploitable.

The whole barrage of parasexual space junk which plays on the fact that many men never move beyond masturbatory adolescence is now aimed at us too; 'erotica for women'on shelf and screen, Chippendales, amateur porn, self-help books on 'hot monogamy', sex-toy parties – the whole sad, soft parade. Perhaps the most tragic thing I've seen in recent years was an expensive lace bodysuit with a cheesy little pocket to hold a condom; now, not only is a working woman expected to blow her wage packet on some corny whore drag which will tickle the jaded joystick of some overworked salaryman, but she must be ready, like a geisha, to soil her hands with a stinking slimeball of latex just in case she's screwing someone who has a fatal disease which could kill her.

Sex used to be the one area of life where a woman could just lay back and let men, the lazy bastards, do the work. But now even this lay-by has been closed, and we have to slog away like stevedores in the sack as well as out. Sex as play; sex as safe; sex as jolly good wheeze. 'Sex is natural/Sex is good/Not everybody does it, but everybody should,' was probably the dumbest, numbest line George Michael ever wrote, though admittedly one is spoiled for choice. Yet this is now the party line on '90s sex; one nation under a moronic groove.

Everyone is meant to be having a certain moderate but regular amount – say three times a week – of a certain sort of sex – playful, non-sexist and preferably non-penetrative. No one is meant to be celibate. No one is meant to be a total self-loathing slag. No one is meant to harbour mean, moody, miserable crushes on aloof objects of desire (shows lack of self-respect) and no one is meant to have magnificent obsessions ('No one person can fulfil the needs of another'). But once you've taken all of this away from sex – the famine and the feast, the agony and the ecstasy, the bad and the beautiful, the wild, the innocent and the E Street Shuffle – it isn't really sex any more. It's blancmange for the genitalia.

It's the myth that good sex can be non-penetrative which really gets up my nose right now. Sex without penetration isn't sex at all. it's courtship, it's seduction, it's foreplay; it's a single that's all intro, a meal that's all hors d'œuvres.

The AIDS lobby have done more in five years to reduce us to a state of nervous fumbling and nonconsummation of lust than the Christian Church managed over the last four decades. And I particularly resent being lectured by male homosexuals on the 'correct' way to have sex. Until recently, queers were the most sexually promiscuous group the world has known; in the bath-houses of New York City, it was possible to fuck 50 men a night. And these men believed – with admirable honesty and lack of hypocrisy – that happiness was invariably nine inches of hot salami served straight up the tradesman's entrance. This is what makes it so incredible that they are now lecturing us about the subtle joys of tickling each other stupid while wearing head-to-toe latex diving suits. It's a bit like having Woody Allen telling you how to bring up your daughters.

Even worse than the AIDS Brigade are the Erotica Nerds; broads, this time. Erotica is the bastard child of Political Correctness and the profit margin. Sometime in the '80s, Andrea Dworkin finally drove it home to the big boys that women found pornography unpleasant and depressing. But as every publisher knows, sex sells; erotica was a good bet to turn a fast buck from faint-hearted fuck.

But erotica is a false friend to women, drawing seven veils of silence over a dirty business and seeking to persuade us that fucking is a delicate, cosy experience, like sitting in a Jacuzzi with a feather up your twat. Women get enough soft soap from romantic fiction writers; the sex-is-fun posse are nothing more than Mills & Boon for the pierced-nipple set. Quite simply, if sex really is healthy, harmless and wholesome for you, you're doing it wrong. ●

1993

We craved glamour so we either lusted after supermodels and boy bands or lost some weight and became androgynous neo-glam-rockers.
The K-Foundation burnt a million quid but it was all the rest of us could do to find 50p for the meter.

January
Czechoslovakia becomes the Czech and Slovak Republics.

February
Baby Jamie Bulger is abducted and murdered.

Over 300 people are injured and seven killed when a bomb explodes underneath the World Trade Centre in New York.

April
Tennis star Monica Seles is stabbed by Gunther Parche at a tournament in Hamburg.

The siege on David Koresh's Branch Davidian cult ends in disaster when agents of the Bureau of Alcohol, Tobacco and Firearms attempt to enter the compound. Nearly 90 people perish.

The Grand National ends in chaos as the race is abandoned after two false starts.

May
The Queen Mother is airlifted to a hospital after swallowing a fishbone.

Nurse Beverley Allitt is convicted of killing four babies in a Grantham hospital.

August
An emotional Dave Lee Travis resigns on air from Radio One.

Guided tours are introduced to Buckingham Palace.

September
BSkyB is launched.

October
Film star River Phoenix dies after collapsing outside LA nightclub the Viper Room.

November
Robert Thompson and Jon Venables are convicted, at the ages of eleven, of murdering Jamie Bulger.

Sleepless In Seattle
This variation of the 'him and hers' schtick comes complete with another of Meg Ryan's ditzy romantics and a fine cameo from Harry director Rob Reiner.

Jurassic Park
Spielberg is still supreme as an action director, and when the T Rex makes beefburger of the jeep, the film inspires wonder and awe.

Schindler's List
The elastic editing and grainy camerawork lend an immediacy as surprising as the shockingly matter-of-fact depiction of violence and casual killing.

Suede - Suede (Nude)
Whether this is the first time you've thrilled to boys letting themselves get out of control, or if it brings

on a wave of nostalgia, Suede is eminently shaggable.

Björk - Debut (One Little Indian)
Debut is a brilliant piece of work; as empty as a landscape, and consequently as full as a book, and it's not often you can say that about records made for dancing.

Jamiroquai - Emergency On Planet Earth (Sony)
Imagine Smash Hits doing a colour spread on '70s soul and funk, explaining the attitudes, fashions and sounds that shaped the groove of the of the day. Now imagine what the record sounds like. It sounds like this one.

Take That

from 'Boys keep singing' in T.O. 1217, by **Paula Yat**

We're all in Birmingham. It's 2am, and in the hotel corridor five huge bodyguards sit on five small chairs. It's their usual nocturnal routine. Inside the rooms, Take That sleep. Outside about 400 anguished, freezing girls huddle by the gates of the remote country hotel. It's another sexless night for everyone. Night after night, according to Take That. In my frozen bed I occasionally hear the girls whisper their beloveds' names. The sound carries on the icy November air, the mass pining of every young girl in Britain for the five beautiful boys who through lack of guile, intense good humour, glorious bodies, determination, dancing and sheer ability have become not just this year's big thing but next year's massive thing Take That and their manager Nigel Martin Smith seem to have cracked it in the way all the others only dreamed of.

It's four in the morning and I'm tossing and turning, with a brisk breeze whistling from the north face of the Eiger straight up the front of my Take That T-shirt. I'm seriously thinking of sleeping with Nigel just so we can get some body heat going, but I can't remember his code name – there are more code names on a Take That tour than at the Pentagon. I put on my Take That woolly hat and my Take That socks, resolving to get myself a Take That anorak for tomorrow night…

'Of course it's everyone's dream,' says their laconic lead singer and songwriter Gary Barlow by the pool the next morning. 'We're really calculating about everything we do, partly because everyone is waiting for it to be over, and we've been knocked so much. But it is hard for us to know what's happening sometimes – we're oblivious to so much that's going on around us; when I go home I just think there's another week's work over with.'

I'm lying trying to conserve heat swathed in all my clothes,

Suddenly, the littlest fan wets herself in time to the music.

with the *Independent* spread over the top.'You know,' says Gary, 'My nan used to say I had the ugliest bum in the world.'

But they're all almost impossibly perfect and cute when they're wet. Gay guys must kill for them. Everyone wants to kiss them and all they do is moan about trying to have sex by the year 2000 and how much they miss their mums. Of course, in the time-honoured tradition they can now no longer go anywhere unaccompanied, no girls are allowed to hang out backstage for fear of hurtful 'stories', there's careful planning needed all the time in case of the crazed hysteria the sight of them provokes. It gets to be lonely sometimes, but they can't believe their luck – and as a group they are remarkably homogenous, constantly supportive of each other; they don't bitch, are exhaustingly enthusiastic and really do love their fans. It's like a whole group of Pauls without a John, George or Ringo…

'You're aware of always been watched,' says Barlow. 'When I bought my house I hadn't any money, so it's in the middle of loads of other houses and now it's impossible to live in. I get ratty of course: phone calls all the time, people going round to my parents' house. The other day I was in the lean-to at the back of my house, standing there in my underpants waiting for the spin-dryer cycle to finish, and I suddenly saw this bloke in the darkness. He was obviously a photographer, and my first reaction was to chase him, like I leap-frogged the front gate and ran down the street after him, and then I suddenly thought, "well, what am I going to do if I catch him?" so I came back again. It makes my blood boil.'

Howard Donald has raging flu, is charmingly shy, has a pierced nipple, a washbasin in his bedroom and the endlessly useful ability to sing in tune and spin on his head simultaneously…

'Robbie's pulled out my nipple ring three times and there was blood everywhere. Last time I didn't even know and it started to heal up so I had to borrow an earring, but I was screaming with pain trying to get it in.

'I don't know why girls think I'm so sexy, I don't think like that at all, I put myself down a lot. I'm very lucky to be in the position I'm in and I do feel quite important – I just wish girls would be more forward with lads.'

Every schoolgirl in Britain is in love with Mark Owen. He has it all: the pouting lips, the perfect cheekbones, the lithe 12-inch hips and he says things like: 'I really want a baby so if any girls want a baby, can they call me tonight.

'When I'm at home I've got girls I can see, nothing serious. I don't really want to settle down, I'd like to spend time with a girl, but it's difficult – the other day I went shopping with my sister and I was thinking: girls are going to think this is my girlfriend. You've always got to be careful.'

If any of Take That can be said to look mildly threatening, Jason's the one who musters it up, he has that loose-limbed sexy insouciance that all popstars should possess; in fact he looks like he'd have very rough sex with you and then leave with your stereo speakers. This is where appearances are deceptive. He wouldn't. He'd go to his room, try and be alone, probably write a poem on the back of an envelope and sit around being Take That's resident dark brooding soul, playing his guitar and not sleeping very well. 'I've never felt really, really happy,' he says. 'I can laugh loads but I'm never letting go of my worries. But then what are the things that make people happy? I don't think I've got those things yet.'

Robbie says he's only had sex three times this year but assures me he was 'really good' one of those times. He's only 19, very

clever, has a ton of attitude and is sort of naughty, like the wicked nephew at every wedding, the one who puts his dick in the trifle and gooses the bridesmaids during the wedding photos. 'I'm extremely happy today,' he says, throwing himself down. 'I was just buzzing my tits off on stage last night, but I am also the one who gets told off a lot by everybody in the world but I don't care.'

At Wembley, Elton John and I are swaying in time to the music, occasionally gazing mistily at each other as we mouth the words to a 'Million Love Songs'. I'm cross I didn't bring a handbag because then we could have both danced round it. The entire audience cries, sweats, swoons and emits a high-pitched squeal every few seconds. It's the same frequency that Russian spies always use in movies down the phone to the American president so that he falls to his knees in the Oval Office and his eardrums burst.

'Gary sings beautifully, he plays piano beautifully,' says Elton. 'If he nurtures that talent he could be a George Michael.' We watch as Gary flings himself down on the lid of the Steinway and vanishes into the bowels of the arena.

Some girls erect their king-sized duvet cover and wave it frantically at the stage. One side says 'SHAG ME ROBBIE' and the other side says 'SHAG ME GARY'. It is making sure that the right side is being waved at the right band member that is giving them nervous exhaustion as they struggle with their origami style folding and semaphoring; by the time Mark Owen comes on, all three look like they wished they'd written their love messages on a hand towel. Suddenly, the littlest fan wets herself in time to the music. The duvet cover is hastily put to use mopping up and I'm happy to see it's now too wet to wave. ●

Pulp

from 'Specs appeal' in T.O. 1213, by **Laura Lee Davis**

'I consider it a personal triumph over sexiness,' confesses Jarvis Cocker, the lanky lead singer of Pulp. In a short space of time, he has made the transition from cult status as one of Sheffield's indie music eccentrics to major sex-god worship. He smiles behind his thick-rimmed, geek-strength glasses as guitarist Russell Senior observes that Jarvis being in any way 'sexy' is a relatively new thing. 'Definitely '90s,' he drawls in a similar south Yorkshire accent. 'Never heard of Jarvis being sexy before then.'

'I would've said that the raw materials I was dealt at birth had me marked out for a "Blockbusters" contestant,' Jarvis adds. 'You know, slightly studious, wear glasses, bit tall, have a bit of a stoop, go to university, get a job in a library. I've always considered it a mission to try and rise above that. I know I couldn't be sexy in a normal way because I haven't got the physique of Mel Gibson. I can't do the macho thing; I wasn't brought up that way, me dad left and there were no male figures to base meself on. So I do consider it a triumph if someone considers me attractive.' His laugh reveals two rows of stunted teeth. 'I find that satisfying.

'I've always had a bit of a hang-up that songs and films feed you a delusion which makes you dissatisfied with real life before you've lived it yourself,' considers Jarvis. 'I don't know if I was particularly naïve when I watched telly, but I gave it a lot of credence, probably more than me mother, because she was only a person just like me. That's why it was important to attempt something that's more a reflection of

human behaviour.

'But we also want to be quite glamorous, not "Sunday looking at cracks in the pavement". We want to elevate everyday things to something exaggerated and a bit exciting.'

'Rave did us a lot of favours,' suggests Russell. 'It was a big bonfire, people didn't want personalities at all, they wanted anonymity. It was a purifying thing and now people are seeking that excitement and glamour again.'

'We've got inadequate personalities so we need to be bolstered up by seeking approval,' says Jarvis. 'We've always said we wanted to be popular. We don't consider ourselves to be cool, though,' he says, crossing his maroon corduroy-decked legs. 'The idea of cool is a joke, in't it? Being out of it – "I'm so cool that I can't function as a human being". I don't think there's anything interesting in that.'

'Cool is like money,' Russell adds. 'You build it up in order to blow it.' ●

A month or so before 'Bullets Over Broadway' receives its world première at the Venice Film Festival, Woody Allen is in London to audition actresses for his next movie. Dressed casually, he seems both warmer and more relaxed than might be expected; he's happy to answer any question, frequently laughs that strange, nasal, breath-catching laugh familiar from his movies, and speaks openly – albeit with sadness and, yes, some bitterness – about reactions to events in his personal life a couple of years ago. Far from the portrayals of him as depraved monster, neurotic schlemiel or shy, high-minded genius, he's… well, disarmingly normal.

Audiences' perceptions of Woody have always been complicated by the fact that his films – confessional in tone, set in the upper middle-class New York milieu he himself inhabits, and usually revolving around the artistically inclined characters he plays – inadvertently encourage us to draw parallels between the real man and his fictional creations. Ever since 'Annie Hall', in which he first played a character not so different from himself, involved with a woman not so different from his real-life lover Diane Keaton, movie-goers have often felt that his work contained clues to his off-screen existence; that they somehow 'know' him in a way they'd never presume to think they understood any other filmmaker. Hence the disappointment when he elects to do something that doesn't conform to his fans' expectations – when he makes a serious drama, say, or doesn't himself appear in a movie. Hence, too, the hysterical sense of betrayal felt by many when it was revealed that he'd taken up with Soon-Yi, or that Mia Farrow had accused him of child molestation in her fight to deny him custody of their children.

Woody's reaction to the controversy surrounding his private life has been sensibly pragmatic; he has simply carried on working, hopeful that the hysteria would eventually die down and that we'd get back to appreciating his films as movies rather than as putative films-à-clef. And so the fact that 'Bullets Over Broadway' gleaned seven Oscar nominations – including best direction and screenplay for Woody, and best supporting performances for Dianne Wiest (who deservedly won), Jennifer Tilly and Chazz Palminteri – not only suggests that he's firmly reinstated as a major player in the movie world, but shows that his work hasn't suffered from his recent trials and tribulations. With several genuinely great movies to his name ('Zelig', 'Hannah and Her Sisters' and 'Husbands and Wives' are my top three) and many more that tower head and shoulders over most other American screen comedies of the period, as one of the most consistently rewarding filmmakers of the past 25 years, Woody Allen is to be cherished, regardless of whatever one may feel about his off-screen life.

'I didn't feel I should be repentant for anything; it was the world thatshould be repentant to me.'

Geoff Andrew: 'Bullets Over Broadway' moves from John Cusack's opening line, 'I'm an artist', to his denying at the end that he's an artist. And he's a better man for it. Is the movie about life being more important than art?

Woody Allen: Not to me. All I wanted to show was that the artist has to be a natural-born artist. There are people who have all the outer trappings of art – they study it, live in the Bohemian section of town and surround themselves with other pretentious people who argue about art – but they're not artists, they just live that life. Whereas the genuine artist can be anything. Chazz [Palminteri], in the movie, is like that; though he's a gangster, he happens to have been born with a gift. It's easier to see in music – like Errol Garner in jazz, who never learns to read but just sits down at the piano and has a huge, a huge amount to say with it – but it's true in writing and acting or any other art form.

So is your film partly an attack on art that is cut off from reality? In which case, that's also a charge that has been levelled against your own depiction of New York.

True. That's partly what the film's about – Chazz instinctively has a greater sense of, and connection with, how people sound and feel than Cusack does. And it's accurate to say I only deal with a limited side of New York life, but I don't regard that as a valid criticism. I can only write about what I know, and what I write does accurately reflect that stratum of society I have contact with. It's like my acting: I have an incredibly limited range. What I can do I can do, but ask me to go beyond that – say, to play in Chekhov – and it'd be preposterous. So there's only a certain area I can write about – when it comes to more realistic New York things, that is. It'd be tough for me to do a movie like Spike Lee or Scorsese, just as it'd probably be difficult, I think, for them to do movies like mine.

Recently, you've made lighter films that seem rather more distanced from your personal life. Is that a deliberate move on your part to prevent that equation of fiction and reality?

People have done that from the day I started. No, it's not a conscious thing. You know, when you finish a film, you just feel lucky to have an idea for the next, and it could be anything. It's not like I have 20,000 ideas I just pick up. And the worst time in a writer's life – you may know this – is when you're between ideas; when you have something to work on, it's not so bad. So I'm just thrilled to have an idea.

I don't want to go over old ground. But has what happened changed your attitude to life or affected your work?

I don't see it if it has. When you were outside of all that, it looked like it was something that was all-consuming; but inside, at the epicentre of the blast, it wasn't that time-consuming for me. It was in the hands of lawyers all the time. Now naturally, I'd speak to my lawyer, sometimes every day, for 15 minutes or half an hour on the phone, but the rest of the

Spike Lee

from 'Malcolm X' in T.O. 1172, by **Brian Case**

In the dynamite political atmosphere of the '60s, many anticipated the sort of carnage patented by the slave Nat Turner, who in 1831 rampaged through Virginia's colonial mansions with his fellow slaves, butchering 57 whites in their beds before the Army caught and hanged him. 'There's a shit-storm coming,' warned Norman Mailer.

However, to date the storm is still hovering over the USA in a holding pattern. Over a quarter of a century later, racial tensions appear essentially the same. The Rodney King beating – 'This gorilla's in a mist,' quipped an LAPD officer – resulted in leaderless riots not dissimilar to the riots in 1965, 1967 and 1968. The crop of charismatic black leaders and spokesmen that the '60s threw up have either been killed or driven into exile; certainly they haven't been replaced. The new generation is dimly aware of Martin Luther King and Malcolm X, but reserves its veneration for black heroes in sport and showbiz. 'Yeah, but who was Malcolm IX?' asked a Harlem teenager. Aiming to dispel this ignorance is Spike Lee's $33 million biopic, 'Malcolm X', starring Denzel Washington and based on an original screenplay by James Baldwin.

'Angela Davis, Huey Newton, Bobby Seale, Stokely Carmichael – destroyed by the police, FBI, CIA, got killed, run off, put in jail, the movement discredited, all the rest of it,' recounts Lee. 'Black history isn't taught in schools and parents don't teach their children, so it's gonna be lost. There's a whole lotta stuff now about black-Jewish conflicts, but any Jewish kid in the world, the first thing he's gonna learn about is the Holocaust. That's one thing I respect Jewish people for. They make sure their history is passed down. Malcolm is in a long line of people. Booker T Washington, WEB DuBois, Marcus Garvey, Adam Clayton Powell Senior, Dr King and – who did the movie end with? – Nelson Mandela. I hope "Malcolm X" broke down that door and films about African-American history can be made now.' Promoting the film in the States, Lee demanded a public holiday so black families could see his film and learn.

Spike read Malcolm's autobiography at Junior High School, though the bias was towards Martin Luther King whose non-violent Civil Rights movement was more convenient to the authorities. 'A *lot* more convenient. Not that there was any love for Dr King either, but his methods were less of a bitter pill to swallow.'

'*Saw?*' exclaimed Spike when I told him I'd seen Malcolm here towards the end of his life. At that time, Malcolm was in the throes of yet another transformation, and closing the gap with King. 'I'm man enough to tell you that I can't put my finger on exactly what my philosophy is now,' he was telling reporters, 'but I'm flexible.' Spike looked at me as if I shouldn't have been there.

Malcolm started life as Malcolm Little, became the hustler Detroit Red and drifted into street crime after his father was killed by the Ku Klux Klan. In prison, with time to read, he became converted to the Nation of Islam, a Black Muslim sect led by Elijah Muhammad. On release, he soon became the movement's star orator, and hot copy for the media who saw him as a dangerous black supremacist. 'By any means necessary' spread dread. Commenting on the assassination of JFK, he caused another storm. 'Being an old farm boy myself, chickens coming home to roost never did make me sad; they've always made me glad.'

The Nation of Islam censured him, and during the growing rift, he travelled to Mecca and revised his views on race, later telling Dr King's wife that it was his extremism that made the middle ground possible. He condemned Elijah Muhammad for his 'religious fakery' and personal immorality. 'We had the best organisation the black man's ever had – niggers ruined it!' he told Alex Haley bitterly. He became a marked man. His home was firebombed. He was assassinated in 1965, aged 39, while speaking at Harlem's Audubon Ballroom, by what looked like a firing squad. 'They know I didn't harm Malcolm but he made war against me,' protested Elijah Muhammad, as his following dwindled. 'His foolish teaching brought him to his own end… He was a star who went astray.'

And Malcolm became a martyr. Spike Lee, who was six

> **'Black history isn't taught in schools and parents don't teach their kids.'**

when Malcolm died, loves him. 'Yes, that's a fair statement. There's nobody like that now. I mean, how many people today are comparable with Winston Churchill? People like that only come around once every 50 years.'

White liberals may find some of the Nation of Islam's doctrines unpalatable. You can see the point in refusing to vote or be conscripted, though the latter cost Muhammad Ali – 'no Viet-Cong never called me nigger' – his world heavyweight crown. The theology, however, is something else: rapprochement between the races is impossible; blacks originally inhabited the moon; trillions of years ago, black scientist Dr Yakub made the white man by mistake, while trying to make a devil.

'But you can say that about any religion,' says Spike. 'The parting of the Red Sea and Noah's ark? How's that any different to Yakub, the evil scientist? If you believe it, you believe it without any reservations. But this was a great deviation from Islam, and that's why Muslims never considered the Nation of Islam to be the real thing.' Spike has never joined any organised religion, though he's used Nation of Islam bodyguards – the Fruit of Islam – as security on his films since 'Do The Right Thing', and flew to Chicago to get clearance to make his film from Minister Louis Farrakhan, current head of the movement.

'We declare our right on this earth to be a man, to be a human being, to be respected as a human being, to be given the right of a human being, in this society, on this Earth, in this day, which we intend to bring into existence by any means necessary.' (Malcolm X)

'The United States could be brought down to its knees with a rag and some gasoline and a bottle.' (Black Panther spokesman)

'Will the machine-gunners please step forward.' LeRoi Jones

1993

Spike Lee

The abstemiousness of Islam appeals to him. 'No one has devised a programme with relation to drug addicts and alcoholics the way the Nation of Islam did. Elijah Muhammad was a marvellous teacher. He built it into a great organisation, self-help, buy black, do for ourselves, black business – but at the same time he was a human being, he wasn't a god, and he had faults. He had flaws.' One flaw was multiple adulteries, a discovery which tested the faithful Malcolm to his limits. 'Elijah wasn't at all charismatic as a public speaker. He didn't have the oratorical skills that Malcolm had. He had a bad speech impediment. The way that Al Freeman Jr portrays him in the film, that's the way Elijah Muhammad spoke.'

The racial conflicts of the '60s were never settled. Burn, baby, burn! White Americans watching the 1968 Olympics were shaken when legions of black American medallists ascended the podium – Gold, Silver, Bronze – and drew on black gloves to raise their fists in the Black Panther salute to 'The Star Spangled Banner'. On the Southside of Chicago a black in a pith helmet walked the length of a supermarket aisle to stand on my foot and told me I was standing on his.

There's plenty of residual fear out there. Critics had feared riots in the wake of 'Do The Right Thing'. 'Malcolm X' is out of the same bag. 'Somebody could definitely be killed behind this movie. Hopefully it won't be me,' Lee told *Vanity Fair*. Professionally provocative, today he was Mary Poppins. 'There's no need for the white audience to be frightened. Come and see this film and be entertained and enlightened. People who love cinema, who love big movies, I think it will knock them out.'

But there are problems beyond the three hours 20 minutes running time. 'How many speeches to include, that was always a big issue.' And feminists will not be pleased. 'We must protect our most valuable property: our women' went the slogan. 'You can never fully trust any woman,' Malcolm told Alex Haley. Vanity was their downfall. Spike nodded 'Feminists'll have a big problem with that but that's the role of women in the Islamic religion altogether. Wearing veils, never showing your body, walking behind your man. It would be very hard to be a feminist and be a Muslim.'

Did *he* trust women?

'Women can be trusted.'

White men?

'Some white men. I don't trust Clarence Thomas and he's black,' he snickered.

In one scene we see the young Malcolm impressing his gang with Russian roulette, and later confessing that he'd palmed the bullets. He hadn't wanted this in the autobiography lest the deception confused the faithful. Spike overrode that. 'We were wavering about what should we show? In the end Denzel decided we'd show him palming the bullets. Shows he wasn't stupid.'

Far from revolutionary in appearance, Malcolm was indistinguishable from an Ivy League executive. His message comprised family values, abstinence, no sport, prayer. 'Stuff like that doesn't go in or out of fashion,' says Lee. 'Being educated, being healthy, not using drugs or smoking, stuff like that – that's beyond being trendy.'

Drugs destroyed a generation of blacks from Bird down. 'There look – I got my scars just like those Jews had their numbers. This was *our* Holocaust,' a jazz musician once told me, rolling up his sleeve to show me his tracks. It is widely believed that hard drugs entered the ghetto in the '40s via the Mafia, courtesy of the US government, as part of the reward to Lucky Luciano for leaning on the waterfront unions and aiding the Allied invasion of Sicily. Born into a jazz household, Spike saw the effects of drugs himself. His father, bassist Bill Lee, took a fall in 1991 for buying heroin.

'Yes. There's a scene where Denzel says, "There would not be drugs in Harlem if white men didn't want them to be there. There would not be alcohol, prostitution. Every time you open up that bottle, that's a government seal you're breaking." Remember in "The Godfather" where all of the Family are sitting together talking about getting into narcotics and Don Corleone says, "Okay, I'll go in as long as long as you keep it in the black community," and someone else says, "They're animals anyway. Let them lose their souls." That's why drugs for a long time wasn't thought of as a problem, but the minute it started to invade into white suburbia, then it becomes a propblem, then… Same thing happened with AIDS. As long as AIDS was detained among hispanics, gays and blacks, it was not on the national agenda. Then it hit heterosexual white suburbia – then it becomes a problem. Then you get the money to find the cure!'

Black music powerpacks much of the film. John Coltrane's widow, Alice, allowed him to use 'Alabama' for the footage in 'X' of Dr King's march on Montgomery. 'Yeah. That's what he wrote it for.' Perhaps out of the cultural imperialism that drove Spike to wrest the project from Norman Jewison, the director is no fan of Tavernier's 'Round Midnight' nor Eastwood's 'Bird'. 'I had objections but I realised at the same time they are artists and they pursued their artistic vision. I just found it odd that the Red Rodney character had a much more significant part than the Dizzy Gillespie character in "Bird" and that the part played by Dexter Gordon seemed to be a child. I'm just tired of this image of the great jazz musician always ending up being an alcoholic or a broken-down heroin addict. You never really saw any humour in those films – so dark and sombre, always raining outside. It wasn't always so down.'

Amusing to learn that when Lee shot a video on Miles Davis, he met his match in truculence. 'He cursed me out left and right during the making of that video. He could be gruff. He was like that. He knew my father, he was joking around.'

To Miles, all whites were muthafuckers. 'Well, he used to say that about Cicely Tyson too – it wasn't just white men he was talking about. But for me the funniest thing Miles Davis ever said was, he was being interviewed, and they asked him, "Miles, if you were about to die, what would your last act be?" "I would grab the nearest white person and choke the shit outa him!"'

For the first time, Spike laughs uproariously. 'Think he'd make a good movie?' he asks, slyly. ●

'There's no need for the white audience to be frightened. Come and see this film.'

Derek Jarman

from 'Blue yonder' in T.O. 1200, by **Paul Burston**

'All I see in AIDS films is sentimentality,' Derek Jarman disclosed to me in October 1991. 'That isn't how I feel about it at all.' The occasion of our meeting was the release of his 'Edward II', a film referred to by at least one critic as 'Jarman's death work' – an intimation of the fact that, having battled with the HIV virus for almost five years, few people really expected him to make another feature. What I wanted to know was why, as someone who had taken the bold decision to go public about his illness, he still hadn't addressed it explicitly as a film director. Jarman was adamant: 'The experience of AIDS is simply too wide for anyone to put into one film. For all its talk of death, at least "Edward" arrives with its flags flying. I honestly think that if I had gone and made a film about AIDS it would have put an end to my film-making.'

Two years (and two remarkable feature films) later, Derek Jarman has finally made his 'AIDS film', simply entitled 'Blue': 75 minutes of poetry and extracts from personal diaries, read out against an unchanging blue screen. The monochrome blue symbolises both 'infinite possibility' and his descent into AIDS-related blindness (blue is the colour Jarman saw when he was administered eye drops for a viral infection).

'I really haven't changed my mind about these things,' he insists. 'And I honestly don't think I've been ducking the issue. What always held me back was that it really was going to have to be a very good film. It was always going to have to be the best film I had ever made. And to make matters even more complicated, there was never a situation that presented itself as the obvious scenario. I was always stuck with images. I could have made a film with actors, I suppose, but there's always the question of whether the audience will identify with them. You'd have to get past that hurdle before you even came close to the experience. I simply wasn't prepared to short-change myself. The key to "Blue" was to

do away with images altogether and to make it personal by integrating diary entries into the script. I suppose it's a bit like hearing someone telling stories to keep illness at bay. People do tend to keep watching the blue though, and even to see things that aren't there.'

When 'Blue' was shown as part of the Venice Biennale in June this year, audiences were delirious in their approval. 'It was the first time in my life that I've experienced that kind of unanimous feedback,' Jarman recalls happily. 'I felt like Maria Callas taking a bow at the end of an aria. Really, it was incredible. Everyone stood up and cheered. It's a tough film to watch, and yet I don't think I've ever seen such an enthusiastic response from an audience – certainly not for one of my films. It just confirms to me that it really is the best film that's been done about HIV.'

Seven years after he was first informed that he had been exposed to the HIV virus, Derek Jarman says he doesn't feel he can keep going for very much longer. 'I can feel it all sliding,' he says wearily, perched in an enormous armchair in his flat overlooking Charing Cross Road. 'I've hit this new level of illness, which makes it very hard to concentrate. Even walking down the street is difficult. Some days I just can't get up. I just lie here all day. It's annoying when I want to do a bit of gardening, or some housework, but otherwise I suppose it's quite a relief. It's been such a struggle coping with all of this, always putting a brave face on the world. The thing is, I'm really not worried about kicking the bucket. I just don't want to waste away in hospital for months and months. I'd much sooner just get it all over with quickly. And I have to think of my friends. I don't want them sitting around a hospital bed for months on end.'

> **'It was always going to have to be the best film I had ever made.'**

Similar sentiments echo throughout 'Blue', culminating in Jarman's cool, disembodied declaration that 'I shall not win the battle against the virus, in spite of slogans like "Living With AIDS" – symptomatic of a society that cannot come to terms with death.' He's looking frail these days; the viral infection in his eyes has left him almost totally blind. Daily appointments at the hospital prevent him from escaping to his beloved Dungeness. But 'Blue', he says will, 'in all probability' be his last film: 'I really haven't got the energy or the focus to get something else together. I'm too involved with the daily drips and blips of illness.' Besides which, he says he has grown 'quite tired of the fictions of cinema'.

But for now there is 'Blue', a film quite unlike any he has ever made, a film in which the director who built his reputation on the manipulation of visually arresting images risks it for the quiet simplicity of a blank canvas. 'I always said I would end up painting,' he says with a chuckle. 'And I suppose in a sense that is what I'm doing. I'm sure there will be some people who won't like "Blue", or who won't appreciate why I had to do it. It is very much the kind of film where what you get out depends on what you bring with you. I just hope that people will think about what's happening, even if it's only for the length of the film. I hope they'll get some sense of extra fun and sadness that comes with this illness.' Considering that the physical and emotional agonies that AIDS has put Derek Jarman through, he can't really mean 'extra fun' surely? He laughs. 'Oh, absolutely! There is a strong sense of humour in there. Actually I think it's very important that you stress that.' ●

Kith
and Kinski

Nastassja Kinski interviewed in T.O. 1244,
by **Tom Charity** and **Sheila Benson**,
originally published in **INTERVIEW** magazine Dec 1993

1993

Nastassja Kinski

Nastassja Kinski has the kind of face an artist might paint for a lifetime and still come away unsatisfied. Draped in a python and nothing else, in Richard Avedon's famous photograph, she exudes the same cool, challenging poise: thus far and no further; look but don't touch. Whatever the promise of that voluptuous mouth, she's not giving anything away – just those lips, those eyes…

She was born in 1960, the daughter of a poet, Ruth, and the notorious actor, Klaus Kinski. If she inherited much from her father, it is not immediately apparent on the screen: he is *Sturm und Drang*, Herzog's manic alter ego, she is entirely passive, Wim Wenders' gentle muse. Wenders discovered her dancing in a disco when he was casting the part of a mute teenager in his film 'False Movement': 'She was truly beautiful,' he recalls. 'There was something in the eyes… she was 14 during shooting, she kept laughing in the middle of a take – but she was magnificent. Half the crew fell in love with her, and it was clear from the first rushes that she was all actress, even if she hadn't taken that decision yet.'

She made three more films before Roman Polanski 'discovered' her anew, and launched her to international stardom with the title role in 'Tess' (1979). A beautiful, bloodless adaptation, 'Tess' was shaded by the director's troubles with the American authorities – his affair with the 17-year-old Kinski just the latest in a line of teenage liaisons. For her part, Kinski has shown a complementary predilection for older men – often her directors – that armchair psychologists have been quick to label a father fixation (not that they lack hearsay: Nastassja's first husband – her long-term manager and 17 years her senior – complained he was 'more a father than a husband', and she sued Klaus for libel when he hinted at incest in his scandalous autobiography. Current husband Quincy Jones is 60).

In 1985, after 12 films in five years, Nastassja Kinski all but vanished. She married, had children, worked intermittently in Europe. Presented with Hollywood's semblance of immortali-

ty, she chose real life for herself. Now she's back, working with Wim Wenders for the first time since 'Paris, Texas' in his follow-up to 'Wings of Desire'. Appropriately enough, she's cast as an angel: a spiritual companion to mankind, and an omnipresent observer of human endeavour – but insensible to taste and touch and smell. Perhaps this is as close as we'll come to Nastassja, or any star. Far away, so close…

What feelings did you have playing the guardian angel Raphaela in 'Faraway, So Close'?

I often feel with God and humans and angels that it's up to us to make something or to break it, to do things or not do them. The angels in 'Faraway, So Close' are observers, and they are frustrated because they can't do anything: they can be there, they can soothe, they can speak to people's souls and hearts, but they can't prevent things from happening unless they become human. So their role is kind of a sad one. They say to the humans, 'You think we're far away, but we're really so close. We are nothing, and you are everything to us, and everything's in your power.' I could really understand this – I've always thought it was that way. Faith is important, and yet it's here on earth with each other that we have to do our best.

Wenders says that few films dare to ask 'how to live' and 'what to live for'. What do you live for?

I live for being with the people I love and to live as happily as possible. And you must dare to do as many things as you dream of.

What kind of things?

Anything. Everything. It's important not to treat your dreams as, Oh, they're just dreams. I tell my kids that something can start with a dream and that, more often than not, you can really go for something if you believe in it. I live for my family, and for us to be together and to stay together, even if there are obstacles and the road is rocky. Often there are so many reasons one could go one's own way rather than try to work things out.

> ## 'You must dare to do as many things as you dream of.'

And, if I do things that that are not okay I live for getting up in the morning to make them better and change them, and not to let myself drown in those things. A very dear friend of mine told me this story: There are two brothers. One is ready to be executed – he has basically messed up his life. His brother has had a very beautiful life. It's been hard, but he has done what he has wanted to do. They're both asked 'How did this happen?' The unlucky one says: 'I had a father who was a criminal, who drank, who beat us up and beat my mother up – so what else could I be?' Then the other brother tells the same story about the father and says, 'Well, what else could I be?'

You see, there's a definite choice we all make. Sometimes you see people who've really got it together, and you think, Wow, I bet they had a really cool upbringing. And sometimes they did, but often they didn't at all – and that's the second brother.

Obviously, you made a decision to have a life and not just a career.

'That idealisation, or wanting to idealise your director, is pretty mathematical.'

It wasn't a decision. It's just the way I wanted to live. Often, when you're on a job you're far away, and you know you can't be there with your children, but you want to do both. It's really hard.

You have said you need to idealise your directors.

That, I guess, is how you are when you don't have a father to turn to. When I was little and my father used to work a lot, we always led a very hectic life, a life I didn't particularly like. He was nervous, he couldn't sleep, he was never there. For me, directors were like father figures most of the time. A director tells you what to do and what's right, and he's there when you need him and he's someone you can argue with! He's the father I – and millions of other kids – didn't have. So that's where that comes from.

That idealisation, or wanting to idealise your director, is pretty mathematical. It's also a little bit of an obstacle because you want to grow up and do a movie for what it is. I grew up very fast, and yet part of me was always a child longing for that father figure. But I'm very grateful for my job because it helps me fill the void, at least part of it. Even though things happen by accident, you also unconsciously choose things that help you. I'm sure one reason I chose to do movies was because it enabled me to be part of a family where everybody's trying to work toward the same goal. Another reason is that when I was little I was very quiet – I didn't express myself.

In your first film, Wim Wenders' 'Wrong Movement', you were mute.

Yes, that's true. That's funny!

I remember you juggling in it.

I remember when Wim and his wife asked me to do that film. Wim was so calm he was almost slow-motion – he's less so now than he was then – and I thought that was so different and so nice. He was imaginative when he spoke to us, and everybody really got along, it was just the opposite of what I thought it was

like to do movies. He treated me with a lot of respect and Hanna Schygulla, who was the main actress in the film was like that, too. They created an atmosphere that was like a nest for me, very, very warm.

I felt Wim really cared. We didn't speak much in the next few years, but when he told me the story about this character in 'Paris, Texas' who had had a child and how her relationship with her husband [Harry Dean Stanton] had fallen apart, it really touched me, because I had my baby growing inside me. Wim said, 'I want you for this role because I feel we really know each other. I know you're waiting for your baby and it's a special moment for you.' I'm truly lucky that he saw me and believed in me and truly lucky to have worked with him three times.

Looking at your roles overall, do you see a touch of melancholy, a slight sadness? I know I do a little bit.

(Pause) Maybe. I guess. If you feel that…

Well, few of your characters have been upbeat.

(Giggles)

The circus girl you played in 'One from the Heart' was different. She was just magical.

That was fun to do, but I was so nervous! Coppola is another figure who is devoted to his family. Back then I knew his films, of course, but I was also greatly impressed by the man he was, is. When you went to his house, he was always with his wife and kids; it was never just him. To be there was a dream. Then we worked and did the film, and I was no less happy, but to be with the family was so special. You take one look at a family like that and, no matter what happens, you know that nothing could ever break them apart. Quincy is the same with his children.

In 'Maria's Lovers' you share a lovely scene with Robert Mitchum. I think you brought out a real tenderness in him that you don't see very often.

First of all, I really admired him, but I didn't know him. He didn't talk much. You could tell he needed time to warm up. But Robert was extremely helpful to me and told me things, which I wrote down, and, of course, I sat and listened to his stories and just loved to be there. Then he gave me a little ivory elephant – I think it was an antique – with a chain at the tail and a teeny, little baby elephant attached. In the story of 'Maria's Lovers' the son comes home from the war and tries to have a baby with my character, Maria, but they can't have a baby. Robert said that baby elephant was the little baby. And right after that film I had my first baby.

I think people are fascinated by who you are. There is something about you that is very special to them.

Why?

I think they see you as your own person, as somebody who strikes a balance. How do you feel about living in America again?

I'm happy to be here. You know the Tao? It says all is one, and only what is one can succeed. Because of the things that happen everywhere, far away from you and close to you, we all know at any one moment what's going on. And you cannot escape that. It brings us apart, and it brings us together to enable change. And these two extremes are always there, everywhere. ●

HP
Source

Harold Pinter interviewed in T.O. 1204, by **Steve Grant**

Given the importance of territory in the works of Harold Pinter, it's an unsettlingly tight fit as the two of us peruse the pictures in his toilet. There are just three, which provide a pleasing shorthand to the life and inspirations of our greatest living dramatist: a painting of Sir Len Hutton, Ashes hero and Pinter's favourite cricketer; a photograph from the mid '60s when Pinter had 'The Caretaker' and 'The Homecoming' playing simultaneously at theatres across Broadway. And, most imposingly, smack over the seat, a poster: a commemorative poem by John Berger sitting underneath a photograph of one-time Socialist Chilean Defence Minister, Orlando Letelier, tortured, exiled and, in Washington DC in 1976, car-bombed.

Cricket. Theatre. Politics. 'Look at that! Amazing!' mutters HP as we survey the scene of the pencil-slim, pensive Letelier walking down some steps in Santiago, surrounded by heavily-armed military. 'I'm never going to take it down as long as I live,' and yes, you do feel a sense of the terror, menace and desolation lying at the heart of Pinter's most powerful work in that juxtaposition of one man among many thugs.

The khazi in question is in the lavish mews house in Holland Park which adjoins the Pinter home and which functions as den, study and also a repository of Pinter's life and works. We have gazed lovingly at his full set of 'Wisden' volumes going back to 1862 ('though the first few are facsimiles, I'm afraid'), the bookshelves devoted to cricket books which Pinter notes are more numerous than a similarly impressive collection of poetry, his first creative love. There is the drinks tray, a sofa, the spacious writing desk complete with yellow pads for his writing, more books, and a fetching photograph of Lady Antonia Fraser. Outside there is a bookcase stacked with the latest Faber editions of Pinter's works; downstairs a fax machine and other instruments of mass communication for a man who currently has productions on or in preparation in New York, Osaka, Berlin, Paris, Stockholm, Amsterdam and throughout the People's Republic of China, where the Youth Theatre of Shanghai are touring with 'The Lover', a teasing sexual comedy first seen here in 1963.

'I want to put something on the record,' Pinter declares in that famously rich voice which once belonged to a jobbing actor called 'David Barron' 44 years ago. 'The record seems to imply that I haven't written anything since 1978. I looked it up the other day; I read that I'd been blocked for 15 years. I've actually written six short plays, but *plays*, including "A Kind of Alaska" which won an award somewhere. I've also written seven film scripts which were important to me, including "The French Lieutenant's Woman", so that's seven and six, I make 13. It's about time that was recorded. To say that I've been doing fuck-all for 15 years is a slight exaggeration.'

Perusing the Pinter cuttings file in preparation for an interview is rather like being marked down for a kamikaze run or a raid on the Emperor's bunker. The tantrums are well documented, violent rows at the drop of a dictator's name; an assault on an American ambassador's ear; reducing friends and strangers to tears; denouncing the jackals of the press; celebrated fallings-out with loyal friends like Simon Gray and Sir Peter Hall. And yet the chance of a rare audience with a man who made us redefine our attitude to communication, gave an adjective to the dictionary, and jolted our belief in a playwright's control over his creations, is worth the risk.

> **'I can't be sacked, you see, because I haven't got a job. Therefore, I'll continue to say whatever I like.'**

As it turns out, Pinter is ever the courteous host, even if the initial seating arrangements seem to resemble stage directions from 'The Caretaker'. Pinter has never really forgiven the intrusions into his private life when his marriage to actress Vivien Merchant broke up spectacularly in 1975 after his affair with Lady Antonia. The latterday brickbats of 'Champagne Socialist' and 'Angry Old Man' haven't helped either, though some of the maturer critics have been perceptively tolerant of Pinter's increasing political activity, an interest which dates from the overthrow of the Chilean Allende government in 1973. The *Independent on Sunday*'s Irving

Wardle remarked that 'it is easy to leap on to the barricades when you are 20, to ascend them with the creaking joints of late middle-age is an altogether more heroic act; it also means you are unlikely to climb down again in a hurry.'

This doesn't mean that Pinter doesn't have to answer for his actions occasionally; one close associate who wished to remain anonymous talks of 'a tendency with so many politicos to care more about mankind as a whole than the feelings of people in particular', while his undoubted wealth and some of his more emotional political statements do give some ammo to his snipers. But it's also unheard of for the people of Germany, Peru or Eastern Europe to question the actions of Günter Grass, Mario Vargas Llosa or Pinter's close friend Vaclav Havel just because they are writers.

Pinter: 'The attacks represent a well-established tradition of mockery of the artist in this country. I was going to say "intellectual", but I'm not that, I'm just a working writer; but any writer who pops his head over the trenches and dares to speak in this country is really placed outside the pale. I suppose it stems from the fact that a writer is supposed to be some kind of entertainer; it's true in the United States too. But this has never been the case in Europe or Latin America. All that I can say is that if they have contempt for me it is as nothing to the contempt I have for them, and I really mean that. Not because they are insulting me, but because they are insulting standards of truth and seriousness which I believe should obtain in any civilised society.

'There was a time when I was attacked by everyone in sight and I've survived that. So there's no way I can go under. I did a programme on Channel 4, "Opinions", on American foreign policy and I was accused of "ranting", of being a "ranting emotional playwright", the usual accusation the press deliver to someone they wish to discredit. But I got a record number of letters from people who said, "We feel the same way as you do, but we can't say it as a bus conductor or a factory worker because if we do we'll be ostracised or even sacked." But I can't be sacked, you see, because I haven't got a job. Therefore, I'll continue to say whatever I like.'

Pinter says that family relationships and death are at the heart of his new play, 'Moonlight'.

'One thing that's happened to me since 1977 is that my mother died last year, she was 88. But I'm not at all sure the play comes from that fact. Obviously as you're older you think about death more; you have it on your body; but there's so much death about. This is a strong element in my political nausea.'

He says that the 'energy you expend in writing gives you more energy. I feel quickened by it.' Certainly he's not all gloom; the joys of cricket calm this man, so much so that I suggest if 'the past is a mist', as the dying man in 'Moonlight' avers, then cricket with its emphasis on holding the moment by the use of statistics, is a thrice-blessed activity. Pinter shows me the fixture list for his own team, the Gaieties, for which he manages, captains and participates. 'Get this right: won 9, drawn 9, lost 0. And this is a high-quality fixture list with Oxted and Sidcup left. We've got two fellows opening for us, Falkus and Smith, they made 264 in two hours 20 minutes for the first wicket. Make what you will of that, but I reckon they could open for England.' Messrs Atherton and Fletcher have been warned. ●

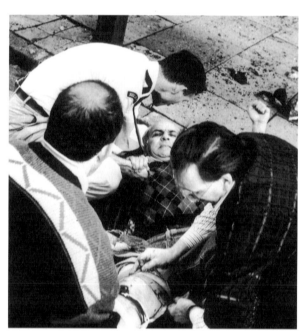

Why?

an **IRA officer** interviewed in T.O. 1176,
by **Denis Campbell**

They frisked me quickly, put me into the back of a car, then sealed my eyes with two pieces of Sellotape – 'If we're stopped, just say we're showing you the area.' Ballymurphy, a staunchly Republican stronghold in west Belfast, early 1993: such is the routine involved in meeting the Provisional IRA.

A two-minute drive, with none of my three minders saying a word. Then a 30-second stumble: first, stony ground, somewhere windy and open; then smooth concrete; guided all the way at both elbows by unseen arms. Next: helped up a step into a house, directed into a side room, eased into a chair and told to wait. About ten minutes later: 'Okay', Sellotape removed and a nod from the burly one, his moustache the only distinct feature of a face hidden by a navy blue parka, motioning me to go upstairs. As I climbed the stairs, my minders turned to face the wall; I looked straight ahead. He was waiting in an upstairs bedroom, wearing a cream-coloured balaclava with only his eyes and mouth visible, a green army-style jacket, well-worn jeans and trainers. There was no hand-shake or greeting, just a nod of recognition and a hand raised to show me to sit down on the single bed opposite. No tape recorder, naturally; shorthand only.

'I'm a member of the General Headquarters staff of the Irish Republican Army,' he said. 'I am active in the IRA. I am here today as a representative of Oglaigh na hEireann [the Irish Volunteers, the IRA's name in Irish]. But in my words the British Government will find echoed the words of IRA volunteers right across the arena of conflict.'

London in 1993 is a city on a permanent war footing. Armed roadblocks, daily transport disruptions caused by 'security alerts', businesses unable to get insurance against bomb damage, public paranoia about carrier bags mistakenly left on tube platforms – all proof of the insidious effects of IRA terrorism, or just the threat of it, on the everyday lives of millions of Londoners. And all because of the efforts of maybe only a dozen IRA activists. Unpalatable though it may be, 1992 witnessed some of the IRA's most spectacular 'successes' in its 20-year-old campaign against London. In April, its massive Baltic Exchange blast caused an estimated £800 million worth of damage and prompted insurance companies to withdraw bomb cover for London businesses. In November, it launched a car-bomb attack on Downing Street, not long after security in Whitehall was increased after a previous assault by mortar-bomb. Meanwhile, leaked minutes of a top-level Scotland Yard meeting revealed that it had 'little intelligence' about IRA activities in London.

No wonder the IRA man opposite me, reflecting on 1992, expressed such satisfaction with the year's operations. They, and IRA strikes since, 'are demonstrating to the British Government that they haven't learned the lessons of Belfast: that regardless of what they do to harden so-called "security" in London, which in itself brings massive disruption, we will continue to strike at the heart of their government and administration.

'There's clearly no alternative to the use of force because the British Government have consistently proved, not only in Ireland but elsewhere, that they do not listen to the force of argument. The argument of force is forced upon us,.'

Over the next 75 minutes, he discussed in unprecedented detail the Provos' campaign of terror in London last year, apologised for the IRA 'inadvertently' killing four civilians and answered Scotland Yard accusations about 'vague' bomb warnings with a counter-claim that the police in London 'play with people's lives' by deliberately ignoring certain warnings. In the light of the Camden Market bomb last weekend, the IRA's claim now seems even more suspect.'It is not our intention to kill or injure members of the civilian population, in Britain or the Six Counties or anywhere else. Were it our intention to do so, the death toll would be appalling. Let's not forget that the IRA don't go to the lengths of delivering warnings if it's their intention to kill and injure.'

So what would the IRA say to the families of the four people who died last year as a result of their actions?

'We would offer sincere apologies. We would tell them that having suffered similar loss ourselves in a very personal sense, we understand what they're going through. And we in no way attempt to remove from ourselves the blame for those deaths. But they are victims of this conflict just as much as we are, and we are victims of this conflict just as much as they are. The people with the power to resolve this conflict ultimately share the responsibility for all deaths arising from it. That will cut no ice with the families; we don't expect it to. We have robbed those families of loved ones. It's highly unlikely that any words of ours will be of any comfort to them, but we apologise unreservedly for those deaths and any other civilian deaths which occur as a result of our operations.' ●

1994

By '94 we were all confirmed ravers, so when the Criminal Justice Act kicked us indoors, we scraped the mud off, carried on dancing and let them invent the superclub. Kurt hurt. Jungle started its piratical rumblings and they finished off the hole that went to France.

January
Michael Jackson reaches an out of court settlement after being accused of child sexual abuse.

February
Stephen Milligan MP dies, apprently as a result of a sex game gone wrong.

Frederick and Rosemary West are arrested and charged with murder as bodies are dug up in their Gloucester home.

Age of consent for gay sex is cut from 21-years to 18-years.

April
Kurt Cobain, lead singer with Nirvana, commits suicide at his Seattle home.

May
Brazilian racing driver Ayrton Senna is killed during the Italian Grand Prix.

The ANC and Nelson Mandela win the first multi-racial elections in South Africa taking nearly two-thirds of the vote.

The Channel Tunnel is opened by the Queen and President Mitterand of France.

July
Tony Blair becomes the latest Labour Party leader, after the death of John Smith.

Brazil win World Cup, after beating Italy on penalties.

OJ Simpson goes on trial accused of murdering his ex-wife and her friend Ronald Goldman.

November
Serial killer Jeffrey Dahmer is beaten to death in jail.

George Foreman becomes one of sport's most improbable heroes when he defeats Michael Moorer at the age of 45 to take the heavyweight title.

December
Russian troops occupy Chechnya.

Pulp Fiction
There's plenty of sharp, sassy, profane dialogue, and there are plenty of acute, funny references to pop culture, though the talk sometimes delays the action.

Four Weddings And A Funeral
A British comedy that's classy and commercial - and, most important, very funny. Genuine feel-good entertainment.

The Shawshank Redemption
This is an engrossing, superbly acted yarn, while the Shawshank itself is a truly form-idable mausoleum.

Massive Attack - Protection (Circa)
Protection is a work of power and spartan charm and another classic work from Bristol. Blue Lines

was an expressive classic; Protection leaves it standing.

Blur - Parklife (Food)
At the moment, Blur remain a better idea than a band. But when their execution becomes as deft as their vision, they'll be untouchable. Parklife confirms that it's a matter of when rather than if.

Oasis - Definitely Maybe (Creation)
Be Here Now is the sound of a band who think that just because they are important, they should *sound* impor-tant. But that was never the point. It's a superb 40-minute album lost inside a quite good 72-minute one. Too much sonic, not enough super.

The boy with the ice cream face

He was mobbed by gangs of fans so desperate for souvenirs he had suits made with detachable sleeves.

Tony Curtis interviewed in T.O. 1230, by **Maria Lexton**

The once raven-black hair is now a distinguished shade of grey; the famously piercing blue eyes are hidden behind a pair of dark glasses; he's carrying a few extra pounds and he's a little shorter than I'd expected, but there's no mistaking the swagger in his walk. Tony Curtis, living legend of the silver screen, is an instantly recognisable figure, his image engraved on our memories as a solid-gold twentieth-century icon.

His film career began in the late '40s at Universal Studios where he was known as 'the boy with the ice cream face'. With his pretty-boy good looks and 100 per cent beefcake physique, he was swooned over by screaming teenagers and mobbed by gangs of fans so desperate for souvenirs he had to have suits especially made with detachable sleeves. Before Dean, before Presley, Curtis was the ultimate teen dream, the prototypical '50s pin-up. 'Yes,'

> **'We could do what we liked. I could pick up any girl in the world I wanted. And yes, I picked up a lot!'**

he agrees in his hard-bitten Bronx accent, 'I was. And I loved it all. I was the first. The beginning of it all in a movable feast. There wasn't any great novel; I didn't write a great song; I didn't give a great performance in a movie. I came along with a hairstyle and jeans… into perpetuity. Hey, I'll take that!'

The smile that plays constantly round Curtis's curling lips breaks into a broad grin; his chuckle is low, throaty and infectious; he's lost none of the charm that carried him through his chequered career and, though his looks may have faded with his 68 years, the Greek God profile is as captivating as ever. This is the man who influenced a generation; as much a part of '50s culture as blue jeans, Coca Cola and rock 'n' roll. Curtis pioneered the Italian look that dominated that decade: the sharp suits and the slick hairstyle that characterised the chisel-faced spiv spawned a stream of imitators who in turn became teen idols – Paul Anka, Frankie Avalon, Dion – and brought the incidental artefacts – espresso bars, Lambretta scooters, stiletto heels and winkle-picker shoes –into the fashion forefront. Heady days for a young man in Hollywood.

'The whole era was very glamorous,' he recalls, 'and we all believed that bullshit. We all thought we were bigger than life

– as though they were shooting stock footage of us all the time. Every time we moved somebody was photographing us. I was never sure I was alone. I was so convinced there was always someone with a camera looking at me I thought I'd better be careful I didn't make any unusual noises and please let me shave properly because I'm being photographed… forever.' He chuckles delightedly at the memory. 'At the time it was an élite group – if I may call us élite – of us hanging out together at the time. We were élite because there wasn't anything we couldn't get; anything we wanted was ours. There was RJ Wagner, Rory Calhoun, Tab Hunter, Rock Hudson, Barbara Lawrence, Debra Pagett, Mara Corday, Natalie Wood came a little later, Jimmy Dean was at Warner Bros, Marlon got there a year before us. I got in the movies in the summer of '48. From the winter of '48 to the spring of '50, those 18 months I remember them so clearly.' He leans in close, his eyes now the colour of faded denim. 'We socialised with each other; we finished work, and at the end of the day couldn't wait to get in our cars, go home, clean up; eight o'clock we'd eat at Dolores' Drive-in, then hit the clubs: Morocco, Ciro's, Mocambo, Lucy's, and the Club Gala, where Spago's restaurant is now. All-night madness – we didn't know there was a tomorrow.

'We could do what we liked. I could pick up any girl in the world I wanted. And yes,' he smiles. 'I picked up a lot! I did indeed. Hallelujah! I was sure it said somewhere in small print in my contract that I was allowed the privilege of making out with any of the er, non-leading ladies on the set. Anything that moved actually; though certainly not a Buick,' Curtis is now laughing uproariously, 'but close. There were a lot of girls and it was a lot of fun for all of us. Post air-conditioning and before television was a great period, and our behaviour was created by the times. There was no great rush for cocaine; it wasn't available. We'd never heard of it. We smoked joints, marijuana, we'd all puff away. It was a wonderful time.

'There were casualties. I took out Suzan Ball, a beautiful, dark-haired girl with a magnificent figure, for a while. We'd go for drives down to the beach and talk about what we would do if we achieved success in the movies. We both wanted to

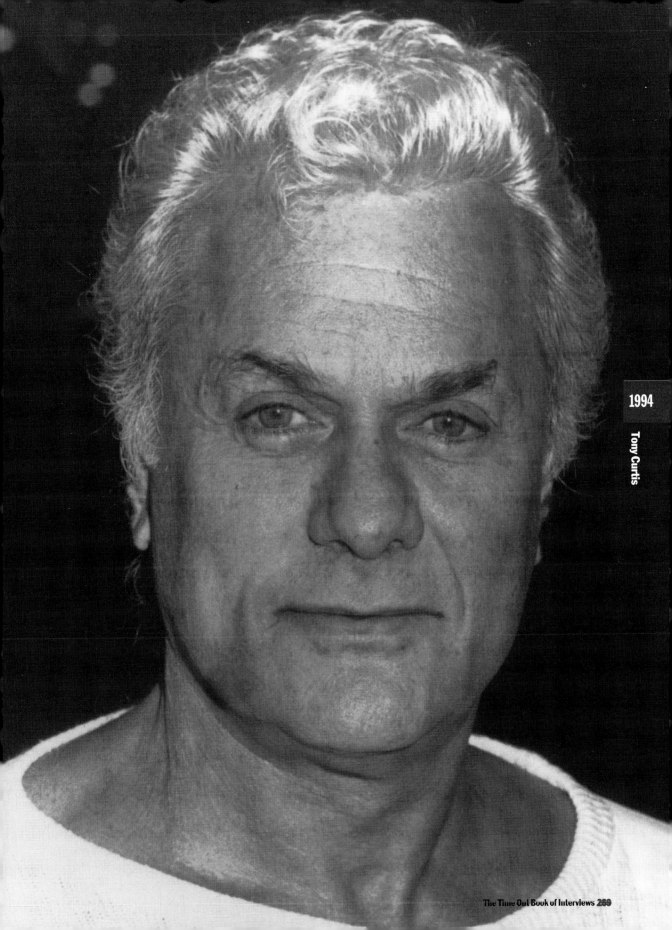

1994

Tony Curtis

be movie stars in the most intense way. She was cast as a dancer in a Jeff Chandler movie but she fell during one of the rehearsals and injured her knee. A few months later they diagnosed the pain in that leg as cancer. They had to amputate her leg, and a year later she was dead at 22. I often think about her. Susan Cabot was another lost soul from those days. She was going with Prince Hussein, the future king of Jordan, until he found out she was Jewish. She also went with Rock Hudson, which shows you how smart she was. Her son killed her with a weight-lifting bar in 1986, claiming she'd driven him to it.

'They arranged for me to go out with Ann Blyth for a time, and then Wanda Hendrix, who was married to Audie Murphy.

'They say that licking frogs will end your depression. Well, it certainly doesn't hurt the frog any.'

After she and Audie separated, I, like a fool, called Wanda and started taking her out – the Congressional Medal winner's wife – I wasn't only stupid, I was dumb. He was the war hero of America, who'd blow your fucking head off quicker than he'd look at you. My brain was in my dick. She was a lovely woman, but I had to avoid Audie for months. These were the women I went out with. All Hungarians are crazy about women, you know, and I knew all those beautiful girls.

'About a year after I got to California, in 1949, I met Marilyn Monroe for the first time. She was still trying to get a contract at Universal, or anywhere else. When she'd walk down the street, everybody would look at her. She was wearing see-through blouses then, which was shocking in those days – a fantastic-looking woman. We had an early relationship, an affair then. I took her out and in a weekend the relationship was over. There's something very intimate about that experience that I just don't want to share with anybody.

'I liked Marilyn. I didn't hate working with her on "Some Like It Hot", that got all out of proportion. She was okay. We were good friends. But after that film she was finished. All those stories about her and the Kennedys couldn't possibly be true. Just look at the chronology. After "Some Like It Hot" in 1959, Marilyn was going downhill fast – she was slovenly and unappealing. Kennedy was elected in 1960. She busted up with Arthur Miller just about a year later. Who would want to have an affair with her then? If she had an affair with the Kennedys, it had to be in 1955 or maybe 1956. After that she was unmanageable, unpleasant, dirty – no one wants to acknowledge that. People have a time warp. They imagine the Marilyn that the Kennedys were supposed to be jumping on was the Marilyn of the early '50s. But she wasn't.

'Let me tell you: The Kennedys didn't murder Marilyn. The Mafia didn't murder Marilyn. Marilyn killed Marilyn. Why would a man like Jack or Bob Kennedy go out with a half-drunken, out-of-control woman, particularly when she was married to Joe DiMaggio and Arthur Miller? There were no Kennedys around her in 1957. So when did she start fucking around with the Kennedys? When did they shovel her into an airplane to Washington or to the beach? I heard on TV that the Kennedys gave her poison suppositories. Give me a fucking break. She was such a great cocksucker? Forget it. Nobody's that good.

'By 1959, when "Some Like It Hot" was finished, I predicted she'd never make another movie. It was truly my feeling that she would commit suicide. And I only missed it by a film and a half. "The Misfits" was made in 1960. She was living alone, the poor girl. Where were all her friends then? Where were all those fucking people who love her so much? Where were all these girlfriends of hers, letting her die in that stinking little room, in that stupid little house? There was the sex goddess of our time and she's living alone like an exaggerated bag lady. A lot of us were very depressed over her demise. It was so unnecessary. When she took those pills she always had somebody to call and they'd rush over, take her to the hospital, pump her out... She always had checkpoints. That night, the checkpoint was Peter Lawford. What she didn't know was that Peter was drunker than she was. By the time he realised what she'd been saying it was too late.' Curtis shrugs. 'I know it sounds cynical but I don't give a fuck. I'm just telling you the truth.'

Curtis's autobiography is candid throughout. In the late '70s his alcohol intake increased considerably and he discovered the mind-numbing effects of cocaine, a drug he indulged in until the early '80s when he checked into the Betty Ford clinic. 'There I was, sitting with all these guys – 22, 18, 31 – and the therapist says, "This is the only 58-year-old fuck-up you guys will ever see so you'd better take a good look." That shook me up quicker than anything, I can tell you. I was in a lot of pain. I was angry and frustrated. I didn't like the idea of getting old, I didn't like the idea that I wasn't getting those parts that I wanted any more, I didn't like the idea that I didn't like my wife any more. Whoever it was.' He laughs till the tears fall, then continues softly: 'I was so depressed and so unhappy. I'd started out with such great hopes and aspirations... It wasn't as if I did something deliberately to get it out of hand. I just wasn't smart enough. Right from the start I didn't have the wherewithal or the intelligence or the drive to promote myself in anything other than "The Prince Who Was A Thief" or "The Son of Ali Baba".'

Alexander Mackendrick, director of 'Sweet Smell of Success', the film which saw Curtis in his first real adult film role, once said: 'Tony Curtis has fantastic vanity but no ego.' Would Curtis agree? 'Yeh! Exactly!' he cries, then asks sweetly, 'What does he mean by that? I kind of feel it, though. Instantly, when I read that myself, I looked in the mirror (he poses, hand on hip, and preens like a high school beauty), and said, "Yeah, I can see what he means." I don't propel myself. I'm propelled.'

Tony Curtis may sigh over the might-have-beens but today he's happy about actualities. 'It's a shame we don't start out old and become young,' he mutters thoughtfully.

If that were so I'd be talking to the boy with the ice-cream face. What does that mean? 'I don't know,' he replies. 'Something you lick, if you'll excuse the vernacular. Have you heard about licking frogs? They say that licking frogs will end your depression. Well, it certainly doesn't hurt the frog any.' ●

Jon Ronson at the Brits

from T.O. 1227

Here at Ally Pally – at 'The Brits' Media Room, a squalid, tiny hole jam-packed with frenzied stringers – questions and answers are being volleyed around like a tennis game between the Care Bears. If there were any more complicity between journalist and subject, they'd be cutting straight to the post-coital cigarette. Not that, of course, any investigative probing of 'Two-eyes-one-patch' Gabrielle or Tori 'I'm a dolphin' Amos would trigger an especially scintillating discourse. But still, it'd be nice to hear a line of questioning

'It's nice to know that there are still cunts in the industry and not just vegans.'

slightly more inquisitive than: 'Gabrielle. What does your boyfriend do?'

'Don't want to talk about it.'

'Oh go on.'

'Runs a fast food restaurant.'

'McDonalds?' I yell.

'No,' says Gabrielle.

'Burger King?' shouts Rick Sky from the *Daily Mirror*, smelling a scoop.

'No,' says Gabrielle.

'Kentucky Fried Chicken?' I shriek, warming to my theme.

'Wendy's?'

'No, no,' says Gabrielle.

There is a long, long pause, in which everyone tries to think of something to say. And finally: 'McTuckys?' Silence. 'It's McTuckys!' I yell, in triumph. 'We've got her!'

The glittering prize of the night is a ticket to the after-show party, where there's free salmon, Tori 'I'm a blade of grass' Amos, and John McCarthy who's appearance here amongst the drag queens and pre-teen sensations is a wholly weird coup. The winner of the much hyped Brits v Brats battle has become, I'm afraid, a foregone conclusion with the appearance of this celebrated radiator hugger. Had the NME dumped Bikini Kill and got

in, say, Stephen Hawking to announce Best Male Vocalist, there'd still be a contest.

Furthermore, in employing an appalling, balding, power-crazed asshole called Bernard Docherty to distribute the after-show invitations, the Brits have pulled off a coup. There's more than a sniff of the school bully at work in Docherty's methods. He refuses, for instance, to reward the *Smash Hits* journalist with

a ticket until she admits that she's overweight. 'I'll give a fucking ticket to who I fucking want to,' he says to me, when I interview him on the subject. It is rare – a breath of fresh air – to witness a twat of these dimensions at work, now that the pop world is all Huggy Lovey Boy Next Door. It's nice to know that there are still cunts in the industry and not just vegans.

When I finally make it to the Brits party, a mighty and prominent rock 'n' roll manager corners me, clicks his fingers, a youngster scuttles over, and he proclaims: 'Give Jon some drugs.'

The whole experience is terribly depressing in one respect and not at all depressing in another.

Then somehow, security is breached, and the party is invaded by a horde of screaming fans (the screaming and the frostbite is the only way to distinguish them from this year's crop of teen-sensations: the stars here appear to have been picked at random). I follow a group of youngsters as they scurry around the tables, attempting to locate Take That. Behind us, security are catching up. One of the youngsters gives up, and is ejected. On the way out, I ask her why she gave in so easily.

'I thought it would be different in there,' she explained. 'But it's all fat businessmen.'

Naomi Campbell

from 'Belle, book and scandal' in T.O. 1255, by **Maria Lexton**

It's mid-afternoon, August Bank Holiday Monday, and the carnival crowds are converging on Notting Hill. Music, laughter, shouts and shrieks pierce the ether, producing as much noise as a flock of migrating birds heading for the sun. But not one sound from the streets penetrates the secluded sanctuary of the exclusive Halcyon Hotel on Holland Park where Naomi Campbell is based between transatlantic flights. The silence is suddenly broken by the entrance of the supermodel, gushing greetings with a smile that widens into a huge grin. 'Oh!' she squeals in delight, pointing one long, slender hand down to my feet. 'You're wearing black nail varnish! That's great! Really great! I just lurrve dark polish! What do you think of the colour I'm wearing?'

In an instant she has kicked off her shoes and is wiggling her toes in my direction, simultaneously waving her immaculately manicured, elegantly tapered fingers up to my face, awaiting approval of her wine-red painted nails. She beams with pleasure when complimented, and some sort of bonding process seems to have taken place as she leans towards me to confide: 'I used to mix colours to get this dark red,' she sighs, 'but it never really worked. Mac do one similar… Vino, isn't it…? but this is the best.' She nods emphatically. 'It's new from Chanel!' She sits back for a moment, hands before her face, utterly lost in admiration for this season's shade. ●

Killing Joke

Cannes' hottest ticket on pop-culture
assassins and the comedy of violence.

Quentin Tarantino interviewed in T.O. 1257,
by **Geoff Andrew**

When a big film – a really big film, from a name direc- tor premières in Cannes, the conscientious critic will ensure he's in the queue outside the Palais des Festivals half-an-hour or so before the film begins. But by the time 'Pulp Fiction' made it on to the screen last May, the keen- est members of the audience had been waiting more than 90 minutes; when the doors first opened half an hour earlier, well over 1,000 hacks had been pushing and shouting at each other in their desperation to catch the festival's hottest ticket. On that hot, clammy, crazy Friday evening, it couldn't have been clear- er that Quentin Tarantino had arrived, and that was still a few days before it was announced, to the surprise of many, that the film had carried off the coveted Palme d'Or

Not bad for a 31-year-old who'd directed only one previous film – 'Reservoir Dogs'. True, he's also written two others: 'True Romance' directed by Tony Scott, and 'Natural Born Killers' (so changed by Oliver Stone that Tarantino asked to be credited only for the story, not for the screenplay). Still, it's a pretty meagre CV, given the fanaticism displayed on the Croisette; then again, the cult that's grown up around Tarantino since 'Reservoir Dogs' first burst, brash, bloody and bravura, into the movie world is quite extraordinary.

But what, exactly, is all the fuss about? Well, there's the violence, of course. It's always been a staple of cinema, but in the current puritanical climate, Tarantino's imaginative facil- ity with the stylishly brutal set-piece and his readiness to go beyond what is normally deemed acceptable by the Hollywood mainstream mark him out as something of an iconoclast; and even though the violence in his films is seldom graphically explicit (the notorious ear-lopping scene in 'Reservoir Dogs' was actually shot with considerable discretion, with the cam- era turning away from the razor-cut at the crucial moment), the mood of aggression is often so intense that the viewer will imagine he's seen something that's not in fact shown. What's more, he'll play violence, at times, for comedy, not in some sick cheapo-horror way, but with sudden shifts in tone than can make us gasp in surprise at the confusion of emotions he's arousing in us; he hardly allows us time to think, let alone get sentimental over the victims.

'I'll have the Douglas Sirk steak.' 'How d'you want it? Burnt to a crisp or bloody as hell?' – Hitman Vincent Vega and waiter in 'Pulp Fiction'.

But there's more to Tarantino than the bloody belly, the stylised point-blank standoff Jacobean carnage. There's his obsessional love of movies, born of a childhood and adolescence spent bunking off school to go to the cinema and, later, of five years' work at an LA video store, where he mainlined on just about every tape he could get his hands on. Then there's the colour and wit of the dialogue he writes: fast, sharp, profane, vividly memorable, and packed with hip allusions to everything and anything in pop-culture (he also makes much of choosing the right music for his films). Remember the arguments over the meaning of Madonna's 'Like a Virgin' and the ethics of tipping in restaurants at the start of 'Dogs'? All part of the delirious pleasure Tarantino takes in the spoken word, and of his (sensible) contention that when hoodlums aren't actually committing illegal acts, they're just as likely to talk about non-criminal topics as the rest of us.

And then, finally, there's his ambivalent approach to genre. Though he likes to play fast and loose with conventional 'rules', he steers clear of pastiche and parody. Rather, he seems fasci-

'I don't think you can go too far with violence if what you're doing is right for the movie. What's too far?'

nated by narrative structure – 'Dogs', a heist-movie, never showed the robbery, instead creating suspense through a complex alternation of before and after scenes (including flashbacks within flashbacks) – and by the causes and consequences of traditional crime-movie action, rather than by the action itself. Hence all the talk; hence, too, the feeling among the growing number of his fans that Tarantino really is doing something fresh and different, and is even the most exciting new figure to arrive in the movie world since Scorsese.

'C'mon, let's get in character' – Hitman Jules Winnfield to partner Vincent Vega in 'Pulp Fiction'.

'In real life, I have a moral stance towards violence, but in films, no. I feel completely justified in saying that I get a kick out of violence in movies while I abhor it in real life – just like I feel exhilarated watching Gene Kelly dance in the rain, whereas if I saw someone really doing that, I'd think they were kinda barmy, a bit daft! Actually, I make it a strong point never to put forward any overall moralistic view or agenda I might have. When you have a director making, say, anti-war statements, it's like, "We know that!" When a film just becomes a mouthpiece for the director, like in "Born on the Fourth of July" where the Tom Cruise character didn't seem like a character but like that truck in "Nashville" which just goes round spouting those political ideas… I'm not taking a dig at Oliver Stone – I love "JFK" and "Salvador" – but I don't do that. I just follow the characters. So when Jules, the hitman in "Pulp", has his epiphany, there was no big dicta-

"1994"

"It's not dying about which I have any great worry, it's not living any more."
François Mitterrand

"Elvis Presley landing a UFO on top of the Loch Ness Monster."
William Hill's Graham Sharpe on your chances of winning the newly launched National Lottery

"If he was a member of the Church he would probably be facing excommunication on grounds of heresy."
Arthur Scargill on Labour's new leader, Tony Blair

"I think he is very, very beautiful, ravishingly attractive."
Auberon Waugh on Tony Blair

"Not many executives actually read books in Hollywood. Their lips get tired after ten pages."
Richard Sylbert, who optioned Anne Rice's 'Interview With A Vampire'

"Yeah, it's getting very easy now. Rachel pushes it into the middle and I nod 'em in. We're two up so far."
Rod Stewart explains childbirth

"I look on my friendship with her as like having a gallstone. You deal with it, then there is pain, and then you pass it."
Sandra Bernhardt on ex-pal Madonna

"Just think, nobody thought this would last."
Michael Jackson, kissing his three-month long wife, redefines long-term relationship

"Insomnia and cocaine."
Pedro Almodovar, on what keeps him awake at night

"It rumbled very loudly and we thought: "God, this is a great special effect"."
Pink Floyd fan on the seating collapse at an Earl's Court concert

"Below stairs has nothing to do with social class. Dame Barbara Cartland has defined it succinctly."
Jane Clark

"Below stairs means appalling people, like in 'Coronation Street'."
Barbara Cartland gets under the stairs

tion on my part he'd end up that way; it was his decision, that's how he had to end up. I never force that moral stuff on my characters.'

For the most part, to be sure, 'Pulp Fiction' is a gleefully amoral genre exercise. An intricately constructed, two-and-a-half-hour epic of hard boiled tack, it comprises a prologue, three stories (seemingly separate but as it transpires, closely linked) and an epilogue, all set in the LA underworld. As their creator confesses: 'The three stories you've seen a zillion times before, they're the oldest chestnuts in the world: the boxer who's supposed to throw the fight but doesn't, the mobster who's supposed to take his boss's wife out but not touch her, and that familiar situation from the start of Joel Silver movies where a couple of guys do a killing… only we go on and just hang out

'The problem with the majority of movies made nowadays is they're not so much stories as situations, the equivalent of situation comedies.'

with them for the rest of the morning. The fun part was to take these familiar situations and go to the moon with them.'

The hyper-energetic Tarantino speaks quickly, leaving sentences unfinished or peppering his comments with nervy, rat-a-tat laughter and endless interruptive phrases like 'Y'know', 'Okay', 'All right', 'I mean', 'The fact is'. Whatever; his down-to-earth friendliness, enthusiasm and readiness to talk about movies till the cows come home make him immediately likeable. At the same time, however, while he apparently has no social pretensions, he's not entirely modest; what occasionally sounds like arrogance may merely be self-confidence, but you do sometimes wonder whether he ever really entertains doubts about his work.

'I very much consider myself a storyteller,' he declares. 'Storytelling has become the lost art form, and I think part of the problem with the majority of movies made nowadays is they're not so much stories as situations, the equivalent of situation comedies. I look back at movies of the '30s, '40s, '50s or even the '70s – I'm not talking about "Chinatown" but even an exploitation movie like "Macon County Line" – and I'm shocked I'm actually hearing a story told to me.'

'You kill anybody?' A few cops. 'No real people?' 'Just cops.' – Mr Pink and Mr White in 'Reservoir Dogs'.

As far as Tarantino's own attempts to develop the art of storytelling go, they seem to centre partly on his knack for unexpected, witty, semi-naturalistic dialogue digressions, partly on balancing the more violent elements with comedy. But does he ever worry that he might misjudge the tone in this latter respect? Or that he might be taking the violence a little too far?

'I think I got the tone perfect. So I'm not worried now and, to tell the truth, I wasn't worried when I was making the film. If the tone's right in the script, it'll be right in the movie. If I didn't get in right on the page, I wouldn't even attempt it in the movie; to me, that'd be like working without a net. But with "Pulp" when I read the script, it was harrowing and

it was funny as hell – and that's what I was trying to do. The biggest problem with doing that comes with, the territory: you get misunderstood. People might reject the comic notion out of hand, but the audience, they're not rejecting it. When I watch it with an audience, it's terrific – to hear people diving under seats over here, others laughing their asses off over there. That's a movie! The images don't just glaze over you.'

It's wrong, anyway, to take Tarantino to task for the violence in his films, since they are very much movie-movies, inspired by cinematic tradition rather than by reality. Nevertheless, he insists 'Pulp Fiction' has 'a lot to do with real-life crime. I'm taking genre characters and applying them to real-life circumstances. I guess the master of that is Elmore Leonard. And real life ends up fucking up the best laid plans of mice and men: all the humour in my films comes from the absurdity of real life rearing its head.

'And I don't think you can go too far, or too short, with violence if what you're doing is right for the movie. What's too far? What would my characters never do? Well, I'm not playing God with them, so I don't know what they'd never do. But oddly enough, I don't actually show very much: "Dogs" is not that violent, it's intense. Actually it's a major fuckin' drag talking about violence, but at the same time I can only take it as a compliment. Like Brian De Palma has said many times, working in a violent medium you get penalised for doing it well; they don't complain when hacks do violence, because it has no effect.'

'I bet you're a big Lee Marvin fan, aren't you? Me too. I love that guy.' – Mr Blonde in 'Reservoir Dogs'.

But is there perhaps a limitation in making films that have more to do with movie lore and fan-boy allusions than with everyday life? Tarantino immediately goes on the defensive. 'No. I don't think my passion for movies will get in the way of artistic growth or whatever: that's like saying you love something too much, it'll screw you up. Well, I don't agree with that. in what I've done so far, all my stuff is very, very personal. Like when I was writing "Pulp", I was in Europe for the first time, taking in European culture, and I was fascinated by it. And that worked its way into the script, when you get the hitman Vincent just back from Europe and talking about it. And if I was writing a swashbuckler and all of a sudden I broke up with someone, that'd work its way into the piece. To deny that, I'd be a robot or something.

'And I'll do anything I wanna do. When I was writing "Pulp" I didn't want to be known as the gun guy. It was going to be a get-it-out-of-your-system kinda movie, a goodbye to the genre, and I'd go off and do other things and then revisit it from time to time. But when I thought about it recently, it was like, "Fuck that!" For sure, there are three or four things I wanna do away from the crime genre, but I'm not gonna predestine myself; I'm too young, I've got my whole life to make movies. And I think I can expand myself by doing crime films; the genre opens itself to so many different things. So you know what? If I come up with a crime-story I wanna do next, I'm gonna do it.' ●

Joanna Lumley

from 'One of a kind' in T.O. 1233, by **Alkarim Jivani**

As television approaches the end of its first half century, it is becoming clear that its most enduring characters are comedic: Hancock's hangdog humorist, Leonard Rossiter's hapless Reginald Perrin, Harry Enfield's You Don't Wanna Do That! The latest addition to this gallery is Joanna Lumley's Patsy Stone – the monstrous fashion editor from 'Absolutely Fabulous' with a red gash for a mouth and a hairdo that could knock an elephant unconscious.

Patsy's appeal cuts through class, age and nationality. For a character whose ambit extends only as far as Groucho's, the Caprice and Harvey Nicks, she has remarkable legs – both literally and metaphorically.

Last month at the Sydney Mardi Gras parade there was an 'Absolutely Fabulous' float. At an event where eye-popping sights are ten a penny, the most extraordinary spectacle was a dozen drag queens with tight, tight skirts, towering beehives and teetering heels clip-clopping down the street with ciggies dangling from their lips.

'I was sent a photograph of them and I wrote back with due gravity,' says Lumley, that unmistakeable gravelly voice supressing a slight giggle. 'I suppose they chose Patsy because it's easier for drag queens to impersonate someone like me who is tall and has big shoulders.'

Jon Plowman, producer of 'Absolutely Fabulous' recalls Jennifer Saunders giving a warning to Lumley during the show's first rehearsals. 'Jennifer said to Joanna, "You realise this will completely change your fan base?" Whereas before it was colonels writing in to say "I admire your work immensely, my dear," now it will be drag queens saying "Can I borrow your frock?"' He chuckles, 'and that's exactly what happened.' Lumley has somehow managed, in defiance of conventional wisdom, to be a cult

'Patsy doesn't know when she's gone over the top... and she doesn't care.'

icon and a figure of mass appeal. When 'Absolutely Fabulous' moved to BBC1, cynics thought that it would sink in the mainstream – in fact it averaged more than ten million viewers.

Alec Guinness once claimed the key to a character lies in getting the shoes right. With Lumley it's hair. 'My instinct is, "What sort of hair would she have?" And it's so simple; you get Nice 'n' Easy or Recital from Boots for a few pounds and 20 minutes later you are transformed.' Patsy Stone took shape when Ruby Wax asked Lumley to be interviewed, in character, on her chat show 'The Full Wax'.

'Rather than be a film star person I though it would be nicer to be a slut', she says. 'I thought it would be amusing to contrast this angelic public image with a ghastly bitch behaving in that rather snappy, disagreeable way at home with rotten flowers, filthy food on the floor and whisky bottles everywhere.' With Wax as the script editor on Absolutely Fabulous and with Plowman and Saunders both impressed with Lumley's performance on the West End stage in 'Vanilla', the next step was inevitable.

'When I read the first script I thought, this is going like smoke. The character was born without brakes: she doesn't know when she's gone over the top – and doesn't care. I wanted to do it not least because I've never been offered anything like it. I've always been drawn to anarchic humour and playing elegant women gets very boring.'

Saunders was so impressed during filming of the pilot that she began to expand Lumley's role. 'Although Jennifer had always seen Patsy as Edina's best friend, it wasn't conceived as a double act,' explains Plowman. 'But Joanna threw herself at it with such gusto that it would have been a shame not to develop it.' It's easy to see why Lumley was so enthusiastic: not only did it give her a role she could get those gleaming gnashers into, it brought her back on TV in a series with more profile than Barry Manilow. 'People thought I'd died or was rotting in an old people's home somewhere,' she laughs. 'And this exhumed me.' ●

Stung!

Sting interviewed in T.O. 1266, by **Peter Paphides**

There aren't many things Sting gets to do that you don't hear about, be it saving the rainforests or doing Amnesty benefits with Bruce Springsteen. Hell, even when he decided to make 'Bring On The Night', a feature film of his world tour with some respected jazz blokes, Sting didn't just stop at some backstage footage and in-depth interviews. Oh no. We got gory footage of his wife Trudie Sting giving birth to their third child, grandly accompanied by 'Russians', his Prokofiev-pilfering ode to the Cold War. Cheers, Sting.

So it's understandably with some trepidation that I meet the freshly stubbled superstar at the 'Top Of The Pops' studios, where he's singing 'When We Dance', from his current album 'Fields Of Gold: The Best Of Sting'. When I arrive, he's in his dressing-room, sifting through some old photos. Nervously attempting conversation, I pick up a photo which features him dressed as Billy Idol wearing a bulbous false nose. 'Sting, why are you wearing a comedy nose?' I jovially enquire. A tiny eternity follows. I look at his face. I suddenly realise. Shit. Shit shit shit shit shit. 'It's not a false nose,' he replies, roughly one nanosecond after I remember about that nose job he apparently doesn't like to talk about.

At this point the Sting I've read about would storm out in a chauffeur-driven huff, spitting obscenities. Fortunately, the Sting I've read about doesn't really exist. Instead, I ask him what he's been up to and, perhaps a little conscious of his image as global do-gooder, he quips: 'I've just returned from South Africa. I went over there to free Nelson Mandela, but when I arrived they told me he was already free! What a wasted journey!'

In fact, Sting is a terribly nice chap. I can't even kid myself that he's pretending to be a nice chap, because we all know what a shit actor he is. Crumpled and well-chiselled, just as a million housewives imagine him, he's self-effacing too: 'I enjoy celebrity,' beams the 43-year-old Geordie, crouched on the floor next to his sofa, 'Even the negative bits. If someone wants to shout "Sting, you're a wanker" as I walk down the street, that's fine too. The only alternative to that is shutting yourself off from everyday living. And once you do that, you may as well give up altogether.'

Sometimes, though, Sting seems so into what he does that he doesn't think about how clumsy it looks. For instance, his love of jazz led him to hire the talent of respected jazz musicians like Branford Marsalis and Omar Hakim for his first two solo albums. Then on top of the jazz-rock fusion experiments, Sting would make a point of crow-barring Jung and Nabokov into his songs. It's almost as if he was getting more abstruse because he was embarrassed about being a pop singer.

'I think that's a good summing up, actually,' he says. 'I enjoyed working with those people, but in the past few years I've concentrated on simplifying things again. When you appear to be complex, it's really just a disguise for not knowing what the fuck you're doing. The song "Fields Of Gold" is a case in point. There's a valency about it that all manner of time changes and odd keys couldn't cover. Having said that, I was never really into pop from the age of 20. The Police merely served to curb my interest in jazz and classical music.'

That may be true, but Sting wasn't averse to doing the Spinal Tap bit in his days with the Police. Long before he was set on preserving large quantities of South America, reports suggest that he was sticking them up his nose. On stage too, his new role as messianic stadium star saw him in some unlikely situations. In a bid to bring the Police to all the classical civilisations that so fascinated him, Sting arranged a tour of Bombay, Cairo, Athens and Rome. In Cairo, Sting was dismayed to discover that the Police were actually playing the American University in Cairo – a gig populated, naturally, by American college kids. Striding on stage purposefully, Sting commanded, 'Throw open the doors and let Cairo in!' The security men duly did so, at which point, a couple of Egyptians had a look to see what was going on, decided they didn't much like the look of it, then left. Sting tells me that towards the end of the Police's days, the animosity between him and Stewart Copeland had intensified so much that Copeland took to writing 'FUCK... OFF... YOU... CUNT' on his drums.

These days, perhaps, people get resentful because they see Sting using the paraphernalia of wealth and fame to right the world's wrongs. The rich pop star dancing with the widows of the Pinochet regime in the stadium where their husbands were shot; the rich pop star forming the Rainforest Foundation and hanging out with Chief Raoni from the Kayapo Tribe (aka The Bloke With The Plate-Sized Lower Lip). Presumably, if you're Sting, you watch the news on TV, see vast expanses of land are being destroyed, and think, 'I'm Sting – I can help!'

'Well, something like that,' he chuckles, rubbing his huge forehead. 'There were lots of negative insinuations in the press about my involvement in the rainforest; that I was doing it for the publicity; that the Indians had been ripped off. Seven years on, though, I'm still involved. We've managed to save an area the size of Switzerland.'

You became good mates with Chief Raoni, didn't you?

'Erm yes,' hesitates Sting, 'I took him around the world. He'd never been outside Brazil.'

Really?

'Yes. He's a warrior.'

What do warriors do, then?

'They hunt... erm, you know...'

Er, right. How did he react to the joys of non-rainforest life?

'Well, I'd show him the Eiffel Tower and he would say, "It's OK". He found traffic jams funny. I'd say, "Why are you laughing?" And he couldn't understand why anyone would want to be here when they could be in the jungle. The only things that impressed him were the ocean and Mont Blanc. He saw that and thought he'd just met God. Which I suppose he had.'

And all this, because you're a pop singer...

'Isn't it weird!' laughs Sting, rubbing his eyes in exasperation, 'That's exactly the thought I have a lot of the time: "I'm a pop star. What the hell am I doing here?"'

But that's what your critics say about you too.

'Well, you know... I'm not afraid of taking chances. I'm brave.'

That's going to look terrible in print.

'I don't care. I am.'

Right you are, sir. While Sting was busy saving the planet, his world fell apart in 1988 when his father died of cancer. Sting reacted by writing an entire album, 'The Soul Cages'. It was, by most accounts, a truly dreadful record – a maudlin plod through Sting's self-pity, alleviated only by the beguiling 'Mad About You'.

'I had to make "The Soul Cages",' he pleads. 'I was bereaved.'

Making it is one thing, I counter; putting it out is quite another. It should have had a warning sticker on it.

'I needed to get those songs out the way,' he mutters a little defensively. He's now left his trousers and seems to be trying to unravel his jumper. 'Once I did, it was time to get a bit more light-hearted.'

You have made some staggeringly shit records though.

'Such as?'

Such as that dreadful thing with Bryan Adams and Rod Stewart, from 'The Three Musketeers'. You can't expect to be taken seriously and appear on corporate, airbrushed bollocks like that.

'Oh, right! You mean "All For One", or "All For Wad", as I called it. Bryan Adams phoned me up and said, "Do you want to sing on this song I've written?" And Bryan's a good mate. I'm not the sort of bloke who says, "What is it?" or whatever. If someone asks me to sing on their song and they're a mate, I say yes.'

Do you not think it's one of the worst songs you've ever heard?

'I don't like it, to be honest with you, but the kitschness of working with Rod Stewart was just too attractive to turn down.'

So he's not really a pompous prat. The real prima donnas in the business are the ones you never find out about, because they're too precious to let it show. Sting does what he likes, rather than what he's necessarily good at. That makes for a likeable, well-rounded human being but, once in while, a lousy recording artist. He's a 43-year-old man with four children, so perhaps he can be forgiven for not having heard of China Black, Green Day, East 17 or any of the other artists in this block of dressing-rooms. He's heard of Nirvana, though: 'My son Joe, who's studying in America, was a massive Nirvana fan, so as you can imagine, he was very affected by Kurt's suicide. There were a lot of phone calls that weekend, I can tell you. Kurt's death was a terrible psychic event for an entire generation of kids. I was sympathetic to Kurt.'

Why's that then?

'I think he had a difficult life...' Sting laughs nervously '...but anyone who blows themselves away like that... it's a very selfish act. Particularly for the people who have to mop up after you!' Stopping only to remove his foot from his mouth, he concludes... 'It's a real "fuck you" to everyone around you.'

Right. What do you think people would say if you died then?

'What? You're asking me to write my own obituary? "Consider Him Gone". It's gotta be,' he roars, delighted at his punning suggestion. 'I don't really know. I'd like to think there'd be kind of a warm upswing of approval! That Tom Sawyer fantasy of being at your own funeral appeals to a lot of pop stars. Pop is such an approval-seeking thing anyway. I want to live, though. I wanna be old!! I'm not ready for that obituary just yet.'

Bad news then, for those eager to write it. ●

'When you appear to be complex, it's really just a disguise for not knowing what the fuck you're doing.'

The monocled mutineer

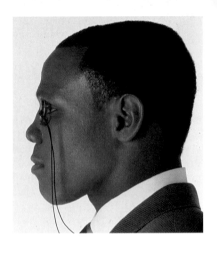

Chris Eubank interviewed in T.O. 1247, by **Andrew Shields**

An unbeaten fighter who has made millions from a sport he professes to hate.

The map room of the Royal Geographical Society in Kensington Gore: starting point for many of the world's most famous expeditions. Looking down from its cream and pink-painted walls, portraits of purposeful-looking men create an atmosphere of due solemnity, a feeling that history has been made here. Now, a frock-coated Dr David Livingstone surveys the scene as a modern-day adventurer launches his own voyage of discovery.

Attired in the immaculate pinstripes you would expect from someone twice voted Britain's best-dressed man, Christopher Livingston Eubank – the use of his middle name reveals the persona he has today chosen to adopt – deals with the rough-and-tumble of a press conference with his usual élan. He is here to announce a pugilistic passage around the globe, involving eight defences of his WBO super-middleweight title inside 12 months, in what Eubank's promoter, Barry Hearn, declares will be 'a mission to spread the gospel of Eubankism'. It's a formidable challenge to the champion's stamina, both mental and physical. No wonder that Hearn then asks, with a rhetorical flourish and nod towards the picture on the wall, 'In a year's time, will we still be saying "Christopher Livingston Eubank, world champion I presume?"'

After the nation's boxing writers have chewed over the details of opponents and training schedules, a guy with a pony-tail sitting at the other side of the room suddenly announces that he's from a bike magazine and fires a question to Eubank about his spirituality. Then another, about his philosophy of life. Whether he meditates. What he feels he has been put on earth to achieve. The hack pack are nonplussed, embarrassed even – this, after all, is their territory. They start to mutter among themselves, masking Eubank's thoughtful response to queries he takes pains to listen to. Caught off guard, Hearn quickly decides the best thing to do is to call a halt: 'These are really questions for a one-to-one interview,' he raps. 'Anyone else want to ask anything? No? Then, good day, gentlemen.'

'I wish my press conferences were more about spirituality and less about boxing,' says Chris Eubank three hours later. It's a warm, sunny day, but he's still wearing his suit and tie, and the curtains of his suite are half-drawn. Run-of-the-mill banter with the press clearly bores him, but his distaste for one of boxing's more wearisome commitments is mild compared to his professed hatred of the sport itself. Boxing, Eubank insists, is a mug's game and a fearfully dangerous one at that: any man who claims to love fighting is either a liar or a fool.

Yet it's a game which has made him extremely rich, and given him the chance to indulge a passion for expensive clothes and Harley-Davidsons. His tour is backed by Sky TV, which has paid £10 million for the privilege. When he unlaces his gloves in a year's time and contemplates retirement, his career earnings will have topped £15m. Eubank's philosophy can sometimes sound like a bag of contradictions, but underpinning it is a firm belief that such enormous sums of money are the right of anyone brave enough to step into the ring in the name of 'sport'. The last word comes with a sneer. For Eubank, boxing is business pure and simple.

'I wasn't born rich, I don't do this for fun or because I love it. I do it because it is necessary.'

'If I had looked at boxing as a business a year after I had begun my career,' he says, 'it would have been a year too late. I wasn't born rich, I don't do this for fun or because I love it. I do it because it is necessary. Nothing can be considered a sport where there is no alternative. If you can't lose – if you have to win – then it's not sport. There's too much on the line, too many people who want to see me lose, too many people who don't want to see me break the mould, for what I do to be considered sport. Putting on the line your self-esteem, your pride, your… manhood: that, for the participant, is no sport. If you do consider it a sport then you are not a thinker, and if you aren't a thinker then you won't be at this level anyway.

'Boxing is great for discipline. You have to get into that ring and produce. You have to live a clean life or you're going to get beaten up. You have to follow the rules, and the rules do work. I speak from experience. You have to lose weight, there are things you can't do, you have to go into a period of purdah before a fight. You only get out of it what you put in.'

Eubank is still unbeaten after 39 contests, testimony to his belief that boxing is '85 per cent mental and only 15 per cent physical' – and that he has the capacity to do just enough to win each time. 'A man can learn to fight, but the physical aspect is very small. It's whether you are willing to take the pain and come back. If you are a weak-hearted man or a weak-minded man you would quit. It's not the body what does the work, it's the mind that endures.' Even with a rare grammatical slip-up, you know what he means.

But does his chosen pursuit ever excite him? Does he gain any intellectual satisfaction from literally outwitting either opponents or the sharks who infest the sport's murky waters? It seems not. 'People use words like "fascinate" and "excite", but nothing ever grabs me that way. I got excited yesterday when I saw my little baby girl. I hadn't seen her for ten days and her milk spots had gone and her eyes were wider open. That was exciting. Something is exciting only when you're not used to it, and I'm now an old dog in this business. A boxing match may be exciting to the spectator, but to the participant it becomes mundane when you have done it so many times.'

Nevertheless, the rewards of this 'mundane' business have enticed him into slugging and slogging it out for eight more fights. He is impatient of those who doubt whether he can sustain peak fitness for such a long period: 'Everyone is thinking of eight fights, but I'm just thinking of one. Eventually eight will pass. When you are a warrior, you don't do it part-time.' And anyway, as he says without even a hint of self-deprecation on his face, 'I am not a normal man physically.' An unbeaten fighter who has made millions from a sport he professes to hate. ●

1995

It's a disaster! whether it was capitalism collapsing, Japanese cults nerve-gassing the subways, west-country serial killers or ebola eating its way through the tabloids, everything was pretty disastrous this year. Nevertheless, the New Lad found time for spiritual questions: Which washes whiter, Blur, Oasis or OJ's defense team?

JANUARY

Mass murderer Fred West is found hanged in his cell.

Master humourist Peter Cook, dies.

Eric Cantona launches a kung fu kick at an abusive fan.

FEBRUARY

Richey Edwards of the Manic Street Preachers disappears.

Barings Bank collapses with debts totalling £860m. Fingers are pointed at 28-year-old Nick Leeson.

MARCH

Gangland legend Ronnie Kray dies.

The Aum Shinrikyo sect attacks Tokyo's underground system with nerve gas.

'Forrest Gump' wins six Oscars.

NWA rapper Eazy E dies of AIDS.

APRIL

168 people are killed in the explosion of a federal office block in Oklahoma City, USA .

Brookside's Mandy and Beth Jordache go to jail.

JULY

Robbie Williams leaves Take That. Fans bombard Samaritans phone lines.

Uber-hippie Jerry Garcia of the Grateful Dead dies.

'Raving vicar' Rev. Chris Brain of Sheffield's Nine O'Clock Service is revealed to be a sexually-obsessed cult leader.

OCTOBER

Football star and crap actor OJ Simpson is acquitted on two counts of murder.

NOVEMBER

Teenager Leah Betts dies after taking ecstasy at her 18th birthday party.

Rose West, wife of Fred, receives ten life sentences.

To Die For
A sharp, funny blend of black comedy and satire on the deleterious effects of TV complete with Van Sant's oddball appeal. Enormous fun.

The Usual Suspects
Director Singer's magnificent thriller, aided by a gloriously complex screenplay; a hugely challenging labyrinth, always a few steps ahead of the audience.

Babe
World's apart from the junior consumer research approach of Disney. Babe should have whole families chuckling.

Pulp - Different Class (Island)
Too passionate to justify the dumb 'kitsch' allegations; they've never sounded this ferocious.

The Chemical Brothers - Exit Planet Dust (JBO)
Armed with an iridescent inventory of breakbeats, they've melted down everything they've ever thrown on a turntable as DJs and created the monster that Primal Scream couldn't be bothered to finish when they made Screamadelica.

Black Grape - It's Great When You're Straight, Yeah! (Radioactive)
It doesn't sound remotely straight. Shaun tattoos his chaotic-yet-gentle worldview on the whole thing. Should Ted Hughes pop his sneakers, we won't have to look too hard for a new poet laureate.

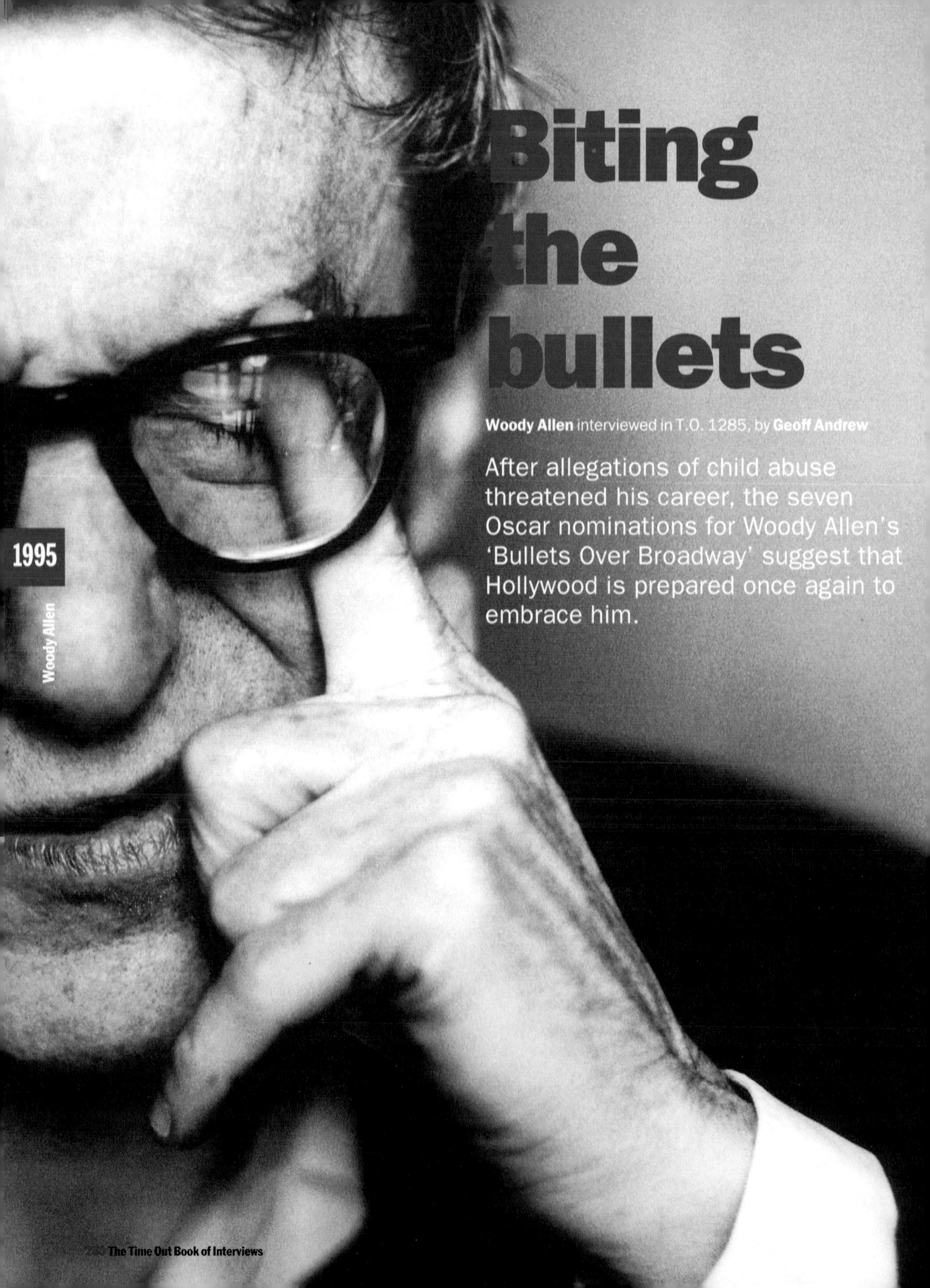

Biting the bullets

Woody Allen interviewed in T.O. 1285, by **Geoff Andrew**

After allegations of child abuse threatened his career, the seven Oscar nominations for Woody Allen's 'Bullets Over Broadway' suggest that Hollywood is prepared once again to embrace him.

1995

Woody Allen

day there was nothing I could do to influence events in any direction. So I just worked on. I finished 'Husbands and Wives', wrote and directed 'Manhattan Murder Mystery' and 'Bullets', adapted 'Don't Drink the Water', and wrote a one-act play for Broadway.

Did you find hard work a help in facing such unpleasantries?

Work has always been a life-saver to me, from when I was 20 years old. People ask, 'Why work so much, doing one film after another? You're a workaholic,' but that's something I've done my whole life. It's a sense of taking control over the chaos of life. I've always found it's better to be obsessed with the problem of what I'm going to do with my second act

'I'm not sure I've been in the right business.'

than with the problem of what I'm going to do with my life when I turn 80 or something. The problems of theatre or film are stimulating and difficult, but at least you can cope with them; and they keep your mind off those problems you can't cope with.

Clearly some of the opprobrium in the press arose because you were famous. But weren't people also angry because you refused to play the game of parading the usual emotions, because you seemed rather detached, rather than displaying some sort of repentance?

Well, I didn't feel I should be repentant for anything; it was the outside world that should be repentant to me. I was falsely accused of something, and that accusation was fed and stimulated, shamelessly, by the press. To this day there are people who think Mia and I were married, and that I had some kind of affair with my daughter. Not only were we never married, but we never lived together, and in 13 years of dating Mia I never slept at her house; we had a very unusual, unconventional rela-

tionship. Truth is, she lived in a house with 11 kids, I lived in a different part of town. We saw each other, did a certain amount of work together, had one child together and adopted another.

Then suddenly I found myself, at the height of an acrimonious child-custody thing, accused of child-molestation – a standard ploy in these situations. And everybody jumped on that, it was all over magazines and newspapers, and I was not about to betray my sense of integrity, for the sake of ameliorating public relations, by confessing to or apologising for something I hadn't done. I feel the apologies are owed me. To this day, because of an abysmal judicial system in the United States, I have not been able to see my daughter for two years. This is ridiculous; I was never charged with anything, and the groups hired by the police and District Attorney all came to the conclusion that absolutely no molestation had taken place. I'm allowed to see my son every week – though only for six hours, which is insanity – but not my daughter. So this poor little girl, who was seven when it started… from where she sits, I just dropped off the face of the earth. People who are in jail, in jail for killing people, get to see their children, and I was never even charged with anything. So all I can do is fight as hard as I can.

Are you annoyed that people so often equate fiction and reality, when thinking about you?

It has in the past, but I've given up fighting that, because I can't win. Poor Clark Gable used to say how in a bar some guy'd come up and say, 'I don't think you're so tough,' and Gable'd say, 'Hey, I'm an actor.' It's the mythological power of the movies – unlike the stage, where it's clearly acting. And with Chaplin, who made an extreme change of costume and persona for his films, it wasn't hard to believe he was a different person.

Tracey Emin

from 'Open Art Surgery' in T.O. 1305, by **Sarah Kent**

'I imagined that, if ever I had my portrait taken, it would be in the bath,' says Tracey Emin, 'because it's intimate and personal – naked without being naked.' Emin is keen to share intimate moments with her public. She planned a month-long, round-the-clock exhibition in which anyone could join her at home – eating, sleeping, washing, watching TV. Like all her work, it would be 'a live-in show; living autobiography… When I'm dead,' she says, 'my work won't be half so good.' Now she is planning a modified version – the Avery – in an old cab office, which she intends to open every day for a year. 'It will be an Emin Museum, where I'll present myself and my work – every moment of creativity can be shared, everything I think or make will be on view.'

No matter what the medium, everything Emin does is autobiographical. 'Why I Never Became a Dancer' is a video explaining why she left Margate. It's a small-town story with a twist. At 13, Tracey discovered sex: 'Something you could just do and it was for free… on a beach, down an alley, a green, a

But with me, the characters I play dress like I dress, they live in New York, so they can easily be perceived as me. But they're not. Right from 'Annie Hall', I've said that I didn't meet Diane Keaton that way, we didn't have these experiences, I didn't grow up in Coney Island under an amusement centre.

But people who don't create – and this is not a criticism – who can't fathom an act of imagination, they don't realise I sit in a room, by myself or with somebody else, and make up a story. I just do anything that is dramatically effective, whether it's funny or serious. The ideas in the films are autobiographical, not the plots. It's true I'll make my character a writer or a comedian rather than a rocket-scientist, because I don't have the patois, but it's still totally fabricated.

Are your films in any way cathartic for you?

Making them, yes; it's like a wonderful working-out at a gym. The catharsis comes after you write it. Tennessee Williams said it's a shame you have to produce your play; it'd be great if you could just write it and throw it in the drawer. As you probably know, you've transcended something as soon as you write it. But in theatre and film, you write and transcend it, then you have to spend a year making the thing. But that's physically cathartic. Shooting is the hardest part of the film: up at 5.30 in the morning, standing on some freezing corner, wondering if the light's gonna suddenly change – it's a nerve-racking thing. I prefer writing and editing, when you're in a warm space with your friends, with thousands of feet of film to put together. That's a good feeling.

And is artistic freedom a sine qua non for you?

Absolutely. If I didn't have it, I wouldn't make films. I don't think it's possible to make films without it. Obviously some people do, but they go through such struggles. I don't believe in film being a committee affair; it's gotta be one person's vision – not because of ego or arrogance, but because you can't do it any other way.

What ambitions are left for you to fulfil?

I'd love to make what I considered a great film. I've never done that. I'd love to make a film and think afterwards, Gee, this is right up there with 'Bicycle Thieves' or 'La Grande Illusion' or 'Rashomon' or something.

And regrets?

Sure, plenty. I'm not sure I've been in the right business. (Laughs) If I had my life to live over, knowing what I know now, I might not go into film-making. I might wanna be a musician, or maybe I could have been more productive if I'd just written books, because you finish writing then write again, and write again; whereas in film there's a year of down-time before you get to write again. And it's not that I wanted to be a director: I wanted to be a writer, and I directed my films in order to get them done properly.

Do you still feel serious films are worthier than comedies?

Yes, I always felt that. I'd love to do more serious films, and I don't feel straitjacketed by other people's expectations; I feel no obligation to the press or the public except to try and do good work. But it has to come naturally. Unfortunately, most of the ideas that occur to me are comic.

So why, in the end, do you go on making films?

I wish the decision was taken out of my hands; that someone would come along and say, 'We're never giving you money to make a film again', then I could get on with working quietly on a novel or a play or something. But as long as people are standing in line saying, 'We'll give you $15 million to make a film', I can't say no, because everybody wants that opportunity. It's not a good reason to make films, but it's like I'm on a roller-coaster and can't get off. And I'm hoping someone will stop the ride. ●

park, even a hotel… a wild escape from all the shit that surrounded me.'

At 15 she gave up sex for dancing and entered the local finals of the British Dancing Championship. If she won, it would be her route to freedom. The crowd clapped as she twirled round the floor. Then a gang of local lads, the ones she'd had sex with, started chanting – 'SLAG, SLAG, SLAG, SLAG' – so loudly they blotted out the music and so insistently they drove her off the dance floor. 'Shane, Eddie, Tony, Doug, Richard... This one's for you,' says Tracey over a shot of her dancing round and round.

People got to know her when she ran a shop in Bethnal Green Road for six months in 1993, with fellow artist Sarah Lucas. On Saturdays they stayed open all night and the shop became the place to hang out and buy weird things made by the artists, such as Emin's 'Rothko Comfort Blankets, for Private Views and State Occasions' – pieces cut from a favourite childhood blanket fringed in yellow blanket stitch and cornered with a comforting piece of satin. 'The shop was like my family, doing it meant so much,' recalls Emin. 'We didn't get any sleep and lived on Guinness and Indian takeaways.'

Through the shop she met Jay Jopling, Damien Hirst's dealer, who invited her to show at the White Cube. She had six weeks to prepare what she ironically called 'My Major Retrospective', assuming that it would be her one and only show.

Emin is a hoarder; she opened the cardboard boxes gathering dust under her bed, sorted the trolls, the teapots, the diaries, letters and family snaps, put them into frames and installed them as a wall of memorabilia. The death of her uncle Colin, decapitated in a car crash, was recorded with the newspaper story, family snaps of him and his midnight blue E-type Jaguar and the pack of Benson & Hedges that he had, screwed up in his hand, when he died. The cabinet commemorating her abortion made some people cry. It contained a phial of bloody tissue, her hospital wrist band and a letter describing the foetus sliding down her thigh as she got out of the cab returning her to hospital, and the process of forgiveness – coming to terms with the guilt. Then there were the lyrical watercolours – full of pastels, flowers and hearts – that she did as a means of mourning the lost baby. There were photo-badge reproductions of her art school pictures, the first-class BA which, against the odds – having dropped out of school at 13 – she got at Maidstone College of Art, and the MA from the Royal College where, she says, she was treated like a 'weird retard' for doing figurative paintings.

'Being an artist is a 24-hour thing; it isn't a veneer,' she says. 'I don't want to hide behind a screen – the work.' It's this openness that makes Tracey Emin special. It's the directness of her work, the lack of evident artifice, that makes it so affecting. People end up in tears, sharing their own stories with her.

I'm running out of space and I haven't even begun to tell you about her childhood in the International Hotel, Margate; her three-day-a-week father who had another family, lusted after her and went bankrupt; her twin brother Paul, with whom she played sexual games in the bathroom and who head-butted out her front teeth, and… ●

Boys keep swinging

David Bowie & Brian Eno Interviewed in T.O. 1306, by **Dominic Wells**

Q. Does it hurt you if a lot of people are saying, 'David Bowie, what a pretentious tosser'?

A: I don't know of a time when it was never said.

David Bowie & Brian Eno

The first thing that happens when I finally meet David Bowie is I break his arm. Almost. As I shake his hand, too hard, a resounding crack sounds from inside his elbow. He doesn't seem to feel it, but it's alarming all the same when his limbs are as achingly thin still as when Candy Clark carried him, bloody-nosed and unconscious, down the hotel hallway in 'The Man Who Fell To Earth'. It's an Oedipal moment: Bowie is the only pop star to have visited my dreams (I was hitch-hiking, he pulled up in a black stretch limo, we chatted amiably about Japanese culture), the only one I've pinned to my wall – not counting Debbie Harry, where the attraction was purely hormonal. As with an astonishing number of my peers, my golden years were played out to a Bowie soundtrack. Always more than just a pop star, he introduced me to the films of Nic Roeg through 'The Man Who Fell…', Nietzsche through 'Oh You Pretty Things' ('Gotta make way for the homo superior'), pop art through 'Andy Warhol', Jean Genet through 'Jean Genie', and performance art through 'Joe The Lion'. The mime, admittedly, I could have done without.

'Let's Dance', in 1983, was the turning point – his first album to be of the times rather than ahead of them. Since then, barring small upwards blips such as 'Blue Jean',

When I finally meet David Bowie, I break his arm.

he's lagged pitifully behind. There was his reciting of the Lord's Prayer at the Freddie Mercury tribute; the wedding photos in *Hello!*; the desire to be considered an artist, my dear; the Laura Ashley wallpaper… And that's what makes me nervous as I sink into a sofa: not so much meeting the man of my dreams, but the very real possibility of finding him a complete prat.

I arrive in the midst of a discussion between Bowie and his collaborator, the producer and ambient musician Brian Eno, about satellite TV (which Eno strangely does not possess), and Bowie inquiring about some Polish film-maker whose name Eno cannot remember. They make a good double-act, this diminutive duo of rock intellectuals, these laughing gnomes. Brian Eno (anag. Brain One), often referred to jocularly as The Professor – by virtue of his balding dome, measured lecturing

tones and generally planet-sized mind – has recently become one for real, at the Royal College of Art. David Bowie (anag. Ow, I Bed Diva) is dapper, goateed, relishing his new role as English gentleman-artist. His mismatched eyes are indeed disconcerting: as Desmond Morris would tell you, the one that is permanently dilated says to your subconscious, 'You're fascinating, I want to sleep with you'; the other, contracted, signals, 'You bore me, worm.'

Dominic Wells: *There's an assumption that rock musicians shouldn't be doing art, shouldn't be acting and shouldn't be writing books.*

David Bowie: There are more and more people moving into areas they're not trained for, especially in America. I've just been doing this film with Julian Schnabel ['Basquiat', in which Bowie plays Andy Warhol], and he's making movies, having just made an album… I think that's fantastic.

Brian Eno: One of the reasons it's possible now is that for various technical reasons, anybody can do anything, pretty much. I can, sitting in my studio, put together records with basses and drums and choirs, or I can put together a video in a similar way. So the question then becomes not, 'Do I have the skill?' It's not an issue.

DB: The skill hasn't been an issue in art for 50 years. It's really the idea. Picasso said, I think, when someone said to him a child of three could do what you're doing, he replied, 'Yes, you're right, but very few adults.'

I think he said: 'It took me 16 years to paint like Raphael, but 60 years to learn to paint like a child.'

BE: Einstein said, 'Any intelligent nine-year-old could understand anything I've done; the thing is, he probably wouldn't understand why it was important.' That's the other side of that coin: to be free and simple and child-like, but to be able to understand the implications of that at the same time. To be Picasso is not suddenly to become a three-year-old child again, it's to become someone who understands what's important about what the three-year-old child does.

I understand much of your new album 'Outside' was improvised, and that Brian would hand out cards to different musicians saying things like: 'You are a disgruntled member of a South African rock band. Play the notes they won't allow', or 'You are the last survivor of a catastrophic event. Play to fight the loneliness. Is that to strip everything down, remove everyone's preconceptions and start again from scratch?

BE: There are certain immediate dangers to improvisation, and one of them is that everybody coalesces immediately. Everyone starts playing the blues, basically, because it's the one place where everyone can agree and knows the rules. So in part they were strategies designed to stop the thing becoming over-coherent. The interesting place is not chaos, and it's not total coherence. It's somewhere on the cusp of those two.

The rhythm is very strong throughout the album. That's what holds things together…

DB: Something we really got into on the late-'70s albums was what you could do with a drum kit. The heartbeat of popular music was something we really messed about with.

BE: And very few people had done. It was, 'Right, bass and drums, get them down, then do all the weird stuff on top.' To invert that was a new idea.

DB: The great thing about what Brian was doing through much of the improvisation is we'd have clocks and radios and things near his sampler, and he'd, say, find a phrase on the French radio and keep throwing it in rhythmically so it became part of the texture. And people would react to that, they'd play in a different way because these strange sounds kept coming back at them.

BE: Yeah, and he was doing the same thing lyrically. We had a thing going where David was improvising lyrics as well; he had books and magazines and bits of newspaper around, and he was just pulling phrases out and putting them together.

DB: If I read some to you, some you'd find incomprehensible.

I did try that, in fact. I read the lyrics out loud and thought, 'He's gone off his rocker.' Then when I heard it ▶

"1995"

"I've seen bigger and I've seen smaller. But his was cute."
Divine Brown on Hugh Grant's member

"Shouldn't you be in the boot?"
Taxi driver to John McCarthy

"It was like going to a club but it had a better sound system."
Kate Francis, who went to the rave vicar's Nine O'Clock Service on Easter Sunday

"That boy wanted to sue him for millions of dollars… I'd have been quite pleased if Michael Jackson had touched me at 15."
David Hockney on the Jordan Chandler scandal

"If it falls to me to start a fight to cut out the cancer of bent and twisted journalism in our country with the simple sword of truth and the trusty shield of fair play, so be it. I am ready for the fight."
Jonathan Aitken, after the Guardian/World in Action programme made allegations against him

"We regret that Rabin was killed by a Jew because he should have been killed by a Palestinian."
Ahmed Jibril from the Popular Front for the Liberation of Palestine

"Go Mad This Weekend –
Buy Some Beef"
Notice in Scarborough Safeways

"I'm nobody in LA because I'm only half the size of the breasts of other women."
Pamela 'Flat-Chest' Anderson

"It wasn't a riot. It was a few people who wanted to grab some trainers or a hi-fi."
An eye-witness reflects on Brixton rioting

"I don't see why I should subsidise his greed, just because he has a divorce to pay for and has just had all his teeth redone."
AS Byatt, on Martin Amis' lucrative book deal for 'The Information'

"Last year you said you had three bastards in the Cabinet. I don't think you can count."
Dennis Skinner asks John Major about the people who wanted rid of him.

with the music, it made sense.

DB: Exactly. There's an emotional engine created by the juxtaposition of the musical texture and the lyrics. But that's probably what art does best: it manifests that which is impossible to articulate.

If an English student on a poetry course sat down and tried to analyse your lyrics, would they be wasting their time?

DB: No, because I think these days there are so many references for them in terms of late twentieth-century writing, from James Joyce to William Burroughs. I come from almost a traditional school now of deconstructing phrases and constructing them again in what is considered a random way. But in that randomness there's something that we perceive as a reality – that in fact our lives aren't tidy, that we don't have tidy beginnings and endings.

So you'd be very happy if I and another journalist had different ideas of what the songs were about?

DB: Absolutely. As Roland Barthes said in the mid '60s, that was the way interpretation would start to flow. It would begin with society and culture itself. The author becomes really a trigger.

In rock music, the lyrics you hear are sometimes better than they turn out to be. In 'Stone Love', a line I adored was 'in the bleeding hours of morning'; I finally discovered it was 'fleeting hours of morning', which is much more prosaic.

'I work because it's such a great way to escape having to work in a shop.'

DB: That's right. Frankly, sometimes it's a let-down to discover what the artist's actual intent was.

You've now got a computer program, apparently, to randomise your writing. But you've been doing cut-ups since the '70s, inspired by Burroughs.

DB: As a teenager I was fairly traditional in what I read: pompously Nietzsche, and not so pompously Jack Kerouac. And Burroughs. These 'outside' people were really the people I wanted to be like. Burroughs, particularly. I derived so much satisfaction from the way he would scramble life, and it no longer felt scrambled reading him. I thought, 'God, it feels like this, that sense of urgency and danger in everything that you do, this veneer of rationality and absolutism about the way that you live…'

It's a drugs thing as well, isn't it? When I was a student and took lots of drugs, suddenly all kinds of things would make sense that otherwise wouldn't; or rather, you'd see connections between things you otherwise wouldn't.

BE: That's what drugs are useful for. Drugs can show you that there are other ways of finding meanings to things. You don't have to keep taking them, but having had that lesson, to know that you're capable of doing that, is really worthwhile.

DB: But you know, I think the seeds of all that probably were planted a lot earlier. Think of the surrealists with things like their 'exquisite corpses', or James Joyce, who would take whole paragraphs and just with glue stick them in the middle of others, and make up a quilt of writing. It really is the character and the substance of twentieth-century perception, and it's really starting to matter now.

BE: What I think is happening there is it removes from the artist the responsibility of being the 'meaner' – the person who means to say this and is trying to get it over to you – and puts him in the position of being the interpreter.

DB: It's almost as if things have turned from the beginning of this century, where the artist reveals a truth, to the artist revealing the complexity of a question, saying, 'Here's the bad news, the question is even more complicated than you thought.' Often it happens on acid I suppose – if I remember! – you realise the absolute incomprehensible situation that we're in… *(Bowie, who has been gesturing with dangerous animation, knocks an ashtray full of chain-smoked Marlboros on to the carpet)… like this kind of chaos! (Eno kneels to sweep up the ash and butts from Bowie's feet.)* Why are you doing that, Brian? That's immensely big of you.

BE: Just so you can finish your sentence.

DB: I didn't need to. I illustrated it! *(Hilarity)* The randomness of the everyday event. If we realised how incredibly complex our situation was, we'd just die of shock.

You designed a wallpaper for Laura Ashley. A lot of people found the idea a little surprising.

DB: Well, it's not very original. Robert Gober and a number of others, even Andy Warhol, did them. It's just part of a tradition.

You also had your first solo art exhibition recently. Was it frightening to open up your work to public scrutiny?

DB: No, it wasn't at all.

Why not?

DB: Because I know why I did it. Ha!

BE: The thing is when you show something, or you release a record, you open it up to all sorts of other interpretations which don't belong to you any longer. By putting something out you actually enrich it, I think, and you enrich it for yourself. You get it reflected back in a lot of differently shaped mirrors.

DB: I was just a bit late. The reason I wasn't afraid, either, is I'm an artist, a painter and a sculptor. Why should I be afraid? Seemingly the only other thing I'm supposed to be afraid of is whether other people thought it was any good or not, but I've lived that life ever since I began, publicly, of whether I'm any 'good' or not, for nearly 30 years, so that comes with the territory.

Does it hurt you if a lot of people are walking around London saying, 'David Bowie, what a pretentious tosser'?

DB: I don't know of a time when it was never said, though. What's the difference? It's just a different colour overcoat. Not at all.

BE: If you do something different from what you did last time, there is going to be a band of people who'll walk around saying you're a pretentious tosser but after a while you just have to accept *(Bowie is laughing too)*, both of us just have to accept that we're good at what we do. The record proves it. We've both influenced a lot of things, a lot of things that are going on can be traced back to what we did, as we would trace ourselves back to other people.

DB: The history of any art form is actually dictated by other artists and who they are influenced by, not by critics. So for me, my vanity is far more interested in what my contemporaries and peers have to say about my work. A lot of it just comes from pure pleasure, you know? I work because it's such a great way to escape having to work in a shop – to be a songwriter, and a musician and a performer and a painter and a sculptor – it's so cool to do all this stuff, I can't tell you how exciting it is. It really is great. ●

Miranda Sawyer

rings your bell

Oral sex is a question of personal taste – still, have you ever talked someone into coming? It's 3.52am on Sunday and I am doing my motor-mouth damnedest with Aidan from Illinois. We, or rather I, have discussed: my underwear (black, lacy, conventionally undersized), my body shape (tall, trim, yet heavily breasted, with 'hot ass'), how I go about arousing myself

(nothing too emasculatingly mechanical), and what we could get up to if only we weren't separated by a) the Atlantic Ocean and b) our differing opinions *vis à vis* the best use for my toasty posterior.

'You want it up there, don't you?' huffs Aidan. We spend some merry moments in synchronised 'ooh'ing and 'aah'ing (I, embarrassedly covering the mouthpiece with both paws; he, using his free hand more freely, I suppose) before it happens. Aidan ejaculates. I can tell this because he half-growls, half-yelps, 'I'm coming', goes 'uhuhuhuh' like an early-morning VW and then hangs up without so much as a 'fancy a fag?'. They're not big on postcoital manners in Illinois.

Long-distance orgasms: safe, cybernetic and rarely simultaneous. I'm left both tetchy and triumphant. Tetchy because it's tiring making virtual love to ingrates; triumphant that I've finally lost my telephone cherry. My first climax. Victory! Timber! Gooooooaaaal!

The other girls, each in her own booth, are all on the phone. Most are reading; some have their feet up; one is standing, making gestures for a cup of tea. They're all talking quietly, just a bored moan or the occasional 'harder', 'yes', 'really?' discernible above the chug of humour-him chatter. One girl puts her phone on the desk, winks at me, lights up, then picks up again to whisper: 'I've taken my panties off now.'

Model planes

Having two supermodels in bed together was enough to make 'Big Breakfast' bosses quiver beneath their baseball caps last week when they enticed both Kate Moss and Naomi Campbell to the house on the same morning. But they nearly filled their pants when Kate told them that her boyfriend, Johnny Depp, was coming along to meet her after the show and that he'd probably come on and have a chat. But he couldn't make it until after 9am, when the show finishes. Not wanting to miss a great moment in TV history, 'BB' producers got on the Michael Grade hotline to ask his permission to extend the show for half an hour. Amazingly he said yes, and Johnny's appearance was eagerly anticipated. The only snag was that Streatham's Naomi had to leave at 9am exactly to catch an Air France flight to Paris for one of those tedious modelling assignment thingies. 'I'll stay on with Johnny and Kate,' she yawned, much to the delight of all at 'The Big Breakfast'. 'The plane will wait.' And — *sacré bleu!* — it did.

Trump card

Super-rich Ivana Trump was seen laden with food and wine in Harrods' food hall having her credit card refused. When the shop assistant informed our Ivana that she had surpassed her limit, Iv was heard to say some comment along the lines of: 'Limit? I don't have a limit.'

Goldie

from 'Golden Nugget' T.O. 1299, by **Peter Paphides**

Jutta is annoyed, but no one knows what about. So we – The Entourage – keep our distance and sober up a little, because we're silly, excitable buggers and she's a German promotions woman. Not so Goldie, the peerless graffiti artist, failed mugger, fleeting film star, occasional DJ, and (eventually) bona fide musical maverick. The breakbeat wizard who – under his trading name Metalheadz – has just made the definitive electronic album of 1995, seems to have made it his mission to defrost Jutta with his Crazy English Sense of Humour. Hence stories like: 'You know what this one journalist said to me today? He said, "Why do you wear all this cheap gold?" I said, "Listen, mate. First of all, it's not cheap. All this stuff is 14-carat. Secondly, it would be a lot fucking cheaper if

your economy hadn't fucking exploited it in the first place. Thirdly, sort out those trousers before drawing conclusions about me!"' If looks could kill, this hotel lobby would be the Somme.

For someone so likeable, Goldie seems to rub an awful lot of people up the wrong way. Yesterday, on a flight from Heathrow to Hamburg, his mobile phone rang while the plane was on the runway. A worried steward ordered Goldie to switch off the accessory at once, lest it interfere with radio contact between plane and control tower. 'I didn't know it was dangerous to bring phones on to planes,' sighs the exuberant Walsall-born 29-year-old. 'And in any case, why the fuck are they letting me bring it on board if it's dangerous? Isn't that the point of all those expensive X-ray machines?' That

wasn't the end of the matter either: 'Well, I had me mate chatting away in one ear and the steward telling me off in the other. By the time I've turned the thing off, the pilot's making an announcement on the intercom.' Switching effortlessly to olive-in-the-mouth poshspeak, Goldie continues: '"There will be a delay of 50 minutes due to the inconsiderate behaviour of one of the passengers. At a cost of several thousands of pounds, we will have to turn the aircraft back to the terminal, where police are waiting to escort the passenger off the plane."'

Christ! What did you do? 'What could I do?' he exhales sharply. 'I just got up out of my chair and said to everyone, "It's me he's fucking talking about, all right? Anyone got a fucking problem with that, they can talk to me. GOT IT?"' ●

Slave to the rhythm

♀/**Prince** interviewed in T.O. 1282, by **Peter Paphides**

Prince has always been a bit weird, but lately he seems to have lost it completely. He's changed his name, declared war on his record company and scrawled 'SLAVE' on his cheek. What the *@*! is ♀ playing at?

1995

Prince/♀

'**N**O FOOTBALL. There's NO FOOTBALL allowed in here. Can we switch it off?' The Wembley catering staff are looking decidedly agitated. It's not clear whether or not the directive concerning the backstage TV has come from higher up, but you can sense the relief when the offending footy fans switch back to Bugs Bunny. Royalty is in the vicinity. Consequently, even though The Artist Formerly Known As Prince/♀'s minders are taking it easy over some lunch and a coffee, there's a palpable tension about the place.

Minder One: 'Did you see what she called him?'

Minder Two: 'She didn't call him Prince, did she?'

Minder One: 'She did, you know! She was in the studio and she said, "And now we're going to Wembley for Prince!" She said it!'

Minder Three shakes his head, incredulous. Staring at his pizza for inspiration, he reflects for a moment and inhales sharply: 'Heads will roll.' Before anyone has time to work out whether or not he's joking, the door opens. A voluptuous young woman in cycling shorts strolls in. Clearly, this is some kind of sign. Six minders grab their radios and jump to attention just as ♀ follows behind her, heading for the canteen. However, by the time they've come to their senses, he's gone again, evident-

> '**Prince is dead–they've killed him, so writing "SLAVE" on my face doesn't seem so strange**'

ly not peckish. Then the summons. 'He's ready,' shouts his publicist, avoiding at all times the dilemma of having to address ♀ by his new name. More minders line the walls as I pass through another layer of security blokes, until finally I'm faced with a small subcontinent in trousers. I offer it £10 following a somewhat erotic body-search, but it seems this is no time for funnies. The point, of course, isn't that I might be an assassin, more that ♀ is one of the most famous pop stars in the world. And – along with 15 albums, an entire Minneapolis studio complex, several other solo careers launched on the back of his patronage and an untouchable respect within and beyond the music industry – such is the paraphernalia of that fame.

As you may have heard, ♀ wants to wrest ownership of his songs from Warner Bros Music. Warners has responded to ♀'s dissent by refusing to release his new album – 'The Gold Experience'. So he's taken to writing 'SLAVE' on his face, changed his name and refrained from performing any 'Prince' songs at his current shows, opting instead for songs from 'The Gold Experience'. As long as Warners owns his songs, it is claimed, you won't get to hear the album on record. Terrible shame, really, as it's his finest album since 1987's 'Sign O' The Times'. ♀'s recent Wembley set comprises almost entirely unreleased material, yet it's only upon going home you realise he didn't play 'Alphabet Street', 'Gett Off' or '1999'.

So: ♀ wants to talk. About 'The Gold Experience' and about his 'enslavement', and he wants to talk about these things to me. The last time I saw ♀ speaking was his acceptance speech at last month's Brit Awards. This is what he said: 'Prince? Best? "Gold Experience", better. Get wild. In concert, perfectly free. On record, slave. Peace.' Can you see why I'm nervous?

'Sorry about the glasses. We were up kind of late last night,' smiles ♀ pointing to his Bono-style 'Fly' shades. In terms of fame, he may be bigger than Minneapolis, but right now he's smaller than my mum. His dressing room is tiny, rendered claustrophobic by the sheer volume of patterned drapes and velour hangings that frame the dim light. Sifting through the awe, I remind myself that I've been summoned here for a reason. ♀ is using *Time Out* to tell everyone how oppressive his record company is.

When I suggest to ♀ that he's only decided to talk to the press because he has a vested interest in doing so, he snaps, 'Well, Prince never used to do interviews. You'd have to ask Prince why he never used to do interviews, but you're not talking to Prince now. You're talking to me.'

Okay then. So why are you doing interviews at the moment? 'We have to free the music,' explains the pantalooned sex dwarf opposite me. 'I don't own my music at the moment. That's why I'm in dispute with the record company.'

Apparently, ♀'s record company thought he was releasing too much material. This is why it claimed to be putting off the release of 'The Gold Experience'. According to Warners, if it released ♀'s albums as aften as he wants, they'd swamp the market and everyone would lose interest in ♀. Aesthetically too, it might make more sense for ♀/Prince to release fewer records: many critics have commented that if he was more selective and released fewer albums, they would be stupendous rather than merely very good. ♀ unsurprisingly, has little time for either line of thinking.

'There's a lot of things that critics don't understand,' he responds conspiratorially, as if I'm not one of those critics. 'Like the second song in our set is a track called 'Jam', and what people don't realise is that in America that's the number one track at house parties. Now, the audience know that, they respect that! But that's not something that most critics are down with, you know what I'm saying? So when people say I make too many records, I just show them the Aretha Franklin catalogue in the '60s, when she made a new record every four months.'

That's the kind of work ethic you aspire to then, is it?

'That's right. I work hard, with the best musicians in the world. We work all day, you know what I'm saying? But those people at the record company who own my music, they go home at 6pm! And they're the people that control my music. Can you see how there's no room for debate between myself and them?' ♀'s eyes peer up from beneath the shades as if to punctuate the assertion: 'You know, they still call me Prince.'

Is that so surprising?

'No! That's my point! They have to! It's the name that's written down in the contract. If they acknowledge that I'm not

Prince, that ♀ is different to Prince, then they can't hold me to the conditions of their contract.'

One's initial reaction to ♀'s tale of semantic crosswits is to laugh in disbelief, but the point beneath his almost whimsical reasoning is a serious one: 'The concept of ownership of music by record companies is senseless. Like, you know the singer Seal? He's a wonderful talent, but how do I go about telling him and all the other brothers about the battle that we have to fight, when I don't own my music?'

The more you talk to ♀ the more you begin to feel that he's been planning this whole stunt for a long time, just waiting to reach a position of sufficient power from which he could pull it off. Look at the sleeve to Prince's 'Purple Rain' album, made 11 years ago. You'll see a primitive version of the ♀ sign clearly emblazoned on the side. It's been appearing since then with increasing regularity. Presumably, that was the point of the Paisley Park studios and pressing plant, to create the beginnings of a separate infrastructure in the music industry. One that doesn't have to go through the existing white multinationals, and ultimately exists as an alternative to them.

♀ sits upright in affirmation: 'That's what the live show is about. I've done it! And if you look around at the fans, so many of them are waving signs with the new symbol. It's such a beautiful sight.'

You can see why Warners is worried. ♀'s commitment to the promotion of a separate infrastructure is no longer a distant dream. Far from the patronising jests of certain broadsheet writers who see endless comedy mileage in referring to ♀ as Squiggle Man, the motivations behind the name change are, to a degree, political. Sure, ♀ doesn't need the extra money. But if he's making you question the ownership of intangibles like music (and the political implications thereof) then ♀ deserves much respect.

'That's exactly what it is,' smiles ♀. 'Do you see how suddenly writing "SLAVE" on my face doesn't seem as strange? It's a gesture that communicates my position very well. It's like this is what my record company has reduced Prince to. So now, Prince is dead – they've killed him. ♀, on the other hand is beyond contracts. They can talk about contracts till they drop, but they're Prince's contracts, not mine. The record company can't afford to accept that though.' Now the relish on his face is palpable… 'They're still expecting me to do "Purple Rain", a cabaret set.

'The important thing is that my fans hear this music, whether it be through duplicating cassettes, or if we press up 10,000 CDs after the show and charge $5 each, just to cover costs, you know? Even if we do what Pearl Jam do – just turn up at radio stations and play the people our music. That's what these shows are about, communing with the fans. I go to a club and I see fans dancing to my records. They wave to me, I wave back and I realise that this is why I make music. Not for record companies.'

♀ is always quick to mention how his fans 'understand'. While I don't doubt he's genuinely moved by the adulation he receives, it also strikes me as a pretty basic ploy of

'Prince is dead–they've killed him, so writing "SLAVE" on my face doesn't seem so strange' testing the commitment of the diehards while bringing the waverers closer to you. As long as the majority of your fans are prepared to, ahem, die 4 U, there's never too much need to worry about what critics say. So when I start asking ♀ anything more probing than 'Why are you so wonderful?' he clams up visibly.

Anyone with a passing familiarity with Prince's canon will already know the three main themes of his music: shagging, humping and fucking. An elementary knowledge of psychology tells me that anyone so eager to impress upon the world his sack prowess ('you jerk your body like a horny Pony would' and 'there's a lion in my pocket and baby it's ready to roar' are my personal faves) must be motivated, in part, by a deep-rooted misogyny. It's also worth bearing in mind that early in his childhood the young Prince Rogers Nelson ran away from his mother in order to be with his father, a musician. For the first time in our little meeting, ♀ stumbles on his words: 'Aah… oh, well, that's a whole concept that, aah… you know, I could say something about that, and you could take a line out of context that might change the meaning entirely. It's all in the songs anyway.'

Yes, but you do see, don't you, that the sheer volume of fucking that goes on in your songs, is frankly bizarre. Don't you?

'Um, sometimes hate can be love and love can be hate.'

'We have to free the music'

'Gett Off' boasts your, sorry, Prince's ability to assume '22 positions in a one-night stand'. Any chance of passing a few tips on to a mere novice like myself?

' Oh…' ♀ is now visibly buckling beneath the ignominy of having to entertain a question this moronic. 'That's not what all this is about… That's not something I, aaah…'

All what?

'Aaaah.' Big pause. He looks away. All right then. What about marriage, then? Any plans to singlehandedly put Durex out of business by having lots of little ♀s?

'Not really,' he smirks. 'I decided that things like family don't have a big part to play in my future. I'm dedicated to music, to the point that I see all of life through it.'

What would seem like a flippant, sentimental declaration from any other pop star becomes a fierce declaration of humanism from the mouth of ♀. The past two weeks have seen him deliver night after night of rumbustious boilerhouse funk while the psychedelic harems of his mind are recreated on stage around him. 'A couple of years ago perhaps,' he concludes, 'I had a spiritual, uh… rebirth. I was lacking direction for a very long time. But I saw a light which I realised I had to follow. At that point I became…' ♀ points to a drape bearing his hieroglyphic name.

By the way, how do you pronounce that?

'It isn't pronounced. It just is.' ●

Kin hell

Noel Gallagher interviewed in T.O. 1315, by **Laura Lee Davies**

A couple of weeks after Blur's single, 'Country House', beat Oasis's 'Roll With It' to number one in the charts, guitarist and songwriter Noel Gallagher was asked on MTV if he considered Oasis to be a failure. 'Listen to me,' he replied. 'I'm 28 years old, right? I've got about a quarter of a million quid in the bank, right? I'm healthy, I've had six hit singles, one of which got to Number One, three of which made the Top Three and four of which made the Top Ten. I've got a record-breaking album in the fucking Guinness Book Of Records, more discs on my walls than I'd care to mention. Some failure!'

With the new Oasis album, '(What's The Story) Morning Glory?' having sold a staggering 350,000 copies in its first week, Noel Gallagher is unlikely to lose sleep over coming in second to Blur over the sales of one single. However, the much-discussed marketing duel – an election campaign with Oasis as 'oop the workers northerners' and southerners Blur as 'the bosses' sons' – did get heated enough for Noel to say he hoped the members of Blur would die of AIDS.

'Two years ago, everyone would've started laughing and saying, "Oh you fucking ruffians" if I'd said that,' he says, clearly tired of the continuing fall-out. 'I took it back immediately, but the journalist chose not to print that. People want the controversial quote, so it's sort of half our fault and half them fishing. We came along at a time when pop stars were all nice people. Everybody was trying to say something. We came along, pissed as arseholes, singing about yellow submarines and fucking dogs who sniff Alka Seltzer. If you write about social issues, you're gonna get asked about them. Fortunately for us, we were writing about drinking, so we get asked about drinking and shagging birds and taking drugs. At the end of the day, I'm just a musician with a big mouth. The press cultivated our image and we had to deal with it.'

Noel, 'a complete fucking cunt' in the studio, speculates that he would've 'disintegrated into a fucking yobbo' if Oasis hadn't happened, though he proclaims to be something of a pussycat the rest of the time, putting the Gallagher Bros' reputation as the Krays Of Pop down to Liam's less rational outbursts.

'Our Kid offered the crowd out at Glastonbury – all 90,000 of them! Someone was throwing eggs and one of them hit my monitor and splashed all over me new dufflecoat, so I stopped the song just to wipe down. And Our Kid jumps off stage shouting, "Fucking come on, dickheads!"' Noel shakes his head.

Surprisingly though, he seems finally to have acquired some humility…ish. 'We used to say, "We want to be bigger than the Beatles", and then somebody wrote, "They think they're better than the Beatles". Now it's, "They think they're the new Beatles." Some of our stuff is up there, but we'll probably never be as good as they are. Until I get into a black cab and the drivers constantly know who I am, I'll consider us an average, run-of-the-mill group. Until I get in a cab in New York and the driver says, "Hey, Oasis!", then, compared to U2, we're just tiny kids rolling tyres around.' ●

1996

In a flurry of snogging and shagging, the New Lass burped her way to the bar, leaving her lad behind, though she did eventually come home (whereas football didn't). Rappers dropped like flies, Prozac was dropped like vitamins, cows went mad and there was more life on Mars than here back home.

January

François Mitterrand dies.

Earvin 'Magic' Johnson returns to the basketball court after retiring four years previously, the result of a HIV-positive diagnosis.

February

Protesters against the Newbury by-pass are evicted from the site after occupying it for a month.

Jarvis Cocker cocks a snook (and an arse) at Michael Jackson and becomes instantly popular.

March

Scientists link the eating of beef with Creutzfeldt-Jakob Disease, also known as 'Mad Cow' Disease.

Disgruntled gun-enthusiast Thomas Hamilton mows down 16 children and a teacher in Dunblane.

April

Michael Bryant guns down 34 people in Tasmania when he opens fire on tourists at a holiday resort.

May

The Duke and Duchess of York divorce.

June

Germany beats the Czech Republic in the final of the European Championships.

July

TWA flight 800 explodes shortly after take-off in New York killing all 230 on board.

August

The Prince and Princess of Wales divorce.

September

Tupac Shakur dies when he is gunned down in Las Vegas. Gangs are alleged to have been involved.

Seven

Serial killers and mismatched cops overcoming antagonism are seldom fruitful subjects, but this exceptionally nasty thriller blends genres to grim and gripping effect.

The English Patient

The performances are flawless; more surprising is the fluency, poetry and scale of Minghella's direction.

Romeo & Juliet

Sticking with the original dialogue, Luhrmann makes the central element visual. Fine as the rest of the cast is, it's DiCaprio and Danes who steal the honours.

Beck – Odelay (Geffen)

It feels like pop's melting pot future and

a funked-up flamboyant contender for album of the year.

Spice Girls – Spice (Virgin)

When Take That abdicated, in swooped Spice Girls like heroines from a Russ Meyer movie. Furthering their universal appeal as role models, this quivers with infectious tunes.

Underworld – Second Toughest In The Infants (Junior Boys Own)

Second Toughest... could be read as an embracement of confusion through the fluidity of the breakbeat. What it definitely *is*, is an object lesson in how to make your most surreal ideas into a masterpiece.

Looney tunes

Björk Interviewed in TO 1326, by **Laura Lee Davies**

'm a bit funny,' comes Björk's voice from somewhere beneath the white puffball jacket with which she's taking up the best part of the back seat of the taxi. 'Cos I've been dead all day.'

Until five minutes ago, Björk was spending the best part of a Tuesday pretending she was dead at the bottom of a cliff. Michel Gondry, the video director who made her 'Human Behaviour' and 'Army Of Me' promos so startlingly magical, is putting on another epic production for her new single, 'Hyper-Ballad'. Now we're speeding through the streets of north London to her home, where an interview has been squeezed into the tiniest window in her schedule. Remarkably, despite having allowed herself only a couple of days off to return to Iceland for her birthday, Björk has gone straight from a major American tour into the hectic build-up to her biggest-ever London gig, playing Wembley at the end of this month.

'I lost my voice in the middle of the tour,' she explains. 'I've been singing professionally since I was 11 years old. I've been spoilt rotten – I could shout and scream and my voice was always there. I had to rethink something I've always taken for granted. I had to make choices, like did I want to socialise or sing ? I've always been the biggest rebel ever, I was brought up

by a mother who, if I told her I wanna eat 97 bananas, she'd say "Okay, cool." I would dress myself, there was no discipline, just complete anarchy in the most hippy, happy way. I could do all those things and always believe in a spontaneous way of living. Like if you want to eat five pounds of carrots, eat it, if you want to jump into a bathtub of honey, do it. Don't even think about it. On this tour, I was only out of my bus cabin for two hours a day, while I was on stage. There were all these special things I had to eat. I had such a disciplined schedule I felt like one of the Olympics people. Coming out the other side of that, I feel like I've just done an Indiana Jones – I fucking killed the tiger, killed the Nazis, I've done everything and now the titles are rolling. It was a happy ending and I'm just ecstatic, in heaven. I've got my voice back and I'm tripping, big time.'

Okay, so there are people out there who would prefer a world without Björk grunting and howling her way through old jazz standards and spacey pop songs, but without her two solo albums, there'd be nothing but those two dodgy geezers Britpop and Trip-hop to brighten our charts... oh, and Robson and Jerome, natch. Instead, a solo career which started with what Björk calls her 'funny little personal album' in 1993, has proved one of the most innovative and successful musical projects of the '90s. By last year's 'Post', anyone who still consigned her to Pixie Corner deserved to have their head boiled. However, you're still hard pushed to unearth footage of Björk which doesn't shove her in the weirdo pen. Her striking looks, her knack of dressing like something that sprang from a Quality Street box (today it's an orange and black jumpsuit affair, a kind of jazzy orange cream cluster) and her instinctive avoidance of video cliché stand so far apart from the T-shirt parade that putting her into any context within our planet's range seems to be an uphill struggle. However, if she did own a British passport, she'd have breezed the Mercury Music Award for both 'Debut' and 'Post'. Her worth as an artist shouldn't go unrecognised as the price for good copy. Far from trading on a wacky image to boost her career, Björk is, first and foremost, a serious musician.

'The most dramatic gig on the tour was San Diego where, instead of a few octaves range, I had one. We had to change all the melodies, I was crying at the end of it. What annoyed me most was that the crowd were so brilliant. They clapped for encores and I was so offended: "How dare you, this is the worst gig I've ever done! To think it doesn't matter if I sing well or not, it's still the same for you. Can't you throw tomatoes at me? At least then we'd have honesty. I ended up apologising that I wanted to sing them 900 songs, and then, typically over-emotional of me, I started crying. And of course, were in America. Honey, I'm in California, so they all fucking cried with me. Then they were all waiting for me outside, to give me 900 throat medicines.'

Once when the Sugarcubes supported the Swans at the Town And Country Club, a young indie punter clambered onto the stage, not to hurl himself at the diminutive singer, or indeed at the rest of the crowd, but just to touch her, as if he couldn't believe the stellar sound cooing through 'Birthday' was coming from a real person. The miracle still seems to take place every time Björk breaks into song, yet being treated like a prized museum treasure is something which still baffles her. 'I still get it in the strangest places. I might be at a photo shoot and somebody offers me a drink, so I ask for water. But they don't tell me they have everything but water, instead they run a mile to get water when I would've been happy with an orange juice. I can't get my head around that shit .I usually find what people expect of me hilarious. If I go out to eat with people from my record company in America, they just stare at me. I end up playing along, telling stories about transvestites and dinosaurs. But I don't take it personally. If I met David Attenborough I'd be talking about fucking insects.

'I'm almost religious about the fact that no two people are the same, I get absolutely no kick out of being surrounded by yesmen. I want people who are equals to me, even stronger than me, 'cos I'm still learning – from photographers, harpsichord players, lawyers. Sometimes, if there's football on the Pay TV, and I might not even be watching, I'll be just cleaning or walking around, and a lot of people are clapping, I start crying. Just that idea of unison, it's basically what I'm about. A lot of people yawn and say, "Give me a break, you're too utopian, Björk." But that's truly what I like.'

One of Björk's smartest moves since parting with her former indie-rock outfit the Sugarcubes was to be open to the influence of other producers, mixers and musicians. On both albums, Nellee Hooper's sweeping, string-drenched production, Graham (808 State) Massey's vibrant studio work and, more recently, Tricky's inimitably sensual co-writing have all contributed to a sound which remains undoubtedly Björk's own.

'The people I identify with tend to be English or Scottish or Irish. But I work more with characters. Just listen to my accent: it's Howie B from Glasgow, it's Graham Massey from Manchester (the first English accent I learned) and it's the Bristol lot (so there's all this mat'er, but'er rubbish in there), then it's south London. That's the people I work with. When I go to America, they look at me as as a British artist. It was never my ambition to become English or anything. In fact I moved here against my will in a way. I'm just always on a mission to find the world's best song, and I always end up back listening to people who are from here.

'My first band wasn't planned, but I ended up with players from Iran, Turkey, India, Barbados and a couple of English musicians. That to me is England today. all these different races, so many immigrants, I can't put my finger on it because it's still in the making, but the diversity is incredible. The idea today of people from Brazil only making Brazilian music doesn't exist. No way do kids only hear Peruvian music in Peru. No way do people in London only hear "Greensleeves" and the Beatles.

'I took my son to America, he thought the car alarms were the animals who lived between the skyscrapers.'

People worry that they'll lose their individuality if they share their ideas with other people, but if you've got a strong identity, you could hang out with aliens. In Iceland I'm just Björk, over here I'm Icelandic. Even putting the pink dot amongst the green ones makes you what you are. Working with people is just like love. You can't say: "Okay, I'm not going to love anybody for 14 days because I wanna save it for this person who I will love very much on the fifteenth day!" You can't be stingy with your ideas because the more you give, the more you get back. It's arrogance to think that all the ideas you get are yours, it's bollocks. People who get a lot of ideas are those who've got their antennae out. Like today, with Michel: to start with I give him all my ideas and he brews it and gives it back to me. It's like one plus one equals three. People say, "You're mad, Björk, you're back in your dream world", but sorry, honey, this is what life is about. You get a man and a woman and you get a child.'

Sitting on her sofa, peeling satsumas in front of the fire, there is something in the 30-year-old's tone which gives perfect sense to these cosmic ramblings. Aware of her public persona, she occasionally stops herself rephrases her points so they won't sound 'too hippy'. And despite images of a semi-cartoon songstress flying through the decade, and despite a 'Spitting Image' caricature that would have her getting a riff off a boiling kettle, Björk's music is distinctly earthy. From slamming toilet doors and lyrics about one-weekend stands, to the rumble of rhythmic Eastern ▶

thunder and the incurably romantic orchestral sparkle of her albums, there is something warm and very human to her work.

'Most people in Britain have telephones, they know the sound when you put a video in the machine. They know car alarms, fire alarms. I know, you're gonna say "Oh, 'Spitting Image'", but I totally believe these affect us. The first time I took my son to America when he was one year old, he thought the car alarms were the animals who lived between the skyscrapers. He was saying: "Mummy, mummy, where are they? Are they hairy?" A day in my life is car noises, the toaster, but it's also the wind, the rain, the cold, the human voice – the greatest influence on us all. That's why, in my music, I want the humanity, the wind, birds, rain, nature, the sun and the moon, the ocean, the earth, because you could live in the middle of fucking Manhattan and you'd still have all these things.

'Some people listen to my albums and say: "It's got no consistency." Fuck that. What are my musical roots? In a way, there is no such thing as traditional Icelandic music, especially not pop music. I was brought up on many things, why should I stick to one? It's like saying I'm gonna just wear sneakers and jeans for the rest of my life, never a skirt, never a Christmas dress… we've got all these sides to us, it's about time pop music got more human.'

Björk is so open when she talks that conversation seems a lot more intimate than it actually is. She has absolutely no hesitation at setting a journalist down in the middle of her own home, and the appearance of her son, Sindri, home from school does not break her concentration, but she has chosen carefully the parts of her private life that must necessarily be public, and those she is going to keep to herself.

'I used to give 900 per cent to everyone. I thought: Okay, I'm a goody, I can't lose, I'll go into every situation and give 900. But I realised I did that because then I could walk away without feeling guilty. I had to learn to be subtle and not always be on 11 out of ten, which is just boring. Sometimes you go to two, five, nine or minus seven. It gets easier as I get older.

'I'm quite lucky because I got big in Iceland when I was 11 years old and I had to learn the hard way, by instinct instead of brain, that there is privacy and there are outside things. But no two people see the same thing the same way, so even though I'm not telling you the last time I had my period, I'm still not lying to you. There's just a side you show to the man in the corner shop, a side you show to your grandmother and a side to show to your lover.

'It doesn't bother me that different people like different things. I love to be surrounded by people who like celery, but I hate celery. I find it funny to meet people who are obsessed by Queen; I'd never buy their records. I didn't plan to be Björk the pop star/singer. I could start writing string arrangements or play a pipe organ in a church in the Czech Republic. I'm not desperate for this, it just kinda happened. But I'm gonna be doing music till I'm 85.' ●

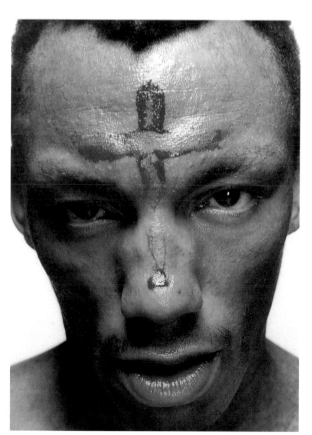

God's gift

When his first album, 'Maxinquaye', went ballistic last year, the trip-hop messiah started believing he was God.

Tricky interviewed in T.O. 1337, by **Peter Paphides**

Last year, a German journalist opened an interview with the words, 'So, Tricky: tell me what it's like being God… well nearly God?' and Tricky's new album – both titled and credited to 'Nearly God' – was born. If you want to establish some truth between Tricky's desire to alienate all the people who found 'Maxinquaye' so accessible and his later admission that he'd have liked to win a Brit, 'because business-wise it's good – I can sell more songs', 'Nearly God' is a pretty good place to start.

Today, he's no-where to be seen. Admittedly, I'm late, but he'd surely have waited for me. 'Five o'clock outside Sticky Fingers in Kensington.' That was what he said… or perhaps it was inside – although quite why credder-than-thou trip-hop practitioner Tricky would want to be seen inside Bill Wyman's saucy west London restaurant is anyone's guess.

Sure enough, he's not there. That's because he's keeping watch from his flat just across the road: 'Oi! Over here! OI! PETE!' Oh, right. Tricky's cries have actually attracted three of us – two Sticky Fingers waitresses on their coffee break and yours truly. And by the time I've parked the car, they're all bunched up on the sofa of his spacious apartment. A joint, as ever, is doing the rounds.

'This is fucking amazing,' croaks Tricky in his West Country brogue, as the video for Michael Jackson's 'Earth Song' reaches its 'Superman II'-style conclusion. 'Don't you think this is amazing? I think he's fucking incredible.'

The waitresses nod uneasily, waiting for a punchline. But Tricky – whose stunning début disc, 'Maxinquaye', has adorned the CD player of every cred bohemian pad in London – isn't joking. He genuinely likes Michael Jackson. He even spoke to the guy who did Jackson's 'Scream' about doing one of his videos. You see, that's the thing about Tricky. Even when he's being needlessly contrary, you kind of delude yourself into agreeing with him. He keeps you on your toes. And women, it seems, like to be kept on their toes. He asks one of the waitresses to make him a cup of tea, and she gladly obliges. Five minutes later, she's off back to Sticky Fingers, serving people for money.

But Tricky hates it when people go along with him too readily. When he played Shepherd's Bush Empire last year, he introduced a song by asking if there were 'any fans of trip-hop in the house…' When a naïve section of the crowd roared in the affirmative, Tricky simply hissed, 'Well, you can fuck off home then.'

'What it is,' he explains between sips, 'is that I look at a crowd like that and I think: These people can't honestly be into it. So it's just a way

of testing them, really. And if they knew anything about me, they'd know I fucking hate the word trip-hop. But they don't. They're just brainwashed sheep.'

Isn't that a little bit cruel?

'Oh yeah, it's cruel. Similarly, if a girl comes up and talks to me in a club, it would be a one-sided conversation. It's boring when people pay you those compliments, so I just end up taking advantage of it. I'll do things like telling them to get me a brandy and coke when I don't even want a drink. They go off and buy it. And if I'm with my mates, we start taking the piss.'

Last year – shortly after the release of his rapturously received 'Maxinquaye' and the birth of a daughter to Martina, his girlfriend whose piercing vocals sealed that album's brilliance – Tricky got it into his head that he was God. Perhaps if enough critics and people in bars tell you you're a deity, you start to believe them. Perhaps if you were able to conjure somnambulant hip-hop noir like 'Aftermath' and 'Ponderosa' out of a sampler, a turntable and some keyboards, you'd think you were God too. Tricky himself puts it down to a combination of the latter and 'too much spliff. It's a common psychosis experienced by heavy cannabis smokers. Have you heard of it?' he asks me. I can't say I have.

'Yeah, you get devil complexes and Jesus complexes. First of all I thought I was the devil. Have you seen "Rosemary's Baby"? It's fucking brilliant. This woman's having the devil's baby, and this guy says, "You have to have this baby. It is the devil's son and he shall be called Adrian" – my real name.'

And the God thing – how did that come about?

'Well, with my lyrics, I feel really God-like.'

This assertion is delivered flatly, in a manner more common to old women who complain of recurring migraines.

'Well, I watch MTV and I feel like there's no one out there doing anything to do with what's real. Nothing's real, and I just feel like God compared to these artists. Part of it is because everyone's trying to suss where my stuff comes from, and I don't know where it comes from. So you ain't gonna get any clues from me.' ●

"1996"

"Who really cares whether I'm gay or straight? Do they really think they've got a serious chance of shagging me or something?"
George Michael gives it to us straight

"I don't know what goes on behind closed doors, but I think we all give the wife a smack once in a while."
George Best offers Paul Gascoigne some advice on wife-beating

"People see it as an indecent race between me, the Pope and Boris Yelstin."
Sir John Gielgud, 92, ponders death

"She's the first Spice Girl; the pioneer of our ideology – Girl Power."
Geri Spice on Margaret Thatcher

"They're not lesbians are they?"
George Walden, MP for Buckingham, when asked what he knew of the Spice Girls

"Young persons' light music combo have spat."
Independent headline on Gallaghers brotherly squabbles

"We've recorded two tracks. Just the same old boring pub rock bollocks."
Noel Gallagher on new Oasis material

"I'm your number one fan."
Michael Jackson on Nelson Mandela

"I can see who the world leader is."
Nelson Mandela observing the paparazzi clamour over Jackson

"You'd be there on stage and there'd be banners saying 'Robbie, shag me', 'Jason, blow me a kiss', 'Mark, show us your bum', and 'Gary, we like your music'."
Gary Barlow on his lack of sex appeal

"Terry went in optimistically and came out misty optically."
Sun headline, after England v. Germany game

"Why didn't you just belt it, son?"
Gareth Southgate's mum's first words to him after missing the penalty against Germany

"Is it a bird, is it a plane…? No, it's a Circle Line train."
Tannoy announcement on strike day

Spike Milligan

Look back in anger

At 77 Spike Milligan, the grandfather of British comedy, is still peeved with the Beeb.

Spike Milligan interviewed in T.O. 1338, by **Steve Grant**

The Spike Milligan experience begins with his address. It's not quite as exotic as Wuthering Heights, but involves a meadow, a district of the small Sussex town of Rye, and something called 'Dumbwoman', which turns out to be a tiny lane named after a medieval local who was, er, dumb, or 'spoke-challenged', as the Middle Ages' politically correct may have put it. I'm not breaking any confidences in telling you this: once you get to Rye, any local cabdriver can tell you where the Godfather of British Comedy lives. I approached one and asked him if he knew Spike Milligan's gaff. His eyes narrowed: 'Is he expecting you?' 'Er, yes.' 'Because if he's not, he'll probably chuck you out.'

It turns out that Dave used to ferry Spike around, and knows him quite well. And Milligan is very pally with Dave's wife, who collects ornamental elephants. Irish Spike, who grew up in India, gave her one that had been hand-carved by his grandfather. 'You'd be surprised,' says Dave. 'We've had calls from his wife saying can you come out here and rescue someone, and we've found reporters wandering the roads five minutes after they've arrived. I like Spike. He's normal, basically. He tells you what he thinks and he doesn't suffer fools. If they irritate him, he just tells them to sod off.'

Milligan is sitting in a chair facing a large window in his log-fired living room; he spends hours each day looking over the fields towards the coast. At one point, he interrupts and waves an arm in the direction of a flock of seagulls wafting across the horizon. 'Look at them, they're like the sky's children.' Milligan's love of nature is well known. In the summer, he can be seen in the fields picking up litter; he once threw a brick through an ICA window in protest at an art installation which electrocuted goldfish. The world has, he considers, been finished by overbreeding. 'The population of the planet increased by 100 million in the last year. I did my bit, I had four kids. If I'd have known what I know now I wouldn't have had any. I don't like traffic, but I bought them each a car, created my own personal traffic jam.' As a lapsed Catholic, did he blame that Church's teaching on contraception? 'Not really. People just like to fuck.'

Milligan bought each of his children a Mini Minor with £15,000 he received some years ago from an auction of his original 'Goons' scripts, which were mouldering in a drawer. Elton John bought them. It was writing these groundbreakers, the launch pad for post-war British comedy, that brought on the first of his many breakdowns, although in one moment of genuine rapture he recalls the days when he 'started at nine in the morning and worked all day until after midnight. That went on for months at a time. It was such a lot of passion, so much driving energy, we really took it seriously, doing away with jokes and one-liners, all the usual crap. We were very serious about it. Sellers and I used to have this anti-one-liner routine. "That dog's got no nose." And he'd reply: "That was no lady, that was my wife."'

It's a truism that Spike Milligan is the comic guv'nor – a man whose comedic genius inspired a whole generation of up-and-coming Oxbridge undergraduates. Milligan's impact on the comedy of the Monty Python team was obvious and has never been denied, but here the acrimony starts. Milligan has never hidden his disgust at the BBC's refusal to repeat his television comedy work, notably his nine 'Q' series which stretched through the '60s. 'It's an outrage, because that's what gave the Monty Python lot their idea. They'd all been flops up until then and then "Q" came along and it fitted their format completely.' Was this homage? 'No, it's called copying. I get fed up to the back teeth with all these comparisons. Reeves and Mortimer? I'm nothing like them. I saw one of their shows and it was just a lot of noise to me. I didn't do noise humour, it was nonsense humour, it was in the tradition of people like Edward Lear.'

Milligan believes 'Q' and some of his other TV work was groundbreaking. 'It was completely new, complete anarchy. I'd do a sketch where someone would produce a door, and someone else would say, "That's a good place for it," and then someone else would knock on that door and say, "Hello, we are

Jehovah's Burglars and we are being persecuted by the Church for our beliefs. We believe there is a lot of money here." I went to Australia recently and they were playing the Goons stuff every day on the radio and no matter what people say, I don't think it's dated much at all. There was a bit where Eccles and Bluebottle are talking. Eccles says: "What time does it say on your bit of paper?" "3.32." "My bit says 9.20, so how am I going to tell them the time?" "Don't show them the paper."'

If asked what his occupation is, he says 'author', but this extraordinary man is also a poet, painter and musician. His happiest times, he says, were spent playing the trumpet in his army band, and one of the saddest signs of the passing of time is that he can no longer perform: his embouchure went in the middle of a reunion concert a few years ago. I ask him if he's ever taken drugs. Not an unusual question when you consider that this man has written sketches in which insects prepare to audition for a David Attenborough wildlife special; or a monologue where a man convincingly believes himself to be a four-poster bed. He says he hasn't, but without much fervour. 'I remember trying to score some smack once for Stan Getz,' he offers, referring to the recently deceased tenor-sax giant. 'We ended up at one of those beautiful-people parties where everyone was naked from the waist down and someone offered me some grass instead. They called it tea. So I said, "That's all very well, but my friend prefers milk. Where's the milk?" "In the fridge," somebody said!'

> 'This is your friendly local rapist, do you have an appointment?'

Milligan isn't nearly as grouchy as some of his remarks may suggest. For a start, he speaks in a soft voice that sometimes sinks to a bare whisper; he also loves laughter, even if he sometimes dares you to explain the joke in question. Intriguingly, though, he's happy to discuss his depressions, which have led to him being heavily sedated in a hospital ward, and even trying to hang himself. He isn't so forthcoming about the 'manic' side of his illness, presumably unwilling to imply that his comic genius owes anything to a clinical condition. Once, the mania led him to attack and try to kill Peter Sellers with a potato knife after Sellers insisted on borrowing his record player when Milligan, deep in one of his depressions, had a blinding headache. Sellers took the threat seriously and fled. Milligan's standard response, when asked what would have happened if he'd succeeded, is: 'He would have died.' Similarly when I ask him what he would like as an epitaph, he comes up with: 'I told you I was ill.' I laugh and he adds, 'I've only just made that up.' The dark side again: he hasn't just made it up, and he knows that I know it. He once told *The Observer* the same thing. But it's still funny.

The phone rings: it's another charity. Milligan answers with 'This is your friendly local rapist, do you have an appointment?' but soon gets fed up and starts waving the phone in my direction. 'If only people would be brief, and stick to the point,' he mutters as he signs up for yet another bout of good works. Don't bet against that knighthood just yet. ●

Trainspotting

from 'the other side of the tracks' in T.O. 1328, by **Tom Charity**

Drugs movies are downers: is there anything intrinsically less entertaining than watching some skinny wretch sticking a needle in their already pock-marked arm – unless of course it's seeing the same sad sack shivering through prolonged cold turkey (invariably the prelude to yet more drugs and degradation)? Think about 'Christiane F', 'Basketball Diaries', 'Rush', or any one of a dozen cautionary tales nobody ever sat through twice.

On the set of 'Trainspotting' back in August, it looks at first as if the film adaptation of Irvine Welsh's 1993 cult novel will be of this cautionary, realist strand. Outside, the sun is beating down so hard the Glasgow tarmac is melting. But it's cool and quiet within the cavernous Victorian Wills cigarette factory – now a makeshift studio for the team who made 'Shallow Grave': producer Andrew Macdonald, director Danny Boyle and screenwriter John Hodge. Macdonald, a gangly 30-year-old, conducts me round a rabbit warren of flats and bedsits, each smaller, dingier and damper than the last. In one, streams of locomotives press

down from ersatz, mildewed wallpaper. In another, cat shit covers every surface. This is the flip-side of the affluent yuppie Edinburgh depicted in 'Shallow Grave'. It's so poor, so barren, so mired in terminal neglect – it could drive a man to drugs.

In the corner of the temporary shanty-town there's a plumbing graveyard, a discarded heap of toilets, urinals and bogs. These are cast-offs from the movie's first big scene: 'The Most Horrible Toilet in Scotland'. In the book, Macdonald explains, congenital heroin addict Mark Renton, the more-or-less hero, is reduced to inserting opium suppositories to relieve his withdrawal pains. No sooner are they safely in place, however, than Renton's constipation breaks. When the shits hits the pan, the suppositories go down with it, and 'Rent Boy' dredges through the excrement to retrieve them: '...panhandling the shite ay many good Muirhouse and Pilton punters. Ah gag once, but get ma white nugget ay gold.' Apparently this wee stomach-churner does not go far enough for Hodge, Boyle et al. In the movie, Renton's up to

his armpits in crap - and then his head goes in, his neck, his torso, his jeans and sneakers until he's swimming in the stuff. 'Tomorrow we're shooting the dead baby crawling on the ceiling...' offers Macdonald, gratuitously. He's made his point. Social realism it ain't. Social surrealism, perhaps. ●

Wannabe my lover?

Sporty, Posh, Ginger, Scary and Baby offer their Valentine's advice

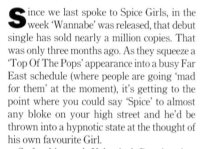

The Spice Girls interviewed in T.O. 1315, by **Laura Lee Davies**

Since we last spoke to Spice Girls, in the week 'Wannabe' was released, that debut single has sold nearly a million copies. That was only three months ago. As they squeeze a 'Top Of The Pops' appearance into a busy Far East schedule (where people are going 'mad for them' at the moment), it's getting to the point where you could say 'Spice' to almost any bloke on your high street and he'd be thrown into a hypnotic state at the thought of his own favourite Girl.

So for this year's Valentine's Day, in scientific in-depth research stylee, we asked five of the nation's young females (who just happen, conveniently, to be in the most successful British pop outfit of the moment) to give us their tips on what the '90s girl is looking for. The results were impressive. I mean, these girls could seduce a rubber plant if you gave them five minutes and a bottle of brown ale. And don't go thinking it's all hunks and high-flyers when you're in music's fast lane; all you sour-faced stand-up comedian types, there's hope for you yet…

Right, let's start with the chat-up line: reliable turn-on or relic of bygone blokedom?
Mel C: 'Ooh, I don't really believe in chat-up lines, although sometimes they're so obvious they're quite cool. Your first line is gonna be the ice-breaker, so it should be a funny one.'
Emma: 'I can't believe it, but I have had: "Do you come here often?"'
Mel B: 'Can I just add that not a lot of people chat me up so I'm really open to offers, all right? A nice bit of conversation, even if it might not go anywhere.'
Victoria: 'Someone came up to me once and said: "You've got really good dress sense, I really like your clothes, they'd look great on my bedroom floor."'
Mel C: 'A bloke's best chat-up line with me would be an invitation to a football match. I'm not really interested in restaurants and romance and all that bollocks.'
Victoria: 'Being in a gang does boost your confidence. We were at some awards party last

night and there was this bloke there that I really fancy and Mel B just went up to him and said: "My mate fancies you!" Embarrassing as that is, it certainly breaks the ice.'

Is it a question of location, location, location? Should men really waste their time throwing half a kilo of talc down their trousers before heading off to the local disco?
Emma: 'If you're out clubbing, everyone's on a good vibe.'
Mel B: 'I disagree, everyone there's just on the pull. It's better if you meet that special someone when you're in traffic, or on the tube, or in a supermarket queue.'
Emma: 'The back seat of the cinema's a good place.'

Don't you think you should know someone before you get that far?
Emma: 'Weeell, you don't have to do everything, you could just have a fondle… ha ha.'
Mel C: 'The ideal place is the Kop, that way you know they support the right team.'
Geri: (instructively) 'Well, a bad place would have to be the STD clinic, I suppose. But a good place? Anywhere. Everywhere.'
Victoria: 'I tell you what, I was down the pub the other day, and I thought, if I didn't have a boyfriend, is there anyone here that I'd wanna talk to? It was like, no! They're all standing there with their Ralph Lauren shirts undone, bit of fake tan. It was like a uniform. I like a bit of individuality. That's why Jack Dee really turns me on.'

Well, you never know your luck.
Victoria 'Nah, he's married, with kids… maybe that's why he's so miserable.'

And if you do wake up one morning and realise that the guy making toast isn't the one for you, how do you get rid of them?
A chorus of Spice Girls: 'Tell it like it is.'
Mel C: 'Cruel to be kind.'
Victoria: 'The nastier you are to some of the creeps who try and chat you up, the more keen they get! If you tell them to piss off, they don't get it, so it's better just to ignore them.'

Do you think that it's easier to be honest these days? Do men still run a mile if you simply say how you feel? Or can you command the truth from the two-faced lovehound?
Geri: 'It's easier for women to say what they want these days because they can admit that they like sex. Whether it's a one-night stand or something permanent, as long as you're aware of the situation, it's okay. And you have to remember that there are blokes out there who get more attached and women who are less committed.'

So does the New Lass really exist or is it merely a notion dreamt up in an ad company's boardroom?
Mel B: 'I think the New Lass has been around a long time. Some guys mistake it for either being too loud or being a bit tarty or a bit upfront, and they can be afraid of it because they're getting a taste of their own medicine. They've treated us like little girls, and the new lasses are more prepared to fight back. It's been happening anyway… for some girls it might have only been when they're pissed or when they're with the gang, but every girl's got a right to stick up for herself, especially with so many leery perverts out there.'
Geri: 'People are more conscious of the New Lass, but there have always been strong women prepared to chain themselves to railings to get the vote. Maybe men are accepting it more now.'

Okay, so any parting shots, pearls of dating wisdom?
Geri: 'People can smell desperation, it's the biggest turn-off. It's important to be natural, personality is like a muscle: they have to use it and work it for it to grow.'
Mel B: 'There are opportunities all the time, it's just that people aren't aware of them. Instead of just going out and saying to yourself that you're going to pull, you should just be open to other people. It could happen in two hours or two weeks, it's just a question of daring to say, "Look, I fancy you, how about a drink, Wednesday, 7.30, down the pub?"' ●

1997

Di died, but Chris Evans lived, discuss… We came over all emotional and with our new touchy-feely-weepy sensitivity, we almost let Tony Blair's New Labour convince us we were Cool Britannia. Cool? We caught trench-foot at Glastonbury, we retuned our videos for Channel 5, and we still couldn't tell a teletubby from a spice girl.

January
Tony Bullimore is rescued after spending five days trapped underneath a capsized yacht.

February
Edinburgh scientists claim a breakthrough in cloning techniques when they announce the arrival of Dolly.

Timothy Leary, having turned on and tuned in, finally drops out.

March
39 people from Heaven's Gate cult commit mass suicide in San Diego.

Tiger Woods becomes the youngest golfer ever to win a US Masters at 21-years-old.

Channel 5 is launched.

May
Labour win their first election in 24 years.

June
Mike Tyson is disqualified after biting the ear off opponent Evander Holyfield.

July
Hong Kong is handed over to the Chinese.

Italian designer Gianni Versace is gunned down in Florida.

September
Diana, Princess of Wales, is killed when her car crashes in a Parisian underpass. Dodi Fayed is also killed.

Scotland and Wales vote in favour of devolution.

November
Louise Woodward, having been found guilty of the murder of baby Matthew Eappen, has her sentence commuted to manslaughter and is immediately released.

December
Rock singer Michael Hutchence is found hanged in a Sydney hotel room.

Nil By Mouth
Gary Oldman's debut as writer/director is so uncompromisingly honest, it makes other portraits of British working class life look like sour caricature or misplaced idealism.

The Full Monty
You could get all metaphorical about it, but as these former steel-workers go into their dance, it's just bloody funny.

LA Confidential
Subtle, shocking, compelling and enormously assured, this is one of the most accomplished American films of the decade.

Erykah Badu - Baduism (Kedar)
Baduism is the kind of record that makes me want to write essays on each track, so accomplished is

its blend of sensuality and intellect, restraint and instinct.

Cornershop - When I Was Born For The 7th Time (Wiija)
There's something so good humoured and deeply funky about Cornershop's global pop. A masterful demonstration of the correct use of everything that's great about British music.

Daft Punk - Homework (Virgin)
This is definitely homework from the old skool, fusing snappy electronica with rare groove and a generous dollop of tongue-in-cheek style. There are moments of brilliance and, on the whole, this is prep with pep. Le techno-funk, *c'est chic.*

All hail McQueen

Why is this London Fashion Week the biggest ever?
Just ask its undisputed star: the East End tailor turned
head of Givenchy who puts the shock into frocks.

Alexander McQueen interviewed in T.O. 1414, by **Lorna V**

A s he studies his eyes, charcoaled to black for our photo-shoot, the man known as the bad boy of fashion, the designer world's self-styled yob, chuckles. What would his Givenchy couture clients – just 2,000 ladies in the world who pay a minimum £10,000 for an outfit – say to this? 'They never see me,' he laughs. 'If they did, they wouldn't buy!'

Like most of what Alexander McQueen says, this is more than just a throwaway remark. For behind what seems to be a self-deprecating joke, there is a punchline. He explains: 'Why should these women who've been buying from established French couture designers change to a twentysomething British designer? They buy the clothes because they like them, not because of who I am.'

So who is Alexander McQueen? He may not command the same international advertising budgets as Calvin Klein and Giorgio Armani, his label might not have the same status as Gucci and Prada, and he's not yet a mainstay of successful wardrobes, like Nicole Farhi or Agnès B. Instead, McQueen's status is unique; more rock star than designer, he has propelled fashion from the catwalks onto the front pages, and in the process put London back on the fashion map.

While most designer catwalk shows are sedate affairs with pretty models vacantly pirouetting to an audience of press and buyers noting shapes, lengths, colours and fabrics, McQueen's shows are a cross between performance art and installations, with models acting out his particular vision to a dumbstruck audience. His autumn/winter '97/'98 show was appropriately titled 'It's a Jungle Out There'. At a typically offbeat venue, Borough Fruit Market, away from the usual razzmatazz of the British Fashion Council tents, the show was something between a riot and a rave. Voguettes and fashion luminaries were submerged in the crowds as McQueen fans tore through security. The show itself was astounding: set against a 40 foot screen of corrugated iron drilled with 'bullet' holes, models styled as animals strutted like urban warriors.

His spring/summer '98 show, 'Untitled', on September 28, promises to deliver another stunning spectacle, following on from his last spring/summer show in '97, when he used technicians including movie lighting expert Steve Chivers ('Alien' and 'Highlander'). 'It'll be shocking,' he promises, ready to be photographed with model of the moment, Karen Ferrari. The show's innovations include a collaboration with ICI who are providing futuristic materials to build the set, and a special scent for the venue to put people in the appropriate mood. At a cost of £70,000, it will be McQueen's biggest to date.

The show will also feature a gold suit designed for American Express, to be donated to the Terence Higgins Trust for auction. 'Here's the most cutting-edge designer with the biggest mouth, backed by a huge corporation,' announces McQueen proudly. 'American Express aren't idiots. They wouldn't put up money if they thought this designer was a bad penny. It's really courteous of them to give us so much money, when they've got no say in the show.'

An East End boy, Lee Alexander McQueen, the son of a cabby and the youngest of six children, grew up in Stepney, loved drawing frocks, and left school at 16 with an 'O' and 'A' level in art. After a spell working in a pub, he found his vocation at a Savile Row tailors after seeing a TV report about the lack of new apprentices. (Famously, it was here he scrawled obscenities in the linings of suits, some allegedly destined for the Prince of Wales.) Deciding to move into designer fashion, McQueen bought a plane ticket and headed for Milan with nowhere to stay, and with a job with designer Romeo Gigli top of his wish list. Gigli offered him a job as a pattern-cutter on the spot.

Almost a year later, aged 22, he returned to England, and was offered the chance to do an MA at St Martin's. He couldn't afford the fees until an aunt, convinced of his talent, lent him £4,000. With added emotional support from his mum, who gave him food when he had spent all he had on cloth, McQueen channelled his energy into his designs and shows.

The youngest recipient (at 27) of the British Fashion Council's Designer of the Year award, McQueen had only produced eight collections when last October he was appointed to French couture house Givenchy, succeeding fellow homegrown talent John Galliano, who departed for Dior. He now designs both for Givenchy and for his own label, using his earnings from Givenchy to finance his own two yearly collections. The division is clear. 'Givenchy is about the client.

McQueen is all about me,' he declares. As for a McQueen look dominating the high street, he shudders at the thought: 'I wouldn't like to see my designs on everyone, I'd go fucking mad.'

His rise from working class London to the catwalks of Paris may sound like a fairytale, but his success is based on far more than a few outrageous shows and a vocabulary sprinkled with four-letter words. It may have been his infamous bumster trousers (which revealed a 'bum cleavage') which propelled him into the public eye, but McQueen's career is based, more than anything, on hard work.

'People have to understand my background,' he says. 'Before Saint Martin's I'd worked for seven years in the business. I wasn't some student who jumped into couture. The wives of the customers I made suits for in Savile Row are the women who buy couture. I already knew that world.'

McQueen's view of himself as a designer is as an architect of clothes, rather than a frock-maker. 'I'm about construction and manipulation,' he explains. The intention, for example, behind his trademark bumsters was not to shock or titillate, but to elongate the body by cutting the trousers closer to the hip bone. At a time when both the high street and designer fashion are dominated by a retro look, McQueen is one of the few modernist designers along with names like Rei Kawakubo of Comme des Garçons and Martin Margiela (both of whom he admires), who are seeking new ways to

'The shows are mindful. I don't wanna do a cocktail party, I'd rather people left my shows and vomited. I prefer extreme reactions.'

wrap and present the body.

Although the media have gone for the yob image, there's a finesse to McQueen which often goes unnoticed. Quite unexpectedly, he is polite and nice in an unaffected way that is at odds with the kissy-kissy fashion world. In person he is an effervescent, unpredictable bundle with a pretty face, sensitive eyes and an honest handshake. If he didn't like you, you'd certainly know it, but he wouldn't dislike you just for the sake of an image.

McQueen is full of contradictions, hating the bourgeoisie, yet designing for a couture label; looking for comfort in clothes for himself, yet designing aggressive showpieces; being anti-monarchist, yet crying over Diana; creating shows which shock the system, yet going home to watch soaps. And therein lies the fascination. It's not that McQueen is supremely intellectual or intelligent, rather that he is supremely imaginative, fuelled by every field of artistic endeavour. 'I'm about what goes through people's minds,' he says. 'The stuff that people don't want to admit or face up to. The shows are about what's buried in people's psyches.'

'The shows are mindful,' he adds. 'Not in-yer-face obvious. I don't just stick a dick and a cleavage in people's faces. I don't wanna do a cocktail party, I'd rather people left my shows and vomited. I prefer extreme reactions.'

So, just what is the connection between his shows and his clothes? He laughs:

'Fuck all!' ●

Secrets & lies

If humanity is a zoo, then 'The Jerry Springer Show' is what happens when the animals escape.

Jerry Springer interviewed in T.O. 1409, by **Steve Grant**

I t's about to hot up on 'The Jerry Springer Show'. Reno, a perky young black male, is about to reveal his secret to Monique, a gorgeous babe who he's been dating for several months. 'I'm a girl,' he declares. Monique laughs, holds her face in her hands, and shudders. The audience moans with glee; through their ranks roams the blow-dried Springer in the usual black designer suit, holding the mic like a deadly weapon. He begins to scent blood. Later it transpires that Reno has had sex with Monique by turning her round, cuffing her to the bed and then strapping on a dildo which he proudly refers to as 'my man'. Monique says she had no idea: 'It's not as if I went down there with my face.'

'My Guy's A Girl' is a staple title for 'Springer' which is a hugely successful talk-show in America, where the man is an idolised household name. In the now rapacious field of tabloid-television, Jerry is King. So far there have been 200 shows in seven series, and he's been signed for another five years, his show syndicated to 127 different stations across the USA. Other programmes include 'I'm Having Your Husband's Baby', 'I Can't Live With My 680lb Mom', 'I'm In Love With A Serial Killer', 'Stay Away From My Man', 'I Can't Stand Your Sexy Job', 'Kristmas With the Klan', 'Tijuana Sex Dancers' and the catch-all ever-present, 'I Have Something to Tell You', which usually involves a woman telling her boyfriend ('You know that I love you… but') that she is seeing another person, the other person often turning out to be a woman who will then kiss and fondle her lesbian mate in full view of the baying studio watchers. Like Howard Stern before him, Jerry has long seen the market in designer dykes, but it could just as easily be a pair of canoodling guys. On the sex front, Springer is a decided liberal.

Increasingly Britain is awash with these close encounters: everything from the pallid 'Kilroy!' to the perky Ricki Lake, to the self-righteous heart-throb 'Geraldo', corporate secretary from hell 'Sally Jesse Raphael' and the chuckling Doris Day lovechild lookalike that is Jenny Jones. Of them all, it's the 'Jenny Jones Show' that has caused the biggest headache yet: last year, Jonathan Schmitz, a 24-year-old waiter from Detroit, met a man who had come on to declare his 'secret love' for Schmitz (who had assumed eagerly that his secret admirer was a

woman). 'But I'm straight,' protested Schmitz, who after being taunted by neighbours, went round to gay barman Scott Amedure's home three days later – and shot him dead.

'That could never happen on our show,' says Springer. 'We always take care to tell people the general parameters of the programme and all guests are given the opportunity to edit any section they're not happy with. Sure it can be cruel, but the news is far more cruel, the news intrudes on the lives of strangers in a sometimes hideously unfair way. What we do is entertainment pure and simple. It's not serious, and we have literally thousands of people who are desperate to get on the show every week.'

Springer's show no longer condones violence between guests, but full-scale brawls and punch-ups were once de rigueur: women take off their shoes to fight, men roll about on the floor, four-letter-words and explicit sexual terms are bleeped out with laughable lack of success. But then if you team up the Ku Klux Klan with a bunch of black militants who dress like extras from 'Aladdin' you are asking for more than a frank exchange of views.

There is much talk about how 'true' these stories are: there's even the discovery of an agency which signs up potential guests who can vary their own set of problems according to demand: today's daughter coping with a dad who weighs 1,200 lbs (the 'Springer' weight record) can be tomorrow's 'slut-pants' dating a married man twice her age who is really a woman and has sex with sheep in 'his' spare time. Springer says 'we have a very tough approach to cheats. Guests sign forms before they come on, if they are found to be lying we will sue them for the

Death of a Princess

1961-1997

The tragic death of Diana, Princess of Wales, on the morning of Sunday 31 Aug 1997 resulted in media chaos, followed by the same intrusive reporting that is alleged to have led to her death.

from T.O. 1411, by **Peter Paphides**

I t was a fine line that the TV journalists had to tread on Sunday. On one side of that line, the paparazzi and paper editors. On the other, eager to stress their detachment from the seamier side of the industry, the indignant anchormen, Peter Sissons and the hysterical Nicholas Owen, whose job it was to express the anger of their viewers. And for the main part, they negotiated it like a herd of blind elephants.

The useful thing about an all-encompassing term like 'the media' is that there's always some other bit of 'media' to push the buck to. On Sunday, we saw newspaper editors blaming the public for buying their papers, the public attacking photographers outside Buckingham Palace; journalists blaming editors for buying paparazzi photos and – most poignantly of all

cost of the show which is around $80,000. It usually works.' Indeed, he once exposed such a trio, although the man (who was told he was the father of his best friend's girl's baby) didn't help his scam by the absurd response: 'But we only had sex four times.'

There's more to Springer than meets the eye, and his biggest plus is that, despite the nature of his material, he's actually undeniably likeable, off-air and on. A former lawyer and CBS anchor man, he was a decidedly left-wing mayor of Cincinatti for several years, pushing forward tough programmes on housing and education reform. He says that he never watched these sorts of shows before he was hired to present his own. 'As long as it's true and outrageous, we're interested,' he says. 'If anything our show demonstrates the First Amendment, freedom

applies to racists as well as holocaust victims.' He's also proud that, despite the inevitable assortment of lard-butts and saddies, his show appeals to 'young, intelligent and curious people, particularly females'.

He adds that maybe the British have been unknowing vanguards in the move towards telly outrage: 'I think you people paved the way by writing about your royal family and celebrities in such a frank and often insulting way. You have naked women in your newspapers, we don't, ours tend to be more conservative. My theory, for what it's worth, is that ordinary people want to be part of all that, want to be part of that 15 minutes of fame thing, think that if famous people can share their secrets or be exposed, then why not them?' ●

● ●

– Diana's brother blaming the paper editors and proprietors who, he had always believed, would be the death of her. The BBC and ITV, of course, were only too happy to show them fighting among each other. It deflected from the actions of their very own news rooms, who positioned their zoom lenses on the road from the Royals' Balmoral home to church to focus on the grieving Princes William and Harry.

It didn't get any better, either. As people who had met Diana once at a charity function, tinpot pundits and plain opportunists were wheeled in, Sunday turned into exactly the kind of gauche voyeurism conducted 'in the public interest' that Chris Morris's 'The Day Today' and 'Brass Eye' set out to lampoon. *Daily Mail* writer Ann Leslie cheerfully implied that Diana had, in a way, met a rather fitting end. After all, said Leslie, 'Diana made a Faustian pact' with a media which she used just as keenly as they used her.

The more you discuss something, the less sensitive you become to it, and it took the media mere hours to descend to the depths of idle conjecture. By 9pm, having long exhausted hard

news, the focus had turned to Diana's contribution to the fashion industry: Bruce Oldfield blithely slagging off her wardrobe; a quick word with Elizabeth Emmanuel, co-creator of Diana's wedding dress.

What might have been deemed unpalatably tasteless on Sunday was constituting good TV on Monday morning. 'The Bigger Breakfast', broadcasting from a desk outside Buckingham Palace, had finally reduced the Princess of Wales's life to a one-minute soundbite: 'Her death,' concluded their report, 'echoes the violent deaths of Marilyn Monroe and James Dean. But whether, like Elvis, she'll remain a twentieth-century icon remains to be seen.' But it was on the same programme that the only words of sense throughout the whole two days were spoken.

Phoning in from his home, an angry Bob Geldof launched an offensive: 'Ridiculous people like James Whitaker exist by writing nonsense about this woman. People should mount some kind of demonstration by not buying these papers for 31 days…' Needless to say, he was cut off. ●

"There's a difference between the Spice Girls and a porn movie. A porn movie has got better music."
Phil Spector

"I think Andrew Morton will go down in history as a far more important writer than Martin Amis."
Julie Burchill puts it into perspective

"I always believed the press would kill her in the end. But not even I could imagine that they would take such a strong hand in her death."
Earl Spencer reacting to his sister's death

"It was the paparazzi who did it."
Frank Johnson of the *Spectator* on what finally killed columnist Jeffrey Bernard

"She leaves behind two saris and the bucket she used to wash in."
Daily Telegraph report on Mother Teresa's death

"I think it devalues all the other blue plaques."
Arch snob Brian Sewell on the erection of a blue plaque for Jimi Hendrix

"It'll be a long time before it's seen in the same way as, say, Morris dancing."
'Groovy' Norman Tebbit on the Notting Hill Carnival's place in British culture

"Is that twat tall? 'Cos if he is, it'll look better when I bleeding batter him. I hate him. Lanky, moaning, posh…"
Shaun Ryder fosters good relations with Brett Anderson

"I mean, if you mix with gay boys in Miami, this is what you leave yourself open to."
'Clothes Show' presenter Jeff Banks explains the death of Gianni Versace

"I think Noel was misquoted. I think he was saying the band was bigger than Rod – meaning Rod Stewart."
George Harrison on Noel Gallagher's assertion that Oasis are bigger than God

"Why didn't Hong Kong just buy England?"
PJ O'Rourke offers a solution to the Hong Kong question

The hole story

Living in a tunnel for a week made Swampy Britain's most wanted eco-warrior. We dig him out to find out what motivates the man behind the mud.

Swampy interviewed in T.O. 1393, by **Tony Thompson**

In the woodland next to Manchester Airport, down the muddy banks of Camp Flywood, along the mud-spattered walkways that flank the River Rats site and then up over the mud-caked escarpment that leads to Camp Sir Cliff Richard OBE, Daniel 'Swampy' Hooper, Britain's most famous eco-warrior, is going through the vegan equivalent of cold turkey.

'I'm trying to give up smoking, but it's not easy,' he says while shovelling a plate of baked beans on toast into his mouth with muddy fingers. 'If I have a drink in the evening, then I really feel like a smoke afterwards. But I shouldn't. It's bad. Really bad.' I nod in agreement and begin to talk about health problems, before being interrupted. 'Oh, not that,' says Swampy. 'You don't understand. For the average smoker, one tree a week has to be cut down for the drying process. It's destroying the planet. I feel really contradictory every time I light up.'

If 23-year-old Swampy comes across as a tunnel-obsessed, single-issue campaigner, it is the fault of the media, not the man. The truth is that he cares about pretty much everything.

Five years of campaigning started with an anti-fascist group, which defaces racist posters and generally causes mischief: 'I used to ride trains without paying – not as a protest, just because I could never afford the fares. When I used to get caught, I'd give the inspectors the name and address of the local National Front candidate.' He also joined an anti-porn group, steaming into newsagents, grabbing magazines off the top shelf and ripping them up. 'Pornography is totally unnecessary. If people don't have imaginations… well, they're pretty sad, aren't they?' He has also been a vegan since the age of 17, having first spent a few months as a vegetarian. 'I used to think vegans were extremists, but now I think that vegetarians are really half-hearted. In many ways, just as bad as meat eaters. 'In the column [for the *Sunday Mirror*], I write about a lot of other issues, but they get cut out. There's the fact that they lied about the number of jobs that will be created by the airport. They started out saying 50,000, but

now they say 8,000. And what kind of jobs will they be? Not pilots and engineers, but toilet cleaners. Demoralising, low-paid work. Nothing empowering. I've also written about the wildlife that will be destroyed; about problems with public transport; about air pollution – but none of that ever makes it in.'

One of the few things that Swampy doesn't care about is the election, despite the publicity generated by his April Fools' joke that he would be standing as a candidate: 'People are voting for a party that they think are going to change things, but whoever wins will still be controlled by the same multinationals who control things now. They have the power, not the politicians, not us. Money talks.'

But not to him. Last month, Swampy was offered around £500,000 to record a cover version of 'I Am A Mole And I Live In A Hole'. Despite the boost such a sum could have given the cause, he had no hesitation in turning it down. 'The record would have been a load of bollocks,' he says. 'It wouldn't have helped to get the message across. Besides, we don't need money that badly. We get £550 each week from the *Sunday Mirror*. The problem now is that people find it easier to remember that I turned that down than that I'm involved in a campaign against the airport.'

Tunnels are where Swampy feels most at home and, as he and his colleagues have previously demonstrated, they prove highly effective in delaying developments. 'The ultimate goal would be to stop the whole runway development,' he says. 'But we accept that that is unlikely. They have been talking about a third runway and if they scrap that idea, then this will be a victory.' Swampy shows me the way into his latest tunnel. I crawl in. It is barely big enough for my shoulders to fit through, pitch black, terrifying and looks distinctly unsafe. 'Of course they're dodgy,' says Swampy. 'That way they can't come after us without shoring it up themselves.'

The problem worrying Swampy is not falling earth but failing air: 'We've gone high-tech, using car fans and computer fans to keep it circulating. A couple of nights ago, me and Merry [his Finnish girlfriend] were asleep down there and someone turned the fan off. I woke up and tried to put the lighter on, but it wouldn't work. There wasn't enough oxygen. It was starting to get really difficult to breathe – the air was really stale. I don't worry about a collapse, but I do worry about going to sleep down there and not waking up again.'

With eviction expected any day now, Swampy and co are spending more and more time underground. And as with the A30 protest in Devon, Swampy is expected to be the last to emerge: 'I'm glad I only did a week last time. That means I only have to do two in Manchester. After all, I've got to break my record, haven't I?' ●

Knowing E, knowing you

He's seen what drugs can do to a human life. And it's not very nice at all.

from T.O. 1419, by **Alan Partridge**

I have to admit I was very unsure when asked to contribute an article on drugs for fear of giving the subject publicity. However, after *Time Out* assured me they would take a responsible approach and would only glamorise drug use as much as was strictly necessary in order to get people to buy their magazine, I agreed. And if my article risks being surrounded by pictures of sexy, crop-haired young women in tight T-shirts and impractically small rucksacks (fine in a disco, but for fell-walking in Cumbria, forget it – you'd be lucky to get a penlight torch and a barleysugar stick in there!) then so be it.

Personally, if I go to a disused aircraft hangar, it's to visit the RAF museum on a bank holiday. On the subject of rave-ups by the way, I think they've had a bad press. A few years ago I became concerned about my son Fernando, who was suffering from mood swings – animated and chatty one day, aggressive and sniffly the one after that. So I followed him one night to a dance at an old hangar near Diss and the bar was selling nothing stronger than bottled water!

So what does Alan Partridge think of drugs? Well, not the knee-jerk reaction you may expect from a 43-year-old radio presenter ('Up With Partridge' 04.30-1.00am, Mondays to Saturdays Radio Norwich 106.5FM). Although I personally get all the highs I need from a week in Malta or the sight of a well-preserved Victorian folly on a crisp March morning, I am aware that certain drugs have medical benefit: marijuana has been known to relieve arthritis, and Disprin is unbeatable for indigestion. And believe me, the day they ban Setlers is the day I head off to Hyde Park with a banner, chanting 'STOP THIS SETLERS BAN INSANITY!' All the same I still deeply oppose legalisation for recreational use – Holland is a terrifying example of where the decriminalising of cannabis has led to people experimenting with hardcore pornography.

Drugs hurt everyone and I'm not just talking about the countless young lives wrecked or ended prematurely, although that certainly gets on my wick. What about the untold damage to hundreds of perfectly good cars torn apart by customs officers in their search for the ultimate high?

Radical problems require solutions – why not allow police to re-sell confiscated drugs on the black market to raise cash? Yes, in the short term this will result in an increase in the number of addicts, but in the long term it will lead to smarter uniforms and shorter working hours.

Another solution is to rip up pavements in areas where pot-pushers are known to operate (indeed for numerous reasons not entirely related to drugs, I would immediately call a halt to all urban pedestrian schemes, especially in Norwich, where the proposed extension to Bridge Street is nothing short of a very sick joke).

Drugs are not the answer. We've all had our moments when we'd like to shut out the pain, such as when my wife threw me out and moved in a fitness instructor called Lee. He drinks that yellow stuff in tins. He's an idiot.

And here's where those of us in the public eye can set an example. Bands like The Oasis should look to those they claim to emulate – great groups like ELO who only spat in countries where it was customary to do so after a meal, such as in Japan. I think. But there is still the occasional shining example – Boy George who once said he'd prefer a 'cup of tea' and Keith Richards who, despite experimenting briefly with drugs in his youth, has these days learnt to channel his energies into mountain biking and CB radio (handle: 'Jumping Jack!').

Sadly, however, Paul McCartney still occasionally allows his name to appear in full-page advertisements for big newspapers read by middle-class people to promote the legalisation of pot. That the man who wrote 'Mull of Kintyre' can behave so appallingly I find deeply depressing. The great irony is that while his wife Linda opposes the testing of drugs on animals, Sir McCartney openly advocates putting drugs in humans, who are technically animals. Something to 'Mull' over (Mull as in 'Mull of Kintyre'). Sir Mc.

One way we can all battle against high-class drugs is by reclaiming certain words that have been vandalised by the druggists. For example, we should use 'joint' once more to mean simply somewhere you hang out. 'Crack' is something you attend to with Polyfilla; 'Coke' a drink that youngsters would have with a bag of crisps; 'weed' something you've been planning to get rid of in the garden; and finally 'acid' which can mean either a kind of wet something you'd find in a car battery, or by far the best way of disposing of a corpse. ●

Pills, thrills and bellyaches

from T.O. 1408, by **Julian Kossof**

While out clubbing, have you ever looked across the floor and wondered how many of your fellow dancers are on drugs? As you suspected, the answer is just about everyone – and that's official. According to interviews conducted with over 500 clubbers at 18 venues by Release, the independent drug advice group, 87 per cent intended to use drugs (probably bought from a friend) that evening.

Who's had what?

Young London clubbers who had ever tried these drugs

Cannabis	91%
Ecstasy	81%
Amphetamines	81%
LSD	74%
Poppers	61%
Magic mushrooms	60%
Cocaine	57%
Temazepam/Valium	29%
Ketamine	28%
Crack	17%
Heroin	15%
Methadone	9%

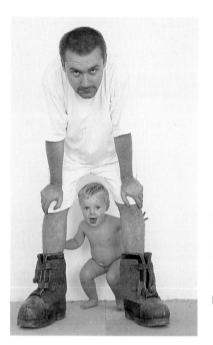

Hirst among equals

I'm hanging on to being an *enfant terrible*.
Later I can be an *adulte terrible* – for ever.

Damien Hirst interviewed in T.O. 1412, by **Sarah Kent**

Damien Hirst's pickled shark – 'The Physical Impossibility of Death in the Mind of Someone Living'– is the first piece you will encounter in the Royal Academy's 'Sensation' exhibition. Suspended in a tank of dark green liquid, the predator looks as though it is swimming in the sea. It bares its teeth as though about to rip your arm off and, although you know it's dead, its potential to kill still remains riveting. Looking death in the face (its and yours) makes you keenly conscious that – miraculously – you are alive.

It is five years since the shark swam into view at the Saatchi Gallery, in the gallery's first exhibition of Young British Artists (YBAs). It attracted phenomenal publicity, and immediately became a symbol of the radical new art. Hirst was cast in the role of the Bad Boy who everyone loves to hate; but he is not just a figurehead. 'I'm still hanging on to being an *enfant terrible*,' he says. 'Later I can be an *adulte terrible* – for ever; that's what art's about. Secretly, though, I'm a traditionalist – you can be a traditionalist without being establishment.'

It's hard to think of him as a traditionalist. The shark is simple, stark, literal and effective – that's why it arouses so much interest and so much hostility. People can't see the art in it and Hirst's detachment seems callous, when he is only being matter-of-fact. He doesn't tell you what to think; he simply shows you something and lets you get on with it. 'I want the viewer to do a lot of the work and feel uncomfortable,' he says. 'They should be made to feel responsible for their own view of the world rather than look at an artist's view and be critical of it.'

But critical they are. Hirst has become as much a phenomenon as his shark – an object on display. Each time he was photographed he looked wilder; his hair grew longer and more

> **'I'm going to die and I want to live for ever. I can't escape the fact, and I can't let go of the desire...'**

unkempt and the designer stubble thickened, as though he were becoming a deranged anthropoid – one rung up from the animals he exhibits. In 1994 he shaved his head and chin for *Esquire*, donned a suit and brandished a chainsaw. A bloody close-up shows him slicing a pig's head in half. The butcher of the art beat – exotic and dangerous; no wonder he receives hate mail. 'I like the idea formally of trying to cut something in half,' he says, as though it were an innocent pastime. He also sliced in half a cow and calf.

'Mother and Child Divided' won him the coveted Turner Prize in 1995. Sawn in half lengthways and preserved in formaldehyde, the animals are displayed in glass tanks; you walk between the two halves and marvel at the intricacies of their vital organs, wondering how you would look sliced open to view. Death is ameliorated by the awesome beauty of the internal landscape. These are not bloody corpses; the body fluids had been drained away and the flesh is bleached into a pallid semblance of life. Decay had been halted and time stopped; the creatures have been given a spurious immortality.

'Decay is more horrifying than death,' says Hirst; but death is the subject dearest to his heart: 'I'm going to die and I want to live for ever. I can't escape the fact, and I can't let go of the desire... I want a glimpse of what it's like to die, trying to understand death when you only know life is impossible.' His solution is to look death in the face – repeatedly. As a student he visited the morgue: 'After the first two weeks they ceased to be corpses; death was removed, just a little bit further.'

This week sees the launch of Hirst's handsome book, 'I Want to Spend the Rest of My Life Everywhere, with Everyone, One to One, Always, Forever, Now' – a retrospective from student collages through to the spin paintings which, in recent years, he has made with celebs such as David Bowie. It's the mixture of detachment and mordant humour that makes his work so powerful; it has the impact of an advert.

Several pages are devoted to cigarettes which, for Hirst, symbolise death and the life cycle .'Every time I finish a cigarette I think about death,' he declares. Exquisite images of lighters and cigarettes are sandwiched between 'Dead Ends', a sculpture of dog ends elegantly arranged on shelves, and 'Party Time', a giant ashtray filled with butts that has the aura of a graveyard.

Beneath the morbid, wild boy façade, though, Hirst is a romantic: 'Everything I do is celebration... I'm really obsessed with life, and death is the point where life stops... Art's about life and it can't really be about anything else. There isn't anything else.' When presented with the Turner Prize, he declared his best artwork to be Connor, his newly born son. In the book, Damien is joined by his son and his girlfriend Maia for a group portrait. Each one is pickled in their own tank, as though they were sculptures, eyes closed as if they were dead.

'The steel and glass cases came from a fear of everything in life being so fragile,' says Hirst. 'I wanted to make a sculpture where the fragility was enclosed. We get put in boxes when we die because it's clean. And we get put in a box when we are born. We live in boxes.' The glass containers have hit a nerve in the national psyche, inspiring cartoons and even adverts. The Ford Company sliced a saloon car in half and displayed it in a Hirst-style vitrine – so you know that it's art.

Life and death co-exist in Hirst's work. In his first West End show – in an empty shop, off Oxford Street in 1991 – gorgeous Malaysian butterflies hatched from pupae attached to canvases and spent their lives in the simulated climate of a tropical rainforest, sipping sugar water, mating, laying eggs and dying. 'I wanted these paintings to be more real than a Wilhelm de Kooning,' says Hirst, 'where the colour leaps off the canvas and flies around the room. Downstairs, though, butterflies were embedded in the gloss of monochrome paintings as though they had got stuck and slowly died. Hirst understands the power of empathy: 'You have to find universal triggers; everyone's frightened of glass, everyone's frightened of sharks, everyone loves butterflies.'

'A Thousand Years' (1990) is a more macabre example of the desire for moving elements. One chamber contains a box of maggots that mature into flies and buzz lazily about; some find their way through holes in the glass partition, attracted by a dead cow's head in the next chamber. Above the rotting meat hangs an Insect-O-Cutor, each execution is announced by a flash and crackle before the body joins the corpses in the tray beneath.'I wanted an empty space with moving points within it, moving like stars.' Such a formalist description of this grizzly sculpture is strange; it ignores the disgust engendered by the spectacle.

Hirst is aware, though, of the power of brute reality: I couldn't say what I wanted to with a painting or a photograph of an object. I wanted the real thing.' Yet it was a painter who most influenced him. Picture a painting by Francis Bacon: a distorted figure writhes in existential agony on a chair, bed or lavatory, overwhelmed by the anguish of life and the knowledge of death, a transparent box, stage or elegant interior frames and dramatises the anguish.

Translate this into three dimensions and you have the basis of a Damien Hirst sculpture. He replaces the human subject with an animal, fish or insect – 'I like metaphor,' he says. 'People need to feel distanced. You can look at a fly and think of a person'– and encases them in a glass and steel chamber that performs a similar function to Bacon's space frames. By designating the object as an artwork, the tank neutralises and also dramatises the fearsome vulnerability of the victim. I visited the Royal Academy while 'Sensation' was being installed. A man was kneeling inside one of Hirst's tanks polishing glass. It was an incredible sight. 'That,' said Saatchi, 'is what Damien would really like to put inside his sculptures.'

> '**Art is like medicine – it can heal. Yet many people who believe in medicine don't believe in art**'

Like smoking, drugs are an obsession. Hirst fills medicine cabinets with pills and potions arranged as mirrors of the body – those for the head on the top shelf, those for the feet at the bottom. Some cabinets contain drugs that are so old they are poisonous; most contain new ones that, in time, will become toxic, or useless. All are symptoms of our eagerness (and failure) to fend off degeneration and death.

In the frontispiece of the book, 'Damien Hirst' is printed as though it were the name of a drug on a packet of pills. Above the name is a hand preparing an injection and on the flyleaf a photograph of the inside of an ambulance. The book is obviously meant to save lives. 'Art is like medicine – it can heal,' says Hirst. 'Yet I've always been amazed at how many people believe in medicine, but don't believe in art, without questioning either.'

Hirst has become a symbol of the generation he has done so much to promote and publicise. Having assiduously cultivated his image, he has gained the kind of media attention usually reserved for pop stars. Is he the 'real thing' though or, having buzzed so brightly, will he fizzle and fall like one of his electrocuted flies? His book is magnificent, but it is retrospective – as though it marked the end of a career, rather than its midpoint; and recently there have been terrible lapses in taste. In the past two years, Hirst has made a clichéd pop video for Blur's single 'Country House' and an appalling, sub-Peter Greenaway film. Later this year he is opening a restaurant in Notting Hill Gate called Pharmacy, featuring waiters dressed in lab coats. But he is immune to criticism. 'I've learned that you must never compromise; you must get on with it, and have a laugh. I'm working on a car crash. There'll be no bodies, but I want that feeling of absolute horror, just after a crash – the wheels turning, personal possessions spilling out, the radio on, the horn going. I'm using a red car and a corporation grey car and calling it 'Composition in Red and Corporation Grey'. I'm a traditional colourist at heart!'

'I'll stop when I'm bored or when I'm barking like a dog in the gutter on my hands and knees...' ●

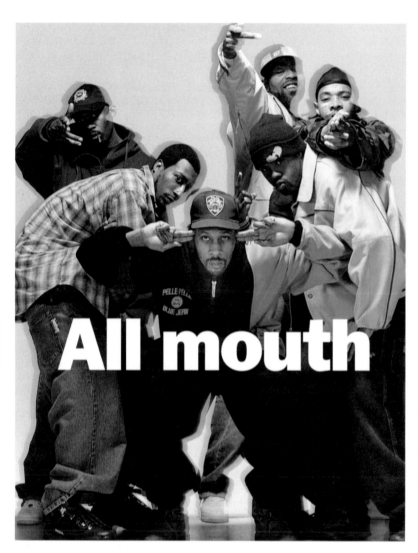

All mouth

They're certainly out of this world, but are they out of their minds?

Wu-Tang Clan interviewed in T.O. 1395, by **Garry Mulholland**

t is Friday evening in Camden, and strange things are happening. Things that may never be fully explained. In a small room in the HQ of MTV Europe, six members of a hip hop group are submitting to standard interrogation. The three men at the back are silent and visibly bored. The three in the front are more animated and familiar. The dark-skinned, hang-dog-looking guy on the right is holding forth about the excellence of his group. The equally dark, oddly childlike bloke next to him is staring wildly around, finally settling on the air-conditioning fans. He taps his cousin, the leader of the band, until he stops talking, and then turns to the interviewer and crew.

'Excuse me?' He begins with theatrical politeness. 'If you put on these fans, would you be unable to manipulate the negatives of this film?'

Confused silence. Finally, a cameraman pipes up: 'Erm, it would screw the sound up.'

'Ah!' – the childlike one – 'Can you put them on then, please?'

The interviewer is getting impatient. 'Well – no,' he blurts.

'So!' The face of his nemesis brightens. 'Your plan really is

the destruction of The Fathership!' He strokes his chin. 'I like that – keep on doin' it.'

An uncomfortable silence falls. Is this the end of the interview? A signal for the six to display their mastery of martial arts? The childlike one pauses, then suddenly beams and spreads his hands.

'It's okay. I love all my children.' His band mates burst into giggles. The interviewer coughs nervously. And the man they call Ol' Dirty Bastard stares ahead innocently, seemingly unaware that he's said anything other than a self-evident truth.

This man has made a record with Mariah Carey.

The Wu-Tang Clan, named after a martial arts sword style, were formed in 1992 by Robert Diggs (re-titled RZA, pronounced 'Rizza'), in New York's Staten Island. Together with core members Method Man, Ol' Dirty Bastard, and Genius/GZA (pronounced 'Jizza'), RZA declared his aim of creating not just a band, but a whole musical empire. Their debut album, 'Enter the Wu-Tang (36 Chambers)', released the following year, sold over a million in the US alone and the Wu were the talk of the hip hop scene. Following that, true to his word, RZA put out records by Method Man, Ol' Dirty Bastard, Genius/GZA and fellow clan members Raekwon and Ghostface Killah. Each sold over half a million copies. The Wu-Tang masterplan was taking effect.

The second full Clan album, 'Wu-Tang Forever', is perhaps the most eagerly awaited hip hop set of all time. The press in the black music mags has been just this side of religious fever. People are already talking of 'Wu-Tang Forever' being the greatest hip hop album of all time. Smart trick, considering that at the time of going to press nobody except some of the band had heard it all through. So, as they visit London, the question is: are the Wu-Tang Clan the most important group in hip hop, maybe even music? Or are they just blinding us with science?

Our attempt to find out begins in a hotel on the Edgware Road. It is one of those conveyor-belt press calls, despised by hacks, photographers and bands alike. In attendance – along with various disgruntled press – are Method Man, Ol' Dirty Bastard and lesser-known Clan members U-God and Inspektah Deck. RZA arrives later in the week. Almost immediately, I am whisked off for a private audience with The Dirty One. The only way I can do justice to this bizarre experience is to just write it as it happened.

So, ODB. The album…

'The Wu-Tang album gonna be banging. We got a lot of special shit in there. Things dealing with the world today. And the world yesterday. When people speak things they feel, it's like a threat to society sometimes. So sometimes you gotta watch the things you say. Just keep the train on the two-way street.'

Would you prefer not to do interviews?

'Yeah, personally.'

Why? The music speaks for itself? Or you just hate journalists?

'No. I love speaking. I speak to all of my human fans on the planet Earth. It's just that… the things that I say is sometimes against me. I say things that travel like sound, like all across the world. Matter of fact, to the universe. Things that are just not supposed to be said. I gotta respect that 'cos I got children.'

How many?

'A few. I can't even count 'em…'

Are you surprised by the success of the Wu masterplan?

'Erm… no… no [sighs]. What I'm really surprised at is how much I'm worth. Not everybody else. I got something nobody don't have. And this [drops voice] makes me a threat to society. They want me to keep it quiet. 'Cos this "what I have" might cause a lot of… pain. It might cause a lot of uncomfortableness. They say I'm an enemy to the mind. These little atoms that I get – it's like bombs. Enough to blow up Hikoshima… I mean, Hiroshima. And Japan. And um… all parts of the world. So they tell me to be quiet and that's what I gotta do.'

Who tells you?

'I mean… I mean… like… the government.'

Really? How? Are they tapping your phone?

'A lot of strange things been happening. But I respect their word. 'Cos they're respecting mine, in a way. You give

respect, you get respect. I don't wanna be known as no troublemaker, 'cos there's no time for trouble. Everything was already predicted and planned. So nothin' can mess up this plan for the future.'

You were arrested last year.

'I went to jail 'cos I was a bad boy. I was fuckin' up. I was on probation… but they don't want me in jail. They fear me in jail. If I'm in jail – ha! – I may cause a riot or somethin'. Or a prison break-out. And I know they're gonna send me to the crazy house, 'cos they already did that to my father.'

Really?

'Yeah. They'd rather have me killed. Or I just shut the fuck up. I know I talk a lot in these interviews, man. I'm just trying to teach my children.'

If teaching the truth meant you stopped selling records, would you carry on teaching?

'It's impossible for me to stop sellin' records, man. They can't stop that. I'm loved by too many. Can't stop that. Cannot stop that. If they tried to stop that, they'll know something's wrong.'

He hollers into the tape machine. 'They tried to stop Public Enemy! BUT THEY CAN'T STOP THE REALITY OF RIGHT-EOUS!!! Just like you can't stop the reality of unrighteousness.

'They wanna know what moves we're making. They wanna know what baths we take.'

But both sides gotta be respected.' And then, bizarrely, without pause: 'I know my woman fucks other men. But I gotta respect that. Fuck it, what the fuck I'm a do? She gotta respect me.'

He yawns dramatically. 'That's all them babies that I got pregnant, don't worry about it. The woman that I got pregnant having them babies, I mean. Word.

'The Wu-Tang album is gonna be a smash. It will be loved by many. I got about five cuts up on there myself. I didn't put too much on it 'cos I don't wanna have too many people hearing me. 'Cos when I start talkin', man, I don't know what the fuck starts happenin'. All types of cars running up on me in the street tellin' me, "Yo, yo, yo! You'd better shut the fuck up!" Every time I turn my head I'm being watched [sighs]. I'm tired of this shit, man. I'm tired of it.'

Will it stop?

'No. I just have to tone it down. We're all being watched. They wanna know what moves we're making. They wanna know what baths we take. They wanna know every fucking thing. Oh, let me shut the fuck up!'

Erm… RZA?

'He taught me everything I know. As for me, I'm a mental martial artist. I got some mental telepathy shit goin'… I don't know where it came from, but I like it. But RZA – he bear witness too. Even he told me to shut the fuck up.'

So, the fateful meeting in 1992 when RZA explained the whole masterplan and, in a blinding flash, you were transformed into swordwielding rap superheroes. Is this legend true?

'Zzzzzz'

Erm, ODB?

'Zzzzzz'

He's fallen asleep. The poor geezer's snoring away, looking about 12. I have to resist the temptation to pick up the duvet and tuck him in. ●

Anyone for Tennison?

Find out what it's like to be kissed by the beloved ball-buster of 'Prime Suspect'.

Helen Mirren interviewed in T.O.N.Y. 72, **by Stephan Talty**

Have you dreamed of Helen Mirren yet? Many people have. If you're a man who likes women, chances are she didn't leave the dream without offbeat sex entering the picture. If you're a woman, she was probably the British girl who wouldn't be messed with, the one who made the bad people whimper.

'In America, women mutter in my ear,' says Mirren. She imitates the urgent whisper: '"I love you."' She cracks up. 'I just hear "I love you" as they go past, and I turn around and there's this woman walking away, going "Oh!", clasping her hands, saying, "You're a goddess!" And it's not a sexual thing, I hasten to add. It's like I represent some sort of dream ideal of a successful ball-breaker.'

That's her Tennison, the driven cop from 'Prime Suspect' – the show that makes you embarrassed to think 'N.Y.P.D Blue' is considered good TV. But the actual Mirren is quite different: The star of 'The Cook, The Thief, His Wife and Her Lover' and 'The Madness of King George' is dressed in a jean jacket, white nubby blouse and long blood-red skirt. She looks younger, happier, tan. She is Tennison's younger sister, the one who didn't have to prove herself.

Over a plate of scrambled eggs, Mirren delivers some shocking news: 'Prime Suspect 5' is to be the last instalment of the popular series. What if people start getting Beatlemaniac about the show – holding candlelight vigils, demanding a reunion?

She laughs, a slow, luxuriant woman's laugh. 'I don't think it will happen; it's not the nature of television. But I wouldn't mind coming back if there was that sort of reunion. I want people to think, especially me to think, that I've moved on to something else.'

Perhaps she's right; it is time to give 'Prime Suspect' a rest. PS5, whose subject is youth gangs, is merely decent, not brilliant and revolutionary like 1 or 3.

'Youth crime is huge in England,' says Mirren. 'My sister and I lived in different middle-class London neighbourhoods ten years ago. I was broken into about four times and physically attacked once in my house. My sister was broken into at least 15 times – once she woke up and there was a guy at the end of the bed. And Americans think of England as being like 'Sense and Sensibility'.

One of the new episode's subtexts is, as always, Tennison's sexual anarchism. The detective's clinical mind disguises a healthy taste for men – though her choices are often ill-advised. In PS5 she sleeps with her boss, a happily married cop.

Mirren found that hard to swallow. 'I don't think my character would sleep with him in the same bed where he sleeps with his wife,' she says. 'And on the first date! It worried me terribly.'

But in sleeping with the boss, Tennison also gets to whip the sexual roles into reverse. Here, it's the man who ends up feeling confused and wanting. 'I enjoyed that, and I enjoyed the fact that Jane Tennison enjoyed it,' says Mirren with a saucy grin. 'She loves putting the boot in. When she's confronted, she has a smart-ass remark, and she's so pleased with herself in a rather nasty way. As I would be.'

This is what makes people – especially women of a certain age – love Mirren's detective. Her No to the world men want. Her brutal honesty and even more brutal self-honesty.

I test her: 'What is your best erotic feature?'

'My nose,' Mirren says, touching it with her finger. 'It's so out there, poking erotically into the nooks and crannies where it shouldn't be. Taylor [the director Taylor Hackford, her companion] says my nose is always cold and my lips are warm. It's the most extraordinary experience being kissed by me.'

Eroticism brings us to the sexual debate of the moment: Larry Flynt. Mirren jumps right in. 'I did go on record in the '70s saying I much prefer *Hustler* to *Playboy* because at least Hustler is not hypocritical. *Hustler* is a wanker's magazine – get that sperm out, get it over and done with. It's disgusting but honest. And there's nothing wrong with a good wank every now and then, is there, Steve?' She cocks an eyebrow, laughing.

Women love Mirren the way men love Bogart. Bogie is almost a male counterpart to Tennison: the exhausted look, the wise eyes, the sexiness of command. Mirren makes a face. 'I do hate Humphrey Bogart, I have to say. Sorry, Lauren – I like you so very much. But I thought Bogart was a terribly bad actor – and he was a coward in real life. He dumped the McCarthy era people in the shit in a major way.'

To call Bogie a rat is to court a little controversy, which is nothing new to Mirren. The latest storm she's endured was over her role in an IRA drama, 'Some Mother's Son'.

'The right-wing tabloid press in England did a couple of hate pieces on me, saying I was an idiot and a fool and a wishy-washy liberal, which I didn't altogether disagree with,' she says. 'Not because I did the film, but just in general.'

The interview is over, but Mirren isn't ready to leave. She picks up my list of questions and finds one I've skipped – about her best years coming in her forties. It's a lucky choice: she has a story about it.

'When I was about 25, I was really depressed and uptight and fucked up. I went to a hand reader, this Indian guy in this funky neighbourhood. He said, "The height of your success won't happen till you're in your late forties." From that moment on, I felt much better, because I realised I didn't know what was going to happen. I just wanted to get on with it.' So she took the sheet with the rest of the palm reader's predictions, balled it up and tossed it into the trash. Tennison would have nodded, slightly, in approval. ●

1998

We were easily led. Spin, spun and spiralled, in fact. How else do you explain Feng Shui? After agonising over the best place to hang our melon ballers, we were sold speed garage and trainers that induced altitude sickness. The tension and tragedy of England's World Cup script scooped an Oscar and the country's weather was committed to a psychiatric institution.

January
President Clinton denies having an affair with 21-year-old Monica Lewinsky, a former White House worker.

May
A man is sued for $2m after leaving his wife of 20 years for a younger woman. He had been taking new wonder-drug, Viagra for four days.

Arsenal wins the Double under Arsene Wenger, the first foreign manager to lead a team to the Championship.

Ginger Spice quits the Spice Girls.

The Lennon offspring, Julian and Sean, slug it out in the charts as both release LPs at the same time.

June
Elections take place in the Northern Ireland Assembly.

Frank Sinatra dies.

July
In a shock result, France wins the World Cup for the first time, beating favourites Brazil 3-0.

Russell Weston guns down two police officers in Capitol Hill, Washington DC. He claims that the FBI have been spying on him.

Nelson Mandela marries for the third time.

August
The Queen Mother is 98.

Monica Lewinksy strikes a deal with the Grand Jury that will grant her immunity.

Ex-MI5 employee David Shayler is arrested in France and reveals a plot to assassinate Gaddaffi.

Terrorist bombs explode in American embassies in Africa.

The Big Lebowski
It's almost impossible to think of a recent movie more enjoyable than this comic update of the world crystallised by Raymond Chandler.

Jackie Brown
This may not please those who adore violent set-pieces or bravura grand-standing, but it's probably his finest, certainly his most mature movie to date.

Good Will Hunting
Like its title, the patent 'sincerity' comes capitalised and bearing inverted commas – which is not to deny it's some-times honest and mo-ving, in its own way.

Madonna - Ray Of Light (Maverick)
It's as complex, contradictory and contrary as main-stream pop gets.

Madonna conveys this without ever sounding self-pitying, and that's why this is her best album yet.

Massive Attack - Mezzanine (Virgin)
You'll bathe in Mezza-nine over and over again, drown in this confusion, sadness and sensuality. They set the standards the others can't match.

Air - Moon Safari (Virgin)
Philadelphia, Detroit, Nashville, *Versailles*? Who'd have thought the first slice of musical grooviness this year was going to come from a place more often associated with games of pre-Revolution excess and cheeky cake comments?

Porn Cocktail

A hard man is good to find

from T.O. 1430, by **Louis Theroux**

Three days into my stay in the San Fernando Valley in Southern California, the call came. I had been cast in a gay porn flick. This was not entirely unexpected. I was in town shooting a documentary for BBC2 on male performers in porn, the third episode in a four-part series on subcultures on the American fringe called 'Louis Theroux's Weird Weekends'.

The call had been set up in advance. The movie was called 'Snowbound' and it was shooting in the mountains a few hours out of Los Angeles. The plot had a convict breaking out of jail and taking refuge with two gay couples in their ski lodge. The convict is straight, but soon finds himself enmeshed in a five-way gay orgy. I was to play the part of a park ranger who warns the couples about the escape:

Ranger: Good evening, gentlemen. I'm just out telling everyone that they should be on the look-out for an escapee from Jordan Valley Prison.

Man 1: (Looking at a photo of escapee) Hello!

Man 2: Is he as cute as his picture?

I am not much of an actor at the best of times. My park ranger's uniform was much too small; my lines were unaccountably hard to remember. The writer/cameraman, an excitable young man called Darren, seemed to be under the misapprehension that he was Martin Scorsese the Second.

We ended up doing about six takes. Only three of them were because of my screw-ups.

The porn business is not glamorous. I was discovering this the hard way. Not only is it not glamorous, it's also ridiculous and embarrassing and, by showbiz standards, low-paying (I got $50 for my 'Snowbound' cameo). And I got off easy. Mine had been a non-sex role, so I'd been spared the toughest, most stressful, most crucial part of the job of porn stud: actually getting an erection and coming (preferably in that order).

In the industry, the act of a man becoming aroused is called 'getting wood'. It's a phrase you hear an awful lot. It's a man's chief qualification to be in the business. Nothing else really matters – looks, punctuality, penis size, cer-

tainly not acting ability. 'Just keep it hard,' said one female performer when I asked what she looked for in male co-stars. Having kept it hard for the requisite number of hours – permitting the director to get his shopping list of positions and shots – the male performer must then deliver the so-called 'money shot', or 'pop shot'.

'You don't come, you don't get paid,' porn talent scout and sometime performer Steve Austin told me. (For the record, the fee for a scene – one 'pop' – is from $250 to $500.) 'If you don't do the shot, then they hire somebody called the "stunt cock" which is a guy that comes in and just pops. And usually you give that stunt guy anywhere from $50 to $75 to $100 for fixing the scene. I started a long time ago and I needed many a stunt cock to fill in for me. It's not a very good feeling.'

What this kind of pressure does to you psychologically can only be imagined. And of course, the fear of being unable to perform only compounds the problem. I saw this myself on

the set of a movie called 'Twisted'. I was there learning the ropes from a 23-year-old up-and-comer called JJ Michaels. Though a neophyte, JJ came highly recommended: in the first scene of his career, he'd carried off a double penetration – 'one anal, one vadge,' as he explained it to me, without a hitch.

But on 'Twisted', for whatever reason – and I have a hunch the presence of a BBC camera crew didn't help – JJ had wood problems. Any lingering belief I had that being a porn guy might be fun was dispelled seeing JJ desperately trying to arouse himself while the crew huffed and sighed and muttered about 'woodless wonders'.

On top of this, not insignificantly, you've got the risk of catching AIDS. Performers in porn movies generally do not wear condoms, though they are required to take HIV tests every 30 days. And yet, in spite of the sordidness and the pressure and the health risks – or maybe because of them – there are many winning

Jean Paul Gaultier

from 'Vive la différence' in T.O. 1439, by **Alkarim Jivani**

Should Barbara Cartland ever feel the need for a makeover, Jean Paul Gaultier is itching to get his hands on her.

'Alors! Something needs to be done!' he says in a charming language which is English only by default – the words are all recognisable, but the syntax, the inflexions, the body language and the accompanying facial movements are as French as the 'Marseillaise'. 'I would take off the hat and put a wig that is as extravagant as her hat or put a wig that is bald. And I would put her in black. She is always very colourful so now she has to change her look, she has to wear black – a black corset and rubber leggings.' There is a contemplative pause as he cocks his head and pictures the effect. Then he is struck by sudden inspiration. 'And I want to dress also the dog! I make the same outfit for the dog with the rubber and the corset.'

qualities to those involved in the porn business. This is something the new movie 'Boogie Nights' is good on: porn virtues. One is the sense of the industry as a family, albeit a highly dysfunctional one.

There is also something to be said for the way the porn world allows people to reinvent themselves. 'Everyone's blessed with one special thing,' the young Mark Wahlberg character says early on in 'Boogie Nights'. Later, he takes the name Dirk Diggler and enters porn full-time, and we root for his success because we know he likes doing it and that he's good.

JJ Michaels had a similar quality. I don't doubt that for most, porn is a last resort. But for a few, like JJ, porn is an actively desired destination. Having dropped out of the Air Force, JJ was approaching the job of professional penis with the seriousness and zeal of an aspiring Rhodes Scholar. Before I met him, I'd been expecting six feet of buff beefcake: I found a nerdy little guy with flicked hair and a collection of 'Godzilla' toys who used to run the John Carpenter fan club and whose only dream in life was to be good at making porn. You could argue with his choices. I thought he was misguided. But he was trying to be the hero of his own life and there was something touching about it.

I saw JJ again a few weeks ago. When we first met, JJ had done about 15 films. He'd now made about 88. He told me that one of the porno producers we'd interviewed, a man called Israel Gonzalez, had died in a shoot-out with the police after having a run-in with his girlfriend.

JJ was upbeat and happy. And yet I thought he seemed different: coarser. Whether the industry had changed him or whether he was just more confident, I don't know.

The movie I was in had its title changed to 'Take A Peak'. They sent me a copy: I couldn't help noticing that they'd given me no close-ups and that they'd used a take where I fluffed my line. Amazingly, it appeared on the counter of my local video store in New York, showing that there's no escaping a past in porn films, even when that past is limited to the role of a park-ranger. ●

Jack Nicholson

from 'Grin reaper' in T.O. 1438, by **Geoff Andrew**

In 'As Good as it Gets' my character Melvin's the kinda guy who wouldn't find this politically incorrect: one of my friends during the original onslaught of the AIDS epidemic, said, "God, Who'd've thought three years ago that getting fucked in the ass seven times a day would be bad fer ya?"'

Stop this state rock madness

from T.O. 1429, by **Linton Chiswick**

It's June 2001, and time for the fourth 'Rock for Diana – Dance on Her Grave' charity gala concert spectacular on Diana Island. Sir Cliff Richard, Sir Chris de Burgh and Sir Jimmy Nail are all waiting in the wings, but right now, the Prime Minister is on with his band Blair, which he formed after ousting ex-lead singer Damon Albarn for failing to toe the Britpop line. 'New singer, new band,' Albarn was told. 'Now fuck off ... I'll build a house, a nice Barratt house, in the caantry.'

Complementing the sharkskin suit and black shirt he wore to his first ever Brit Awards, Blair is sporting a slim, leather, piano-keyboard tie and is punching the air. 'Hello, Islington,' he shouts, as executives from Sony, PolyGram and EMI look on in approval. Creation's Alan McGee is so overcome he can't hold back the tears. 'I love you, Tony,' he sighs, before passing out into the arms of a St John's ambulanceman. Because ever since Tony took an interest in what we call 'pop', and what he calls 'a massive part of our social and economic infrastructure', Britain's middle managers have rediscovered classic rock 'n' roll.

First, Blair tests the future popularity of an act by what he calls the 'Euan test': if his son thinks it's cool, it must be cool with the youngsters. Then he invites the band round to Number 10 and subtly infiltrates them, so that the public thinks the Government has nurtured the group from the start.

'I am a Christ-i-an,' leers Blair, finishing his tribute to the Sex Pistols (now the Sensible Fiscals); and starting his best of Motown set. 'My Cherie Amour... lovely as the NHS.'

Is that what you want? Because that's what's going to happen.

Getting the Ball rolling

'Why can't women go out and have a good time?'

Zoë Ball interviewed in T.O. 1443, by **Elaine Paterson**

The phrases 'I really don't drink very much' and 'I was so drunk' co-exist quite happily in Zoë Ball's up-all-night anecdotes. In fact, her scatter-gun chatter tumbles over with contradictions, as in: 'I don't get too abusive when I'm drunk… although I do get quite abusive, actually'; or: 'I have this really weird cut-off point where it's like, I am too drunk now to know what I'm doing, I have to go home', followed swiftly by: 'I can't control myself when I'm drunk', used, as it has been by drinkers for centuries, to punctuate some painful recollection.

It doesn't feel like a conscious ploy to come across as open and garrulous while giving very little away, more like a genuine identity crisis: the result, perhaps, of a career that places her in a weird limboland between childhood innocence and teenage rampage. Even here, at our photoshoot, there's some anxiety over the appropriate image for the 27-year-old Zoë Ball. The BBC PR woman is concerned that her charge and a pint of beer should not go hand in hand on the cover. We've got those school-age 'Live And Kicking' viewers to think of, while on the other hand, TO is considered to be perfectly placed to enhance Ball's Radio One girl-about-town persona. The subject of this debate copes by simply being as easygoing in temperament as she is physically flexible and gangly.

It's a good job Ball was a party girl before she became a professional party girl, otherwise she would surely have burnt out by now. She seems to be everywhere at once. A couple of weeks ago she made her first big-screen appearance, in the rock comedy 'Still Crazy', with Jimmy Nail, Timothy Spall and Billy Connolly, and unveiled her first clothing line, clubby teen fashions for Littlewoods catalogues. All this and she gets up at 5.30 every morning, sometimes after only about an hour's sleep. Yet Ball can truthfully claim that, unlike her notorious R1 predecessor, Chris Evans, 'I've never missed a day. Plus I tend to find that if I've been out and had an hour's sleep, or no sleep, I've kind of got this weird, funny, exciting buzz that comes before you crash, usually at about 10 o'clock.'

Evans, a long-time acquaintance, has tried to derail her in drinking competitions, but while the Virgin king may be catching up in the breakfast-show ratings war, his drinking victories over Ball have been less impressive. 'I did have one afternoon, it was a Chris Evans day, where I ended up going home at about seven when I was supposed to be there at two, and I fell in the door, said, "I've got to be sick", knelt down to throw up and fell over, smashed my head on the sink and knocked myself out,' she laughs, a little shamefacedly. 'But I was fine. I kind of got dragged into bed and left for dead by Louis [Jones of the Warm Jets, a boyfriend, recently ex-ed].

'Chris is such a bully, he will literally sit you down and make you drink – I've seen him do it to so many people. The next day he told his listeners to tune in to our show. He said, "Turn over and see what kind of a hangover she's got." But I went to bed at 7 o'clock!'

Fame has curtailed her clubbing enjoyment; 'I can find myself dancing up against a wall of

Bob Flanagan: **supermasochist**

from 'Death becomes him' in T.O. 1433, by **Sheila Johnston**

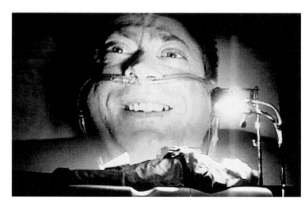

By rights, Bob Flanagan ought to have been long dead. At the ripe age of 40, he had by far outlived expectations for someone suffering, as he did, from cystic fibrosis, a severe and hereditary disease. But Bob Flanagan was very far from dead. Instead, he was busily occupied nailing his penis to a board. A fighter determined to not go gently into the night, Flanagan had quelled his illness in a highly original fashion. By becoming an extreme sexual masochist, he turned pain into a source of pleasure and empowerment: an incentive for survival.

As an artist, he transformed his plight into a series of outrageous videos, installations, poems, photographs and performance pieces celebrating, immortalising and, not least, mocking his own increasingly decrepit body. Among his creations was Visible Man, a scatological cousin of the transparent manikin used in science classes. Modelled on its inventor, this version emits a constant stream of bodily fluids: faeces, ejaculate and the faces,' but she likes the current trend in DJ bars, 'So at the moment I tend to go to places like that. You can have a drink and socialise and dance as well, without it being a hassle or uncomfortable.'

But the thing that's done more than fame or anti-social working hours to inhibit Ball's behaviour is the fear of accusations of 'laddism'. Loaded Man couldn't have found a better way to humiliate women into feeling guilty about enjoying themselves than by co-opting us into his own boorish lifestyle. 'One journalist described me as "degrading myself with my laddism",' says Ball, frustration rising. 'The thing is, I've never professed myself to be anything other than what I am. I've always been out with the lads, having a good time, and I've never been particularly ashamed of myself for doing so. I don't do it to be in with the crowd and impress male listeners on the radio. Why can't women go out and have a good time?'

Ball dates her current capacity for drinking heavily back to a year and a half ago – probably, not so coincidentally, to around the time she quit 'The Big Breakfast' following a hail of harsh criticism. She drinks shorts, Jack Daniels or Jamesons, and blames drink for an (imaginary) physical deterioration. At one point in the interview she pulls down her trousers, bends over, clutches a bony buttock in each hand and gives them a good jiggle to demonstrate encroaching flab (There's only the merest hint of a mud-flap tendency, if you must know). She freely admits to being a flirtatious drunk. 'I'd like to be able to say that I'm discriminating, but I don't know if I am really,' she muses. 'I generally only flirt with men…

> ## 'I really don't drink that much, I just get drunk very easily.'

but I have been known to flirt with women. Especially if they're very beautiful, I sort of become obsessed with beautiful women.' Embarrassing drunken moments include telling actor Ben Chaplin they were meant to be together ('I staggered up to him and said, "I love you", and he just said, "No you don't", and I said, "You don't know, but I really do love you." And he just said, "Ha ha ha"') and trying to abduct Jonny Lee Miller: 'I thought, "Oh my God, Sick Boy!" and then I started dragging him across the bar… I was yelling, "You're lovely!" and he's only about this big [she indicates the top of her thigh – about five-feet off the floor].'

And still Ball keeps coming back to her original claim that 'I really don't drink all that much, I just get drunk very easily'. Therein lies the crux of her appeal – the vulnerability that lies just below the sunny surface. She's more famous than any of the current crop of media blondes (Melinda Messenger, Denise Van Outen, Ulrika Jonsson), but unlike them, Ball hasn't convinced herself that being blonde and beautiful is a talent in itself. She's still the same scatty, insecure media wannabe she ever was; she works harder than any of the babes she's unfairly lumped in with and does a better job. Ball refers often in interviews to her lack of tangible talent. She doesn't even get to spin the records on the breakfast show. Right now, she's riding the scary rollercoaster of her career as far as it will take her, but you wonder what goes through Zoë Ball's head in the slow moments. Fortunately, there aren't many of them: 'If I don't go out, not only do I get a bit depressed, I also have bugger all to talk about on the radio.' ●

• •

thick green phlegm that is a hallmark of CS. Plans for a posthumous artwork involved persuading a wealthy collector to sponsor a video camera in his coffin, to allow the patron to 'see how I'm coming along'.

Film-maker Kirby Dick, has captured all this and more in an astonishing and audacious documentary, 'Sick: The Life And Death of Bob Flanagan, Supermasochist'. 'I'd been interested in making a movie about somebody dying because of its narrative impact on an audience. As soon as you have a camera, there's an intimacy, and over a period of time it becomes very intense.

'Some people walked out, but most stayed and really loved it. There's a whole cult of body modification and piercing, and so S&M is more in the mainstream culture. And because of AIDS we're more aware of the link between illness and sexuality. One thing that's interesting about Bob is that he looks at that issue from another angle: it's a different illness and a different sexuality.'

Even the impaled penis survived these test screenings and is revealed in 'Sick' in all its glory. 'The scene's in there and it's in for a minute: it's the whole thing. It was Bob's signature gesture, and I had always intended to make a film in which, by the time the audience got to that point, they would accept and understand it. I couldn't rest until that had been achieved. Besides, I'll never have a shot like that in one of my films again.' ●

"Quentin wants to be black. He's like my daughters' little white hip-hop friends. They're basically black kids with white skin."
Samuel L Jackson on Tarantino

"So, does this prove once and for all that size does matter?"
James Cameron, director of 'Titanic', picking up a Golden Globe

"I've kind of reached the stage now where, if there's any reference to drugs or music on the dust jacket of a book, I'll put it straight down."
Irvine Welsh gets bored of post-'Trainspotting' publishing

"Saddam Hussein is a nasty dictator, sitting on an awful lot of nasty stuff."
Tony Blair makes that public school education count

"The king is dead, long live the king."
Chelsea chairman Ken Bates on replacing Gullit with Vialli

"I'm just going to find a woman who hates me and give her £1 million – cut out the middle bit."
Jim Davidson, leaving court after his fourth divorce settlement

"Take away the illegality of drugs and you take away their sexiness. Why do 19-year-old kids shun alcohol? Because it's legal."
Creation Records' Alan McGee, arguing for the legalisation of drugs

"Princess Diana? It's complete nonsense to say that she could have been an international supermodel. She didn't have the looks."
David Bailey

"It would be great to walk into a club like John Travolta does in 'Saturday Night Fever' and have everyone give you a high five and yelp hello, but the reality is having some pissed-up bloke going, 'How's your mate Michael Jackson, eh?'"
The price of fame for Jarvis Cocker

"Half the population of the US over 30 were conceived while their parents were listening to his records."
Gore Vidal assesses the impact of Frank Sinatra

Cruel for cats

Is this freak show the future of cinema?

Harmony Korine interviewed in T.O. 1443, by **Tom Charity**

I have seen the future of cinema – and he's barely five feet tall. Harmony Korine is a nerdy looking Jewish kid with unruly hair, a beaky nose and a whiny voice. When we meet, he's wearing a canary yellow tank top over a nasty striped towelling shirt, a black tie which really should know better, and baggy blue jeans which run short above the ankle, revealing white socks and Patrick Cox Wannabes. He's 23 years old but a movie veteran, having scripted Larry Clark's controversial 'kids' when he was 18. Now he's written and directed his own film, and he believes that cinema will never be the same again.

If 'Gummo' had a plot, it would be the story of Foot-Foot, a cat who strays into the wrong part of town. But it doesn't have a plot, it isn't that kind of movie. In fact, it's like no movie you've seen before. Set in Xenia, Ohio, site of America's worst ever tornado once upon a time, but shot on the wrong side of the tracks in Nashville, Tennessee, it's an impressionistic, poetic, absurdist, punk collage of teenage enervation – a country cousin to 'kids', without the melodramatic fix which cheapened the earlier film. Picking out half-a-dozen youngsters, most of them at a dead loss, all of them freakier looking even than himself (you can't help wondering about in-breeding in the Midwest), Korine takes off with the tornado idea to twist from cinéma-vérité to improvisation to pre-scripted material, often within the same scene, surfing between video, film, super-8 and still images, throwing heavy metal, punk rock, Bach, Buddy Holly and mumbled, confessional doggerel into the mix. The result is breathtaking, provocative, and often repellent.

Here are some of the lowlights: two teens scrape money together by selling dead cats to the local Chinese restaurant. They hunt strays with BB guns; drown them; lay poison by trash cans; or put glass in tuna-fish. When they're not catnapping, these kids are sniffing glue, messing with life-support machines, or paying for sex. Then there's the boy who wanders around wearing pink bunny ears, gobbing on passing cars. And the retarded girl who puts on a show for the camera by shaving her eyebrows. Toto, we're not in Kansas any more.

Harmony's on his eighth cigarette, he tells me.

> ## 'There were dead bodies. I found a finger in a toothbrush.'

As in, his eighth, ever. He took up smoking yesterday. Why? 'I dunno, I like vices, I think addiction is good, as long as it doesn't control you.' While I'm figuring this one out, I ask what his other vices might be. 'Cinema,' he says, without hesitation. 'Horse-riding. And riding unicycles. And trying to find that Jerry Lewis movie, "The Day the Clown Cried". There's only one print in the world, and that's my goal, to see that movie. It was produced by some Iranian oil baron, and Jerry Lewis plays this Pied Piper character who leads children into the gas chambers. And it's like pro-Hitler propaganda, Wagnerian cinema. To me, the idea that this movie exists, that's what makes America great.'

He claims he went to school in Nashville, but his family travelled around a lot – his father was a documentary film-maker, 'very much into circus clowns and children who rode bulls… then he started firebombing empty houses across the South. That was when I broke away.' For all we know, some of this may be true. It hardly matters – that amalgam of circus, documentary and subversion is as good a starting point for discussing 'Gummo' as any. (The title is in honour of the other Marx brother, by the way.) I tell him I feel guilty when I tell people I like his film. In fact, I say, 'like' is the wrong word… it's a troubling, problematic film, it puts you on the spot.

'But isn't life problematic?' he retorts. 'I won't make movies that are simple, that don't deal with people's lives, that don't affect you in an emotional way. There's not a point to "Gummo", it's not saying one thing. Where people go wrong, they try to dissect its logic. If you saw the movie and hated it, if you didn't understand it and had nothing to reference it to… if you thought it was empty, anti-human, immoral – then you're right. But if you thought the opposite of that, then you're right as well. It's open, and it's free. That's what cinema should be. That's what great art is. People now want propaganda. They want to be told this is a good person, this is a bad person. It's Gumpification. I won't be a part of it.'

But doesn't the artist have a responsibility to take a moral position?

'No, because there's no responsibility in art, period. Why does art have to be moral? Why does it have to say anything? Morality comes in increments, in small doses. But there's morality in "Gummo". What could be more moral than real people doing real things?'

But it's not reality when you put a camera in front of these people…

'It's not reality, it's trickery. I'm obsessed with truth, but I'm aware it's a fallacy. Any time there is a camera in a room, it's a lie – 24 lies a second. This is what upsets people, because it's a movie, right, it's not a documentary. And movies aren't supposed to be reality. It's like a different kind of vernacular, like a different way of thinking… When I first met Werner Herzog, he told me people will hate my movies for the same reason they hate his films, because they say it's aestheticising mental illness, or aestheticising poverty… "Realism is the enemy of the people," he told me. They don't want to be reminded, I guess. Hopefully they'll tire of emptiness.'

Watching the film, often it's impossible to know where performance ends and reality begins – the finished film was maybe 50 per cent scripted, Harmony says. 'What I do, I write a script, and the script is a dead piece of shit. Then you have living people, tell them what you want, what goes on in your scenario – where the magic is, for me, is when the characters leave the script and bring something of themselves. Like when you hear the girl talk about putting a cat in a microwave and watching it melt… she wouldn't say that if there were 40 people around her. But she will when there's a camera sitting on my lap and we're having a conversation. The reason I switch formats, and it jumps around, is because it affords that. Eventually I think

cinema will change. You can make films now on video by yourself. You can get to places and feelings that have never been touched, because of what's prohibited by crews, money, commerce and all the other shit that goes along with the movie industry.'

I ask him about the scene in which he appears, apparently intoxicated, pathetically chatting up a black, gay dwarf – who rejects him. 'I can't watch it,' he admits. 'It was the last scene in the shoot, and it had to be me, because it wasn't scripted, and I wanted to be rejected. I can't work intoxicated. I do no drugs at all while I work, I don't even drink. But in order to do that scene, to give the love, to take it to that point, I had to lose myself. So I was definitely under the influence of alcohol. We finished at two in the morning, and everyone was crying, and my sister came to give me a hug and I threw her through a glass window because I was so drunk. I took off all my clothes and vomited into a plastic yellow bucket – and cut off my pubic hair with scissors and smoked a huge Havana cigar. I get sick of myself watching that scene – I almost cut it out, because I was so disgusting and bloated and drunk and awful, but, I think it works in the movie.'

So, I say, taking a deep breath, where did you get the dead cats?

'We had 'em made,' he shrugs, irritated. 'And Chloë [Sevigny, who appears in 'Gummo' and 'kids', and who is sitting quietly behind me during the interview], Chloë found one on the side of the road. I read about how many cats are slaughtered in my movie. There's one scene in the film, where they whip a dead cat, which lasts 45 seconds. Cat-killing has almost nothing to do with my movie, it's just the way these kids survive, it's their commerce, they're American, they're capitalists – they don't know right from wrong. I don't find anything in the movie shocking – there's not one thing in the movie done out of a sense of evil. There isn't one character who you can say is evil.'

Well, there's the paedophile journalist…

'Oh, that's true. I was just getting my own back… But the movie has nothing to do with shock. What's shocking is you've never seen these images projected, only in life. There's no one murdered in the movie…'

Except the granny?

'Yeah, well, but I mean, that's like, she was dead already. She's on a life-support machine, she wasn't alive. There's no violence in the movie except to cats. No cursing except for little boys. The only drug use was glue. The MPAA tried to destroy my movie because I sustained shots. They tried to kill my film because they said it was so nihilistic and anti-social that it would destroy the minds of young people. The youngest person on the board was 68 years old. He was having bowel movements during the screening.'

And what's this about your crew staging sit-down strikes?

'We filmed in a house, full of bugs, the most disgusting, inhuman, god-awful place anyone could ever imagine living. I found a piece of a man's shoulder in a pillow-case, there was a full jaw in a chandelier with a slightly shaved beard, I found a petrified turd in a sock. I'm totally not kidding. Ask her!' He gives Chloë the floor.

'There were dead kittens…', she says, feebly.

Harmony (firmly): 'There were dead bodies. I found a finger in a toothbrush.'

Chloë: 'It was awful though. We actually had to clear it up a bit to make room for the camera.'

Harmony: 'That's why I used the house. A family really lived there, that little boy with his legs eaten up by the bugs: that's America, and those bourgeois bullshit city critics accuse me of being a New York hipster, they want to pretend it doesn't exist. It does exist. My movie isn't a documentary or a social statement on poverty in America, but everything in the movie is based on some kind of truth. I know these people, I grew up with them.'

So the crew went on strike because they didn't want to be in the house?

'Jean-Yves [Escoffier, the cinematographer] said "Fuck 'em all", and we bought 'em nuclear asbestos outfits, and they shot the rest of the scenes in them, which really freaked out the residents of the household. Jean-Yves and I were so pumped we bought flip-flops and Speedos, and directed the rest of the scenes like that. The scene where the kid eats the chocolate bar in the bathtub? There were bugs falling in his food. He stayed in there eight hours. He was puking into plastic buckets. That's why I don't use actors, actors would never do that. A real person will give you himself.

'My whole life has been life, and cinema – that's why I'm so pale,' Korine tells me, and this time I believe every word. 'The first time I saw Buster Keaton's face I knew there was a poetry in cinema, a living poetry, and it was the greatest thing I ever saw in my life. And it's all I ever wanted to do. I knew I would make movies when I was a little boy. Yes, "Gummo" is uncomfortable, yes it's messy. That's life. Movies are too neat, now. Don't you think things need to change? I go to movies now and I feel nothing. When you watch "Boogie Nights", do you feel anything? Or Tarantino: does anything resonate? Nothing. It's all about air. When Lumière first made movies he was making films about people riding horses, or climbing trees, just capturing life. It was about the poetry of life. For me, "Gummo" is the first new movie. It's what I call a "mistake-ist" art form. You learn from your mistakes. Things fall from the sky. It's like science projects. Like explosions. This is the future, and it's chaos.' ●

King of the road

Would you buy a used Ferrari from this man?

Jeremy Clarkson interviewed in T.O. 1429, by **Bruce Dessau**

Jeremy Clarkson has got the largest big end in television. Propped precariously on an electric scooter in a corridor of the Hilton, it blocks out much of the light. It makes Robbie Coltrane resemble Kate Moss. If the photo-shoot was outdoors, it would cause an eclipse. But the arse is nothing compared to the outfit. Without a shadow of a doubt, Jeremy Clarkson is the worst-dressed star I have ever interviewed: jeans that must drain the blood are merely part of an onslaught of denim. And then he goes and puts a scarf on. In the Hilton. A scarf.

So there you go: a bit of Clarkson-style hyperbole to give him a taste of his own medicine and get you in the mood for the man who kicked BBC2's 'Top Gear' into the '90s. The show now outrates the channel's flagships such as 'Have I Got News For You', and the memory of Noel Edmonds hosting it has long since faded. Another ex-presenter ended up in a Buddhist monastery in Scotland, which, after working with Edmonds, was probably a doddle.

While 'Top Gear' has its annual service, the Keegan-curled critic returns to TV with 'Jeremy Clarkson's Extreme Machines'. Forget four wheels and a chassis: Clarkson calls the show,

He flies an F15 jet.
He vomits in the cockpit.

which features the fastest, largest and most expensive gadgetry on the planet, 'hardcore television'. He goes for a shunt in a Canadian combine harvester. He races an F1 speedboat that is so fast it nearly takes off. He flies an F15 jet. He vomits in the cockpit.

That last scene is, in fact, more than a little ironic, as Jeremy Clarkson apparently makes a lot of people sick. While it's true that he's an unreconstructed lad who smokes 40 Marlboros a day and drives a red Ferrari 355GTS, he's also one of the most amusing TV presenters around, and an excellent writer to boot: who else would be versatile enough to write a column for both

the *Sun* and the *Sunday Times*? The quote of the week box in the 'Wheels' section of the Guardian would be permanently empty without him. In fact, last November it ran an apology: 'Jeremy Clarkson wrote nothing of interest this week. We wish him a speedy recovery from this uncharacteristic blandness.'

Instinct decrees I should hate him. That haircut alone is an abomination. But he's simply a bloody nice bloke, with a wry sense of humour and even – despite sartorial appearances – a touch of irony. He's also very professional and extremely industrious: this 10.30am interview was my first work of the day, but was already his third meeting. He doesn't even want to talk that much about cars or heavy machinery, and would rather banter about the soundtrack for the series. Unfortunately, his taste in music mirrors his taste in clothes. 'The row we've had is phenomenal, because the director and producer are both into bands like Blur and Portishead, which I think are largely shite. My taste is Bad Company and Led Zep, but this director raises one eyebrow if you just say Led Zep.' I raise an eyebrow too, but I don't think he noticed it through the fug of cigarette smoke.

Clarkson is keen to dispel the myth that he is car-crazy. 'I could say "Maserati" before I could say "mummy", but then it went away when I got into girls. I couldn't drive, so there was no point being into cars.' The teenage Clarkson didn't even have Scalextric. 'We were so poor I had to play with twigs.' So maybe the motormania is revenge for years of deprivation? Clarkson

paedophilia. You can't go up to someone and say "Hey! I like little girls!" either.'

Clarkson hates the Germans ('flatulent people and their BMWs'), doesn't trust the Welsh, and loathes John Prescott ('he wants to stop people driving after one wine gum'), but he made his new series to annoy another demographic. 'I did it to shut motorcyclists up. They're always going on about bikes being so marvellous, I thought I'd find 30 things that would make bikes look positively ridiculous.'

The six-part series was made very much on the hoof: at the Reno air race, for example, the team just turned up and hitched. 'You just find someone with a two-seater who'll give you a ride. I didn't know if they were psychotic or not. The previous year there was a collision and two pilots were killed. When it happened to distract the grandstand, they had a wing-walker on standby, who did his bit to keep the crowd occupied. His finale was to fly upside down past the grandstand, but the pilot misjudged the height and took the guy's head off and smeared his shoulders along the runway. And this was to take people's minds off the carnage on the other side of the track.'

There is no glee to this storytelling. Despite his prejudices, Clarkson is likeable because there is an honesty to him. 'What you see on the screen is me. The only thing missing is the swearing. I was on a Swedish snowmobile in a frozen river race and the director said: "For heaven's sake, don't swear." I got two words out. "Fucking" and "hell". You can't always come out with something witty when you're afraid of dying.'

There's one final question I've been dying to ask this proud owner of a very priapic red Ferrari, but thought best to save to the end. Does he adhere to the theories about links between powerful thrust and sex? He pauses for a moment and teeters on the edge of his electric scooter.

'I can't think of a link. There was never a moment when I swelled in the whole series: no sexual thrill at all. All that stuff about E-type Jags looking like a big penis? I can't say I've ever mistaken a penis for a Jaguar.' And with that, he dismounts from the scooter and disappears into his hotel room. Jeremy Clarkson's big end is gone. ●

demurs. 'No. I left the *Rotherham Advertiser* to become a freelance journalist in London. I thought I'd write about cars. But if you showed me a shock absorber, I wouldn't have a clue. The AA exists for when the car goes wrong. I've got no idea how things work.' These days he talks about cars with an almost missionary zeal. 'With films, music or books, you can find common ground with most people, but with cars, people want to be in another room when a car fan starts talking. It's almost like

from T.O. 1131, by Kipper Williams.